W9-COO-773

World Empires, World Missions, World Wars

A BIBLICAL WORLD HISTORY CURRICULUM
NAPOLEON TO KOREA

1:1
answersingenesis®
Petersburg, Kentucky, USA

by DIANA WARING

World Empires, World Missions, World Wars: Teacher Guide

Copyright © 2012 Diana Waring. No part of this book may be reproduced, stored in a retrieval system, or transmitted in any form or by any means—electronic, mechanical, photocopying, recording, or otherwise—without written permission from the publisher.

Second printing: July 2013

For more information, contact
Answers in Genesis
2800 Bullittsburg Church Rd.
Petersburg, KY 41080

All Scripture quotations are taken from the New King James Version, © 1979, 1980, 1982 by Thomas Nelson, Inc., Publishers. Used by permission.

Map Keys copyright © 2012 Answers in Genesis and its licensors

For Student Manual image credits, see Student Manual.

Cover Design: Brandie Lucas
Text Design: Diane King
Editors: Gary Vaterlaus, Anneliese Rumminger, Stacia McKeever

ISBN: 978-1-60092-647-1

Printed in China

www.answersingenesis.org

"Jesus answered and said to him, 'Blessed are you, Simon Bar-Jonah, for flesh and blood has not revealed this to you, but My Father who is in heaven. And I also say to you that you are Peter, and on this rock I will build My church, and the gates of Hades shall not prevail against it.'" Matthew 16:17–18

Special Thanks to:

This Teacher's Guide is a tool for the teacher intent on guiding students along their voyage of discovery in the amazing subject called history. I am indebted to many people and sources for insights into biblical education which have formed the foundational core of our approach to studying history:

- Rosalie Pedder, late friend, mentor, and international teacher in the areas of learning issues, for her invaluable ministry and encouragement;

- Terry Small, "The Brain Guy" and international speaker/educator, for his insight into best brain practices and his constant encouragement;

- Lois LeBar, foremost Christian educator in the 1950s, whose book *Education that is Christian* has been highly valued in creating the structure of this curriculum;

- Dr. David Aikman, journalist, author, and history professor at Patrick Henry College, for his scholarly insights and critique of the manuscript;

- Dr. Tracy McKenzie, history chair at Wheaton University, for his wisdom and ongoing encouragement to approach history with humility;

- Dr. Paul Hawkins, international educator, for his continued and vocal support of this curriculum;

- Kevin Havens, AIA architect and Senior Vice President at Wight & Company, for his fascinating insights in architectural history;

- Catherine Levison, author and speaker on the Charlotte Mason approach to education, for her invaluable willingness to merge a Charlotte Mason schedule with this curriculum;

- Dan Zordel, Dale Mason, and Gary Vaterlaus of Answers in Genesis, for their kindness, patience, and willingness to "go the extra mile" for this project;

- Isaac Waring, my son and graduate of Cornish College of the Arts, for his extraordinary help with theater, pantomime, and conceptual design suggestions;

- My other children, Michael and Melody, who have been a constant source of insight and encouragement for this project, along with my daughters-in-law, Ashley and Lissy, who have brought new zest to my life;

- My beloved husband, Bill. Without his counsel and editing, and his willingness to live with poster-sized easel sheets lining our living room, this book would still be in process!

Contents

Introduction

Sometimes, people work for a paycheck.

> "Not enough to get tired,
> Just enough to not be fired."

> Ho-Hum.

In the same way, students often work for a grade.

> "Not enough to really learn,
> Just enough to get the grade and move on."

> Ho-Hum.

But is that what God intended?

> "And whatever you do, do it heartily, as to the Lord and not to men . . ." Colossians 3:23

> "Whatever your hand finds to do, do it with your might . . ." Ecclesiastes 9:10

> " . . . not with eyeservice, as men-pleasers, but as bondservants of Christ, doing the will of God from the heart, with goodwill doing service, as to the Lord, and not to men." Ephesians 6:6–7

Rather than a ho-hum approach to life and learning, He created us to be *passionately* involved:

> "And you shall love the Lord your God with all your heart, with all your soul, with all your mind, and with all your strength!" Mark 12:30

Recognizing that we cannot crawl inside the student's mind and heart, throw a switch, and create a passion for learning, how on earth do we get students involved in the process? How do we help them move beyond spectator to active player?

The solution we and many others have discovered is a new model: **we must work with the design of God**.

Our Creator uniquely designed each of us with strengths and styles of learning, so we must respond to this by developing an educational approach which gives opportunities for these differences. Realizing that our students are made in the image and likeness of God, and recognizing that we are working under God, we begin to comprehend that our labor in ministry is nurturing handcrafted masterpieces, not assembly-line, Dollar Store merchandise!

A basic, practical, and attainable method for accomplishing this is to provide variety in the learning environment. With that in mind, the *World Empires, World Missions, World Wars* curriculum was designed with a broad variety of opportunities for pursuing information. Without the teacher having to analyze every student or to create a dozen different activities, the program offers suggestions for creating that variety.

Honor and respect your students

Allow them to be whom they were designed by God to be: physical? verbal? interactive? daydreamer? hands-on? logical? artistic? musical? quiet? attention-getter? leader?

The many-faceted suggestions within each section of the curriculum allow students to actively and personally pursue learning—no more spectator education! The students will purposefully be involved in setting the direction of each Unit through their exploration, discovery, discussion, hands-on activity, and creative expression. Engaging them this way honors and respects the unique approach to learning, which God has set into each student. This impacts the entire course—not just by providing real opportunities for the students, allowing them to joyfully and actively learn the content, but by also providing real structure, a valid paradigm of structure and organization, enabling teachers to move forward within the content of the course. By approaching lessons this way, teachers are given the opportunity to be partial to *every* student (rather than partial to the linguistic and math/logical students whose successes normally dominate the classroom); to be fair and just in assessing student accomplishment by giving opportunities and honoring all the different types of learners; to be creative in the areas that appeal personally to the students; and to keep all the students motivated and moving along in their studies.

This curriculum encourages each learner to become self-motivated: through choosing specific learning activities; through choosing how to creatively share what has been learned; through team projects as well as individual accomplishments; through visual, auditory, and kinesthetic learning opportunities; and through the integration of multidisciplinary learning (which sometimes appeals to the student beyond the actual subject of history).

> "Learning is not always FUN. Most of it is very hard work, but it does not also have to be unpleasant. Gardening in spring is delightful—it's hard work, but pleasant. Only a fool would try to carry out the same activities in winter. Why

add unpleasantness to something already difficult? But we do that in learning all the time. Something hard but satisfying often unnecessarily becomes something both hard and unpleasant." Rosalie Pedder

Our intent is keep learning delightful, even if demanding and challenging. We have endeavored to present a rich variety of creative activities for you to access for your students.

Teach history as HisStory

A biblical perspective in history means seeing God as central to our understanding. In this curriculum, we do not add a few Hebrew dates into an otherwise typical presentation of history and label it "biblical." Instead, we want to see history from His point of view; to view all of history—all cultures and events—in the light of God's revelation of Himself and of His ongoing redemptive purpose pursued throughout the world's existence. Encountering God in the affairs of men, distinguishing the good leader from the bad leader—the hero from the villain—and making those determinations based on the Bible, is teaching history from a biblical perspective. (See "Worldviews in the Study of History" on page xxv for an illustration of this principle.)

To gain this perspective, the student is frequently asked to consider, *"What was God doing in this moment of history?"* The answers are found and explored in the Bible, the archaeological record, the writings of experts, and historical source documents. This overlapping of what are often described as "secular" history and "sacred" history gives us a front row seat to observe the incredible events, the amazing people, and the fascinating imprints of God's interaction in our world. This

Teaching History From A Biblical Perspective . . .

- Letting students learn history in ways that honor and respect their individual design;

- Letting them be inspired by the greatness of who God is and what He has done;

- Letting them meet the great heroes of world history and see the great villains;

- Letting them be mesmerized by the incredible adventures and cliffhanging tight spots;

- Inspiring them to jump in with both feet and discover whatever is unexplained, curious, awe-inspiring, funny, fascinating to THEM!

. . . IS TEACHING HISTORY FROM A BIBLICAL PERSPECTIVE.

provides not only insight into history but revelation of the Maestro of HisStory. With this perspective, students will not only gain academic understanding of history, but more importantly, they will grow in their personal understanding of God's faithfulness and wisdom.

The highest purpose and ultimate goal of this curriculum is to see the lives of students change as they come face to face with the reality of God's amazing faithfulness throughout all time.

May you find great joy in this study!

In Jesus,

Diana Waring

The Foundation Beneath the Structure . . .

There are three foundational building blocks undergirding this curriculum—three approaches to learning, which help explain some of the differences in the ways people learn:

» Four Learning Styles

» Three Learning Modalities

» Eight Intelligences

Four Learning Styles

Learning Styles refers to the categorization of how a particular personality style best learns. The method we refer to was developed by Myers-Briggs. Here is a brief description of each of the four learning styles:

THE FEELER	THE INTUITOR
This is the "people person" learning style. A Feeler wants to know the people perspective, i.e. how this subject affects people; how does this impact our lives now; who were the people of history, as opposed to the events or things. These learners need to be in good relationship with the people around them—their teacher, siblings, friends, etc. They love to be with other people in one-on-one conversations and in group activities, especially when they are part of a "team effort."	"Wait! I have an idea!" The Intuitor is the one brimming over with ideas about how this might have happened, or about how you might put on a play for the whole city portraying an historic event, or about what it must have been like to live in ancient times, and on and on. This learner is very good at coming up with suggestions, but is not as strong at seeing things through to completion. The Intuitor needs a lot of flexibility in schedule, and a "safe haven" for suggesting and trying out ideas.
THE THINKER	THE SENSOR
"Give me the facts, ma'am, just the facts." The Thinker has a black & white approach to knowledge, wanting authoritative input, not just someone's opinions. This learner truly enjoys using textbooks, encyclopedias, charts, and diagrams. There is a need to know exactly what the rules are in the class, when assignments or projects are due, what is required for good grades. Thinkers are organized and expect organization.	The "hands-on," get-it-done-now person. The Sensor is the one who can make projects happen—taking them beyond the blueprint stage and into production. This learner does NOT enjoy sitting for long periods of time, looking through books for information, or discussing things for hours on end. Instead, the Sensor prefers to be involved with things that can be efficiently accomplished with physical effort.

Three Learning Modalities

Learning Modalities refers to the approach learners use to take in new information, how they best concentrate, process, and retain. Here is a brief description of each of the three modalities:

VISUAL	AUDITORY	TACTILE/KINESTHETIC
learn best by seeing, whether through reading, looking at pictures, watching a documentary, observing.	learn best by hearing, whether through audio recordings, conversations, lectures, or reading out loud.	learn best by touching objects or moving, whether through hands-on projects or physical action, such as jumping, running, dancing, even wiggling.

Eight Intelligences

Eight Intelligences refers to natural potential and areas of talent. Howard Gardner of Harvard University theorized that intelligence is made up of more than verbal and mathematical skills, and that people can strengthen their natural giftings and improve their weaknesses. Here is a brief description of each of the eight intelligences:

INTRAPERSONAL This could be described as Self-Smart. It is the ability to enjoy being alone, working independently, and relying on self-motivation. This person needs solitary time in order to think.	**NATURALIST** This could be described as Nature Smart. It is the ability to observe, investigate, experiment, and discover the natural world, including weather, animals, plants, and geologic structures. This person needs to go outside!
BODILY-KINESTHETIC This could be described as Body Smart. It is the ability to use one's body through touch and movement to accomplish what is desired. It includes being able to process knowledge through bodily movement or through sensation, enjoying physical activity, and being constantly in motion even while sitting down. This person needs to move!	**SPATIAL** This could be described as Picture Smart. It is the ability to see in pictures rather than words, and includes drawing and design, three-dimensional constructing (such as LEGO® bricks), and other visual arts, such as photography, sculpting, and painting. This person needs pictures, maps, diagrams, charts, photos, and other visual/spatial material.
MUSICAL This could be described as Music Smart. It is the ability to learn through rhythm and melody, sing or play musical instruments, enjoy listening to music, remember songs, and study more effectively when music is played. This person needs music, whether it is music lessons or musical recordings.	**INTERPERSONAL** This could be described as People Smart. It is the ability to understand and enjoy people. A person who is interpersonal learns best when other people are involved, whether through games, team work, or cooperative learning sessions. This person needs people.
MATH/LOGICAL This could be described as Number Smart. It is the ability to reason mathematically, discover abstract patterns, classify and organize, enjoy mathematical computations, and think logically. This person needs to see the logic and organization in what is being learned.	**LINGUISTIC** This could be described as Word Smart. It is the ability to enjoy and use language through word games, books, recordings, trivia, poetry, papers, discussion, and other forms of using words. This person needs words in order to communicate.

Structural Overview

The Course of Study

- » Unit 1: *Napoleon & Early Missions*
- » Unit 2: *Industrialization & the Church's Response*
- » Unit 3: *The British Empire & Awakenings*
- » Unit 4: *Napoleon III & Christian Outreach*
- » Unit 5: *Alliances & Revivals*
- » Unit 6: *World War I & the Russian Revolution*
- » Unit 7: *Fascism & Fundamentals*
- » Unit 8: *World War II & Miraculous Deliverances*
- » Unit 9: *Early Cold War & Renewed Vision*

SCOPE

The Structure of Each Unit

WEEK ONE: INTRODUCTION

- » Discuss Key Concepts
- » Read the Unit article
- » Listen to the appropriate recordings
- » Consider and discuss opinions
- » Choose interesting books or Internet search

WEEK TWO: EXPLORATION & DISCOVERY

- » Research a topic of your choice
- » Learn the Words to Watch
- » Construct the time line
- » Report findings on your research

WEEK THREE: HANDS-ON

- » Geography mapping
- » View art & architecture
- » Design art projects
- » Conduct science experiments
- » Music suggestions
- » Cook the recipe

WEEK FOUR: EXPRESSION

- » Linguistics: journalism, prose, poetry, playing with words
- » Art: painting/drawing, graphic design, sculpting, cartooning
- » Music: compose, practice performance
- » Drama: comedy, tragedy, reality, reader's theater, puppetry
- » Movement: pantomime, dance, action
- » Conceptual design

STRUCTURE

Explanation of Structure

Based on the Myers-Briggs definitions of Learning Styles—Feeler, Thinker, Sensor, Intuitor—*World Empires, World Missions, World Wars* has been designed so that each Unit proceeds through a four-week cycle of one week per learning style. This means that students will have the opportunity to learn history in his or her own style, as well as from other approaches.

Complementing this approach is the opportunity for students to learn new information from a combination of visual, auditory, and kinesthetic presentations. This insures that your students have the occasion to learn in the way they learn best. This curriculum has already designed this multi-modality approach into every Unit. Hopefully, you will utilize aspects of each one in every Unit.

Week #1 will appeal greatly to the Feeler Learning Style, as students gain the "people perspective" by listening with you to auditory recordings, reading the Scriptures and other history materials, and discussing together what they are learning. The discussion suggestions range from open-ended questions with many possible answers to discovery questions, which require studied consideration.

Week #2 is designed to capture the interest of the Thinker Learning Style by appealing to the authoritative and factual perspective through chronological work with a time line, vocabulary drill, and research & reporting projects. Since the students are allowed to each select their own research project and the manner in which they will report what has been learned, there is an intrinsic motivation factor—they choose what they want to learn about!

Week #3 provides the often neglected hands-on learning opportunities which will allow the Sensor Learning Style to thrive. This week focuses on the geography of a historic time through mapmaking, and gives place to the fine arts. Students are given exposure to great art, architecture, and music, and given hands-on experiences with creating art and preparing food. Science experiments round out this week, connecting the historic moment in time with its scientific inventions, explorations, and discoveries.

Week #4 gives the idea-loving Intuitor Learning Style a platform and an audience for creative expression. The possibilities include creative writing, journalism, poetry, short stories, political cartooning, posters, illustrating, sculpting, skits, puppetry, music performance, role playing, pantomime, dance, conceptual design, and more. Students have the opportunity to be creatively involved as deeply or as casually as their interests and time constraints take them.

Goals for the Teacher

Through this flexible, multidisciplinary, learning-style-centered approach to history, teachers will be enabled to:

- impart history instruction in ways that will be retained and comprehended;
- facilitate and guide the students' active participation in learning;
- recognize the value of each student's unique design of God in learning;
- validate the particular thread of history which the student is interested to learn;
- provide encouragement as needed;
- offer a safe atmosphere for discussion and creative problem-solving;
- help students choose appropriate projects and resources;
- give opportunities for students to demonstrate what has been learned;
- evaluate students' progress based on direct experiences and actual learning.

Goals for the Student

Through this in-depth look at human history from the Napoleon to the Korean War, students will learn to:

- understand and trust God's faithfulness;
- view other cultures and peoples from His perspective;
- gain an understanding of some of God's intimate and overarching work in human history through nations and individuals;
- understand the importance of worldviews in interpreting history;
- gain a solid foundation in apologetics, using the Bible as literal history;
- comprehend the relevance of the Modern Era and world missions to today's headlines;
- understand the chronology, as well as the cause and effect of world history;
- have a critical and in-depth understanding of each of these cultures through various disciplines, such as art, science, literature, geography, music, warfare, agriculture, religion, family life, government, economics, architecture, communications, and history;
- understand these civilizations' unique impact on other cultures;
- learn how to approach, appreciate, and apply the study of history.

Icon Key

 Teacher Tip: From time to time in each Unit, there are suggestions or ideas that can make your work as a teacher easier, more creative, or more successful. This icon highlights these suggestions and ideas.

 Question: Several questions have been provided for you to ask your students during the course of each Unit to spark more stimulating class discussions. This icon emphasizes these questions.

 Spiritual Emphasis: Since this curriculum seeks to understand history in light of what God has done—tracing the history of redemption—and since the object of the curriculum is to not only gain knowledge of the content but also an understanding of God's character and nature, there are opportunities in each Unit to engage your students on a spiritual level. This icon can include areas for prayer and discussion, as well as suggestions for activities with a spiritual purpose.

Phase One: The Introductory Week

◉ Informally discuss the Key Concepts

Pretests to discover what students already know generate either excitement or panic, depending on the learning style of the student ! Instead of a formal pretest, simply engage your students in an informal discussion by asking them what they've read, heard or thought about these concepts. This is not intended to make them feel stupid or ignorant but to activate their interests and generate ideas, so keep the session open and non-threatening. Avoiding the common shame-based questioning is critical in this opening exercise. Feel free to read excerpts of the expanded concepts to the students, after they have shared their own knowledge, if it will help generate more discussion.

Discussing the Key Concepts is not the same as exhaustive learning. It is merely an introduction—a chance for students to share what they know and to have their interest piqued concerning the information they will encounter through the rest of the Unit.

Feel free to choose a small sampling of these concepts to discuss, or even, if the discussion is interesting, focus on only one. The students will be introduced to all of the concepts as the Unit progresses.

REMEMBER:

Students learn:

10% of what they **read**

20% of what they **hear**

30% of what they **see**

50% of what they **see** & **hear**

70% of what they **say**

90% of what they **say** & **do**

THEREFORE:

Encourage them to make mind maps or outline. This is not to be graded!

◉ Read the article

◉ Listen to the audio recordings

Because some students receive new information better by seeing it, the articles have been included. Because other students receive new information better by hearing it, the audio recordings have been produced. Some students receive new information best by moving, so we encourage you to allow students the opportunity to quietly walk or do some other inconspicuous movement during the audio portion, if that will assist them.

◉ Read the Scriptures

◉ Recap the material with an activity

After the students have read the article, listened to the appropriate recordings, and read the Scriptures, it is vital that they have an opportunity to process and review. God has designed many different types of learners, so offer the students a choice of several alternatives for process and review. Though it is more comfortable for us to regulate, control, and officially streamline our students' activities, we must honor and respect God's design in each student (which may be quite different than our own design). We can do this with the recap activities by setting up eight different stations—one for each of the eight suggestions provided. Each activity represents one of the Eight Intelligences. (For more information, consult page xii.) Allow each student to choose which station would be most helpful.

In order to facilitate all eight stations for the recap activities, you will need to occasionally gather a few materials, such as poster board and colored marking pens.

◉ Talk together

Remember: the point is to process and review, so don't encumber this session with other goals, or make it an instruction time for new material.

Individual Preparation

It is important to give students a chance to think about their answers to these questions before discussing them in class. Though some students generate answers spontaneously and verbally, other students require time to internally process answers before speaking. For this reason—to honor the different ways learners think—we ask that you give all the students time to ponder, consider, seek the Scriptures, and think about the possible answers prior to a class discussion. Give the students the assignment to write out their answers, whether partially or thoroughly, which will help them during the class discussion. These answers are not to be graded, although you could certainly give credit for having completed the assignment.

Class Discussion

It is important to create a safe environment for good class discussions. Prior to beginning, set the ground rules for each student, including taking turns, no sarcasm, etc.

Good class discussion is quite different from a good lecture! As the teacher, see yourself as the moderator of the discussion, seeking to keep it positive, interesting, and creative; allowing students to interact; encouraging further thought without giving lengthy answers. In pursuing this activity in the Introduction Phase, we are still developing a sense of wonder that will propel the students through the rest of the Unit.

Students must realize that people see from their own point of view, and, though someone's idea may seem dumb at first, if we give the person a chance to speak without fear of ridicule, we may hear some treasures! If someone's idea is not clearly stated, respectfully ask questions until the meaning is understood.

◉ Choose books of interest/ internet search

This is one of the places in this Unit where students have the opportunity to explore the specific areas in which they have an interest. Not everyone will find the same subjects fascinating, so allow the students as much leeway as possible as they explore potential topics.

◉ Conduct a review and evaluation

You might choose to evaluate your students based on their participation in the class discussion and in their participation in the recap activity. For further ideas on assessment and evaluation, please see page xxii.

One of the greatest drawbacks to using the Internet for research, apart from the obvious dangers of pornography, is that many of the articles are filled with such arrogance (even some of the ones written by Christians). Our students may find themselves in a quandary trying to manage conflicting interpretations and even conflicting facts! My encouragement is to teach the students to beware of arrogance and embrace humility. Arrogant writers might or might not have correct knowledge, but they will certainly be lacking God's wisdom:

"But the wisdom that is from above is first pure, then peaceable, gentle, willing to yield, full of mercy and good fruits, without partiality and without hypocrisy." James 3:17

If students can simply be made aware of the arrogance, it will help them considerably in understanding some of the raging debates among Christians. Teaching students to remain humble and teachable even while expressing their opinions earnestly means that if they examine an argument and choose one side, then later hear something which sheds new light on the issue, they can graciously let go of the wrong idea. It is always a good idea to embrace humility, as God "resists the proud but gives grace to the humble." James 4:6

Phase Two: The Exploration & Discovery Week

◉ Choose a topic and begin research

Students may conduct research in a variety of ways, including library research, internet research, interviewing experts, field trips, etc. If a student has a difficult time finding materials or information on a chosen topic, you can either help with the search, or suggest another topic for research.

Students may report what they have researched by writing a research paper or doing an oral report. However, for some students, having a creative alternative for reporting what they have discovered could make the difference between enthusiastically digging in and merely complying with the assignment.

◉ Construct the time line

The point of doing a time line is not to burden the student with needless labor. Instead, it is to begin to create a mental bulletin board on which to organize the people, the events, and the flow of history. Encourage your students to see this exercise as the start of a jigsaw puzzle, which will eventually display for them a very clear understanding of the chronology of history, which will in turn help them discover for themselves some of the cause and effect relationships between actions and subsequent reactions. Also, it will give the Christian student a much broader understanding of God's interaction with the people and nations of history.

Students using the time line provided in the Student Manual may utilize their preferred system for marking people, events and dates. Some commonly suggested systems: use a bullet point to mark the date, then write the event or name; create a series of symbols for entering dates to distinguish between biblical and non-biblical, and to distinguish events versus persons versus locations; draw a sketch of the person or event; cut out a magazine photo to represent an event or date; use some other system which appeals to the artistic style of the student.

◉ Practice vocabulary

Vocabulary is important in that it allows students an opportunity to gain a better grasp of some of the concepts in a time period—concepts which are expressed in particular terms. We must not turn vocabulary practice into an arduous chore which breeds a hatred and contempt for the magnificence of language. Therefore, we have included in each Unit of the Teacher Guide a suggested activity highlighting one of the eight intelligences. This allows students a greater enjoyment of the process of learning the pertinent vocabulary, and results in improved retention and comprehension. See Appendix B for definitions.

◉ Complete research projects and share in class or turn in

Remember that timing is everything! Do NOT criticize a student immediately after their presentation, unless, of course, you desire that they would never again make the attempt to share their thoughts, except in a safe, boring, mediocre way. If there is a criticism to be given, wait until a later moment to give it, as the moment of sharing is a tremendously vulnerable time, and we have the power to crush our students if we do not honor the value of what they have labored to accomplish.

Remember the Rule of Sandwich:

1. Begin with appreciation and honor
2. Kindly give any pertinent critique
3. Finish with appreciation and honor

◉ Conduct a review and evaluation

You may wish to evaluate your students based on their efforts in the Research and Reporting projects and their active participation in the Vocabulary and time line exercises. For further ideas on assessment and evaluation, please see page xxii.

Phase Three: The Hands-On Week

These activities, though not strictly within the normal confines of a history class, will allow the students who learn best through hands-on and sensory activities to thoroughly learn cultural material relevant to this Unit. The teacher does not need to be well-versed in art, architecture, music, or science in order for the students to learn deeply during this phase. Every student will find new insights and understanding about the time period of this Unit, so we recommend that all students participate, regardless of learning style. With all the options provided, students should be able to find something that looks interesting. The teacher need only facilitate the experience—the students will do the work.

◉ Create a map and discuss the issues in teams

It is amazing to discover how greatly the geography of a location has impacted the history of that location. Help your students recognize that they won't understand their subject as well if they don't know where it is and what it is like geographically! A huge mountain range can have a daunting effect on invading armies; a river can be a source of irrigation in a dry place; a swamp can affect the health of the settlers; and more.

If students have good, sharp colored drawing pencils, they may enjoy making artistic maps, showing, for instance, mountain ranges as a series of peaks, rather than functional maps indicating mountain ranges merely with words. See Appendix A for an answer key to the maps.

◉ Examine and discuss art and architecture

There are no right and wrong answers to the questions listed in the Student Manual and the Teacher Guide concerning these art forms. Give the students permission to have their own ideas about what they are seeing, rather than herding them into conformity—even a "Christian" conformity.

◉ Do an art project

Give one day for the start of any one of the art projects suggested, and then encourage the students to complete their art project on their own time. Depending on your resources, you may be able to offer students their choice of all of these art projects, or maybe only a few. If students find interesting art suggestions that you are not able to offer, encourage them to access the needed materials and accomplish the projects on their own for credit and for enjoyment.

Remember, some students will be naturally talented in art projects, but this is not an art class, so evaluate them based on effort rather than on the level of skill evidenced.

◉ Do a science experiment or field trip

Science is seldom seen in its historical moment of time but is instead relegated to a strict area of experimentation, vocabulary, and rules. However, if students can discover the interrelationship between science and history, each subject area will be enhanced and enriched. Science-loving students might discover that history is worth knowing and history-loving students might embrace science as a fascinating subject!

◉ Listen to and discuss the music

For students with strong intelligence in music, this exercise will help make the connection for them into history.

◉ Cook the food

For some students, smelling and tasting food related to the Unit will be the difference between boring and memorable. If you are in a classroom setting, you may

> Though it should be obvious that this small amount of scientific experimentation is not a substitute for a thorough science curriculum, it is presented for the obvious motivation that it can help students, especially the kinesthetic learners, enjoy their history studies more and possibly spark a greater understanding. In other words, it's worth doing!

either bring in a sample of the food for the students to taste, or encourage them to make it at home. For students in a homeschool setting, be sure to take the time to make the recipe (or something similar). Make it part of the celebration of what has been learned thus far!

◉ Conduct a review and evaluation

You may wish to evaluate your students based on their class participation in these hands-on activities. For further ideas on assessment and evaluation, please see page xxii.

Phase Four: The Expression Week

 Students may want to select their expression early in Phase One, in order to have adequate time to prepare their presentations.

◉ Choose an area of expression

·This week is the culmination of the Unit. Allow students the freedom to choose which area(s) they prefer to use as the expression of what they have learned. It may be that one selection will take a student the entire week to accomplish. On the other hand, a student might appreciate the opportunity to do several selections during the week. Students may work together in teams or individually—though this decision should be made at the beginning of the week for those wanting to do a selection from the drama or movement areas.

Linguistics

There are many possibilities of creative expression within the linguistics area. Some students who are intimidated by writing a paper might find delight in being able to express what they have learned in this phase through humor. Others will delight in the opportunity to write a first person narrative, or a children's book. Remember that this is *creative expression*, so be careful to not quench their exploration of creativity.

Art

Students who are attracted to painting, drawing, sculpting, graphic design, illustrating or cartooning will have the opportunity to share their enjoyment of art AND their insights into the history topics studied. This might provide spatially intelligent students the rare experience of successfully expressing what they have learned, since, traditionally, students are required to share what they know solely through linguistics. Provide a warm, welcoming atmosphere for these artistic students!

Music

To have the opportunity to use music to express what has been learned in history is another unusual form in traditional settings. However, if musically intelligent students can be released to share their knowledge of history through their instruments, it might motivate many other students to actually "dig deeper!" Be sure they take adequate time for practice, so that the performance is as polished as possible.

Drama

Encourage any students who wish to use drama as their means of expression to use the "Prop needs/Costume ideas/Role-player/Set suggestions" worksheet in their Student Manual to adequately prepare for their presentation. Although it is cute for five-year-olds to put on an "instant play" for guests, it is not appropriate for upper elementary through high school students. If students are planning to do solo presentations, encourage them to work carefully on writing their lines and memorizing them. If a team of students is going to work together, have them write out their lines and memorize them. Be sure to give adequate time for practice!

Movement

For students who are strong in the Bodily-Kinesthetic intelligence, this area will prove to be a tremendous blessing in allowing them to express what they have learned in the way they were designed. Encourage students to work in a team if they are going to do the Action selection. Again, it is not worthy of a student's effort to do an unrehearsed, poorly planned presentation. Remind the students to practice until the movements communicate effectively, and until the students have memorized the actions.

Conceptual Design

Some students will excel if given a chance to create something that has never been seen before. Encourage these students to reflect on what they are creating, and to work on it until it is of very high quality.

Create Your Own Expression

There may be some other avenue of expression which your student will decide best expresses what has been learned. Have students submit their ideas to you to ascertain the appropriateness and difficulty level. Encourage them to reach a high standard in their creative expression!

◉ Share creative expressions in class

Create a safe environment for the presentations. Set ground rules prior to the presentations for all the students, so that they know each one will be honored and respected in their work by all those observing.

Remember that timing is everything! Do NOT criticize students immediately after their presentation, unless, of course, you desire that they would never again make the attempt to share their endeavors, except in a safe, boring, mediocre way. If there is a criticism to be given, wait until a later moment to give it, as the moment of sharing is a tremendously vulnerable time, and we have the power to crush our students if we do not honor the value of what they have labored to accomplish.

Remember the Rule of Sandwich:

1. Begin with appreciation and honor

2. Kindly give any pertinent critique

3. Finish with appreciation and honor

◉ Conduct a review and evaluation

You may wish to evaluate your students based on their effort in the Creative Expressions, either as individuals or in teams. For further ideas on assessment and evaluation, please see page xxii.

Traditional Weekly Schedule for Each Unit

Teachers can choose to have students do one or two activities, rather than the entire week's schedule. Please use what works for you in your unique setting.

	Week 1: Feeler	Week 2: Thinker	Week 3: Sensor	Week 4: Intuitor
	Students will be introduced to the time period and to the Scriptures relating to the Unit.	Students will explore topics of interest through research and reporting, learn new vocabulary, and construct a time line relating to the Unit.	Students will gain cultural understanding through sensory activities as they explore interrelated subject areas pertaining to the Unit.	Students, through creative self-expression, using one or more creative activities, will present some aspect of what they have learned in the past three weeks. Areas of expression include linguistics, art, music, drama, movement, and conceptual design.
Monday	Informally discuss the Key Concepts Listen to the *What in the World?* audio recording(s)	Choose topic and begin research	Create a map and discuss the issues in teams	Choose an area of expression and begin work either individually or in teams
Tuesday	Read the article Listen to the other audio recording(s) Read the Scriptures		Examine and discuss art masterpieces & architectural structures	
Wednesday	Recap the material with an activity Talk together	Construct the time line	Do an art project*	
Thursday	Conduct class discussion	Practice vocabulary	Do a science project or field trip**	
Friday	Choose books of interest/Internet search Conduct a review and evaluation	Complete research projects and share in class or hand in Conduct a review and evaluation	Listen to and discuss the music Cook the food listed in the recipe, if desired Conduct a review and evaluation	Share creative expressions in class Conduct a review and evaluation

*Art project will need to be planned ahead of time to acquire materials.

** Field trip will require extra planning time.

Charlotte Mason Method Schedule

Catherine Levison has been homeschooling with the Charlotte Mason Method since the 1990s. She has a wealth of information about the Charlotte Mason philosophy, and possesses a talent for helping homeschoolers apply CM methods in practical ways. She has written several books on Charlotte Mason, including *A Charlotte Mason Education*, *More Charlotte Mason Education*, and *A Literary Education*. Catherine was kind enough to review *History Revealed*, and offers the following for those who use a CM approach in their homeschool education:

> Charlotte Mason parents will immediately see compatibility between the teaching approach of *History Revealed* and many of the elements with which they are already familiar.

> There are two elements to education: "how" to teach and "what" to cover. *History Revealed* does the work for you and gives you everything you'll need in the way of "what" to study and even provides much of the information. Both the Charlotte Mason method and Diana Waring's approach incorporate chronological order, original eyewitness accounts, art, field trips, plays and costume-making, student illustrations, time lines, map work, and the always-important springboard to literary books. Both approaches use hands-on learning, avoid boredom, and make history come alive.

See Catherine Levison's suggested Charlotte Mason Method Schedule at the online resource page (www.HistoryRevealed.org) to see how to easily incorporate the Charlotte Mason method with *History Revealed*.

University Approach Schedule

For some families, a University approach to scheduling might prove helpful. Universities often have more of a block schedule, which allows more in-depth exploration than the typical high school schedule. An example for how you might structure your week in this way can be found at the online resource page (www.History Revealed.org).

Other Scheduling Suggestions

Semester Schedule

For teachers confined to one semester for this course, we suggest that you complete for each Unit the Introductory Phase plus either the Exploration & Discovery Phase or the Hands-On Phase. This would allow you to finish *World Empires, World Missions, World Wars* in 18 weeks.

Alternatively, you could choose to use only one or two activities per Phase, accomplish two Phases per week, complete an entire Unit in two weeks, and the entire course in 18 weeks.

*For Homeschooling Parents:

If you are going to go through each of the four Phases in every Unit, we suggest that you consider doing Math, Language Arts, etc., in the mornings prior to starting *World Empires, World Missions, World Wars*. This will allow your children the freedom to dig into the material to their hearts' content, without concern for wrecking the schedule by following interesting rabbit trails. (We discovered, in conversation with a math teacher, that it is not only possible but beneficial to do mathematics on Monday, Wednesday, Friday, which leaves Tuesday and Thursday for language arts. This schedule worked well for our family, and our university-aged children have thrived in both areas, as well as in history!)

Evaluation & Assessment

"I have often asked a teacher what it means if their student receives 13 out of 20—what was missing? What would a 14-out-of-20 assignment look like? Where is the assessment key the student worked from? It has horrified me that so many teachers have no idea what an assessment key is, and are marking a student's assignment more on the basis of how recently they had a good meal and a cup of coffee, than on the basis of an unchangeable set of criteria.

"This is an issue of justice we need to address. Many of our students have come from educational systems that are unjust. We must be different, and providing students with a clear set of expectations is a demonstration of justice. As students mature, the guidelines can become more headlines than details, leaving room for personal interpretation and expression that a student can be expected to defend.

"Much of a poor assessment practice can be attributed to the fact that the teacher often doesn't really know what he wants as he sets the assignment and can fall into the trap of letting the most interesting or visually attractive answer set the standard. This is completely unjust to everyone else. Everyone needs to know and be able to reach the unchanging target."

From *Thinking Well* by Rosalie A. Pedder

For Classroom Teachers

Proverbs 20:10 says, *"Diverse weights and diverse measures, they are both alike, an abomination to the Lord."* What does that mean to us as we consider the serious issue of evaluating and assessing what students have learned in this course? With a nontraditional curriculum like this, which allows students a wide range of choice and creative expression, in what is traditionally such a staid subject, what activities are available to teachers for assessing measurable growth and for evaluating a student's work for a grade? Combining the obligation of providing an evaluation that is not "diverse weights and diverse measures" with the reality that God has designed students as unique learners who do not display their knowledge in exactly the same ways, how do we find a system that is both just and manageable?

I have asked Dr. Julia Harper, a professor of education at Azusa Pacific University—and the mentor of Rosalie Pedder, my own mentor—to share what she has learned about evaluation and assessment through her many years of teaching in the classroom, as well as her doctoal studies and graduate level instruction. Her wisdom in this area is experienced, practical, and eminently usable. Please take time to read her excellent thoughts and ideas on the online resource page.

For Homeschool Parents

We have found, in our twenty-plus years of homeschooling, that evaluations can and should be informal rather than formal. Tutors do not need the same type of testing procedures for one or two students as teachers need for thirty students. One on one interaction will speak volumes regarding what has been learned (and what has NOT been learned). I discovered this when I studied French with a tutor during my university years: Sister Consuelo knew immediately if I had not prepared for my lesson, as there was no one to hide behind!

As you provide the enthusiastic audience for what your children are learning, what they are reading, what they are thinking, what they are creatively sharing, you will readily discover what they have learned in this course. As you watch them interact with new ideas, grapple with their own questions, use higher level thinking skills to apply what has been learned to a creative expression, you will have a firm grasp of their measurable growth in this subject.

Assigning grades to our own children can be a daunting task. My husband and I looked for mastery of content in conversations and reporting projects, for effort as they worked on maps and art projects, for participation in discussions like the ones around the dinner table, and for the level of creativity they exhibited in their final projects. Because this course was, in general, so much fun for my children, they dug deeply into the areas that interested them and devoured the information. So we gave them *As* on their high school transcripts for the subjects covered in this course. Our children then demonstrated their competence in history as they went on to study politics, international relations, New Testament history, and more at university. And, the retention continues—it amazes me to listen to them today discuss issues they learned many years ago during these studies. When we enjoy what we are learning, we remember far more far longer.

Worldviews in the Study of History

Our Approach to History

While attending a secular university, I took some anthropology courses. Anthropology is the scientific study of mankind, especially its origins, development, customs, and beliefs. At the very introduction to General Anthropology, I was alarmed and put on guard because it was announced that Christian missionaries were always destructive to the cultures they went to convert; that by changing the primitive peoples' belief systems and destroying their uniqueness with a western religion, the missionaries had ruined them. In sharp contrast, the anthropologists were engaged in the "scientific" study of these people groups and wouldn't think of changing anything about them (much like a "nature" photographer will take pictures of predators killing a baby elephant without doing anything to help preserve the life of the baby.)

One particular people group that we studied extensively in this class made a deep and lasting impression on me. They were the Dani of Irian Jaya (Papau New Guinea shares the same South Pacific island). The anthropologists studying the Dani had filmed them during the time that a small argument between a few escalated into a violent battle with many men killed. Throughout the film and the documents prepared on the Dani, we were "treated" to a look at a "Stone Age" tribe that was brutal, violent, aggressive, and dominated by a religion of evil spirits. This "scientific study" of the Dani left me with a sense of darkness and hopelessness because of the despair and depravity in this people group.

Twenty years later I picked up the book *Torches of Joy* by John Dekker (YWAM Publishing). Can you imagine the astonishment and delight when I discovered that this book was about a Christian missionary family that devoted themselves to the Dani people?! It described a complete, miraculous turnaround for these precious "Stone Age" people. The Dani burned their fetishes, forsook tribal warfare, and began to walk in the joy and freedom of their deliverer, Jesus Christ. The missionaries taught them basic medical knowledge, hygiene, nutrition; built fish ponds and imported fish so the Dani could increase the protein in their meager diets; helped set up trade stores, which the Dani owned and oper-

ated; taught them how to read, so they could read the Bible in the newly written form of their oral language; discipled them in biblical principles so the Dani men began to truly love their wives (rather than treating them as slaves), as well as loving their neighbors as themselves; appointed native leadership for the young church, which resulted in Dani missionaries actually going out to other tribal peoples in Irian Jaya!

The difference between these two approaches, between the "scientific study" of a "Stone Age" tribe by the anthropologists, and the compassionate, life-giving ministry of the Christian missionaries, is the difference between darkness and light; the difference between secular humanism and biblical Christianity; it reveals how godless man looks at cultures and how God looks at people. Seeing with God's heart will prevent bigotry and hate, replacing it with outreach and compassion.

As we study Church history and the modern age together, please remember this illustration because it will be the difference between

- learning merely the facts and figures of a people group,

  OR

- seeing fully the loving heart of God toward those people.

The first will give head knowledge of important data that may impress our audience and make us think that we really know a lot. However, the second will give heart understanding of God's involvement in human history, so that we might be effective ministers in obedience to the Lord of all.

As we learn the details of history, of civilizations, of kingdoms and empires, scientific discoveries, explorations, missions, and more, we will begin to see God's fingerprint on the lives of people and cultures. History will become a window of adventure as we observe His faithfulness and provision for those who seek Him, His timing in raising up one nation and bringing down another, His perfect ability to work through imperfect people, and His wonderful plan revealed in Jesus—to bring us to Himself—all of which is revealed in the Bible.

Teachers As Followers of the Lord

My journey in teaching history has taught me far more than the date Julius Caesar was assassinated. As the Lord has taken me on an amazing adventure of discovery, I have encountered the most unexpected sources in the most unusual places:

- While visiting the British Museum, I noticed a small untitled sculpture. On my return to the U.S., during a Bible study on Abraham, Genesis 22:13 stood out: "Then Abraham lifted his eyes and looked, and there behind him was a ram caught in a thicket by its horns." My thoughts exploded as the small sculpture in London jumped back into my memory. Though unmarked in the exhibit, it was titled by the archaeologist who discovered it in a burial pit of ancient Ur, "The Ram Caught In The Thicket." Realizing that God might have placed a prophetic witness of His provision for Abraham in the pagan culture of Ur, I rushed home to research the dating of the sculpture, to see if Abraham had lived prior to its creation. Amazingly, it was dated at least 200 years before Abraham walked the earth!

- At a small country museum in Maine, a book title grabbed my attention: *Nineveh and Its Remains* by Austen Layard. I had only a brief glance to see if it was useful in my studies. Opening the book at random, I began to read the author's description of how nineteenth century intellectuals had discounted the truth of Scripture, in part because of its description of the ancient Assyrians—who were totally unknown through any other source. With Layard's discovery and excavation of Nineveh, the Bible stories leaped squarely onto the pages of history AND shut the mouths of the critics! This opened my eyes to the amazing place Assyria has held in both world history and biblical apologetics.

Through these experiences, as well as many others, my eyes were opened to the fact that, though I was limited in my knowledge, God was actively leading me to keys of understanding—all I needed to do was follow Him. What an amazing discovery! He wants to lead us—you as much as me—to teach us, show us, and open doors of knowledge for us. If we ask, we will receive. If we seek, we will find. If we knock, the door will be opened.

You see, I find that God did not relegate the subject of education to a closed academic system (which would be similar to the evolutionists' view that we live in a "closed system"—one without God). Learning was intended by God to be revelational—because He, the source of all wisdom and knowledge, is intently involved in it:

> "However, when He, the Spirit of truth, has come, He will guide you into all truth . . ." John 16:13

As dearly beloved followers of Jesus Christ, we who are teachers need to understand this: the essential truth at the very foundation of education is that God is the True Teacher, the Master Teacher, the Actively-Changing-Lives Teacher. To teach as a "student teacher" under His authority and His leading will transform our hearts and attitudes; it will dramatically affect our students' experience, and, in the final analysis, it will reflect the heart of God.

Instead of a mere dispenser of facts, requiring our students to regurgitate the same facts back to us, we can teach with anticipation and a sense of wonder, expecting God to show us new insights, new connections, and new understandings we never had before. We can enthusiastically and humbly share with our students what and how God has taught us, eagerly encouraging them to watch for His involvement in their own lives.

Practically, here are some points we need to consider as we follow God in teaching:

#1 Education that conforms to God's ways will first of all be relational, because He has called us to be His children (a profoundly intimate relationship with our Father), and He has set us in one Body (a necessarily cooperative, healthy, and interdependent relationship with each other).

We learn about all subjects in relationship to Him. We see all fields of knowledge (biology, mathematics, physics, music, literature, history, architecture, etc.) as having their beginnings in God:

- He created all things (the sciences);

- He set order into the universe (mathematics);

- He created ears to hear the sounds of birds singing, leaves rustling, water swishing, AND He created voices for singing (music);

- He spoke the universe into existence AND gave us His Word (literature);

- He created man in His own image and likeness (the start of our history);

- He designed the world (architecture);

- . . . and on and on and on.

We teach our students relationally, not as mechanical computers intent solely on transmitting facts—with no heart, no artistry, no intuition, no comprehension of others, no lively debates, no symbiotic learning, no creativity, no opportunity to defend oneself—but as brothers and sisters in the Body of Christ:

- We honor them

- We allow individuality to them
- We listen to them
- We ask them
- We learn from them
- We respect them
- We humble ourselves before them
- . . . and on and on and on

#2 Education that conforms to God's ways will also be revelational because God actively leads us and guides us into all truth. We facilitate the students' learning, but He is the One who can communicate and bring illumination to the students in ways that will change their lives. God's revelation as the foundation of Christian education is dramatically opposed to the common system of education, which looks no higher than human reason, and sets teachers as the authoritative experts in charge of distributing knowledge. This has its foundation in the Greco-Roman worldview:

> "The ancient Greeks believed that humans could, by using their ability to think rationally, discover and understand the fundamental order of the universe and everything in it. They developed the belief that humans could equal (and even exceed) the gods in understanding." Dr. Perry Seymour, astrophysicist

In other words, the ancient Greeks (and later, the Romans) depended solely on human reasoning rather than on God's revelation. This viewpoint is diametrically opposed by Scripture:

> "For Jews request a sign, and Greeks seek after wisdom; but we preach Christ crucified, to the Jews a stumbling block and to the Greeks foolishness, but to those who are called, both Jews and Greeks, Christ the power of God and the wisdom of God." 1 Corinthians 1:22–24

The Greeks enthroned human reason, educating and indoctrinating their students in this point of view. As Christians, we must choose a different path.

> "Beware lest anyone cheat you through philosophy [such as, ancient Greek philosophy] and empty deceit, according to the tradition of men, according to the basic principles of the world, and not according to Christ." Colossians 2:8

We must enthrone Jesus Christ—the power of God and the wisdom of God—educating and discipling children in a biblical worldview. We can open doors for the students into their own personal adventure of discovery with the Lord. We can be their enthusiastic audience and wise advisors, encouraging them to learn in light of God's active and intimate revelation.

Teachers who follow the Lord, who teach under His Lordship, need to consider that biblical education:

- is both relational and revelational;
- leads us beyond mental comprehension to life application;
- has its beginning and ending in the character and nature of God;
- finds its true test, not in a graded essay question, but in a life lived in obedience—a life well-lived.

> "Happy is the man who finds wisdom,
> And the man who gains understanding;
> For her proceeds are better than the profits of silver,
> And her gain than fine gold.
> She is more precious than rubies,
> And all the things you may desire cannot compare with her.
> Length of days is in her right hand,
> In her left hand riches and honor.
> Her ways are ways of pleasantness,
> And all her paths are peace.
> She is a tree of life to those who take hold of her,
> And happy are all who retain her."
> Proverbs 3:13–18

Napoleon & Early Missions
(1790–1815)

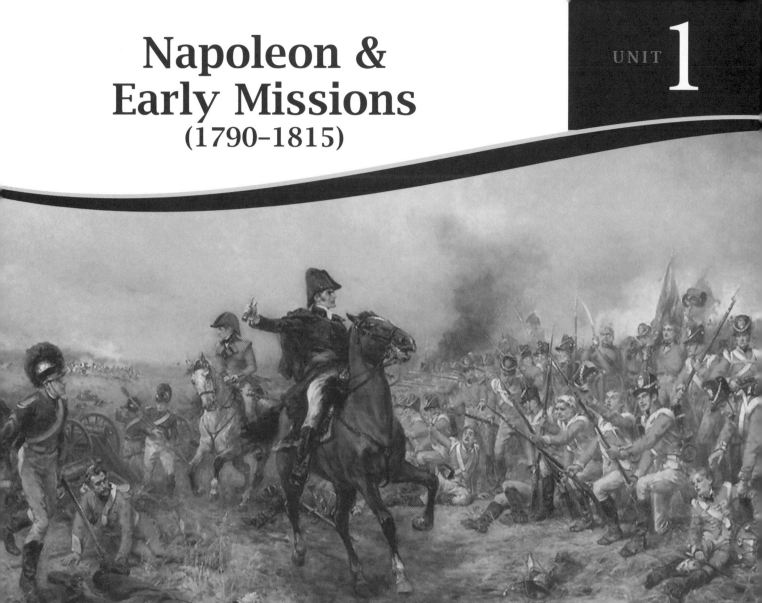

Pray with the students at the beginning of each Unit.

Enthusiasm and delight are the best ways to capture a student's interest and jump-start motivation, so:

» **For the Auditory Students:** To capture their attention at the very beginning of class, consider playing a recording of "La Marseillaise," the French National Anthem. (A link to a YouTube video of this recording—with French and English subtitles—can be found at the online resource page.)

» **For the Kinesthetic Students:** Have the students play "follow the leader" as one volunteer takes them through physical actions to represent traveling from England to India at the end of the 1700s (a sea voyage and then an astonishingly different culture at journey's end).

» **For the Visual Students:** Play a trailer from the movie *Amazing Grace*, the story of William Wilberforce. (A link can be found at the online resource page.)

» **For the hearts of all:** Pray with them at the beginning of the Unit, that God would help them discover what He has for each one to learn in this Unit.

◉ Learning Style Emphasis

Teachers can choose to have students do one or two activities, rather than the entire week's schedule. Please use what works for you in your unique setting.

	Week 1: Feeler	Week 2: Thinker	Week 3: Sensor	Week 4: Intuitor
	During this week, students will be introduced to Napoleon & Early Missions, and start reading through the book of Acts. You may follow this suggested schedule or adapt it to meet your students' needs:	Students will explore topics of interest through research and reporting, learn new vocabulary, and construct a time line relating to Napoleon & Early Missions. They should continue reading the book of Acts.	Students will gain cultural understanding through sensory activities as they explore interrelated subject areas through sensory activities pertaining to Napoleon & Early Missions. They should continue reading the book of Acts.	Through creative self-expression, using one or more creative activities, students will present some aspect of what they have learned in the past three weeks relating to Napoleon & Early Missions. Areas of expression include linguistics, art, music, drama, movement, and conceptual design. They should finish reading the book of Acts.
Monday	Informally discuss the Key Concepts Listen to the *What in the World?* audio recording(s)	Choose topic and begin research	Create a map and discuss the issues in teams	Choose an area of expression and begin work either individually or in teams
Tuesday	Read the article Listen to the other audio recording(s)		Examine and discuss art masterpieces & architectural structures	
Wednesday	Recap the material using activities Talk together	Practice vocabulary	Do an art project*	
Thursday	Conduct class discussion	Construct the time line	Do a science project or field trip**	
Friday	Choose books of interest/Internet search Conduct a review and evaluation	Complete research projects and share in class or hand in Conduct a review and evaluation	Listen to and discuss the music Cook the food listed in the recipe Conduct a review and evaluation	Share creative expressions in class Conduct a review and evaluation

*Art project will need to be planned ahead of time to acquire materials.

** Field trip will require extra planning time.

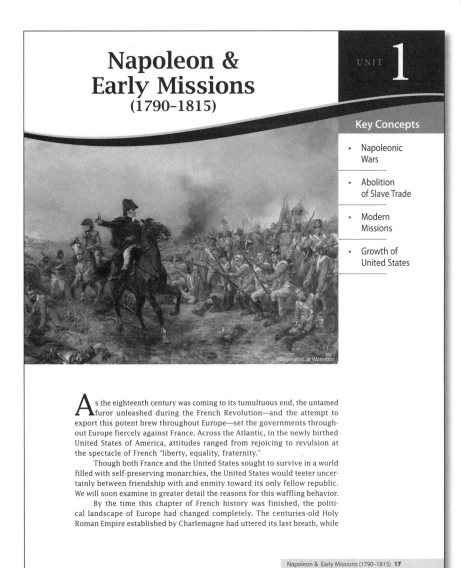

Napoleon & Early Missions (1790–1815)

Key Concepts

- Napoleonic Wars
- Abolition of Slave Trade
- Modern Missions
- Growth of United States

Wellington at Waterloo

As the eighteenth century was coming to its tumultuous end, the untamed furor unleashed during the French Revolution—and the attempt to export this potent brew throughout Europe—set the governments throughout Europe fiercely against France. Across the Atlantic, in the newly birthed United States of America, attitudes ranged from rejoicing to revulsion at the spectacle of French "liberty, equality, fraternity."

Though both France and the United States sought to survive in a world filled with self-preserving monarchies, the United States would teeter uncertainly between friendship with and enmity toward its only fellow republic. We will soon examine in greater detail the reasons for this waffling behavior.

By the time this chapter of French history was finished, the political landscape of Europe had changed completely. The centuries-old Holy Roman Empire established by Charlemagne had uttered its last breath, while

Napoleon & Early Missions (1790–1815) **17**

◉ Informally discuss the Key Concepts with your students

KEY CONCEPTS Background Information

These are the main objectives of the Unit. As you proceed through the four weeks, your students will be given various ways of understanding each of these objectives. Explanations of these Key Concepts follow.

England had become the unequivocal master of the seas, its own empire stretching and growing around the globe. France's expanding empire had acquired the continent of Europe, then shriveled again at Napoleon's defeat, while across the Atlantic that tiny sliver of coastline known as the United States had skyrocketed in size, wealth, and power. This growth was an unexpected feat, accomplished partly through one of the best land deals ever made—if one ignores the illegality—and partly through those special merchandising "goldmines" only available during wartime, like shipping supplies to combatants on both sides. This was not a carefree existence, however. By the time the Napoleonic Wars (1792–1815) had run their full course, the embryonic United States had faced dangerous entanglements with the great powers of Europe in the Quasi-War with France and the full-fledged War of 1812 with Great Britain.

The United States had skyrocketed in size, wealth, and power.

Snippets of the Big Picture

To properly set the stage for this unfolding drama, let us take a brief look at some of the developing political issues of the early 1790s across the map.

- France, embroiled in its own revolution and staggering under the instability it produced, had succumbed to the violence of mob rule. One of their most prolific and influential authors, Marat, said, "We must establish the despotism of liberty to crush the despotism of kings." (Despotism is defined as a government exercising absolute power, especially in a cruel and oppressive way.)
- England's youthful prime minister was eager for peace. He needed it in order to rebuild the economy, which was shattered after years of war with the rebellious American colonies. However, he was dragged into the continental struggle of Europe when revolutionary France declared war on England in 1793.
- The United States was bitterly divided, not only between those who favored France and those who opposed her, but also between two political theories, Federalist and Republican. The Federalists sought a strong, central government, preferring the British Parliament model rather than the French mob rule. The Republicans, on the other hand, sought freedom of the individual and states' rights, and supported the underlying causes of the French Revolution.
- In India, the British East India Company was gaining such notoriety for its freewheeling practices that Parliament found it necessary, after more than one hundred fifty years of the company's operation, to step in and begin exerting government control. However, the policy that prohibited Christian missionaries from entering East India Company

? To get an informal discussion started on this Key Concept, ask a simple leading question, such as, "Can you name some of the events that took place during and as a result of the Napoleonic Wars?"

Napoleonic Wars— EXPLANATION

The Napoleonic Wars were born out of the French Revolution, as Napoleon advanced through the military ranks during the tumult of the decade-long upheaval to the highest position in France. They were a continuation—and yet, in another sense, an utter reversal—of the French Revolution. Napoleon waged war against the rest of the world under the tricolor flag of revolutionary France, but without the liberty, fraternity, or equality it promised.

If you picture a juggler trying to keep a dozen balls in the air, you have a good idea of the internal and external dynamic of the Napoleonic Wars as Napoleon exerted tremendous effort to keep several different spheres under his control at the same time:

- Dealing with his foreign enemies
- Restructuring his nation
- Making himself emperor
- Controlling the continent

First and foremost was his unrelenting focus upon his perceived enemies, especially Great Britain. He was plagued because their navy seemed unbeatable and their island nation impenetrable. As Napoleon successfully waged war across the European continent, he was constantly aware of the danger posed by what he called "that island of shopkeepers." At the same time, Napoleon was seeking to bring all of the other European countries under his power. When they made alliances and amassed vast armies against him, he quickly swung his nearly invincible armies around and crushed them. With his brilliant military strategies and the decisiveness with which he moved his armies, he trounced them all, time after time. One of the most noteworthy results, and perhaps the most unintended consequence of Napoleon's victories, was the fierce resolve of the Prussians to never suffer defeat again. That laid

1

lands was still in place. The merchants feared that the preaching of the gospel might destabilize the status quo and interfere with the profit of their lucrative trade.

- The horrendous trade of African slavery continued, supplying the slave workforce to the Caribbean and the Americas, though abolitionist movements in France and England had recently begun. There was a brief moment of hope when slaves in Haiti rose up to establish a nation of their own.
- On the northern coast of Africa, the Barbary States of Morocco, Tunis, Algiers, and Tripoli, subjects of the Ottomans in theory, found great profit in acts of piracy on the Mediterranean and the North Atlantic. Their piracy was restrained only when formidable nations brought overwhelming firepower or when the wealthy paid exorbitant bribes.
- Russia, during the reign of Catherine the Great, increased both its size and its control—annexing the former Ottoman territories (giving Russia a toehold on the Black Sea in the Crimea) and binding the Russian serfs more firmly to the land.
- Recent victories over the Ottoman Empire had given Russia authority over Orthodox people living under Ottoman domination. Though this centuries-old Muslim empire was continuing to decline in power, the statesmen of Europe were less aware of that fact than the Russians were, and continued to tread warily when it came to the East.
- Under Qianlong, the long-lived Qing Dynasty emperor, China grew to its widest extent, receiving tribute from Nepal, Burma (Myanmar), and Annam (Vietnam). Unlike in Japan, where Christianity was utterly forbidden, in China, Roman Catholic missionaries were tolerated and even employed as astronomers and artists.
- Australia, recently brought to European attention by Captain Cook, was viewed by the British government as the new ideal spot to transport convicts, since England's prisons were full to overflowing and the former American colonies were no longer available to them.

In China, Roman Catholic missionaries were tolerated and even employed.

1793—The Year of Two Opposite Men

As the governments in Europe and America focused more and more narrowly on their own momentous struggles, God expanded more and more greatly one man's vision for the countless people of the world. William Carey, an English shoemaker-turned-preacher, was increasingly convinced that the task of sharing the gospel throughout the world remained God's intention for believers. This startling concept was in stark contrast to the widespread belief that the Great Commission had ended with the apostles. Carey's avid

the foundation for the great German military machine that would eventually crush France and, in the 1900s, bring the whole world to war.

That was still in the misty future, however. In the year 1802, France and England agreed to lay down their arms. With the long-awaited peace announced, Napoleon began juggling the national needs for economic stability, for an overhaul of the nation's legal code, for architectural monuments suited to the prestige of his nation, and even restyling himself as emperor and rebranding the nation as an empire with a new hereditary family (Napoleon's, of course). Much to the chagrin of the European community, they learned less than two years later that all of this activity was just a momentary intermission between acts of war.

Because of Napoleon's continuing enmity toward England, he built a flotilla of ships to carry his war to England's shores. Defeated by the unceasing labors of the British navy and his own ignorance of naval tactics, Napoleon had to cancel the invasion and turn his focus once again to the concrete actions of his army. This change, coupled with a lack of seagoing wisdom, led to the annihilation of the French fleet at the hands of Admiral Nelson in the Battle of Trafalgar in 1805.

Napoleon, stung by his oceangoing defeat, devised another plan to render Great Britain weak and ineffective. Knowing that England depended heavily on trade for its goods and economy, he proposed the Continental System, which was a trade blockade to keep England's goods out of the continent of Europe. Though this system was not successful, Napoleon continued to try to support it, rushing his armies here and there to plug the leaks, especially in Portugal and Spain.

When Russia refused to comply with the Continental System, Napoleon attacked with half a million soldiers, during what is known as the War of

1

William Carey

study of geography, cultures, and languages fueled his growing urgency to motivate Christians to go— to actually travel to all the world and tell the Good News. The powerful message of his book, *An Enquiry into the Obligations of Christians to Use Means for the Conversion of the Heathens*, and his persuasive preaching on this subject resulted in the formation in 1792 of the Baptist Missionary Society, the first of its kind.

In the following year, Carey displayed the depth of his commitment to God's heart for those who had never heard the gospel—he and his family sailed from the relative security of England to the utterly foreign land of India. The Careys, after living for several years inland, eventually settled with other missionaries in the Danish colony of Serampore, near British East India Company land. A short time later, Carey was hired by the governor-general of the British East India Company as the new Professor of Oriental Languages at Fort William College in Calcutta because of his acknowledged expertise in Indian languages. This was truly an extraordinary appointment, given that Carey had never attended college (his formal education ended at age fourteen). Even beyond his lack of academic background, though, it is astonishing to consider that the East India Company had explicitly prohibited missionaries from coming to India. Yet God's plan to extend the influence of this man's work overruled these earthly difficulties.

By the time of his death in 1834, William Carey had translated the entire Bible into Bengali, Sanskrit, and Marathi. Together with the mission workers at Serampore, he founded 26 churches and 126 schools, including Serampore College, which trained native leaders for ministry. Though his never-ceasing purpose was to see the light of the gospel illuminate and transform lives, yet he also held a deep appreciation for the Indian people, their culture, and their literature. These were the motivations for his careful effort to eradicate the murderous practices of sati (widow burning) and infanticide while leaving the rest of the culture intact. His life is a study in the astonishing ways people inspired by God's heart can leave a legacy of goodness.

During the same year another man embarked on a career which would also deeply affect nations, though for markedly different reasons. This man, who would cause the nations of Europe to tremble, was Napoleon Bonaparte. Born to Corsican patriots, Napoleon demonstrated early on that

> *By the time of his death in 1834, William Carey had translated the entire Bible into Bengali, Sanskrit, and Marathi.*

1812. In the same year, Great Britain and its Canadian colony went to war with the United States largely over issues that had arisen from the Napoleonic Wars, with the most highly-charged issue being the impressment of US citizens into the British navy. Napoleon lost his Russian war to the bitterly cold "General Winter," while the United States/Canada/Great Britain war was settled diplomatically after a series of inconclusive battles on land and sea.

Meanwhile, the British army was waging an increasingly successful war against the French in the Peninsular War (on the Iberian Peninsula where Portugal and Spain are located). Though the British had landed first in Portugal, the Duke of Wellington determinedly took his troops beyond that land and into Spain. The news of the defeat in Russia gave heart to those who opposed Napoleon, and Wellington's successes greatly contributed to diminishing the legend of Napoleon's invincibility.

In 1814, the European and British armies finally brought Napoleon to a standstill. He fled to Paris, where he abdicated his throne in exchange for the small island kingdom of Elba. As the allies breathed a huge sigh of relief, Napoleon began to consider the possibilities of staging a comeback. In one of the most remarkable scenes of history, Napoleon clandestinely left Elba and returned to France. The people of France, heartily sick of their new Bourbon king, welcomed their former emperor with great enthusiasm. That enthusiasm undoubtedly waned when Napoleon took their remaining men and boys to fight his final battle.

The allies were stunned to learn that Napoleon was loose once more. They were still settling the diplomatic details of reestablishing the nations of Europe after having been forced into the Napoleonic empire. They quickly gathered their armies and marched to the inevitable war. The Battle of Waterloo was the last act of Napoleon's military show, as he tried once again to use his strategic genius to its greatest effect. It almost worked— almost, but not quite. As they say in the books, "He met his Waterloo."

1

his peculiar path to glory lay in devising tactics and commanding troops. Displaying his military genius on the battlefield, Napoleon advanced up the ladder of success to a height that would have been impossible during the old regime. The rigid rules of the aristocratic society were utterly reconstructed during the French Revolution so that the non-aristocratic standing of his family was not a barrier. Napoleon did not stoop to something so mundane as ponderously climbing the ladder in the usual way. Instead, he shot meteorically in only a few short years to the highest position in the land.

Napoleon Bonaparte

It began in 1793 when he was appointed artillery commander for the Revolutionary army during their siege of Toulon. Royalists (those who sympathized with the monarchy rather than the Revolution) had been protected by British naval ships in the harbor of this port city. Captain Napoleon's study of military tactics in old history books, along with his natural tactical genius, gave this thirty-year-old the moves of a chess master. Setting the French cannons on a strategic hill overlooking the harbor, Napoleon was able to checkmate the British naval squadron, who quickly left the constricted deathtrap for the safety of open water. With their vital support gone, the royalists were unable to adequately defend themselves. The French Revolutionary army quickly took the royalist city, resulting in not only victory for the republican government but also a brigadier generalship for Napoleon.

This was but a foretaste of the military brilliance of this leader of men. It gave him an appetite for victory, regardless of the consequences, that would not be quenched for more than two decades. His power at home and abroad increased to the point that, for a time, he was the undisputed master of the European continent. The far-from-bloodless victory in Toulon would also foreshadow the savage, total-war destruction that would follow in his wake.

Napoleon shot meteorically in only a few short years to the highest position in the land.

The Nations and Napoleon's Wars

Not everyone was checkmated by Napoleon's hunger to rule the world, however. The one nation that brought more frustration to Napoleon than any other was that unconquerable "nation of shopkeepers," the island country of Great Britain. As a devout student of the art of war, Napoleon knew that, historically, the route to conquering enemies lay on the land: mighty

To get an informal discussion started on this Key Concept, ask a simple leading question, such as, "Why do you think the British, after centuries of lucrative African slave trade, ended it in 1807?"

Abolition of Slave Trade—EXPLANATION

One must always keep in mind both the context and the personalities of a historic event. In the case of the African slave trade, the context of Great Britain's decision is somewhat startling. As we have just noted in the Key Concept above, the British were in a life and death struggle with the conqueror of Europe. As Napoleon ably noted, they were utterly dependent upon trade for their economic stability, and the African slave trade was the most lucrative of all. When one discounted the suffering and misery of the Africans (which many easily did), it was an incredibly profitable source of revenue for an extremely eager market.

As difficult as it is for us to understand today, few people in Western societies saw any problem with the slave trade. They viewed Africans as a commodity, much like sheep or cows, so it did not bother European consciences to trade in human life—as long as it was African life. Even the Great Awakening, though it influenced many areas of British society, did not permeate deep enough to make a difference in this issue. Perhaps that is not surprising, since Scripture tells us that the love of money is the root of all kinds of evil.

In God's amazing grace and timing, the root of this evil was about to be exposed. When the life of one member of the British Parliament was transformed by the gospel, the repercussions were felt throughout the halls of power and throughout the country. William Wilberforce was a man gifted by God with tremendous oratory skills, and he put those gifts to use in service that would benefit millions of the poor, needy, and oppressed.

Psalm 72 says, "For He will deliver the needy when he cries, the poor also, and him who has no helper. He will spare the poor and needy, and will save the souls of the needy. He will

1

armies squared off in battle. However, during the upheaval of this new and revolutionary age, the rules of warfare also changed. Now, more than Europe had ever before experienced, the route to disabling your opponent lay upon the oceans: mighty navies out-maneuvering each other across the horizon. On this storm-tossed field, Napoleon soon discovered that he had a lot to learn. An Englishman, Lord Horatio Nelson (Admiral of the British fleet), would supply the lessons at the upcoming battles of the Nile and Trafalgar.

As war escalated, the French and British navies sought to supply their own countries with trade goods and war supplies while capturing the other side's heavy-laden merchant ships. It was during this contest of naval strength that the United States (the "new kid on the block") found itself caught on the high seas between two implacable enemies. Since its own revolutionary victory over England had been partially due to the military assistance of France, the United States now found itself uneasily divided between loyalty to this ally and abhorrence of France's reprehensible slaughter of its own people.

The Americans had no desire to enter this foreign war and had been vigorously set on a path of neutrality by the first president of their republic, as clearly seen in his Farewell Address of 1796. However, for willing ears, money talks. Eager for the enormous profits of carrying trade goods to Europe and Europe's Caribbean colonies, American merchants plunged into the fray, styling themselves as law-abiding traders intent only on making an honest dollar. Neither France nor England saw them in this light, however. Both belligerents immediately turned in anger against the audacious nation that had dared to profit from their misfortune and to obstruct their plans against the enemy. France captured American ships with goods headed to British ports, while England interfered with American ships headed to French ports. It was an impossible and highly volatile situation for a young country with only three ships in its navy.

American merchants plunged into the fray, styling themselves as law-abiding traders intent only on making an honest dollar.

The United States managed to calm the waters and avoid war with England through the signing of the Jay Treaty of 1795. It was not quite as easy with France. Though President John Adams sought a peace treaty with France, his diplomats in the wild-west atmosphere of revolutionary Paris were told that, before negotiations could even begin, enormous bribes would have to be paid. The President's response—which utterly amazed the French—was to recall the diplomats and expose the French demands to the American Congress in what became known as the "XYZ" affair.

The response to this perceived insult to American honor was national outrage and strong support for preparing for war. The first preparation was equipping the navy for engaging enemy ships, protecting American merchant ships, and patrolling the North American coast. In May 1798, when the Navy

22 Napoleon & Early Missions (1790–1815)

redeem their life from oppression and violence; and precious shall be their blood in His sight."

It seems from Scripture that the wisest explanation for the ending of the British slave trade in 1807 is that God moved on behalf of those who were oppressed. He raised up an incredibly determined politician who persevered through enormous difficulties and failures, and who eventually rallied the conscience of an entire nation on behalf of African slaves. In a stunning reversal of previous votes of Parliament—and in the very midst of the Napoleonic Wars—the majority voted to abolish the African slave trade.

To God be the glory, great things He has done!

1

began to capture French naval ships hovering on the coast of America, the United States entered into the "Quasi-War" with France. This was a tactical cat-and-mouse game, fought largely in the Caribbean, as American naval ships engaged French naval ships and privateers (private ships authorized by their government for purposes of war). The infant US Navy showed extraordinary prowess in sea battles, which helped cause France to desire a peace treaty as much as did John Adams. The treaty was finally signed in 1800, after France's navy and army had both suffered defeat in Africa and Asia.

"Europe is but a molehill—all the great reputations have come from Asia."

Two years earlier, in the same year that France and the United States began their unofficial war in the Caribbean, the French fleet in the Mediterranean momentarily eluded the ever-vigilant British Navy and landed 40,000 soldiers in Egypt under the command of General Napoleon. Egypt may seem an unlikely spot for a European conflict, located as it is in North Africa—far from the English Channel or the Caribbean. However, to a chess player, unexpected moves may be the best way to gain one's objective. Napoleon's grand scheme was that France would imperil Britain's wealth by first seizing Egypt and from there threatening India, Britain's most lucrative colony. Venturing off to Egypt was not solely for the glory of France, however, as can be discerned from the statement Napoleon made to one of his friends: "Europe is but a molehill—all the great reputations have come from Asia." This would not prove true in his case.

Though they successfully captured Alexandria and were victorious in the Battle of the Pyramids, the French army was suddenly left high and dry when the British fleet under Admiral Nelson, who had been tirelessly hunting them, discovered the elusive French ships in Egypt's Aboukir Bay. This naval action is known as the Battle of the Nile, though it was more of a rout than a battle, as the experienced British sailors demolished the French ships. With his ships burned and his army stranded in North Africa, Napoleon nevertheless determined to wrest glory out of defeat. He marched four divisions to Syria and began a siege of the city of Acre, which was an uncharacteristically poor move since the city had both excellent strategic defenses and the assistance of the British Navy. The "unbeatable" Napoleon was unable to dislodge the defenders of Acre and had to retreat ignominiously after months of frustrated effort—though he always maintained that he had achieved victory! Shortly after returning to Cairo in 1799, Napoleon boarded a small vessel, eluded the British Navy, and sailed back to France. His reputation, though not enhanced by his African-Asian escapade, was, nonetheless, still intact.

It is always instructive to look at the ongoing effects or "fruit" of someone's actions. In the case of William Carey, many benefits continued to come to the people of India—and in fact, to many nations—from the work he had done. For Egypt, however, Napoleon's short occupation had a shattering

Modern Missions— EXPLANATION

In order to answer this question, we need to consider the results of William Carey's life and work that caused the church to change its thinking about missions. Prior to Carey, there were a few small groups of believers, such as the Moravians and the Danish-Halle Mission, who emphasized missions to the far-flung peoples of the world. But overall, the Protestant church seems to have interpreted Jesus's Great Commission as being applicable only to the apostles in the New Testament.

William Carey, whose imagination was fired by accounts of Captain Cook's travels, began not only to learn more about the world and its people but also to study the Scriptures to better understand God's intention toward these "heathen" peoples who were outside the realm of Christendom. What, for instance, was God's desire for the multitudes of Hindus in India? What did He desire His people to do to share the good news with those who had never heard it?

These types of questions began to have deep ramifications in his life. It is reported that at a meeting of church leaders, when Carey shared what he believed God was showing him from Scripture, he was rebuked by an

To get an informal discussion started on this Key Concept, ask a simple leading question, such as, "Why do you think Protestant church historians designated William Carey the "father" of a new missionary movement when there had been Protestant missionary endeavors at least since the late 1600s?"

1

effect upon the internal political structure of that country. Though Egypt had been ruled in name by the Ottomans for centuries, a powerful group of slaves called the Mamluks held the real power. When Napoleon invaded Egypt, he fought against Mamluk armies. When they were defeated, a vacuum of power was created, and from this void emerged a young Albanian military officer named Muhammad Ali—born the same year as Napoleon. Through a series of strategic moves, including the infamous massacre of the remaining Mamluk leaders in 1811, he gathered the reins of power into his own hands. He became the Ottoman viceroy (or ruler) of Egypt and is known as Muhammad Ali Pasha. He was the founder of the modern Egyptian nation, and his family continued to rule Egypt until 1952.

The Rise of Haiti

Back in the Caribbean, the status quo was giving way to what would become the first independent black state. To better understand what was involved, it is important to recognize that one of the cornerstones of the French Revolution had been the "Rights of Man," which included the statement "men are born and remain free and equal." This declaration was written in such a way that it seemed to address the rights of all. However, it is one thing to *say* everyone is free and equal. It's another thing to be moved to the point of action. When applied to African slaves in the French colonies of the Caribbean, these rights became a subject of fierce debate. While those French citizens who used slaves to work the plantations thought it absolutely necessary to uphold slavery for economic reasons, others who were striving to throw out the whole system of class, aristocracy, and privilege intended to free slaves so that these concepts of equality would move from theory into actual practice. The debate was ended in February of 1794 when the French National Convention voted to abolish slavery. Unfortunately, there was less response in the colonies than the theorists intended.

It is one thing to say everyone is free and equal. It's another thing to be moved to the point of action.

Even before the official abolishment of slavery by the French, the slaves had understood the implications of the Rights of Man for themselves. In the French colony of Saint-Domingue (Haiti), their hunger for freedom under the Rights of Man, underscored by their barbaric living conditions under the French plantation owners, led to a slave revolt in 1791. It is not surprising that, having always been on the receiving end of the savage violence inherent in slavery, the slaves used brutality and violence against the white plantation owners in this explosive struggle. The unsuccessful revolt was brutally suppressed, but the seething hatred between white and black continued. Therefore, when the abolition of slavery became law, many white slave owners fled Saint-Domingue in fear for their lives.

older minister, who said, "Sit down, young man. When God pleases to convert the heathen, He will do it without your aid or mine."

However, the idea that Scripture actually commanded believers to take the gospel to the four corners of the earth was so firmly cemented in Carey's soul that he published a booklet explaining these concepts, entitled *An Enquiry into the Obligation of Christians to Use Means for the Conversion of the Heathens*. The written word has always spoken volumes. The transformed life, which led Carey to leave England and move his family to India, spoke even louder.

Though the majority of the people of India did not embrace Christianity as a result of Carey's work, yet he had significant impact on a few individual Hindus, and his influence was subtly felt in various aspects of the culture. Beyond his specific work in India, however, William Carey's writings and work opened the floodgates of Protestant Christian missions. From that point on, multitudes of Christian missionaries would leave their homes in Europe and America and go to the ends of the earth—all for the sake of fulfilling the Great Commission.

And Jesus came and spoke to them, saying, "All authority has been given to Me in heaven and on earth. Go therefore and make disciples of all the nations, baptizing them in the name of the Father and of the Son and of the Holy Spirit, teaching them to observe all things that I have commanded you; and lo, I am with you always, even to the end of the age." Matthew 28:18–20

1

Others continued slavery but changed the terminology so they would be in compliance with France, while still others ignored the new ruling completely.

The change that the slaves had so desperately anticipated was finally set in motion in 1794 as they took matters into their own hands under the leadership of a former slave named Toussaint L'Ouverture. A brilliant military strategist, he was able to defeat his enemies and bring a measure of peace and prosperity back to the island, ruling as governor for a few short years. He established trade with Great Britain and America—no small triumph since these countries were constantly nervous that he might export something more volatile than sugar and coffee. If he exported ideas of freedom and the rights of man to the slave-holding plantations in Jamaica and the American South, they feared that revolt and uprising would follow.

The specter of slave revolt in the British colonies was frightening to English plantation owners.

Wilberforce—Carrying the Torch of Abolition

The specter of slave revolt in the British colonies was frightening to English plantation owners—and very relevant. Great Britain was in the midst of a fierce political struggle whether to abolish their lucrative slave trade, and the attack was relentlessly led by a Member of Parliament (MP) named William Wilberforce.

At the outset of his political career, Wilberforce showed himself to be one of the best orators in Parliament, using his decisive wit and linguistic abilities to verbally skewer the opposing party. He had friends in high places, including William Pitt, who became England's youngest prime minister. Wilberforce's ambition at this point was to rise along with these friends to the top level in politics. Indeed, he later wrote of his motivation during this time, "Distinction was my darling object." However, *distinction* was not what a politician would receive if he dared to take on the powerful and well-funded slave traders.

You might ask, "What happened to change this man's heart so dramatically that, rather than pursuing a self-centered desire

William Wilberforce

Growth of United States—EXPLANATION

For those alive in the twenty-first century, it may be inconceivable to consider just how frail and tenuous the United States was at the beginning of its history as a nation. But, as evidenced in the writings of European diplomats, many fully expected this experiment in civil liberty to quickly fail and were somewhat amazed when it survived.

During the American Revolution, representatives of the thirteen colonies-become-states came together to establish a governing agreement. They created a system that gave sovereign rights to each state while allowing a measure of authority to a "confederated" government, which would address issues for all the states. These "Articles of Confederation" included the right to negotiate diplomatic agreements such as treaties, the prerogative to make war when necessary, and the ability to resolve issues arising over the newer western territories that were not part of the original thirteen colonies.

Within two years of the end of the American Revolution, the American people were suffering tremendous economic hardship due to high taxes, bankruptcies, farm foreclosures, and a shortage of hard currency. A revolt

> **?** To get an informal discussion started on this Key Concept, ask a simple leading question, such as, "What do you think the first few decades were like for the new nation known as the United States of America?"

1

for personal glory, he devoted himself to the poor, needy, and oppressed?" In the case of William Wilberforce, it was a road trip. After successfully winning his election in Yorkshire (giving him one of the most powerful positions in Parliament), Wilberforce decided to celebrate by taking a leisurely tour of Europe. To his chagrin, the man he had invited to accompany him turned out to be a thoroughgoing follower of Jesus Christ. Throughout their travels, these two men discussed, argued, and considered the claims of Christianity. By the time the trip was finished, William Wilberforce was convinced that it was all true. What remained was to surrender himself entirely to God, which he assumed would mean becoming a minister in the church. Just like many in our day, many people in Wilberforce's day equated "really serving God" with "full-time ministry." Fortunately, a wise pastor that Wilberforce had known as a boy set him straight. John Newton, writer of the hymn "Amazing Grace," helped Wilberforce to see that one could serve God as fully in the political arena as in the church.

John Newton helped Wilberforce to see that one could serve God as fully in the political arena as in the church.

It was with this heart of service that Wilberforce undertook the abolishment of the most vile—and most profitable—enterprise in the British Empire, the African slave trade. Believing that God had set before him this formidable task, Wilberforce made the first of many impassioned speeches in Parliament in 1789. Some MPs were favorable to his ideas, but the proposal to abolish the slave trade was beaten each year that it was attempted, over and over again through the 1790s. It is debilitating to face defeat after defeat, yet Wilberforce tenaciously kept fighting past the turn of the century until passage of the bill was finally secured in 1807. Through his extraordinary perseverance, the slave trade throughout the British Empire was ended, though it would take many years and much patrolling by the British Navy along the coast of West Africa before slave ships became a thing of the past. Complete abolition of slavery was not accomplished in the British Empire until 1833.

Back to Napoleon — Carrying the Torch of Empire

Wilberforce's success was still in the future, however, when Napoleon, safely home from his adventures in Egypt, assumed control at the end of 1799. The French Revolution formally ended—as did many of the "Rights of Man"—when a new form of government, known as the Consulate, was instituted, giving Napoleon a virtual dictatorship. Napoleon's victories on the battlefield and France's increasing stature helped persuade the French people to overlook the loss of their freedoms. (For any who were not convinced, the French secret police had other methods.) Napoleon's domestic policies in France, including systematizing the law (known as *codification*)

took place because debtors were being imprisoned. An American Revolutionary War captain named Daniel Shays, who had become a bankrupt farmer, led a group of armed men to shut down a court session in Massachusetts. Things got out of hand, and suddenly there were thousands of soldiers involved in "Shays's Rebellion."

To many, the system under the Articles of Confederation seemed to be falling apart. That prompted the states to call for a new convening of representatives who would, hopefully, find a way out of the mess.

It was this convention that wrote the Constitution used in the United States today. It provided far more authority to the central—or federal—government, including the ability to tax. In addition, the Constitution formed a new type of government divided into three mutually dependent and equal branches: legislative, executive, and judicial.

Though this new government proved to be much more functional, the young nation was not yet out of trouble. Those who liked the idea of a stronger central government were known as Federalists, and those who opposed the idea were first known as anti-Federalists, and later as Republicans (in identification with the aims of Revolutionary France).

These two groups had competing and vastly different ideas of what was best for their country.

Compounding the troubles, France—America's former friend and ally—underwent a major upheaval as the French Revolution overthrew the established monarchy, and eventually descended into the anarchy of the Reign of Terror. Those in America who approved of the Revolution saw similarities between the two countries: that each had sought liberty from the oppression of monarchies.

1

and reordering the structure of the government, were warmly welcomed by the nation because they brought a new stability to France.

The greatest stability, though, comes when a country is at peace. After nearly a decade of war, Great Britain and France finally signed the Treaty of Amiens in March of 1802, which was jubilantly celebrated on both sides of the English Channel. For the first time since the French Revolution began, English travelers flocked in vast numbers to the continent, especially to Paris. It must have felt like such an enormous relief to no longer be at war, to no longer be isolated and alone. It would be, unfortunately, a short-lived sentiment.

With Napoleon's military victories on the continent securing him virtual rule of Europe, and a peace treaty signed with his remaining enemy, Great Britain, he was ready to advance an even more ambitious plan, extending his rule over yet another continent—North America! In 1801, Napoleon discovered, through diplomatic channels, that the new American president would not only welcome a French invasion to overthrow Toussaint L'Ouverture but would go so far as to assist French troops with American supplies. President Thomas Jefferson was concerned that Haiti's model of slaves ruling their own country as free men might stir up American slaves, and was thus willing to consider supporting France in this endeavor. Unbeknownst to Jefferson, however, Napoleon had his eye on far more than Haiti. With the French firmly in charge of their former prosperous colony, Napoleon would have a well-equipped army in the Caribbean, ready for its next assignment in the vast Louisiana Territory of North America.

It was no longer promoting the interests of the United States to help Napoleon, since he was obviously seeking to gain an aggressive presence in North America.

This immense territory—stretching from Canada all the way to the mouth of the Mississippi River at New Orleans, and from the west bank of the Mississippi River to the Rocky Mountains—had once been part of the French empire in the New World. In the 1763 Treaty of Paris, which ended the Seven Years' War, France had given the Louisiana Territory to Spain in order to compensate them for their losses in the war. Then in 1800 Napoleon had signed a new, secret treaty with Spain, which legally returned the Louisiana Territory to France with the written promise that France would never "cede" (sell, give, or trade away) this land to any other country.

Political secrets seldom remain concealed, and Napoleonic France was no exception. Rumors that Napoleon had plans for re-establishing the Louisiana Territory as a part of France's Empire—complete with French immigrants and a French army—began to drift across the Atlantic to the American government. This put an entirely different light on the matter of French interference with Haiti. It was no longer promoting the interests of the United States to help Napoleon, since he was obviously seeking to gain an aggressive presence in North America. They refused to feed the French army aboard their

Those in America who were horrified by the Revolution saw the anarchy of mob rule and feared that it might come to American shores. Again, these were two opposing views of reality. They led to a significant splintering in American politics, especially after the much-honored George Washington ended his second term as president. Those who came after him were not given the same measure of esteem, and regardless of the actions of subsequent presidents, there were many who vocally and relentlessly derided their decisions in public. Jesus had said that a house divided against itself cannot stand, and it must have appeared to many outsiders that the American experiment was so divided against itself that it was doomed to fall.

Add to the young nation's difficulties one more issue: commerce.

The ongoing enmity between France and England during the French Revolution and Napoleonic Wars, much of which was carried out on the high seas and in the trade routes, could have been a recipe for disaster for the fledgling nation seeking to gain a foothold in the extremely lucrative business of merchant shipping—which was especially good in a time of war. It nearly undid the United States, as it led to the Quasi-War with France and the War of 1812 with Great Britain and Canada.

Amazingly, despite all of these troubles, the United States managed to emerge from its first few decades with more land, more people, a better economy, an effective navy, and a greater stature among the powerful nations of the world.

1

Toussaint L'Ouverture

ships in the Caribbean or to give them a loan with which to buy food.

Despite the lack of promised supplies from the United States, the French army was finally able to force Toussaint L'Ouverture to surrender in 1802, then treacherously captured him and sent him to a frigid prison in the mountains of France. This powerful man, who had lived his entire life in the tropics of the Caribbean, died the following year. Though Toussaint L'Ouverture was not able to defeat the double-minded French, a small mosquito named *Aedes aaegypti*, with its deadly cargo of yellow fever, proved to be more successful. The French general in charge of retaking the island, Napoleon's brother-in-law Leclerc, along with the majority of his soldiers, died from this dread disease, but not before Napoleon had announced that slavery was being reinstituted in the French Empire.

Driven by their fury at being betrayed by Napoleon, and their fury over the capture of their trusted leader, the former slaves of Haiti gave themselves to an all-out assault against those who would re-enslave them. This brutal conflict might have yet resulted in a French victory, since Napoleon was not averse to spending tens—even hundreds—of thousands of soldiers' lives to obtain his goals. However, as time continued to march on, circumstances deteriorated until Napoleon recognized that creating a French stronghold in North America was not worth the price he would have to pay.

> Napoleon recognized that creating a French stronghold in North America was not worth the price he would have to pay.

Suddenly, much to the amazement of the American envoys in Paris, who were trying to buy the city of New Orleans and the Spanish lands of Florida from the French, Napoleon offered to sell the entire Louisiana Territory to the United States. Through fast and furious work behind the scenes, the US diplomats managed to negotiate this massive real estate deal for $15 million. All of this was speedily accomplished despite the fact that the treaty signed between Spain and France specifically forbade selling Louisiana to a third party.

News of the Louisiana Purchase was announced to the people of the United States during the Fourth of July celebrations of 1803—the same day that Captain Lewis left Washington, DC, to rendezvous with Lieutenant Clark and begin the famous Lewis and Clark Expedition—their epic journey of discovery. While the news thrilled many Americans, the French inhabitants of New Orleans were distressed by the US acquisition of their land, and the incensed Spanish officials emphatically proclaimed that Napoleon had no legal right to sell any part of the Louisiana Territory.

28 Napoleon & Early Missions (1790–1815)

The article for Unit 1 is designed to help students learn about Napoleon and Early Missions, and to cause them to consider the implications for people today of the events of this time period. The materials covered in the audio recordings offer another look at this historic moment, covering slightly different information. In the article and recordings, along with introducing the basic understanding of history we are also bringing in the biblical worldview.

You may choose to have your students read the article first and then listen to the audio recordings, or vice versa.

◉ Read the article

◉ Listen to the audio recordings in Listen to This

- The main concepts and chronological flow are contained in *What in the World?* Volume 3.

- Discover more amazing stories about William Carey, the father of modern missions, and William Wilberforce, who brought about the end of the slave trade in the British Empire, in *True Tales* Volume 3.

- Learn about the the desperate state of affairs in America in the late 1700s, the "Concert of Prayer" that sought God's deliverance, and the revival that came, in *Digging Deeper* Volume 3.

1

The End of the Era

Meanwhile, recognizing the alarming and growing signs of Napoleon's military buildup (meaning war was on the horizon), England took the initiative and declared war on France in May. Who could have possibly foreseen that, after only a year of peace following nearly a decade of war, this unremitting and vicious struggle would continue for another twelve years—until Napoleon was utterly vanquished at the Battle of Waterloo in 1815? The battles would be fought on land (won by the unstoppable Grande Armée of Napoleon) and sea (won by the unsinkable Royal Navy of Britain). Before it was over, England and Russia would both be threatened—England, as Napoleon gathered a flotilla to transport his seasoned troops across the English Channel (displaying his lack of knowledge of the sea) and Russia, as Napoleon marched nearly half a million soldiers all the way to Moscow (displaying his foolhardy ignorance of the Russian winter). It would involve the entire European continent in the *Continental System*, which was a trade blockade against English goods that ended up being disastrous for both Britain and France. It would increase tensions between the British and the Americans to the point of war, especially over the issue of *impressment*. (To be impressed is to be taken against one's will to serve on a British naval ship.) The British had an unrelenting need to impress able-bodied—meaning "still breathing"—sailors to man their huge navy in fighting the French, while the Americans had a strong sensitivity to anything Britain might do that affected their liberties, particularly the impressment of American citizens. The result of this increasingly bitter issue was the War of 1812.

In Napoleon's efforts to brand himself a legend in his own time, we see these changes: the prime-time news story of Napoleon crowning himself emperor; the soap-opera story of his divorcing Josephine to marry a real princess; and the reality-TV story of his island escape and victorious march on Paris to reclaim his throne. Finally, there would be a showdown between an international group of armies, determined to take Napoleon down for good, facing the still-dangerous remnant of Napoleon's Grande Armée at an unlikely spot in Belgium called Waterloo. Described by the Duke of Wellington, commander of the British forces, as a "near run thing," the Battle of Waterloo ended not only the threat of Napoleonic ambitions but an entire epoch as well. ◀

Described by the Duke of Wellington, commander of the British forces, as a "near run thing," the Battle of Waterloo ended not only the threat of Napoleonic ambitions but an entire epoch as well.

◉ Read the Scriptures in Read For Your Life

The Scriptures are central to our understanding, our character, and our decisions. Therefore, we must give the greatest weight possible to them.

Help your students gain this perspective as they watch you handle the Scriptures with reverence and awe.

Pray that your students will gain a greater understanding of God's heart for the nations, tribes, and people groups of the world as they consider the Great Commission's significance to and impact upon Christians in the late 1700s.

◉ Recap the material with an activity

In different parts of the room, set up stations for the Eight Intelligences Recap Activities. Then allow students to work alone or together in small groups to accomplish THEIR CHOICE OF ONE of the following suggestions. At the start of the next class, ask for 3–4 groups of volunteers to share.

Homeschoolers: rather than setting up all eight stations, allow student(s) to choose which activity they would most enjoy, and do it.

Recap Suggestions:

Spatial: Create an advertisement to attract new recruits for Napoleon's army, emphasizing the glamour of travel and of being on the winning side. Be sure to deemphasize how many soldiers Napoleon loses each month.

Bodily-Kinesthetic: Physically illustrate, through pantomime or some physical action, some of the most compelling reasons for the War of 1812 between Great Britain (with its colonial ally, Canada) and the United States. Have others guess which reasons you are illustrating.

Interpersonal: In a small group, hold a discussion concerning the influence of William Carey on India and on the modern missions movement. Also consider whether you think his life is a good model for Christians today.

Musical: Sing together "Amazing Grace," written by John Newton, a former slave trader turned preacher.

Phase 1

Key People (Church)

William Wilberforce
Successfully fought slave trade

William Carey
Father of modern missions movement

Robert Haldane
Ministered in the French revival

Hans Nielsen Hauge
Ministered in Norwegian revival

Adoniram Judson
Missionary to Burma

▶ Listen to This

What in the World? VOL. 3

DISC ONE:

- » Introduction to Modern History (track 1)
- » Young Napoleon (track 2)
- » Napoleon's Rise to Power (track 3)
- » Emperor Napoleon (track 4)
- » Napoleon's Downfall (track 5)

True Tales VOL. 3

DISC ONE:

- » William Carey (track 1)
- » William Wilberforce (track 2)

Digging Deeper VOL. 3

DISC ONE:

- » The Protestant Era (track 1)
- » The New Rationalism (track 2)
- » Faith in Universities (track 3)

▶ Read For Your Life

The Holy Bible

- » **The Great Commission**—Matthew 28:18–20
- » **The Prediction of War**—Mark 13:7–8

30 Napoleon & Early Missions (1790–1815)

Afterward, talk together about the most interesting or important facts studied in this Unit concerning the abolition of the slave trade in the British Empire.

Linguistic: Create a short rhyming poem that will help students remember the main points of Napoleon's life, his rise to power, and his sudden descent.

Math-Logical: Analyze the similarities and the differences between the French Empire under Napoleon and the British Empire. Make a simple chart to show this information.

Intrapersonal: Brainstorm ways you personally might have been able to assist Toussaint L'Ouverture in his struggle to keep Haiti free from foreign control, while maintaining a vibrantly Christian approach to the difficult issues facing this new republic.

Naturalist: Allow outdoor-loving students to go outside and find a place that could represent one of the major sea battles between the British navy under the command of Lord Nelson versus the French navy. If you can find a shallow bit of water and reconstruct the Battle of the Nile, so much the better!

Or . . . Activity of Your Choice: What would you like to have your students do for a review activity concerning this week's introduction to Napoleon & Early Missions?

▶ Talk Together

Opinion Column

- » What did you find to be the most interesting aspect, or the most fascinating person, you encountered in your introduction to the time period of Napoleon & Early Missions?

- » Imagine you were living in Austria during the time of the Napoleonic Wars. What do you think your impression of Napoleon would have been? Contrast that with this question: What do you think your impression of Napoleon would have been had you been a citizen of France?

- » Why do you suppose the Russians relied mainly on "General Winter" to fight Napoleon when he invaded Russia in 1812? What kinds of things could a brutal winter do to an army unprepared to face it?

- » Imagine you were living in the United States during the time of the Napoleonic Wars between France and England. What do you think your attitude would have been toward each of the two countries? Which one would you have wanted to win? Why?

- » When Napoleon escaped from the island of Elba and returned to France, his enemies frantically prepared for an aggressive war. If you had been living in England at the time, what do you think your attitude would have been toward this earth-shaking news?

- » Why do you think William Carey is considered the father of modern missions? With the things you have learned about his life and work, what do you think might have been some of the more difficult parts of Carey's time in India? What ideas do you have to explain why he was so successful in his endeavors?

Key People (World)

Thomas Jefferson
American president

Toussaint L'Ouverture
Led Haitian slave revolt

Lord Horatio Nelson
British naval commander

Tecumseh
Native military leader in War of 1812

Napoleon
Military genius & French emperor

Duke of Wellington
Victor at Battle of Waterloo

Muhammad Ali Pasha
Founder of Egyptian dynasty

Ludwig van Beethoven
German composer

Alexander I
Russian czar

◉ Talk together

Individual Preparation

After completing their recap activities, students may begin to consider the questions in the Opinion Column and Critical Puzzling.

Class Discussion

Use the questions under Talk Together to get the students primed and to create a discussion environment in the classroom. You may also want to draw from the open-ended questions listed here.

? The British and Foreign Bible Society was founded in 1804 to print Bibles in different languages. Imagine what it would be like for you to not have a Bible in your own native tongue but only in a language that you barely understand. With this in mind, how do you think this organization made a difference in missions?

? Do you think the War of 1812 would have occurred between the United States and Great Britain if Napoleon had not been aggressively seeking to master the European continent?

? In 1816, the "Réveil," or Awakening, took place in France and Switzerland under the ministry of Robert Haldane. Why do you think the people of post-Revolutionary, post-Napoleonic France might have been hungry for the things of God? Can you think of other times in history when God has moved mightily among people in deep need? How does Psalm 107:4–22 describe God's response to deep needs?

Critical Puzzling

» Why do you think Napoleon was never able to invade England? What are the difficulties involved with invading this island kingdom? What factors were present in 1066 that allowed William of Normandy to be successful in his invasion of England, but which were unavailable to Napoleon? Who else in history tried unsuccessfully to invade England?

» In 1804, President Thomas Jefferson sent Lewis and Clark on their historic expedition to explore the newly purchased Louisiana Territory. In what ways would this journey eventually impact the native people living in this territory and the nations they represented? In what overall ways did it impact the United States?

» Many historians point to the Spanish Peninsular War as Napoleon's greatest mistake. Why do you think this might be true? In what ways did Napoleon's losses in the Peninsular War impact the rest of Europe?

» The tensions between France and England were demonstrated visibly in the blockade of trade goods from England to the European continent, and in the blockade of imports and exports from the continent to the rest of the world. These tensions led directly to the War of 1812 between the United States and England/Canada. How did Napoleon benefit from this war? Who else materially benefited from this war?

» Native American tribes fought against the British and on the side of the French during the French & Indian War in America, then divided during the American Revolution, with some tribes fighting for the British while others fought for the colonists. In the War of 1812, the tribes united to fight on the side of the British and against the Americans. What issues do you think were at stake to explain their alliance with the British?

» William Wilberforce was able, in 1807, to secure passage of a bill in Parliament that outlawed the slave trade to England and her colonies. For what reasons do you think English merchants bitterly fought this bill?

» The Church Missionary Society, founded in 1799, helped to oversee and support missionaries on the field. What factors do you think contributed to the new understanding of and new emphasis on world missions among the European and American churches? How would having a society specifically devoted to helping missionaries aid in recruiting new missionaries?

» The French Revolution granted the slaves in French colonies their freedom; then Napoleon decided to re-enslave them, which led to a slave revolt in Haiti. What relation, if any, do you see between this slave revolt and the outlawing of slavery in England?

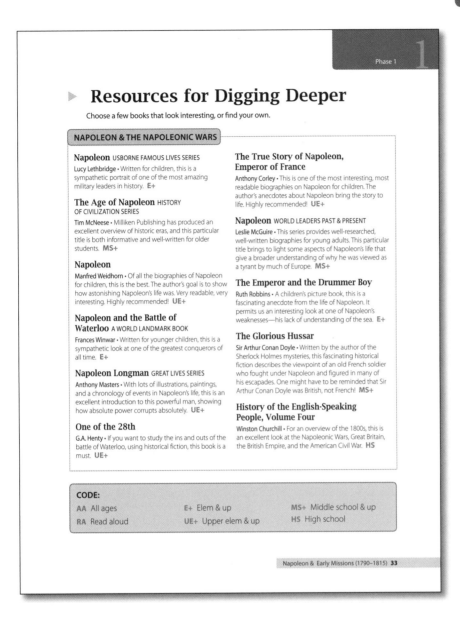

▶ Resources for Digging Deeper

Choose a few books that look interesting, or find your own.

NAPOLEON & THE NAPOLEONIC WARS

Napoleon USBORNE FAMOUS LIVES SERIES
Lucy Lethbridge • Written for children, this is a sympathetic portrait of one of the most amazing military leaders in history. **E+**

The Age of Napoleon HISTORY OF CIVILIZATION SERIES
Tim McNeese • Milliken Publishing has produced an excellent overview of historic eras, and this particular title is both informative and well-written for older students. **MS+**

Napoleon
Manfred Weidhorn • Of all the biographies of Napoleon for children, this is the best. The author's goal is to show how astonishing Napoleon's life was. Very readable, very interesting. Highly recommended! **UE+**

Napoleon and the Battle of Waterloo A WORLD LANDMARK BOOK
Frances Winwar • Written for younger children, this is a sympathetic look at one of the greatest conquerors of all time. **E+**

Napoleon Longman GREAT LIVES SERIES
Anthony Masters • With lots of illustrations, paintings, and a chronology of events in Napoleon's life, this is an excellent introduction to this powerful man, showing how absolute power corrupts absolutely. **UE+**

One of the 28th
G.A. Henty • If you want to study the ins and outs of the battle of Waterloo, using historical fiction, this book is a must. **UE+**

The True Story of Napoleon, Emperor of France
Anthony Corley • This is one of the most interesting, most readable biographies on Napoleon for children. The author's anecdotes about Napoleon bring the story to life. Highly recommended! **UE+**

Napoleon WORLD LEADERS PAST & PRESENT
Leslie McGuire • This series provides well-researched, well-written biographies for young adults. This particular title brings to light some aspects of Napoleon's life that give a broader understanding of why he was viewed as a tyrant by much of Europe. **MS+**

The Emperor and the Drummer Boy
Ruth Robbins • A children's picture book, this is a fascinating anecdote from the life of Napoleon. It permits us an interesting look at one of Napoleon's weaknesses—his lack of understanding of the sea. **E+**

The Glorious Hussar
Sir Arthur Conan Doyle • Written by the author of the Sherlock Holmes mysteries, this fascinating historical fiction describes the viewpoint of an old French soldier who fought under Napoleon and figured in many of his escapades. One might have to be reminded that Sir Arthur Conan Doyle was British, not French! **MS+**

History of the English-Speaking People, Volume Four
Winston Churchill • For an overview of the 1800s, this is an excellent look at the Napoleonic Wars, Great Britain, the British Empire, and the American Civil War. **HS**

CODE:

AA All ages	**E+** Elem & up	**MS+** Middle school & up
RA Read aloud	**UE+** Upper elem & up	**HS** High school

◉ Choose books of interest/ internet search

A list of possible books for further reading is given in the Student Manual. Encourage your students to look for books or videos concerning Napoleon's day and early missions from this list and from other sources. You may want to gather a selection of further resources prior to beginning Unit 1, or you may encourage the students to be treasure hunters and find them on their own. It would be helpful and time-saving before the Unit begins to check availability of these titles on your local library website.

Remember:
Beware of Arrogance,
Embrace Humility!

THE BRITISH NAVY & THE AGE OF SAIL

Hero of Trafalgar: The Story of Lord Nelson A WORLD LANDMARK BOOK

A.B.C. Whipple • The World Landmark series provides excellent biographies for children. In this title, we meet Lord Nelson, who was England's hero and Napoleon's nemesis. **UE+**

Lord Nelson IMMORTALS OF HISTORY

Herbert J. Gimpel, Commander, USN • A very in-depth look at England's most famous admiral, this book also delves into Lord Nelson's "blind spot"—Lady Hamilton. **MS+**

Nelson and the Fighting Age of Sail A HORIZON CARAVEL BOOK

Oliver Warner • This is an excellent book in the Horizon Caravel series. Lots of illustrations, diagrams, maps, and paintings, as well as in-depth text about Nelson and the strategies he used to defeat Napoleon at sea. **UE+**

The Navy That Beat Napoleon A CAMBRIDGE TOPIC BOOK

Walter Brownlee • For one interested in the sea, this is a must-have! It explains many different aspects of ships-of-the-line and other nautical information that is not readily available for younger students. Plus there are easily understood descriptions of the important sea battles that destroyed Napoleon's French fleet. Highly recommended! **UE+**

Two Years Before the Mast

Richard Henry Dana Jr. • While you are reading about Lord Nelson and the British Navy, pick up this true story about life at sea for a young American who ships out on a sailing vessel in 1840. Classic literature and a can't-put-it-down story! **MS+**

ABOLITION OF SLAVERY

A Journey Through the Life of William Wilberforce

Kevin Belmonte • The author was the consultant for the movie *Amazing Grace*, and this book reflects his knowledge of and appreciation for the English abolitionist. Highly recommended! **UE+**

William Wilberforce and the Abolition of the Slave Trade, *Christian History*, Issue 53 (Vol. XVI, No. 1)

This entire edition of *Christian History* is dedicated to William Wilberforce and the Clapham Community, which tremendously impacted England for good in the 1800s. **UE+**

The Slave Who Freed Haiti: The Story of Toussaint L'Ouverture A WORLD LANDMARK BOOK

Katharine Scherman • Absolutely fascinating! This is the biography of the man called "The Black Napoleon," who led the successful rebellion against France by the slaves of Saint Domingue (Haiti). **UE+**

Toussaint L'Ouverture WORLD LEADERS PAST & PRESENT

Thomas and Dorothy Hoobler • This book is an in-depth look at a remarkable man. It chronicles the developments from the time of the French Revolution through the reign of Napoleon in France's most successful (read: profitable) colony. **MS+**

LOUISIANA PURCHASE

The Louisiana Purchase

Thomas Fleming • For older students, this amazing little book will help to set one of America's most unlikely stories into its proper context in the Napoleonic Wars. In this book, history reads like fiction! **MS+**

What's the Deal? Jefferson, Napoleon, and the Louisiana Purchase

Rhoda Blumberg • This is worth the search. Learn more about how Napoleon swindled the Spanish king for the Louisiana Territory, and how he broke his promise to never sell it to anyone apart from Spain. **UE+**

WAR OF 1812

War of 1812
PERSPECTIVES ON HISTORY SERIES
Mary Alice Burke Robinson, ed. • A brief overview of the War of 1812, this excellent guide provides students with source documents—letters and speeches—that help explain the war's motivating factors. Highly recommended. **MS+**

The Story of the War of 1812
Colonel Red Reeder • In order to better understand the events taking place in Europe in the early 1800s, it is helpful to learn about the war between the United States and England/Canada that began in 1812. The seeds of conflict lie deep in the affairs of Napoleon! This is an excellent introduction to the war as seen from all sides. **UE+**

Tecumseh, Shawnee Warrior-Statesman
James McCague • Written for younger children, this biography describes one of the key people of the War of 1812. **E+**

General Brock and Niagara Falls A WORLD LANDMARK BOOK
Samuel Hopkins Adams • General Brock, an English soldier, first fought against the French forces in Holland, then sailed with Lord Nelson to fight the Danes. Hoping to be sent to the Peninsular War in Spain, he was instead assigned to Canada. Read more about this British hero of the War of 1812 in this excellent biography. **UE+**

New Orleans BATTLEFIELDS ACROSS AMERICA
David C. King • This fascinating little book shows the connection between Andrew Jackson and the British soldiers who were veterans of the Napoleonic Wars. Remember, it's all connected! **E+**

BEETHOVEN

Bold Composer: A Story about Ludwig van Beethoven
Judith Josephson • Beéthoven's story is fascinating, and this title does an excellent job of communicating both the genius and the struggles of this composer. **UE+**

Ludwig van Beethoven
WHY THEY BECAME FAMOUS SERIES
Noemi Vicini Marri, translated by Stephen Thorne • Isn't it amazing to learn that Beethoven composed a symphony (Eroica) in Napoleon's honor? When he learned of Napoleon's intention to crown himself emperor, Beethoven furiously scratched out his name from the title! Learn more about this epoch-shaping composer in this excellent biography. **RA**

The Life & Times of Beethoven
PORTRAITS OF GREATNESS SERIES
Gino Pugnetti • This is an excellent overview of the life of the great composer. Filled with paintings, illustrations, and more, it describes the many facets and events of Beethoven's life. **UE+**

HISTORICAL FICTION

Mr. Midshipman Hornblower
C. S. Forester • The Hornblower series is set in the time of the Napoleonic Wars. While the later books in the series show Hornblower's character becoming increasingly unappealing, the first several titles are an amazing window onto the world of the British Navy. One actually begins to comprehend the British view on the necessity of impressment! **MS+**

Pride and Prejudice
Jane Austen • Wonderful classic literature, this is a story of English society in the early 1800s. Highly recommended! **MS+**

For more books, use these Dewey Decimal numbers in your library:

Napoleon, Trafalgar: 940–944

Biography:

B section, found between 919 and 920

B B for Beethoven

B N for Napoleon and Nelson

B T for Toussaint L'Ouverture and Tecumseh

Slave trade: 382

Louisiana Purchase; War of 1812 in North America: 973

Beethoven: 780.92

Haitian history: 972

MISSIONS

From Jerusalem to Irian Jaya A BIOGRAPHICAL HISTORY OF CHRISTIAN MISSIONS

Ruth A. Tucker • This is the best book available on the history of world missions and has recently been re-released as a second edition. Included are short biographies of missionaries all over the world, categorized by their geographical area of service. An indispensable resource for the study of *World Empires, World Missions, World Wars*. For this chapter, read pages 117–139. **UE+**

Imprisoned in the Golden City TRAILBLAZER BOOKS

Dave & Neta Jackson • This historical fiction for children presents the story of Adoniram and Ann Judson who went to Burma as missionaries in the early 1800s. **UE+**

William Carey CHRISTIAN HEROES THEN AND NOW

Geoff & Janet Benge • Wonderfully written, this series of Christian biographies is fascinating, factual, and historically accurate. William Carey can be considered the father of the modern missions movement since it was his willingness to venture out to India in the late 1700s that opened the eyes of many Christians to the possibilities of missions in foreign lands. **UE+**

William Carey MEN OF FAITH SERIES

Basil Miller • This biography was developed from the actual letters and journals of William Carey. It was William Carey's "Expect great things from God; attempt great things for God" that electrified nineteenth century Christians. **MS+**

VIDEO

Amazing Grace

A powerful film, this is the well-researched story of William Wilberforce and his struggle to end the slave trade in the British Empire. (Depictions of his illness, and of the cruelty of horse handlers of the era, may not be appropriate for younger viewers.) Highly recommended!

War and Peace

This film, made during the 1950s and based on Tolstoy's novel, is very long and somewhat depressing. However, it does portray the burning of Moscow during the French invasion, as well as the conditions of battle, and the retreat of Napoleon's army during the winter.

Horatio Hornblower

This A&E swashbuckling adventure does a great job of showing aspects of the Napoleonic Wars from the viewpoint of the British Navy. (Due to the graphic nature of some of the scenes, not recommended for younger students.)

Beethoven Lives Upstairs

Produced in 1992, this wonderful movie directed by David Devine shows a young boy's gradual acquaintance with the "madman" who lives upstairs, the genius composer Beethoven. (Also available as an audio CD under the same title, part of the Classical Kids series.)

What books did you like best?

_____

_____

_____

_____

The Internet also contains a wealth of information about Napoleon & Early Missions.

What sites were the most helpful?

_____

_____

_____

_____

continued next page

◎ Conduct a review and evaluation

In this Phase of Unit 1, your students should have had the opportunity to explore Napoleon & Early Missions through reading, listening, thinking, and discussing by completing a selection from the following:

- informally discussed the Key Concepts;
- read the article;
- listened to the audio recordings;
- read the online articles;
- read the Scriptures;
- explored the recap activities;
- considered the Opinion Column and Critical Puzzling answers on their own;
- participated in class discussion;
- chosen books of interest or searched the Internet;
- completed their self-evaluation for this Phase.

Record student hours: _____

Assess student participation:

Create an evaluation system of your own, or refer to the evaluation rubric in the introduction, as a tool for assessing participation. The categories you will probably find most useful are *"Introduction," "Process: Teamwork"* and *"Process: Originality."* To help students develop good discussion skills, encourage them to participate actively, ask content-based questions, and stay focused on the discussion at

hand. Students demonstrate a higher level of discussion skills when they incorporate comments and questions from others into their own questions, and draw out opinions or ask for points of clarification from others.

Do not critique the self-evaluation page your student completes and do not direct the answers the student gives to the questions. Instead, allow sincere and personal completion of the evaluation, then discuss the responses and incorporate those comments into your evaluation.

Determine a grade for this Phase, if using grades: _____

Teacher Self-Evaluation:

Evaluate your own use of materials and teaching opportunities: what worked and what did not; how effective was your time-management; how were your responses to the needs of your student; did you make your expectations clear; in what ways would you like to improve your approach for the next Unit? Incorporate suggestions from your students in your own evaluation *(this requires humility!)*.

---

1 Phase 1

▶ **Student Self-Evaluation** UNIT 1, PHASE 1

Dates and hours:_____

Key Concepts

Rephrase the four Key Concepts of this Unit and confirm your understanding of each:

- Napoleonic Wars

  _____

- Abolition of Slave Trade

  _____

- Modern Missions

  _____

- Growth of United States

  _____

Tools for Self-Evaluation

Evaluate your personal participation in the discussions of this Phase. Bearing in mind that a good participant in a discussion is not always the most vocal participant, ask yourself these questions: Were you an active participant? Did you ask perceptive questions? Were you willing to listen to other participants of the discussion and draw out their opinions? Record your observations and how you would like to improve your participation in the future:

_____

_____

Every time period is too complex to be understood in one Phase of study. Evaluate your current knowledge of Napoleon & Early Missions. What have you focused on so far? What are your weakest areas of knowledge?

_____

_____

Based on the evaluation of this introduction, project ahead what you would like to study more of in the following Phases.

_____

_____

38 Napoleon & Early Missions (1790–1815)

Phase 2

▶ Research & Reporting

Explore one or more of these areas to discover something significant!

Napoleon

Compare and contrast Napoleon with other notable conquerors in history, such as Alexander the Great, Julius Caesar, or Genghis Khan. In what ways did Napoleon follow their patterns of conquest, and in what ways did he diverge?

Research and report on the Napoleonic Wars, detailing the rise of Napoleon, the major battles (both land and sea), Napoleon's tactical mistakes, and his defeat at the Battle of Waterloo. Describe the reasons why Napoleon is considered to be one of the greatest military minds in history.

Investigate the Spanish Peninsular War. What were the tactics of the British under the Duke of Wellington? What were the policies of the French armies in Spain? Describe how the Spanish reacted to having Napoleon's brother on the throne. How did this differ from the reaction of the other countries in Europe who also had a member of Napoleon's family ruling?

Beethoven

Describe the life and work of Beethoven. How did his childhood experiences and deafness contribute to both his music and his rough personality? Describe Beethoven's attitude toward the French Revolution and Napoleon. How did this attitude change?

Lord Nelson

Study the naval genius of Horatio Nelson. Describe his naval battles, showing how he defeated the French fleet at the Battle of the Nile, defeated the Danish at Copenhagen, and defeated the French again at the Battle of Trafalgar. Why is Lord Nelson considered to be one of the greatest naval tacticians in history?

Toussaint L'Ouverture

Discover more about Toussaint L'Ouverture. Why was he called the "Black Napoleon"? What significance did his ability to read have for the slaves of Haiti? What were the three different groups of people and the two cultures on the island? Describe Toussaint L'Ouverture's battle tactics and his strategies for improving life on the island.

Egyptology

Research and report on Napoleon's conquest of Egypt, particularly its effect on the study of Egyptology. Include the Rosetta Stone, Jean François Champollion, and the impact of the researchers who accompanied Napoleon to Egypt.

◉ Choose a topic and begin research

Allow the students the freedom to choose one of the topics listed under research & reporting in the Student Manual, or to suggest their own area which they would like to research.

Motivating Suggestions:

Especially for Non-linguistic students, and those who are not motivated by written or oral reports, here are suggestions for alternative ways of reporting what has been researched.

Napoleon

Two students can work together to create a television news-style program for an audience. This edition: an interview with Napoleon Bonaparte. One of the students will act the part of Napoleon while the other is the interviewer. Be sure to question Napoleon himself on how he views his accomplishments when compared with other great conquerors from history. The interviewer may want to allow questions from the studio audience.

This reporting project will be like going on a Napoleonic treasure hunt, naming the battles based on the clues given. First, set up different sites, inside or outside, that will represent each of the major battles in the Napoleonic Wars. Then place objects at each site that will be helpful clues to the identity of that battle. These clues could reflect the name of the battle (such as Waterloo) or the nature of the battle (such as, the overwhelming obstacle of the Russian winter). Give participants a "cheat sheet" that tells them the names of the battles, two or three relevant facts concerning each, and blank spaces in which to write the identity of each as they recognize it in your prepared site. As soon as everyone understands what is expected, it will become a race to see who can correctly identify the sites first.

Consider how you would have felt as a Spaniard when Napoleon set his brother on the throne of your beloved country. Then write a description of the motivations you believe were present among the betrayed and suffering Spanish people during the Peninsular War. How did these affect the final outcome of the war? As an addendum, write about how you think a believer, fully devoted to serving Jesus, should react if placed in a similar situation.

Lord Nelson

Create a flip chart that will illustrate the daring tactics used by Lord Nelson in each of his successful sea battles against the French navy. In order to get a sense of how you might create this chart, look at the ways a football coach shows on paper what each member of his team needs to do during each play. The goal is to have Lord Nelson's methods become perfectly understandable to your audience!

Go outside and recreate these sea battles on land. You will either need groups of volunteers who are willing to become the British Royal Navy ships and the French Navy ships, or you can use ships you make out of materials found in nature. Once you have adequate representation of the two navies, set the scene and reenact the battles for interested bystanders. If you are working with live "ships," encourage them to make appropriate sounds of cannons, splintering wood, etc. (You might want to watch a bit of the *Horatio Hornblower* series to learn the types of sounds that would be appropriate.) If you are using nature "ships," you might consider creating a soundtrack to go with the reenactment.

Toussaint L'ouverture

Using paints, photographs, or other pictorial aids, make a large poster that will give others a graphic representation of the life and struggles of Toussaint L'ouverture. Be sure to address each of the issues listed in the Research & Reporting question.

Find or create a selection of music that represents to you the life of Toussaint L'ouverture. Write up program notes for the audience, explain to them what you would like them to listen for in the music—what has spoken to you personally—and why you chose this music to represent Toussaint L'ouverture. Be prepared to answer questions on his life after the short concert is over.

Beethoven

Write a book for young children that will describe, appropriately for their age, the life and musical genius of Beethoven. You have the choice to make him a very sympathetic figure or a very strange and hard-to-live-with man, since he was both! Don't forget the difficulties he faced due to his increasing deafness.

Choose a short selection from your favorite composition by Beethoven. Your assignment is to explain to your audience how this composition reflects his "cutting-edge" musical genius. You will want to give a short synopsis of Beethoven's life prior to playing and explaining the selection. If you are able to create a PowerPoint

---

Louisiana Purchase

Discover the circumstances surrounding this land deal between Napoleon and Thomas Jefferson. Why would the United States have preferred Spain to be the owner of the Louisiana Territory rather than Napoleonic France? Why did Napoleon abandon his plan to occupy it? What had Lewis and Clark been commissioned to do in the Louisiana Territory?

War of 1812

Investigate the war that took place between Great Britain, the United States, and Canada. What were the causes of this war from the viewpoint of the Americans? The British? What was the United States' intention toward Canada? Why were Native Americans involved in this war, and who were they fighting? What were the results of this war?

Compare and contrast the War of 1812, fought in North America and the Atlantic, with the other War of 1812, the one Napoleon was waging in Russia. What, if any, were the connections between these two wars?

William Carey

Research and report on the life and ministry of William Carey. Include information on his life in England, his accomplishments in India, the "Serampore Trio," and his tragic family life.

Adoniram Judson

Adoniram and Ann Judson were among the first American missionaries to go to a foreign field. They traveled to India in 1812, then on to Burma. Discover more about their life and ministry in Burma (now known as Myanmar).

William Wilberforce

Learn more about William Wilberforce, his life's work (including the "reformation of manners"), and the abolitionist movements in different parts of the world.

---

presentation, the visual aids will greatly assist many in the audience to understand the points you make.

Egyptology

Create a solo performance depicting the difficulties surrounding the deciphering of the Rosetta Stone by dramatizing Jean François Champollion's amazing success.

Hold a debate with three other people. The topic to be discussed is this: Did colonizing countries have the right to remove valuable antiquities from the country in which they were found? Be sure to include examples both for and against this topic from Napoleon's trip to Egypt, along with

its impact on Egyptology.

Louisiana Purchase

Using a large wall map of the United States, explain to your audience where the Louisiana Territory was located, how Spain came to possess it, who lived there, why France initially took it in a secret treaty from Spain, what caused Napoleon to relinquish it, and Thomas Jefferson's reasons for sending Lewis and Clark on their epic journey. It would be appropriate to make this presentation in the guise of a National Parks ranger, preparing guests for the journey they are about to take. Be prepared to answer their questions!

Find materials from nature for a "show and tell" that will represent the American/British/Canadian War of 1812, as well as different materials that will appropriately represent Napoleon's War of 1812 in Russia. Then present your work, helping your audience understand the vast differences between these two wars and the reasons they were intrinsically connected.

William Carey

Perform a series of pantomimes to depict the three or four most significant events in the life of William Carey, showing the reality of his ups and downs. Demonstrate the obstacles he faced, both in England and in India. Be sure to express his trust in the faithfulness of God through it all. (It might be helpful to enlist a narrator who could give some background to prepare the audience for what they will see.)

With two or three other students, discuss whether you think William Carey was justified in taking his wife to India, knowing she was very fearful and timid. Should he have remained after the death of their child, as she became more and more unbalanced? In this discussion, be sure to consider the long-term results of his life and ministry in India and his effect on the modern missions movement.

Adoniram Judson

Imagine you are a Burmese living next door to Adoniram and Ann Judson. Write about what you have been hearing them describe concerning their God and how Christianity is so different from your own religion. If you are almost persuaded that they are right, explain what you have been realizing—how this would not only change your own relationship to God, but would also dramatically change the way your family and culture respond to you.

Create a visual display of Myanmar (Burma) that shows the beauty of the land and people along with the religious beliefs in that country. Next,

---

> ## Brain Stretchers

Napoleonic Code

Napoleon, in his exile to St. Helena, remarked that his best work, and what the world would remember about him, was the Napoleonic Code of Law. Research and report on this work. Be sure to include the prior history of law in France, the implementation of the Napoleonic Code throughout the French-speaking world, and some of the most significant aspects of the Code.

Father of Modern Germany

Napoleon has been called the father of modern Germany. Research and report on the impact of Napoleon's actions in the Holy Roman Empire, the Confederation of the Rhine, and the defeat of the Prussians.

Clapham Community

Research and report on the Clapham Community, of which William Wilberforce was a member. What were the effects of the Clapham Community on Great Britain? On the world?

Create Your Own Research Topic

_____

_____

_____

Analyze the costs and benefits (or pros and cons) to Spain in "owning" the Louisiana Territory. Do that same cost and benefit analysis for France, keeping in mind that they saw it as a way to rebuild a vast North American empire. Do a third analysis for the United States as they recognized the huge opportunity to extend their nation. To make things really interesting, create a fourth cost and benefit analysis for the Native American tribes who inhabited most of this land. Then, comparing all four of these, make a spreadsheet or chart to show your work.

War of 1812

Putting yourself in the shoes of the British Admiralty, write a defense of the policy of impressment. Then, considering the sentiments of the citizens of the United States, write a defense of their decision to go to war. In addition, think about the very difficult position of the Native American nations that went to war against the United States, and write a defense of their actions. Finally, explain or write a statement of what you would have believed to be the right answer to the issues during this very volatile time, as a British navy officer, an American worker, and a Native American warrior.

create a visual display of Adoniram Judson's life and work and the obstacles he faced in ministry. Make another one to show the results that are visible on this side of eternity. You may choose to do this as a series of posters, as a PowerPoint presentation, or using any artistic medium you prefer.

William Wilberforce

Set up a museum of William Wilberforce's life, showing the many aspects of British society and culture he impacted. Then be a museum curator and explain what the different objects in the museum mean and how they represent the "reformation of manners" in Great Britain, and the abolition of the slave trade in the British Empire and its far-flung colonies. Be prepared to answer the museum guests' questions.

Compose a hymn of praise to God that expresses what William Wilberforce experienced and believed. You may choose to compose a new tune for this hymn, or you may want to rewrite the words from another hymn such as "Amazing Grace." Remember, the focus of the hymn must be, as was the focus of William Wilberforce's life, the glory of God alone. *"Not unto us, O Lord, not unto us, but to Your name give glory, because of Your mercy, because of Your truth."* Psalm 115:1

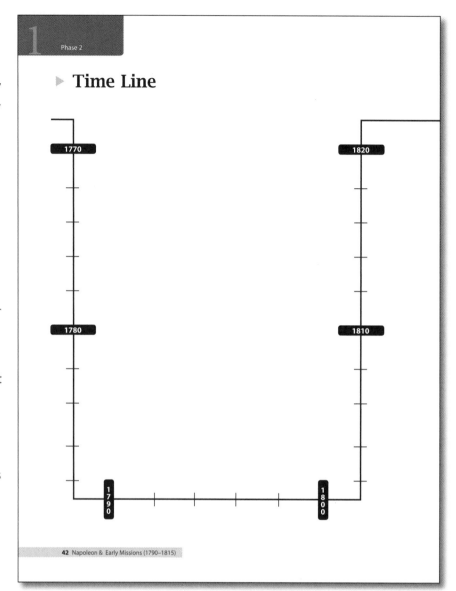

▶ **Time Line**

1770
1820
1780
1810
1790
1800

42 Napoleon & Early Missions (1790–1815)

◉ Construct the time line

Read the information listed with the Key Events in the Student Manual. Dialogue with your students about the issues involved.

Find the dates for the Key People and Key Events listed.

Consider this for your time line

The Napoleonic Age was the first time the entire European continent had been united since the days of Roman Empire, though the man responsible wreaked havoc in culture after culture to accomplish this goal. Across the Atlantic, the United States, a newcomer in the world of nations, was becoming a force to be reckoned with. In this same time period, the man considered to be the father of the modern missions movement imparted a new way of seeing Christian responsibility toward the peoples of the world through his writing and his work. And the diabolical African slave trade, which had been operating for centuries, was finally outlawed. All in all, this was an eventful two decades!

Key Events

- Battle of the Nile
- Quasi-War
- Abolition of the slave trade in the British Empire
- Battle of Trafalgar
- Peninsular War
- Continental System
- War of 1812
- Battle of Waterloo

Be sure to include the people listed in Key People in Phase 1.

Key Events

- Battle of the Nile: 1798
- Quasi-War: 1798–1800
- Abolition of the slave trade in the British Empire: 1833
- Battle of Trafalgar: 1805
- Peninsular War: 1808–1814
- Continental System: 1806–1814
- War of 1812: 1812–1815
- Battle of Waterloo: 1815

Time Line Key

Key People in the Church

- William Wilberforce: 1759–1833
- William Carey: 1761–1834
- Robert Haldane: 1764–1842
- Hans Nielsen Hauge: 1771–1824
- Adoniram Judson: 1788–1850

Key People in the World

- Thomas Jefferson: 1743–1826
- Toussaint L'Ouverture: 1743–1803
- Lord Horatio Nelson: 1758–1805
- Tecumseh: 1768–1813
- Napoleon: 1769–1821
- Duke of Wellington: 1769–1852
- Muhammad Ali Pasha: 1769–1849
- Ludwig van Beethoven: 1770–1827
- Alexander I: 1777–1825

When we look back, we recognize that Napoleon was in power for less than two decades and his continent-wide empire fell apart after his death. But the people who were alive in Europe during that time did not have the luxury of our perspective. To them, he undoubtedly seemed like a superman—a nearly unbeatable dictator who was able to conquer everything he set his sights on. In light of this, read Psalm 73 with your students and talk with them about how our perspective changes when we evaluate current events in light of eternity.

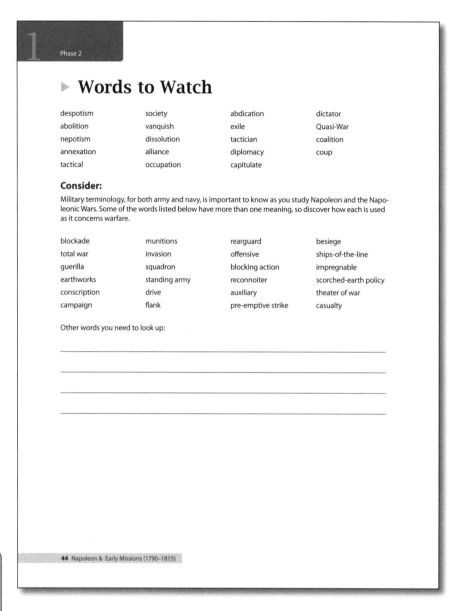

▶ Words to Watch

despotism	society	abdication	dictator
abolition	vanquish	exile	Quasi-War
nepotism	dissolution	tactician	coalition
annexation	alliance	diplomacy	coup
tactical	occupation	capitulate	

Consider:

Military terminology, for both army and navy, is important to know as you study Napoleon and the Napoleonic Wars. Some of the words listed below have more than one meaning, so discover how each is used as it concerns warfare.

blockade	munitions	rearguard	besiege
total war	invasion	offensive	ships-of-the-line
guerilla	squadron	blocking action	impregnable
earthworks	standing army	reconnoiter	scorched-earth policy
conscription	drive	auxiliary	theater of war
campaign	flank	pre-emptive strike	casualty

Other words you need to look up:

_____

_____

_____

_____

◉ Practice vocabulary

You may find other words in this Unit that are especially appropriate for younger children. Feel free to substitute another vocabulary list for the one provided.

◉ Complete research projects and share in class or hand in

Create a safe environment for the presentations. Set ground rules prior to the presentations, so that students know how much time is available for each of them, and so that they know they will be honored and respected by all those observing.

Here is one idea for making vocabulary study interesting and fun: These vocabulary words all have to do with politics in a time of war. So, incorporating the list of words, write a stirring campaign speech that you will use to try to win the election by emotionally swaying the voters who tend to vote with a different political party. If more than one student is involved, have them read their speeches and then have the group vote for the politician they think will do the job and get this war won!

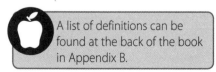

A list of definitions can be found at the back of the book in Appendix B.

> # Student Self-Evaluation UNIT 1, PHASE 2

Dates and hours:_____

Research Project

Summarize your research question:

_____

_____

List your most useful sources by author, title, and page number or URL where applicable (continue list in margin if necessary):

_____

_____

Now take a moment to evaluate the sources you just listed. Do they provide a balanced view of your research question? Should you have sought an additional opinion? Are your sources credible (if you found them on your own)? Record your observations:

_____

_____

_____

Evaluate your research project in its final presentation. What are its strengths? If you had time to revisit this project, what would you change? Consider giving yourself a letter grade based on your project's merits and weaknesses.

_____

_____

_____

Letter grade: ____

You have just completed an area of specific research in the time of Napoleon & Early Missions. Now what would you like to explore in the upcoming Phases? Set some objectives for yourself:

_____

_____

_____

Napoleon & Early Missions (1790–1815) **45**

◉ Conduct a review and evaluation

In this second Phase of Unit 1, your students should have had the opportunity to explore Napoleon & Early Missions through researching, thinking, and reporting by completing a selection from the following:

- done a research project;
- learned the vocabulary;
- constructed a time line;
- created a project report on what was researched;
- completed their self-evaluation procedure for this Phase.

Record student hours: _____

Assess student effort in the research and reporting projects.

Create an evaluation system of your own, or refer to the evaluation rubric in the introduction, as a tool for assessing research and reporting. The categories you will probably find most useful are *"Introduction," "Task," "Process: Teamwork"* (if students are working together), along with Grammar, Format, and Spelling. As a tool for helping your students develop better research skills, pay attention to their evaluation of sources. Older students should learn how to make a "Sources Cited" list according to academic standards—refer them to English usage books or websites for formatting rules. Younger students should learn how to obtain a balanced view of their research subject; if they use more than one source they will get a bigger picture of what was happening. Encourage your students to make use of their self-evaluations for their next research projects, in order to practice good research skills.

Do not critique the self-evaluation page your student completes in the Student Manual—spelling errors are not to be considered in such an exercise. Students should feel free to humbly evaluate themselves without that added complexity. Instead, discuss with them the intention of their written comments and incorporate those into your evaluation.

Determine a final grade for this Phase: _____

Teacher Self-Evaluation:

Evaluate your own use of materials and teaching opportunities: what worked and what did not; how effective was your time-management; how were your responses to the needs of your student; did you make your expectations clear; in what ways would you like to improve your approach for the next Unit? Incorporate suggestions from your students in your own evaluation (*this requires humility!*).

The Hands-On Week

Phase 3

▶ Maps and Mapping

Physical Terrain

» Label as many as possible of the major mountain ranges, rivers, and seas affecting Napoleon's troops. (Don't forget Egypt and Russia!)

» Label the major mountain ranges, deserts, plains, and rivers of India. As you look these up, discover also the four general climatic zones in this vast subcontinent.

Geopolitical

» Shade France in one color, then shade with a different color the area of Europe that was brought into the Napoleonic Empire.

» Mark and label the sites of Napoleon's victories. Mark and label the sites of Napoleon's defeats.

» Mark the places in India where William Carey lived and ministered. Locate Burma (Myanmar) and show the area where Adoniram Judson ministered.

Explore

» *Who's in Control:* Mark the areas that were, during the time period of this unit (1790–1815), under the jurisdiction of the British East India Company, the Dutch East India Company, and those areas ruled independently by Indian royalty.

» *Strategies:* Consider the impact of the various terrains and climates Napoleon faced in his bid for empire. In what ways was he helped by the terrain? In what ways was he hindered? What part did the seas and oceans play in this political drama? Mark the map with symbols to show where his troops were favored by these factors and conditions and where they were hindered.

» *Christian Outreach:* What is the status of evangelical outreach today in India? What opportunities and what difficulties face those who share the gospel in these areas?

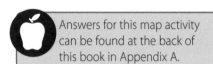
Answers for this map activity can be found at the back of this book in Appendix A.

◉ Create a map and discuss the issues in teams

The students each have an outline map in their manuals. They will be given assignments for drawing in the rivers, mountains, cities, and regional boundaries that are listed. For details on where these things are, please consult Appendix A, a historical atlas, an encyclopedia, or another source of geographic information.

Upper elementary students might be satisfied to accomplish only this portion:

• **Physical terrain:** This part of the mapping exercise will help students locate and mark the Eurasian countries involved in the Napoleonic Wars, including Russia. Students will also locate the major regions of India.

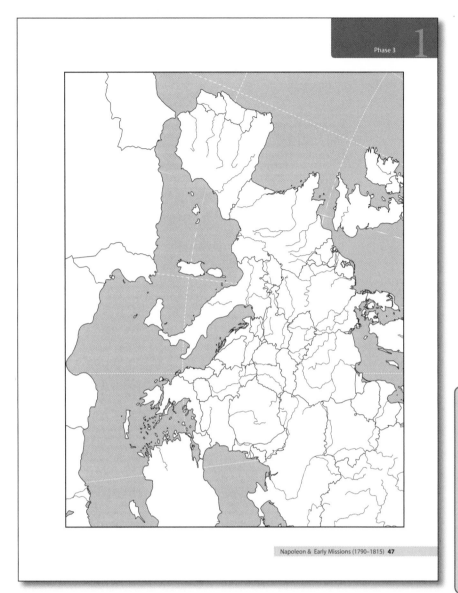

Napoleon & Early Missions (1790–1815) **47**

Middle school students might be satisfied to complete both the previous mapping exercise and this exercise:

• **Geopolitical:** This section of the mapping exercise will provide students an opportunity to locate and mark the specific sites where Napoleon conquered various European nations, as well as the cities where William Carey and Adoniram Judson served as missionaries.

High school students might be satisfied to complete both the previous mapping exercises and at least one exploration topic of this exercise:

• **Explore** a selection from this portion of the mapping exercise in teams.

WHO'S IN CONTROL **?**

Students might find it helpful to see where the boundary lines were between the British and the Dutch East India Company lands and the lands governed by independent Indian rulers. It will give them greater insight into the dynamics that produced the British Raj in India, the time from 1858 to 1947 when the entire subcontinent was governed by the British.

STRATEGIES **?**

Encourage students to think about these dynamics in each of Napoleon's military moves, including Egypt, Haiti, Russia, England, and Europe, as they consider this geographic puzzle.

CHRISTIAN OUTREACH **?**

Students might wish to locate information about current missionary endeavors in India or Bangladesh. If possible, interview someone who has worked in these fields to provide more help and insight.

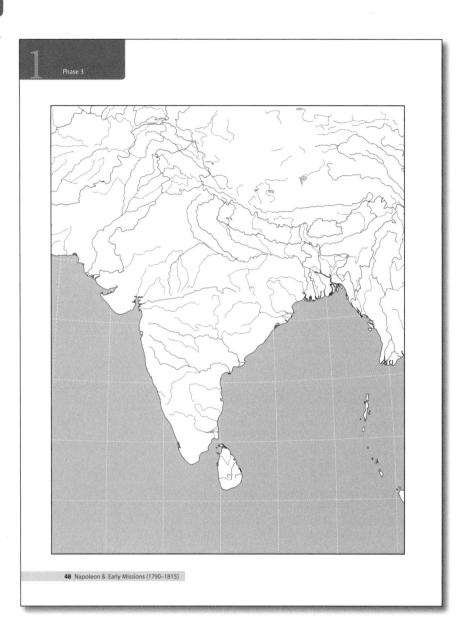

48 Napoleon & Early Missions (1790–1815)

▶ Art Appreciation

Napoleon at the St. Bernard Pass
by Jacques-Louis David

You can find links to see these paintings at the online resource page.

» What sense of Napoleon's accomplishment does this painting convey to you? In what ways does it convey the message of triumph in the undertaking? In what ways could you compare this image of Napoleon with Alexander the Great and his horse, Bucephalus?

» Would you describe this painting as realistic? What other terms could be used?

» Compare this with Paul Delaroche's painting of the same event, *Bonaparte Crossing the Alps*. In what ways are the paintings similar? In what ways are they different?

The Third of May, 1808 by Francisco de Goya

This is one of Goya's most powerful paintings. It shows Napoleon's army carrying out retribution for an uprising of Spaniards against Napoleon in Madrid.

» Goya might have been an eyewitness to the massacre of Spanish citizens in Madrid. How does this painting differ in style, content, and message from David's painting?

» In what ways could you describe this painting to someone who had never seen it? For what reasons might you recommend this painting to someone studying Napoleon's military career?

CONSIDER:

The French Revolution and the reign of Napoleon had a dramatic effect upon art, especially on the continent of Europe. It ushered in neoclassicism—a return to the classical style of ancient Rome and Greece. In painting, this meant that figures would resemble sculptures in form and simplicity, objects would have very defined outlines, and colors would be kept to a minimum (though bright colors could be used).

The online resource page at www.HistoryRevealed.org contains many helpful Internet links to artwork, architecture, music, project helps, and more.

The online resource page at www.HistoryRevealed.org contains many helpful Internet links to artwork, architecture, music, project helps, and more.

When we idolize someone (apart from God), we lose sight of who they truly are. With your students, consider the differences between David's painting of Napoleon crossing the Alps and Delaroche's painting. Then pray together that you each might be equipped by the Holy Spirit to see people as they really are and to not be deceived by the perceived glamour of "stars."

◉ Examine and discuss art and architecture

The online resource page at www.HistoryRevealed.org has links to view each of the items listed. Allow the students time to observe the paintings without any conversation, and then, when they are ready, engage them in some or all of the questions listed below or in the Student Manual.

Art Appreciation

Napoleon at the Saint-Bernard Pass by Jacques-Louis David

Jacques-Louis David was not only an artist, but also a passionate follower of the French Revolution and, subsequently, of Napoleon Bonaparte. His painting style, which was Neoclassical, was used in the service of politics to give his subjects an almost religious quality. He was the most influential French artist of this very unstable time.

The Third of May 1808 by Francisco de Goya

Francisco de Goya started painting in the Rococo style but eventually changed to Neo-Baroque (the style of Rembrandt and Velazquez). He created portraits for the Spanish royalty prior to 1808, when Napoleon's troops occupied Spain. Goya had hoped that the French Revolution would bring a long-awaited liberty, equality, and fraternity to the Spaniards, but found, much to his shock, that the French were interested in control rather than freedom. His paintings from 1810 until Napoleon's final defeat are dramatic testimony to the type of treatment Spaniards experienced at the hands of the French.

Architecture

The Pantheon, Paris by Jacques-Germain Soufflot

After the French Revolution began, the exterior windows of the Church of Saint Genevieve were walled up, changing the transparency of glass at the outer walls to the cold blankness of stone, as the church was converted to its new use as a mausoleum to honor dead French heroes.

Try to locate a photo of the Pantheon, the first neoclassical building built in Paris. Discuss with your students the majestic nature of this architectural style. The location of the Pantheon is also a significant part of its importance to Paris. Ask students to discover why this is so.

Park Crescent, Regent's Park

Though this park was originally envisioned to be a beautifully landscaped setting for the Prince Regent's palace, as well as a site for fifty-six villas, amazingly, no palace was ever built and few villas remain.

You can see a photo of the beautifully curved building known as *Park Crescent* in Regent's Park at the online resource page. There is also a link to a photo of the Royal Pavilion in Brighton, also designed by Nash. Discuss with students the contrast between these two buildings, both originally part of a design for the Prince Regent.

▷ Architecture

The neoclassical style was evident in architecture beginning in the mid-1700s and continuing into the 1800s. This was due in part to the excavations at Pompeii and Herculaneum, which provided architects with excellent models of Roman architecture. You can find links to see these buildings at the online resource page.

The Pantheon, Paris by Jacques-Germain Soufflot

» Built originally to be the Church of Saint Genevieve, the patron saint of Paris, this building was not completed until 1789. With the French Revolution at hand, the building was renamed and used as the most esteemed burial site for France's heroes. How does this building reflect a classical style of architecture? How would you describe the exterior? The interior draws from the Gothic style of architecture. What are some terms you could use to describe the inside of the Pantheon?

In England, the beginning of the 1800s ushered in the Regency Period, which saw a revival of Greek architecture. The main architect of this time was John Nash. His most famous classic architectural design is Regent's Park in London.

Park Crescent, Regent's Park

» What are some of the possible reasons you can imagine for creating this type of structure? In what ways does it resemble the classical architecture of antiquity?

▷ Arts in Action

Select one or more, and let your artistic juices flow!

Neoclassical Art

Create an artistic piece in the neoclassical style! You may wish to draw, paint, or use modeling clay or LEGO® blocks. Create a backdrop with simple Greek or Roman columns, stairs, marble flooring, and other classical touches. Add a few subjects, dramatically posed, and compose a title, such as "Dianacus Awaiting Inspiration." Have fun!

Realism

Choose an adventure from your life (or from one of your family members). Create a stylized depiction of the adventure, showing the heroic nature of the central character. This is not an exercise in realism; it is to emphasize the dramatic nature of the event, similar to David's painting of Napoleon crossing the Alps.

50 Napoleon & Early Missions (1790–1815)

◉ Do an art project

Neoclassical Art

To gain a better understanding of how Neoclassical art is connected to classical Roman and Greek art, look at Jacques-Louis David's painting *The Oath of the Horatii* at the online resource page. It depicts a story, well known to the Romans, of the sacrifice willingly made by three brothers for the sake of the Roman Republic.

Painted in 1784, during the years leading up to the turbulent French Revolution, this painting had a dramatic effect upon the French people, as it hearkened back to the Romans. Encourage students who are interested in these art projects to observe the stark simplicity of David's paintings and study the way he creates "heroic" scenes.

> # Science

George Cuvier (1769–1832) was a scientist in France during the time of the Revolution, Napoleon, and the "Restoration" (when the Bourbon kings regained the throne). He is best remembered for his work in establishing the sciences of comparative anatomy and paleontology (the study of fossil remains). He maintained that the fossil record showed clearly the reality of Creation (no in-between species), and he carefully refuted the notion of evolution.

Visit a Fossil!

» The Creation Museum, natural history museums, paleontological digs, zoos, and fossil shops all have interesting fossil specimens to examine. Ask yourself these questions: Is this a marine animal, land animal, or plant? Is it extinct? Where was it found? Is it an unusual fossil? (*Dry Bones and Other Fossils* by Dr. Gary Parker is an excellent introduction to fossils for younger students. *The Fossil Book*, by Dr. Gary & Mary Parker, is appropriate for ages 12 & up.)

> # Music

The music of Ludwig van Beethoven predominated during the early 1800s—the Napoleonic era. It is the bridge between the classical style of music (Haydn, Mozart) and the romantic style (Schubert, Berlioz, Mendelssohn, Schumann, Liszt, Chopin, Tchaikovsky). The neoclassical movement in painting and architecture, with its emphasis on form, simplicity, and control, gave way to romanticism and realism (with their emotion, imagination, and lack of restraint). Beethoven's music moves similarly from classical to romantic. You can find links to listen to the music at the online resource page.

Symphony No. 5 in C minor, Op. 67 by Beethoven

Beethoven's Fifth Symphony is one of the most popular symphonies ever written. After listening, talk together about why this might be so. What is the famous theme, or *motif*, in the second movement of the symphony? Can you sing it?

"The Year 1812," Festival Overture in E flat major, Op. 49 by Tchaikovsky

Though composed long after the actual event, the 1812 Overture by Pyotr Ilyich Tchaikovsky is an amazing musical celebration of the Russian victory over Napoleon's troops. The piece was first played in 1882 in Moscow.

» Listen carefully to this entire piece, thinking about Napoleon's experiences in Russia as you do. Did you find any particular messages that the composer was trying to convey within the music?

◉ Do a science field trip

If your students can speak with *agape* and not arrogance, the curators and shopkeepers might be responsive to questions.

◉ Listen to and discuss the music

Beethoven actually dedicated his third symphony to Napoleon until he learned that his "hero of humanity" had betrayed the Revolution and crowned himself emperor!

Listen

Fifth Symphony

In its form, the Fifth Symphony is similar to the symphonies of the classical era, but the emotion that is displayed in its famous theme—"da da da DAAA"—is indicative of the emotional and expressive sound that was to come in the Romantic era.

This motif was played by the BBC to introduce their radio news broadcasts during WWII—because those four notes resembled the Morse code for "V" (three dots and a dash), which stood for Victory. A German composer's music was used to represent Allied efforts. Isn't that ironic?

1812 Overture

Understanding the historical background of the time enriches the listening experience. It helps us know what to listen for in the music. The online resource page has a link to an article that is particularly easy to understand.

▶ Cooking

According to tradition, Napoleon demanded a meal after the Battle of Marengo. His chef had to make do with the scanty items he could find: a chicken, some eggs, tomatoes, olive oil, garlic, herbs, onions, and crayfish. From these ingredients (plus some of Napoleon's cognac), the chef came up with a dish that pleased Napoleon. In fact, he considered it lucky and refused to have the recipe altered on future occasions. Fix some for yourself, and see why Napoleon was to taken with this dish.

Chicken Marengo

½ cup flour	2 cups canned tomatoes
¼ cup butter	1 tsp dried tarragon
1 tsp salt	1 clove garlic, finely chopped
1 cup dry white cooking wine	3 lbs. chicken, cut in pieces
(or substitute 1 cup of chicken broth)	10 mushrooms, sliced
½ tsp black pepper	¼ cup olive oil

Preheat oven to 350° F. Mix flour, salt, pepper, and tarragon, then dredge the chicken in this mixture. In a frying pan, heat the olive oil and butter together. When it is sufficiently hot, brown the chicken on all sides. Place the chicken in a heavy casserole dish. Whisk the remaining flour mixture into the oil and butter until smooth, then gradually add wine until sauce is thickened and smooth. Pour it over the chicken and add the tomatoes, garlic, and mushrooms. Cover casserole with an ovenproof lid, and bake until chicken is tender (about 45 minutes). If you would like, sprinkle fresh parsley over the chicken just before serving. Serves 6.

Be sure to serve with French bread and a salad. Bon appetit!

If you can obtain fresh tarragon, use that instead, substituting one tablespoon of chopped fresh tarragon for the one teaspoon of dried. Fresh herbs are absolutely the best, if you have them available!

◉ Cook the food

▶ Student Self-Evaluation UNIT 1, PHASE 3

Dates and hours:_____

Evaluate your projects

- List which of the activities listed in this Phase you did:

  _____

  _____

- Rate your enthusiasm: _____

  Explain: _____

  _____

- Rate the precision of your approach:_____

  Explain: _____

  _____

- Rate your effort toward the completion of the project: _____

  Explain: _____

  _____

- Ask yourself what worked and what did not. What would you do differently in the future, and what would you repeat?

  _____

  _____

- How specifically did these hands-on activities enhance your knowledge of Napoleon & Early Missions? What made them worthwhile?

  _____

  _____

- In the first three Phases of this Unit, what aspect of the time period has most captured your imagination? What would you like to creatively pursue to conclude your study?

  _____

  _____

◉ Conduct a review and evaluation

In this Phase of Unit 1, your students should have had the opportunity to explore Napoleon & Early Missions through various hands-on and creative sessions by completing a selection from the following:

- completed a mapping section;

- observed and discussed art & architecture;

- worked on an art project;

- experimented with a science project or taken a field trip;

- listened to music;

- tasted a food related to this Unit;

- completed their self-evaluation procedure for this Phase.

Record student hours: _____

Assess student involvement in the hands-on activities.

Create an evaluation system of your own or refer to the evaluation rubric in the introduction as a tool for assessing participation. The categories you will probably find most useful for evaluating projects are *"Task"* and *"Process: Teamwork."* Consider specifi-

cally the enthusiasm, the precision of approach, and the efforts toward improving skills and completing activities, rather than rating the project as compared to a masterpiece.

Do not critique the self-evaluation page your student completes in the Student Manual—it is acceptable for students to occasionally leave lines blank if a question does not apply. Instead, discuss with the student the intention of the written comments and incorporate those into your evaluation.

Determine a grade for this Phase, if using grades: _____

Teacher Self-Evaluation:

Evaluate your own use of materials: what worked and what did not? Consider your time management. Were you able to recognize and respond to your students' needs? Did you make your expectations clear? In what ways would you like to improve your approach for the next Unit? Incorporate suggestions from your students in your own evaluation (*this requires humility!*).

◎ Choose an area of expression

Students may work either individually or in teams.

Linguistics:

Journalism

Exposé is a term that means a report, especially a journalistic report, that reveals something scandalous. There are many examples of this type of reporting that students could examine for this project. A fascinating online report on the valuable role played by investigative reporters in a free democracy, "The Withering Watchdog," can be found at the online resource page.

To find current interviews of international politicians, students might consider going online to reuters.com. Once there, search for "interview" to see how professional journalists handle this type of article.

Encourage students to scan local newspapers for the "Letter to the Editor" section. That is a great place for taking the "pulse" of a community about various issues.

Poetry

Though the subject is serious, students may choose to do this project in the style of Dr. Seuss, with interesting rhymes and a humorous telling of truth.

Prose

To better understand how one might address Napoleon, whose power to swallow a country was legendary, encourage students to observe

---

Phase 4

▶ In Your Own Way...

We have seen the newly forged empire of the French Revolution rise to European dominance while the centuries-old Holy Roman Empire fades to a mere memory in the history books; the British Navy become the formidable ruler of the seas through the genius of admirals and the power of impressment; William Carey powerfully share the gospel as he wends his way through the difficulties of missionary life; the United States successfully navigate its first three decades of existence while growing in size and power, despite two wars; the creation of the first black republic; and a near-miraculous end to the African slave trade. Now, choose a selection of these activities, or create your own, which will best express what you have learned from this Unit.

LINGUISTICS

Journalism

As an investigative reporter for the hard-hitting monthly magazine *The Christian Persuader,* you have been given the job of uncovering the dark secrets and exploitive reasons why the British East India Company refuses to allow Christian missionaries to live or work within their territories. Remember, in this era shortly after the Great Awakening, you have a chance to impact policy by mobilizing British opinion on this issue—if people are sufficiently outraged.

As a reporter for the *Island Insider*, interview Toussaint L'Ouverture to discover the volatile situation in Haiti. In your article, analyze his chances of holding out against the Napoleonic Empire. What does he have going for him? What things are working against him?

Write a letter to the editor of the *Empire Herald* expressing your views of Napoleon's decision to divorce Josephine and marry Mary Louise. Are you shocked? Tell the readers why, but remember to couch it in such a way that the imperial temper is not provoked!

Poetry

Create a rhyming poem about the possible anticipated invasion of England by French troops. You may write it either from the viewpoint of the

English, who are fearful but trusting in the prowess of the British Navy, or from the viewpoint of the French soldiers, who are eager to go but frustrated by their lack of seamanship.

Prose

You are the king of Spain. When you turned over the Louisiana Territory in the Americas to Napoleon, you required that it never be transferred to someone else unless it was back to you. You just learned that he had the audacity to sell it to Thomas Jefferson of the United States. Write Napoleon your thoughts on this action (in the language of a king). Be sure to remind him of your former agreement. Remember, your desire is to influence him to cancel the deal with Jefferson before it's too late!

Write a job application to William Carey or Adoniram Judson. Tell him why you would like to work alongside him in ministry and how your skills and experience would qualify you, being careful to display your familiarity with the work he has accomplished in his ministry country, whether India or Burma.

In the style of Aesop's fables, tell the story of the rise and fall of *The Very Important Person*, using what you have studied of Napoleon's life as the model and the lessons learned as the moral.

---

the protocol and etiquette used by Columbus as he wrote to King Ferdinand and Queen Isabella. A link to the letter can be found at the online resource page.

There are excellent resources online for writing your résumé. These might be helpful for students to consider as they write a fictional job application for Carey or Judson, since a résumé would be an essential part of the package.

A fable is a short allegorical tale, written with a proverb or moral at the end. Jacob Grimm, one of the two Brothers Grimm, said this about the crafting of fables: "In the first place,

the fable must exhibit the animals as being endowed with human reason, and initiated into all the customs and conditions of our mode of living, so that their behavior has nothing at all odd in it." Students would find it helpful to read some of Aesop's fables in order to better understand how to write their own fable. See a link at the online resource page.

Art:

Painting/Drawing

Students interested in gaining ideas for a painting or drawing could do an online image search for "Battle of the Pyramids." There are many depic-

ART

Painting/Drawing

Create a visual presentation of the Battle of the Pyramids, with the backdrop of antiquity setting the stage for Napoleon's famous engagement with the Egyptian Mamluks.

Graphic Design

As a captured British sailor/artist, you have been given the opportunity to win your freedom. The price? Design an award-winning T-shirt graphic for use by members of Napoleon's Grande Armée, which was unbeatable on land at the height of the French Empire. If you are extremely careful, you may be able to work in a visual reminder that your country's navy is unbeatable on the seas.

However, if it's too obvious, your design will be disqualified. Good luck!

Cartooning

Draw a political cartoon of Napoleon's exile on Elba. Remember that he didn't stay long—as a kingdom, it was much too small for a conqueror of his stature!

Sculpting

With clay or another sculpting medium, create a piece of symbolic or abstract art that expresses your thoughts on the long-awaited and hard-won victory achieved by William Wilberforce in outlawing the African slave trade in the British Empire.

MUSIC

Compose

Sea shanties are a time-honored form of folk music—actually work music—for sailors. A song like "Blow the Man Down" is an example of a sea shanty. Compose your own sea shanty with lyrics focused on the British Navy's habit of impressing unwilling sailors into their fleet during the Napoleonic Wars.

Performance Practice

With your teacher's help, select an appropriate piece of music that expresses a particular aspect studied in this Unit, whether from the Napoleonic Wars, William Carey's experiences, the abolition of slavery, or the struggles of the United States during this volatile time.

---

tions of this very famous battle and its ancient setting. A link to some of them can be found at the online resource page.

Graphic Design

A trip to a clothing store might provide inspiration for this project, if students take careful note of the use of color, design, images, and wording on popular T-shirts.

Cartooning

Ask students to consider the elements of political cartooning that would provide the most interest for viewers, and those areas that would best lend themselves to lampooning Napoleon's visions of grandeur. (One suggestion would be to discover who went with Napoleon to Elba and who, noticeably, did not.)

Sculpting

If students need inspiration for this project, suggest that they watch the historical retelling of Wilberforce's work in the DVD *Amazing Grace*. Beyond that, there are many powerful images online for African slavery and its abolition that may give ideas.

Music:

Compose

A well-known sea shanty sung about

Napoleon is "Boney." Though you can find the lyrics online, it is much more satisfying to listen to the actual shanty. A music store online would be one source. At the online resource page you can find a link where you can listen to a 30-second clip for free or purchase the song for a small price.

Performance Practice

For musical students, this selection may be a wonderful opportunity to express what they have learned. Make sure they have selected a piece that they have adequate time to prepare.

Drama:

Comedy

This is a wonderful opportunity for students to learn the "Rule of Three:"

> If something happens once, it is an accident. If it happens twice, it's a coincidence. If it happens three times, it's a comedy. Commonly used in theater, as well as dance, visual arts and music, this is a technique which will allow students to create a comedic moment. What makes it work is that the third time it happens, something has to change. (Find further comments regarding this principle in Unit 4 Phase 4 Dance.) In this particular example, students could build the scene repeating some element of things going wrong as Carey keeps ruining shoe leather. The comedy will work if the timing is right as his boss walks in during the third repetition.

If students want some ideas to add a touch of slapstick to this comedy, they could watch a 3-minute clip from the *I Love Lucy* show, where Lucy and Ethel wrap candy at the chocolate factory. You can find a link to the video on the online resource page.

Puppetry

Students interested in this drama might find it helpful to use a "chorus."

Greek tragedy had a very definite

style with a chorus that served as a collective, often poetic voice. The chorus commented on the story as it progressed, using a variety of techniques including singing, dancing, narration, and acting. Since it is more interesting to set people in triangles on stage rather than straight lines, students will find it helpful in this puppet show to add a chorus group along with the two opposing sides of the struggle. This chorus will be ones the opposing sides are trying to convince, which gives the chorus an opportunity to repeat after them, to take what they say and turn it into quick songs, etc. This will not only add dramatic interest, it will also help interpret the action to the audience.

There are online resources for crafting your own puppets, from sock puppets to more complex papier-mâché head puppets. Puppet patterns for sewing are also available for purchase online. Students who enjoy this form of theater may find it motivational to create their own puppets for long-term use.

Drama

In theater, the use of height and vertical levels can be used to depict emotional states and social status. Just as a judge in court is seated in the highest place to depict authority, just as fighting a battle from the high ground takes advantage of gravity, and just like arrogant persons raise their chins in disdain, the physical act on stage of growing taller or stepping higher communicates emotions and circumstances effectively.

So, in this drama, consider using changing levels and heights to visually represent the transformation that occurs among the French and the Russians.

In her book *Jack and Jill*, Louisa May Alcott describes a theatrical performance by children portraying the winter at Valley Forge during the American Revolution. Students searching for inspiration for this project might find it helpful to read how this group of students created such

---

DRAMA

Comedy

Depict the scene from William Carey's life when his employer asked him to stop ruining his good shoe leather and to focus on preaching the gospel. Be sure to set the scene with Carey trying to make shoes while at the same time diligently studying a world map and learning several languages!

Puppetry

With puppets, portray the story of the tension in America between those who supported the French Revolution (like Thomas Jefferson)

and those who opposed it (like John Adams). Remember, men (and puppets) should wear powdered wigs to represent the fashion in those days.

Drama

Dramatize the War of 1812 in Russia. Half of your actors should play the part of the French army (which was smug going into Russia) and the other half should play the part of the Russian peasants (who were smug when the Russian winter destroyed the French). Remember that Napoleon made it to safety in his comfortable coach.

Prop Needs

_____

_____

Costume Ideas

_____

_____

Role/Player

_____

_____

Set Suggestions

_____

_____

---

a moving drama about the effects of winter on a group of soldiers. A link to this chapter can be found at the online resource page.

Movement:

Miniature Action

You can do this either two-dimensionally or three-dimensionally. For two-dimension, use color to depict the different levels of terrain and the physical elements. For three-dimension, find creative ways to depict hills or valleys and natural elements like trees, rivers, etc.

With the assistance of the Internet, you can actually get a satellite view of

the land where the Battle of Waterloo was fought! You can find a Google Maps link at the online resource page. Zoom in to see the details.

Pantomime

In English-speaking countries, center stage is the most powerful. In a spiral effect, upstage right (audience left) is the second most powerful, upstage left (audience right) is third, downstage left is fourth, and downstage right is the weakest, most vulnerable position. Audiences tend to be more sympathetic with actors on their left. So suggestions for this pantomime of William Wilberforce's work could be: when students wish to depict a slave

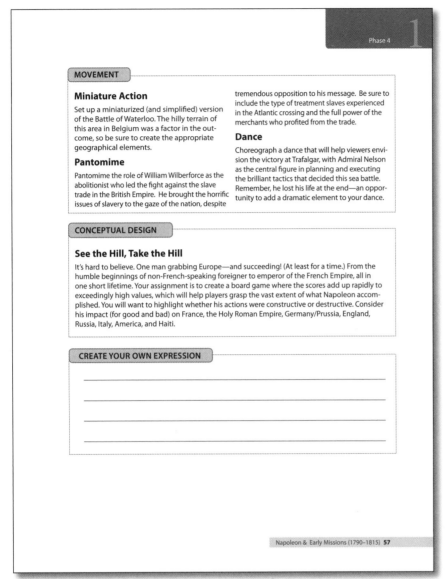

MOVEMENT

Miniature Action

Set up a miniaturized (and simplified) version of the Battle of Waterloo. The hilly terrain of this area in Belgium was a factor in the outcome, so be sure to create the appropriate geographical elements.

Pantomime

Pantomime the role of William Wilberforce as the abolitionist who led the fight against the slave trade in the British Empire. He brought the horrific issues of slavery to the gaze of the nation, despite tremendous opposition to his message. Be sure to include the type of treatment slaves experienced in the Atlantic crossing and the full power of the merchants who profited from the trade.

Dance

Choreograph a dance that will help viewers envision the victory at Trafalgar, with Admiral Nelson as the central figure in planning and executing the brilliant tactics that decided this sea battle. Remember, he lost his life at the end—an opportunity to add a dramatic element to your dance.

CONCEPTUAL DESIGN

See the Hill, Take the Hill

It's hard to believe. One man grabbing Europe—and succeeding! (At least for a time.) From the humble beginnings of non-French-speaking foreigner to emperor of the French Empire, all in one short lifetime. Your assignment is to create a board game where the scores add up rapidly to exceedingly high values, which will help players grasp the vast extent of what Napoleon accomplished. You will want to highlight whether his actions were constructive or destructive. Consider his impact (for good and bad) on France, the Holy Roman Empire, Germany/Prussia, England, Russia, Italy, America, and Haiti.

CREATE YOUR OWN EXPRESSION

_____

_____

_____

_____

in a merchant ship, use the downstage right corner of the stage; when they wish to depict a court listening to William Wilberforce, put them upstage left; when they wish to depict a slave trader, put them downstage left; when they wish to depict William Wilberforce praying by himself, place it upstage right. Reserve center stage for Wilberforce's attempts to convince the Parliament that the slave trade is wrong.

Olaudah Equiano, the former African slave who was part of the fight to abolish the slave trade in the British Empire, wrote this about his experience of the dreadful Atlantic crossing: "I was soon put down under the decks, and there I received such a salutation in my nostrils as I had never experienced in my life; so that, with the loathsomeness of the stench and crying together, I became so sick and low that I was unable to eat." Students choosing to pantomime this project will need to read some of the descriptions of the crossing in order to have a good understanding of what they are to portray.

Dance

A beautiful and expressive tool in dance can be "order versus chaos." Students wishing to create the choreography of this battle might use straight lines for the British patterns of movement but carefully choreographed chaotic circles to depict the confusion of the French and Spanish ships. Because one of the primary British strategies was to cut off the French flag ship from its fleet, appoint two dancers as admirals—one British, one French—and show how the British managed this, throwing the remaining French and Spanish forces into chaos. A visual clue that would help the audience could be to dress in costumes that clearly identify the British from the French and Spanish forces.

To better understand the dynamics and strategies of the Battle of Trafalgar, students intending to choreograph a dance might find a certain BBC article very helpful. A link to this article can be found at the online resource page.

Conceptual Design:

If students wish to combine geography with history in this game, they can start with a laminated map of Europe and move their players along the battle lines in various countries. Another idea is to set up a Monopoly-style game, where players can move around a board that includes different categories pertinent to Napoleon's empire. As always, great inspiration can come from seeing what others before you have done: visit a well-stocked game shop to discover some of the ways game-makers craft successful sellers.

◉ Share creative expressions in class

Create a safe environment for the presentations. Set ground rules prior to the presentations, so that students know how much time is available for each of them, and so that they know they will be honored and respected by all those observing.

Conduct a review and evaluation

In this Phase of Unit 1, your students should have had the opportunity to express what they have learned about Napoleon & Early Missions through one or more various creative selections of their own choosing. These include:

- Linguistics;
- Art;
- Music;
- Drama;
- Movement;
- Conceptual Design.

Record student hours: _____

Assess student effort in the creative expressions, as individuals or as teams.

Create an evaluation system of your own, or refer to the evaluation rubric in the introduction, as a tool for assessing participation. The categories you will probably find most useful for evaluating their projects are *"Task," "Process: Teamwork," "Process: Originality,"* and Grammar, Format, and Spelling.

In this Phase especially, do not critique the self-evaluation page your student completes in the Student Manual—consider how the very soul of an artist has been exposed and vulnerable, so be encouraging and not belittling. Again, consider enthusiasm, precision of approach, and efforts toward improving skills and completing the activity, rather than rating the project as compared to a masterpiece. Instead, discuss with the student the intention of the written comments and incorporate those into your evaluation.

Determine a grade for this Phase, if using grades: _____

Teacher Self-Evaluation:

Evaluate your own use of materials and teaching opportunities: what worked and what did not; how effective was your time-management; how were your responses to the needs of your student; did you make your expectations clear; in what ways would you like to improve your approach for the next Unit? Incorporate suggestions from your students in your own evaluation (*this requires humility!*).

Take a moment now to evaluate the whole Unit. What would you like to remember if you taught this subject again? What do you recognize that your students gained most—either as students of history or as creative individuals? What did you learn about Napoleon & Early Missions or about teaching?

▷ Student Self-Evaluation UNIT 1, PHASE 4

Dates and hours:_____

Evaluate your projects

- What creative project did you choose?

  _____

- What did you expect from your project, and how does the final project compare to your initial expectations?

  _____

  _____

- What do you like about your project? What would you change?

  _____

  _____

In Conclusion

Revisit the four Key Concepts from the beginning of this Unit. Explain how your understanding of and appreciation for each has grown over the course of your study.

- _____

  _____

- _____

  _____

- _____

  _____

- _____

  _____

Record your concluding thoughts on Napoleon & Early Missions:

_____

_____

58 Napoleon & Early Missions (1790–1815)

Industrialization & the Church's Response
(1800–1850)

Pray with the students at the beginning of each Unit.

Enthusiasm and delight are the best ways to capture a student's interest and jump-start motivation, so:

» **For the Auditory Students:** Play music with the sounds of Latin America, such as the wonderful Colombian song "Soltarlo" performed by artist Claudia Gomez. (A link to listen to it on YouTube can be found at the online resource page.)

» **For the Kinesthetic Students:** Select a student to be the leader in a game of Simon Says. The task to be performed? Building a railroad! (Don't forget the blasting powder.)

» **For the Visual Students:** Bring a Greek flag, or an image of one, to show students the colors and design of the flag that was adopted shortly after Greece gained its independence during this era.

» **For the hearts of all:** Pray with them at the beginning of the Unit, that God would help them discover what He has for each one to learn in this Unit.

◉ Learning Style Emphasis

Teachers can choose to have students do one or two activities, rather than the entire week's schedule. Please use what works for you in your unique setting.

	Week 1: Feeler	Week 2: Thinker	Week 3: Sensor	Week 4: Intuitor
	During this week, students will be introduced to Industrialization & the Church's Response, along with the appropriate Scriptures. You may follow this suggested schedule or adapt it to meet your students' needs:	Students will explore topics of interest through research and reporting, learn new vocabulary, and construct a time line relating to Industrialization & the Church's Response.	Students will gain cultural understanding through sensory activities as they explore interrelated subject areas through sensory activities pertaining to Industrialization & the Church's Response.	Through creative self-expression, using one or more creative activities, students will present some aspect of what they have learned in the past three weeks relating to Industrialization & the Church's Response. Areas of expression include linguistics, art, music, drama, movement, and conceptual design.
Monday	Informally discuss the Key Concepts Listen to the *What in the World?* audio recording(s)	Choose topic and begin research	Create a map and discuss the issues in teams	Choose an area of expression and begin work either individually or in teams
Tuesday	Read the article Listen to the other audio recording(s) Read the Scriptures		Examine and discuss art masterpieces & architectural structures	
Wednesday	Recap the material using activities Talk together	Practice vocabulary	Do an art project*	
Thursday	Conduct class discussion	Construct the time line	Do a science experiment or field trip**	
Friday	Choose books of interest/Internet search Conduct a review and evaluation	Complete research projects and share in class or hand in Conduct a review and evaluation	Listen to and discuss the music Cook the food listed in the recipe Conduct a review and evaluation	Share creative expressions in class Conduct a review and evaluation

*Art project will need to be planned ahead of time to acquire materials.
** Field trip will require extra planning time.

Industrialization & the Church's Response (1800–1850)

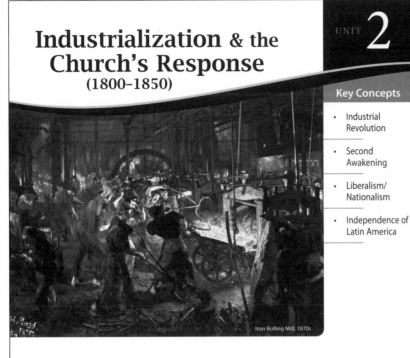

Iron Rolling Mill, 1870s

Key Concepts

- Industrial Revolution
- Second Awakening
- Liberalism/ Nationalism
- Independence of Latin America

Changes

As smoke cleared from the battlefield at Waterloo, the victorious nations breathed a collective sigh of relief at having finally vanquished the monster—Napoleon Bonaparte, the embodiment of all their problems, the disturber of their peace. After seeing him securely imprisoned on the extremely remote Atlantic island of St. Helena, these nations now faced the urgent diplomatic business of unraveling the mess from twenty years of constant battle. The sovereign heads of state were each anxious to return to the "good old days," restoring their national boundaries and reestablishing their royal prerogatives as all-powerful leaders. It is not surprising, given the disastrous results in France and across the Continent, that the kings and emperors of each country viewed the turbulent results of revolution— whether American or French—as a potent menace, to be avoided at all costs.

Industrialization & the Church's Response (1800–1850) **59**

◉ Informally discuss the Key Concepts with your students

KEY CONCEPTS Background Information

These are the main objectives of the Unit. As you proceed through the four weeks, your students will be given various ways of understanding each of these objectives. Explanations of these Key Concepts follow.

The Industrial Revolution— EXPLANATION

To understand the immensity of the changes to people and nations, to business and church, and to the concepts of time and power, we need to look back at the way things were done before this revolution. Let's consider how cloth was made, for instance, since the Industrial Revolution had a major impact on the manufacture of textiles. In England, where sheep were plentiful, wool was regularly shorn from the sheep. From that raw substance, spinners in a home would spin the yarn into skeins. At a weaver's home, those skeins could then be woven by hand into lengths of woolen fabric. Next, a tailor would carefully cut, piece, and sew the fabric into articles of clothing. Obviously, this was a lengthy process, and clothing was a treasured commodity.

With the advent of the new power-driven machinery of the Industrial Revolution, however, all of this began to change. The first of the new technologies in textiles was invented by John Kay of England in 1733. It was a "flying shuttle," which allowed a weaver to single-handedly weave a broad length of cloth rather than the narrow length that was common. (If two weavers worked together, they could manage broad cloth, but it was not nearly as efficient as this new machine.) Though the weavers of woolen fabric were up in arms about the flying shuttle—since it would put many of them out of business—weavers of cotton were not such dyed-in-the-wool traditionalists. Beginning around 1750, cot-

The dawn of the nineteenth century saw the birth of the Industrial Revolution.

But the world was simply not the same as it had been before Napoleon. Common people on both sides of the Atlantic now knew, and their kings feared, that the potential existed for them to have a voice in their own governments, to be ruled by the laws of a constitution rather than the whims of an absolute monarch, to have a free press, to have a choice in their religious beliefs, and to rise in society without limitations of birth or class. From the humblest African workers on Caribbean plantations to the Catholic priests in Mexico to the German academics at European universities, there was an increased vision and desire for change in the circumstances of the world.

These intense yearnings were mutually exclusive. Either life would return, as the monarchs desired, to the good old days, or life would change, as the people desired, in radical new ways—they simply could not both have what they wanted. And the political tension throughout Europe and Europe's American colonies arising from this struggle was one of the most significant factors in the events of this time period.

However, just as it is today, there were more factors at work than merely the theories of politics. The dawn of the nineteenth century also saw the birth of the Industrial Revolution, which would bring unprecedented changes to the world. This revolution in technology would eventually shatter centuries-old concepts of power, of space, and of time. To illustrate, consider how impatient we become if our washing machine breaks, our plane is delayed, or our Internet connection is too slow. Contrast this with the expectations of people prior to the Industrial Revolution. They were familiar with the power of water to turn wheels, of yoked animals to move stones, and of strong men to shape iron by powerful strokes of the hammer. They had no notion that you could move faster than the wind could propel your ship, or your horse could gallop, or your legs could run. They recognized that communication with someone far away required weeks or even months of waiting, as a letter had to go through the process of traveling across land or water to be delivered and then the same process reversed for a reply to be received. But all these were about to change dramatically.

In the midst of the struggle and changes in nineteenth century politics and technology, people's lives were deeply affected. Poor people became even more desperate in their needs and desires, while rulers and leaders were faced with an increasing tumult among the masses. It is precisely at this point, interwoven through all of these upheavals, that we discover the significant story of God's presence and power on the earth. He sent men and women to bring comfort to those affected by the Industrial Revolution, and, beyond that, He sent revival—the explosive, supernatural work of God known as the Second Awakening. Throughout the early to mid-1800s, and layered within the everyday work of the church, the Second Awakening

ton weavers began using the flying shuttle. This meant, however, that these weavers were much faster than they had been, and now the cotton spinners could not keep up. New machines were then invented to spin cotton more efficiently. With Eli Whitney's invention of the cotton gin in 1793, which simplified and sped the process of separating the cotton from its pod, the southern United States became one of the main suppliers of raw cotton to the vast cotton textile industry of Great Britain. Output grew from 2,000 tons of cotton in 1795 to 96,000 tons in 1830 and 550,000 tons by 1860, the year before the American Civil War began.

As you can see by these numbers, the manufacturing of textiles was big business indeed and was greatly increased by the use of machinery. But what were the costs to the people who had been spinners and weavers? For some, the cost was unemployment, since the machines replaced many of the workers while creating a greater output of product. In England, this led to the riots of the "Luddites" between 1811 and 1818, which were harshly suppressed by the authorities. For those who kept their jobs, the place of employment shifted from the home—where hand-powered looms and spinning wheels were used—to the factories,

2

brought this wide-scale revival to America, Great Britain, France, Germany, Switzerland, Scandinavia, and realms beyond.

The Second Awakening broke out initially on the American frontier at the turn of the century, before making inroads into other nations and cultures. If we could peek back before the War of 1812 or Napoleon's Battle of Waterloo, we would discover that the westward migration in America had resulted in a wild frontier, where the law was based more on "might makes right" than on the Ten Commandments. Christianity, according to letters and journals from the time, had made very little headway in this rugged land. Circuit riders, going on horseback hundreds of miles per week, preached a Christian message throughout the isolated communities.

Bishop Francis Asbury, a famous Methodist circuit rider in America, wrote in his journal concerning the people he had met in the churchless wilderness, "When I reflect that not one in a hundred came here to get religion, but rather to get plenty of good land, I think it will be well if some or many do not eventually lose their souls." The need to "know the Lord" was not uppermost on people's minds in the West, nor were they steeped in Scripture or church traditions. However, what God was about to do was not limited by their education or their goals.

In June 1800, a Presbyterian preacher named James McGready organized a communion service at Red River in Kentucky for those who attended the three backwoods churches he pastored. Nearly five hundred people attended this three-day event, which was a huge number for the sparsely populated wilderness. As the various ministers present saw the response of the people to the preaching of the Word, they recognized that something quite astonishing was taking place—a move of God beyond what they had ever seen before. Another preacher, Barton Stone, heard of the revival and decided to hold a similar lengthy camp meeting at Cane Ridge, Kentucky, in August 1801, which was well advertised. It is estimated that between ten thousand and twenty-five thousand people came, some from as far away as Ohio and Tennessee. That is a staggering number of people, given that the largest city in Kentucky at that time had fewer than two thousand inhabitants! There was a tremendous response to the preaching, and people throughout the camp meeting were dramatically changed by the gospel.

This time of revival had far-reaching effects on the American West.

Though there were excesses and odd behaviors among a few, this time of revival had far-reaching effects on the American West. One well-respected eyewitness observer of this Second Great Awakening, George Baxter, president of Washington College in Virginia, wrote after touring Kentucky in 1801:

On my way I was informed by settlers on the road that the character of Kentucky travelers was entirely changed, and that they are as remarkable for sobriety as they had

---

Take the time to talk with your students about the way technology and industry continue to have an effect on people around the world. Encourage them to pray and ask the Lord to raise up many who would bring His compassion, justice, and mercy to those who are beaten down and oppressed—especially those in third world countries who are now suffering some of the same effects from the Industrial Revolution that laborers in England, the United States, Germany, and France experienced in the early to mid-1800s.

To get an informal discussion started on this Key Concept, ask a simple leading question, such as, "What do you think it looks like in societies when God 'awakens' His people?"

---

where power-driven looms and spinning machines were located. This meant a significant change for families, because the workers needed to live close to their employment (mass transit had not even been envisioned yet!). From small villages in rural areas, workers moved to growing industrial cities where factories were located. These burgeoning cities were not designed with beauty, sanitation, or the health of the inhabitants in mind. Instead, they were go-for-broke, get-rich-quick manufacturing towns that swelled in population as desperate people flocked to find work. The infrastructure necessary for maintaining a healthy city—like

housing, markets, garbage removal, and pest and disease control—were not yet in place, which led to horrific slum conditions. And the churches, which had been the center of village life, could not possibly keep up with the huge influx of laborers to these cities. Where Christian compassion could have been ministered through the local pastor to the known needs of a village family, the faceless mass of humanity in these industrial centers seemed to be known only to God Himself.

A God-breathed answer to the deep needs of the people displaced by the Industrial Revolution was on its way, as we'll see in the next Key Concept.

The Second Awakening —EXPLANATION

"The Second Awakening" is the term loosely used to describe the moving of God among Protestant churches in the early- to mid-1800s, with the Great Awakening its predecessor during the 1700s. Though we will continue to learn about revivals in following Units, it is instructive to consider how the Second Awakening impacted the responsiveness of individuals not only to their Savior but also to their fellow man.

First, it is important to realize that God was bringing revival to many areas of the world. Immediately

2

The culture was changing for these Americans of the untamed wilderness, because of the radical changes in their personal lives.

formerly been for dissoluteness and immorality. And indeed I found Kentucky . . . the most moral place I have ever seen. A religious awe seemed to pervade the country. Upon the whole, I think the revival in Kentucky the most extraordinary that has ever visited the church of Christ; and all things considered, it was peculiarly adapted to the circumstances of the country into which it came. Infidelity was triumphant and religion was on the point of expiring. Something extraordinary seemed necessary to arrest the attention of a giddy people who were ready to conclude that Christianity was a fable and futurity a delusion. This revival has done it. It has confounded infidelity, awed vice into silence, and brought numbers beyond calculation under serious impressions.

The culture was changing for these Americans of the untamed wilderness, because of the radical changes in their personal lives, and, in the same decade, the culture was changing for the Spanish-speaking people in Mexico, because of changes in their king's life. The change began when Napoleon toppled King Ferdinand VII and the royal house of Spain in 1808. Though his intentions had been focused on Europe, the political tremors in Spain traveled all the way across the ocean to her colonies in North, Central, and South America. Fiercely loyal to their deposed king, Spaniards in the Americas rejected the idea of being ruled by any other Europeans, even another one from Spain. Instead, these colonials preferred to rule themselves in the "name of the king." That opened the door to the concept that a colony might be equal to its colonizing country, and no longer subservient to it. This was a radical departure from the way things had been for nearly three hundred years—since Cortez had conquered the Aztecs in 1521.

Though all of the Spanish and Portuguese colonies in the Americas would eventually be affected, it is instructive to focus on Mexico, where the banner of freedom was first raised. In 1810, a Roman Catholic priest in northern Mexico named Father Miguel Hidalgo preached revolution to his flock. Hidalgo, who was a Creole (meaning a native-born descendent of Spanish settlers), told the peasants that their battle was with the European-born usurpers who were trying to rule over Mexico, enemies of their rightful king, Ferdinand VII. He inflamed them with the rhetoric, "Long live the Virgin of Guadalupe, and death to the Spaniards!" (He was referring to

Miguel Hidalgo

after Napoleon's exile to St. Helena, a Scotsman named Robert Haldane felt that God would have him go to France and French-speaking Switzerland to minister. The result was revival that brought hope and grace to a war-weary people. In Germany, there were revivals throughout the early to mid-1800s in various areas: 1816 in the Lower Rhine, 1835 in Saxony, and 1843 in Stuttgart. According to Christian historian J. Edwin Orr, in 1834 such a powerful work of God took place in the Pacific island of Tonga that Tongans began to go out as missionaries to other islands; in the islands of Hawaii, a revival in 1838 brought thousands of native Hawaiians into the kingdom. In the United States, revivals took place at the turn of the century in Kentucky (the camp

meetings described in the article for Unit 2) and in the 1830s and 1840s in the Northeast under the ministry of Charles Finney and others. In Scotland, a great revival in 1839 spread throughout the nation. In Ireland, the bishops saw such a powerful response to this same revival that they called it "a Second Reformation." In England, an increasing hunger for God was recorded by Lord Shaftesbury, who, when he considered the lack of religious interest among the schoolmates of his own day, was surprised to note the earnest seeking after God and devotion to Christianity among his children's friends only a few short decades later.

Care for others, especially the poor and downtrodden, was the common response to these revivals. Kenneth Scott Latourette, an authoritative chronicler of Christianity's history, wrote of English evangelicals during this era, "Believing . . . in salvation through faith in the unmerited grace of God in Christ and the obligation to lead a life which would display the fruits of salvation, they gave themselves to the propagation of the faith, to fighting social ills, and to serving the victims of those ills."

A tailor in London, Thomas Cranfield, opened schools for children who were too raggedly dressed to attend the church-sponsored Sunday

2

European-born Spaniards living in Mexico.) Within a short time, the angry peasant mob swelled to sixty thousand or more. The result was that many Spaniards as well as Creoles were killed in the violence. But it was a short-lived phenomenon, as Hidalgo was captured and executed and his leaderless mob disbanded within a few months.

This new idea, however, did not die with Hidalgo. The torch for freedom was briefly raised again by another Roman Catholic priest, Father José Morelos. He organized an army aimed at abolishing slavery and ending the caste system that oppressed the majority of the people (who were either of mixed parentage—Mestizos—or indigenous). Morelos said that all who were born in Mexico were "Americanos," regardless of what people group they descended from. This concept of "Americanos" versus "European foreigners" became an increasingly powerful image to those living throughout Spanish- and Portuguese-speaking America. In 1813, Morelos declared Mexico to be independent and led his army for two years before he too was caught and executed by Spanish authorities. That King Ferdinand VII was restored to his throne in the midst of this helped dampen the enthusiasm of the common people, but the tantalizing idea of freedom from foreign rule would not go away. As was the case in Europe during this time period, it merely went underground to await a more opportune moment.

Their efforts at diplomacy kept Europe from Napoleon-style wars for nearly one hundred years.

At the diplomatic Congress of Vienna in 1815, the "great powers" (Russia, Great Britain, Prussia, and Austria) sought to deal with the aftermath of Napoleon's empire and his wars—devastation over much of the Continent of Europe. Though France was represented at the table, it was still viewed as the enemy and was treated much as an outsider. Of all the sovereigns and diplomats who had come to the dazzling splendor of Austria's capital city, three were the moving forces behind the treaty and alliances that would be signed and formed because of this Congress: Czar Alexander of Russia, Lord Castlereagh of Great Britain, and Prince Metternich of Austria. Each had the interests of his own country in mind but hoped that it would be possible to blend these interests in such a way that a balance of power would prevent further major wars in Europe, at least for a generation. Russia wanted, as always, more territory. Great Britain wanted to ensure that neither France nor anyone else would ever again be in a position to dominate the Continent. Austria, whose policies were masterminded by Metternich, wanted to go back to the way things were done prior to the American and French Revolutions, and to erase the very idea of revolution from people's minds by giving them peace and tranquility in their daily lives.

As we will see over the course of this book, changes did not go exactly as these men had hoped, even in their own lifetimes. However, their efforts at diplomacy, in fact, kept Europe from Napoleon-style wars for nearly one

Pray that God will give your students a hunger to serve those who are in need, especially as they examine the lives of such models as Lord Shaftesbury and William Wilberforce.

To get an informal discussion started on this Key Concept, ask a simple leading question, such as, "What do you think these two terms meant during the early to mid-1800s?"

schools of industrial England. His vision was picked up by many others, and soon there were "ragged schools" throughout the nation. A young Scottish Christian, David Nasmith, was so moved by the poverty of people living in the slums of Glasgow that in 1826 he started the Glasgow City Mission to minister to their practical and spiritual needs. Other city missions were soon opened in Dublin, London, Paris, and various industrialized cities in the United States, with wide-ranging results.

Orphanages were opened and operated by Christians who were moved with compassion for the victimized children of the Industrial Revolution

like those immortalized in Charles Dickens's *Oliver Twist*. Christians involved in politics, such as Lord Shaftesbury, worked tirelessly to change the laws of the land for the protection of women and children who were being worked, literally, to death.

With a high regard for the Bible as literal truth and a deep sense of God's command for them to love others as they loved themselves, the Christians of the Second Awakening had a tremendous effect on the lives of countless individuals, on the church itself, and on society as a whole. Their example should stir us profoundly.

Liberalism/ Nationalism— EXPLANATION

It may be surprising for many Christians today to learn that "liberalism," which is often fiercely attacked as being contrary to their worldview, drew its original meaning from the concept of liberty as exemplified by the democratic form of government in the new United States. Liberty and freedom—what a stunning concept to those who had long lived under censure and authoritarian rule! It was the stuff of their dreams: freedom of speech, freedom of the press, freedom of religion, constitutional

2

hundred years, a major accomplishment. What did come out of this meeting in Vienna was a pair of alliances that would encourage a judicious balancing act between the great powers of Europe until the dawn of WWI in 1914.

The first alliance was simply the nations who had stopped Napoleon: Great Britain, Russia, Prussia, and Austria. After France's good behavior for three years under the restored Bourbon monarchy, it was also allowed into this alliance. The second alliance was known as the Holy Alliance. It was the brainchild of Czar Alexander, who desired to unite all of the Christian monarchs of Europe in a committed brotherhood. As it turned out, the commitment of this brotherhood was not to encourage vibrant Christianity in their realms but to stomp out fires of political revolution, even if they arose in someone else's country. It was an alliance of *reactionaries* (those who oppose political reform).

The Holy Alliance formalized its position in 1820 when it authored a document that explained its fundamental reason for existing:

> States which have undergone a change of government **due to revolution**, the result of which threatens other States, ipso facto cease to be members of the European Alliance, and remain excluded from it until their situation gives guarantee for legal order and stability. . . . If, owing to such alterations, immediate danger threatens other States, the Powers bind themselves by peaceful means, **or, if need be, by arms,** to bring back the guilty State into the bosom of the Great Alliance. (emphasis added)

This revolution monitoring and international meddling by the Holy Alliance was not applauded by all.

The first opportunity for this Holy Alliance to demonstrate that this was its resolve came when it sent an army against the people of Spain who had revolted against the repressive policies of King Ferdinand VII.

This revolution monitoring and international meddling by the Holy Alliance was not applauded by all. Great Britain reacted strongly against this idea. Lord Castlereagh wrote:

> England stands pledged to uphold the territorial arrangements established at the Congress of Vienna. . . . But with the internal affairs of each separate State we have nothing to do. We could neither share in nor approve, though we might not feel called upon to resist, the intervention of one ally to put down internal disturbances in the dominions of another. We have never committed ourselves to any such principle as that, and we must as a general rule protest against it.

Britain's response notwithstanding, in 1823, with the blessings of the Holy Alliance, France marched an army of soldiers into Spain to restore Ferdinand VII once more to his absolute monarchy. This followed Austria's

freedom—with the right to vote and to be heard. All of these were new and revolutionary ideas to the people of the early 1800s.

Of course, considering the view of liberty expressed in the French Revolution, many on the European continent were appalled by the legacy of these "freedoms." Especially among the ruling classes and monarchies, the concept of liberty and freedom was something to be curbed, even crushed, since this experiment in democracy (government of the people, by the people, and for the people) was largely unproven and potentially disastrous. And much of what happened during the early- to mid-1800s was a result of the clashing interests between the ruling monarchs and the liberty-seeking people.

Some notable examples of this clash of interests occurred in 1821, in 1830, and again in 1848. Spain, which had suffered the loss of its king under

Napoleon, found the return of the king so onerous that it rose in revolt in 1821 against his absolutist policies. Other countries, such as Portugal, Greece, and the southern area of Italy also rebelled against their rulers during this significant year. In 1830, the people of France rose up in earnest against King Charles X's resistance to those liberties he deemed unsafe for the country, like freedom of the press. Having tasted liberty, the people were loath to give it up. Thus, Charles X lost his throne in a revolution to a new, more pliable constitutional monarch, King Louis Philippe. England, too, was nearly upended as the people of the new industrial

cities began clamoring for the right to vote for their own representatives. If the Reform Bill of 1832—which gave them what they wanted—had not been passed, revolution might have truly occurred there. Known as The Year of Revolutions, 1848 saw France once again tossing out its reigning monarch, choosing instead a new president from the family of Napoleon. The tremors of revolution in Austria were so strong that they caused the powerful Prince Metternich to fall from power, as well as causing the Austrian emperor to abdicate. In many areas of Italy, revolution broke out as the people increasingly sought both liberty for

2

earlier example of marching into the south of Italy to restore order and absolutism.

Two other countries in revolt brought unexpected complications to the Holy Alliance's position, however. In 1821, Greece raised the flag of revolt against its Turkish overlord, the Sultan of the Ottoman Empire, while in the same year Mexico once again declared its independence from Spain, though this time with the full backing of the Mexican people.

Two revolts, two problems. First of all, though Russia was traditionally the champion of Orthodox people, and, though Greece was religiously Orthodox, yet the Greeks were revolting against the established order! For Russia, the spectacle of revolution outweighed the obligation to protect Orthodox interests. This put Russia in the very unusual and uncomfortable position of supporting the Muslim Ottomans. It was unable to protect Orthodoxy against Islam because it could not support subjects— even Orthodox subjects—who turned to revolution. In the midst of this turmoil, Russia lost the opportunity to grasp one of its long-desired goals: to become the most influential, powerful presence in the Balkans. The separate problem of Mexico was that, though the Holy Alliance was ready, willing, and able to send an army of soldiers to restore Spain's control of Mexico, neither Great Britain nor the United States was willing to accept that scenario. In fact, in response to threat of European intervention in the Spanish Americas, President James Monroe issued a warning in 1823 that came to be known as the Monroe Doctrine. It stated, "Any interference on the part of the great powers of Europe for the purpose of oppressing or controlling the destiny of the Spanish American States, which had declared their independence, would be dangerous to the peace and safety of the United States, and would be considered as the manifestation of an unfriendly disposition towards them."

In the end, the Holy Alliance was unable to stop either the Greek revolt or Mexican independence. For the Greeks, who had looked unsuccessfully to the Americans as their comrades-in-revolutionary-arms, it was Britain, France, and, surprisingly, Russia under its new czar who helped them to eventually gain their freedom. For Mexicans, independence was gained through their own efforts unhampered by invading armies. The

In the end, the Holy Alliance was unable to stop either the Greek revolt or Mexican independence.

President James Monroe

Industrialization & the Church's Response (1800–1850) **65**

themselves and freedom from foreign rule—especially Austrian rule.

This leads us to the second term we need to define: nationalism. Your feelings about your country may differ depending on which country you live in, but for all of us there is an identification with the land we call home. If your land is governed by people who speak your language, worship in the same way you do, and share your culture and history, then there will be a stronger sense of patriotism, a belief that this is the way it should be. If, on the other hand, the people governing your land don't speak your language, don't worship as you do, and don't share your culture or history, then

you will feel that outsiders are in charge and that it is wrong for them to be there.

Though this has been true throughout history (for example, the Israelites cried out to God for deliverance when their land was ruled by Hellenistic Romans), it became an even more powerful issue in the 1800s as people saw others successfully revolting against their foreign rulers. In 1821, the Greeks, who had lived under Ottoman domination for centuries, rose up in revolt, inspired by the principles of liberty espoused by the American and French Revolutions. The Poles, who had long been fighting a losing war for their liberties, rebelled

unsuccessfully in 1830 against the Russians who ruled them. Many people groups sought freedom from the far-reaching empire of Austria, including the Hungarians, the Czechs, and the Italians. The sense of nationalism was defined by continent when the Spanish- and Portuguese-speaking people of North and South America sought independence from their colonizing masters. Though the language of colony and colonizer was the same, birthplace began to have a huge effect on the concept of who belonged and who was foreign, and was very significant in the separating of Latin America from its European rule.

2

requirements Mexico faced, though, in governing itself as a non-colonial country brought about the same type of political struggle that was facing various nations throughout Europe.

What did these struggles that were upsetting European and Spanish-American nations look like? To better understand the situation, it might be helpful to consider the issues specifically facing Mexico after independence. On one side were the people known as "liberals," who wanted the types of radical change to their society that the United States' revolution exemplified (freedom of the press, religious freedom, freedom of speech, popular vote, etc.). On the other side were the "conservatives," who wanted the comfort of the familiar status quo: a monarch to lead the country and the Roman Catholic Church to be the official, national religion. In the early days of independence, the Mexican conservatives had the upper hand politically, so they eagerly sought for someone from the Spanish royal family to come be their king. For better or for worse, their search was in vain. Remember this, because the search for a European royal to lead the Mexican nation would come to the forefront again a few decades later, but the next time it would have disastrous results.

They had experienced firsthand that the poor got poorer as the rich got richer.

Just as the conservatives of Mexico valued having a national religion, so did many of the conservatives of Europe. Freedom of religion, or freedom to choose a religion other than that held by the monarch, was not acceptable to conservatives on either continent. The concept of a national religion was common throughout Europe during this era, whether it was the Roman Catholicism of southern Europe or the Protestantism of northern Europe. And, as is always the case with national religion, the rulers of the nation subscribed to and were thus identified with that religion. (A case in point would be the Prussian King Fredrick William III, who was a devout Protestant. He encouraged the voluntary union of Lutheran and Reformed churches—both established churches in his realm—a notable and sincere attempt to bring unity to the Body of Christ in Prussia.) However, when monarchs and their reactionary policies were linked to the state religion, many of the common people, workers in the Industrial Revolution, rejected the religion of the state (whether Catholic, Orthodox, or Protestant). They had experienced firsthand that the poor got poorer as the rich got richer. To these laborers, who worked impossible hours under appalling conditions, Christianity was seen as the religion of their exploiters.

Christianity in Action

What a sad and twisted caricature of God's amazing redemption! Instead of Christians being the bearers of the good news, they were identified with greed, repression, and heartless cruelty. But Christ-followers, those who

? To get an informal discussion started on this Key Concept, ask a simple leading question, such as, "When Napoleon attacked Spain and Portugal, what effect do you suppose it had on their colonies in North and South America?"

Independence of Latin America—EXPLANATION

As we consider this question, it is helpful to first understand the way colonial society was divided up into classes. At the very top of the pyramid, with the highest standing, power, and prestige, were the peninsulars, people born on the Iberian Peninsula (Spain or Portugal). Next came the Creoles, who were of European descent but born in the Americas. These two classes had the wealth, the power, the education, and the respect, though the peninsulars had more than the Creoles. The Mestizos, people who had mixed parent-age (belonging to both European and American Indian), were considered superior to the native and tribal people of the Americas, though definitely inferior to "pure" European stock. At the bottom of colonial society's heap were the people known as Indians.

The significant message of the American and French revolutions, which was evidenced in the neighboring Caribbean island of Haiti, was this: things are changing. One's status in society could potentially change—even dramatically—if independence were attained. People throughout Europe and the Americas took note of this, and many took heart.

2

have truly picked up their cross to follow Jesus, will always care for the welfare of others—especially the poor, the needy, and the oppressed. So it should not be surprising that during the upheaval of the Industrial Revolution, many of those caught in its merciless hold found relief and comfort through the service and ministry of Christians, both small and great. James 1:27 states, "Pure and undefiled religion before God and the Father is this: to visit orphans and widows in their trouble, and to keep oneself unspotted from the world."

Here are some examples of the people who responded to the needs of those hurt by the Industrial Revolution.

In the German city of Hamburg, a devout Christian man named Johann Wichern opened a home for destitute children in 1833. Though he had ministered diligently as a Sunday school teacher in a poverty-stricken area of Hamburg, Wichern came to believe that helping only one day a week was simply not enough for the many waifs who had no homes and were in trouble with the authorities. So, with the help of his mother and sister, he started a home for these "throwaway" children that was consciously and purposefully filled with joy. With the guiding principles of love, trust, community living, self-respect, and learning useful trades, this home—with its transformed children—became such a success that others took note.

A more familiar story, though similar in many ways, is that of the orphanages started in Bristol, England, by a Prussian Christian named George Müller. Beginning in 1835, he set about the work of caring for destitute orphans through both practical and spiritual means. With his wife and eventually many other helpers, Müller provided a loving home, food and clothing, training for work, and Christian discipleship for numerous children. What is unusual and noteworthy about his story is that, throughout the history of this work, it was entirely funded through the prayers of the Müllers and their fellow workers. They had no fundraising letter or advertising or spokesperson calling for support. Even when the ministry grew to five huge orphan houses containing two thousand children, the Müllers relied solely on God's faithful provision and perfect timing.

As was noted in the previous unit, William Wilberforce was another shining example of a Christian caring for the needs of those who had no voice. His final victory, though carried to completion by others, was the

George Müller

The Müllers relied solely on God's faithful provision and perfect timing.

Since the development and independence of Portugal's one American colony was quite different from the experiences of Spanish America, we will consider it here separately. When Napoleon's army invaded Portugal in 1807, the royal family escaped to the Portuguese colony of Brazil in South America. While the royal family was still living in Rio de Janeiro, the new capital city of the Portuguese Empire, they decided to raise the status of Brazil from colony to independent kingdom. When the ruler, Prince John, returned to Portugal in 1821, he left his son Pedro to rule in his stead. The following year, Pedro declared Brazil to be independent and was crowned emperor in 1824. The bid for independence came from the top and was easily attained.

It was not so for the Spanish colonies of America. When Napoleon deposed Spain's king in 1808, new possibilities for freedom were envisioned by those living in its colonies. In 1810, Mexico, one of the richest and most profitable Spanish colonies, made its first bid for freedom. It was short-lived and violent. Venezuela, one of the poorest colonies, was the first South American colony to revolt, declaring independence from Spain in 1811. That was also short-lived. However, when the famous Venezuelan Simon Bolivar took up the flag of

2

complete abolition of slavery in the vast British Empire. Following in his parliamentary footsteps was an Anglican Evangelical, Lord Shaftesbury, who used his position in politics to bless those who had no voice, though at great personal cost to himself. The Duke of Wellington, hero of Waterloo, had taken the young man under his personal patronage, with the intent of grooming him as a future prime minister. But Lord Shaftesbury's convictions as a Christian gave him an unceasing and vocal concern for the rights of the poor, which eventually made him unacceptable to England's political power brokers. To the hopeless poor, to the penitent thieves, and to the brutally overworked laborers, Lord Shaftesbury was treasured. For his tireless work on their behalf, he became known as the "poor man's earl."

As we have seen, the Industrial Revolution, with its accompanying technological and societal changes, significantly affected the lives of everyday people. In the political landscape of England, the foremost constitutional monarchy in Europe, this revolution also resulted in a challenge to the centuries-old system of wealthy landowners representing the nation in Parliament. Now, with growing urban industrial centers such as the city of Manchester, a new dynamic was being unleashed. People of these industrial cities wanted a voice—not of a noble landowner, but one of their own—to represent their interests at the center of governmental power. It was no longer acceptable to them, in this burgeoning awareness of liberty and rights for the common man, to have the upper crust of society create the laws that ruled them all. The issue was one of extending the *franchise* (the right to vote). But it was not only a matter of having the right to vote; even more it was an issue of having the right to vote for someone from their area, someone with an understanding of their concerns, someone who would then take a seat in Parliament to affect the laws of the land for their benefit.

> *People of these industrial cities wanted a voice.*

This volatile question, which was beginning to shake England to its core, rose during the same time that France was undergoing another turbulent shaking. The Count d'Artois, powerful leader of the extreme conservatives since the restoration of the Bourbons, had become King Charles X in 1824. His actions as king, which threatened to undo all that the French Revolution had accomplished, were viewed increasingly as the death knell to constitutional monarchy and liberty in France. Thus it was that at the end of July 1830, the people rose up in revolt against him. Within a few days, Charles X abdicated, and the elected representatives of the people chose a new king, one who would understand and keep his constitutional place. This revolution is known in history as the July Monarchy, with a *Citizen King*, Louis Philippe, at its head.

The effects of this political upheaval in France went way beyond the French borders. Poland revolted against Russia, Germans took to the streets to demonstrate for a liberal and nationalist agenda, people of Italy revolted

revolt, greater progress was made. It would take him until 1821 to finally see his home country set free from European control.

In 1816, Argentina was freed from Spain's yoke by an Argentinean named José de San Martin. He joined forces with a Chilean named Bernardo O'Higgins, and the two men and their armies were then successful in bringing Chile to independence. While this was taking place in the southern region of South America, Simon Bolivar continued his efforts in the northern area, successfully freeing Colombia in 1819. It was here that

a congress was held and a constitution written to establish the Republic of Gran Colombia, with Bolivar as its president. This republic included both Colombia and Venezuela, eventually adding Panama and Ecuador.

In North America, Mexico finally gained its independence in 1821—exactly three hundred years after Cortez conquered the Aztecs—when the general in charge of the Spanish army chose to meet with the leader of the rebels. Together, they declared Mexico's independence from Spain, and the general

2

against their Austrian overlords, and Catholic Belgium sought independence from the Protestant Dutch, with whom they had been united into the Kingdom of the Netherlands by treaty in 1815. Of these revolts, only the Belgians realized their goals, due to the strong assistance of England. Knowing that without their own independence, Belgians might seek to unite with France (with whom they had much in common), the English Foreign Secretary labored long and hard to bring about a state of affairs that would be acceptable to all and would prevent France from owning this strategic piece of land. In the end, Prince Leopold of Saxe-Coburg, who had recently endured the death of his wife the Crown Princess of England, was offered the opportunity to become king of newly independent Belgium, and he accepted in 1831. We will hear more about him in the next Unit.

England's victory in this international chess game was sweet, but the country's internal strife was threatening to unravel into its own revolution. Amid melodramatic scenes in Parliament and in the palace, the voice of the people finally conquered the entrenched policies of landowners with the successful passage of the Reform Bill of 1832. This hard-won bill allowed far more people to vote, and changed some of the seats in the House of Commons from representing the lightly populated lands of the nobility to representing the densely inhabited industrialized cities.

The gain to the United States was more than 500,000 square miles, including the Pacific coast territory of California. And gold.

A similar voice was about to be heard across the Atlantic in Texas, though with a crucial difference: this time it would be the revolt of English-speaking Americans who had been permitted to settle in this sparsely populated territory of Mexico. When Santa Anna, the newly styled dictator of Mexico, changed the government of this republic in such a way that all power would now be centralized under his control, American expatriates and Mexican liberals living in Texas raised the standard of rebellion, declaring Texas to be an independent republic in 1836. Defeated at the famous Battle of the Alamo, the rebels won the Battle of San Jacinto later that year and gained their independence, though the government of Mexico continued to dispute it. After nearly ten years as an independent republic, Texas was annexed by the United States, and then joined the Union as the 28th state. Since Texas's independence was not officially recognized by Mexico, this act provoked a war between the United States and Mexico. The end of the war in 1848 resulted in Mexico's loss of nearly fifty percent of its territory. The gain to the United States was more than 500,000 square miles, including the Pacific coast territory of California. And gold. It was in this highly coveted land that gold would be discovered the following year.

In an interesting twist of history, in the same year that Texas revolted against Mexico, a young Frenchman raised a revolt against the government of France. For his treason, he was banished to the United States. The

Industrialization & the Church's Response (1800–1850) **69**

went on to become Mexico's emperor for a very short time.

Peru, whose silver mines made it one of Spain's most profitable colonies, was the last region of Spanish control in South America. San Martin from the south and Bolivar from the north both envisioned their continent free from Spanish control and, in an unusual scenario, worked in tandem to accomplish this feat. San Martin first brought an invading army of Argentines and Chileans into Peru in 1820, and began the process of setting Peru free. Declaring independence for that country in 1821, San Martin then left to Bolivar the task of vanquishing the Spaniards in the highlands and completing the process. With an army of Venezuelans and Colombians, Bolivar marched into Peru in 1823, becoming its ruling dictator in 1824.

Though Bolivar had dreams of a union of South American nations, similar to the United States, functioning on both a federal and a state level, it was impossible to attain. But the vision for independence, through the extraordinary efforts of Bolivar and many others, had finally been realized.

2

Napoleon III

young man's name? Louis Napoleon Bonaparte, nephew of Napoleon and now heir to the family expectations. He would return again to France to raise another unsuccessful revolt. This second treason resulted in imprisonment, from which he escaped. But in the Year of Revolutions, 1848—the same year the United States won the war against Mexico—revolutionary embers flamed into an incendiary blast across Europe, toppling Louis Philippe from his French throne and Metternich from his grip on Austria's policies. It was in that year that Louis Napoleon would finally be allowed to set his feet on the pinnacle of French power. Elected as president by the will of the people because of his famous name, Louis Napoleon would eventually stage a coup d'état in order to make himself Emperor Napoleon III. In the midst of his own machinations within France, he also began meddling in international politics. This included sending a French army to restore the pope to power in Rome in 1849, enmeshing the European allies in an unwanted and unjustified war in the Crimea in 1853, and, with the help of Mexican conservatives and French soldiers, enthroning a Hapsburg prince as the new emperor of Mexico in 1863.

The French-dominated Mexican Empire, displacing the Mexican republic by force, ended violently only a few years after it began. And as we shall see in Unit 4, Napoleon III's Second Empire of France would manage to survive just three short years beyond that.

In the meantime, the great powers would soon find that one of their number had outstripped them all in trade, in manufacturing, in colonies, and in power. Great Britain, the cradle of constitutional monarchy and of the Industrial Revolution, was just hitting its stride. That story and its implications will be told in the next Unit. ◀

70 Industrialization & the Church's Response (1800–1850)

It is important that we allow God's Word to permeate our hearts on the issue of poverty, without robbing these Scriptures of their power to bring significant changes in our own habits of thinking and spending. Pray with your students about a specific and practical way they might do something to minister to the needs of the poor, whether in their local area or in remote areas of the world. And then *do it*!

You may choose to have your students read the article first and then listen to the audio recordings, or vice versa.

◉ Read the article

◉ Listen to the audio recordings in Listen to This

- The main concepts and chronological flow are contained in *What in the World?* Volume 3

- Learn more about James Watt, one of the early leaders of the Industrial Revolution, in *True Tales* Volume 3.

- To learn more about the European policies of this era, as well as some of the dynamics of Latin American independence, listen to the amazing stories of Metternich, Napoleon III, Benito Juarez, and Simon Bolivar on *True Tales* Volume 3.

- Learn more about the effects of revival upon social reform and aid to the poor in *Digging Deeper* Volume 3.

Phase 1

Introduction Week

▶ Listen to This

What in the World? VOL. 3

DISC ONE:

- » Reactionaries (track 6)
- » Liberals (track7)
- » The Industrial Revolution (track 8)
- » Response & the Age of Revolution (track 9)

True Tales VOL. 3

DISC ONE:

- » Von Metternich (track 3)
- » James Watt (track 4)
- » Napoleon III (track 5)

DISC TWO:

- » Benito Juarez (track 1)
- » Simon Bolivar (track 2)

Digging Deeper VOL. 3

DISC ONE:

- » Revival on the Frontier (track 4)
- » The Revival Spreads (track 5)
- » Charles Finney and Social Reform (track 6)

▶ Read For Your Life

The Holy Bible

- » **Caring for the Poor and Needy** (seen in the lives of Christian reformers of this time)—Proverbs 14:21, 22:22; Isaiah 58:6–11; Luke 6:38; Galatians 2:10

Key People (Church)
Elizabeth Fry *Reformed prisons in England*
Charles Finney *American revivalist*
Lord Shaftesbury *Christian statesman*
George Müller *Cared for orphans*
Florence Nightingale *Founded Red Cross*

Industrialization & the Church's Response (1800–1850) **71**

◉ Read the Scriptures in Read For Your Life

The Scriptures are central to our understanding, our character, and our decisions. Therefore, we must give the greatest weight possible to them.

Help your students gain this perspective as they watch you handle the Scriptures with reverence and awe.

KEY PEOPLE

More of the main characters in this Unit. They are listed in the Student Manual, along with a brief identifier, so that the students can familiarize themselves with these people.

◉ Recap the material with an activity

In different parts of the room, set up stations for the Eight Intelligences Recap Activities. Then allow students to work alone or together in small groups to accomplish THEIR CHOICE OF ONE of the following suggestions. At the start of the next class, ask for 3–4 groups of volunteers to share.

Homeschoolers: rather than setting up all eight stations, allow student(s) to choose which activity they would most enjoy, and do it.

Recap Suggestions:

Spatial: Brainstorm and then draw some simple images that you could use to represent the Key Concepts of this Unit: the Industrial Revolution, the Second Awakening, Liberalism/ Nationalism, and the Independence of Latin America.

Bodily Kinesthetic: The Independence Race: Divide your group into two teams, one team labeled "the Reactionaries," who are the older players, and the other labeled "the Liberals," who are the younger ones. Players each choose the country they want to represent (for instance, on the Reactionary team a player may choose Prussia, Russia, Austria, Spain, or one of the other countries described as reactionary during this era, while individuals on the Liberals team might choose Mexico, Italy, France, Germany, etc.). The players must put signs on their backs indicating which country they represent. Then have a race, with the appropriate Reactionary countries racing to catch the Liberal countries, who are racing to a goal line labeled "Independence." The Reactionaries are staged twice as far from Independence as the Liberals. The race starts when the Liberals revolt (start running!).

Interpersonal: In groups of two, take turns teaching each other the most interesting fact learned so far from this Unit. Keep in mind that you want to describe this fact in such a way that the person listening will find it as fascinating as you do!

Musical: In a small group, decide what the Industrial Revolution would have sounded like to the people of the day (crowded cities, railroads, machinery, telegraph, etc.). Once you have chosen the type of sounds that will best reflect this revolution, organize your team to make a rhythmic and discernible set of sounds, paying attention to rhythm, loudness, and pitch. Can onlookers identify your sounds?

Linguistic: Write a short, catchy slogan for Mexico's independence from Spain, designed to appeal to all the different classes of people.

Key People (World)

James Watt
Redesigned steam engine

Robert Fulton
Designed steamship

Klemens von Metternich
Architect of Congress of Vienna

Simon Bolivar
"The Liberator"

Samuel Morse
Invented Morse code

Benito Juarez
Restored Mexican Republic

Napoleon III
Second emperor of France

Maximilian I
Emperor of Mexico

▶ Talk Together

Opinion Column

» What did you find to be the most interesting aspect, or the most fascinating person, you encountered in your introduction to this time period, which includes the Industrial Revolution, the beginnings of nationalism, and the independence of Latin America?

» Many poor farmers moved to industrial areas looking for work as their harvests failed, or as it became impossible to make a living in their villages after factories changed the place of labor. Imagine that your family moved to one of the cities in industrialized England. What do you think your living conditions would have been like? Your working conditions? Why do you suppose slums developed in these areas?

» Think about the changes that occurred when people could travel a mile a minute, as they were able to do on British railroads beginning in 1847. How would that affect the way you saw the world?

» George Müller was deeply concerned for the orphans of industrialized England. What do you think motivated him to trust in God alone for the support of these orphans? In what ways might God's miraculous provision have made an impact on the people of Bristol? If you had been an orphan living at one of Mr. Müller's orphanages, how might you have felt when one of these miracles occurred?

» Imagine you were living in a European country that had a firm policy against all of the new-fangled liberties exported during the French Revolution. Why do you think you would want freedom of the press, freedom to vote for rulers and policies, freedom of religion, and other liberties that had been whispered about in your neighborhood?

Math-Logical: List three reasons why the Holy Alliance justified the repression of the types of liberties fought for during the American and French Revolutions. List three reasons why countries with democracy or constitutional monarchies justified the expression of these same liberties. Compare and contrast these reasons.

Intrapersonal: Consider and then journal the most important points or the greatest revelations you have had for your own life as you have learned about the dedicated service of Lord Shaftesbury to the poor.

Naturalist: Choose a spot outside to represent the setting of the Kentucky Camp Meeting revivals of the early 1800s—feel free to add to the scene to make it more realistic. Then take a group to the spot and tell them briefly about this time of revivals, using the most interesting stories you have learned.

Or . . . Activity of Your Choice: What would you like to have your students do for a review activity concerning this week's introduction to Industrialization and the Church's Response, Nationalism and the Independence of Latin America ?

» If you had been living during the mid-1800s, knowing that people of the higher levels of English society looked down on those who extended care to sick and hospitalized patients, what would you have thought about Florence Nightingale leaving her affluent home to nurse the wounded in the Crimea? Can you think of any reason that this would be shocking to people? Is there any place or activity that a young person could pursue today that might be similarly shocking?

» Why do you think José de San Martin, who fought *for* Spain against the French invasion during the time of Napoleon, might go back to his native land of Argentina and fight for its independence *against* Spain?

Critical Puzzling

» Why do you think the Second Awakening caused people to feel such a direct connection between a vibrant personal faith and a deeply committed care for the poor and downtrodden?

» At the beginning of the Industrial Revolution, canals had to be built in order to transport large, heavy quantities of materials to and from factories. Why do you suppose factories were not built right next to the supply of raw materials? Why wouldn't they have used existing rivers for transportation? How difficult would it be to build a canal in that time period?

» The year 1848 was known as The Year of Revolutions in Europe. Some of the European monarchs used force to stop revolution from happening in their domain, while others agreed to make concessions in order to slow down the revolutionary fervor. What would give one of these approaches more impact and better possibilities of success?

» The Crimean War brought together armies from the Ottoman Empire, France, and England on one side, and Russia on the other. Why do you think that Catholic France and Protestant England would join forces with the Muslim Ottomans against the Orthodox Russians? In what ways might this provide a "balance of power" in the eyes of Europeans?

» Why do you think Spain relinquished its hold on the Spanish colonies in the Americas? What part did Napoleon play in this? For what reasons do you think Simon Bolivar was considered to be the George Washington of South America? In what ways did he resemble him?

» Why would Napoleon III think it was his right to find a European "royal" to rule Mexico? What benefit would it bring Napoleon III?

◉ Talk together

Individual Preparation

After completing their recap activities, students may begin to consider the questions in the Opinion Column and Critical Puzzling.

Class Discussion

Use the questions under Talk Together to get the students primed and to create a discussion environment in the classroom. You may also want to draw from the open-ended questions listed here.

Why do you think the Monroe Doctrine was issued by the president of the United States? What impact might it have had on the United States to have European nations putting down revolutions in Latin America?

Napoleon III was originally brought to power by the vote of the people of France. In what ways do you think his name and relation to Napoleon Bonaparte affected the election? Can you think of any people in politics who have been elected because of their name and family relations? Would you consider that to be a sufficient reason to vote for a candidate? Explain your reasoning.

▶ # Resources for Digging Deeper

Choose a few books that look interesting, or find your own.

THE INDUSTRIAL REVOLUTION

The Industrial Revolution
Sean Connolly • Part of the Witness to History series, this informative little book not only tells briefly the story of various aspects of the Industrial Revolution, but also includes source documents from this time. **UE+**

Nineteenth-Century Inventors
AMERICAN PROFILES
Jon Noonan • Though this book focuses on Americans, the inventions of Robert Fulton, Samuel F. B. Morse, Thomas Edison, Alexander Graham Bell, and others changed the world for all of us. **UE+**

21 Great Scientists Who Believed the Bible
Ann Lamont • From Johannes Kepler to Wernher von Braun, this book of short biographies is an excellent resource to use throughout *World Empires, World Missions, World Wars*. **MS+**

Samuel Slater's Mill and the Industrial Revolution TURNING POINTS IN AMERICAN HISTORY
Christopher Simonds • "Since 1774, it had been illegal to send textile machinery, or the plans for it, out of England." And so is told the pivotal experience of the first Englishman to smuggle plans out of England (in

his head!) for the construction of cotton-spinning machines. Thus was born the Industrial Revolution in America. **UE+**

The Man Who Transformed the World: James Watt
William D. Crane • James Watt perfected the steam engine, which started the Industrial Revolution. This fascinating biography gives many of the details of his life and inventions, including the fact that he was homeschooled! **UE+**

Inventors of the World
I. O. Evans • This is a delightful children's book presenting short biographies of several inventors. It includes the Morse code that Samuel Morse developed. **UE+**

Men of Science, Men of Invention
AMERICAN HERITAGE JR. LIBRARY
Michael Blow • Learn about the Industrial Revolution in America, the impact of the development of internal combustion engines on machines and people, the attempts of Edison to develop a light bulb (lamp), and splitting the atom (both for good and for destructive purposes). This book provides an excellent overview of the scientific developments of the 1800s and early 1900s. **UE+**

THE SECOND AWAKENING

The 100 Most Important Dates in Church History
A. Kenneth Curtis, J. Stephen Lang, and Randy Petersen • Beginning with the year 64 in Rome and continuing to 1967, this book is filled with short descriptions of events and people within the church. Read the articles on Charles Finney and Elizabeth Fry. **UE+**

Charles Finney MEN OF FAITH SERIES
Basil Miller • Published by Bethany House, these Men

of Faith and Women of Faith biographies are excellent. This book tells the story of Charles Finney and his prayer partner, Father Nash. **MS+**

The Autobiography of Charles G. Finney: The Life Story of America's Greatest Evangelist—In His Own Words
Charles Grandison Finney had an enduring impact upon America as the leading figure in the revivals of the Second Awakening. Fascinating account! **MS+**

Remember:
Beware of Arrogance,
Embrace Humility!

◉ Choose books of interest/ internet search

A list of possible books is given in the Student Manual. Encourage your students to look for books or videos on Industrialization and the Church's Response from this list and from other sources. You may want to gather a selection of further resources prior to beginning Unit 2, or you may encourage the students to be treasure hunters and find them on their own. It would be helpful and time-saving before the Unit begins to check availability of these titles on your local library website.

CHRISTIANS WHO TOUCHED THE POOR

George Müller CHRISTIAN HEROES THEN AND NOW

Janet & Geoff Benge • Wonderfully written, this series of Christian biographies is fascinating, factual, and historically accurate. George Müller was the man who believed God was able to provide all the needs for orphan houses. He ministered to the orphans of the Industrial Revolution around the same time that Charles Dickens wrote *Oliver Twist*. **UE+**

The Autobiography of George Müller

George Müller • This is an amazing, detailed recounting of God's faithfulness in answer to Mr. Müller's prayers. Life-changing! **MS+**

The Bandit of Ashley Downs TRAILBLAZER BOOKS

Dave & Neta Jackson • Historical fiction for children, this title describes the ministry of George Müller to orphans in England during the mid-1800s. **E+**

Shaftesbury: The Poor Man's Earl

John Pollock • Though out of print, this excellent biography provides an amazing view into the life of one who made a huge difference in the lives of the poor in England. Highly recommended! **MS+**

CHARLES DICKENS

Tales for Hard Times: A Story about Charles Dickens

David R. Collins • A Creative Minds Biography, this book describes the life of one of the most widely read authors in Victorian England. **E+**

Charles Dickens: The Man Who Had Great Expectations

Diane Stanley & Peter Venema • Diane Stanley's books are wonderful, and this title is no exception. With wonderful illustrations, the biography of Charles Dickens is well presented. **RA**

Charles Dickens: His Life

Catherine Owens Peare • Charles Dickens was a fascinating man. Read about his life—his successes and failures—in this excellent biography. **UE+**

Oliver Twist

Charles Dickens • This classic in literature is one of the great depictions of life in early industrialized Great Britain. If the book is too difficult, watch the movie or the musical *Oliver*. **MS+**

WORLD-CHANGING WOMEN

Florence Nightingale WHY THEY BECAME FAMOUS

Donnali Shor • Learn about Florence Nightingale's childhood, including the time her family fled Switzerland during a European tour because Louis Napoleon was seeking refuge there; about her heroic work during the Crimean War; and about her incredible influence in the medical field. **UE+**

The Thieves of Tyburn Square TRAILBLAZER BOOKS

Dave & Neta Jackson • Historical fiction for children, this title describes the work of Elizabeth Fry in reforming the prison system in England. **UE+**

Florence Nightingale THE SOWER SERIES

David R. Collins • Learning people's motivations makes a huge difference in how we interpret the events and choices of their lives. Florence Nightingale was a devoted Christian who, in following God, broke societal customs of her day in order to serve as a nurse in war. This book explains some of this dynamic in her life. **UE+**

Florence Nightingale A WORLD LANDMARK BOOK

Ruth Fox Hume • As is the case with all of the World Landmark Books, this biography is an excellent look at its subject—the "Angel of the Crimea." **UE+**

POLITICAL FIGURES

Klemens von Metternich
WORLD LEADERS PAST & PRESENT

John von der Heide • A biography of the Austrian architect of Europe after the fall of Napoleon, this book is a must-read if you can find it. It was Metternich's philosophy of government that ruled in Europe until 1848—the year of revolutions. It will greatly help you understand this era. **MS+**

Simon Bolivar WORLD LEADERS PAST & PRESENT

Dennis Wepman • Considered to be the George Washington of South America, Simon Bolivar was a man who never gave up. This is an excellent biography of the man who liberated South America, almost single-handedly, from Spain. **MS+**

Simon Bolivar: The Great Liberator A WORLD LANDMARK BOOK

Arnold Whitridge • This is an excellent introduction to one of the most important figures in South American history. It is very readable and very interesting! **UE+**

The French Foreign Legion
A WORLD LANDMARK BOOK

Wyatt Blassingame • Created in 1832 by King Louis Philippe of France, the French Foreign Legion was a very special army that played a significant part in many wars around the globe, including the attempt to conquer Mexico, and later WWI and WWII. **UE+**

Ashes of Empire: Carlota and Maximilian of Mexico

Marguerite Vance • The story of the emperor and empress of Mexico from 1864 to 1867, this book sympathetically describes the tragedy of this royal couple. **UE+**

Juarez, the Founder of Modern Mexico

Ronald Syme • This is a fascinating story of the first Zapotec Indian to become president of Mexico. He fled to the United States when Maximilian came as emperor, but returned at his downfall. **UE+**

The Execution of Maximilian, June 19, 1867 A HAPSBURG EMPEROR MEETS DISASTER IN THE NEW WORLD

Robin McKown • Straightforward and factual, this children's book gives the basic overview of France's attempt to set up a colonial empire in Mexico with a Hapsburg as emperor. It has a clear explanation of the reasons for both France's involvement in and departure from Mexico. **UE+**

Juarez, Man of Law

Elizabeth Borton de Trevino • Another excellent biography of Juarez, focusing on his commitment to the law. The author writes, "He is regarded as a hero because he was stubbornly devoted to the idea that strict observance of the law is what makes men worthy, that law is the greatest achievement of men in their efforts to live together peacefully on this earth, and that justice must be the same for everyone." **UE+**

VIDEO

Oliver

This musical presentation of Dickens's *Oliver Twist* is memorable. There are some scary people (at least, they scared me!), so parents may want to preview this before allowing younger children to watch it.

What books did you like best?

_____

_____

_____

_____

The Internet also contains a wealth of information about Industrialization & the Church's Response.

What sites were the most helpful?

_____

_____

_____

_____

For more books, use these Dewey Decimal numbers in your library:

Industrial Revolution: 941

Biography:

B section, found between 919 and 920

B B for Simon Bolivar

B F for Charles Finney

B F for Michael Faraday

B J for Benito Juarez

B M for Klemens von Metternich

B N for Napoleon III

B N for Florence Nightingale

History of Mexico: 972

Crimean War: 947

Inventions: 607, 608, 670s or 680s

◉ Conduct a review and evaluation

In this Phase of Unit 2, your students should have had the opportunity to explore the rise of Industrialization & the Church's Response through reading, listening, thinking, and discussing by completing a selection from the following:

- informally discussed the Key Concepts;
- read the article;
- listened to the audio recordings;
- read the online articles;
- read the Scriptures;
- explored the recap activities;
- considered the Opinion Column and Critical Puzzling answers on their own;
- participated in class discussion;
- chosen books of interest or searched the Internet;
- completed their self-evaluation for this Phase.

Record student hours: _____

Assess student participation:

Create an evaluation system of your own, or refer to the evaluation rubric in the introduction, as a tool for assessing participation. The categories you will probably find most useful are *"Introduction," "Process: Teamwork,"*

and *"Process: Originality."* To help students develop good discussion skills, encourage them to participate actively, ask content-based questions, and stay focused on the discussion at hand. Students demonstrate a higher level of discussion skills when they incorporate comments and questions from others into their own questions, and draw out opinions or ask for points of clarification from others.

Do not critique the self-evaluation page your student completes and do not direct the answers the student gives to the questions. Instead, allow sincere and personal completion of the evaluation, then discuss the responses and incorporate those comments into your evaluation.

Determine a grade for this Phase, if using grades: _____

Teacher Self-Evaluation:

Evaluate your own use of materials and teaching opportunities: what worked and what did not; how effective was your time-management; how were your responses to the needs of your student; did you make your expectations clear; in what ways would you like to improve your approach for the next Unit? Incorporate suggestions from your students in your own evaluation *(this requires humility!).*

▷ Student Self-Evaluation UNIT 1, PHASE 1

Dates and hours:_____

Key Concepts

Rephrase the four Key Concepts of this Unit and confirm your understanding of each:

- Industrial Revolution

  _____

- Second Awakening

  _____

- Nationalism/Liberalism

  _____

- Independence of Latin America

  _____

Tools for Self-Evaluation

Evaluate your personal participation in the discussions of this Phase. Bearing in mind that a good participant in a discussion is not always the most vocal participant, ask yourself these questions: Were you an active participant? Did you ask perceptive questions? Were you willing to listen to other participants of the discussion and draw out their opinions? Record your observations and how you would like to improve your participation in the future:

_____

_____

Every time period is too complex to be understood in one Phase of study. Evaluate your current knowledge of Industrialization & the Church's Response. What have you focused on so far? What are your weakest areas of knowledge?

_____

_____

Based on the evaluation of this introduction, project ahead what you would like to study more of in the following Phases.

_____

_____

Phase 2

▶ Research & Reporting

Explore one or more of these areas to discover something significant!

Four C's of the Industrial Revolution

Discover and report on the "Four C's" that made it possible for the Industrial Revolution to occur—coal mining, canals, capital, and cheap labor.

Scientists of the Industrial Revolution

Compare and contrast the early giants of the Industrial Revolution, including James Watt, Robert Fulton, and Samuel Morris. Describe their lives, their scientific inventions, where they secured funding for their research, public reception of their inventions, and how these inventions changed the world.

The Telegraph

Research and report on the development of the telegraph, which was one of the significant scientific developments during the Industrial Revolution and which led to great changes in communication.

Canal Building

Learn more about the building of canals, such as the Erie Canal in the United States and the canals of England. What was their purpose? How did they improve transportation? What was required to build one? What effect did they have on commerce and manufacturing?

Steamships

Investigate the development of steam-powered ships. How did the use of steam power change the shipping industry? What impact did this change have on the economies of England and the other developing nations?

Railroads

Discover the story of the technology and building of railroads in the 1820s and 1830s. Be sure to include the story of the Liverpool & Manchester railway, which was the first public railway to use steam alone. How did the development of the railways in England and the United States change these two nations?

Charles Finney

Research and report on Charles Finney and the Second Awakening in America. Finney is described as the "father of revivalism." What does that mean? Describe Father Nash and his importance to Finney and the revivals. Describe the impact of these revivals upon the northeastern part of the United States.

George Müller

Study the life of George Müller. Describe his childhood, his life before he became a Christian, and his ministry. Report on his careful recording of prayer and God's provision through the years, as well as his method of dealing with obstacles and difficulties.

Industrialization & the Church's Response (1800–1850) **79**

◉ Choose a topic and begin research

Allow the students the freedom to choose one of the topics listed under research & reporting in the Student Manual, or to suggest their own area which they would like to research.

Motivating Suggestions:

Especially for Non-linguistic students, and those who are not motivated by written or oral reports, here are suggestions for alternative ways of reporting what has been researched.

Four C's of the Industrial Revolution

Compose a piece of music or write new lyrics to an existing song to describe these Four C's. Aim to create catchy words that will help your audience remember the song.

Create an exercise routine that will identify each of these four areas. The movements may mimic reality or may be entirely symbolic. Make sure that it is an authentic workout: your audi-

ence should be puffing by the time they finish!

Scientists of the Industrial Revolution

Make a chart that will visually depict the information you have discovered about these various scientists. You may want to use a flip chart, creating a different chart for each of the suggested areas.

In a small group, debate the relative importance of each of these scientists. Who is the most significant to the Industrial Revolution in your opinion? Be prepared to defend your choice.

The Telegraph

Choose props and perhaps a costume to help you do a first-person presentation of Samuel Morse, the successful developer of the telegraph. You might consider showing the history of the telegraph by first reenacting all the scientists whose discoveries led to Samuel Morse's amazing technology.

Learn and demonstrate the Morse code so that your audience can understand how it was used for communicating. Be prepared to answer questions about this fascinating method of disseminating information.

Canal Building

Draw a picture or a series of pictures to illustrate how canals were built and how they were used. Remember to show how boats on these canals were powered!

With a small group, hold a historic debate over the relative merits of canals versus railroads. Research the perspectives that people held during this era concerning this issue, learning the strength of the arguments from each side.

Steamships

Imagine you were one of the first passengers to travel across the Atlantic ocean on a steamship, having crossed many times previously by sail. Write a journal of your experiences, sharing your thoughts on the benefits and perils of this new technology.

Create a game to be played outdoors that will help your audience grasp the difference between a ship powered by wind and one powered by steam. The goal is to have them recognize the immensity of the change steam power brought to the world.

Railroads

Taking into account the very real fears people had concerning the new technology of railroads, create a poster for the late 1820s to advertise the wonders and health benefits of traveling on a train. Remember, your goal is to reduce resistance and increase awareness!

Set up a railroad museum, in which people can learn the history of how railroads came to be built and used. You will be the curator of this museum, so be prepared to take tours through it and to answer any questions that arise.

Charles Finney

Do a live interview with this controversial figure from history. You might want to include Father Nash, who was the intercessor for Finney's preaching campaigns. Perhaps you can find someone to include who takes an opposing point of view regarding Finney's revivals, such as Asahel Nettleton.

Create a map to show the locations where Finney preached, illustrating it with some visual representations of the stories and events connected with those specific locations. Be prepared to describe the meaning behind the map and its images for your audience.

George Müller

In a small group, analyze the way Müller's life has impacted the church and the world. Some of the areas to be considered might include prayer, finances, service to the poor, distribution of Scripture, education, and ministry in the church. Discuss

---

Metternich & His Policy

Research and report on Klemens von Metternich of Austria. Describe the Congress of Vienna in 1814–1815. What was Metternich's policy? How did this policy influence the monarchs of Europe and Russia? What was Metternich's policy toward Italy? What caused Metternich's influence to end?

The Year of Revolutions

In Europe, the year 1848 was known as the Year of Revolutions. Study to show the conditions of the various cities that were involved in these revolutions. What was the effect of revolution in each of these cities and countries?

The Crimean War

Study the military strategies of the Crimean War. What did Napoleon III introduce into naval warfare? How did the Industrial Revolution affect the Crimean War? What were the particular tactics of this war, and what results did they produce? What was the overall impact of the Crimean War upon Russia, the Ottoman Empire, France, and England?

Florence Nightingale

Research and report on the life of Florence Nightingale. Show the effect she, with her group of nurses, had on British soldiers wounded during the Crimean War, and describe the state of nursing in England prior to Florence Nightingale's involvement. Consider how Christianity made a difference both in Florence Nightingale's work and in the nursing profession.

Simon Bolivar

Discover the life and work of Simon Bolivar. Why was he called the George Washington of South America? What countries did Bolivar "liberate"? What countries did Bolivar govern? What happened to these countries after his death?

Mexican Independence

Study the history of Mexico from the time of its independence in 1821 through the dictatorship of Santa Anna to the liberal government of Benito Juarez. As part of your study you may wish to include the loss of Texas during the war between the United States and Mexico, or the Empire of Mexico under Maximilian.

The Independence of Brazil

Discover the story of how Brazil won its independence from Portugal during this time period. How was Brazil's experience of independence different from what was experienced in the other Latin American countries? What impact—for better or worse—did independence have on Brazil?

---

together how Müller's life challenges and instructs your own.

Both George Müller and Charles Dickens were concerned with the orphans of the Industrial Revolution. Compare and contrast their lives and work, including what you can discover of the lasting effects of their labor.

Metternich & His Policy

Create a board game that, in a lively and competitive way, helps others learn about Metternich, the countries that followed his policies, the countries that did not, and some of the historic results of his ideas. You might want to use a European map for the board on which to play the game. Re-member, you want people to want to play it, so craft your creation in such a way that it is compelling and fun!

What kind of law would be enacted, and what kinds of results might take place, if a Metternich-style political theory were in power in your nation? To illustrate what you have learned about Metternich and his policy, write a modern-day version of what this type of governing policy would look like in your country, or in the group of nations with whom your country functions (such as NATO).

The Year of Revolutions

Using different hats or coats to represent each different city or country

▶ Brain Stretchers

Industrial Revolution

The increased output of manufacturing during the Industrial Revolution required a corresponding increase in markets. Learn more about how trade, and the theories behind it, changed as a result of the Industrial Revolution.

Earl of Shaftesbury

Learn more about the seventh Earl of Shaftesbury, the great Christian statesman known as the "poor man's earl." What laws did he help to effect in Parliament? What organizations for the poor did he serve and champion? What overall effect did Lord Shaftesbury have on England?

Napoleon III

Research and report on Napoleon III. What political theory did he follow? How did the Second Republic become the Second Empire? Analyze the factors leading to the success of the Second Empire, and the factors leading to its downfall.

Create Your Own Research Topic

_____

_____

_____

Prussia and Germany

Learn more about the increase of Prussian influence in German affairs—and the corresponding decrease of Austrian influence—during this era. Describe the unsuccessful bid for a constitutional monarchy, with the Prussian king as its ruler, that the German confederation attempted in 1849.

Greek War of Independence

Research and report on the Greek War of Independence against the Ottoman Empire. What factors led to this revolt? How were the Greeks able to gain their independence from the Ottomans? In what ways did the great powers differ in their opinions on this issue?

Holy Alliance

Learn more about the Holy Alliance. What were its purposes? How did it develop its policies toward revolutions? What affect did the Holy Alliance have on Europe? What affect did it have on the United States and Latin America?

---

affected by the revolutions of 1848, reenact the role of an observer—such as a journalist—who watched these revolutions and their aftermath occur.

Create a collage of the various places and issues represented in the revolutions of 1848. You may choose to use magazine photos, printed images from the Internet, or your own drawings. Be prepared to answer questions as people look at your collage, remembering that the point of this is to help others grasp some of the dynamics at work in that troubled year.

The Crimean War

Create a flip chart or PowerPoint presentation of the Crimean War. Be sure to include the unfolding political and religious tensions leading to this war, as well as some of its unusual features and legacies.

Though many people are familiar with the term Crimean War, few have any idea where it actually took place or how the unique geographical aspects challenged the warring armies. Create a salt-dough relief map that will show some of these dynamics, and then as a well-traveled tour guide explain to your audience the details of what they are seeing.

Florence Nightingale

Write and illustrate a book for children that will teach them about the amazing life of this Christian woman, whose lifework continues to minister to people in hospitals as well as to those helped by the Red Cross.

Create a diorama that will depict the work of Florence Nightingale and the nurses who served with her in the Crimean War. Remember that she was known to wounded soldiers as "the lady with the lamp."

Simon Bolivar

Set up a space, whether indoors or outside, to represent all of the different countries owing their independence to the work of Simon Bolivar. If you can create interesting props, add photos or posters, and play authentic South American music in the background, it will really help visitors capture the feeling of being on Bolivar's continent. Then, as a tour guide, take groups of people through this display of nations he impacted, explaining along the way why Bolivar was considered to be South America's version of George Washington.

In the same musical style as a familiar folk song, compose a song to tell the story of Simon Bolivar and his astonishing accomplishments. You may use an old familiar tune and write new lyrics, or, if you prefer, compose both the lyrics and the melody.

Mexican Independence

As a TV host, interview an Anglo-Texan and a Mexican-centralist regarding their opposing views of the Texas declaration of independence. Be sure to give both sides equal time to express their opinions and to defend themselves against the accusations of the other.

Create a series of posters that will clarify and simplify for viewers the history of Mexico from independence through Juarez. Take the mindset of one who honors and loves Mexico as you draw these posters, rather than as a foreigner who disdains what he does not understand.

The Independence of Brazil

"Become" the nation of Brazil, and, in your own words, describe what happened before, during, and after independence. You are the largest and most populous nation in South America, so present your story with the appropriate magnificence and command that such a position would bestow to you.

Compare and contrast Brazil's experience of independence with that of the other South American nations. It might be very helpful to include a map of South America to show the various countries.

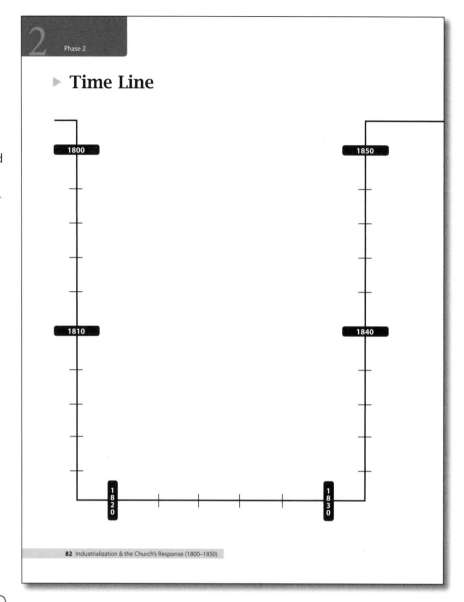

▶ **Time Line**

1800
1850
1810
1840
1820
1830

82 Industrialization & the Church's Response (1800–1850)

Proverbs 13:23 says, "Much food is in the fallow ground of the poor, and for lack of justice there is waste." Talk with your students about the meaning of this verse as it applies to providing the poor with opportunities for education, for better shelter, and for hope to improve their lives. How was this lived out during this era, as Christians sought to help, serve, clothe, feed, educate, train, and care for the poor of the Industrial Revolution? What would life be like for your students if not for the blessings of food, shelter, nurturing, parenting, education, and, most especially, knowing the love of God for us in Christ Jesus?

◎ Construct the time line

Read the information listed with the Key Events in the Student Manual. Dialogue with your students about the issues involved.

Find the dates for the Key People and Key Events listed.

Consider this for your time line

This is an era of revolution and reaction, politically as well as technologically. Changes were taking place that are still affecting our modern world—changes that people living prior to that time would not have imagined in their wildest dreams. It was also a time of Christians making significant differences in the lives of the poor as they enacted laws and gave themselves to serve those who were being crushed under the weight of the Industrial Revolution. It is a time upon which we should reflect carefully, as there are lessons in it for us today.

Be sure to include the people listed in Key People in Phase 1.

Key Events

- Firsts of the Industrial Revolution: railroad, steamship, telegraph

- Independence of Mexico

- Independence of Brazil

- Independence of Venezuela, Colombia, and Argentina

- Various revivals of the Second Awakening

- Greek War for Independence

- Belgian independence

- July Monarchy of France

- Year of Revolutions

- Crimean War

Time Line Key

Key People in the Church

- Elizabeth Fry: 1780–1845
- Charles Finney: 1792–1875
- Lord Shaftesbury: 1801–1885
- George Müller: 1805–1898
- Florence Nightingale: 1820–1910

Key People in the World

- James Watt: 1736–1819
- Robert Fulton: 1765–1815
- Klemens von Metternich: 1773–1859
- Simon Bolivar: 1783–1830
- Samuel Morse: 1791–1872
- Benito Juarez: 1806–1872
- Napoleon III: 1808–1873
- Maximilian I: 1832–1867

Key Dates

- First railroad: 1758 (the English Parliament established the Middleton Railway); 1830 (the Liverpool and Manchester railway was built—the first railway to provide scheduled passenger service)

- First steamship: 1787 (first operable steamship created by John Fitch); 1807 (Robert Fulton built the *Cleremont*—the first commercially successful steamship)

- First telegraph: 1833 (the first electromagnetic telegraph was built for regular communication)

- Independence of Mexico: 1810 (Mexico declared its independence); 1821 (Mexico independence was formally recognized)

- Independence of Venezuela: 1811

- Independence of Colombia: 1811

- Independence of Argentina: 1811

- Independence of Brazil: 1822

- Various revivals of the Second Awakening: 1790s (earliest beginning; lasted till the 1830s, some say 1870s)

- Greek War for Independence: 1821–1832

- Belgian independence—1831 (Belgium declared its independence); 1839 (Belgium's independence was formally recognized)

- July Monarchy of France: 1830–1848

- Year of Revolutions: 1848

- Crimean War: 1853–1856

▷ **Words to Watch**

mechanization	smelting	censorship	concession
industrialized	manufacture	canals	repression
invention	textiles	liberal	confederation
telegraph	orphanage	slum	liberate
charcoal	status quo	urbanization	reactionary

Consider:

The Industrial Revolution, with its accompanying technology, gave rise to many new words. Here are some terms that add an interesting glimpse into this new world.

flying shuttle	cotton gin	iron ships	steam locomotive
spinning jenny	steam hammer	paddlewheel	wrought iron
power loom	coke	steam carriage	

Other words you need to look up:

_____

_____

_____

_____

◉ **Practice vocabulary**

You may find other words in this Unit that are especially appropriate for younger children. Feel free to substitute another vocabulary list for the one provided.

◉ **Complete research projects and share in class or hand in**

Create a safe environment for the presentations. Set ground rules prior to the presentations, so that students know how much time is available for each of them, and so that they know they will be honored and respected by all those observing.

Here is one idea for making vocabulary study interesting and fun: Group the vocabulary words into categories. For example, you might have a "political" vocabulary group into which you would place words such as *reaction* and *repression*. On index cards, with a separate card for each, write the vocabulary words on one side and the meaning of the words on the opposite side. Also on index cards, with a separate card for each, write in large letters the name of each category. Then take turns timing each other to see who can place the vocabulary words into the appropriate categories the fastest. If you forget what a word means, read the definition on the back of the card. Keep working at it until everyone can group the cards into their categories in less than a minute.

A list of definitions can be found at the back of the book in Appendix B.

> ## Student Self-Evaluation UNIT 1, PHASE 2

Dates and hours:_____

Research Project

Summarize your research question:

_____

_____

List your most useful sources by author, title, and page number or URL where applicable (continue list in margin if necessary):

_____

_____

Now take a moment to evaluate the sources you just listed. Do they provide a balanced view of your research question? Should you have sought an additional opinion? Are your sources credible (if you found them on your own)? Record your observations:

_____

_____

_____

Evaluate your research project in its final presentation. What are its strengths? If you had time to revisit this project, what would you change? Consider giving yourself a letter grade based on your project's merits and weaknesses.

_____

_____

_____

Letter grade: _____

You have just completed an area of specific research on the time of Industrialization & the Church's Response. Now what would you like to explore in the upcoming Phases? Set some objectives for yourself.

_____

_____

_____

Industrialization & the Church's Response (1800–1850) **85**

◉ Conduct a review and evaluation

In this second Phase of Unit 2, your students should have had the opportunity to explore Industrialization & the Church's Response through researching, thinking, and reporting by completing a selection from the following:

- done a research project;
- learned the vocabulary;
- constructed a time line;
- created a project report on what was researched;
- completed their self-evaluation procedure for this Phase.

Record student hours: _____

Assess student effort in the research and reporting projects.

Create an evaluation system of your own, or refer to the evaluation rubric in the introduction, as a tool for assessing research and reporting. The categories you will probably find most useful are *"Introduction," "Task," "Process: Teamwork"* (if students are working together), along with Grammar, Format, and Spelling. As a tool for helping your students develop better research skills, pay attention

to their evaluation of sources. Older students should learn how to make a "Sources Cited" list according to academic standards—refer them to English usage books or websites for formatting rules. Younger students should learn how to obtain a balanced view of their research subject; if they use more than one source they will get a bigger picture of what was happening. Encourage your students to make use of their self-evaluations for their next research projects, in order to practice good research skills.

Do not critique the self-evaluation page your student completes in the Student Manual—spelling errors are not to be considered in such an exercise. Students should feel free to humbly evaluate themselves without that added complexity. Instead, discuss with them the intention of their written comments and incorporate those into your evaluation.

Determine a final grade for this Phase: _____

Teacher Self-Evaluation:

Evaluate your own use of materials and teaching opportunities: what worked and what did not; how effective was your time-management; how were your responses to the needs of your student; did you make your expectations clear; in what ways would you like to improve your approach for the next Unit? Incorporate suggestions from your students in your own evaluation *(this requires humility!)*.

Phase 3

▶ Maps and Mapping

Physical Terrain

» Locate and label on a map two of the five great powers of this era: Great Britain and France. Shade each country a different color.

» Locate and label on a map a third great power, Russia, along with the Crimean peninsula, the Black Sea, and Turkey. (The Ottoman Empire during this time included a larger area of land than the modern-day nation of Turkey, but it will be acceptable for this Unit to simply understand the basic geographical location of two of the combatants in the Crimean War.) What type of terrain is the Crimean peninsula? Shade these countries as well.

» Locate and label on a map the country of Mexico, which won its independence during this era. Shade it a warm, vivid color appropriate for a tropical country.

Geopolitical

» In addition to locating Great Britain, France, and Russia on a map as listed above, locate and label on a map the other two great powers of this era: the Austrian Empire and Prussia. Because the boundaries of these two nations in the early- to mid-1800s were different than they are today, this will be a challenging activity. Be sure to shade each of the five great powers a different color on your map so it will be easier to understand some of the geographic realities of their alliances and arguments.

» Locate and label on a map the other Latin American countries that received their independence during this era: Venezuela, Colombia, Bolivia, Ecuador, Peru, Argentina, Chile, and Central America. (British Honduras—Belize—received its independence at a later date.) Shade the Spanish-speaking countries similar but slightly different tones of one color, and shade the Portuguese-speaking country (Brazil) an entirely different color.

Explore

» *Geographical Impediments to Trade:* When Mexico won its independence, it was in a position to begin trading—importing and exporting—with countries other than Spain. However, Mexico's terrain does not lend itself to moving goods throughout the country. With this in mind, research to find out where Mexico's mountains, deserts, rivers, tropical forests, and coastlines are located. Try to discover what happened to the economy after independence and how this was connected to Mexico's geography.

» *Christian Outreach:* What is the status of evangelical outreach today in the Ukraine (Crimea)? In the countries of Latin America? What opportunities and what difficulties face those who share the gospel in these areas?

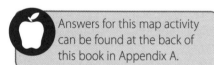

Answers for this map activity can be found at the back of this book in Appendix A.

◉ Create a map and discuss the issues in teams

The students each have an outline map in their manuals. They will be given assignments for drawing in the rivers, mountains, cities, and regional boundaries that are listed. For details on where these things are, please consult a historical atlas, an encyclopedia, or another source of geographic information.

Upper elementary students might be satisfied to accomplish only this portion:

- **Physical terrain:** This part of the mapping exercise will help students locate three of the great powers of Europe, the region of the Crimean War, and the country of Mexico, which was the first to revolt against its Spanish ties.

Middle school students might be satisfied to complete both the previous mapping exercise and this exercise:

- **Geopolitical:** This section of the mapping exercise will provide students an opportunity to locate and mark the boundaries of the Austrian Empire and Prussia, which were the other two great powers of the era. In addition, they will

discover the locations of many of the newly independent countries of Central and South America.

High school students might be satisfied to complete both the previous mapping exercises and at least one exploration topic of this exercise:

- **Explore** a selection from this portion of the mapping exercise in teams.

GEOGRAPHICAL IMPEDIMENTS TO TRADE

At the time of independence, Mexico had inadequate infrastructure for transportation of goods and people. With almost no navigable rivers—which throughout human history had been the main "highway" for transporting goods—the wealthy colonialists had contented themselves with small, highly profitable trade goods such as silver (transported on the back of a donkey). Encourage students to discover how this lack of transportation affected the economy of the newly independent Mexico, which had been a most profitable Spanish colony.

CHRISTIAN OUTREACH

Students might wish to locate information about current missionary endeavors in the Ukraine and Central and South America. If possible, to provide even more help and insight, interview someone who has worked in these fields.

▶ Art Appreciation

The Hay Wain by John Constable

This painting, with its beautiful lights, shadows, and colors, is perhaps one of the most famous English landscape paintings. Interestingly enough, many people who saw this painting did not understand what the white highlights were doing in the painting. They called it "Constable's snow"! You can find a link to see this painting at the online resource page.

> How would you describe it? What similarities do you see between Constable's portrayal of nature and the following poem by William Wordsworth?

Written in March

The cock is crowing,	Like an army defeated
The stream is flowing,	The snow hath retreated,
The small birds twitter,	And now doth fare ill
The lake doth glitter,	On the top of the bare hill;
The green field sleeps in the sun;	The plowboy is whooping—anon-
The oldest and youngest	anon:
Are at work with the strongest;	There's joy in the mountains;
The cattle are grazing,	There's life in the fountains;
Their heads never raising;	Small clouds are sailing,
There are forty feeding like one!	Blue sky prevailing;
	The rain is over and gone!

CONSIDER:

Because the Industrial Revolution was causing cities to grow larger and uglier, decreasing the everyday experiences of beauty in the English countryside, painters were drawn to creating gorgeous landscape scenes. In fact, during the first half of the 1800s, landscapes were the prevalent subject for artists in Great Britain.

The online resource page at www.HistoryRevealed.org contains many helpful Internet links to artwork, architecture, music, project helps, and more.

◉ Examine and discuss art and architecture

The online resource page at www. HistoryRevealed.org has links to view each of the items listed. Allow the students time to observe the paintings without any conversation, and then, when they are ready, engage them in some or all of the questions listed below or in the Student Manual.

Art Appreciation

Hay Wain by John Constable

In reaction to the strict, controlled forms of Neoclassicism, many artists, poets, architects, and musicians sought a more imaginative, emotional, free-flowing style of art—Romanticism. In painting, this can be seen in the luxurious use of color, less defined outlines of objects (objects barely recognizable because of the indistinct, hazy outline), and an emphasis on nature and simple, homey scenes (rather than Roman or Greek history). Art historian Frederick Hartt wrote that Romanticism "became a way of life, affecting not only art but also conduct, an elevation of emotion

The online resource page at www.HistoryRevealed.org contains many helpful Internet links to artwork, architecture, music, project helps, and more.

above intellect, content above form, color above line, intuition and passion above judgment."

John Constable wrote, "It will be difficult to name a class of landscape in which sky is not the keynote, the standard of scale, and the chief organ of sentiment." In fact, he was deeply influenced by scientific studies of cloud formations and types that had just been conducted by a fellow countryman, Luke Howard. He made his own artistic study and systematic observations of clouds in 1821–22. However, he did not stay strictly within the confines of the reality of nature: "It is the business of the painter . . . to make something of nothing, in attempting which he must almost of necessity become poetical."

Constable's gentle, soothing landscapes have been compared to Wordsworth's comforting view of nature. Ask students whether they agree with this comparison, and the reasons for their point of view.

Look at Joseph Turner's painting *Snow Storm: Hannibal and His Army Crossing the Alps.* Ask students how they would describe the differences between Turner and Constable.

▷ Architecture

In 1836, with the commencement of the building of Parliament, Gothic Revival became a pronounced style of architecture in England. It had powerful champions in two men, John Ruskin and A. W. Pugin. Ruskin, an influential art critic of the nineteenth century, believed classical architecture was pagan and immoral, declaring Gothic to be morally superior, even "Christian." Pugin, a noted English architect, also believed and wrote that Gothic was truly the Christian style of architecture. You can find a link to see this building at the online resource page.

Houses of Parliament by Sir Charles Barry and A. W. Pugin

» Look at photos of this excellent example of Gothic Revival architecture—in fact, the largest example of this style. You can find a link at the online resource page. How would you describe this building? What are some of the unusual features that you notice? How does it differ from a building in neoclassical style?

» The Royal Throne inside the House of Lords was also designed by Pugin. Look at some of the photos using the link at the online resource page. What are some terms you would use to describe this throne and its setting?

▷ Arts in Action

Select one or more, and let your artistic juices flow!

Landscape Diorama

Create a diorama of a pastoral landscape near your home, or an English landscape if you prefer, to imitate the style of John Constable. Rivers, hills, sheep, trees, flowers, and clouds are all good choices to include. Experiment with "fuzzy" materials—like cotton balls for the clouds, wool for the sheep, and moss for the grass—to create the look of the Romantics. Be creative!

Seascape

Try your hand at creating a picture of the sea in the style of Joseph Turner, one of the most famous English Romantic artists. You may use colored pencils, watercolors, crayons, tempera, or oil paints. Use lots of color, a fluid style, and light and shadow.

Architecture

Houses of Parliament by Sir Charles Barry and A. W. Pugin

The architectural style of Gothic Revival was initiated by the Tractarian revival (also known as the Oxford movement) in the Church of England. Their concern was to once again elevate and honor the ancient church traditions, especially in protest against the perceived political intrusion of the state in church affairs.

Discuss with your students how this Gothic style might have been associated with a trend toward elevating the traditions of the early and medieval church.

◉ Do an art project

Landscape Diorama

Students interested in this project might benefit from viewing also the artwork of Hans Heysen, a German-born Australian artist who wrote, "I cannot help feeling that my heart lies with these men who see intense and almost religious beauty in simple Nature that surrounds us in the beauty of the skies and the mystery of the earth."

Seascape

Have students study Turner's painting *The Shipwreck*, and then discuss some of the dynamics they have observed. Using those dynamics as a basis, encourage them to create a seascape that touches the emotions (one of the tenets of Romanticism).

▶ Science

Steam Power

James Watt was not the inventor of the steam engine, but his refinements made it practical and useful. Since the first steam engines replaced the work done by horses, the strength of the engine is measured in "horsepower."

» Discover what happens to water when it turns into steam. (Adult supervision required.) Place a pan filled three-quarters full of water on the stove. Cover the pan with a lid and bring the water to a boil. Watch what happens to the lid. Does it move? *The steam's force that pushes against the lid is the same force that causes a steam engine to work.*

Mechanization

The use of industrial power in spinning thread and weaving cloth brought about tremendous changes to the textile industry. Instead of families working together in their homes to produce small amounts of fabric through spinning and weaving, mechanized factories were set up, greatly increasing the output of material but also resulting in urbanization and slums.

» Try this: Wind thread by hand onto an empty bobbin (the type used in sewing machines). Time yourself to see how long it takes to completely fill the bobbin. Next, with adult supervision, thread an empty bobbin using a sewing machine. Time how long this takes. Compare the time and effort you expended to fill the bobbin by hand to what it took to fill the bobbin by machine.

◉ Do a science experiment

Steam Power

At the Bureau of Land Management website, there is a hands-on experiment where students can actually build a low pressure steam engine. You can find a link at the online resource page.

Mechanization

Discuss with your students what they have learned about the Industrial Revolution and its impact from this demonstration of human power versus machine power.

▶ Music

The Romantic Period

Emotional!   Expressive!   Innovative!

Poetry in musical form!   Idealizing nature!   Larger than LIFE!

A time of contrasts: large orchestras—solo pianos; instrumentals—vocals; stormy—sensitive

The major composers of the Romantic time period are:

Rossini   Mendelssohn   Berlioz   Schumann   Chopin   Donizetti   Liszt   Schubert

You can find links to listen to the music at the online resource page.

"A Midsummer Night's Dream" by Felix Mendelssohn

This is Mendelssohn's delightful musical rendition of Shakespeare's play. As you listen, can you imagine the scenes that are being depicted through the music? Is this an effective way of expressing emotion musically? Can you explain the different ways Mendelssohn uses the orchestra to tell the story?

"Italian" Symphony by Felix Mendelssohn

Mendelssohn also created musical "landscapes," much as John Constable painted them. Listen to this symphony, imagining the scenes the composer is portraying musically.

▶ Cooking

Studying Mexico's independence would not be complete without this satisfying taste of Mexican food!

Chile con Queso (Cheese Dip)

2 tbsp oil
1 8-oz. can stewed tomatoes, chopped
1 cup chopped onions
8 oz. Monterey Jack cheese, grated
2 garlic cloves, minced

8 oz. sharp cheddar cheese, grated
1 4-oz. can chopped green chilies
(not jalapeño, much milder)
1 cup sour cream

Heat oil in a large saucepan. Add onions and garlic, cooking until tender but not browned. Add chilies and tomatoes. Lower heat. Add cheese and cook until melted. Stir in sour cream. Cook just until heated—do not boil! Makes 4 cups of dip.

Prepare to be amazed at how delicious this is! Serve with crisp tortilla chips.

◉ Listen to and discuss the music

Listen

Felix Mendelssohn brings us into the Romantic era through his use of "program music"—instrumental music that conveys an imaginative description of a scene or story. The concept of program music was pursued by many composers across Europe throughout the 1800s.

Students might enjoy watching a presentations of the "Italian" Symphony by Mendelssohn. A link to one by the Cologne New Philharmonic Orchestra in Germany can be found at the online resource page.

◉ Cook the food

You can actually make your own tortilla chips. Start with fresh corn tortillas and cut them into sixths. With adult supervision, carefully fry several at a time in hot oil until crisp.

Alternatively, you can spray the corn tortilla wedges with oil and bake them in a 425°F oven for approximately ten minutes. Turn wedges over halfway through the cooking time and spray the second side with oil. Cook until golden and crisp.

▶ **Student Self-Evaluation** UNIT 1, PHASE 3

Dates and hours:_____

Evaluate your projects

- List which of the activities listed in this Phase you did:

  _____

  _____

- Rate your enthusiasm: _____

  Explain: _____

  _____

- Rate the precision of your approach:_____

  Explain: _____

  _____

- Rate your effort toward the completion of the project: _____

  Explain: _____

  _____

- Ask yourself what worked and what did not. What would you do differently in the future, and what would you repeat?

  _____

  _____

- How did these hands-on activities enhance your knowledge of Industrialization & the Church's Response? What made them worthwhile?

  _____

  _____

- In the first three Phases of this Unit, what aspect of the time period has most captured your imagination? What would you like to creatively pursue to conclude your study?

  _____

  _____

Industrialization & the Church's Response (1800–1850) **93**

◉ Conduct a review and evaluation

In this Phase of Unit 2, your students should have had the opportunity to explore Industialization & the Church's Response through various hands-on and creative sessions by completing a selection from the following:

- completed a mapping section;
- observed and discussed art & architecture;
- worked on an art project;
- experimented with a science project or taken a field trip;
- listened to music;

- tasted a food related to this Unit;
- completed their self-evaluation procedure for this Phase.

Record student hours: _____

Assess student involvement in the hands-on activities.

Create an evaluation system of your own or refer to the evaluation rubric in the introduction as a tool for assessing participation. The categories you will probably find most useful for evaluating projects are *"Task"* and

"Process: Teamwork." Consider specifically the enthusiasm, the precision of approach, and the efforts toward improving skills and completing activities, rather than rating the project as compared to a masterpiece.

Do not critique the self-evaluation page your student completes in the Student Manual—it is acceptable for students to occasionally leave lines blank if a question does not apply. Instead, discuss with the student the intention of the written comments and incorporate those into your evaluation.

Determine a grade for this Phase, if using grades: _____

Teacher Self-Evaluation:

Evaluate your own use of materials: what worked and what did not? Consider your time management. Were you able to recognize and respond to your students' needs? Did you make your expectations clear? In what ways would you like to improve your approach for the next Unit? Incorporate suggestions from your students in your own evaluation (*this requires humility!*).

Phase 4

▶ In Your Own Way…

We have seen the increasing tumult of liberty-hungry people and regions, the advances and yet the refuse of the Industrial Revolution, the moving of God in and through His people during the early years of the Second Awakening, and the struggle for the Spanish-speaking people of the Americas to gain their independence. Now, choose a selection of these activities, or create your own, which will best express what you have learned from this Unit.

LINGUISTICS

Journalism

Klemens von Metternich has hired you to "flush out revolutionary scum." You landed this lucrative job because of your proposal to place advertisements in newspapers throughout Europe that would lure politically active liberals out into the open. Your reputation is on the line, so write the ad! (Remember, of course, if the ad is too obvious, the censors—who do not know about your deal with Metternich—will remove it.)

It is the year 1825, and England has 75,000 power looms and 250,000 hand looms for weaving spun yarn into cloth. The editor of your newspaper just learned, to his astonishment, that these two are running neck and neck—producing the same output of fabric, though the hand looms vastly outnumber the power looms. He has assigned you the task of interviewing hand weavers, power loom weavers, and "the man on the street" to get their opinions on whether the new technology is here to stay, and the impact it will have on their lives and society if it remains.

Poetry

Write a soul-stirring, patriotic poem about Mexico's struggle for independence. You may want to craft it in the style of Henry Wadsworth Longfellow's "Paul Revere's Ride," which tells the story of America's battle for freedom. You can find a link at the online resource page.

Prose

You have been accompanying the Finneys for some time now as they have been invited to various cities and towns in the Northeast for revival services. You have seen many unusual, even spectacular, changes in people's lives. Now write a letter to your family at home, who do not understand what is going on or why you are such a vagabond, to share your observations concerning God's activity in this mighty work.

Write and illustrate a children's book that will show how wonderfully the "ragged schools" of England, organized by devout Christians, ministered to the needs of the poor children whose lives had been traumatized by the Industrial Revolution.

◉ Choose an area of expression

Students may work either individually or in teams.

Linguistics:

Journalism

Encourage students to look through several magazines and newspapers, especially ones that deal with politics to get a better idea of the types of advertisements used to attract this kind of politically active readers.

Students interested in writing this project might benefit from reading about the Luddites of England, who protested and actually destroyed machines that were putting them out of work.

> A mind map is a diagram with a central key word or idea at the top or center, which is then used to develop connections with other appropriate words or ideas by linking them together in some way. It is a visual tool, and very helpful in the creative process!

Poetry

Encourage students to make a mind map of the most significant and important events of Mexican independence. On the mind map, the student can link together the fragments of story that will be expressed in the poem.

Prose

Reading a good article or book on Finney will be very helpful for this project. One possibility is the book *Revival Fire* by Wesley Duewel, which contains very helpful information and details about not only Finney but also many other people connected to the revivals from the time of the Great Awakening to the 1970s. It would be a valuable addition as a reference throughout *World Empires, World Missions, World Wars*.

ART

Political Cartoon

In order to assist the Earl of Shaftesbury in his difficult struggle to limit the workday of children to only ten hours, create a stinging political cartoon showing how greed and profit are what stand between these child laborers and justice. Many people follow your political cartoons, so you have a chance to really make a difference this time. Don't hold back—tug their heart strings.

Painting/Drawing

Create a drawing or painting that will show some of the changes to transportation that came during the Industrial Revolution. You may want to juxtapose the old manner of travel with the new technology, and, perhaps, include people's responses to each newfangled means of transport!

Illustrate graphically the reign of King Cotton in the southern United States after the development of the cotton gin. You may wish to show how the bales of cotton were eagerly awaited by English textile manufacturers as well as how the back-breaking labor of African slaves on the southern plantations powered this particular reign.

Graphic Design

Louis Philippe, the Citizen King of France, is perceived by his countrymen as a somewhat boring king. Historians have actually credited part of his fall from power to this very issue. Your job is to create a revitalizing ad campaign designed to excite the French about the wonderful job their king is doing. Your main vehicle for the ad campaign will be posters, since that is an enormously effective method of political communication in this era.

MUSIC

Performance Practice

With your teacher's help, select an appropriate piece of music that expresses a particular aspect studied in this Unit, whether Latin American independence, European reaction to revolution, American camp meetings and revivals, the Industrial Revolution, or the Christian response to the needy.

Compose

Compose a song for this era that will express the hearts of those who yearned for freedom and liberty, whether Latin Americans seeking independence, African slaves seeking liberty, Germans seeking a constitutional monarchy, Greeks waging war, or any of the other people groups and nations studied in this Unit. You may choose to combine all of these in one song or to focus on a specific group.

Art:

Political Cartoon

Arizona State University's ArtsWork website has an excellent article about how to create a political cartoon. A link can be found at the online resource page.

Painting/Drawing

If students need some visual inspiration, suggest they do an Internet search for images of railroads and steamships during the Industrial Revolution.

Online there are a number of historic images showing "King Cotton" and its attendant problems. Students might benefit from seeing what other artists were creating during that time.

Graphic Design

Louis Philippe was the one in power when France went through its own experience of the Industrial Revolution and when education was extended to more than two million French children. He was a constitutional monarch, in the style of the British kings, and he sought to live as an accessible "citizen king." These factors, if well presented, might assist students in their advertising project.

Music:

Performance Practice

For musical students, this selection may be a wonderful opportunity to express some aspect of what they have learned. Make sure they select a piece that they have adequate time to prepare.

Compose

Students might find it helpful to listen to songs of the African slaves in America as they contemplate composing their own song. Two suggestions: "Wade in the Water" and "Follow the Drinking Gourd." A link to these can be found at the online resource page.

DRAMA

Puppetry

With puppets, tell the story of Simon Bolivar, the George Washington of South America. Your goal is to help children understand how much he did and the vision he had for the people of his continent.

Comedy

Act out the scene from the orphanages of George Müller when the children are called to eat, yet the servers bringing food know there is no food for them. Though the humorous possibilities are enormous, be sure to show the miracle of God's goodness and provision to them with the baker and the milkman both showing up at the door just after George Müller gives thanks to God for the meal!

Drama

Dramatize the life of Florence Nightingale. Include her privileged childhood, her struggle to go into nursing, and the obstacles she faced in the Crimean War. Show her determination as a Christian to make a real difference in the world!

Using the story line from Charles Dickens's *Oliver Twist*, write and perform five or six short scenes that will tell the tale, giving your audience a taste of the troubles poor orphans faced during this time.

Prop Needs

_____

_____

Costume Ideas

_____

_____

Role/Player

_____

_____

Set Suggestions

_____

_____

Drama:

Puppetry

Encourage students to use the story about Bolivar playing tennis with the future king of Spain (he really did!) and beating him at the game. This was a powerful prelude to what would happen in Bolivar's quest for South American independence!

Comedy

Timing is everything in physical comedy. It is fascinating to recognize that there are many similarities between staging comedy and tragedy. The difference is that tragic timing is very slow and resonant while comic timing is quick and unexpected. In order to have good comedy, the tragedy of the situation—no food—must be emphasized. Encourage students to display the extreme difficulty of hunger and suspense so that when a resolution comes they can show genuine surprise.

Drama

If this is to be done as a solo performance, it might be useful to tell the stories from different periods in time, so feel free to experiment, playing Florence at different ages of her life. It would be a dramatic challenge, but it would make the story more engaging.

As students prepare by reading the novel, have them find and consider the one central theme of the story that affects all the characters and is present in every chapter. Choose five or six scenes from the story that communicate this theme most effectively.

Movement:

Pantomime

Use a variety of tempos and heights or levels to explore the variety of the actions.

Dance

Explore the use of objects in the dance, incorporating them into the

MOVEMENT

Pantomime

Show us how it's done! Build a railroad, drive a train, all in the style of the 1820s and 1830s. You might want to even pantomime the astonishing event of the mile-a-minute English train in 1847.

Dance

During this era, when the rulers of the reactionary countries were professing Christians, many of the people laboring in the factories and mines of the increasingly industrialized countries identified Christianity with those who oppressed them, rejecting it for that reason. Choreograph a dance that will show this tension and how God's people responded to it.

Action

With dramatic action, depict the major scenes from the life of Napoleon III, from his youth and exile to the United States all the way to his debacle in engineering the Mexican Empire with the Hapsburg prince Maximilian.

CONCEPTUAL DESIGN

With what you have learned from this Unit about the impact of the new industrialized cities, especially upon the poor and helpless, design a factory system for the early to mid-1800s that will be functional and profitable while providing the workers a healthy environment. Include the workers' dwellings (which need to be located nearby), the educational facilities (like a library and rooms for teaching literacy to the workers), the food sources (gardens, orchards, bakeries, butchers, greengrocers), the church with its accompanying services to the workers, the utilities, and whatever else would contribute to the overall beauty and productivity of this factory-town.

CREATE YOUR OWN EXPRESSION

_____

_____

_____

_____

choreography. Also, and perhaps even more effectively, explore proximity—being close to or far away from the audience or dance partners—to demonstrate oppression, the separation between the workers and the rulers, and their perception of Christianity.

Action

Napoleon III was in many locations and influenced many regions, so utilize a number of areas in your performance space to represent the countries he affected. While he is present in those locations, engage in an activity with a strong visual metaphor, such as building a tower out of blocks and then knocking it over, to show the effect that he had on that location.

Conceptual Design

Students who desire to do this creative project will need to do research on what is considered a healthy wage (translated into 1800s money), how to provide good nutrition, and the optimum hours for working. Also find out what kind of physical space is required for a garden to feed a family and how much room is needed for residences, for recreation, and for the factory. In order to find that information; you could encourage students to start with Wikipedia and follow the links at the bottom of the page to find the sources cited in the article.

"Zoning" and "city planning" would be good keywords to look up.

◉ Share creative expressions in class

Create a safe environment for the presentations. Set ground rules prior to the presentations, so that students know how much time is available for each of them, and so that they know they will be honored and respected by all those observing.

◉ Conduct a review and evaluation

In this Phase of Unit 2, your students should have had the opportunity to express what they have learned about the Industrialization & the Church's Response through one or more various creative selections of their own choosing. These include:

- Linguistics;
- Art;
- Music;
- Drama;
- Movement;
- Conceptual Design.

Record student hours: _____

Assess student effort in the creative expressions, as individuals or as teams.

Create an evaluation system of your own, or refer to the evaluation rubric in the introduction, as a tool for assessing participation. The categories you will probably find most useful for evaluating their projects are *"Task," "Process: Teamwork," "Process: Originality,"* and Grammar, Format, and Spelling.

In this Phase especially, do not critique the self-evaluation page your student completes in the Student Manual—consider how the very soul of an artist has been exposed and

vulnerable, so be encouraging and not belittling. Again, consider enthusiasm, precision of approach, and efforts toward improving skills and completing the activity, rather than rating the project as compared to a masterpiece. Instead, discuss with the student the intention of the written comments and incorporate those into your evaluation.

Determine a grade for this Phase, if using grades: _____

Teacher Self-Evaluation:

Evaluate your own use of materials and teaching opportunities: what worked and what did not; how effective was your time-management; how were your responses to the needs of your student; did you make your expectations clear; in what ways would you like to improve your approach for the next Unit? Incorporate suggestions from your students in your own evaluation (*this requires humility!*).

Take a moment now to evaluate the whole Unit. What would you like to remember if you taught this subject again? What do you recognize that your students gained most—either as students of history or as creative individuals? What did you learn about Industrialization & the Church's Response or about teaching?

▷ **Student Self-Evaluation** UNIT 1, PHASE 4

Dates and hours:_____

Evaluate your projects

- What creative project did you choose?

  _____

- What did you expect from your project, and how does the final project compare to your initial expectations?

  _____
  _____
  _____

- What do you like about your project? What would you change?

  _____
  _____
  _____

In Conclusion

Revisit the four Key Concepts from the beginning of this Unit. Explain how your understanding of and appreciation for each has grown over the course of your study.

- _____
  _____

- _____
  _____

- _____
  _____

- _____
  _____

Record your concluding thoughts on Industrialization & the Church's Response:

_____
_____

98 Industrialization & the Church's Response (1800–1850)

The British Empire & Awakenings

(1830–1870)

Pray with the students
at the beginning of each Unit.

Enthusiasm and delight
are the best ways to capture
a student's interest and
jump-start motivation, so:

» **For the Auditory Students:** To capture their attention at the very beginning of class, consider playing a sample of African music to get a musical sense of this continent. (The online resource page has a link to some samples of Christian music of Africa.)

» **For the Kinesthetic Students:** Building the Suez Canal took ten years, 20,000 Egyptian laborers, and shovels. Now, you provide shovels and a place to dig a small trench. The exercise is complete when the students realize how difficult it was to build the Suez Canal.

» **For the Visual Students:** Bring a visual object to stimulate their interest in the new Unit, such as pictures of Queen Victoria.

» **For the hearts of all:** Pray with them at the beginning of the Unit, that God would help them discover what He has for each one to learn in this Unit.

◉ Learning Style Emphasis

Teachers can choose to have students do one or two activities, rather than the entire week's schedule. Please use what works for you in your unique setting.

	Week 1: Feeler	Week 2: Thinker	Week 3: Sensor	Week 4: Intuitor
	During this week, students will be introduced to the British Empire & Awakenings, along with the appropriate Scriptures. You may follow this suggested schedule or adapt it to meet your students' needs:	Students will explore topics of interest through research and reporting, learn new vocabulary, and construct a time line relating to the British Empire & Awakenings.	Students will gain cultural understanding through sensory activities as they explore interrelated subject areas through sensory activities pertaining to the British Empire & Awakenings.	Through creative self-expression, using one or more creative activities, students will present some aspect of what they have learned in the past three weeks relating to the British Empire & Awakenings. Areas of expression include linguistics, art, music, drama, movement, and conceptual design.
Monday	Informally discuss the Key Concepts Listen to the *What in the World?* audio recording(s)	Choose topic and begin research	Create a map and discuss the issues in teams	Choose an area of expression and begin work either individually or in teams
Tuesday	Read the article Listen to the other audio recording(s) Read the Scriptures		Examine and discuss art masterpieces & architectural structures	
Wednesday	Recap the material using activities Talk together	Practice vocabulary	Do an art project*	
Thursday	Conduct class discussion	Construct the time line	Do a science experiment or field trip**	
Friday	Choose books of interest/Internet search Conduct a review and evaluation	Complete research projects and share in class or hand in Conduct a review and evaluation	Listen to and discuss the music Cook the food listed in the recipe Conduct a review and evaluation	Share creative expressions in class Conduct a review and evaluation

*Art project will need to be planned ahead of time to acquire materials.
** Field trip will require extra planning time.

The British Empire & Awakenings (1830–1870)

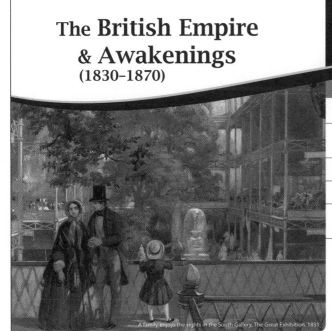

A family enjoys the sights in the South Gallery, The Great Exhibition, 1851.

Key Concepts

- The British Empire
- Africa: Christianity/ Colonies
- Great Prayer Revival
- American Civil War
- The Intellectual Revolution

Queen Victoria

Something momentous occurred in England in 1837—though few at the time could have realized it was to have such a long-lasting effect. William IV, the final reigning son of King George III, died without a direct heir. Since the English kings of the first decades of the 1800s had lived such openly scandalous lives, many wondered whether the monarchy could, or even should, survive. In fact, Winston Churchill wrote, "indeed the vices and eccentricities of the sons of George III had by this time almost destroyed its [the monarchy's] hold upon the hearts of the people."

As we discovered in the previous Unit, this was a time of great unrest and tension throughout Europe as reactionary governments sought to extinguish revolutionary ideas and activities, while revolutionaries sought to bring down established governments. Into this politically charged atmosphere

◉ Informally discuss the Key Concepts with your students

KEY CONCEPTS Background Information

These are the main objectives of the Unit. As you proceed through the four weeks, your students will be given various ways of understanding each of these objectives. Explanations of these Key Concepts follow.

3

Queen Victoria

came a young, untried teenage girl who would be queen of one of the great powers of Europe. And, due to the rigid seclusion her mother had deemed necessary for Victoria, this eighteen-year-old was an absolutely unknown personality to the British people.

It is fascinating to read what Victoria wrote in her diary when she became queen: "Since it has pleased Providence to place me in this station, I shall do my utmost to fulfill my duty towards my country; I am very young, and perhaps in many, though not in all things, inexperienced, but I am sure that very few have more real good will and more real desire to do what is fit and right than I have."

This was not the mere musings of a young girl. It was, in fact, her determination to live in a vastly different way as the sovereign than her recent predecessors had. She was greatly assisted by her marriage a few years later to Prince Albert of Saxe-Coburg, who not only held similarly high ideals but lived conscientiously and uprightly. It was Prince Albert who helped Queen Victoria recognize the plight of the poor and distressed in their midst, who organized the Great Exhibition of 1851 to display Great Britain's scientific and technological achievements, and who sought with his wife to model the joys of home life and family for a nation in need of encouragement and fidelity.

"Since it has pleased Providence to place me in this station, I shall do my utmost to fulfill my duty towards my country."

It is fascinating to see that the Earl of Shaftesbury, whom we met in the previous unit, was well acquainted with the Queen and her Prince Consort. According to biographer John Pollock, the Earl had the opportunity to freely converse with Prince Albert one day. He took that opportunity to suggest that "if the Prince put himself at the head of all social movements in art and science, especially as they bear on the poor, he could do more than if he were king because he was not restricted by constitutional forms; yet his presence would be virtually that of the Queen, and would show the interest of Royalty in the happiness of the kingdom."

It says much of Prince Albert that he endeavored to do just that. In fact, between the obvious care that these two had for the people of Britain and the happy marriage they enjoyed with each other, Victoria and Albert were able to win for the British Crown once again the respect, even devotion, of their subjects.

100 The British Empire & Awakenings (1830–1870)

? To get an informal discussion started on this Key Concept, ask a simple leading question, such as, "What do you think the phrase 'The sun never sets on the British Empire' means?"

The British Empire— EXPLANATION

Though England was relatively small and situated on an island off the coast of Europe, it was able to create a massive empire around the world through colonizing settlements, aggressive trade, and, as a result of the Napoleonic Wars, the most powerful navy in the world. With the advent of the Industrial Revolution, another factor was added into the mix. Through the wealth and opportunities presented by manufacturing, trade, and finance, England became the center of commercial power in the world.

In short, though small in appearance at its native island home, England was a force to be reckoned with all over the world—from Europe to North America, the South Pacific, Asia, and Africa.

Great Britain's colonies did, in fact, extend right around the globe. Let us now consider some of the major ones. Though Britain had lost the American colonies during the 1700s, its North American colonies in Canada continued to grow in population and territory throughout the 1800s. Legislation enacted in Britain in 1867 merged several of the colonies into one large federation. Surprisingly, the colony of Newfoundland remained a separate colony all the way to 1949!

In the South Pacific, Captain Cook's favorable reports of Australia in the 1770s had led to the establishment of a penal colony on the southeastern coast, which was called New South Wales. From there, other British colonies in Australia were established, including Tasmania (known first as Van Diemen's Land), Western Australia, Southern Australia, Victoria, and Queensland. When gold was discovered in Victoria (1851), hopes were raised for a new source of income for the colony. However, agriculture continued as the more certain and long-lasting way to make a living. The same was true for Australia's island neighbor, New Zealand, which had even more remarkable resources in lumber, horticulture, and sheep. In 1840, it became a British colony through the Treaty of Waitangi (which was favorable to the indigenous

3

Colonies and Racism

Because the British Empire was growing by leaps and bounds in both land and people, it was an opportune time for this royal couple to restore the monarchy's tarnished image. With the wisdom born of experience, Great Britain developed a new colonial model where a colony would function almost entirely independently of its mother country, yet retain relationship and viable connection to it. This new model began for Canada with the British Parliament proclaiming the Act of Union in 1840. The success of the new model would prove, in time, to be enormously effective for many other British colonies, especially those of the South Pacific.

In these South Pacific colonies, changes were occurring. Though English convicts had been sent to the Australian colony of New South Wales since 1788, in 1840 this practice ceased. By 1841 there were more than 100,000 free settlers living in this colony, while the other Australian colonies of the time—Tasmania, West Australia, and South Australia—were growing and developing as well. In that same year, their South Pacific neighbor, New Zealand, became a British colony through the Treaty of Waitangi. There would be much stiffer resistance on the part of the indigenous people in this colony than in most of Australia (with the notable exception of Tasmania). The Maori reacted forcibly to the English settlement of their land. Much of the tribal land was purchased in private agreements, although this was in conflict with the treaty, which decreed that the land belonged permanently to the Maori. This violation led to the Maori wars, which ran intermittently from 1843 to 1869.

Wars between European settlers and native tribes were not limited to New Zealand and Australia, however. The Dutch settlers of the Cape Colony of southern Africa came into conflict with the Xhosa people over cattle raiding at the boundary of the colony, Fish River. This began a series of wars known as the Xhosa Wars which continued off and on for one hundred years. The Dutch settlers, better known as Boers, struggled not only against the native people but against the British who took over permanent control of the Cape Colony in 1806. The British flexed their colonial muscle by giving British settlers generous tracts of land, by changing the official language of the colony from Dutch to English, by changing the currency and the legal system, and by setting up British schools and churches. Beyond these unsettling developments for the Boers, however, a far more significant challenge to the status quo was evident throughout this area. British missionaries to South Africa held a view of the native peoples—that they were the equal of the Europeans—that conflicted greatly with the beliefs of the Boer farmers, who had Africans working on their farms under conditions very nearly like slavery.

British missionaries to South Africa held the view that the native peoples were the equal of the Europeans.

The British Empire & Awakenings (1830–1870) **101**

To get an informal discussion started on this Key Concept, ask a simple leading question, such as, "Do you know any of the changes that took place on the continent of Africa during the 1800s?"

Maori and continues to be a powerful protector of their rights).

India, as a British colony, was quite different from the others listed, in that the British did not become "settlers"—they did not move to India for life, raising families who would continue there—but instead functioned as administrators and traders. However, through the East India Company the British gained increasing authority, annexing more and more territory to themselves through the mid-1800s. When Governor-General Lord Dalhousie set up the "Doctrine of Lapse" (if a ruler were to die without an heir, the territory would pass to the East India Company), it brought many new princedoms under British control. However, this policy violated the long-standing Indian tradition that allowed a ruler to adopt an heir, and became one of the grievances leading to the Indian Mutiny of 1857.

At the southern tip of Africa, the Cape Colony passed temporarily from the Dutch to the British as a result of the Napoleonic Wars. When the transfer was made official by means of a treaty, European settlers, who had themselves brought foreign ways to African land, found their own traditions disturbed by the foreign ways of this new colonizing power. More on this in the next Key Concept.

Africa: Christianity/ Colonies—EXPLANATION

The 1800s would prove to be an immensely significant century, both for good and for evil, to the people of Africa. It was during this time that explorers trekked and mapped much of the interior of the continent, places hitherto unknown to Europeans. It was the century when Protestant missionaries would go in increasing numbers to the land with the well-earned reputation as the "white man's graveyard." It was in this historic era that revival, which had been sought in prayer for decades, brought new life in Christ to thousands across

3

One missionary from Scotland, John Philip, who was to become highly controversial in his stand on behalf of the African peoples, wrote concerning this issue: "So far as my observation extends, it appears to me that the natural capacity of the African is nothing inferior to that of the European. At our schools, the children of Hottentots, of Bushmen, of Caffres, and of theBechuanas, are in no respect behind the capacity of those of European parents: and the people at our missionary stations are in many instances superior in intelligence to those who look down upon them, as belonging to an inferior caste."

"So far as my observation extends, it appears to me that the natural capacity of the African is nothing inferior to that of the European."

The effects of emancipation, with the outlawing of slavery in the British Empire in 1833, were soon felt in the Cape Colony. In response to this perceived outrage, along with the numerous other grievances imposed on their culture and way of life by British rule, many of the Boers decided to leave the colony and make their own way in the wilderness beginning in 1836. This departure and subsequent journey is known as the Great Trek, which led to the founding of Natal, the Orange Free State, and the Transvaal. Those venturing out on the Great Trek, though, faced great dangers and difficulties, not least of which was a disastrous encounter with the powerful Zulu people where hundreds of Boers were slaughtered.

It is instructive to read what one woman, Anna Steenkamp, wrote of the reasons for the Great Trek. She said of the native Africans, "It is not their freedom that drove us to such lengths, as their being placed on an equal footing with Christians, contrary to the laws of God and the natural distinction of race and religion . . . wherefore we withdrew in order to preserve our doctrines in purity." This perspective, with its racist philosophy seamlessly interwoven with Christian doctrines, would continue to affect and influence countless lives in South Africa, even through the twentieth century.

We must stop and ask, is that truly what the Bible teaches? In Acts 17:26, we learn from the Apostle Paul, "He has made from one blood every nation of men to dwell on all the face of the earth." Rather than a lofty superiority that looks down on other cultures or people groups, we need to acknowledge that He has created us all—which gives us a common ground of *humility*. Whether our ancestors are from Argentina, Ireland, or Zaire, our bloodlines all go back to Noah, making us each distantly related members of the same family. If we have heard and believed the good news of redemption in Jesus, what might the result be if we lived like 2 Corinthians 5:20 describes?

"Now then, we are ambassadors for Christ, as though God were pleading through us: we implore you on Christ's behalf, be reconciled to God."

102 The British Empire & Awakenings (1830–1870)

cultural and racial boundaries. And, tragically, it was in the late 1800s that European nations and individuals scrambled to take as much African land as possible, dividing it among themselves for their own colonial use and, in many cases, abuse.

It is fascinating to see how exploration of Africa combined seamlessly with Christian mission in the person of David Livingstone. This Scottish missionary came to Africa to work with an established missionary, Robert Moffat, in 1840. It was Moffat who had inspired the new missionary candidate with his tantalizing description—he had "sometimes seen, in the morning sun, the smoke of a thousand villages, where no missionary had ever been." In his more than three decades in Africa, Livingstone did far more exploration than evangelization, resulting in books and subsequent fame that focused the attention of the world on Africa more powerfully than anyone before him.

As mentioned in this Unit's article, the Great Prayer Revival that had so impacted North America and Great Britain had tremendous effect on regions of Africa as well. Indeed, though Christianity in sub-Saharan Africa took root slowly, that area has grown in our current day to be one of the most vibrant centers of Christianity in the world. Andrew Walls, noted historian of Christianity in Africa and Asia, wrote that African Christianity should be seen as "potentially the representative Christianity of the twenty-first century." He is indicating that our western experience of church and Christian living, though obviously still vital, might find that African Christianity rises up to a much larger and more significant role in spreading the kingdom of God across the world.

Europeans, bent on enlarging their territories through colonization in the 1800s, focused on Africa. At the Berlin Congress of 1884, fourteen European nations gathered to divide up the continent in what became known as the Scramble for Africa. Prior to this European scramble, the vast majority of Africa was under local and traditional control, with more than one thousand separate cultures and regions. But when these European

Motivated by the love of God, we would humbly recognize that we are not intrinsically better than others. We would be as starving beggars who, finding a vast supply of life-giving nourishment, eagerly run to share this good news with the other beggars we meet.

Tragically, when those who identify themselves as Christians don't live as Jesus lived (see Philippians 2:5–8), others get a fractured and false concept of Christianity. The repercussions of this in South Africa were grim. Yet, as we shall soon see, when the mercy of God brought revival to people in this region, it leapt across the cultural and racial divide, uniting Boers and blacks in worship to the God who had made them both.

The competing ideologies of *equality for all* versus *superiority over another* were producing fearful results in the United States as well. Though tensions had been steadily rising between North and South regarding slavery (and the accompanying power struggle in the Congress between "free states" and "slave states"), things became inflamed when a decision was reached by the US Supreme Court in 1857 on the *Dred Scott v. Sandford* case. Dred Scott, a slave, had sued for freedom based on his having lived for a time in the free state of Illinois, as well as in the free Wisconsin Territories. Supreme Court Justice Roger Taney wrote that, under the Constitution, Scott had no right to sue at all because, as a descendant of Africans, Scott was not a citizen. He wrote:

Dred Scott

They are not included, and were not intended to be included, under the word "citizens" in the Constitution, and can therefore claim none of the rights and privileges which that instrument provides for and secures to citizens of the United States. On the contrary, they were at that time considered as a subordinate and inferior class of beings, who had been subjugated by the dominant race, and, whether emancipated or not, yet remained subject to their authority, and had no rights or privileges but such as those who held the power and the Government might choose to grant them.

Rather than the powerful, indeed revolutionary, American declaration that "all men are created equal," Taney wrote of this specific phrase, "The general words above quoted would seem to embrace the whole human

"They are not included, and were not intended to be included, under the word 'citizens' in the Constitution."

The British Empire & Awakenings (1830–1870) **103**

Ruth Tucker, in her book *From Jerusalem to Irian Jaya*, wrote, "It is true that missionaries were often closely tied to colonialism, unashamedly identifying European civilization with the Christian message. But they, more than any other outside influence, fought against the evils that colonialism and imperialism brought. They waged long and bitter battles (sometimes physically) against the heinous traffic in human cargo. And after the demise of slave trade, they raised their voices against other crimes, including the bloody tactics used by King Leopold to extract rubber from the Congo. The majority of missionaries were pro-African, and their stand for racial justice often made them despised by their fellow Europeans. Indeed, it is no exaggeration to say that without the conscience of Christian missions, the crimes of colonialism might have been even more horrific."

Talk with your students about the implications of the gospel for issues of justice. Pray together that the Lord will give His people wisdom, compassion, and courage to stand up for those who are currently in slavery or who are experiencing the injustice of ethnic prejudice in the world.

To get an informal discussion started on this Key Concept, ask a simple leading question, such as, "What do you think the Great Prayer Revival, which began in 1857, was like?"

Great Prayer Revival— EXPLANATION

In history, each supernatural move of God within the church, though sharing certain characteristics with all other revivals, has its own distinctives that make it unique. The Great Prayer Revival was no exception. One of the most outstanding features was that, by and large, it was a revival of prayer. As we have noted in the article for

nations were done divvying up the map of Africa, fifty countries were created without any correlation to the one thousand people groups, languages, or cultures. This meant that many new national borders actually divided homogenous people groups while at the same time forcing hostile tribes together in the same geographic entity.

Why did the European countries take it upon themselves to do this? There are many and varied answers, but the simple one is that they could. They possessed the new maps from explorers such as Henry Stanley (whose work allowed the infamous King Leopold II of Belgium

to plunder the Belgian Congo), the firepower, the technologies, the new medical breakthrough of quinine for malaria, and the overpowering desire to command new colonial markets for trade and for raw materials to supply the ever increasing industrialization of Europe.

Many of the complex problems facing Africa today can be traced, in large part, to this colonization by several European nations, including France, England, Portugal, and Germany. We will gain greater understanding in the next Unit of the part Germany played in the Scramble for Africa, and how its goals would affect not only Africa but Europe as well.

3

family, and if they were used in a similar instrument at this day would be so understood. But it is too clear for dispute, that the enslaved African race were not intended to be included, and formed no part of the people who framed and adopted this declaration."

Beyond the Court majority opinion concerning the lack of rights for Africans and their descendants (who, if enslaved, were considered to be "property" rather than people), the Supreme Court ruled that it was unconstitutional to legally limit the spread of slavery in the United States, since a person's constitutionally protected right of property would be affected.

Though the proponents of slavery in the South agreed with the Supreme Court, the opponents in the North were outraged. In fact, this was one of the significant steps leading to the savage American Civil War, which was just a few years over the horizon. The issues before the nation were ones where people held fiercely passionate and divided opinions. They were multifaceted and complex questions, including not only slavery, with its accompanying struggles of territory and profit, but also the sovereignty of states versus the power of the federal Union, and a massive struggle for economic dominance between the agrarian wealth of the South and the industrial wealth of the North. When it erupted, it became one of the most devastating and fury-driven wars of the 1800s—surpassed only by Napoleon's battles—with more than 600,000 killed, where brother would literally fight against brother.

Prayer Revival

God's mercy and goodness are bigger than our largest conflicts, however. In 1857, the year of the Dred Scott decision, an awe-inspiring move of God began in the United States and Canada, then spread across the world to Great Britain, South Africa, India, China, and Jamaica. Known as the Prayer Revival or Second Evangelical Awakening, it was a tremendous and life-changing movement that, in the short space of three years, ushered more than two million people into the kingdom of God! Organizations were founded out of this revival that ministered powerfully to the poor and distressed, and a new missionary agency—the China Inland Mission—was started which would become the largest in the world, releasing thousands to the mission field.

How did it start? With prayer. People in many areas of the world had been praying for years that God would send revival. When He did, it began in the noticeably humble setting of a local prayer meeting. In September 1857, a Christian worker in New York City, Jeremiah Lanphier, felt led of the Lord to post a notice for weekly noon prayer

The Prayer Revival was a tremendous and life-changing movement that, in the short space of three years, ushered more than two million people into the kingdom of God.

this Unit, there was an outpouring of prayer among large masses of people during the time of the revival, which was quite a noteworthy change from the norm (even within the churches). A second feature, which is connected to the first, is that newspapers told stories of the revival. They featured articles and information concerning this dynamic move of God and His impact upon people—and they were mostly favorable! Quite noticeably, there was also a tremendous spirit of unity across denominational boundaries. Excepting the preaching of Charles Spurgeon in London and Andrew Murray in South Africa, this revival was considered a "lay revival"

because it was not led by particular personalities or full-time ministers. It was, instead, a spiritual movement of prayer among everyday men, women, and children.

If we were to look at the specific number of conversions in North America and Great Britain during the first three years of the Great Prayer Revival, we would see that a significant percentage of the population of the various countries was impacted. According to J. Edwin Orr, academic historian of this revival, there were one million conversions in the United States and Canada, which included both the northern and southern regions of the US (who would soon

face each other in civil war) as well as the western territories. In Ireland, there were approximately 100,000 converts, giving this revival the greatest Christian impact to the land since St. Patrick! Scotland had 300,000 converts, including Mary Slessor, who would go as a missionary to western Africa and have a tremendous effect upon the people and culture of Calabar. In Wales, of the 100,000 people converted during this great revival, it was noted fifty years later that most had continued in the Christian faith. England itself had 650,000 converts, and saw such famous preachers minister during this revival as William and Catherine Booth (who would soon

3

meetings at a church on Fulton Street. The first day of the advertised hour-long prayer meeting, he prayed alone for thirty minutes, which must have been incredibly discouraging. But by the end of that particular prayer meeting, six men from four denominations had joined him. The next week, twenty people came. In the third week, forty people attended, and afterward decided to hold the prayer meetings on a daily basis. Within a week, there were more than one hundred people coming to pray, including unbelievers. And within six months, more than ten thousand people were meeting to pray in various churches and halls throughout the city.

Within six months, more than ten thousand people were meeting to pray in various churches and halls.

Newspapers began to report on the phenomenon; such unusual behavior was considered newsworthy. As the rest of the country began to hear of the amazing revival, prayer meetings began to spring up in other cities throughout America. Listen to this description from the March 13 edition of the *Chicago Daily Press.*

Chicago has shared in the general religious awakening that has been one of the most marked events of the year, throughout the entire country, East and West. In the larger cities of the East and in New York City especially, this movement, in the increased zeal of Christians and the awakening and conversion of those previously unconcerned and careless in religious matters, has become a prominent topic among the news of the day, so large a portion of those communities have been sharing in and yielding to the influences at work which has had steady, silent and solemn progress, without noise or excitement.

The British Empire & Awakenings (1830–1870) **105**

Andrew Murray's father had prayed for revival, along with many in Africa, for thirty years . . . and it came! Take heart. Pray with your students that the Lord would send revival once again to our nations. Even better, maintain a regular time of prayer for revival throughout the year.

To get an informal discussion started on this Key Concept, ask a simple leading question, such as, "What was Europe's involvement during the American Civil War?"

start the Salvation Army), and Charles Spurgeon, the "boy preacher."

Many types of ministries, which continue to the present, came into being as a result of this revival and its aftermath. InterVarsity, which began in 1877 on the campus of the University of Cambridge, became an international student ministry with an emphasis on prayer, Bible study, and worldwide evangelism. The China Inland Mission, which will be examined in more detail in the next Unit, was formed in 1865 for the purpose of interdenominational evangelism of the interior provinces of China. Child evangelism became a significant focus during this revival, as can be seen

in the early work of D. L. Moody in his Sunday school in Chicago.

One of the most intriguing aspects of revival is the timing of God in bringing a supernatural work of grace to people and regions. The Great Prayer Revival, begun in 1857 and continuing powerfully for the next few years, would bring many Americans in both the North and the South to a saving knowledge of Jesus immediately before the catastrophic event known as the American Civil War. We will note other instances of God's great timing, particularly several decades ahead in Korea.

American Civil War— EXPLANATION

We need to remember that Europe in the mid-1800s was still very much involved in the struggle between those known as "conservatives" (reactionaries) and "liberals" (revolutionaries). Viewing the American Civil War from European eyes is helpful in understanding the international dynamics of this conflict. Those in Europe who preferred monarchies over republics hoped that the Civil War would end once and for all American democracy in the world. On the other side, those striving for liberalism and nationalism in their countries saw the American

3

It is instructive to learn, as reported by Dr. J. Edwin Orr, the noted historian of revivals, that this powerful movement affected the people on both sides of the divided United States. It brought massive numbers of people of both African and European descent into church membership (which was a documentable measure of the revival), increasing church attendance throughout all the Protestant denominations by one million in two years. For those who had ears to hear and eyes to see, God was demonstrating unequivocally that "there is neither Jew nor Greek, there is neither slave nor free, there is neither male nor female; for you are all one in Christ Jesus" (Galatians 3:28).

From North America, reports began to flow across the world, which brought about an increased hunger to pray for revival.

From North America, reports began to flow across the world, which brought about an increased hunger to pray for revival. In the Irish city of Ulster, a young man who had been reading George Müller's accounts of God's answers to specific prayer learned about the revival in the United States and wondered, "Why can't it happen here?" He gathered a small group of friends to pray for revival, and by August of 1859, there were 20,000 people gathering for open-air prayer meetings in Belfast, and Irish churches were packed even during the weekday services. In Scotland, in August 1859, there were 20,000 meeting for prayer in Glasgow. In Wales, there was a report given in 1860 estimating that one tenth of the population of the country had been converted in two years. In London, theaters were rented to hold worship services, with more than 20,000 meeting nightly. In South Africa, revival came first to the Zulu and Bantu in May 1859. Then, in 1860, revival took place in the Dutch Reformed Church of Andrew Murray, Jr., who had ministered mightily among the Boers. After the first night of unusual and spontaneous prayer in response to God, one of the eyewitnesses reported:

Andrew Murray

After that, the prayer meetings were held every evening. At the commencement there was generally great silence, but after the second or third prayer the whole hall was moved as before, and everyone fell to praying. Sometimes the gathering continued till three in the morning. And even then many wished to remain longer. . . .

On the first Saturday evening in the larger meeting house, Mr. Murray was the leader. He read a portion of Scripture, made a few observations on it, engaged in prayer, and then gave others the opportunity to pray. . . . Suddenly the whole gathering was praying. That evening a stranger had been standing at the door from the commencement, watching the proceedings.

106 The British Empire & Awakenings (1830–1870)

republic, in the words of Abraham Lincoln, as "the last best hope on earth." In other words, this was not just a distant war of little interest to Europeans. It was a potentially significant battlefield between two competing political ideologies.

At the very beginning of the war, diplomatic recognition of the Confederacy (the new government of states who separated from the Union) was the great need of the South and the equally great fear of the North. Each side was well aware that France's support during the Revolutionary War had been essential to gaining victory. If the Confederacy were officially recognized by European nations, it could lead to financial support, weapons, and even troops, which,

in turn, might defeat the North's industrial superiority. Though the new Confederate government desperately needed this diplomatic recognition, it seems they lacked the necessary discernment to attain it. Perhaps typical of Southern attitudes at the beginning of the war is this remark by the governor of Mississippi: "The sovereign state of Mississippi can do a great deal better without England than England can do without her." In other words, the cotton of the South was more necessary to England's industry and commerce than diplomatic recognition by England was to the Confederacy. However, as events proved, this was not the case.

Cotton was so important, such a vital raw material for manufacture in the textile industry, that it was known as "King Cotton." Imagine this: four-fifths of the raw cotton necessary for the British textile industry was imported from the American South, while France was even more dependent, purchasing ninety percent of its cotton from them. It was neither far-fetched nor naive to believe that cotton might prove to be the most important factor in pushing the nations of Europe into diplomatic recognition. However, when the South placed an embargo on the sale of cotton until Europe gave this formal acknowledgment, the plan backfired.

3

Mr. Murray descended from the platform and moved up and down among the people, trying to quiet them. The stranger then tiptoed forward from his position at the door, touched Mr. Murray gently, and said in English, "I think you are the minister of this congregation: be careful what you do, for it is the Spirit of God that is at work here. I have just come from America, and this is precisely what I witnessed there.

According to Dr. William Lindner, Jr., biographer of Andrew Murray, people of every denomination, age, and people group were flocking to the prayer meetings not only every day, but as much as three times a day! Their only complaint seemed to be when the prayer meetings ended too soon. Again, as in the United States, God's Spirit was tearing down racial divides erected by man, resulting in powerful ministry and changed lives among Boers, Bantu, English, Hottentots, Xhosa, and Zulu.

Indian Mutiny

The year 1857 brought to India, not the spiritual blessings of revival, but rather the horrors of warfare and bloodshed. With increasing unrest and for a multitude of causes, the Indian Mutiny exploded into violence. The British East India Company had implemented a new policy—to take possession of lands where an Indian ruler died without a direct heir. This practice had gained them much valuable new territory, but at the price of growing hostility and dissatisfaction on the part of the Indian people. In addition, as the British brought the new technologies of railway and telegraph to India, many Indians found that their country and culture were being changed into something alien and unrecognizable. These new ways were creating difficult, even insurmountable problems in the Indians' ancient system of *caste* (a complex Hindu system of separating people based on hereditary social class). There were rumors that the British were planning to require their Muslim and Hindu troops—perhaps even all of India—to convert to Christianity, which seemed plausible since Christian missionaries were busily setting up schools and churches throughout the land. The time-honored Hindu practice of *sati* (widows being burned on the funeral pyres of their dead husbands) had been banned by the British, which caused smoldering resentment toward these interfering foreigners.

The spark that finally lit the inferno was in the cartridges for the new Enfield rifle, introduced in early 1857. Rumors began to circulate that the cartridges were greased with the fat of cows (holy to the Hindus) and pigs (forbidden to the Muslims). Seen as a threat to or slur against their religions, these rumors caused many

There were rumors that the British were planning to require their Muslim and Hindu troops—perhaps even all of India—to convert to Christianity.

The British Empire & Awakenings (1830–1870) **107**

England did suffer a few alarming years of economic distress due to this embargo, as factories closed down and workers lost their jobs, but the South was blamed for these financial woes. Refusing to be placed in this position for long, England sought new sources for raw cotton in Egypt and India. Though Napoleon III favored recognizing the Confederacy because of his own agenda in Mexico, he was not in a political position at this point to thwart England, so he followed their lead in doing nothing to favor one side or the other.

Since the British Empire had outlawed slavery nearly thirty years before—while slavery was one of the hotly-defended issues of the South—there was also the ongoing question in England of whether diplomatic recognition of the Confederacy would render them "guilty by association." This came to the forefront when Lincoln issued the Emancipation Proclamation, which seemed to European eyes to give the North a higher moral ground in the conflict. Instead of it being an issue of union versus secession, now the reasons for fighting included the volatile and weighty abolition of slavery. From this point on, Europe had little interest in favoring or helping the Confederacy. In the area of European diplomacy, the North had certainly carried the day.

To get an informal discussion started on this Key Concept, ask a simple leading question, such as, "What are some possible factors that might explain why, with its rejection of Christianity and of a literal belief in the Bible, the Intellectual Revolution would take place in the nineteenth century?"

The Intellectual Revolution— EXPLANATION

In the twenty-first century, the prevailing view in western cultures is *secular humanism* (also known as *scientific humanism*). This may be defined as a philosophy that emphasizes a reliance on human reasoning and specifically rejects religion and the supernatural. It is the culture of our times and the expression of our media. However, up through the beginning of the nineteenth century, religious belief was the prevailing philosophy of the West, whether Catholic, Protestant, or Deist. Something

3

of the Indian soldiers (known as *sepoys*) who served in the British army to rise up in revolt. The ferocious struggle that emerged caught the British by surprise, and many innocent bystanders—women and children—brutally lost their lives because of it. However, it is significant that, despite the culture clashes between the British and the Indians, none of the leaders and few of the Indian people actually joined the mutiny.

In 1858, after the fighting had ended, the East India Company was abolished.

In 1858, after the fighting had ended, the East India Company was abolished. From this point until India's independence, nearly one hundred years later, the British government ruled India, with Queen Victoria as the new sovereign. In fact, she would be given the title "Empress of India" in 1877.

As the fighting was drawing to a close, American missionaries in India, aware of the revival taking place at home, wrote letters asking that prayer be offered up not only for India, but for revival worldwide. Revival came to India in 1858, and as we have seen, the prayers for a larger move of God across the earth were having tremendous effect.

Same Problems, Different Solutions

Charles Spurgeon, one of the most famous preachers in English history, was at the height of his ministry in London during this move of God. He had tremendous influence and drew enormous crowds to hear

Metropolitan Tabernacle

significant happened—a seismic eruption in thought—to bring about an utter reversal of beliefs. Let us consider several contributing factors.

As we have discussed in previous Units, revolutionary ideas were taking hold across a number of areas of life: in politics, as people threw off the age-old concept of monarchy for the new ideas of people governing themselves in a republic; in industry, as machines were increasing the speed of production and changing the location of labor from homes to factories; in communication, as the telegraph made possible nearly instantaneous transmission of news, messages, and ideas across the globe; and in transportation, as the age of steam, on rail and sea, brought vast distances into reach

It was also a time of revolutionary ideas in philosophy, in man's thinking about himself and his place in the universe—what is termed "worldview." An English philosopher of the time, John Stuart Mill, wrote,

The nineteenth century will be known to posterity as the era of one of the greatest revolutions of which history has preserved the remembrance. . . . The first of the

leading peculiarities of the present age is that it is an age of transition. Mankind have outgrown old institutions and old doctrines, and have not yet acquired new ones.

Things that had appeared as certain and knowable as the daily rising of the sun—like the rule of kings and the travel time between cities—were shaken and even toppling. Implicit belief in the Bible, with its authoritative description of life and meaning, was being shaken as well. For many, Christianity had belonged to the status quo in that it was the acknowledged view of "civilized people." Though philosophers of the Enlightenment, such as Voltaire and Rous-

seau, had already discounted a literal view of Scripture and had rejected Christianity, their view had not yet become widely accepted. With all the fast and furious revolutions of the 1800s, however, this was about to change dramatically.

The icons of this philosophic change, this Intellectual Revolution, were Charles Darwin and Karl Marx. Though these two men had distinct messages dealing with their own particular spheres of interest (Darwin in biology and Marx in economics), there were lines of overlap in their views of reality and in the impact of their beliefs upon modern man. Frederick Engels, a close friend of Marx and co-author

3

his preaching. The Metropolitan Tabernacle, which seated 6,000 people for a service, was built in 1861 to accommodate the growing group of believers. And in the revival throughout England, it is estimated that 650,000 people were converted in the space of a few years!

Charles Spurgeon

It is interesting to consider that in this same time and same country, two men lived who rejected not only the revival, but the Creator God who was behind it all. Karl Marx, co-author of *The Communist Manifesto* (published in 1848), lived in London, not far from the Earl of Shaftesbury. Charles Darwin, author of *The Origin of Species* (published in 1859) lived in Kent, only forty miles from London.

Just as people of the industrialized West had lived through the tumultuous changes that came to communities and families with the arrival of factories and mechanization, so they were now to be exposed to the tumultuous changes that would come with the rising tide of evolution and atheistic communism. That the authors of these two revolutionary ideas were firmly set *against* a literal acceptance of the Bible and Bible-centered Christianity is without question.

Consider these fascinating quotes:

Charles Darwin, in his autobiography, wrote about religion:

> I had gradually come, by this time, to see that the Old Testament from its manifestly false history of the world, with the Tower of Babel, the rainbow as a sign, etc., etc., and from its attributing to God the feelings of a revengeful tyrant, was no more to be trusted than the sacred books of the Hindoos, or the beliefs of any barbarian. . . . By further reflecting that the clearest evidence would be requisite to make any sane man believe in the miracles by which Christianity is supported . . . I gradually came to disbelieve in Christianity as a divine revelation.

Charles Lyell presented in his book, *Principles of Geology*, a theory on the age and natural processes of the earth, which played a large part in Darwin's thinking. Of him, Darwin wrote:

> During the early part of our life in London, I was strong enough to go into general society, and saw a good deal of several scientific men, and other more or less distinguished

In this same time and same country lived two men, Karl Marx and Charles Darwin, who rejected not only the revival, but the Creator God who was behind it all.

of the *Communist Manifesto*, saw this overlap. At Marx's death, Engels said in the eulogy, "Just as Darwin discovered the law of development of organic nature, so Marx discovered the law of the development of human history: the simple fact . . . that mankind must first of all eat, drink, have shelter and clothing, before it can pursue politics, science, art, religion, etc."

In 1880, in a letter to Marx's son-in-law, Darwin declined the dubious honor of having Marx's second volume of *Das Kapital* dedicated to him. This letter displays an interesting perspective on his views of science and its eventual effect upon Christianity. Darwin wrote:

I should prefer the Part or Volume not to be dedicated to me (though I thank you for the intended honour) as this implies to a certain extent my approval of the general publication, about which I know nothing. Moreover though I am a strong advocate for free thought on all subjects, yet it appears to me (whether rightly or wrongly) that direct arguments against Christianity & theism produce hardly any effect on the public; & freedom of thought is best promoted by the gradual illumination of men's minds, which follows from the advance of science. It has, therefore, been always my object to avoid writing on religion, & I have confined myself to science. I may, however, have been unduly biassed by the pain which it would give some members of my family, if I aided in any way direct attacks on religion.

It is fascinating and deeply troubling to learn that as young men, both Darwin and Marx *professed to be Christians*. As their lives unfolded, however, they moved—Marx more viciously and Darwin more compellingly—away from acceptance to rejection of Scripture. The heart of this move was an abandonment of the biblical description of God and humanity. In Darwinian evolution, God was no longer necessary to life on earth, and human beings were no longer a unique and special creation. In Marxist communism, atheism was embraced so God was dethroned and denied, and humans were considered simply material beings—stomachs to be filled. As these ideas began to filter down to the common people, many took them as fact and began to live their lives on these utterly false and very precarious foundations.

3

Karl Marx

men. . . . I saw more of Lyell than of any other man, both before and after my marriage. . . . His delight in science was ardent, and he felt the keenest interest in the future progress of mankind. He was very kindhearted, and thoroughly liberal in his religious beliefs, **or rather disbeliefs**; but he was a strong theist. (emphasis added)

Karl Marx wrote in 1844, "Religion is the sigh of the oppressed creature, the heart of a heartless world, just as it is the spirit of a spiritless situation. It is the **opium** of the people." (emphasis added)

Frederick Engels was Karl Marx's close associate and co-author. In the popular Victorian parlor game "Confessions," one of the questions asked was, "Who are the characters you most dislike?" Engels wrote one word: "Spurgeon." His disdaining reference was to Charles Spurgeon, who was called "The Prince of Preachers," and who was widely respected as the most powerful preacher in England at the time.

Karl Marx's son-in-law, Paul Lafargue, wrote, "When Darwin published his *Origin of Species*, he took away from God his role as creator in the organized world, as Franklin has despoiled him of his thunderbolt."

One of the most troubling of these new concepts to gain increasing acceptance was that man, no longer fashioned uniquely by the loving hand of God, was now believed to have descended from animals. In 1863, Thomas Huxley, one of the first to believe and promote Darwin's theory of evolution, published *Man's Place in Nature*. In this book, Huxley attempted to explain the arrival of human beings on earth apart from creation by God.

The nineteenth century Russian author Dostoyevsky wrote, "If there is no God, everything is permitted."

In what would be the logical next step, Francis Galton (a cousin of Darwin), published his book *Hereditary Genius* in 1869. He used Darwin's theory of evolution to "scientifically" promote the idea of *eugenics* (the effort to improve the human population by allowing only the best, fittest humans to reproduce). In other words, someone could create a race of supermen through selective breeding, just as successful breeders do with horses and dogs. As we will see in WWII, this offshoot of Darwin's theory would bear much bitter fruit in years to come.

Without the "fear of God before their eyes" (Psalm 36:1), those enthusiastic about the revolutionary ideas of a godless universe had no authoritative limits on their actions. Might could, indeed, become right because there would be no God to answer to on this earth or in eternity. The nineteenth

110 The British Empire & Awakenings (1830–1870)

Two of the most important spiritual concepts needed in a discussion concerning the Intellectual Revolution and its impact in our own day are humility and love.

"Knowledge puffs up, but love edifies." 1 Corinthians 8:1

"And though I have the gift of prophecy, and understand all mysteries and all knowledge . . . but have not love, I am nothing." 1 Corinthians 13:2

People are seldom won to the Lord by an argument, though they may be touched by a wise answer given in loving humility. Pray with your students that you will each hunger for a heart that reflects godly humility and love as you engage the culture of our day with truth.

You may choose to have your students read the article first and then listen to the audio recordings, or vice versa.

◉ Read the article

◉ Listen to the audio recordings in Listen to This

- The main concepts and chronological flow are contained in *What in the World?* Volume 3

- A fascinating look at the man who brought about the building of the

Suez Canal, Ferdinand de Lesseps, can be found in *True Tales* Volume 3.

- For a specific look at the Great Prayer Revival, be sure to listen to *Digging Deeper* Volume 3.

3

century Russian author Dostoyevsky wrote, "If there is no God, everything is permitted." One of Marx's friends, Max Stirner, who promoted anarchy (a state of lawlessness), wrote, "I am legitimately authorized to do everything I am capable of." In the *Communist Manifesto*, Marx and Engels wrote, "The Communists disdain to conceal their views and aims. They openly declare that their ends can be attained only by the **forcible overthrow of all** existing social conditions." (emphasis added)

Charles Darwin

Ideas are not birthed out of nothingness. Karl Marx, living in London during the ravages of the Industrial Revolution, viewed his world and its problems from a godless, revolutionary, man-centered philosophy, which would eventually bring suffering and death on a scale never seen before. At the very same time and place, the Earl of Shaftesbury viewed the world and its problems from a biblical, Christ-centered philosophy that caused him to work tirelessly on behalf of the workers Marx was talking about. Yet his work produced life and hope and liberty for the multitudes.

While Darwin was crafting an explanation of living things, requiring millions of years and excluding the God of the Bible, that same God of the Bible was demonstrating His reality, bringing millions of people to Himself through the Great Prayer Revival. Where Darwin's theories would lead to increased justification for racism, God's mercies led to increased compassionate action toward other people groups.

Same world, different starting point. Same problems, different solutions. And, as we shall see throughout the remaining units, the unleashed and ongoing theories of communism and evolution would have entirely different results than whole-hearted, Christ-centered service for mankind. ◀

◉ Read the Scriptures in Read For Your Life

The Scriptures are central to our understanding, our character, and our decisions. Therefore, we must give the greatest weight possible to them.

Help your students gain this perspective as they watch you handle the Scriptures with reverence and awe.

Did you realize that the book of Acts describes the gospel being shared with an African man? Read about it in Acts 8:26–39! Discuss with your students the opportunities this highly-placed Ethiopian might have had to share his newfound faith in Jesus with others in his country.

KEY PEOPLE

The main characters in this Unit are listed in the Student Manual, along with a brief identifier, so that the students can familiarize themselves with these people.

◉ Recap the material with an activity

In different parts of the room, set up stations for the Eight Intelligences Recap Activities. Then allow students to work alone or together in small groups to accomplish THEIR CHOICE OF ONE of the following suggestions. At the start of the next class, ask for 3–4 groups of volunteers to share.

Homeschoolers: rather than setting up all eight stations, allow student(s) to choose which activity they would most enjoy, and do it.

Recap Suggestions:

Spatial: Either individually or in a small group, create a mind map of the facts you have learned thus far about the British Empire, including its colonies in Asia, the Americas, the South Pacific, and Africa.

Bodily Kinesthetic: Use as many pipe cleaners as needed to create a representation of Darwin's theory of evolution, his historic voyage, or the effect his theory had upon the nineteenth century.

Interpersonal: In groups of three, with one student acting the part of a European colonist in Africa, one acting the part of an African, and one acting the part of a Christian missionary, communicate honestly the struggles each has with one or both of the others.

Musical: In a small group, list four songs, whether secular or Christian, that remind you of some aspect of this Unit.

Phase 1

Key People (Church)

David Livingstone
Scottish missionary & explorer of Africa

Andrew Murray
South African pastor & author

Charles Spurgeon
"The Prince of Preachers"

Mary Slessor
Scottish missionary to West Africa

Samuel Kaboo Morris
African who impacted America

For fascinating background information, be sure to listen to tracks 1 and 2 from the Bonus CD, *The History of Geology & Darwin: 1750-1925.*

▶ Listen to This

What in the World? VOL. 3

DISC ONE:
» The Victorian Era (track 10)

DISC TWO:
» Charles Darwin (track 1)
» Karl Marx (track 2)
» David Livingstone & Africa (track 3)

True Tales VOL. 3

DISC TWO:
» The Suez Canal (track 3)

Digging Deeper VOL. 3

DISC ONE:
» Materialsm vs. Prayer Meetings (track 7)
» The Great Prayer Revival (track 8)

▶ Read For Your Life

The Holy Bible
» **God's Protection** (consider Mary Slessor)—Psalm 3:3–6
» **Missionaries Described**—Isaiah 52:7–10
» **The Gospel to Africa**—Acts 8:26–39

Linguistic: Imagine and rewrite a different ending to the story of the American Civil War. One option would be that a divided America became the quickest and most surefire way to end the American experiment in democracy. Another option would be that America was divided into numerous countries, much like Europe.

Math-Logical: Make a prediction of what will occur in Africa if the European nations at the Berlin Congress decide it would not be in their best interests to colonize this continent.

Intrapersonal: In reflecting on the Great Prayer Revival and the stories of God moving among people of many nations and ethnicities, write a journal entry where you ponder what it would mean to you personally, and also to our current culture, should God bring this kind of revival once again.

Naturalist: Choose an Australian animal to represent life in Australia or a New Zealand bird to represent life in New Zealand during this era. It may represent the indigenous people, the Europeans, daily life in that land, or some aspect of being colonized. Be prepared to explain why this particular animal or bird was chosen.

Or . . . Activity of Your Choice: What would you like to have your students do for a review activity concerning this week's introduction to the British Empire & Awakenings?

> ## Talk Together

Opinion Column

» What did you find to be the most interesting aspect of what you have learned so far concerning the British Empire, Africa, the Intellectual Revolution, or the Great Prayer Revival?

» What do you think it would have been like to have lived in England when the young Queen Victoria began her reign? After the scandals associated with King George III's reigning sons, what might people think of this young woman who was determined to do the right thing?

» In the 1800s, European countries saw the acquisition of colonies as necessary and even good, whether in Asia, the Pacific islands, the Americas, or Africa. In your opinion, could anything positive have resulted from colonization? If so, what might that have been? Were there any negative results that came from colonization? If so, what were they?

» Imagine you had been with Henry Stanley, looking for David Livingstone in Africa. What do you think it might have been like to travel with someone who didn't know where to search for his quarry? Do you suppose Livingstone was surprised to see Stanley? What impact do you think Livingstone might have had on Stanley? (Hint: Look up the length of time Stanley stayed with Livingstone once he had found him.)

» If you had lived in New York City in 1857, what might you have enjoyed most about the Great Prayer Revival? Looking at this amazing revival from the distance of one hundred fifty years, what impresses you the most? In what ways does it inspire you?

Key People (World)
Ferdinand de Lesseps *French builder of Suez Canal*
Abraham Lincoln *US president during Civil War*
Charles Darwin *Author of Origin of Species*
Karl Marx *Co-Author of Communist Manifesto*
Queen Victoria *Longest reign in English history*
Leopold II *Belgian king who exploited Congo*

◉ Talk together

Individual Preparation

After completing their recap activities, students may begin to consider the questions in the Opinion Column and Critical Puzzling.

Class Discussion

Use the questions under Talk Together to get the students primed and to create a discussion environment in the classroom. You may also want to draw from the open-ended questions listed here.

? What do you think colonies provided to the European colonizer, the "mother country"? What did that country provide to the colonies? Who might have seen this as a mutually beneficial relationship? What do you think the indigenous people of a colony would have thought about this relationship?

? What might have happened in European countries if they had not had access to the raw materials imported from their colonies? How might this have impacted the Industrial Revolution?

? How might Darwin's theory extend beyond the realm of biology? For instance, what was Karl Marx's interest in Darwin's work?

? Mary Slessor, who lived alone in the African bush and away from other missionaries in order to minister more effectively to the African people, was unusual among Europeans. What might this have meant to the people she was serving? To the other Europeans? Why do you suppose the British government made her their first female magistrate in the British Empire?

Critical Puzzling

» During Queen Victoria's reign, the British Empire grew until it encompassed twelve million square miles and one-fourth of the world's population. What are some of the factors that might explain the magnitude of this growth?

» Why do you think the slave trade was continuing in Africa even after the British outlawed it in their empire? David Livingstone believed that both commerce and Christianity would help to eradicate the ongoing evil of slavery in Africa. What might have changed with this two-pronged approach?

» What part did the explorers of Africa, such as Livingstone and Stanley, have in the European "scramble" for this continent? Why do you think the European powers divided up Africa among themselves without concern for tribal boundaries?

» How might the policies of Metternich, which sought to repress revolutionary actions and ideas in Europe, have affected Karl Marx when he was a student in Prussia? Why do you suppose Marx was allowed to live in England with his reputation for revolutionary rhetoric? What role do you think the political freedoms and the industrialization of England played in the development of Marx's ideas?

» What effect do you think Lyell's book *Principles of Geology*, which promoted a theory of geology known as *uniformitarianism*, might have had on Charles Darwin as he made observations of nature on the voyage of the *Beagle*? Can you think of any examples of two people looking at the same fact and interpreting it from different perspectives? What explanation might a scientist who saw the world through the lens of Scripture have given concerning the same animals and landforms that Darwin encountered on his historic voyage?

» In what ways did the Great Prayer Revival impact people and their cultures? Discuss what might have been its effect upon the various cities where throngs congregated each day to pray. Beyond the good it brought each individual, what areas of society were also improved?

▶ # Resources for Digging Deeper

Choose a few books that look interesting, or find your own.

QUEEN VICTORIA

Queen Victoria WORLD LEADERS PAST & PRESENT
Deirdre Shearman • A well-balanced look at the longest-reigning queen in British history, this biography provides an excellent overview of the many facets of Queen Victoria, her family, her policies, and her reign. **MS+**

Queen Victoria A WORLD LANDMARK BOOK
Noel Streatfeild • This is an excellent "primer" for children concerning Queen Victoria's life. Learn about her isolation as a child, her governess, her accession to the throne at the age of nineteen, her prime ministers, Prince Albert, her children, and more. Highly recommended. **UE+**

BRITISH EMPIRE

Europe Around the World CAMBRIDGE INTRODUCTION TO HISTORY
Trevor Cairns • This book is an excellent overview of the growth and development of European colonies around the world, and of how some of them achieved their independence. Though it focuses mostly on events in the 1800s, there are brief descriptions of the British Commonwealth, the South American countries, the development of Japan, the exploration of Siberia, and the Scramble for Africa. Highly recommended! **UE+**

The British Empire and Commonwealth of Nations
Douglas Liversidge • The story told in this fascinating book is of the British Empire becoming the Commonwealth of Nations. Learn how the Commonwealth works, what it means, and what countries belong to it. **MS+**

Focus on Australia
Otto James • One of the World in Focus series, this is an excellent overview of Australia, giving a brief history not only of this land but also of its form of government, landscape and climate, natural resources, and culture. **UE+**

Maori and Settler
G. A. Henty • Following Henty's style for very factual presentation of his fiction, this is a fascinating history of New Zealand, telling the story of the troubles between British settlers and Maori tribes. **UE+**

The British Raj and Indian Nationalism
Margaret Yapp • India and England have been connected for centuries. This book describes both the beneficial and the detrimental aspects of the British Empire in India. **UE+**

Exploration into India
Anita Ganeri • For younger students, this book is an excellent introduction to the history of India. It includes several pages on the British Raj and the movement toward independence. **UE+**

South Africa ENCHANTMENT OF THE WORLD SERIES
R. Conrad Stein • This series gives a brief overview of the country's history, geography, and culture, and this title is excellent for discovering a bit about South Africa and the South African people. Learn more about the struggle between the British and the Boers, the Zulu kingdom, and the impact of apartheid. **UE+**

◉ # Choose books of interest/ internet search

A list of possible books is given in the Student Manual. Encourage your students to look for books or videos on the British Empire & Awakenings from this list and from other sources. You may want to gather a selection of further resources prior to beginning Unit 3, or you may encourage the students to be treasure hunters and find them on their own. It would be helpful and time-saving before the Unit begins to check availability of these titles on your local library website.

Remember:
Beware of Arrogance,
Embrace Humility!

INTELLECTUAL REVOLUTION

Prophet of Revolution: Karl Marx

Alfred Apsler • I was fascinated by this children's book on the life of Karl Marx, including his family's religious background. To understand the growth and impact of communism, it is very helpful to understand the growth and impact of its founder. Highly recommended. **UE+**

Understanding the Times

David Noebel • Read especially the chapter about secular humanist biology and Darwinism. It is excellent! **MS+**

Darwin on Trial

Phillip E. Johnson • This is one of the definitive books explaining the faith factor necessary for Darwinist evolution—faith in naturalism. Highly recommended! **HS**

Karl Marx GREAT LIVES SERIES

Nigel Hunter • This is a much shorter biography than the one listed above. It contains all of the essential information about Marx's life and work, though it does not show the inconsistencies of Marxism or of his lifestyle. **UE+**

Seven Men Who Rule the World from the Grave

Dave Breese • Darwin, Marx, Freud, and Kierkegaard are some of the people profiled in this thought-provoking book. Mr. Breese has done us an invaluable service by showing how the philosophies of these men have dramatically impacted both our world and the church. Highly recommended! **HS**

GREAT PRAYER REVIVAL

The Power of Prayer: The New York Revival of 1858

Samuel Prime • Filled with details about the Prayer Revival in New York City, including specific stories of people who were deeply changed, this book was first published the year after the revival began. Amazing! **HS**

The Great Revival in Ireland in 1859

William Gibson • The fires of revival, first kindled in North America, were soon seen across the Atlantic in Ireland, Scotland, Wales, and England. This book, an excerpt from the much more detailed and lengthy book entitled The Year of Grace, gives an amazing glimpse into a supernatural revival that ushered multitudes into the kingdom of God. **HS**

Charles Spurgeon: The Prince of Preachers

Christian Timothy George • This is the amazing story of one of the great preachers of the nineteenth century, whose height of influence corresponds with the Great Prayer Revival. Highly recommended! **UE+**

Charles Spurgeon MEN OF FAITH SERIES

Kathy Triggs • The story of Charles Spurgeon, including his gift of humor, is well told in this fascinating book. **UE+**

Spurgeon: Heir of the Puritans

Ernest W. Bacon • Published by Christian Liberty Press, this excellent biography is a deeper look at the foundation of Spurgeon's life. He was known as "the Prince of Preachers," and it would be good to understand his motivations for living to the glory of God. **MS+**

AFRICA

Exploration of Africa A
HORIZON CARAVEL BOOK

Thomas Sterling • European exploration of Africa took place almost entirely during the 1800s. This excellent book introduces us to the most important explorers of this continent, including Mungo Park, David Livingstone, and Henry Stanley. We also learn of the various river systems, the mysterious cities (like Timbuktu), and the slave trade conducted in Africa. **UE+**

Shaka, King of the Zulus

Diana Stanley and Peter Venema • A children's biography of a military genius, this is the story of the Zulu who united his people and turned them into the finest warrior nation in Africa. **E+**

The Zulus

Robert Nicholson • Discover fascinating facts about one of the most powerful African tribes of the 1800s in this informative children's book. **E+**

Escape from the Slave Traders TRAILBLAZER BOOKS

Dave & Neta Jackson • Historical fiction for children, this title describes the work of David Livingstone to eradicate the slave trade in Africa. **E+**

David Livingstone CHRISTIAN HEROES THEN AND NOW,

Janet & Geoff Benge • Wonderfully written, this series of Christian biographies is fascinating, factual, and historically accurate. Meet David Livingstone, whose travels through Africa opened up this land to European view. His concern was twofold: that the gospel would be preached and that slavery would be ended. Highly recommended! **UE+**

David Livingstone: Man of Prayer and Action

C. Silvester Horne, MP • Reprinted by Christian Liberty Press, this is an excellent biography of a missionary who was controversial among Christians and non-Christians alike. **UE+**

Trial by Poison TRAILBLAZER BOOKS

Dave & Neta Jackson • Historical fiction for children, this is the story of Mary Slessor and her ministry in West Africa. **E+**

Mary Slessor CHRISTIAN HEROES THEN AND NOW,

Janet & Geoff Benge • Mary Slessor was an amazing missionary who desired to live simply among the unreached people of Calabar (known today as Nigeria). Learn more about her life and ministry in this excellent book. **UE+**

Mary Slessor: Heroine of Calabar WOMEN OF FAITH SERIES,

Basil Miller • Mary Slessor had such an impact on the people she ministered to that she was known as the "Mother of Calabar." She was also the first woman in the British Empire to be appointed vice consul. **MS+**

Samuel Morris MEN OF FAITH SERIES,

Lindley Baldwin • Subtitled "the African boy God sent to prepare an American university for its mission to the world," this book tells the incredible story of a young man who miraculously escaped from a torturous death in Liberia and eventually came to America in the 1880s. **UE+**

Andrew Murray MEN OF FAITH SERIES,

Dr. William Lindner, Jr. • Born in South Africa, Andrew Murray was used mightily by God in a revival that took place in his country in 1860. Many have been blessed and challenged by his devotionals, but the story of his life, in its historical context, is incredible! **UE+**

The 100 Most Important Events in Christian History

A. Kenneth Curtis, J. Stephen Lang, and Randy Petersen • Beginning with the year 64 in Rome and continuing to 1976, this book is filled with short descriptions of events and people within the church. For this chapter read about David Livingstone and Kierkegaard. **UE+**

From Jerusalem to Irian Jaya: A Biographical History of Christian Missions SECOND EDITION

Ruth A. Tucker • This is one of the best books on the history of world missions available. Included are short biographies of missionaries all over the world, categorized by their geographical area of service. An indispensable resource for World Empires, World Missions, World Wars. For this chapter, read pages 147–175. Highly recommended! **UE+**

For more books, use these Dewey Decimal numbers in your library:

Asia: 915

Africa: 916

General history of Africa: 960

Southern Africa: 968

American Civil War: 973.6–973.7

Darwinism: 576.8

Marxism: 335.4

Victorian era: 941

Colonialism: 325

Missions: 266

Suez Canal: 386 and 962

AMERICAN CIVIL WAR

The Emancipation Proclamation: The Abolition of Slavery

Janet Riehecky • For elementary students, this book examines the issue of slavery in the United States prior to the Civil War, the events that led to the Emancipation Proclamation, and the impact on the North and South. **UE+**

Fields of Fury: The American Civil War

James M. McPherson • Written by the Pulitzer Prize–winning author of *Battle Cry of Freedom*, this title will provide students with an overview of the key elements of this war. **UE+**

THE SUEZ CANAL

Building the Suez Canal A
HORIZON CARAVEL BOOK

S. C. Burchell • What a fascinating story! Learn about Ferdinand de Lesseps, the man who built the canal against tremendous odds. This book gives the reader a sense of what was involved—both politically and structurally—to get the job accomplished. Highly recommended! **UE+**

CLASSIC LITERATURE

Jane Eyre

Charlotte Bronte • Classic literature set in Victorian England, this is one of the most celebrated romances of all time—because of the integrity of the heroine. **HS**

VIDEO

Zulu Dawn

This movie shows the battle at Isandlwana (Zululand) between the British and Zulu in 1879. The heavily armed and sophisticated British soldiers were completely overwhelmed and defeated during this battle. **MS+**

(This is the prequel to the film *Zulu*, which depicts the Battle of Rorke's Drift between a small company of British soldiers and several thousand Zulus shortly after the defeat of the British at Isandlwana.)

What books did you like best?

_____

_____

_____

_____

The Internet also contains a wealth of information about the British Empire & Awakenings.

What sites were the most helpful?

_____

_____

_____

_____

◉ Conduct a review and evaluation

In this Phase of Unit 3, your students should have had the opportunity to explore the rise of the British Empire & Awakenings through reading, listening, thinking, and discussing by completing a selection from the following:

- informally discussed the Key Concepts;
- read the article;
- listened to the audio recordings;
- read the online articles;
- read the Scriptures;
- explored the recap activities;
- considered the Opinion Column and Critical Puzzling answers on their own;
- participated in class discussion;
- chosen books of interest or searched the Internet;
- completed their self-evaluation for this Phase.

Record student hours: _____

Assess student participation:

Create an evaluation system of your own, or refer to the evaluation rubric in the introduction, as a tool for assessing participation. The categories you will probably find most useful are

"Introduction," "Process: Teamwork," and "Process: Originality." To help students develop good discussion skills, encourage them to participate actively, ask content-based questions, and stay focused on the discussion at hand. Students demonstrate a higher level of discussion skills when they incorporate comments and questions from others into their own questions, and draw out opinions or ask for points of clarification from others.

Do not critique the self-evaluation page your student completes and do not direct the answers the student gives to the questions. Instead, allow sincere and personal completion of the evaluation, then discuss the

responses and incorporate those comments into your evaluation.

Determine a grade for this Phase, if using grades: _____

Teacher Self-Evaluation:

Evaluate your own use of materials and teaching opportunities: what worked and what did not; how effective was your time-management; how were your responses to the needs of your student; did you make your expectations clear; in what ways would you like to improve your approach for the next Unit? Incorporate suggestions from your students in your own evaluation (this requires humility!).

---

3 Phase 1

▷ Student Self-Evaluation UNIT 3, PHASE 1

Dates and hours:_____

Key Concepts

Rephrase the five Key Concepts of this Unit and confirm your understanding of each:

- The British Empire

   _____

- Africa: Christianity/Colonies

   _____

- Great Prayer Revival

   _____

- American Civil War

   _____

- The Intellectual Revolution

   _____

Tools for Self-Evaluation

Evaluate your personal participation in the discussions of this Phase. Bearing in mind that a good participant in a discussion is not always the most vocal participant, ask yourself these questions: Were you an active participant? Did you ask perceptive questions? Were you willing to listen to other participants of the discussion and draw out their opinions? Record your observations and how you would like to improve your participation in the future:

_____

_____

Every time period is too complex to be understood in one Phase of study. Evaluate your current knowledge of the British Empire & Awakenings. What have you focused on so far? What are your weakest areas of knowledge?

_____

_____

Based on the evaluation of this introduction, project ahead what you would like to study more of in the following Phases.

_____

_____

120 The British Empire & Awakenings (1830–1870)

both her life and the life of the nation during her reign. As a group, evaluate her reign in terms of national, international, and cultural changes.

Queen Victoria's Descendants

Create a flip chart or PowerPoint presentation to show the royal houses and nations into which Victoria's children and grandchildren married. In the generation of the grandchildren, be sure to show visually how these various heads of state—cousins—related to each other.

Write a song, with as many verses as needed, to briefly tell the story of Victoria's history-making children and grandchildren. You might want to make it a tongue-in-cheek version, with a title such as "Round, Round, Get Around, We Get Around!"

The Crystal Palace

Create a collage that will represent the various aspects of this marvelous structure and the exhibits it contained. Be sure to include some of the architectural design elements, types of displays, and overwhelming success of this first World's Fair–style event.

Set up a "Crystal Palace Museum"— with diagrams, photos, descriptions, even miniature displays—to help modern visitors understand some of the amazing dynamics of this Victorian-era event. Then, as a tour guide, take groups through the museum, explaining what is on display and answering any questions they might have.

Colonization of Australia & New Zealand

Either in a team or as an individual, portray two sides of this story. First, as a British settler in either New Zealand or Australia, explain to an interested audience what life is like in your new home and what some of your concerns are about government policies regarding the indigenous people. Then, as a Maori of New Zealand or Aboriginal of Australia, explain your perspective on what has happened to

---

Phase 2

▶ Research & Reporting

Explore one or more of these areas to discover something significant!

Queen Victoria

Discover more about this fascinating woman, along with the time period that took its name from her: the Victorian era. Learn about the challenges she faced, the responsibilities of monarchy in England during this time, Victoria's family, and the extensive changes England experienced during her extremely long reign.

The Descendants of Queen Victoria

Research and report on the descendants of Queen Victoria—her children and grandchildren—and the royal positions they held or married into in various nations of Europe. Consider, as you research, the scope of influence in the world that this one family has had.

The Crystal Palace

Investigate the Crystal Palace Exhibition, which was a celebration of the technologies of the Industrial Revolution in London. Who championed this project? What was on exhibit? What countries were represented? How long did it last? What were the results?

New Zealand

Research and report on British colonization in the South Pacific. What were the reasons for the settlement of Australia and of New Zealand? What was the response of the Aboriginals of Australia and the Maori of New Zealand to this colonization? How were these people groups treated by the British government and by British settlers? What did the colonists of these two countries use for trade with Great Britain?

Colonization of Australia & New Colonial Trade

Discover more about the issues of trade with the colonies, especially the economics of colonial trade (remember the investigative motto: "follow the money"). Discover which parties benefitted and whether it was equal or unequal, which party suffered material or personal loss, and whether there were particular displays of greed or of altruism (generosity). You might also want to consider aspects of trade, such as the merchant vessels used to bring trade goods, the methods of keeping trade routes safe, and the missionaries traveling to the ends of the earth via these merchant vessels.

The Boers & the British

The Dutch were the original European settlers in South Africa. Eventually, however, the British began colonizing the area. Research and report on the Great Trek of the Boers, including its causes and results, as well as the relationship between the British, the Boers, and the Zulu.

European Colonial Empires of the 1800s

Research and report on colonization under a specific European government including its colonies in Africa, Asia, the Caribbean or the Pacific. How did European nations, such as France or Germany, acquire their colonies during this era? How were the indigenous people of a colony treated by their European colonizers? What kinds of raw materials did the European country import from its colonies? What was exported back to the colonies? By

---

◉ Choose a topic and begin research

Allow the students the freedom to choose one of the topics listed under research & reporting in the Student Manual, or to suggest their own area which they would like to research.

Motivating Suggestions:

Especially for Non-linguistic students, and those who are not motivated by written or oral reports, here are suggestions for alternative ways of reporting what has been researched.

Queen Victoria

Imagine you are either one of the Queen's ladies-in-waiting or a Member of Parliament during Victoria's accession to the throne. Journal your thoughts concerning the differences between this young woman and the kings before her. Consider how Victoria's determination to be a good queen might affect the nation over time.

With a group of students, discuss your research on Queen Victoria. Consider the significant milestones of

your homeland and what possible solutions to the problems you envision.

Gather actual materials from nature (or photos when necessary) that will help you illustrate what was so compelling to both natives and settlers about these fascinating countries. You might wish to create a three-dimensional scene outdoors or use these materials to enhance your storytelling of life in the South Pacific colonies.

The Boers & the British

Create a hard-hitting television news report, which tells the story of the Great Trek of the Boers. Your decision will be whether to tell it from the Dutch point of view (favorable to the Boers) or from the British point of view (unfavorable to the Boers) or from the Zulu point of view (antagonistic toward both the Boers and the British).

Compare and contrast the original Dutch settlers of South Africa with the British settlers during the time period being studied. Prepare charts to show the similarities and differences between these two European colonizers. Show the way each group interacted with the native Africans.

Colonial Trade

Create an advertising campaign that will boost sales for merchant traders in both the mother country and the colony. Your challenge is to create incentive on the part of colonists and natives to purchase items from Europe *and* to motivate European businessmen at home to buy the raw imported materials. Be sure to use graphic designs that will actually "move product"!

As an official in the British Empire during the late Victorian Era, you have been given the assignment of assessing colonial trade over the past several decades in order to decide what, if any, policies should be changed. Add your own opinion concerning which policies have been helpful and which have been harmful.

---

extension, you might want to study and describe what happened to the colony after gaining independence from its European colonizer.

The Great Prayer Revival

In 1857, a noon prayer meeting was begun in New York City. The result of this ongoing prayer meeting was revival. Research and report on this revival and on the subsequent revivals that took place in Great Britain, South Africa, Jamaica, China, and India.

The American Civil War

Research and report on the causes leading up to this war, along with its major events and conclusion. What were some of the most notable results of this war? What part did the tension between states' rights and federal rights play? Why was slavery such a critical issue during this conflict, and how did slavery in America affect the European view of the war?

Indian Mutiny

Study the causes and results of the Indian Mutiny of 1857. Consider the issues as seen through the eyes of the Hindu and Muslim peoples of India: new technologies introduced to the subcontinent by the British, as well as the increasing emphasis on Christianity, as evidenced by new churches and schools throughout India.

The Suez Canal

Investigate the building of the Suez Canal by Ferdinand de Lesseps. Discover also the intended strategic use of the Suez Canal. What are the benefits of this technological wonder in the sand, and who receives them?

David Livingstone

Learn more about the life, ministry, and explorations of David Livingstone. Describe his childhood,

his family life, and his relationship with the Africans he served. Discover his unusual strengths and their corresponding weaknesses, and then with great humility analyze his work as a missionary and as an explorer.

Mary Slessor

Research and report on the life and ministry of Mary Slessor. Include such information as her childhood and conversion during the Great Prayer Revival, as well as the groundbreaking work she did among the people of Calabar. What qualified Mary Slessor, the first woman ever to hold this position, to be a magistrate in the British Empire, and what did this require of her?

Karl Marx

Research and report on Karl Marx and his philosophy of communism. Describe his childhood in Prussia, his university days, and his years of exile. What was the purpose of the Communist Manifesto of 1848? Who was Engels? What was the purpose of Das Kapital (1867)? What was the impact of Marx's writings and philosophy?

Charles Darwin

Study and write about Charles Darwin. What were his studies before the voyage on HMS *Beagle*? What did he observe on his voyage? How did he interpret his observations? What response did his publications receive in the scientific, religious, and popular press?

Battle of Isandlwana

Research and report on the Battle of Isandlwana in 1879 between the Zulu kingdom and the British Empire. Why was this battle fought? What was the outcome? How did that affect British morale and policy? Describe the battle tactics of the Zulu. How effective were these tactics? Why is this battle historically significant?

European Colonial Empires of the 1800s

Create a board game, in the style of Monopoly that will help players learn about the issues facing a European colony, the European country which colonized it, the native people, and the settlers. Make it highly competitive with high financial gains possible. The one with the most money and power at the end of the game wins. (Though that is not true from an eternal perspective, it was certainly the way the European rulers saw it!)

Compose a parody using the tune "Oh, Susanna" to tell the story of one nation's experience of colonization

during the 1800s. For each verse, explain a different aspect of colonization, from successes to difficulties to lessons learned. Though much about the colonial empires of this time was not funny, the more you can use humor in the song, the better a learning tool this will be for others!

The Great Prayer Revival

Make a PowerPoint presentation of the Great Prayer Revival to show the growth of this revival throughout the United States, the British Isles, and other nations of the world. Be sure to include some of the outstanding features of this revival (for instance, favorable coverage by the press).

▶ **Brain Stretchers**

British North America Act

Investigate the connection between the American Civil War (and its resulting tensions with Canada) and the British move to create a federal union in Canada, culminating in the British North America Act of 1867.

Creation vs. Evolution

Compare and contrast Darwinian evolution with biblical creation.

Independence

Compare and contrast the independence of the United States (a former British colony) with the British Commonwealth countries of Canada, Australia, or New Zealand. Examine the way the commonwealth country established its own form of independence while remaining within the overall structure of the British Empire.

Valuable Resources

Learn about the effect of the discovery of valuable resources, such as gold and diamonds, on the European colonies of southern Africa.

Congo

Study the colonization of the Democratic Republic of the Congo (formerly known as the Belgian Congo and Zaire). Consider why this was an attractive area to the Belgian king, Leopold II. How did he learn about this land? What was the effect of colonization on the Africans of the Congo? (You might wish to examine the current political situation and compare it with the colonial period.)

Create Your Own Research Topic

_____

_____

_____

_____

Imagine you were there, attending the first prayer meeting held in New York City, at the beginning of the prayer revival. Write your thoughts about what happened that day, how the revival has changed your life, and what you can pass on to future generations concerning the power of prayer to change individuals and nations.

The American Civil War

Make a series of maps, beginning with the United States on the brink of the Civil War. From there, show the unfolding of the separation between the Northern states and the Confederacy, the major battles, the areas affected by the Emancipation Proclamation, and the ending of the war. Enhance your maps with pictures of specific people, various designs of clothing and weaponry, architectural styles.

With a small group, create a series of short dramatic vignettes that will allow an audience to gain a greater understanding of the events and tensions leading up to the Civil War.

Indian Mutiny

Create a time line or diagram showing the various causes and events of the Indian Mutiny. It might be helpful to use separate colors to highlight the English, Indian, Hindu, Muslim, and Christian factors that played a part in this violent confrontation between cultures.

Imagine you are an interested observer living in India during the time when the British Government has replaced the British East India Company as the ruling authority in India. As a Christian who appreciates William Carey's approach to the Indian people and their culture, share your thoughts on the recent tragedy of the Indian Mutiny. Did you see this coming? What do you think might have prevented the violence? What hope do you see for British-Indian relations in the future?

The Suez Canal

Create a diorama that will show the steps of the process of building the Suez Canal in the Egyptian sands. Be sure to include a paper that will show the statistics of this amazing technological feat, such as how long the process took, how many workers were needed, etc.

Write and illustrate a book for young children that will help them discover not only the fascinating tale behind the building of the Suez Canal, but also the strategic place it holds in modern history.

David Livingstone

Host the controversial, hard-hitting Christian talk show "Commerce or Christ?" in which various famous people and ministries are closely examined to discover whether they are more concerned with money, power, and fame or with the kingdom of God. Today's subject? David Livingstone. You will want to air the viewpoints of Africans and Europeans, missionaries and explorers, in order to discover the truth about this famous Christian man.

Create an outdoor action game that will mimic Livingstone's epic explorations of Africa. Remember, there were many difficulties which had to be evaded or overcome, including geographic hazards, wild animals, hostile African tribes, and nasty diseases. Creatively decide how participants will be encumbered by these unusual troubles!

Mary Slessor

Create a first person presentation of Mary Slessor. She was an amazing and unusual woman, so be sure to include such fascinating facts as the type of dwellings she lived in during her time in the jungle of Calabar, how long she worked among the people in the interior of Calabar, her pioneering attitudes, and how she got along with other European missionaries.

Choose a selection of music, or combine several selections of music, that reflect the life of Mary Slessor. Prepare program notes for your audience to help them understand what they are going to hear. Be sure to include a bit of information regarding the region of Africa where she ministered—including the geography, the history, and the culture. You may choose instrumental or vocal music, and whatever styles of music are suited to this subject. Prior to the concert, explain how these selections are, for you, a window into Mary Slessor's unusual life.

Karl Marx

As a news reporter before an interested, and potentially hostile, audience, interview Karl Marx and his co-worker, Frederick Engels. Ask the questions people want to know: Why do they want to tear down existing governments? Why do they think violence is a good solution? Why do they reject Christianity and the Bible? What do they envision for the future?

Some people embraced Karl Marx and his philosophy with a near religious devotion, while others were appalled at his rhetoric and theories. Even today, people still tend to either idolize or revile this influential man. Analyze your research and decide how you will view Karl Marx. Write a reasoned defense of your position.

Charles Darwin

Compare and contrast Charles Darwin with another famous "Charles" of his day, Charles Spurgeon. Both of these Englishmen influenced many people, though in quite different ways. In what ways did the culture of their day affect their work? How did people respond to each of their writings? What are the ongoing effects of each of their lives?

Create an artistic rendering of the voyage of *HMS Beagle* and the wonderfully diverse creatures which Darwin observed. It would be helpful to include Scriptures which present a biblical view of how the varieties of animal life came to be on these islands—in contrast to Darwin's theory of the branching "tree" of evolution.

Battle of Isandlwana

Using appropriate materials, such as modeling clay, create a topographical map of this first major encounter between the Zulus and the British during the Anglo-Zulu war. You will want to include encampments and armies, and perhaps weaponry, supplies, etc.

As a photojournalist, interview a Zulu warrior who was present at the recent battle to ask his perspective on the issues surrounding this battle and war. In addition, interview both a British survivor of the battle and a representative sampling of people back in England to discover their perspective on why this war is being fought, and the way their stunning loss to the Zulus has impacted their nation.

3 Phase 2

▶ Time Line

1830
1840
1850
1880
1870
1860

124 The British Empire & Awakenings (1830–1870)

Consider this for your time line

This time period is one of great contrasts: a spiritual revival bringing millions into relationship with God is taking place in the same year that a book is published refuting the very notion of a Creator God; while slavery is outlawed in the British Empire, other national groups will defend their right to hold slaves; Africa draws European Christians who will lay down their lives to bless the African people, while other Europeans come to this continent to prosper themselves at brutal cost to the African people; and atheistic communism is born in the most freedom-loving country of Europe.

Key Events

- Great Trek of the Boers
- New Zealand becomes a British colony
- Canada receives "Dominion" status
- The Great Exhibition
- Publication of *Origin of Species*
- Publication of *Communist Manifesto*
- The Great Prayer Revival
- The Indian Mutiny
- Suez Canal built
- American Civil War
- Anglo-Zulu War
- Scramble for Africa

Be sure to include the people listed in Key People in Phase 1.

The British Empire & Awakenings (1830–1870) **125**

One of the most amazing revivals of all time occurred during this era. It was ushered in through the prayers of ordinary people. Discuss with your students the significance of prayer and the part it played in the Great Prayer Revival. Go beyond discussion, however, and, with your students, begin to pray for revival for this generation and time!

◉ Construct the time line

Read the information listed with the Key Events in the Student Manual. Dialogue with your students about the issues involved.

Find the dates for the Key People and Key Events listed.

Time Line Key

Key People in the Church

- David Livingstone: 1813–1873
- Andrew Murray: 1828–1917
- Charles Spurgeon: 1834–1893
- Mary Slessor: 1848–1915
- Samuel Morris: 1873–1893

Key People in the World

- Abraham Lincoln: 1809–1865
- Charles Darwin: 1809–1882
- Karl Marx: 1818–1883
- Queen Victoria: 1819–1901
- Leopold II: 1835–1909

Key Dates

- Great Trek of the Boers: 1836
- New Zealand becomes a British colony: 1841
- Canada receives "Dominion" status: 1867
- The Great Exhibition: 1851
- Publication of Origin of Species: 1859
- Publication of Communist Manifesto: 1848
- The Great Prayer Revival: 1857–1860
- The Indian Mutiny: 1857
- Suez Canal built: 1859–1869
- American Civil War: 1861–1865
- Anglo-Zulu War: 1879
- Scramble for Africa: Berlin Conference: 1884–1885

3 Phase 2

► Words to Watch

colonization	trek	sovereignty	civil (as in "civil war")
communism	compromise	ideology	emancipation
evolution	racism	imperialism	exhibition
accession	malaria	free trade	indigenous
naturalism	eugenics	equality	caste

Consider:

Africa. This remarkable continent was described for an eager European audience by missionary and explorer David Livingstone in his book *Missionary Travels and Researches in South Africa*. Here are a few of the words used to describe a place quite mysterious and magical to European ears.

Kalahari Desert	acacia tree	Zambezi	rapids
Bushmen	mirage	banyan tree	manioc root
nomads	inundation	baobab tree	cataract
wadi	tsetse fly	calabash	

Other words you need to look up:

_____

_____

_____

_____

Here is one idea for making vocabulary study interesting and fun:

PARLANCE PERSONIFIED

Your assignment is to find a way to act out the substance of each of these vocabulary words in order to best remember the meaning. You might want to turn this into a Charades-style game, with one person acting the word while everyone guesses from the list of vocabulary words.

A list of definitions can be found at the back of the book in Appendix B.

◉ Practice vocabulary

You may find other words in this Unit that are especially appropriate for younger children. Feel free to substitute another vocabulary list for the one provided.

◉ Complete research projects and share in class or hand in

Create a safe environment for the presentations. Set ground rules prior to the presentations, so that students know how much time is available for each of them, and so that they know they will be honored and respected by all those observing.

▶ **Student Self-Evaluation** UNIT 3, PHASE 2

Dates and hours:_____

Research Project

Summarize your research question:

_____

_____

List your most useful sources by author, title, and page number or URL where applicable (continue list in margin if necessary):

_____

_____

Now take a moment to evaluate the sources you just listed. Do they provide a balanced view of your research question? Should you have sought an additional opinion? Are your sources credible (if you found them on your own)? Record your observations:

_____

_____

_____

Evaluate your research project in its final presentation. What are its strengths? If you had time to revisit this project, what would you change? Consider giving yourself a letter grade based on your project's merits and weaknesses.

_____

_____

_____

Letter grade: ____

You have just completed an area of specific research on the time of the British Empire & Awakenings. Now what would you like to explore in the upcoming Phases? Set some objectives for yourself.

_____

_____

_____

The British Empire & Awakenings (1830–1870) **127**

◉ Conduct a review and evaluation

In this second Phase of Unit 3, your students should have had the opportunity to explore the British Empire & Awakenings through researching, thinking, and reporting by completing a selection from the following:

- done a research project;
- learned the vocabulary;
- constructed a time line;
- created a project report on what was researched;
- completed their self-evaluation procedure for this Phase.

Record student hours: _____

Assess student effort in the research and reporting projects.

Create an evaluation system of your own, or refer to the evaluation rubric in the introduction, as a tool for assessing research and reporting. The categories you will probably find most useful are *"Introduction," "Task," "Process: Teamwork"* (if students are working together), along with Grammar, Format, and Spelling. As a tool for helping your students develop better research skills, pay attention to their evaluation of sources. Older students should learn how to make a "Sources Cited" list according to academic standards—refer them to English usage books or websites for formatting rules. Younger students should learn how to obtain a balanced view of their research subject; if they use more than one source they will get a bigger picture of what was happening. Encourage your students to make use of their self-evaluations for their next research projects, in order to practice good research skills.

Do not critique the self-evaluation page your student completes in the Student Manual—spelling errors are not to be considered in such an exercise. Students should feel free to humbly evaluate themselves without that added complexity. Instead, discuss with them the intention of their written comments and incorporate those into your evaluation.

Determine a final grade for this Phase: _____

Teacher Self-Evaluation:

Evaluate your own use of materials and teaching opportunities: what worked and what did not; how effective was your time-management; how were your responses to the needs of your student; did you make your expectations clear; in what ways would you like to improve your approach for the next Unit? Incorporate suggestions from your students in your own evaluation *(this requires humility!)*.

Phase 3

▶ Maps and Mapping

Physical Terrain

» Locate and label on a map of Africa the major regions of desert, grassland/savannah, and tropical forest/jungle. In addition, locate and label the three major lakes and these four major rivers: the Nile with its tributaries, the Congo, the Zambezi, and the Niger.

» Locate and label the major colonies of the British Empire—including those with Dominion status—particularly Canada, New Zealand, Australia, India, and South Africa. Also locate and label the islands of the Galapagos, which proved to be so significant in Darwin's theory of evolution.

» Locate and label the different terrains found on the Australian continent.

Geopolitical

» Trace the route of David Livingstone's journeys through southern Africa. Also locate the area of Mary Slessor's ministry. *For extra credit: Label and shade the various regions of Africa claimed by European countries during the Scramble for Africa.*

» Trace the journey of the HMS *Beagle* from England to the Galapagos Islands. Be sure to note those places Charles Darwin found most interesting in the development of his theory, including Tierra del Fuego.

» Trace the route colonists took from England to Australia, New Zealand, India, and South Africa.

Explore

» *Geographical Challenges of Africa:* Discover and report on the obstacles facing early European missionaries and explorers who sought to travel inland in Africa. How did specific terrains and climates affect these non-acclimated Europeans? Were the African tribes affected negatively as well? Did any tribal traditions allow indigenous Africans to live in places where European colonists could not survive? If so, what were they?

» *Geographical Challenges of Australia:* Discover and report on the difficulties caused by the terrain and climate colonists faced in Australia. How did the Aboriginals conquer and capitalize on those same difficulties?

» *Christian Outreach:* What is the status of evangelical outreach today in Africa? Also report on the status of evangelical outreach today in North America, Australia, and New Zealand. What opportunities and what difficulties face those who share the gospel in one or all of these areas?

128 The British Empire & Awakenings (1830–1870)

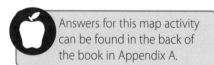

Answers for this map activity can be found in the back of the book in Appendix A.

◉ Create a map and discuss the issues in teams

The students each have an outline map in their manuals. They will be given assignments for drawing in the rivers, mountains, cities, and regional boundaries that are listed. For details on where these things are, please consult a historical atlas, an encyclopedia, or another source of geographic information.

Upper elementary students might be satisfied to accomplish only this portion:

• **Physical terrain:** This part of the mapping exercise will help students locate and mark the African continent. A tremendous resource for locating the rivers of Africa can be found online by doing a search for "major rivers in Africa." In addition, students will locate and mark the major British colonies of this era.

Middle school students might be satisfied to complete both the previous mapping exercise and this exercise:

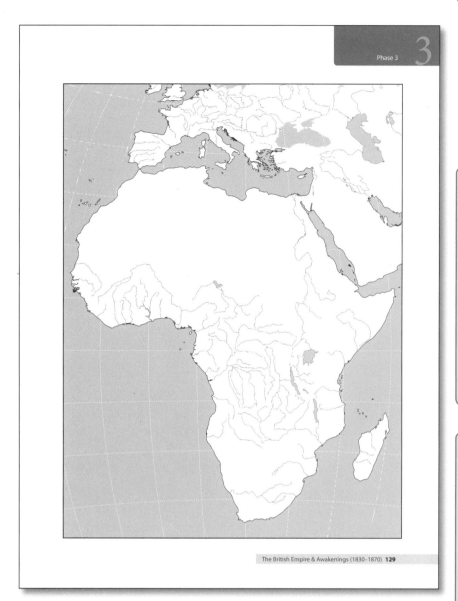

GEOGRAPHICAL CHALLENGES OF AFRICA

Accounts of explorers such as Mungo Park, Henry Stanley, and David Livingstone, in addition to missionary accounts of Africa, are excellent sources for information regarding the physical and geographical challenges faced by Europeans. Livingstone's accounts of his journeys include much information regarding the ways various African tribes were able to flourish in the same areas that challenged Europeans.

GEOGRAPHICAL CHALLENGES OF AUSTRALIA

Australia is the driest inhabited continent (Antarctica is drier but uninhabited), the continent is relatively flat, and the soil is not as fertile as Europe or the Americas. Despite all of this, British colonists still came in droves to farm, ranch, and establish businesses. Compare and contrast their approach with the approach that the various Aboriginal tribes took to living on and from the land.

CHRISTIAN OUTREACH

Students might wish to locate information about current missionary endeavors in Africa, North America (people from other countries are now bringing the gospel to our postmodern nations!), Australia, and New Zealand. If possible, to provide even more help and insight, interview someone who has worked in these fields.

- **Geopolitical:** This section of the mapping exercise will provide the students an opportunity to locate and mark Livingstone's journeys, Darwin's voyage, and the routes of colonists traveling to listed British colonies. Encourage students to discover how Africa was divided up by European countries.

High school students might be satisfied to complete both the previous mapping exercises and at least one exploration topic of this exercise:

- **Explore** a selection from this portion of the mapping exercise in teams.

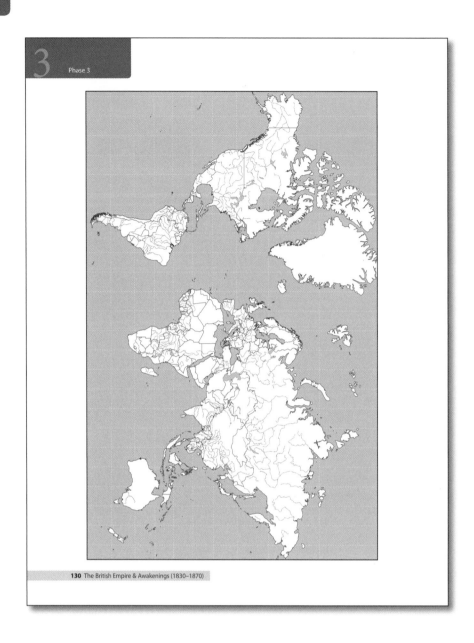

130 The British Empire & Awakenings (1830–1870)

▶ Art Appreciation

The Gleaners by Jean-François Millet

Gleaning is a practice hearkening back to the Old Testament, providing food for the poor from the fields of landowners, and had been the subject of previous paintings. When this painting was first exhibited in 1857, with the marginalized poor painted with sympathetic dignity, it brought many negative reviews—hitting wealthy patrons of art and art critics too close to home to be appreciated. You can find a link to see this painting at the online resource page.

> » Describe what you see. How does Millet contrast the poverty of the gleaners with the wealth of the farm owners? How would you describe the women who are gleaning? What clues do you find that would indicate Millet's esteem of these peasant women? What can you detect in this painting that would cause some to be uncomfortable?

A Farmyard near Fontainebleau by Camille Corot

Camille Corot was the leader of the nineteenth century "Barbizon School" of French landscape artists. Early in his artistic studies, he was advised by his teacher, Michallon, an established artist, "to render with the greatest scrupulousness everything I saw before me. The lesson worked; since then I have always treasured precision." You can find a link to see this painting at the online resource page.

> » Describe what you see in as much detail as possible. Compare this painting to John Constable's *The Hay Wain* (from Unit 2). How are they similar? How are they different?

CONSIDER:

Following in the steps of Constable and Turner, the French development of landscape painting, known as the "Barbizon School," broke with the tradition of classic art by elevating nature and its beauty to center stage. Several French painters, including Théodore Rousseau, Jean-François Millet, Camille Corot, and Charles-François Daubigny, found their inspiration at the Forest of Fontainebleau, just a short distance from Paris. The best known of these, Millet, painted more than landscapes, however. As noted art historian Frederick Hartt writes, "Millet saw them [peasants] as pious actors in a divinely ordained drama—a Catholic counterpart to the dominant role peasants and workers were assuming at that very moment in the thought of Karl Marx, who would have had little but contempt for the supine way in which Millet's peasants accept their humble lot."

The online resource page at www.HistoryRevealed.org contains many helpful Internet links to artwork, architecture, music, project helps, and more.

◉ Examine and discuss art and architecture

The online resource page at www.HistoryRevealed.org has links to view each of the items listed. Allow the students time to observe the paintings without any conversation, and then, when they are ready, engage them in some or all of the questions listed below or in the Student Manual.

Art Appreciation
The Gleaners by Jean-François Millet

Gleaners in this era in France were only allowed to go through the fields at the end of the working day—at sunset—which required haste before dark, and they were only allowed to gather, one by one, ears of corn missed by the harvesters.

Ask students to compare Millet's painting with *Gleaners* by Jules Bret-

The online resource page at www.HistoryRevealed.org contains many helpful Internet links to artwork, architecture, music, project helps, and more.

on, who was a lesser-known painter of the Barbizon school. How do these two paintings compare with one another? Next, have students examine some of Millet's other paintings, such as *The Sower and Angelus*. Ask them to describe in detail the way Millet paints both landscapes and peasants.

Farmyard near Fontainebleau, by Camille Corot

After the death of Millet, Corot gave a tremendous financial gift to his widow in order to help support her children. According to one biographer, Corot's charity was "near proverbial," including financially supporting a day center for children in Paris.

Ask students to compare Corot's painting with the watercolors of Australian artist Hans Heysen. Corot's decision to seldom include people in his landscapes may have influenced Heysen, who studied in Paris many years after Corot's death. What similarities are there between these two landscape painters? What differences?

Architecture

The Crystal Palace, designed by Joseph Paxton

After the exhibition was over, the Crystal Palace was dismantled and moved to a new location, which was opened by Queen Victoria in 1854. The new palace and grounds became the world's first "theme park," offering entertainment, a roller coaster, sporting events, and education to two million visitors a year!

Imagine what it would have been like to walk into this architectural novelty. What kind of effect do you think it would have had on the multitude of visitors to see trees, bushes, flowers, even birds overhead during an international technological and commercial enterprise?

Ask your students to consider the biblical concept of contentment. Do Millet's paintings give them any insight into Paul's statement that he had learned to be content in whatever state he was in, that he had learned to abound and to be in want, able to "do all things through Christ who strengthens me"? What does this mean to them today in a culture largely driven by consumerism?

▶ Architecture

The Industrial Revolution brought about a revolution in architecture. Rather than architects designing only churches, palaces, and government structures, now private industry required their services to design new buildings for factories, railroad stations, warehouses, and more.

The Crystal Palace by Joseph Paxton

In 1851, England astounded the world with its amazing technology and industry during the Great Exhibition (the first commercial and industrial World's Fair) in London. The exhibition was held in the Crystal Palace, a temporary structure of glass panels and iron framework—an extraordinarily large greenhouse! The Crystal Palace covered nineteen acres and was tall enough to house the mighty elm trees standing in Hyde Park. You can find a link to drawings and historic renderings of the Crystal Palace of 1851 at the online resource page.

> » How would you describe this structure? Why do you think it was fitting to hold the Great Exhibition in the Crystal Palace rather than in a neoclassical building?

▶ Arts in Action

Select one or more, and let your artistic juices flow!

Drawing with Perspective

Look at Millet's *The Gleaners*. Do you notice the people in the background? Did Millet paint them the same size as the women who are gleaning? Why not? Try this: sketch a picture of someone working. Add people and a setting in the background (like a park, house, or field). Remember to use perspective to make the items in the background smaller than the items in the foreground.

Drawing the Simple Life

In contrast to Jacques-Louis David's depiction of Napoleon crossing the Alps from Unit 1 (which was classically heroic rather than realistic), create an album of your family that reflects the style of Millet, with a simple, "quiet," industrious piety. If you use black and white or sepia photos instead of drawings, it may be easier to capture this feeling. (You may be able to use old photos from your grandparents.) Be sure to title each photo or drawing—following the style of Millet. Have fun!

◎ Do an art project

Drawing with Perspective

There are many books in the library, as well as online sources, for learning to draw in perspective. YouTube has an excellent 10-minute primer on drawing: How to Draw Two-Point Perspective with Karl Gude, which can be found at the online resource page.

Drawing the Simple Life

Encourage students to analyze the various kinds of activities Millet showed peasants doing as they consider their own album. In the 21st century, what are some appropriate activities that would give the same "feel" for quietness, simplicity, hard work, and piety as is evidenced in Millet's paintings?

▶ Science

Michael Faraday was one of the greatest physicists of history. (Find his biographies listed in Unit 1). His work on electricity and magnetism paved the way for the everyday use of electricity. He was also a devout and humble Christian man—even refusing the honor of being knighted by Queen Victoria, preferring to remain plain Mr. Faraday to the end of his life.

» Faraday was the first to discover that magnetism can produce electricity. Here is a simple experiment to show his discovery: You will need a piece of electrical wire about two yards long, a bar magnet, and a small compass. Peel one inch of covering off both ends of the wire. Loosely wrap one end of the wire around your hand about ten times to form a coil. Slip the wire off your hand, leaving it coiled. Wrap the other end of the wire around the compass about five times, leaving the wire on the compass. Now twist the two peeled ends of the wire together. Move the bar magnet in and out of the empty coils while watching what happens to the compass. Did the needle move? The compass demonstrates that there is a small electrical current being produced. What happens when you leave the bar magnet inside the coils? Outside the coils? Move the bar magnet in and out several times again, using different speeds. What happens?

▶ Music

Nationalistic music:

» Ethnic themes

» Ethnic melodies and harmonies

The major composers of nationalistic music are:

» Wagner » Rimsky-Korsakov

» Tchaikovsky » Smetana

You can find a link to listen to the music at the online resource page.

"The Moldau" by Smetana

This "symphonic poem" is a musical painting, with the composer using the orchestra and sound the way an artist uses brush and paint. The Moldau is a river that winds through Smetana's homeland, through the city of Prague and into the River Elbe. As you listen to this famous orchestral piece, see if you can hear the sounds of the river.

For further study in this time period, you might want to listen to the operas of Giuseppe Verdi (especially *Aida*) and Georges Bizet (*Carmen*).

◉ Do a science experiment

Answers in Genesis has additional biographical information on Michael Faraday. A link can be found at the online resource page.

An excellent and inexpensive book of experiments for this area is *Safe and Simple Electrical Experiments* by Rudolf Graf. The items used in the experiments are household items, while the results are . . . electrifying!

◉ Listen to and discuss the music

Listen

The Moldau by Smetana

Also known as "Vltava," this is the second of six pieces in the symphonic poem "Má Vlast" (My Country). Though Smetana was writing nationalistic music of his own country of Bohemia, you can hear how the music draws deeply from Western European musical tradition. This makes sense when we remember that Bohemia was still part of the Austrian Empire at this time.

Have your students consider the sounds a river would make through the Bohemian countryside. Two flutes musically portray the two streams which flow together to become the actual river, depicted by the strings. Listen for the hunting horns in the forest, a wedding celebration complete with polka, moonlight on the river, then the acceleration and agitation of the river as it crashes over the rapids above the city of Prague, and finally through the great city on its way to the River Elbe. Encourage students to imagine the various pictures being painted musically as the symphonic poem unfolds.

YouTube has some beautiful videos of orchestras playing *The Moldau*. Look for one that begins with the two flutes, then continues on through the well-known string melody.

▶ Cooking

The missionaries to Africa had the opportunity to try many new dishes (it is part of the job description!). Here is a wonderful African meal for you to try.

Bobotie—Meat Timbales

2 tbsp butter
juice of one lemon
1 onion, chopped
¼ cup chopped almonds
1 clove garlic, minced
8 dried apricots, soaked, chopped
1 slice bread
¼ cup raisins

1 cup milk
¼ cup chutney
2 eggs, beaten
1–2 tsp salt
1 lb. ground beef
pepper to taste
1 tbsp curry powder

Preheat oven to 350ºF. Melt the butter in a pan; sauté the onion and garlic until tender and just beginning to brown. Soak the bread in the milk, then squeeze dry. Beat the eggs into the remaining milk. Combine the meat, bread, and onions with the remaining ingredients. Stir in half of the egg-milk mixture. Place the mixture in a greased baking dish. Top with remaining egg mixture and bake until the custard sets, about 45 minutes. Serve with plain rice. Serves 6.

Serve with an accompanying dish of green peas and a salad.

◉ Cook the food

You might enjoy making yellow rice to go with the timbales. Or, if time is of the essence, substitute couscous for the rice. Delicious!

Yellow Rice

1 cup white rice
1½ cups boiling water
½ tbsp butter
2 tbsp brown sugar
1½ tsp turmeric
1½ tsp salt
⅓ cup dark or golden raisins

Place all ingredients in a pan with a cover. Bring rapidly to boiling point, stirring a few times. When the rice comes to a boil, reduce heat to low and cover. Cook until rice is tender, 25 to 30 minutes. Serves 6.

▶ **Student Self-Evaluation** UNIT 3, PHASE 3

Dates and hours:_____

Evaluate your projects

• List which of the activities listed in this Phase you did:

_____

_____

• Rate your enthusiasm: _____

Explain: _____

_____

• Rate the precision of your approach:_____

Explain: _____

_____

• Rate your effort toward the completion of the project: _____

Explain: _____

_____

• Ask yourself what worked and what did not. What would you do differently in the future, and what would you repeat?

_____

_____

• How did these hands-on activities enhance your knowledge of the British Empire & Awakenings? What made them worthwhile?

_____

_____

• In the first three Phases of this Unit, what aspect of the time period has most captured your imagination? What would you like to creatively pursue to conclude your study?

_____

_____

_____

◉ Conduct a review and evaluation

In this Phase of Unit 3, your students should have had the opportunity to explore the British Empire & Awakenings through various hands-on and creative sessions by completing a selection from the following:

• completed a mapping section;

• observed and discussed art & architecture;

• worked on an art project;

• experimented with a science project or taken a field trip;

• listened to music;

• tasted a food related to this Unit;

• completed their self-evaluation procedure for this Phase.

Record student hours: _____

Assess student involvement in the hands-on activities.

Create an evaluation system of your own or refer to the evaluation rubric in the introduction as a tool for assessing participation. The categories you will probably find most useful for evaluating projects are *"Task"* and *"Process: Teamwork."* Consider specifically the enthusiasm, the precision of approach, and the efforts toward improving skills and completing activities, rather than rating the project as compared to a masterpiece.

Do not critique the self-evaluation page your student completes in the Student Manual—it is acceptable for students to occasionally leave lines blank if a question does not apply. Instead, discuss with the student the intention of the written comments and incorporate those into your evaluation.

Determine a grade for this Phase, if using grades: _____

Teacher Self-Evaluation:

Evaluate your own use of materials: what worked and what did not? Consider your time management. Were you able to recognize and respond to your students' needs? Did you make your expectations clear? In what ways would you like to improve your approach for the next Unit? Incorporate suggestions from your students in your own evaluation (*this requires humility!*).

The Expression Week

Phase 4

▶ In Your Own Way...

In this unit, we have watched Queen Victoria choose her path and influence her nation; some self-ishly exploit while others generously serve in Africa; individual lives and even whole countries be changed by prayer; Marx sow bitter seed that will germinate in the nineteenth century, yielding unpalatable fruit in the twentieth; and Darwin provide a new way of looking at differentiation in species, which leads to a non-biblical, wholly mechanistic explanation of their origins. Now, choose a selection of these activities, or create your own, which will best express what you have learned from this Unit.

LINGUISTICS

Journalism

You have been asked to interview Mary Slessor after her appointment as vice-consul—the first woman in the British Empire to be employed in this position. However, before you can speak with her, you must find her—no small feat, given that she lives in an African jungle. Write an eyewitness article describing your adventures in finding and interviewing the "Mother of Calabar."

Karl Marx has been coming daily to the British library in London for years. As a librarian, you try to learn more about your patrons so as to better serve their needs. However, when you read about Marx's philosophy, you are horrified. Write a letter to the editor of the *London Times* expressing your outrage over someone using the resources of the library to try to pull down your government—the same government that funds your library!

Poetry

Create a narrative poem that conveys the reasons for and results of the Indian Mutiny of 1857. It would be helpful for your audience to know

both sides of the story, so be sure to include the dramatic and sometimes traumatic changes that came to India with the English government and Christian missionaries, who played a significant part in the uprising.

Prose

You just recently arrived as a settler in New Zealand. Write a letter to friends back home in England to try to inspire them to come join you. Be sure to include details of the islands of New Zealand, including the climate, the rich agricultural soil, the Maori people, other set-tlers, and whatever else you think might entice them to come. Be truthful when it comes to the difficulties as well, but frame them in the best possible light.

Write a children's version of the life of Queen Victoria. Be sure to include descriptions of her daily life—which may prove startling. Also be sure to mention the lives and the royal positions of her grown children and grandchildren.

136 The British Empire & Awakenings (1830–1870)

◉ Choose an area of expression

Students may work either individually or in teams.

Linguistics:

Journalism

Students might find it useful to examine political interviews from a variety of sources in order to better familiarize themselves with the types of questions asked. A link to an excellent online source for magazine articles focusing on politics can be found at the online resource page.

Writing a letter to the editor or an opinion piece is an important skill to learn. Pay attention to the allotted word count in a newspaper or magazine, and make sure every word is carefully chosen for its maximum "punch." A link to a great online resource for

learning more can be found at the online resource page.

Poetry

Narrative poetry, according to the encyclopedia, "tells stories." The *Iliad* and the *Odyssey* are both epic poems, a form of narrative poem. Ballads are another, shorter form of narrative poem. One humorous example of a ballad, set to music, is "The Arkansas Traveler." Encourage students to look for these or other examples of narrative poetry.

Prose

One source for students wishing to write about New Zealand from a British colonist's perspective is *Maori and Settler: A Story of the New Zealand War* by G. A. Henty. A link to read this book for free online can be found at the online resource page.

A fascinating book by Walter Walsh entitled *The Religious Life and Influence of Queen Victoria* gives insight into her daily life, which would be of great value to students writing about her. It, too, can be read online. A link as at the online resource page.

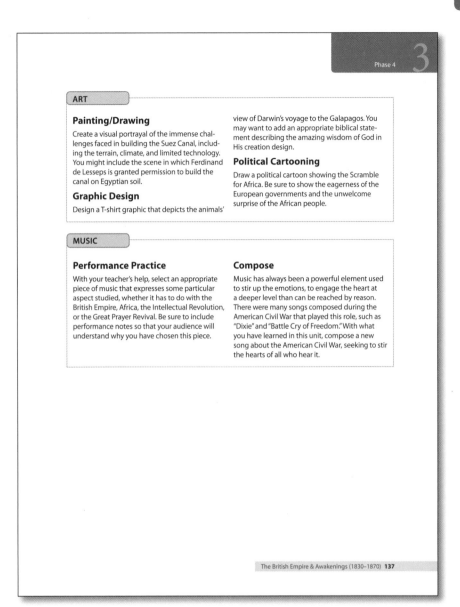

ART

Painting/Drawing

Create a visual portrayal of the immense challenges faced in building the Suez Canal, including the terrain, climate, and limited technology. You might include the scene in which Ferdinand de Lesseps is granted permission to build the canal on Egyptian soil.

Graphic Design

Design a T-shirt graphic that depicts the animals'

view of Darwin's voyage to the Galapagos. You may want to add an appropriate biblical statement describing the amazing wisdom of God in His creation design.

Political Cartooning

Draw a political cartoon showing the Scramble for Africa. Be sure to show the eagerness of the European governments and the unwelcome surprise of the African people.

MUSIC

Performance Practice

With your teacher's help, select an appropriate piece of music that expresses some particular aspect studied, whether it has to do with the British Empire, Africa, the Intellectual Revolution, or the Great Prayer Revival. Be sure to include performance notes so that your audience will understand why you have chosen this piece.

Compose

Music has always been a powerful element used to stir up the emotions, to engage the heart at a deeper level than can be reached by reason. There were many songs composed during the American Civil War that played this role, such as "Dixie" and "Battle Cry of Freedom." With what you have learned in this unit, compose a new song about the American Civil War, seeking to stir the hearts of all who hear it.

Art:
Painting/Drawing

An excellent and comprehensive series of illustrations and photos of the early history of the Suez Canal can be found in the out-of-print Horizon Caravel book entitled *Building the Suez Canal*, by S. C. Burchell. It is well worth the search!

Graphic Design

A link to a list of the animals of the Galapagos Islands can be found online at the online resource page. This site includes photos of each of the animals, which might be useful for this project.

Political Cartooning

These were the European countries involved in the Scramble for Africa: Portugal, Belgium, Germany, Britain, France, and Italy. They are responsible for the dividing up of Africa into colonial units (except for Ethiopia and Liberia—considered to be under the protection of the United States).

Music:
Performance Practice

For musical students, this selection may be a wonderful opportunity to express what they have learned. Make sure they select a piece that they have adequate time to prepare.

Compose

Ask the students to consider what they would like to accomplish with this composition: do they want to rally the North? The South? Or bring reconciliation between the two sides?

DRAMA

Comedy

With comedic style, depict the meeting of David Livingstone and Henry Stanley in Africa, toward the end of Livingstone's life. Remember, Stanley did not know exactly where Livingstone was when he began his search through the vast expanse of Africa!

Puppetry

For children, tell the story of how Canada became self-governing. Be sure to include the fascinating detail that many Canadians were concerned that the United States would—if given the chance—try to take part of Canada after the Civil War ended.

Drama

Retell in dramatic form the story of the 1857 Great Prayer Revival's beginning in New York City. Be sure to create the tension of the scene in which Jeremiah Lanphier waited and prayed alone in the room set aside for the community prayer meeting . . . and happened next!

Prop Needs

_____

_____

Costume Ideas

_____

_____

Role/Player

_____

_____

Set Suggestions

_____

_____

Drama:

Comedy

Shakespeare used "mistaken identity" as a wonderful device for humor in his comedies. Since Stanley has never met Livingstone, perhaps students might enjoy setting up the scene where the famous line—"Dr. Livingstone, I presume?"—is actually delivered to the wrong person, and perhaps more than once!

Puppetry

Since the audience can't see human faces in a puppet show, encourage students to use very distinct voices for the puppets. This would mean exaggerating character voices and finding distinctive ways for each character to say his lines. Students might enjoy even using different accents for different characters, where applicable.

Drama

Drama thrives on conflict and its resolution. What's at stake in this scene? Conflict is enhanced by finding out that there is something the main character risks losing. Why was he doing this, and what was at stake for him? How desperate was his need? How long did he wait for resolution? Encourage students to build the tension by portraying the struggle of Lamphier to trust God even while he is the only person in the room, which would make for good dramatic action. Then the audience can discover his relief as the first person shows up, and his increasing excitement as more people follow into the room. Remind students that this was the start of a massive international revival which saw millions added to the kingdom of God!

MOVEMENT

Pantomime

Create a pantomime that will show David Livingstone traveling with a group of Makololo tribesmen to the west coast of Angola and then returning with them back to their homeland—a journey of several thousand miles that took two years to complete.

Dance

Choreograph a dance that grants the audience a sense of the soaring heights and transparent beauty of the Crystal Palace, built for the Great Exhibition of 1851. Remember that, though it was a massive structure to enclose trees and exhibits, it remained in Hyde Park but a short time.

Miniature Action

Many battles took place during this time period. Choose the most interesting battle to you and depict it through the use of miniature figures. Be sure to include a realistic portrayal of the terrain and temperature that contributed to the challenges of your chosen battle. You might consider a battle from the Maori Wars in New Zealand, the Indian Mutiny of 1857, the American Civil War, or the Anglo-Zulu War.

CONCEPTUAL DESIGN

Charles Spurgeon has a remarkable ministry in London during this era, with thousands coming to hear him speak. A contest has just been announced to pick an architectural design for Spurgeon's new church, since the crowds have grown too large for other buildings to accommodate. If your design adequately handles the various needs of this building (including seating, acoustics, proximity to the speaker, and overall architectural style), you may be able to win the contest. Good luck!

CREATE YOUR OWN EXPRESSION

_____

_____

_____

_____

Movement:

Pantomime

Livingstone kept a journal of his adventures in Africa, including this trip. You can read a portion of _Livingstone's Missionary Correspondence, 1841–1856_ online. A link is at the online resource page. For the pantomime itself, rhythms are important to help define movements. Students wishing to perform this pantomime should be encouraged to create a specific, recurring movement theme, using rhythm and gestures, which would be very helpful in telling this story.

Dance

In order to get the sense of the soaring height of the Crystal Palace, encourage the student to use different levels or varying body movements to show the contrast between high and low. This will enable the audience to "see" what the dancer is seeking to portray.

Miniature Action

Creating a three-dimensional map on which to create the chosen battle scene is quite an interesting experience. Students will need a large piece of cardboard or plywood on which to form the map. Mark directly on the cardboard or wood where any rivers, hills, or mountains may be. Using corrugated cardboard, cut out the shapes of the hills and mountains, then glue these pieces directly to the base. Cut increasingly smaller pieces for the mountains and hills, gluing each layer onto the preceding layer until an adequate height is reached. Once you are satisfied with the basic look of the terrain, cover it with papier-mâché, made from strips of newspaper dipped in papier-mâché solution. After this has dried, paint the map with appropriate colors.

Conceptual Design:

Have students look online at images of the Metropolitan Tabernacle to gain a better understanding of what was important to those who did actually choose the architectural design for the building. Consider what Spurgeon said concerning the desired style, reported in _The British Standard_, Aug. 19, 1859: "That in this city we should build a Grecian place of worship. There are two sacred languages in the world, the Hebrew of old, and the Greek that is dear to every Christian's heart. The standard of our faith is Greek, and this place is to be Grecian. Greek is the sacred tongue, and Greek is the Baptist's tongue. We may be beaten in our own version sometimes; but in the Greek never. Every Baptist place should be Grecian, never Gothic."

◉ Share creative expressions in class

Create a safe environment for the presentations. Set ground rules prior to the presentations, so that students know how much time is available for each of them, and so that they know they will be honored and respected by all those observing.

◉ Conduct a review and evaluation

In this Phase of Unit 3, your students should have had the opportunity to express what they have learned about the British Empire & Awakenings through one or more various creative selections of their own choosing. These include:

- Linguistics;
- Art;
- Music;
- Drama;
- Movement;
- Conceptual Design.

Record student hours: _____

Assess student effort in the creative expressions, as individuals or as teams.

Create an evaluation system of your own, or refer to the evaluation rubric in the introduction, as a tool for assessing participation. The categories you will probably find most useful for evaluating their projects are *"Task," "Process: Teamwork," "Process: Originality,"* and Grammar, Format, and Spelling.

In this Phase especially, do not critique the self-evaluation page your student completes in the Student Manual—consider how the very soul of an artist has been exposed and vulnerable, so be encouraging and not belittling. Again, consider enthusiasm, precision of approach, and efforts toward improving skills and completing the activity, rather than rating the project as compared to a masterpiece. Instead, discuss with the student the intention of the written comments and incorporate those into your evaluation.

Determine a grade for this Phase, if using grades: _____

Teacher Self-Evaluation:

Evaluate your own use of materials and teaching opportunities: what worked and what did not; how effective was your time-management; how were your responses to the needs of your student; did you make your expectations clear; in what ways would you like to improve your approach for the next Unit? Incorporate suggestions from your students in your own evaluation (*this requires humility!*).

Take a moment now to evaluate the whole Unit. What would you like to remember if you taught this subject again? What do you recognize that your students gained most—either as students of history or as creative individuals? What did you learn about the British Empire & Awakenings or about teaching?

▶ Student Self-Evaluation UNIT 3, PHASE 4

Dates and hours:_____

Evaluate your projects

- What creative project did you choose?

  _____

- What did you expect from your project, and how does the final project compare to your initial expectations?

  _____

- What do you like about your project? What would you change?

  _____

In Conclusion

Revisit the five Key Concepts from the beginning of this Unit. Explain how your understanding of and appreciation for each has grown over the course of your study.

- _____
- _____
- _____
- _____
- _____

Record your concluding thoughts on the British Empire & Awakenings:

_____

Napoleon III & Christian Outreach
(1840–1885)

Pray with the students
at the beginning of each Unit.

Enthusiasm and delight
are the best ways to capture
a student's interest and
jump-start motivation, so:

» **For the Auditory Students:** Listen to the music of China, in anticipation of learning about the China Inland Mission. (There are several Internet sites with traditional Chinese music available. A particularly lovely song is "Gao Shan Liu Shui." See the online resource page for a link.)

» **For the Kinesthetic Students:** With strips of red cloth to use as arm bands for each student, have them march 142 steps, to signify Garibaldi's Redshirts marching from Naples to Rome (a distance of approximately 142 miles or 229 kilometers). Marching inside is permissible, though marching outside would be much more liberating!

» **For the Visual Students:** Bring in a print of one of Claude Monet's impressionistic paintings, recognizing that his flight from France to England during the Franco-Prussian War influenced his new style of art.

» **For the hearts of all:** Pray with them at the beginning of the Unit, that God would help them discover what He has for each one to learn in this Unit.

◉ Learning Style Emphasis

Teachers can choose to have students do one or two activities, rather than the entire week's schedule. Please use what works for you in your unique setting.

	Week 1: Feeler	Week 2: Thinker	Week 3: Sensor	Week 4: Intuitor
	During this week, students will be introduced to Napoleon III & Christian Outreach, along with the appropriate Scriptures. You may follow this suggested schedule or adapt it to meet your students' needs:	Students will explore topics of interest through research and reporting, learn new vocabulary, and construct a time line relating to Napoleon III & Christian Outreach.	Students will gain cultural understanding through sensory activities as they explore interrelated subject areas through sensory activities pertaining to Napoleon III & Christian Outreach.	Through creative self-expression, using one or more creative activities, students will present some aspect of what they have learned in the past three weeks relating to Napoleon III & Christian Outreach. Areas of expression include linguistics, art, music, drama, movement, and conceptual design.
Monday	Informally discuss the Key Concepts Listen to the *What in the World?* audio recording(s)	Choose topic and begin research	Create a map and discuss the issues in teams	Choose an area of expression and begin work either individually or in teams
Tuesday	Read the article Listen to the other audio recording(s) Read the Scriptures		Examine and discuss art masterpieces & architectural structures	
Wednesday	Recap the material using activities Talk together	Practice vocabulary	Do an art project*	
Thursday	Conduct class discussion	Construct the time line	Do a science experiment or field trip**	
Friday	Choose books of interest/Internet search Conduct a review and evaluation	Complete research projects and share in class or hand in Conduct a review and evaluation	Listen to and discuss the music Cook the food listed in the recipe Conduct a review and evaluation	Share creative expressions in class Conduct a review and evaluation

*Art project will need to be planned ahead of time to acquire materials.
** Field trip will require extra planning time.

Napoleon III & Christian Outreach (1840–1885)

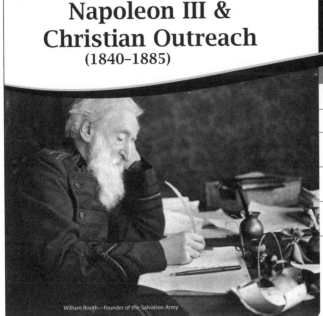

William Booth—founder of the Salvation Army

Key Concepts

- Kingdom of Italy
- East Asia & the West
- Prussia's Rise to Power
- Salvation Army & the Destitute
- The China Inland Mission

The Power in Nationalism

The great powers of the European continent—France, Austria, Prussia, and Russia—continued to be ruled by monarchs despite the revolutions of 1848. Underneath the continuing status quo, however, the dreams of revolution and liberty still burned in the hearts of many. The manner in which each country chose to deal with this internal struggle became one of the significant ingredients in the greater struggle between these powerful nations.

Liberty, or *liberalism*, was not the only ingredient in this churning political mix, however. Loyalty to one's own country, or *nationalism*, was also a continuing element, motivating the masses as well as some of the European leaders. But nationalism was being changed from the original vision—unite people of one language and culture into one nation—into a

Napoleon III & Christian Outreach (1840–1885) **141**

◉ Informally discuss the Key Concepts with your students

KEY CONCEPTS Background Information

These are the main objectives of the Unit. As you proceed through the four weeks, your students will be given various ways of understanding each of these objectives. Explanations of these Key Concepts follow.

4

new, virulent, and aggressive strain of nationalism. This new form would take shape as a country, already united and free, would seek to exalt itself among its neighbors, especially through militaristic means.

Added to these concepts was a growing technical prowess, granted by the Industrial Revolution, which equipped the European armies for fighting each other and for overpowering potential overseas colonies who lacked this level of firepower. Might made right in many industrialized eyes. It also made money, or at least held the promise of doing so, in overseas colonies.

Loyalty to one's own country, or nationalism, was a continuing element, motivating the masses as well as some of the European leaders.

This might was not limited to Europe, however. The United States, with its own Industrial Revolution fully functioning, showed itself just as able as the Europeans to flex its powerful and industrialized military muscle. When Great Britain went to war with China in 1839, because China objected to British support of the opium trade, the resulting treaty opened the massive country of China with five treaty ports for British diplomats and traders. Following their lead, the United States acquired a similar treaty with China in 1844, reaping huge financial benefits. By 1853, American trade with China was worth nineteen million dollars a year! That was heady business indeed for this young government. But it was not the end by any means. The United States, pleased with this first success in Asian trade and hungry for more, sent "the most distinguished and proverbially the most efficient officer in the navy" to do what no one else had been able to do. That is why Commodore Perry sailed to Japan in 1853.

For the previous two hundred years, the Japanese empire had been virtually closed to all nations. In 1638, a Japanese proclamation had been published: "For the future, let none, so long as the sun illuminates the world, presume to sail to Japan, not even in the quality of Ambassadors, and this declaration is never to be revoked on pain of death." The only Westerners allowed into Japan at all were Dutch traders, who were allowed to keep a trading post on a tiny Japanese island. Once a year, their envoys were permitted to visit the Japanese ruler, bringing gifts from Holland and news of the outside world. Though that had been the extent of Japan's international dealings for two hundred years, change was in the wind throughout Asia. Concerning his own diplomatic mission to forcibly open Japan's closed doors to America, Perry wrote while still en route, "The honor of the nation calls for it, and the interest of commerce demands it." And, to a large degree, it was the threat of American military might that procured it.

Commodore Perry

To get an informal discussion started on this Key Concept, ask a simple leading question, such as, "What do you think might have been some of the obstacles to Italy becoming an independent nation in the mid-1800s?"

Kingdom of Italy— EXPLANATION

After Napoleon's downfall in 1815, when statesmen redrew the lines of European boundaries, Italy found itself dominated almost entirely by the reactionary Austrian Empire. Some of its regions were annexed directly, while others were under Austria's "protection." The only Italian state to remain completely free of Austrian control was Piedmont-Sardinia (or simply Sardinia), ruled by the House of Savoy.

Though on the surface this state of affairs looked good to reactionary rulers, Italians were thinking more and more of their "glorious history," when Rome ruled the world. To be under a foreign yoke became burdensome to those who were dreaming of Italian liberty and unity.

Thus in 1848, the Year of Revolutions, many nationalists in Rome began demanding the unification of Italy (which would require a war with its Austrian overlord) and a democratic form of government. After the assassination of one of his officials, the pope fled the Vatican, which gave greater impetus to the "republicans" to form a Roman Republic in 1849, which lasted for a few short months. But when Louis Napoleon, soon to become Napoleon III,

marched his French troops against Rome in order to reinstate the pope, the Republic fell.

Several things resulted from this chain of events. First, Pope Pius IX became a bitter foe of political "liberty" with its goal of Italian unification. Second, the House of Savoy found itself the hero of the nationalists because of its valiant, though unsuccessful, defense of the Italian city of Milan against Austria. And finally, Rome was itself secured and protected by the foreign might of Napoleon III and his French army—a fact that comforted European Catholics but dismayed the nationalists of Italy.

The dream of a unified Italy seemed hopeless since Austria was still holding the reins of power in the Italian areas of Lombardy and Venetia, since the Papal States were governed by the reactionary and French-supported pope, and since the rest of Italy was weak and divided. However, events began to rapidly shift these circumstances—all under the guidance of an Italian statesman named Count di Cavour, prime minister of Sardinia.

Despite Napoleon III's occupation of Rome, Cavour recognized that he needed the assistance of Napoleon III in order to defeat Austrian rule in Italy. It was to help win his favor that Cavour sent Sardinian troops

4

France, another powerful player in East Asian politics, also signed a trade treaty with China in 1844, similar to the Chinese treaty with Great Britain. But France's focus narrowed in on the Southeast Asian peninsula, which would come to be known as French Indochina, (known today as Laos, Cambodia, and Vietnam). The French began a military conquest in 1857 in the northern part of Vietnam and continued southward to the city of Saigon, which fell to the French in 1861. Though successful in war, the French did not find the ongoing possession of French Indochina to be commercially lucrative. However, for nationalist rulers intent on amassing *la gloire* (glory) for their country, the prestige of having foreign colonies surpassed the cost—economic realities were disregarded.

This was certainly true with Napoleon III, emperor of the Second French Empire. Image was everything in this most dazzling nation, from the spectacular architectural restyling of the city of Paris (which became the standard for other capital cities around the world), to the fashionable mode of dress for the rich and richer (which became the yardstick for international fashion, even to this day), to the impressive sight of the French military marching, parading, and drilling throughout Paris. But, as is always the case when image is mistaken for reality, a day of reckoning for this French ruler and his empire eventually came.

To set the scene, let us look back to the Year of Revolutions, 1848. The nationalistic drive for a united Italy had grown to the point that the reactionary pope fled the Vatican, and in 1849 a Roman Republic was proclaimed. Though it was applauded by liberals and republicans, this event horrified loyal Roman Catholics of Europe. Louis Napoleon, the nephew of France's earlier leader Napoleon Bonaparte, newly elected as president of the Second Republic of France, acting consistently as a Catholic ruler but completely out of character for an elected official of a republic, mobilized French troops to reinstate the pope and end the short-lived Roman Republic. French troops would remain in Rome until Napoleon III's ignominious fall in 1870.

As was noted in Unit 2, Napoleon III was the mastermind behind the Crimean War, and it was he who benefited most from the Franco-British-Sardinian victory—at least, in the short term—as nationalistic French patriotism rose to its highest levels since the original Napoleon had waged his wars. The Second Empire also enjoyed enormous international prestige, and Napoleon III was considered to be an extraordinary ruler, calculating and far-sighted. Even Queen Victoria was amazed. After her first meeting with him, she wrote, "He is endowed with a wonderful self-control, great calmness, even gentleness, and with a power of fascination, the effect of which upon all those who become more intimately acquainted with him is most sensibly felt."

In 1849 a Roman Republic was proclaimed. Though it was applauded by liberals and republicans, this event horrified loyal Roman Catholics of Europe.

into the Crimean War on the side of the French and English, where they performed brilliantly. When approached by Cavour in 1858, Napoleon III agreed to an alliance between Sardinia and France in which France promised to help if Sardinia were attacked by Austria.

In 1859, Cavour was able to provoke Austria into a declaration of war, which then brought French troops pouring across the border to help the small Sardinian army. In two battles, Magenta and Solferino, the Austrians were badly beaten, fleeing Lombardy. However, before Venetia was also liberated, France made peace with Austria, ending its part of the war. Without French help, Sardinia could not hope to defeat Austria and entirely remove its presence from Italy. It looked like a crushing defeat for Sardinian and Italian-nationalist hopes. However, the sight of Austrians fleeing Lombardy actually caused an explosion of nationalism and a reawakening throughout the country of the dreams of a united Italy.

It was at this point that Garibaldi, with his thousand "Redshirts," sailed to the Kingdom of the Two Sicilies. This was the largest and most powerful of the Italian states, with a regular army of 100,000 and an excellent navy. Amazingly, Garibaldi won victory after victory as he moved from the island of Sicily to the mainland city of Naples. Many soldiers from the other side deserted to join Garibaldi's small army as they became more and more enthusiastic at the idea of a united Italy. The snowball effect continued until just outside of Rome, where King Victor Emmanuel II of Sardinia intercepted Garibaldi. Since an attack on Rome would mean a declaration of war on France, as it still protected the Eternal City, the king sought to turn Garibaldi aside. Recognizing Victor Emmanuel II as his sovereign, Garibaldi agreed to abide by his will.

The Kingdom of Italy was formally established in 1861, though it still lacked Venetia and the city of Rome. It would acquire Venetia in 1866, as part of a peace treaty after Prussia defeated Austria, and Rome itself in 1870, after Prussia defeated the Second Empire of France (which is described in the article for this Unit).

4

The victorious battles of Magenta and Solferino had so inspired Italian patriots throughout the various cities and states that Italian nationalism exploded throughout Italy.

It was to this powerful man, now the emperor of France, that the Italians of the kingdom of Sardinia appealed when searching for a liberal ally to help oust the ever-present Austrians from Italy. Napoleon III, a proponent of nationalism and liberalism (though these seldom interfered with his own autocratic political actions as the absolute ruler of France), agreed to assist the Sardinians in gaining Austrian-held territory. In exchange, France would receive the desirable areas of Nice and Savoy. In 1859, Sardinia was able to provoke the Austrians into declaring war. Much to the Austrians' surprise, French troops came to the aid of Sardinia, defeating Austria in two major battles, Magenta and Solferino. At this point, before finishing the war, France made peace with Austria—infuriating French liberals who wanted to help Sardinia throw off its oppressor!

France's abandonment left Sardinia alone and in an impossible position. Without French aid, the tiny kingdom of Sardinia could not hope to win a war against the massive Austrian Empire. However, the victorious battles of Magenta and Solferino had so inspired Italian patriots throughout the various cities and states that Italian nationalism exploded throughout Italy. Very quickly, the northern part of Italy consolidated under Sardinia, with the Sardinian king, Victor Emmanuel, as their ruler. The bigger-than-life Italian hero Garibaldi took his thousand "Redshirts" (known for the one distinguishing characteristic of their uniforms) and sailed to the south, conquering the island of Sicily and the city of Naples. Heading north to Rome (which was still protected by French soldiers), Garibaldi met Victor Emmanuel and the Sardinian troops heading south to prevent the Redshirts from attacking Rome and bringing down the wrath of Catholic Europe. Recognizing that for the sake of the yet-to-be-born Italian nation he must submit, Garibaldi yielded to Victor Emmanuel, turned his army away from war with Rome, and disbanded. Though Venetia was still held by Austria, and Rome was still protected by France, the remainder of the Italian states united into the Kingdom of Italy in March of 1861.

The results of the war came as a complete shock to Napoleon III, who had only intended to help Sardinia with their Austrian woes. He had foreseen neither the reaction of French Catholics at the beginning of the war—who were furious that France's support for Italian nationalism might

Victor Emmanuel II

144 Napoleon III & Christian Outreach (1840–1885)

? To get an informal discussion started on this Key Concept, ask a simple leading question, such as, "Why would the industrialized West have wanted the countries of East Asia to be opened to them?"

East Asia & the West— EXPLANATION

In the early 1800s, the countries of East Asia—including China, Japan, and Korea—were either entirely closed to foreigners (particularly from the West) or had extremely limited and restricted contact with them. In the case of Japan and Korea, strict isolation had been in place for nearly two hundred years in order to preserve the culture and religion intact, while China allowed a very limited trade with the West. Previous attempts by Catholic missionaries from Europe to bring Christianity into Japan and China, though initially successful, had resulted in persecution and martyrdom of native believers and a closed door. However, this isolation from the West meant that, as new discoveries were made in industrialization and technology, East Asia did not keep abreast of these

developments. This left them militarily and economically weaker than the West, which they would soon come to regret.

As the industrialized Western nations began looking for new sources of raw materials, as well as new markets to sell the vast amount of manufactured wares that the Industrial Revolution was providing, they turned their eyes to this yet untapped and potentially profitable region of the world. The largest country in East Asia, China, with its policy of limited access and trade, was willing to export tea and silk to hungry Western markets but was not interested in importing Western goods in return. This huge

inequality in trade, particularly with the tea-loving British, motivated merchants of the British East India Company to begin a lucrative trade in opium with the Chinese. Acquiring the opium in India where it was grown, the British then had to smuggle it into China, since the importation of this addictive and destructive drug was forbidden by Chinese law.

It is sobering to consider that the British Empire, which viewed itself as a Christian civilization, was able to choose economic profitability over legality, Christian compassion, and righteousness. This profit-driven approach was powerfully demonstrated during the two Opium Wars, in which

4

imperil the pope and the Papal States—nor the reaction of the French liberals when he left his post before finishing the job. This war was the beginning of his decline, despite the extraordinary popularity he had enjoyed up to this point.

The Prussian Version of Nationalism

The lesson of Italy reminded the crowned heads of Europe that the passionate force of nationalism, once unleashed, could bring about unexpected, uncontrolled, and undesirable results. This lesson was not lost on the Prussians and their conservative monarch. Yet, unexpectedly for their own plans and purposes, they too would soon take up the cause of nationalism. In the hands of the Prussians, a special form of nationalism included a military aggressiveness toward other nations that would significantly affect the world for the next seventy-five years.

The newest crowned monarch, Wilhelm I, King of Prussia, held to the centuries-old view that rule of a nation was a matter of divine right rather than democratic election by the rabble. At his coronation in 1861, Wilhelm declared, "I do not forget that the crown has come to me from God alone and that I have received it from His hands." His opposition to liberalism was a relief to the Prussian aristocracy who approved of neither liberalism nor nationalism. Their loyalty was reserved for Prussia alone: they had no use for a German nation.

"I do not forget that the crown has come to me from God alone and that I have received it from His hands."

In 1815, the Congress of Vienna had established the German Confederation out of the ashes of the Holy Roman Empire, which had been demolished by Napoleon Bonaparte. Thirty-nine independent German states, headed by the Austrian Empire, were loosely organized for mutual defense. Since it had been within the sphere and influence of Metternich, the German Confederation had set itself firmly against liberalism and nationalism; but when he was dislodged from power in 1848, this attitude began to change. The real change, however, was in Prussian attitudes toward Austrian leadership of the German people.

Otto von Bismarck, a Prussian aristocrat, having personally seen Austria's highhandedness toward Prussia in the German Confederation, became a zealous believer in German nationalism—a German nationalism where Prussia would

Otto von Bismarck

Discuss with students what difficulties might arise from the identification of Christians (motivated by God's love, regardless of the personal cost) with merchant-traders (motivated by financial gain, regardless of the cost to others). Beyond what happened in 1800s China, are there any applications that could be made to current issues in other areas of the world?

the British Empire forced the Chinese to open their country to trade and forced them to legalize opium, even though it was causing serious personal, social, and economic difficulties for the Chinese. Not everyone in the empire saw this as a victory, however. Lord Shaftesbury, the Christian statesman who had made such a difference in the lives of England's poor, wrote this concerning the treaty of Nanking: "We have triumphed in one of the most lawless, unnecessary, and unfair struggles in the records of history, this cruel and debasing war."

Christian missionaries, entering China under the same treaty provisions as opium traders, were grateful that

the door was finally open to take the gospel to a previously closed land. Though seen as providential by many, accessing the country under the same treaty caused an identification of self-seeking merchants with self-sacrificing missionaries. This would exact a very high price when secret Chinese societies rose up to eradicate all those who were viewed as Western exploiters of China, merchant and missionary alike.

Japan's story is slightly different, as is told in this Unit's article. However, it was still Western industrialized force that opened the country to trade and to the gospel. In this instance, Japan's acceptance of Western trade,

with the added desire to studiously learn the ways of the imperialists, would lead not only to its astonishing transformation into an industrialized nation but also to an imperialism which would, eventually, nearly destroy it. The gospel, sadly, did not take root and grow as it did in the neighboring country of Korea, perhaps because of its being perceived as a Western religion without value to a Japanese person.

Korea, on the other hand, was remarkably receptive, once the doors to bringing the gospel were opened. That story, however, belongs to the next Unit.

4

lead the German states and Austria would be utterly excluded. In 1862, Wilhelm I appointed him chancellor. This high position of authority, where he was answerable only to the king, allowed Bismarck to deal firmly with the liberal Prussian parliament, who had refused to vote for the huge amount requested for revitalizing and enlarging the Prussian army. The liberals were concerned that a powerful, rejuvenated army could then be turned against them. But Bismarck simply sidestepped them, took the needed money—violating the Prussian constitution—and said, "It is not by speeches and majority resolutions that the great questions of the time are decided . . . but by iron and blood." That was the effective end of Prussian liberalism. Their form of nationalism would now go forth without it.

"It is not by speeches and majority resolutions that the great questions of the time are decided . . . but by iron and blood."

With the masterful military tactics of Chief of Staff Moltke, the brilliant organization of War Minister Roon, and the successful fund-raising approach of Bismarck, the well-equipped, well-disciplined, well-trained Prussian army soon became a formidable force. In fact, with the stunning successes it shortly attained, this incredibly efficient military machine would be emulated by the other great world powers—including the rapidly industrializing nation of Japan.

The first step toward achieving Bismarck's goals came when the Danish king incorporated two tiny provinces, Schleswig and Holstein, into Denmark in 1863. Though few would consider the significance of the event today, it was extremely important politically at the time, with tremendously complex issues. The most notable of these was the fact that Holstein belonged to the German Confederation, and was therefore under its protection. Prussia declared war on Denmark in 1864, ostensibly to protect Holstein and Schleswig from this illegal move on the part of the Danish king. Austria, as head of the German Confederation, quickly joined in the fray, and Denmark was defeated. Schleswig and Holstein were then placed under Prussia and Austria. The awkwardness of this joint-rule arrangement would prove to be just what Bismarck needed to provoke Austria into the war that would make Prussia the head of the German states and make Austria *persona non grata* (a legal term in diplomacy meaning "person not welcome").

To prepare for this upcoming war, Bismarck met with Napoleon III in 1865 to gain the promise of French neutrality. He also made an alliance with the Kingdom of Italy, promising Austrian-held and much-prized Venetia as their reward for fighting with Prussia. Austria, recognizing that war was coming and knowing they would need twice as long as Prussia to mobilize, called up their troops. Bismarck used that as an excuse to send Prussian troops into Holstein, causing the Austrian troops stationed there to flee. Immediately, Austria declared war.

146 Napoleon III & Christian Outreach (1840–1885)

? To get an informal discussion started on this Key Concept, ask a simple leading question, such as, "What do you think caused Prussia's rise to power?"

Great Prayer Revival— EXPLANATION

When the Congress of Vienna, after Napoleon's downfall, created the German Confederation to replace the defunct Holy Roman Empire, Austria became the acknowledged leader and head. This was understandable, since it was the Austrian ruler who for generations had been the head of the Holy Roman Empire. But with the new ideas of liberalism and nationalism taking root throughout Europe, this was no longer automatically accepted. In the revolutions of 1848, German nationalists for a time gained power in a number of places, includ-

ing the Prussian capital of Berlin. Prussia, which was quite militaristic and had spent years honing and refining its education and military systems, was concerned mainly with itself and not with the concept of a unified Germany. You might say that the rulers and aristocrats of Prussia had not yet drunk of the spirit of nationalism (the bringing together of all the peoples of a common language and history under one nation). Because the king of Prussia responded to the 1848 revolutions in his realm by calling for German unification and by forming a national assembly in Prussia, he was seen to be on the side of the nationalists. However, when

asked by the liberal German National Assembly in Frankfurt to become the king of a united Germany, he astonished them by refusing their offer. Being a conservative monarch, he believed that this offer could only rightly come from the German princes, since that is how it had historically been done. With his refusal, the Assembly lost their last hope for creating a liberal German state.

When the German National Assembly, which had replaced the German Confederation, failed, Prussia sought to form yet another group of German states with itself as the head, though with a conservative approach. However, this never came

4

Europe envisioned this war as one which Austria, the powerhouse of Central Europe, would undoubtedly win, though it might be a long and drawn-out affair. The Seven Weeks' War, for so it was named, reversed those opinions rather dramatically. Prussia's troops were relentless in battle against an empire twice Prussia's size, with twice its population. Austria quickly sued for peace, and Prussia was surprisingly charitable in its treaty demands:

- a small war indemnity
- the end of the German Confederation of 1815 with a new Northern German Confederation under Prussia
- the loss of Venetia to Italy

A Different Army

In 1865, the same year that Bismarck was orchestrating behind-the-scenes moves to accomplish his nationalistic agenda, the Holy Spirit was orchestrating an entirely different series of moves with a Kingdom agenda. Two men in England, unknown to one another, each took a significant step of faith to obey what God had placed on their hearts to do. This obedience, in their separate spheres, significantly changed the world. One man was William Booth, founder of the Salvation Army, and the other was Hudson Taylor, founder of the China Inland Mission.

William Booth and his wife Catherine had both been part of the English revival of 1859, preaching first in the church he pastored and then in other areas of England. In 1865, they began a work in East London—a slum area with horrendous poverty, crime, disease, filth, and immorality. Known first as the Christian Mission, this work, which eventually became international in its outreach, was renamed the Salvation Army. Effectively taking the gospel to the masses, the Salvation Army held lively, music-infused meetings in the non-church atmosphere of factories and theaters. William Booth had learned during his early revival years that the masses were most successfully reached by others of their own level of society, so the Salvation Army was staffed mainly with working-class people. And, quite unusual for the time, women were accepted in the Army on the same terms as men—they preached, evangelized, and became officers. The other outstanding concern for the workers of the Salvation Army was the hunger, poverty, and unemployment of those to whom they had come to minister. In great contrast with the governmental system of relief known as "workhouses" (such awful places that only the most desperate of people would go into them), the Salvation Army instead created a network of compassionate Christian relief agencies and homes to

Two men in England, unknown to one another, each took a significant step of faith to obey what God had placed on their hearts to do.

Napoleon III & Christian Outreach (1840–1885) **147**

to fruition. Austria had, by this time, recovered from the staggering blows of the 1848 revolutions and the loss of Metternich, and it now moved to deal with Prussia regarding the German question, "Wer ist hier zuständig?"(which means, "Who's in charge here?").

In November 1850, Austria was able to force Prussia to sign an agreement at the city of Olmutz—known as the Punctuation of Olmutz,"as well as the Humiliation of Olmutz. In this agreement, Prussia submitted to Austria's dominance of the German states, which were reorganized back into the original German Confederation. Though Austria's

victory was momentarily sweet, it led to bitter results: Prussia began to reconsider the benefits of German nationalism—a nationalism under Prussian leadership that did *not* include Austria.

When the king died, his brother became William I of Prussia. He would make Otto von Bismarck the chancellor of Prussia. Bismarck would become the architect of the German Empire, and the king would become the kaiser, as is described in the article for this Unit.

?

To get an informal discussion started on this Key Concept, ask a simple leading question, such as, "What do you know about the conditions of the poor in industrialized countries, such as England, during the 1800s?"

Salvation Army & the Destitute— EXPLANATION

In 1861, a Christian conference was held in London to consider the spiritual needs of the poor living in the slums of the city's notorious East End. Since churches were not proving to be effective in reaching them, ministers at this conference set up a small group, the East London Special Services Committee, to begin working toward bringing the gospel into these dire circumstances. When William Booth, an evangelist who was ministering in the Great Prayer Revival, came to London to seek ministry

4

which the poor could turn in times of need, receiving not only their physical necessities but kindness and caring as well.

Hudson Taylor had felt the call to serve the Lord in China when he was seventeen, only seven years after the Treaty of Nanking had opened the way for British citizens to live in five port cities of China. He sailed in 1853 under the auspices of the Chinese Evangelization Society, their first worker to go. Unfortunately, this mission organization was constantly borrowing money in order to support the mission, leaving Taylor with no funds and many demands. For this reason, he eventually quit the mission, which was an amazingly courageous decision, given that he intended to remain in China and had no other form of support. In 1860, when his health deteriorated to the point that he could no longer function on the field, he returned with his wife to England, where doctors told him that it would take years to recover enough health to return to China. It was during this period that the deep needs of inland China's millions grew ever more compelling to his heart. He realized God was leading him to set up a new interdenominational mission agency, one which would be dependent solely on God for funding—a "faith mission"—and which would go beyond the five port cities into the interior of China. In 1865, he yielded to God and accepted this daunting vision, and the China Inland Mission was officially established.

> *It was during this period that the deep needs of inland China's millions grew ever more compelling to his heart.*

He wrote, "Feeling, on the one hand, the solemn responsibility that rests upon us, and on the other the gracious encouragements that everywhere meet us in the Word of God, we do not hesitate to ask the great Lord of the Harvest to call forth, to thrust forth twenty-four European and twenty-four Chinese evangelists, to plant the standard of the Cross in the eleven unevangelized provinces of China proper and in Chinese Tartary. . . . Our Father is a very experienced one. He knows very well that His children wake up with a good appetite every morning, and He always provides breakfast for them, and does not send them supperless to bed at night. 'Thy bread shall be given thee, and thy water shall be sure.' He sustained three million Israelites in the wilderness for forty years. We do not expect He will send three million missionaries to China; but if He did, He would have ample means to sustain them all. Let us see that we keep God before our eyes; that we walk in His ways and seek to please and glorify Him in everything, great and small. Depend upon it, God's work done in God's way will never lack God's supplies."

When the first party of China Inland missionaries

Hudson Taylor

opportunities as a "home missionary," this committee invited him to become their evangelist. Though it took four years before he was free to accept their offer, William Booth did come at last, in 1865, to London's East End to preach the gospel among the poor, which was the start of what would become the Salvation Army.

Remember what we learned in Unit 2 about the Industrial Revolution? It was not only a transformation of industry and technology, but it also brought about a complete disruption in the fabric of society for those who had traditionally worked in their homes, lands, and villages. As multitudes with high hopes began streaming to the cities for work in the newly constructed factories, they found instead unimaginable poverty, filth, crime, disease, and hopelessness.

Evangelizing among the poor brought about a deepening awareness of what these people were actually facing, so William and his wife Catherine began opening soup kitchens for the poor and establishing shelters and homes for girls who

had been used and abused on the streets. However, in the late 1880s, God began to open William's eyes even more to the plight of what he was to call "the submerged tenth"—the three million who eked out a painful existence while the remaining twenty-eight million of England blissfully went about their productive lives, unconcerned or unaware.

In 1890, Booth published the book *In Darkest England and the Way Out*, which produced a storm of controversy in England (including scathing and outraged letters to the *London Times* from Thomas Huxley, friend and promoter of Charles Darwin and Darwinian evolution). Here is an

excerpt from Booth's introduction to the book:

All the way through my career I have keenly felt the remedial measures usually enunciated in Christian programmes and ordinarily employed by Christian philanthropy to be lamentably inadequate for any effectual dealing with the despairing miseries of these outcast classes. The rescued are appallingly few—a ghastly minority compared with the multitudes who struggle and sink in the open-mouthed abyss. Alike, therefore, my humanity and my Christianity, if I may

4

arrived in Shanghai in 1866, it increased by twenty-five percent the number of Christian workers in this vast land. That was just the tiny beginnings of what was to come in terms of workers and influence. Like the Salvation Army, the China Inland Mission drew its workers mainly from the laboring class, and it viewed women as valuable co-laborers in the field, as is evidenced by its decision to send teams of women into unevangelized districts to establish ministry outposts alone. Obedience to the call to bring the gospel to the entire nation of China was a massive step of faith, and God met the mission with workers, with provision, with conversions, and with a deepening sense that they were dwelling "under the shadow of the Almighty" (Psalm 91:1).

Meanwhile, back with the French . . . and Prussians

In the same year that Hudson Taylor's party of missionaries sailed to China, France, recognizing that war was just over the horizon, began withdrawing its troops from Mexico. In 1866, with the threatening actions of Prussia at his doorstep and a reunited America brandishing its Monroe Doctrine, Napoleon III was forced to bring his veteran troops home. However, withdrawing his troops caused the French Empire in Mexico to collapse, and created increased troubles for him in his own country.

When Napoleon III had originally executed a *coup d'état* in 1851 (illegal seizure of power against the government), he had forcefully repositioned himself from elected president to dictator, establishing a repressive regime. At that point, newspapers were strongly censored, political meetings were banned, and political opponents were jailed. Still, with their ruler owning the magical name of Bonaparte, most people approved of the change, as could be seen in the plebiscite (vote) that was held shortly afterwards. (A notable exception was Victor Hugo, writer of *Les Miserables*, who was such a vocal critic that he was forced to go into exile.) However, in the intervening years, liberty began to slowly make its way back into the political scene of France with the acquiescence of its ruler. In fact, Napoleon III once declared, "March at the head of the ideas of your century, and these ideas follow you and support you. March behind them and they drag you after them. March against them, and they overthrow you."

Uncensoring the press and increasing democracy in France's legislature, however, did not bring about an increased following and support, but rather an escalating disapproval of Napoleon III and his policies. This disapproval reached an all-time high in 1869, when the French elections

"March at the head of the ideas of your century, and these ideas follow you and support you. March behind them and they drag you after them. March against them, and they overthrow you."

I highly recommend that parents/teachers read *When Helping Hurts: Alleviating Poverty without Hurting the Poor . . . and Yourself* by Brian Fikkert and Steve Corbett. It will provide biblical wisdom and experiential insight into this extremely important issue.

Pray with your students about practical ways God would have them begin living out Isaiah 58, especially in regard to the poor of their own neighborhoods and cities.

speak of them in any way as separate one from the other, have cried out for some more comprehensive method of reaching and saving the perishing crowds. . . . Alas, what multitudes there are around us everywhere, many known to my readers personally, and any number who may be known to them by a very short walk from their own dwellings, who are in this very plight! Their vicious habits and destitute circumstances make it certain that without some kind of extraordinary help, they must hunger and sin, and sin and hunger, until, having multiplied their kind, and

filled up the measure of their miseries, the gaunt fingers of death will close upon them and terminate their wretchedness. *And all this will happen this very winter in the midst of the unparalleled wealth, and civilisation, and philanthropy of this professedly most Christian land.*

After the publication of the book, William Booth and the Salvation Army began working out the plans to aid the poor that he had outlined in the book. According to Salvation Army records, nine years later, they had served 27 million cheap meals, lodged 11 million homeless people, traced 18,000

missing people, and found jobs for 9,000 unemployed people.

It truly was putting into action the words of Isaiah 58:6–7: "Is this not the fast that I have chosen: To loose the bonds of wickedness, To undo the heavy burdens, To let the oppressed go free, And that you break every yoke? Is it not to share your bread with the hungry, And that you bring to your house the poor who are cast out; When you see the naked, that you cover him, And not hide yourself from your own flesh? "

4

showed a disapproval not only of the current party in power, but of the Second Empire as well. Recognizing that something radical must be done in order to preserve it, Napoleon III, in a last ditch effort, inaugurated a Liberal Empire with a new constitution.

Unfortunately, with this newfound liberty the legislature voted against his urgent request for money to update, enlarge, and strengthen France's military. Whereas Bismarck, when faced with a similar situation with the liberal Prussian parliament of 1862, simply took the money anyway, Napoleon III was not in a position of enough strength to do so. Instead, he had to be content with inadequate funding for his army. To the casual observer, this might not have seemed like a problem. After all, France looked invincible. Indeed, gorgeously attired soldiers were a significant part of the French landscape. In fact, Karl Marx had written of the Second Empire that, rather than "Liberté, Egalité, Fraternité, it was Cavalry, Infantry, Artillery." But image was not reality, especially in 1870.

> Napoleon III made it clear to Bismarck that France would never accept a Prussian as king of Spain.

The matter that brought things to a head was the vacant Spanish throne. The delicate and complex question was, "Which European royal would become the next Spanish king?" This issue was, of course, an important concern to neighboring France, who did not want a potential enemy behind her if she had to fight Prussia. So when a Prussian relation of King Wilhelm I was asked to accept the throne, Napoleon III made it clear to Bismarck that France would never accept a Prussian as king of Spain. He was assured that the prince would not accept the throne. But some months later, when this Prussian prince was approached again about becoming king, he reluctantly agreed. Before the Spanish legislature could vote to approve their new king, news of this turnabout reached France.

The French Ambassador, traveling to the city of Ems to meet with the Prussian king, demanded, in diplomatic style, that Wilhelm I promise to never allow his young relation to take the throne. When an informative telegram was sent from the king to tell Bismarck of the ambassador's demands, Bismarck was finally able to engineer a humiliating situation where the honor of France would demand satisfaction against Prussia—a duel, if you will, with the armies of both countries drawing their swords against one another. He rewrote an inflammatory version of the telegram and published it to the international press. This slap in the face sent France hurtling into a war for which she was utterly unprepared.

When France declared war against Prussia, she was seen by many as the aggressor, not an unrealistic assumption based on Napoleon III's previous military actions. In fact, the *London Times* wrote that France's attack on Prussia "was the greatest national crime that we have had the pain of recording in these columns since the days of the First Empire . . . the act

---

? To get an informal discussion started on this Key Concept, ask a simple leading question, such as, "How did the China Inland Mission change the face of missions, affecting how missionary work was carried out even to this day?

The China Inland Mission—EXPLANATION

The work of Hudson Taylor, the founder of the China Inland Mission, has been described by missions analyst Ralph Winter in this way: "Taylor almost single handedly broke down the idea that we cannot penetrate inland and with confidence seek to evangelize whole countries. Seventy years after Carey's *Enquiry* was published, token missions, touching only coastlands, was all Protestants could conceive."

Hudson Taylor went as a single young man to China in 1853, under the auspices of the Chinese Evangelization Society. In his early experiences as an unordained non-professional seeking to bring the gospel to a nation where Europeans were considered to be foreign devils, he learned many invaluable lessons.

Reflecting on these lessons brought a hard-won wisdom and insight into how Western missionaries might approach evangelizing that nation: wearing Chinese dress, adapting to Chinese food and living quarters, learning the language fluently, and going inland. After marrying, he returned to England for further medical school, Chinese Bible translation, and, as it turned out, the establishment of the China Inland Mission.

In 1866, Taylor and his family, along with the first fifteen missionaries of his newly formed missions organization, set sail for Shanghai. Not only were these recruits different from other missionaries in China in that they were from the laboring and less-educated strata of English society, but, starting very shortly after their arrival, they also looked very different because Taylor required them to appear in the clothing and hairstyle of the Chinese. The purpose of this was to enable the Chinese to focus on the message rather than the messenger, allowing the gospel to penetrate deeply into all the provinces of China.

Part of the vision for the China Inland Mission concerned the very practical issue of money. Recognizing that God had shown His ability to care for Hudson Taylor's financial needs, even when he was no longer connected to a supporting mission

4

of France—of one man in France." And this one man, with his nation, stood alone. No other European nation came to his assistance, though they might have if the French army had begun to show that it was capable of beating Prussia, since everyone loves to be on the winning side. However, this did not happen. With frightening speed, the French army began to collapse, retreat, and surrender. Within one month, the emperor, along with the bulk of his army, surrendered to the Prussians. Though Paris held out for several months longer, the issue of Prussia's victory was not in question.

Meantime, with the French declaration of war, the southern German states were bound by treaty to come to Prussia's aid. Fired up with the injustice of France's aggressive move, these remaining states, who had not been part of the North German Confederation, were gathered into Bismarck's fold. Ironically, Wilhelm I was crowned emperor of the newly formed German Empire only ten miles from Paris, which was still under siege, at the magnificent palace of Versailles, built by Louis XIV. This new empire, arising at the same time as the French empire was collapsing, would become the central figure in the historic drama to be played out through the end of WWII.

The German Empire, having defeated both Austria and France, each considered to be great powers, now had only Great Britain as its rival in world affairs. In the book *A Short History of Western Civilization*, Harrison and Sullivan state, "The autocratic, militaristic German Empire, which he [Bismarck] welded together, was the world's most powerful and seemingly most efficient nation. These Prussian exploits appeared to bear out the evolutionary teachings of Darwin and Spencer with respect to the survival of the fittest."

With this astonishing success, the German Empire became a model for many governments of how to do business. Banishing liberalism, with its attending nuisances of free speech and a free electorate, would allow rulers to rule efficiently and effectively. And when these same rulers had extraordinary military prowess and technical know-how, they became very dangerous for those with whom they came in contact. One example of this can be seen in the effects of the Congress of Berlin in 1884, which the Germans held in order to organize the dismemberment of Africa into European colonies. There would be other even more wide-ranging examples in future years.

> *The German Empire became a model for many governments of how to do business. Banishing liberalism, with its attending nuisances of free speech and a free electorate, would allow rulers to rule efficiently and effectively.*

A Different Model

A far different model was shown in 1884–1885 as seven young British men—wealthy, cultured, and well-educated university graduates—gave

agency—though his circumstances were often extremely difficult—Taylor set up the new agency as a "faith mission." This meant that they did not guarantee salaries to any of the missionaries, nor did they make any public requests for money. Instead, they sought to "move man, through God, by prayer alone." In practical terms, this meant that they spent a lot of time in prayer, asking God specifically for the material provision—as well as for the increase in personnel—that they needed. It was similar to what we saw in the life of George Müller in Unit 2, who provided homes, food, clothing, and education for thousands of orphans, while depending solely upon God's faithfulness to answer prayer.

In seeking to take the gospel inland, even in very difficult and forbidding circumstances, and in looking to God to provide their every need, the China Inland Mission set a new model for missions that would affect the entire world. Many other mission agencies began to follow their practice, going into the interior regions of East Asia, Africa, and South America. Also, more than forty new missionary groups were established as "faith missions," including the Christian and Missionary Alliance, the Sudan Interior Mission and the Central American Mission.

4

D.L Moody

themselves to be missionaries with the China Inland Mission. This astonishing group chose to walk away from promising careers and the ease associated with their level of society to humbly serve the Chinese people as proclaimers of the good news of Jesus. For the most part nominally religious, many of these young men had not found Christianity to be the single most compelling aspect of their lives until confronted by God through the ministry of D. L. Moody (1837–1899). Moody, a plain-spoken American preacher, had toured the British Isles many years before with amazing results. But it was in 1882, when he preached at Cambridge University, that British university students began to be deeply affected. Coming first to laugh at the uneducated bumpkin, many returned night after night, drawn to the marvelous Redeemer whom Moody preached. As a result, many students, including these seven, consecrated or re-consecrated their lives to Christ. Shortly afterward, first one and then another of the seven friends began to sense God's call on their hearts to the mission field. In the perfect timing of the Lord, Hudson Taylor returned from China to England and held quiet conversations with them concerning serving with the China Inland Mission. Before their departure in 1885, the "Cambridge Seven" toured England to share what God had done in their lives and why they were following His leading to China. This tour created a sensation: people were staggered that Britain's most famous cricket player, the extraordinarily wealthy C. T. Studd, along with other equally distinguished, talented, and promising young men—the veritable cream of the British crop—would give up their lives in this way.

This incredible concept, university graduates serving God on the mission field, took root in Britain and then blossomed even more fruitfully across the sea in America. Known internationally as the Student Volunteer Movement, their self-proclaimed and passionate goal was "the evangelization of the world in this generation." Rather than building empires with a nationalistic "survival of the fittest" doctrine and military prowess, these visionary young men and women held to a biblical "preach the gospel to every creature" doctrine and gave their lives in service to the Heavenly King to demonstrate it. ◀

> You may choose to have your students read the article first and then listen to the audio recordings, or vice versa.

◉ Read the article

◉ Listen to the audio recordings in Listen to This

- The main concepts and chronological flow are contained in *What in the World?* Volume 3

- Learn more about the amazing work of Louis Pasteur, the exploits of Napoleon III, and a brief description of Garibaldi in *True Tales* Volume 3.

- Learn more about interdenominational unity in *Digging Deeper* Volume 3.

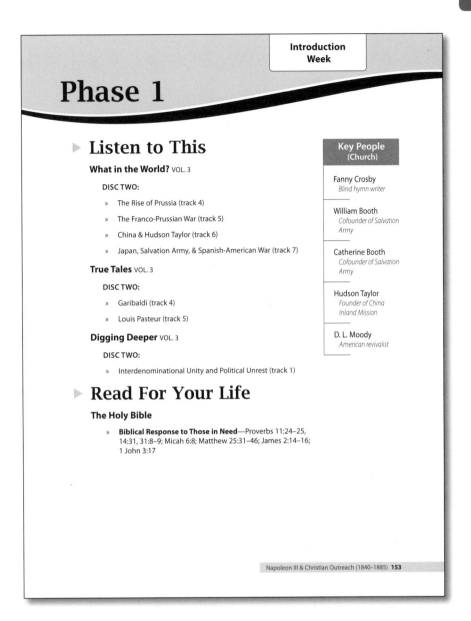

Phase 1

Introduction
Week

▶ Listen to This

What in the World? VOL. 3

DISC TWO:

» The Rise of Prussia (track 4)

» The Franco-Prussian War (track 5)

» China & Hudson Taylor (track 6)

» Japan, Salvation Army, & Spanish-American War (track 7)

True Tales VOL. 3

DISC TWO:

» Garibaldi (track 4)

» Louis Pasteur (track 5)

Digging Deeper VOL. 3

DISC TWO:

» Interdenominational Unity and Political Unrest (track 1)

▶ Read For Your Life

The Holy Bible

» **Biblical Response to Those in Need**—Proverbs 11:24–25, 14:31, 31:8–9; Micah 6:8; Matthew 25:31–46; James 2:14–16; 1 John 3:17

Key People (Church)

Fanny Crosby
Blind hymn writer

William Booth
Cofounder of Salvation Army

Catherine Booth
Cofounder of Salvation Army

Hudson Taylor
Founder of China Inland Mission

D. L. Moody
American revivalist

Napoleon III & Christian Outreach (1840–1885) **153**

◉ Read the Scriptures in Read For Your Life

The Scriptures are central to our understanding, our character, and our decisions. Therefore, we must give the greatest weight possible to them.

Help your students gain this perspective as they watch you handle the Scriptures with reverence and awe.

Discuss with your students what they are discovering about God's heart for the poor and needy as they read through these Scriptures. What changes might each of us need to make in light of God's Word?

KEY PEOPLE

The main characters in this Unit are listed in the Student Manual, along with a brief identifier, so that the students can familiarize themselves with these people.

◉ Recap the material with an activity

In different parts of the room, set up stations for the Eight Intelligences Recap Activities. Then allow students to work alone or together in small groups to accomplish THEIR CHOICE OF ONE of the following suggestions. At the start of the next class, ask for 3–4 groups of volunteers to share.

Homeschoolers: rather than setting up all eight stations, allow student(s) to choose which activity they would most enjoy, and do it.

Recap Suggestions:

Spatial: Create a poster depicting the two or three most interesting aspects of Italian Independence, the Franco-Prussian War, the Salvation Army, or the China Inland Mission.

Bodily Kinesthetic: Set up two sections of a room, one to represent China and Great Britain, the other to represent Japan and America. Consider a short physical activity or a stance in each location that would represent each country's behavior toward the other during this Unit. Then take groups on a tour of these locations, demonstrating the physical action (inviting others to join you) with an explanation of how this shows what was taking place in the 1800s.

Interpersonal: In groups of two or three, decide how you could best present the story of Hudson Taylor

and the China Inland Mission to preschool children so that it would come alive for them.

Musical: Write new lyrics for the tune "When the Saints Go Marching In" to tell the story of William and Catherine Booth and the Salvation Army.

Linguistic: Write a speech for Napoleon III in which he asks for sufficient funds to equip his army, given the fact that Prussia, a potential enemy, is arming itself to the teeth. Remember, Napoleon III is in a difficult spot; his legislature does not trust him, and his army is in shambles. Do your best!

Math-Logical: Make a step-by-step chart showing how Italy managed

to become a unified kingdom in the 1800s.

Intrapersonal: Write a short reflection about the Cambridge Seven. How does their choice to walk away from promising careers and comfortable lifestyles to serve the people of China affect or challenge you?

Naturalist: Using materials found outside, create a visual representation of the new German Empire. Remember, this is not a liberal version of a united Germany, but instead a militaristic version under the command of Prussia. How will this affect the type of materials you use and how you put them together?

Key People (World)

Commodore Perry
Opened Japan to the West

Kaiser Wilhelm I
German emperor

Garibaldi
Fought for Italian independence

Otto von Bismarck
Prussian chancellor

Louis Pasteur
Pasteurization, rabies vaccine

Thomas Edison
Inventor of electric light bulb

Alexander Graham Bell
Inventor of telephone

▶ Talk Together

Opinion Column

» What did you find to be the most interesting aspect or the most fascinating person you encountered in your introduction to the time period of Italian Independence, the Franco-Prussian War, the China Inland Mission, and the Salvation Army?

» Why do you think the Franco-Prussian War of 1870 was important? In what ways do you think Europe was changed by this war? (Consider these two questions: What was Prussia's status at the conclusion of this war? What was France's status at the conclusion of this war?)

» Consider the point of view of the Chinese as the West began to make forcible demands upon China for trade. How do you think you would have viewed European missionaries, since they dressed and lived like other Europeans? For what reasons might the Chinese have called people from the West "foreign devils"?

» Do you think that America was right to force open Japan's closed doors? Explain your reasoning.

» Why, specifically, do you think that European missionaries might have been shocked by Hudson Taylor's decision to wear Chinese clothing and hairstyle? If you had been a missionary in China at the time, do you think you would have wanted to follow suit in wearing Chinese clothing, or would you have continued to dress like other Europeans? Explain your reasons.

» Why do you think it was difficult for the established churches in England to work with people living in slums? What might have hindered them?

» Why do you think the Salvation Army was so successful at meeting the needs of the slum-dwelling poor and the laboring classes? What value can you see in their choice to preach in theaters and factories? What effect do you think the musical bands might have had? If you had been living in England during this time, would you have described the Salvation Army as a "proper" ministry? Why or why not?

» The Student Volunteer Movement was a significant force for missions among university students, especially in America. Considering the impact that the Cambridge Seven had on England when they departed for missionary service to China, what effect do you think one hundred American university students volunteering for missions in 1886 might have had on North America?

Critical Puzzling

» How do you think Commodore Perry was viewed by the Japanese? By the Americans? In what ways might his visit have been beneficial to the Japanese? In what ways might it have been destructive? What were some of the results of his visit?

» Garibaldi was a leader of Italian patriots who wanted to see their country united instead of "parceled out" to various countries. Why do you think he might have seemed to be "larger than life" to many of his countrymen? In what ways was he successful in liberating Italy from foreign rule?

» What benefit did Prussia receive in forming the new German Empire? How do you think the rest of Europe viewed this development? Since Bismarck had shown himself to be a very powerful man, and his policy was "blood and iron," what effect do you think he had on international diplomacy during his tenure as Prime Minister of the German Empire?

» Hudson Taylor, to grow in his understanding that God was absolutely faithful, lived a spartan lifestyle in England when he could have lived in much greater luxury. Evaluate the impact this experience might have had on him when he arrived in China. If you were planning to go to another country as a missionary, in what ways might you train yourself to rely on God's faithfulness before leaving? In what ways would this be valuable for your experience on the mission field?

» Why did Hudson Taylor choose to make the China Inland Mission a "faith mission," depending on God alone to supply the needs of the mission and all its workers? What circumstances was this new mission facing that might have made this a good decision? Do you believe this is still a valid option for Christian workers today? Why or why not?

» William Booth's book, *In Darkest England and the Way Out*, deeply shocked the English public, bringing an awareness of the gut-wrenching poverty, brutal crime, and horrific squalor in which the poor of their country lived every day. How might this book have helped the Salvation Army to fulfill their goals of caring for the poor?

Or . . . Activity of Your Choice: What would you like to have your students do for a review activity concerning this week's introduction to Italian Independence and the Franco-Prussian War, the China Inland Mission and the Salvation Army?

◉ Talk together

Individual Preparation

After completing their recap activities, students may begin to consider the questions in the Opinion Column and Critical Puzzling.

Class Discussion

Use the questions under Talk Together to get the students primed and to create a discussion environment in the classroom. You may also want to draw from the open-ended questions listed here.

In what ways does the phrase "image is not reality" apply to Napoleon III and the Second Empire of France? How might things have gone differently if the people of France had actually comprehended the true state of military affairs in the late 1860s?

Consider Bismarck's success in building up Prussia's army to the point where it became nearly invincible. What Scriptures can you think of that would address his methods?

▶ **Resources for Digging Deeper**

Choose a few books that look interesting, or find your own.

FRANCO-PRUSSIAN WAR

Otto von Bismarck WORLD LEADERS PAST & PRESENT

Jonathan E. Rose • This is the man who, in his first speech to the Prussian parliament, announced, "It is not by speeches and majority resolutions that the great questions of the time are decided . . . but by iron and blood." His governing policy, realpolitik, meant that "any alliance could be broken, any program abandoned, any supporter betrayed in the ultimate struggle for Xpower." Read more about his influence in world affairs in this excellent biography. Highly recommended. **MS+**

Democratic Despot

T. A. B. Corley • This is a compelling, in-depth biography of Napoleon III, nephew of Napoleon Bonaparte and emperor of the Second Empire of France. Through Napoleon III's maneuvering, the Crimean War was fought and won the French and English; Mexico briefly had a Hapsburg emperor, Maximilian; the French navy began to rival the British navy; and the Prussians were able to form the Second German Empire after their defeat of Napoleon III's troops in the Franco-Prussian War of 1870. **HS**

THE OPENING OF JAPAN

Commodore Perry in the Land of the Shogun

Rhoda Blumberg • This excellent retelling of Perry's historic encounter with a feudalistic Japan will help students become better acquainted with this incredible moment in history. **UE+**

Commodore Perry in Japan AMERICAN HERITAGE JUNIOR LIBRARY

Robert L. Reynolds • The story is well told in this interesting book of the "black ships" from America that went to Japan in 1853 and forced open the door of trade which had been closed for two centuries. **UE+**

INVENTORS & INVENTIONS OF THIS ERA

Thomas Edison for Kids: His Life and Ideas

Laurie Carlson • This amazing book not only tells the story of Edison's life (along with short biographies of other notable inventors of his generation), but it also includes twenty-one scientific activities that students can do to learn more about Edison's inventions. Fantastic! **UE+**

The Story of Thomas Alva Edison A WORLD LANDMARK BOOK

Margaret Cousins • The inventions of Thomas Edison changed the entire world! Read about his life and his many inventions, including the phonograph, the electric light bulb, the first motion picture camera, and more in this interesting biography. **UE+**

Alexander Graham Bell: Giving Voice to the World

Mary Kay Carson • One of the Sterling Biographies, this excellent introduction to Bell provides historic insights into his life and work, including the significant influence he had on Helen Keller's life. **UE+**

Alexander Graham Bell GROUNDBREAKERS SERIES

Struan Reid • LEARN THE ANSWERS TO SUCH QUESTIONS AS, "WHY DID ALEXANDER GRAHAM BELL LEARN SIGN LANGUAGE AS A BOY?" IN THIS FASCINATING BOOK FOR CHILDREN. E+

GARIBALDI

Giuseppe Garibaldi WORLD
LEADERS PAST & PRESENT
Herman J. Viola and Susan P. Viola • Garibaldi lived a life of adventure and danger with the purpose of seeing his country freed from foreign rule. This excellent book shows the many facets of his life and work. **MS+**

Garibaldi: Father of Modern Italy A WORLD LANDMARK BOOK
Marcia Davenport • Did you know that Italy had not been united as one country since the time of the Roman Empire—until 1870? This biography is of the man who led his country to independence and unity against the great powers of Europe. Well-written and fascinating to read! **UE+**

LOUIS PASTEUR

Louis Pasteur GROUNDBREAKERS SERIES
Ann Fullick • Pasteur's life is surveyed, including the fascinating fact that in his early days as a student, his main talent lay in drawing! **UE+**

Louis Pasteur
Laura N. Wood • A fascinating biography of one of the greatest scientists of all time. He discovered a cure for

rabies, disproved spontaneous generation, developed vaccines, and gave us pasteurization. Excellent! **UE+**

The Life of Louis Pasteur PIONEERS IN HEALTH AND MEDICINE
Marcia Newfield • This wonderful biography of Louis Pasteur is filled with brief anecdotes about his life and his work. Highly recommended! **E+**

THE SALVATION ARMY

Kidnapped by River Rats TRAILBLAZER BOOKS
Dave & Neta Jackson • Historical fiction for children, this title describes the ministry of William and Catherine Booth, the founders of the Salvation Army. **UE+**

William Booth CHRISTIAN HEROES THEN AND NOW
Janet & Geoff Benge • In this well-written biography,

learn more about William and Catherine Booth's work in bringing the gospel and desperately needed social services to the "outcasts of society." **UE+**

William Booth MEN OF FAITH SERIES
David Bennett •This biography tells the incredible story of a man who ministered to people in the midst of their poverty and hopelessness. **MS+**

FANNY CROSBY & HYMN WRITING

Fanny Crosby: Writer of 8,000 Songs
Sandy Dengler •This is a wonderful biography of an amazing Christian. Fanny Crosby, although blind, became one of history's most gifted and treasured hymn writers. **E+**

101 Hymn Stories
Kenneth W. Osbeck •What a wonderful resource! Though it is not set up chronologically, if you are willing to do a bit of hunting, you will find treasures in the stories of these hymns. This is a marvelous way to bring in another dimension of the story of the church in history— through the singing of hymns to our Lord. **UE+**

Napoleon III & Christian Outreach (1840–1885) **157**

◉ Choose books of interest/ internet search

A list of possible books is given in the Student Manual. Encourage your students to look for books or videos on Napoleon III & Christian Outreach from this list and from other sources. You may want to gather a selection of further resources prior to beginning

Unit 4, or you may encourage the students to be treasure hunters and find them on their own. It would be helpful and time-saving before the Unit begins to check availability of these titles on your local library website.

Remember:

Beware of Arrogance,

Embrace Humility!

D. L. MOODY & STUDENT VOLUNTEER MOVEMENT

D. L. Moody MEN OF FAITH SERIES

David Bennett · Subtitled "The unconventional American evangelist who reached 100 million people with the gospel," this is the story of a man whose ministry profoundly touched both the British Isles and the United States. Flowing out of this ministry were many who ended up on the mission fields of the world. **UE+**

HUDSON TAYLOR, THE CHINA INLAND MISSION, & THE CAMBRIDGE SEVEN

Hudson Taylor CHRISTIAN HEROES THEN AND NOW

Janet & Geoff Benge · Wonderfully written, this series of Christian biographies is fascinating, factual, and historically accurate. Hudson Taylor went to China as a missionary in 1854. His story is one of the most stirring and challenging in all of Christendom. Highly recommended! **UE+**

Hudson Taylor MEN OF FAITH SERIES

J. Hudson Taylor · Hudson Taylor's autobiography, this book is filled with the goodness of God in the midst of life's difficulties. It tells the story of Taylor's life until 1866, and the beginning of the China Inland Mission. Highly recommended! **UE+**

Hudson Taylor's Spiritual Secret

Dr. and Mrs. Howard Taylor ·This book changed my life. It not only tells the story of Hudson Taylor's life, but also tells how he learned to rest in God's abilities, not his own. Highly recommended! **MS+**

C. T. Studd CHRISTIAN HEROES THEN AND NOW

Janet & Geoff Benge · One of the Cambridge Seven, C. T. Studd rocked the British Isles with his departure for China as a missionary. He was a well-known sports figure from an extremely wealthy family, so his willingness to leave it all to serve Christ (giving up his inheritance in the process) made headlines. In later years, he started the Worldwide Evangelization Crusade and served as a missionary in Africa. **UE+**

The 100 Most Important Dates in Church History

A. Kenneth Curtis, J. Stephen Lang, and Randy Petersen · For this unit read about Hudson Taylor, Charles Spurgeon, D. L. Moody, William Booth, and the Student Volunteer Movement. **UE+**

From Jerusalem to Irian Jaya: A Biographical History of Christian Missions

Ruth A. Tucker · This is the best book on the history of world missions available. For this unit read about China (176–200), John Paton (225–227), Korea and Japan (254–272), and Student Volunteers (312–325). **UE+**

China: A History to 1949 ENCHANTMENT OF THE WORLD SERIES

Valjean McLenighan · This is an excellent primer of Chinese history, including the Boxer Rebellion of 1900, Sun Yat-Sen, and the eventual triumph of Communism in China. **UE+**

JOHN PATON & SOUTH PACIFIC MISSIONS

The Man with the Bird on His Head INTERNATIONAL ADVENTURES

John Rush & Abbe Anderson · Published by YWAM Publishing, this is one of the most amazing missionary stories of the twentieth century! If you are going to read about John Paton, you must read this story, too. It concerns a tribal group on Tanna in the South Pacific who became a "cargo cult" after WWII. They were known as the John Frum people because they were waiting for John Frum to tell them of spiritual truths. **UE+**

John Paton MEN OF FAITH SERIES

Benjamin Unseth · The story of a Scottish missionary to the islands of the South Pacific, especially Tanna, this book describes the difficulties early missionaries faced on these lovely islands inhabited by cannibals. **MS+**

FAMOUS ARTISTS OF THIS ERA

Pierre Auguste Renoir
GETTING TO KNOW THE WORLD'S GREATEST ARTISTS

Mike Venezia • Learn about the life and Impressionist paintings of Renoir, whose genuine warmth and interest in all he saw is reflected in his paintings. Full-color reproductions of sixteen of his works are included in this book. **E+**

Linnea in Monet's Garden
Christina Bjork, illustrated by Lena Anderson • This is a delightful book to use for introducing children to the paintings of Monet. **E+**

CLASSIC LITERATURE

Around the World in Eighty Days
Jules Verne • Classic literature concerning a British gentleman who travels around the world, this book is a wonderful glimpse into the time period. **MS+**

What books did you like best?

_____

_____

_____

_____

The Internet also contains a wealth of information about Napoleon III & Christian Outreach.

What sites were the most helpful?

_____

_____

_____

_____

For more books, use these Dewey Decimal numbers in your library:

Kingdom of Italy: 945

East Asia: 951

Opium Wars: 951

Commodore Perry in Japan: 952

Franco-Prussian War: 943.08

Prussia: 943.07

Salvation Army: 287

China Inland Mission / Student Volunteer Movement: 266

Impressionism in art: 700, 750s

Impressionism in music: 780, 781

Art Nouveau in architecture: 709.4, 720.9

Inventions: 384.09, 621.3, 789.9

◉ Conduct a review and evaluation

In this Phase of Unit 4, your students should have had the opportunity to explore Napoleon III & Christian Outreach through reading, listening, thinking, and discussing by completing a selection from the following:

- informally discussed the Key Concepts;
- read the article;
- listened to the audio recordings;
- read the online articles;
- read the Scriptures;
- explored the recap activities;
- considered the Opinion Column and Critical Puzzling answers on their own;
- participated in class discussion;
- chosen books of interest or searched the Internet;
- completed their self-evaluation for this Phase.

Record student hours: _____

Assess student participation:

Create an evaluation system of your own, or refer to the evaluation rubric in the introduction, as a tool for assessing participation. The categories you will probably find most useful are *"Introduction," "Process: Teamwork,"* and *"Process: Originality."* To help students develop good discussion skills, encourage them to participate actively, ask content-based questions, and stay focused on the discussion at

hand. Students demonstrate a higher level of discussion skills when they incorporate comments and questions from others into their own questions, and draw out opinions or ask for points of clarification from others.

Do not critique the self-evaluation page your student completes and do not direct the answers the student gives to the questions. Instead, allow sincere and personal completion of the evaluation, then discuss the responses and incorporate those comments into your evaluation.

Determine a grade for this Phase, if using grades: _____

Teacher Self-Evaluation:

Evaluate your own use of materials and teaching opportunities: what worked and what did not; how effective was your time-management; how were your responses to the needs of your student; did you make your expectations clear; in what ways would you like to improve your approach for the next Unit? Incorporate suggestions from your students in your own evaluation *(this requires humility!)*.

▶ Student Self-Evaluation UNIT 4, PHASE 1

Dates and hours:_____

Key Concepts

Rephrase the five Key Concepts of this Unit and confirm your understanding of each:

- Kingdom of Italy

  _____

- East Asia & the West

  _____

- Prussia's Rise to Power

  _____

- Salvation Army & the Destitute

  _____

- The China Inland Mission

  _____

Tools for Self-Evaluation

Evaluate your personal participation in the discussions of this Phase. Bearing in mind that a good participant in a discussion is not always the most vocal participant, ask yourself these questions: Were you an active participant? Did you ask perceptive questions? Were you willing to listen to other participants of the discussion and draw out their opinions? Record your observations and how you would like to improve your participation in the future:

_____

_____

Every time period is too complex to be understood in one Phase of study. Evaluate your current knowledge of Napoleon III & Christian Outreach. What have you focused on so far? What are your weakest areas of knowledge?

_____

_____

Based on the evaluation of this introduction, project ahead what you would like to study more of in the following Phases.

_____

_____

160 Napoleon III & Christian Outreach (1840–1885)

Phase 2

▶ Research & Reporting

Explore one or more of these areas to discover something significant!

Bismarck & the German Empire

Discover and report on the rise to power of this powerful leader, his political theories (known as realpolitik), and the eventual creation of the German Empire. Consider the means he employed to attain his goals, especially in light of the Scriptures.

Franco-Prussian War

Learn more about the Franco-Prussian War of 1870. Answer these questions: Why did Prussia want to go to war with France? Why did France want to avoid war with Prussia? What was the Ems telegram? In what ways did it provoke the war? What significance did this war have for France, for Prussia, and for Europe?

Garibaldi

Research and report on the life of Giuseppe Garibaldi and the struggle for the unification of Italy. Describe the political division in Italy. Show which European countries governed the different parts of Italy before the unification.

China and the Opium Wars

Research and report on the causes of the Opium Wars between China and Great Britain. What were the results of Great Britain's victory? In what ways did this victory plant seeds for future strife? (Consider the Boxer Rebellion of 1900.)

Commodore Perry and Japan

Learn more about America's interest in opening the closed kingdom of Japan to trade, and how Commodore Perry was seen to be the right man for the job. What were the results of Commodore Perry's success for Japan? For America? (For a fascinating addition to your project, do an Internet search for the "Black Ships Festival" held each year in Shimoda, Japan.)

Hudson Taylor and the China Inland Mission

Research and report on the life and ministry of Hudson Taylor. Discover more about his remarkable life, the way he depended on God for provisions, and the establishment of the China Inland Mission. What were the defining characteristics of this mission? How effective was it in taking the gospel to the inland provinces of China?

William and Catherine Booth

Discover the amazing story of the lives and work of William and Catherine Booth. Learn how they were each uniquely qualified for the ministry God gave them. Consider their children and the part they played in the Salvation Army. How did this ministry affect the family?

◉ Choose a topic and begin research

Allow the students the freedom to choose one of the topics listed under research & reporting in the Student Manual, or to suggest their own area which they would like to research.

Motivating Suggestions:

Especially for Non-linguistic students, and those who are not motivated by written or oral reports, here are suggestions for alternative ways of reporting what has been researched.

Bismarck & the German Empire

Create a solo performance (or "one-man show") of Otto von Bismarck, seeking either to obtain personal sympathy for your cause or to elicit an appropriate fear of your power. Be sure to include quotes from your "Blood and Iron" speech before the Prussian parliament.

With two or three other students, discuss Bismarck's policy of *realpolitik*. Was Bismarck justified in his actions?

Did his actions bring about good or harm for Prussia? For the German Empire? For Europe?

Franco-Prussian War

Imagine you are with Napoleon III's army during the Franco-Prussian War. Journal your thoughts concerning the progress of the war, any surprises that you have experienced, your analysis of why things are going wrong for France, and what you have personally learned through this experience.

Create a map of this war, showing the locations, dates, and outcomes of the various battles, the siege of Paris, and the crowning of Kaiser Wilhelm I.

Garibaldi

In an open outdoor area (like a park or large backyard), section off the separate areas of Italy as they were before its unification. It would be quite helpful to consult a map as you do this so each section is located in a geographically appropriate place in relation to the others. Prepare a talk, in the guise of a national parks guide at a battle site, to explain at each location just what happened there: who had governed it before unification, how circumstances changed, and when it was incorporated into the Kingdom of Italy. Include appropriate physical actions for your audience to do, such as marching from Naples toward Rome to demonstrate Garibaldi's actions. Be prepared to answer questions.

Compare and contrast Italy's unification into the Kingdom of Italy with Germany's unification into the German Empire under Kaiser Wilhelm I. You may want to create a flip chart, PowerPoint presentation, or graphs to explain the similarities and differences.

China and the Opium Wars

Using an appropriate melody, but giving it new lyrics, teach others about China and the Opium Wars. One possibility is the American slave song "Wade in the Water." (Recordings of this song can be found on YouTube.)

Find two plants, trees, or flowers that visually demonstrate the differences between China and Great Britain during the time of the Opium Wars. Then create a "show-and-tell" presentation for an audience, explaining how these plants are illustrative of the showdown between these two nations.

Commodore Perry and Japan

Host a television program where you interview Commodore Perry, the Japanese emperor, a sailor who sailed with Perry to Japan, and a citizen of Japan who watched the ships arrive. In addition to other informative biographical queries, be sure to question each on their views of the foreigners (whether American or Japanese), as well as their overall thoughts of the success or failure of this historic interaction.

Go outside and recreate the historic landing of American ships in Tokyo Bay in 1853. You may want to create a miniaturized version of this spectacle, or an imaginative full-size version. Invite people to visit the site, and explain the significance of what occurred here.

Hudson Taylor and the China Inland Mission

Imagine you accompanied Hudson and Maria Taylor back to China as part of the newly formed China Inland Mission. Write informative letters home that will explain your thoughts on the way the mission is run, on how the Chinese respond to Europeans in Chinese dress, on attitudes you've noticed in missionaries from other organizations, and on what it is like to trust God for all of your provisions.

Hudson Taylor's favorite hymn was entitled "Jesus, I Am Resting, Resting." Using this old hymn, create a presentation (whether a PowerPoint presentation, an artistic presentation, a musical presentation, or an oral report) that will help an audience grasp how Taylor was able to carry such huge burdens (the needs of the missionaries under his care, as well as

The Salvation Army

Learn more about the Salvation Army. Describe its beginning, its leaders, its area of influence, and its purpose. What strategies for ministry were unique (in this time) to the organization? How did it become identified with caring for the poor in practical ways?

Louis Pasteur

Pasteur was one of the greatest scientists of all time. Research and report on the Frenchman's life and work. Working during the time of Napoleon III's Second Empire, how was Pasteur helped or hindered by the politics of his time? Consider his major discoveries and how these continue to affect us today.

Thomas Edison

Edison is the American inventor who said, "Genius is one percent inspiration and ninety-nine percent perspiration." Learn more about Edison's life and work. Describe his childhood, his schooling, his early jobs, and his inventions. What obstacles did he have to overcome?

Alexander Graham Bell

Research and report on the man who invented and patented the first practical telephone, Alexander Graham Bell. Be sure to read about the struggles that resulted from Elisha Gray's simultaneous invention—he was only hours behind Bell in rushing his invention to the patent office!

Fanny Crosby

Study the life of Fanny Crosby, a hymn writer whose heartfelt words continue to bear fruit. How did her blindness affect her ability to minister? Describe her life, her gift for remembering poetry (including her memorization of the entire Bible!), and the process by which she wrote more than 8,000 songs.

D. L. Moody

The life of D. L. Moody is an interesting one to study. Early in his ministry, a good friend said to him, "Moody, the world has yet to see what God will do with a man fully consecrated to Him"—and Moody determined that he would be that man. With that in mind, learn about his background, education, and ministry. What was his focus in ministry? What kinds of opportunities did Moody have to preach? What were some of the effects of his ministry in missions, in education, in evangelism, both in America and abroad?

The Cambridge Seven and the Student Volunteer Movement

Discover the story of the Cambridge Seven, their effect on England, and their lives of service on the mission field. Because of its similarity and connection, learn about the Student Volunteer Movement, which began in the 1880s in America. What were the circumstances that brought about the Student Volunteer Movement? Who was involved? Where did these students go? How did it affect America and the world?

the vast spiritual needs of China) and yet remain calm and peaceful as he truly rested in God.

William and Catherine Booth

Create a collage of the lives of William and Catherine Booth. Be sure to include their work during the Great Prayer Revival in England, their mission in the East End of London, the international growth of the Salvation Army, and their unusual approach to ministry.

Choose what you consider to be the four most pivotal events in the lives of this world-changing couple. Then prepare to do a pantomime or interpretive dance about these events to help

others see what you see. You may find it helpful to use appropriate music.

The Salvation Army

Hold an informal discussion of this question: "What responsibility do Christ-followers have in becoming aware of and giving practical care to the needs of those who live in material poverty?" Be sure to include William Booth's arguments from his book, *In Darkest England and the Way Out*. You can find the entire book online at the online resource page.

Create a flip chart or multimedia presentation to show the various activities of the Salvation Army, the countries in which they worked, and

▶ Brain Stretchers

Scramble for Africa

Compare and contrast the Scramble for Africa with the divvying up of China by Western powers into separate spheres of influence. What were the costs and benefits, if any, to the West? What were the costs and benefits, if any, to these non-industrialized regions?

Compare Rulers

Compare and contrast Klemens von Metternich, Napoleon III, and Otto von Bismarck and the way their policies changed the shape of European politics. What was the state of affairs in Europe during the time of each one's influence? What caused each to fall from his position of power? How was Europe affected by the implementation of each one's policies and by the cessation of these policies?

Military Strategies

Research and report on the military strategies used by the Prussian army to defeat Napoleon III and his Second Empire. In order to do this, be sure to describe how Napoleon III had employed his army before this war, and then contrast this with Bismarck's preparation of the Prussian army before the war. How did this preparation (or lack thereof) affect the final outcome?

Taiping Rebellion in China

Learn about the Taiping Rebellion in China, including the living conditions of people during the late period of the Manchu dynasty. What were the issues of the Taiping Rebellion? In what way was it linked to Christianity? What was the result of this rebellion?

John Paton

Read about John Paton, the missionary to cannibals in the South Pacific. Describe his ministry and the obstacles he overcame. Compare and contrast his ministry with the story of John Rush, the young man who, in the 1990s, had an unexpected ministry to tribal people on the island of Tanna—the same island from which John Paton had fled.

Create Your Own Research Topic

_____

_____

_____

_____

the amount and type of assistance they provided to the poor. Explain to your audience what you consider to be the strengths and weaknesses of this organization during this era.

Louis Pasteur

Set up an exhibition to show Pasteur's many inventions and discoveries. If possible, have three-dimensional objects available, such as a stuffed plush dog to represent Pasteur's rabies vaccine, which could help people really grasp what Pasteur did. Be prepared to answer questions as people see the exhibits.

Create a colorful image-rich time line of Pasteur's life and work. Be sure to include the ongoing events of the Second Empire of France within the time line, so that others will be able to see how they fit together.

Thomas Edison

Storytell the life of Edison, who is considered to be one of the greatest inventors in history. Choose props and costumes that will help you explain to your audience Edison's childhood, education, work, inventions, and unusual habits!

In a small group, consider how our lives have been affected by Edison's inventions. Discuss what life would be like if the electric light, phono-graph, and motion pictures had never been invented.

Alexander Graham Bell

Compare and contrast the lives of two inventors born in 1847: Alexander Graham Bell and Thomas Edison. What are the similarities in their lives? What are the differences? How did each one approach inventing?

Create a "jungle" phone! Study the basic components of Bell's original telephone; then find items in nature that you can use to illustrate the most important parts of the telephone and the principles upon which it relied. (Note: This suggestion recognizes that your "jungle" telephone will not actually work.) Present your findings, allowing the audience to ask questions about the first telephone and its inventor.

Fanny Crosby

Write a journal entry in which you reflect upon Fanny's attitude toward the obstacles and tragedies in her life. How did she respond to her blindness? In what ways did it hinder or, conversely, help her? How does the story of her life inspire and challenge you?

Select your favorite 6–8 hymns out of the 8,000 written by Fanny Crosby. Then organize an old-fashioned hymn-sing, where people can sing her songs and worship God. Either in the program notes or through an oral presentation before each hymn, share how each hymn illuminates some aspect of Fanny's life and what she had learned about God. Your goal in doing this is that by the time the hymn-sing is finished, participants will understand the basic facts and amazing service of this blind woman.

D. L. Moody

Set up a glimpse into the gospel preaching style of D. L. Moody. Learn about Moody's sermon delivery style, choose a portion of one of his sermons (either printed or memorized), and decide in what location and year

"Moody" will preach. You might want to add in a hymn with "Ira Sankey," Moody's constant companion in evangelism. A selection of Moody's sermons can be found at the online resource page.

As a Christian investigative journalist, study the life and ministry of D. L. Moody. Then either prepare a written piece for a Christian magazine or videotape a news report to be used for television. Starting from the premise that Moody had determined to be fully consecrated to God, show as much circumstantial evidence as possible concerning whether he fulfilled this desire or not. (Alternatively, you could do this from the point of view of an agnostic investigative journalist researching to discover whether Moody was the "real deal.")

The Cambridge Seven and the Student Volunteer Movement

Create a public relations campaign for the Cambridge Seven. Your purpose is to raise public awareness of the astonishing story of these young men going to the mission field, in order to draw as many people as possible to hear them before they actually depart for China.

Write and illustrate a children's book about the Cambridge Seven in England and the Student Volunteer Movement in America. Be sure to help them see how this movement impacted not only the sending country but the receiving countries as well.

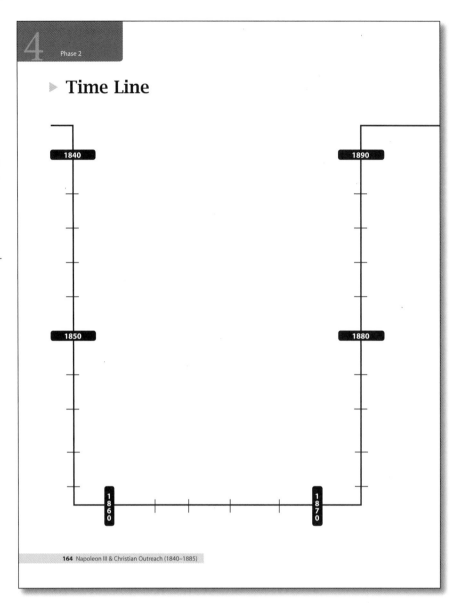

▶ **Time Line**

164 Napoleon III & Christian Outreach (1840–1885)

◉ Construct the time line

Read the information listed with the Key Events in the Student Manual. Dialogue with your students about the issues involved.

Find the dates for the Key People and Key Events listed.

Consider this for your time line

As a new form of nationalism, combined with aggressive militaristic power, steps onto the stage of history in the form of the new German Empire, a new means of serving in the name of Christ is unveiled through the China Inland Mission and the Salvation Army—one as a faith mission to the inland regions of China, the other as a practical ministry to those caught in the mire of poverty, degradation, and crime. It is a time of great concern and great hope.

Be sure to include the people listed in Key People in Phase 1.

Key Events

- Kingdom of Italy

- Opium Wars in China

- Commodore Perry and the Black Ships in Japan

- Seven Weeks War

- China Inland Mission founded

- Salvation Army founded (known first as the "Christian Mission")

- Franco-Prussian War

- Cambridge Seven

- Student Volunteer Movement

Time Line Key

Key People in the Church

- Fanny Crobsy: 1820–1915

- William Booth: 1829–1912

- Catherine Booth: 1829–1890

- Hudson Taylor: 1832–1905

- D. L. Moody: 1837–1899

Key People in the World

- Commodore Perry: 1794–1858

- Kaiser Wilhelm I: 1797–1888

- Garibaldi: 1807–1882

- Otto von Bismarck: 1815–1898

- Louis Pasteur: 1822–1895

- Thomas Edison: 1847–1931

- Alexander Graham Bell: 1847–1922

Key Dates

- Kingdom of Italy: 1861–1946

- Opium Wars in China
  - First Opium War: 1839–1842
  - Second Opium War: 1856–1860

- Commodore Perry and the Black Ships in Japan: 1853–1854

- Seven Weeks War: 1866

- China Inland Mission founded: 1865

The second era of the Modern Missions movement began with the founding of the China Inland Mission, in which Protestant Christians began going to the inland regions of unevangelized lands. These areas were remote, difficult, and potentially dangerous. With your students, discover where the greatest need currently exists for a clear presentation of the gospel. (YWAM Publishing carries titles that address this issue.) Then begin to systematically pray for these nations by name. One suggestion is the Kingdom of Lesotho in southern Africa.

- Salvation Army founded: 1865

- Franco-Prussian War: 1870–1871

- Cambridge Seven: 1885

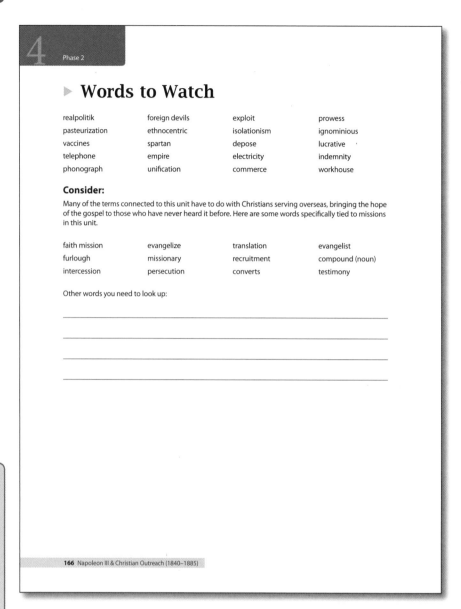

▶ Words to Watch

realpolitik	foreign devils	exploit	prowess
pasteurization	ethnocentric	isolationism	ignominious
vaccines	spartan	depose	lucrative
telephone	empire	electricity	indemnity
phonograph	unification	commerce	workhouse

Consider:

Many of the terms connected to this unit have to do with Christians serving overseas, bringing the hope of the gospel to those who have never heard it before. Here are some words specifically tied to missions in this unit.

faith mission	evangelize	translation	evangelist
furlough	missionary	recruitment	compound (noun)
intercession	persecution	converts	testimony

Other words you need to look up:

_____

_____

_____

_____

Here is one idea for making vocabulary study interesting and fun:

PICTURE CUE!

On a 3x5 card, glue a photo or image cut from a magazine to be a visual clue to the meaning of one of the vocabulary words. On the back of the card, write the vocabulary word. Create a separate card for each word. With all the cards completed, try remembering the vocabulary word by looking at its picture cue. See if you can get to the point where you can say each vocabulary word instantly as you see the picture. Be ready to explain how the picture cues help you to understand the meaning of each word.

A list of definitions can be found at the back of the book in Appendix B.

◉ Practice vocabulary

You may find other words in this Unit that are especially appropriate for younger children. Feel free to substitute another vocabulary list for the one provided.

◉ Complete research projects and share in class or hand in

Create a safe environment for the presentations. Set ground rules prior to the presentations, so that students know how much time is available for each of them, and so that they know they will be honored and respected by all those observing.

▶ Student Self-Evaluation UNIT 4, PHASE 2

Dates and hours:_____

Research Project

Summarize your research question:

_____

_____

List your most useful sources by author, title, and page number or URL where applicable (continue list in margin if necessary):

_____

_____

Now take a moment to evaluate the sources you just listed. Do they provide a balanced view of your research question? Should you have sought an additional opinion? Are your sources credible (if you found them on your own)? Record your observations:

_____

_____

_____

Evaluate your research project in its final presentation. What are its strengths? If you had time to revisit this project, what would you change? Consider giving yourself a letter grade based on your project's merits and weaknesses.

_____

_____

_____

Letter grade: ____

You have just completed an area of specific research on the time of Napoleon III & Christian Outreach. Now what would you like to explore in the upcoming Phases? Set some objectives for yourself.

_____

_____

_____

Napoleon III & Christian Outreach (1840–1885) **167**

◉ Conduct a review and evaluation

In this second Phase of Unit 4, your students should have had the opportunity to explore Napoleon III & Christian Outreach through researching, thinking, and reporting by completing a selection from the following:

- done a research project;
- learned the vocabulary;
- constructed a time line;
- created a project report on what was researched;
- completed their self-evaluation procedure for this Phase.

Record student hours: _____

Assess student effort in the research and reporting projects.

Create an evaluation system of your own, or refer to the evaluation rubric in the introduction, as a tool for assessing research and reporting. The categories you will probably find most useful are *"Introduction," "Task," "Process: Teamwork"* (if students are working together), along with Grammar, Format, and Spelling. As a tool for helping your students develop better research skills, pay attention to their evaluation of sources. Older students should learn how to make a "Sources Cited" list according to academic standards—refer them to English usage books or websites for formatting rules. Younger students should learn how to obtain a balanced view of their research subject; if they use more than one source they will get a bigger picture of what was happening. Encourage your students to make use of their self-evaluations for their next research projects, in order to practice good research skills.

Do not critique the self-evaluation page your student completes in the Student Manual—spelling errors are not to be considered in such an exercise. Students should feel free to humbly evaluate themselves without that added complexity. Instead, discuss with them the intention of their written comments and incorporate those into your evaluation.

Determine a final grade for this Phase: _____

Teacher Self-Evaluation:

Evaluate your own use of materials and teaching opportunities: what worked and what did not; how effective was your time-management; how were your responses to the needs of your student; did you make your expectations clear; in what ways would you like to improve your approach for the next Unit? Incorporate suggestions from your students in your own evaluation (*this requires humility!*).

Phase 3

▶ Maps and Mapping

Physical Terrain

» Locate and label the major mountain ranges, deserts, rivers, and seas of China. Locate and label the major islands of Japan.

» Locate and label the major rivers, mountain ranges, and coastlands as they were in Prussia in the mid-1800s, and also label them as they currently are in Germany.

Geopolitical

» Shade Prussia in a dark color, then shade the German Empire in a lighter shade of the same color. Shade in France and Austria with separate colors to show these two countries who went to war with Prussia and lost.

» Mark the city of Edo (modern day Tokyo) in Japan, where Commodore Perry landed his ships in 1853.

» Mark on your map these cities of China where Hudson Taylor lived and worked: Shanghai, Ningbo, Hangzhou, Yangzhou. Also mark on the map the city of Beijing, which includes within its borders the Imperial City of China.

Explore

» **Alsace-Lorraine:** Discover the natural resources of this region, which France lost to the German Empire at the end of the Franco-Prussian War. In what ways would France have been affected by this loss?

» **Christian Outreach:** What is the status of evangelical outreach today in Northern Asia, including Japan and China? What opportunities and what difficulties face those who share the gospel in these areas?

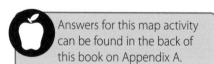

Answers for this map activity can be found in the back of this book on Appendix A.

◉ Create a map and discuss the issues in teams

The students each have an outline map in their manuals. They will be given assignments for drawing in the rivers, mountains, cities, and regional boundaries that are listed. For details on where these things are, please consult a historical atlas, an encyclopedia, or another source of geographic information.

Upper elementary students might be satisfied to accomplish only this portion:

• **Physical terrain:** This part of the mapping exercise will help students locate and mark a few of the major geologic features of China as well as the four major islands of Japan. China is the one of the largest countries in the world, so don't let students feel overwhelmed! In addition, students will locate and mark the rivers, mountain ranges, and coastlands of Prussia and of modern-day Germany.

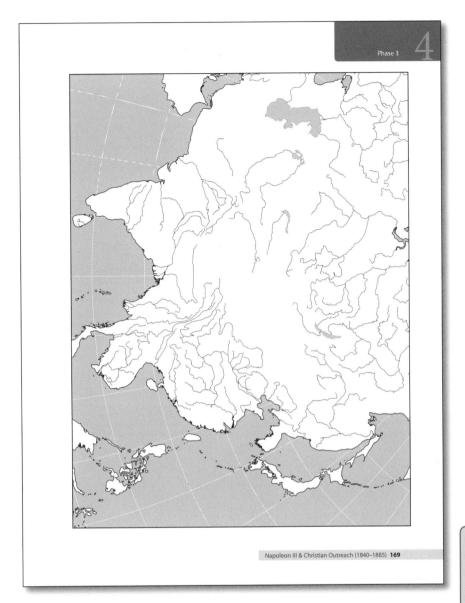

Middle school students might be satisfied to complete both the previous mapping exercise and this exercise:

- **Geopolitical:** This section of the mapping exercise will provide the students an opportunity to locate and mark the areas affected by the Franco-Prussian War, the location of Commodore Perry's historic visit, and the Chinese cities where Hud-son Taylor worked. (Online search engines offer an excellent way to find this information.)

High school students might be satisfied to complete both the previous mapping exercises and at least one exploration topic of this exercise:

- **Explore** a selection from this portion of the mapping exercise in teams.

ALSACE-LORRAINE:

Encourage students to look online for information concerning the strategic and industrial value of the region of Alsace-Lorraine, as this will be a contested area not only as a result of the Franco-Prussian War, but also during WWI and WWII.

CHRISTIAN OUTREACH:

Students might wish to locate information about the state of Christianity in Northern Asia today. (Note: There are many countries in the world today where Christian missionaries are not allowed to go. Yet, the church continues to grow through various means.) If possible, to provide even more help and insight, interview someone who has worked in these fields.

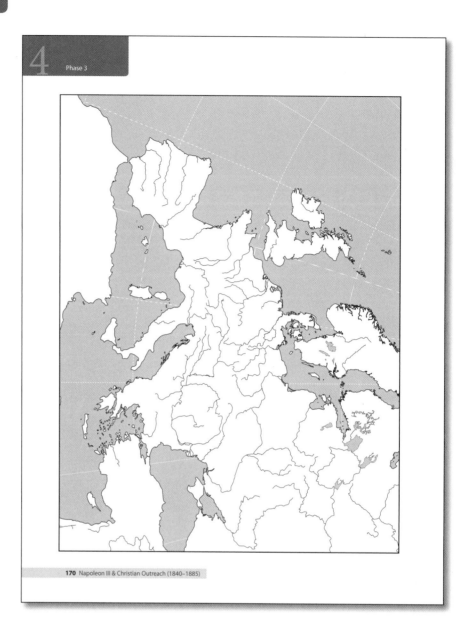

170 Napoleon III & Christian Outreach (1840–1885)

► Art Appreciation

Impression: soleil levant by Claude Monet

This is the painting, created in 1872, from which the Impressionist movement takes its name. Monet fled Paris during the Franco-Prussian War, seeking refuge in England. While there, he studied the works of Joseph Turner and John Constable, which encouraged him in his artistic pursuit of nature and light. You can find a link to see this painting—both a color version and a black and white version—at the online resource page.

» What do you immediately notice about the orb of the sun in the black and white version? How does Monet's use of color, light, and shadow affect this painting?

» Would you describe this painting as realistic? What other terms could be used? Why do you think the paintings of Monet, along with other Impressionists, were originally criticized and ridiculed?

» Compare this with Joseph Turner's painting *The Fighting Temeraire Tugged to Her Last Berth to Be Broken Up.* In what ways are the paintings similar? In what ways are they different?

Le Moulin de la Galette by Pierre-Auguste Renoir

Painted in 1876, this masterpiece of Impressionism has as its subject working-class people enjoying themselves during a typical Sunday afternoon in Paris. Renoir used the effects of dappled light and shadow to create this painter's "snapshot" of a very pleasant scene. You can find a link to see this painting at the online resource page.

» How would you describe this painting to someone who had never seen it before? How does it fit within the Impressionist style of painting?

CONSIDER:

Impressionism was an artistic revolution, completely changing the way artists viewed objects, light, and color. Instead of light establishing the form and color of an object, it was now itself the ephemeral focus, which meant that objects became less substantial and less discernible, even dissolving away.

The online resource page at www.HistoryRevealed.org contains many helpful Internet links to artwork, architecture, music, project helps, and more.

Napoleon III & Christian Outreach (1840–1885) **171**

◉ Examine and discuss art and architecture

The online resource page at www.HistoryRevealed.org has links to view each of the items listed. Allow the students time to observe the paintings without any conversation, and then, when they are ready, engage them in some or all of the questions listed below or in the Student Manual.

Art Appreciation

Impression: Sunrise, Le Havre by Claude Monet

Fascinating Fact: According to art historian Frederick Hartt, a newspaper story described the reaction of a visitor to the first Impressionist art exhibition (at which this painting was shown). According to the newspaper, the man was driven mad by this style of painting—he rushed out onto the street and started biting innocent bystanders!

Monet believed that the most intense optical sensations become possible when mixed—by the eye! So he painted masses of flecks of contrasting pure color to be mixed by the eye of the viewer. For instance, a spot of red next to a spot of yellow creates a vivid orange when viewed from a distance. His technique involved expressing both color and light in new ways. His focus was to capture the fleeting moment of time through his art—his "impressions"—rather than focusing on a particular subject or theme.

Ask students to view other paintings by Monet. What are their thoughts concerning this Impressionist style? Is it interesting? Is it beautiful? Is it effective? What does it communicate to them?

Le Moulin de la Galette by Pierre-Auguste Renoir

Impressionist artist Paul Signac wrote, "The entire surface of the [Impressionist] painting glows with sunlight; the air circulates; light embraces, caresses and irradiates forms; it penetrates everywhere, even into the shadows which it illuminates."

Ask students to give their opinions of Renoir's painting in light of Signac's description of Impressionist art.

Architecture

In response to a query about the Art Nouveau style of architecture, architect Kevin Havens writes:

In my opinion, what was unique and humanizing about the Art Nouveau movement was that it celebrated not only new construction technologies but also the artistic and decorative potential that these new materials offered. Unlike earlier architectural styles that derived expression from the ancient classics, the Art Nouveau architects *took inspiration from nature*, resulting in fluid, curving lines and flourishes derived from plants, animals, and landscape forms. This movement was strongly linked to the Arts and Crafts movement in painting and furniture design that began in England a few decades earlier. Art Nouveau was a powerful departure from anything *previously built*. It represented a revolt from repeating the styles of the past. The Art Nouveau designers were making their own rules and thus developed very personal styles that were difficult for others to copy, thus limiting the longevity of the movement.

Church of the Sagrada (Holy) Family, Barcelona designed by Antoni Gaudi

Antonio Gaudi was a Catholic who renounced secular art in his later years and dedicated most of his life to building the church. When questioned about the lengthy construction period, he would answer, "My client is not in a hurry." One of the most famous landmarks in Barcelona, the church was finally consecrated on Nov. 7, 2010, with Pope Benedict presiding. For a fascinating view of this building, see the link to the YouTube video at the online resource page.

Discuss with your students the Church of the Holy Family. Gaudi took over the design and construction of this building, which had first been planned to be, and was partially built, in the neo-Gothic style. In what ways did this structure obviously change as it moved from neo-Gothic to Art Nouveau?

Casa Milá, Barcelona designed by Antoni Gaudi

As art historian Frederick Hartt writes:

▶ Architecture

Art Nouveau (or "Modern Style") was a type of architecture popular in the late 1800s and early 1900s. Like the paintings of the Impressionists, Art Nouveau broke away from the historical forms and styles of architecture. This transitional phase of architecture was based on curving lines and vegetation-like forms, though eventually it developed into something that looked very different: a style that sought to remove all decoration—expressing, in architectural form, the "Machine Age."

Church of the Holy Family, Barcelona designed by Antoni Gaudi

» You can see a photo of this unfinished church at the online resource page. Gaudi worked on this building on from 1883 until his death in 1926. His design shows Art Nouveau's freedom from historical constraints. How would you describe this amazing structure?

Casa Milá, Barcelona designed by Antoni Gaudi

This apartment building, built in 1905–1907, avoids as much as possible the use of straight lines, flat surfaces, and any sort of symmetry. You can find a link to see photos of this building at the online resource page.

» Consider the roof line and the exterior of this building—what descriptive words could you use to explain its structure?

▶ Arts in Action

Select one or more, and let your artistic juices flow!

Create Impressionist Art

Try your hand at creating Impressionist art by using colored dots (red, yellow, blue) from the store. First, lightly sketch the outline of a simple outdoor scene, such as a meadow or lakeshore. Next, cut the colored dots into halves or fourths, appropriate to the size of your sketch. Finally, position the dots in appropriate places to create the colors you want. *Hint: lay the colored dots very near each other so they will blend well, and remember to "mix" your primary colors to achieve the color you want.*

red + yellow = orange   blue + red = purple   yellow + blue = green

» How far away do you have to stand to be able to recognize the image and the "blended" colors?

» Using orange crayons, tempera paint, or drawing pens, color a large orange (fruit) on paper. On a second piece of paper, create an "orange" using strokes of red with strokes of yellow next to each other. You may use dots instead of strokes if you prefer. Now, set both pictures up against a wall and move to the other end of the room. How far back do you need to go before the red and yellow "orange" blends to become the color orange? Which picture do you prefer? Why? What does it look like close up? Try this experiment with other objects—leaves, flowers, etc.—always using primary colors beside each other so they will blend into other shades when viewed from a distance.

The building is convulsed as if it were gelatin. Balconies ripple and flow, bulge and retract in a constant turmoil; windows reject vertical alignment. . . . Inner courtyards and corridors move with the random patterns of natural caverns, and the interior walls and partitions are so arranged that few are parallel and none meet at right angles.

A link to a fantastic online site for viewing the Casa Milá can be found at the online resource page. After looking through some of the details, ask students what they think it might be like to live in this apartment building.

▶ Science

In 1876, Alexander Graham Bell patented the basic design for a telephone. The ability to use electricity to carry sounds long distances—especially vocal sounds—revolutionized the world. It is important to note that Bell preferred to be remembered as a teacher of the deaf rather than the inventor of the telephone!

» Create a "telephone" with two paper drinking cups and twenty feet of waxed dental floss or fishing line. Make a small hole in the bottom of each of the cups. Then insert one end of the floss through the hole into one of the paper cups, tying it to a paper clip to keep the floss from slipping out. Do the same for the second cup. With students standing twenty feet apart and the line taut, have one hold the cup to his ear while the other speaks softly into the cup. What are the results? Try the experiment again while standing only fifteen feet apart, with the floss not held taut. Is it a different result? If so, how would you explain the difference?

The book *Thomas Edison for Kids* by Laurie Carlson has a number of science activities related to Edison's experiments and inventions. This would be a wonderful resource to own.

» With adult supervision, build an electrical circuit to test various materials to see whether they work as conductors of electrical current or as insulators that impede electrical current. *(Found on page 65.)*

▶ Music

Claude Debussy was one of the most significant composers in music history. He did as much to redirect music as Beethoven. He often wrote music that was as impressionistic as the art of French Impressionist painters like Monet. Art critic Camille Mauclair wrote, "The landscapes of Claude Monet are in fact symphonies of luminous waves, and the music of Monsieur Debussy . . . bears a remarkable resemblance to these pictures. It is Impressionism consisting of sonorous patches." His music left the traditional forms and traditional uses of harmony and melody, and moved toward creating an atmosphere of misty, dreamlike sounds. Though he was a musical genius, and his music shows incredible imagination and beauty, it has been said of his music, "It is the beginning of the twentieth century breakup of music." A convinced atheist, Debussy once said, "I have made a religion out of mysterious nature." Tragically, as his life drew to a close, this view left him without hope. He wrote in a letter, "I am a poor traveler waiting for a train that will never come anymore."

"Prélude à l'après-midi d'un faune"—Prelude to the Afternoon of a Faun by Debussy (1894)

You can find a link to listen to the music at the online resource page.

» How would you describe this music? Can you find the theme of the faun, which is heard several times during the piece? In what ways does this music seem similar to Impressionist paintings?

The online resource page at www.HistoryRevealed.org contains many helpful Internet links to artwork, architecture, music, project helps, and more.

◉ Do an art project

Create Impressionist art

The online resource page has links to a site where you can print a Monet coloring page of *Woman with a Parasol*, and a Renoir coloring page of *A Girl with a Watering Can*. To print, click on the button that says, "Imprimer la page" (French for "print the page").

◉ Do a science experiment

Feel free to choose one of these projects. If students love science, they might want to consider doing all of them!

If you would prefer to find an Internet source for an experiment on insulators and conductors, check out the online resource page for a link.

◉ Listen to and discuss the music

Listen

Debussy's *Prelude to the Afternoon of a Faun* (1894)

Jane Stuart Smith and Betty Carlson, in the book *The Gift of Music*, write of this composition, "Though not loud music, in a sense it broke sound barriers because it was unlike any music of the past. It is fragmented, with shimmering vibrations, and the emphasis is on individual voices."

You can listen to *Prelude to the Afternoon of a Faun* by going to the link at the online resource page.

▶ # Cooking

With the study of Hudson Taylor and the China Inland Mission, let's sample a taste of China. Chinese cooking includes many wonderful foods, though it often requires skill and lots of preparation time. There are relatively few desserts in Chinese cuisine, but this one is *wonderful!*

Almond Cookies

2¼ cups flour
1 egg
⅓ tsp salt
1 tsp almond extract
1½ tsp baking powder
5 dozen whole blanched almonds

1 cup shortening
1 egg yolk
½ cup granulated sugar
2 tbsp water
¼ cup firmly packed brown sugar

Preheat oven to 350ºF. Stir together flour, salt, and baking powder. In a bowl, cream shortening and both sugars until fluffy. Add egg and almond extract; beat until well blended. Add flour mixture and blend well.

Using about 1 tablespoon of the dough for each cookie, roll into a ball and place on ungreased baking sheet, two inches apart. Flatten each to make a 2-inch round. Press an almond into the center of each round. Beat egg yolk and water together; brush over each cookie.

Bake for 10 to 12 minutes, or until lightly browned around edges. Transfer to wire racks and let cool completely. Store in airtight containers. Makes about five dozen.

◉ Cook the food

Blanched Almonds

Blanched almonds are raw almonds with the skin removed. They are not hard to prepare:

- bring a pan of water to boil

- remove from heat

- add raw, shelled almonds and let sit for one minute (too long will make them soggy!)

- drain almonds, then run cool water over them

- place them in a single layer on kitchen towel until cool enough to handle

- squeeze almond between thumb and forefinger until skin slips off

- drain on paper towels or second kitchen towel

▶ Student Self-Evaluation UNIT 4, PHASE 3

Dates and hours:_____

Evaluate your projects

- List which of the activities listed in this Phase you did:

  _____

  _____

- Rate your enthusiasm: _____

  Explain: _____

  _____

- Rate the precision of your approach:_____

  Explain: _____

  _____

- Rate your effort toward the completion of the project: _____

  Explain: _____

  _____

- Ask yourself what worked and what did not. What would you do differently in the future, and what would you repeat?

  _____

  _____

- How did these hands-on activities enhance your knowledge of Napoleon III & Christian Outreach? What made them worthwhile?

  _____

  _____

- In the first three Phases of this Unit, what aspect of the time period has most captured your imagination? What would you like to creatively pursue to conclude your study?

  _____

  _____

Napoleon III & Christian Outreach (1840–1885) **175**

◉ Conduct a review and evaluation

In this Phase of Unit 4, your students should have had the opportunity to explore Napoleon III & Christian Outreach through various hands-on and creative sessions by completing a selection from the following:

- completed a mapping section;
- observed and discussed art & architecture;
- worked on an art project;
- experimented with a science project or taken a field trip;
- listened to music;
- tasted a food related to this Unit;

- completed their self-evaluation procedure for this Phase.

Record student hours: _____

Assess student involvement in the hands-on activities.

Create an evaluation system of your own or refer to the evaluation rubric in the introduction as a tool for assessing participation. The categories you will probably find most useful for evaluating projects are *"Task"* and *"Process: Teamwork."* Consider specifically the enthusiasm, the precision of approach, and the efforts toward improving skills and completing activities, rather than rating the project as compared to a masterpiece.

Do not critique the self-evaluation page your student completes in the Student Manual—it is acceptable for students to occasionally leave lines blank if a question does not apply. Instead, discuss with the student the intention of the written comments and incorporate those into your evaluation.

Determine a grade for this Phase, if using grades: _____

Teacher Self-Evaluation:

Evaluate your own use of materials: what worked and what did not? Consider your time management. Were you able to recognize and respond to your students' needs? Did you make your expectations clear? In what ways would you like to improve your approach for the next Unit? Incorporate suggestions from your students in your own evaluation (*this requires humility!*).

Phase 4

▶ In Your Own Way…

We have seen the successful unification of Italy as a nation; the forcible opening of China and Japan by Western governments; the rise of militaristic Prussia and its success in forming a second German Empire while at that very same moment France experienced humiliating defeat and the fall of its Second Empire; the establishment of the Salvation Army—a new type of evangelistic outreach to the laboring classes along with practical care and help for the poor; and the start of the second era of missions with the China Inland Mission, which took the gospel into the interior of China and looked to God for financial provision. Now, choose a selection of these activities, or create your own, which will best express what you have learned from this Unit.

LINGUISTICS

Journalism

Known for your courageous reporting, you have been assigned by your liberal Prussian newspaper to interview Otto von Bismarck right after his "Blood and Iron" speech to the Prussian Parliament. As you write your article, remember two things: the political wind seems to be shifting, and Bismarck has the wholehearted support of the Prussian king.

The Salvation Army has been gaining a lot of notice this year, 1890, in the English city where you live. Though they have been much maligned recently in the newspaper—especially by those who have been offended by William Booth's new book—you think the Salvation Army is doing a wonderful job for the poor and needy, both in sharing the Good News and in caring for material needs. In the hope that you can win others to your point of view, write a letter to the editor.

Limerick

Finish this limerick about Alexander Graham Bell.

There once was a man named Bell

Who thought it improper to yell…

Prose

Choose three episodes from Hudson Taylor's life and write them into a short, adventure-packed story for young children, illustrating the book with appropriate pictures, maps, photos, and other images.

As one of the thousand Redshirts fighting with Garibaldi for the independence of your beloved Italy, write a letter home to help your family understand the surprising and encouraging things that happened in Sicily and Naples, and to tell about the current rumors concerning Rome and Victor Emmanuel. Tell your story well so others might join!

◉ Choose an area of expression

Students may work either individually or in teams.

Linguistics:

Journalism

Students interested in writing about Bismarck might find it helpful for this article to consider, from an 1860s liberal perspective, what the future for Prussia and Germany might look like if he succeeds with his plan. (A grim consideration of Germany's future would be Hitler, another German leader who possessed some similarities to Bismarck.)

For students who want to write a letter to the editor, you can find at the online resource page a link to a fascinating site to learn more about Salvation Army history.

Limerick

For students who are unfamiliar with this form of poetry, there is a link to a helpful website at the online resource page.

Prose

To better understand how to appeal to young children, students might find it helpful to read a sampling of children's adventure books in a library or bookstore. Notice the way illustrations are used to help explain situations or create suspense in an adventure story. (One example of an adventure book for young children is *Madeline's Rescue* by Ludwig Bemelmans.)

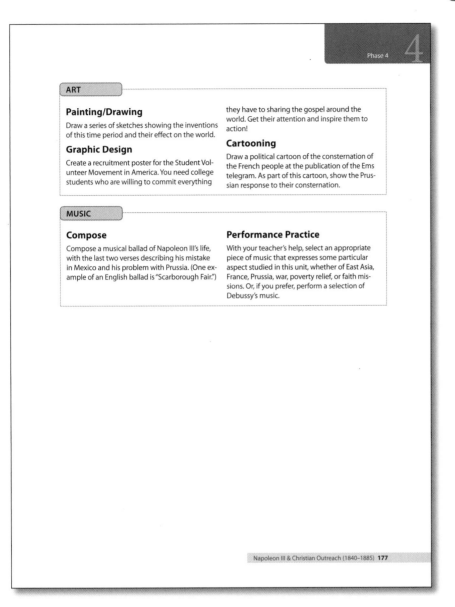

ART

Painting/Drawing

Draw a series of sketches showing the inventions of this time period and their effect on the world.

Graphic Design

Create a recruitment poster for the Student Volunteer Movement in America. You need college students who are willing to commit everything they have to sharing the gospel around the world. Get their attention and inspire them to action!

Cartooning

Draw a political cartoon of the consternation of the French people at the publication of the Ems telegram. As part of this cartoon, show the Prussian response to their consternation.

MUSIC

Compose

Compose a musical ballad of Napoleon III's life, with the last two verses describing his mistake in Mexico and his problem with Prussia. (One example of an English ballad is "Scarborough Fair.")

Performance Practice

With your teacher's help, select an appropriate piece of music that expresses some particular aspect studied in this unit, whether of East Asia, France, Prussia, war, poverty relief, or faith missions. Or, if you prefer, perform a selection of Debussy's music.

Napoleon III & Christian Outreach (1840–1885) **177**

Art:

Painting/Drawing

A link to an astonishing online resource for Edison's inventions can be found at the online resource page. It allows students to see not only written information but also sketches of his inventions.

Graphic Design

The Student Volunteer Movement slogan was "Evangelization of the world in this generation." Ask students interested in doing the recruitment poster what visual images this slogan suggests to them, then encourage them to incorporate those images into the poster.

Cartooning

Students intending to create this political cartoon might benefit from reading the actual telegrams—both the unedited version sent from King Wilhelm to Bismarck *and* the edited version sent from Bismarck to the newspapers. There is a link to a translation of these telegrams at the online resource page.

Music:

Compose

Simon and Garfunkel recorded an excellent version of this English ballad. A link to a live YouTube version is at the online resource page.

Performance Practice

For musical students, this selection may be a wonderful opportunity to express what they have learned. Make sure they select a piece that they have adequate time to prepare.

DRAMA

Comedy

Set the scene for D. L. Moody's talks at Cambridge University. He wrote, "There never was a place that I approached with greater anxiety than Cambridge. Never having had the privilege of a university education, I was nervous about meeting university men." According to revival historian J. Edwin Orr, Moody had good reason to be anxious—"There were many high-spirited students lying in wait for him. There were hoots and cheers, fire-crackers and guffaws, but Moody kept his temper." Be sure to end with the Cambridge Seven committing their lives to serve God on the mission field.

Puppetry

With puppets, create a depiction of a Salvation Army band gathering up folks to hear gospel preaching in a local theater. Be sure to show that not everyone responded favorably to the music or the preaching!

Drama

Dramatize the life and work of Louis Pasteur. Include the discovery of pasteurization and disproving spontaneous generation. The climax should be when he uses his rabies vaccine for the first time to save a young boy who will surely die without it.

Prop Needs

_____

_____

Costume Ideas

_____

_____

Role/Player

_____

_____

Set Suggestions

_____

_____

Drama:

Comedy

Figuring out how the audience might respond to what Moody says will be invaluable for students wishing to perform this comedy. Encourage students to choose a specific sermon (you can find a link to them online at the online resource page), and then to come up with a few jokes and puns that these non-churched young men might have used. See how many of those you can work into a crowd response. Remember, Moody never lost his temper! In fact, his good humor and attitude won the respect of many.

Puppetry

In order to make this scene work with only one or two puppeteers, you may want to consider using recorded music to simulate the band effect. Also, create a few appropriate slogans and catchy invitations in order to convince the crowds to come along with you. With the puppets and these slogans, invite actual people to come watch the puppet show. Then use them to invite the puppets to come to the meeting!

Drama

One way to approach this play is to write the script in the present tense, in which each event is happening at the moment. As Pasteur discovers or invents something, he could talk to the audience as though they were with him at that moment. Then find a way to transition between the various times and events of his life. This transition could be accomplished in various and creative ways: placards, an actor announcing a new time, costume changes, or cosmetic changes (adding a beard or gray hair). Be creative!

Movement:

Pantomime

Use music that would help the actor playing Hudson Taylor make these changes. One suggestion would be to have a dedicated "sound engineer" with traditional Chinese music on one CD player and traditional European music on a separate CD player. Then, by the use of volume on each CD player (whether Chinese music is heard or European music is heard), the audience will be able to comprehend Hudson Taylor's thoughts about what type of appearance is useful in the context of preaching the gospel to the Chinese. Also, it would be

MOVEMENT

Pantomime

Pantomime Hudson Taylor as he makes the critical decision to stop dressing as a European and starts the process of looking as Chinese as possible.

Dance

Choreograph a dance of Commodore Perry's interaction with the Japanese in 1853. In your dance, be sure to contrast the military marching of the US sailors on land with an oriental style of movement that would be appropriate for the Japanese.

Action

With a group of students using stylized action, depict these conflicts and their resolutions: Prussia against Denmark, Prussia against Austria, and Prussia against France.

CONCEPTUAL DESIGN

Design a City

Napoleon III commissioned Baron Georges Haussmann to bring the city of Paris out of its medieval clutter into the modern age: well organized, symmetrical, and classically beautiful. Now it's your turn. With the refurbished Paris as your example, choose a city—whether real or imagined—and design its upgrade.

CREATE YOUR OWN EXPRESSION

_____

_____

_____

_____

visually very helpful to have the two types of clothing in different locations on stage to clarify the action for the audience.

Dance

To gain a better understanding of Japanese movement, do an online search for videos of "traditional Japanese dance." If it is possible to have several dancers, students might want to consider experimenting with "choral movement," where a group of dancers do the same movements. If, for instance, there were three dancers showing the American movement and three dancers showing the Japanese movement, it would be very interesting visually. Also, while this choral work is proceeding, a soloist interpreting Commodore Perry while another soloist interprets the emissary of the Japanese emperor would allow the dance to show both choral and solo movement —fascinating!

Action

It might be helpful for students to understand the rule of three:

If it happens once, it's an accident.

If it happens twice, it's a coincidence.

If it happens three times, it's deliberate.

The way to utilize this rule onstage in movement can be described as setup, setup, payoff. The first two depictions are leading up to the third, but something about the third depiction needs to be surprising and different, even if a similar result occurs. So, in this instance, find a way to change what happens when Prussia goes up against another country so that the third time is a surprise.

Also, experiment with the physical size of the actors. Use their physical stature to help tell the story. (Example: Perhaps the smallest person is Prussia, and yet somehow the smallest person finds a way to overcome the others.)

Conceptual Design:

To better understand what Haussmann did, encourage students to read the article "Haussmann's Paris." A link can be found at the online resource page.

◉ Share creative expressions in class

Create a safe environment for the presentations. Set ground rules prior to the presentations, so that students know how much time is available for each of them, and so that they know they will be honored and respected by all those observing.

◉ Conduct a review and evaluation

In this Phase of Unit 4, your students should have had the opportunity to express what they have learned about Napoleon III & Christian Outreach through one or more various creative selections of their own choosing. These include:

- Linguistics;
- Art;
- Music;
- Drama;
- Movement;
- Conceptual Design.

Record student hours: _____

Assess student effort in the creative expressions, as individuals or as teams.

Create an evaluation system of your own, or refer to the evaluation rubric in the introduction, as a tool for assessing participation. The categories you will probably find most useful for evaluating their projects are *"Task," "Process: Teamwork," "Process: Originality,"* and Grammar, Format, and Spelling.

In this Phase especially, do not critique the self-evaluation page your student completes in the Student Manual—consider how the very soul of an artist has been exposed and vulnerable, so be encouraging and not belittling. Again, consider enthusiasm, precision of approach, and efforts toward improving skills and completing the activity, rather than rating the project as compared to a masterpiece. Instead, discuss with the student the intention of the written comments and incorporate those into your evaluation.

Determine a grade for this Phase, if using grades: _____

Teacher Self-Evaluation:

Evaluate your own use of materials and teaching opportunities: what worked and what did not; how effective was your time-management; how were your responses to the needs of your student; did you make your expectations clear; in what ways would you like to improve your approach for the next Unit? Incorporate suggestions from your students in your own evaluation (*this requires humility!*).

Take a moment now to evaluate the whole Unit. What would you like to remember if you taught this subject again? What do you recognize that your students gained most—either as students of history or as creative individuals? What did you learn about Napoleon III & Christian Outreach or about teaching?

▶ Student Self-Evaluation UNIT 4, PHASE 4

Dates and hours:_____

Evaluate your projects

- What creative project did you choose:

  _____

- What did you expect from your project, and how does the final project compare to your initial expectations?

  _____
  _____

- What do you like about your project? What would you change?

  _____
  _____

In Conclusion

Revisit the five Key Concepts from the beginning of this Unit. Explain how your understanding of and appreciation for each has grown over the course of your study.

- _____
  _____
- _____
  _____
- _____
  _____
- _____
  _____
- _____

Record your concluding thoughts on Napoleon III & Christian Outreach:

_____

Alliances & Revivals
(1860–1913)

*Pray with the students
at the beginning of each Unit.*

*Enthusiasm and delight
are the best ways to capture
a student's interest and
jump-start motivation, so:*

» **For the Auditory Students:** To capture their attention at the very beginning of class, consider playing one of the best-known musical pieces by the Russian composer Rimsky-Korsakov: "Flight of the Bumblebee." (You can find links at the online resource page to hear the US Army Band playing this or watch pianist Yuja Wang play it—wow!)

» **For the Kinesthetic Students:** Have the students warm up as class begins by doing an action that will prepare them for the "balance of power" in this Unit, such as having three students, with straight bodies, feet touching and hands clasped, lean sideways or backwards as far as they can go while still maintaining their balance.

» **For the Visual Students:** Bring a visual object to stimulate their interest in the new Unit, such as a copy of *Starry Night* by Postimpressionist artist Vincent van Gogh.

» **For the hearts of all:** Pray with them at the beginning of the Unit, that God would help them discover what He has for each one to learn in this Unit.

◉ Learning Style Emphasis

Teachers can choose to have students do one or two activities, rather than the entire week's schedule. Please use what works for you in your unique setting.

	Week 1: Feeler	Week 2: Thinker	Week 3: Sensor	Week 4: Intuitor
	During this week, students will be introduced to Alliances & Revivals, along with the appropriate Scriptures. You may follow this suggested schedule or adapt it to meet your students' needs:	Students will explore topics of interest through research and reporting, learn new vocabulary, and construct a time line relating to Alliances & Revivals.	Students will gain cultural understanding through sensory activities as they explore interrelated subject areas through sensory activities pertaining to Alliances & Revivals.	Through creative self-expression, using one or more creative activities, students will present some aspect of what they have learned in the past three weeks relating to Alliances & Revivals. Areas of expression include linguistics, art, music, drama, movement, and conceptual design.
Monday	Informally discuss the Key Concepts Listen to the *What in the World?* audio recording(s)	Choose topic and begin research	Create a map and discuss the issues in teams	Choose an area of expression and begin work either individually or in teams
Tuesday	Read the article Listen to the other audio recording(s) Read the Scriptures		Examine and discuss art masterpieces & architectural structures	
Wednesday	Recap the material using activities Talk together	Practice vocabulary	Do an art project*	
Thursday	Conduct class discussion	Construct the time line	Do a science experiment or field trip**	
Friday	Choose books of interest/Internet search Conduct a review and evaluation	Complete research projects and share in class or hand in Conduct a review and evaluation	Listen to and discuss the music Cook the food listed in the recipe Conduct a review and evaluation	Share creative expressions in class Conduct a review and evaluation

*Art project will need to be planned ahead of time to acquire materials.

** Field trip will require extra planning time.

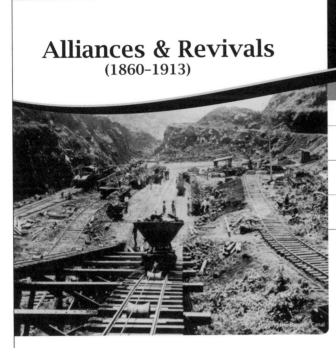

Alliances & Revivals
(1860–1913)

UNIT 5

Key Concepts

- The Balkans

- Turn-of-the-Century Russia

- Upsetting the Balance of Power

- Worldwide Revivals

Digging the Panama Canal

Growing Conflict

What would happen if two strong and determined people worked eagerly to achieve their goals, but each one's goals turned out to be in conflict and incompatible with the other's, even mutually exclusive? If the goals were greatly desired, then tension, strife, and even violence might well be the outcome. What if it were two strong and determined nations seeking incompatible goals? Political tension, aggressive posturing, and even war would result.

With that in mind, consider the effect of more than a dozen nations seeking aggressively to attain their own goals—driven by such powerful motivators as nationalism, economics, and imperialism—while each one's goals are at cross-purposes with the others'. That is the nature of international relationships during the last decades of the nineteenth century and

Alliances & Revivals (1860–1913) **181**

◉ Informally discuss the Key Concepts with your students

KEY CONCEPTS Background Information

These are the main objectives of the Unit. As you proceed through the four weeks, your students will be given various ways of understanding each of these objectives. Explanations of these Key Concepts follow.

5

the first of the twentieth. Empires such as the Russian, British, German, and Ottoman; countries such as the United States, Japan, Serbia, France, China, and the Transvaal (South Africa); regions such as the Balkans; and islands such as Cuba—all pursued their own concerns, their own needs, and their own interests. These often conflicted violently with the needs and interests of others and produced rising tensions internationally.

Into this volatile mix were added three other turn-of-the-century ingredients. The first was vastly improved technologies in transportation and war—indeed, some call this time the Second Industrial Revolution. Second, there was a determined race between various Western nations to grab as much African and Asian land as possible and to create colonial empires for themselves. Third, there was the political application of Darwin's concept of the "survival of the fittest"—that a nation could become strong enough, large enough, and technologically advanced enough to face all opponents in war and emerge as not only survivor, but victor.

> God sent seasons of supernatural revival that resulted in a dramatic awakening of the church and a powerful evangelizing of those outside.

Yet, amazingly, in the midst of these human plans for struggle and conquest, there was One at work who had a greater power and a higher motivation than all. As has been described in earlier units, from time to time and place to place, God sent seasons of supernatural revival that resulted in a dramatic awakening of the church and a powerful evangelizing of those outside. The turn of the century would see unprecedented revival, bringing new life and hope to millions upon millions, but also preparing communities and nations for the wholesale destruction that would soon be unleashed in the world—in Europe and, to a lesser degree, in East Asia.

In attempting to avoid that doomsday scenario—worldwide war—European governments since Napoleon had been constantly maneuvering to build strategic political alliances with one another. As they had painfully learned with Napoleonic France, if any nation had too much power, it easily forced its will upon others. This prompted a political theory that said each nation needed only enough power to be able to protect its own territories. If alliances could be formed between nations, strength in numbers would allow them to dissuade an aggressive nation from rising up to overstep its boundaries and dominate them all. With alliances, they could achieve a *balance of power*. To restrain potential enemies they would befriend even former foes. This meant that, for instance, though England and France had been the bitterest of enemies, in the climate of a newly revitalized and increasingly aggressive German Empire, they agreed to form a friendly political alliance in order to keep Germany at bay. Such an alliance was an abrupt change in policy and a diplomatic revolution between longstanding opponents. All of this and more was done by European nations to maintain a theoretical balance of power.

182 Alliances & Revivals (1860–1913)

? To get an informal discussion started on this Key Concept, ask a simple leading question, such as, "What do you know about the region of the Balkans?"

The Balkans— EXPLANATION

If you were to locate Europe on a globe, you would notice that, just east of the "boot" of Italy, a somewhat triangular peninsula points down into the Mediterranean, between the Adriatic and Aegean seas, then continues up along the western coast of the Black Sea. This is the Balkan Peninsula with its wide diversity of languages, ethnicities, and religions. The Balkans include Greece, Serbia, Montenegro, Croatia, Bosnia and Herzegovina, Slovenia, Macedonia, Albania, Moldova, Romania, and Bulgaria. At the southern tip of the peninsula, you would find Greece and the Greek islands. Directly opposite them, across the Aegean, lies the westernmost part of Asia. You would notice how Europe and Asia intersect in this critical triangle, and you would begin to understand how the Balkans have been so significant

in world history, from the time of the Roman Empire.

With this prime location, you can see why the Balkans were so very desirable to the Ottoman Empire, who had taken the entire Balkan region by 1481 (including Constantinople, which they renamed Istanbul). With the addition of this territory, the Ottomans spanned three continents—ruling not only western Asia and northern Africa, but the southeastern part of Europe as well.

By the 1800s, however, the Ottoman Empire had lost its strength and was in a state of decline. The growth of nationalism, where people who

spoke the same language and shared the same history sought to form their own nation independent from overlords, had a tremendous influence on the Balkan region throughout this century. In 1821, Greece was the first of the Balkans to declare its independence from Ottoman control. In 1876, Serbia and neighboring Montenegro declared war on the Ottoman Turks. This, along with the simultaneous Bulgarian revolt, which was brutally suppressed, drew the Russian giant into yet another war with the Ottomans. (Only two decades earlier, they had been fighting each other in the Crimean War.)

5

One of the most ticklish and long-lived challenges to this balance was the "Eastern Question," which concerned the southeastern part of Europe, known as the Balkans. Ruled for more than four centuries by the Muslim Ottoman Empire, this region of the world was a variety of ethnicities (including Serbs, Croats, Montenegrins, Slovenes, Greeks, Bulgarians, Macedonians, Albanians, Romanians, Jews, Romas, Turks, and Magyars), languages (Serbian, Croatian, Bosnian, Montenegrin, Slovene, Macedonian, Bulgarian, Greek, and more), and religions (Eastern Orthodox, Roman Catholic, Muslim, Jewish, even Protestant). Predominantly Eastern Orthodox and detesting their Turkish overlords, many of the people in the Balkans looked to Mother Russia, which was religiously Orthodox and politically ambitious, as the one most likely to liberate them from the Ottomans. Despite the desires of the Balkan people, England was utterly opposed to Russian involvement, as this would undoubtedly increase Russia's strength and weaken the Ottoman Empire—upsetting the balance of power in the region. Britain's participation in the recent Crimean War— supporting the Ottomans and fighting the Russians—was one example of how strongly they felt about this.

Beyond religious ties, there was another factor of Russian interest in the Balkans. Since the days of Catherine the Great, Russia had been intent on capturing Constantinople (Istanbul), because of it's strategic value in guaranteeing access to the Mediterranean. With most of its ports encased in ice during long arctic winters, Russia needed to be able to freely move in and out of the Black Sea—through Constantinople—in order to function as a world power. Great Britain was intent on preventing Russia from gaining such a port, as a full-time Russian navy might interfere with British interests in maintaining and defending its round-the-globe empire. The balance of power in Europe generally and in the Balkan region specifically was helped, in the British perspective, by having the massive and powerful Russian nation periodically hemmed in by the weather.

The region was not politically stable, however, regardless of the desires of the European great powers. In 1875, peasants in the Balkan area of Bosnia and Herzegovina rose in revolt against Ottoman tax collectors because, although their crops had failed, the harvest tax was still due. This revolt soon escalated into an international conflict, as not only other Balkan groups but European nations took a hand in the proceedings. Then, in 1876, Serbia and Montenegro rebelled against the Ottomans in the western Balkans, while Bulgaria revolted in the east. When an American war correspondent, Januarius MacGahan, described Turkish reprisals in response to the revolt in Bulgaria, the West was horrified, the Ottomans vilified.

> *Since the days of Catherine the Great, Russia had been intent on capturing Constantinople (Istanbul), because of it's strategic value in guaranteeing access to the Mediterranean.*

But Russia's involvement in the Balkans was not solely the role of a disinterested observer rushing to assist a helpless victim. Instead, Russia was motivated by one of its greatest national needs—free access into and out of the Mediterranean from its Black Sea ports. With the control of the Balkans, Russia would gain the port city of Istanbul, which is both ice-free and one of the most strategic ports—for trade and for war—in the world.

The people of the Balkans were not unaware of Russia's mixed motives, but they were glad to avail themselves of any who could rid them of the Muslim Ottomans. As mentioned in the Unit 5 article, Russia was seen by people of the Balkans as the nation most able to help them throw off the yoke of Ottoman control. The largest Slavic country in the world, Russia was also Orthodox in religion—which gave them preeminence in the largely Slavic and Orthodox Balkans. To many, Orthodox Russia was a better choice than Catholic Austria-Hungary (another close and extremely interested neighbor). This attitude would come into play when Austria-Hungary, under the terms of the Treaty of Berlin in 1878, was granted the right to occupy the Balkan area of Bosnia and Herzegovina. The Europeans demanded this occupation in order to balance Russia's increasing power in the Balkans, though it was bitterly opposed by not only Bosnia and Herzegovina but Serbia as well.

The drive to remove the Ottomans from the Balkans, the struggle between Russia and Europe for control of the Balkans, and the fierce nationalism within various people groups inside the Balkans were not solved by the Treaty of Berlin. In fact, this geographical junction between Europe and Asia was becoming an unstable and volatile powder keg. With the Balkan Wars of 1912–13, this powder keg was primed to explode the world into war.

5

These events produced, according to Winston Churchill, "the most difficult and dangerous situation for Great Britain since the Napoleonic wars." Why? Because British public opinion did an about-face—suddenly viewing the Ottomans as the most evil of enemies. With the public enraged by Turkish atrocities in Bulgaria, the idea of Great Britain supporting the Ottoman Empire was no longer politically expedient. Russia, able to take advantage of this moment, determined to come to the rescue of the Christian Balkans by declaring war on the Ottomans in 1877.

Public opinion is fickle, foreign policy changeable. When it was reported in Britain that the Russians, in their war against the Ottomans, were now advancing triumphantly on the city of Constantinople despite a truce to end the war, the British were outraged. It produced a war fever that can be seen in this popular song:

> We don't want to fight, but by Jingo if we do
> We've got the ships, we've got the men, we've got the money too!
> We've fought the Bear before, and while we're Britons true
> The Russians shall not have Constantinople.

Public opinion is fickle, foreign policy changeable.

The result of this *jingoism*, or "belligerent nationalism," was that the British fleet sailed into the waters of Constantinople, where it held the Russian army back from the city for six long months. It was during this uneasy standoff that Russia and the Ottomans signed the Treaty of San Stefano to end the war. The terms of this treaty, however, deeply angered the European great powers, since its provisions would have virtually given control over the Balkans to Russia. War would have been the result if diplomacy had not saved the day. The Congress of Berlin produced a new treaty, which was enthusiastically hailed by Europe, though only grudgingly tolerated by Russia. The Treaty of Berlin was acclaimed by the British Lord Deaconsfield as "peace with honor." This uneasy peace would endure thirty-four years.

Not everyone was satisfied with the results, however, particularly those actually living in the Balkans. For them, the San Stefano Treaty would have finally removed the hated Ottomans from the Balkans—one of their most important and long-standing goals. The European-engineered Treaty of Berlin, with its concern to restore a balance of power, did not keep this provision. Instead, it returned many areas of the Balkans to Ottoman control, including the highly-coveted land of Macedonia. Bulgaria, favored by Russia, would have been greatly enlarged under the terms of the first treaty, but under the Treaty of Berlin, it shrunk to one-third of its size. Bosnia and Herzegovina, rather than being self-governing, as had been decided under the San Stefano Treaty, was now to be occupied by the Austro-Hungarian empire. And Russia, the actual victor in the war, was now humiliated by the peace. It could ill afford this loss of prestige.

184 Alliances & Revivals (1860–1913)

? To get an informal discussion started on this Key Concept, ask a simple leading question, such as, "What do you think conditions were like in Russia as it entered the twentieth century?"

Turn-of-the-Century Russia—EXPLANATION

Since the days when Peter the Great first introduced Western ideas into Russia and Catherine the Great expanded her domain into central Europe, Russia had been one of the major players in European politics. More than three times the size of Europe, Russia was a force to reckon with. This fact had been highlighted when Czar Alexander I's troops chased Napoleon all the way back to Paris after his unsuccessful invasion of Russia in 1812. After the Congress of Vienna redrew the lines of post-Napoleonic Europe, Russia's stature and influence could be seen in the "Holy Alliance," which brought Prussia and Austria into active partnership with Russia.

However, despite its acceptance as a great power in the eyes of Europe, Russia was still steeped in ancient feudal practices, with the majority of its vast number of people living as serfs bound to the land. But by the mid-1800s, the revolutionary concepts of freedom and liberty were being considered. Indeed, Czar Alexander II, in one of the most radical acts in Russian history, emancipated the forty-seven million serfs. Unfortunately, his action lacked the wisdom and foresight to provide adequately for their desperate and growing need for land, which led to injustice and abuses. The former serfs often ended up with the poorest land, for which they had to pay continuous taxes to the government. As you might imagine, the unfairness of the situation and their hopeless yet dire need caused a seething unrest among a huge portion of the population.

The industrial revolution did not fully come to Russia until the late 1800s, but when it came, it produced many of the same horrific conditions that had been experienced in other countries. Extraordinarily long hours, survival wages, awful living situations, being cheated out of one's

5

The ongoing nineteenth-century struggle between reactionaries and liberals in western Europe had its corresponding counterpart in Russia, though this counterpart was, of course, culturally unique. Just as reactionary Europe looked to the historic past for guidance, even so the slavophiles of Russia (lovers of Slavic culture and Russian Orthodoxy) looked to their historic past for solutions to current problems. They traced many of Russia's prevailing difficulties to the westernization of their country, beginning in the early 1700s with Peter the Great. On the completely opposite philosophical side of the table were the Westernizers, the champions of this very same Western culture. They believed that Russia's best hope was to imitate the ways of the liberal West, and considered the "all things Russian" slavophiles outdated and old-fashioned.

A third option was introduced into this polarized debate to be described, discussed, promoted—and suppressed. This was the brand new philosophy of *nihilism* (in its early form, a rejection of *all* authority except science; in its later Russian form, a justification of terror and savagery to gain individual freedom). Elevating scientific reason while rejecting church, government, and family, nihilism sought to discard both the traditions of historic Russia and the liberal innovations of the West. Though nihilism, along with the associated idea of anarchy (a state of lawlessness and disorder), eventually created havoc in the country, at this point it was only a tiny drop in an ocean of Russian autocracy and Orthodoxy.

To better understand conditions in Russia at this point, it is important to note that the Russian czar was the head of the Russian Orthodox Church, and it was his strongest supporter. This in itself was not entirely unique, as the British monarch was also the "supreme governor" of the Anglican Church. But unlike the British monarch, Russia's czar was not only the religious leader of millions of people but also an absolute ruler. This meant that his word was supreme law: there was literally no limit to his power, and Russia had no "bill of rights" to which he must defer. This close identification between Church and State would later bring tragic consequences, as the growing restlessness of peasants and industrial workers eventually led to a revolution that rejected both religion and ruler.

As Russia's humiliation in the Treaty of Berlin became known, revolutionary unrest throughout the country increased, focused especially on the person of Czar Alexander II. In 1881, after many close brushes with lethal anarchists, he was finally assassinated. His son and successor, Alexander III, was thoroughly opposed to Western liberalizing ideas, believing they had encouraged anarchy and nihilism. In fact, his tutor referred to Abraham

Elevating scientific reason while rejecting church, government, and family, nihilism sought to discard both the traditions of historic Russia and the liberal innovations of the West.

rightful wages by greedy bosses— all these and more brought about a desperate hunger for significant change among Russia's industrial and factory workers. This large and discontented group, bound together by their shared experiences of misery and exploitation, was persuaded into believing that the revolutionary and anti-capitalistic works of Karl Marx held the key to a better future.

Adding to the unrest of the peasants and the despair of the workers was Russia's humiliating defeat by Japan in 1905, which displayed to the Russian people and the world that Russia was no longer a great power. This sobering event, along with increas-ing worker strikes, military mutinies, and terrorism, pushed Czar Nicholas II into setting up a constitutional monarchy. He was not happy with the results, however, and sought to limit and restrict the people's power as much as possible.

At this point, the Russians were tired and distrustful of their czar and his autocracy. Instead of continuing to look to him as their political and economic champion, they looked to other solutions in government, other types of leadership or philosophy, that could solve the problems of their immense and unstable country. One group, the enlightened noblemen and industrialists, thought that a parliamentary system such as the British had would be the best answer. A second group, the urban industrial workers and radical intellectuals, were most impressed with Marxist ideas, believing that it held the answers to their troubles. The third group, socialist-revolutionaries, with their philosophy "all the land for those who labor," appealed to the peasant majority. All three groups had mutually exclusive solutions for a complex and intricate problem.

For all those who looked carefully, the end of Russia's status quo was in sight.

5

Alexander III

Lincoln's description of American government—of the people, for the people, and by the people—as the "most terrible heresy since Servitus denied the Trinity."

With this kind of rhetoric ringing in his ears, the new czar decided that the best thing for Russia was to embrace Orthodoxy, autocracy, and Russian culture. In this way, Russia would find its strength and place in the world. Unfortunately, instead of strengthening Russia, this policy—and the accompanying suppression of anything or anyone that disagreed—actually increased the momentum of forces tearing Russia apart.

Going back a few decades and further east, not far from Russia's easternmost boundary, the Asian nation of Japan had taken a completely different approach to solving its problems. Rather than looking to its historic past, it began to look to the West. When Commodore Perry brought Japan face to face with the force of the Western powers during the nineteenth century, it produced a violent internal struggle—between the shogun (the hereditary military ruler) on the one side, and the samurai (the class of military nobility) and the daimyo (the feudal lords) on the other. This struggle to deal with the new foreigners and their demands led to the restoration of the Japanese emperor as the political leader in 1868. Recognizing that the Western powers were strong because of their industrial might and their educational systems (creating soldiers, industrial workers, citizens, and leaders), Japan began to transform itself into a modern state by learning about industrialization and education from the United States, France, and Great Britain. In addition, Japan updated and increased its military power, modeling its navy on Britain's, considered to be the best in the world. But the German Empire, with its increasing brilliance in military arts, science, industry, and education, was increasingly noticed and valued by Japan as well. This gave the Germans great influence during the 1880s and early '90s. With a dedicated and energetic study of Western ideas and technology, Japan had, by the mid-1890s, become an industrialized country with formidable military power.

> *Japan had, by the mid-1890s, become an industrialized country with formidable military power.*

Learning well the lessons of its Western counterparts, Japan went to war with China in the Sino-Japanese War of 1894. The object of this war was the country of Korea, China's most important *client state* (a country that is economically or politically dependent on a larger country). Like China, Korea was experiencing political tension and division over the issue of tradition versus modernization. Japan, with its pro-West approach, supported the radical modernizers of Korea, while China supported the traditional conservatives.

? To get an informal discussion started on this Key Concept, ask a simple leading question, such as, "What do you think upset the balance of power among nations at the turn of the century?"

Upsetting the Balance of Power—EXPLANATION

While the smoke from the Waterloo battlefield cleared in 1815, the newly triumphant European rulers and diplomats resolved to prevent any nation from ever gaining the same power and control over Europe that Napoleon had taken. Balancing the power of each one seemed so appropriate that it became the standard European policy from that time forward.

Imagine a playground teeter-totter (seesaw) as the balance of power: if there was a strong power on one side, several smaller powers might form an alliance on the opposite side in order to even it out, to establish a balance. This, in fact, continued to take place throughout the 1800s and early 1900s as treaties (public or secret) were signed between various nations to form alliances that would protect them from the aggressions of others.

At the conclusion of the Franco-Prussian War in 1870, Bismarck had finally succeeded in forming the German Empire, though it was at France's expense. From that moment, he knew that France would earnestly seek an opportunity for revenge on Germany, especially over the ownership of Alsace-Lorraine. This highly desired region, now a part of the German Empire, was considered by France to rightfully be French territory.

Bismarck was unafraid of a lone France exacting vengeance on a much more powerful Germany, but France in combination with other powers, like Russia and Great Britain, might become far too strong to defeat. It was for this reason that Bismarck worked hard to maintain alliances with Austria-Hungary, Russia, and Great Britain. For Great Britain, he sought to pacify their fears by keeping clear of the imperialist race for colonies (until 1884) and by avoiding a naval rivalry. For the others, he formed the Three Emperors' League

5

When the Korean king appealed to China for assistance in quelling a peasant rebellion, China sent troops. This violated an earlier treaty between China and Japan, however, so Japan decided it was well within its rights to send troops to fight the Chinese—in Korea. That action started a war which foreign observers predicted China, with nearly limitless numbers of soldiers, would easily win. However, this was Japan's moment. All the modernizing, industrializing, and militarizing paid off. Within eight months, the island nation of Japan had shown the world that it had the ability to score overwhelming victories on both land and sea against a much larger enemy. It was the emergence of Japan as a fully functioning modern nation, on par with the nations of the West. And it was also an utterly shocking moment of humiliation for China. To have been beaten by the European great powers would have been humiliating enough, but in a dramatic reversal of China's centuries-old status as the supreme power in East Asia, the winner of this war was one of China's peripheral and much smaller neighbors, Japan.

Japan had shown the world that it had the ability to score overwhelming victories on both land and sea against a much larger enemy.

In the treaty that ended this war, Japan received the Liaodong Peninsula (including the strategic city of Port Arthur) in northern China, the island of Taiwan, and a substantial amount of money from China as a war indemnity. And Korea was recognized as independent of China. The nations of the West were stunned and concerned at this new competent and aggressive rival in the East, not wishing to see a change in the balance of power in the East, which had been centered on China. Indeed, a Russian diplomat wrote, "The nation which controls Port Arthur holds a pistol pointed at the head of China." So, Russia, France, and Germany protested against the terms of the treaty, demanding that Japan give the Liaodong Peninsula back to China. Japan reluctantly complied.

It is interesting to consider that the German Empire, a newcomer to Western intrigues in the East, would be one of those protesting against Japan's spoils of war. Prior to this time, under the guiding hand of Bismarck, Germany had focused on maintaining its gains in Europe through carefully nurtured diplomatic alliances. However, a new wind began to blow as Kaiser Wilhelm II, a determined young ruler, mounted the throne. In 1888, after the death of his grandfather, Wilhelm I, and, three months later, his own father, this militaristic twenty-nine year old took office. Rather than continuing to allow the chancellor to control the affairs of state, Wilhelm II came to power with the intent of not only reigning over the German Empire but ruling as well.

Kaiser Wilhelm II

between Germany, Austria-Hungary, and Russia. It did not last, though, because of conflict between Russia and Austria-Hungary. So he had to replace that with a pair of treaties: the Triple Alliance between Germany, Austria-Hungary, and Italy, and a separate treaty of alliance between Germany and Russia, known as the Reinsurance Treaty. Each of these treaties was to be renewed periodically.

When the young Kaiser Wilhelm II took over the reins of office, he disregarded Bismarck's policies and formed his own. Because the kaiser saw great opportunities available to Germany in the Balkans and the Ottoman Empire, he decided in 1890 to not renew Germany's treaty with Russia. This alarmed Russia, which saw the Balkans as its own sphere of influence, so Russia formed an alliance with France in 1894—the very scenario which Bismarck had been striving to avoid.

Wilhelm II, determined that Germany should be viewed not only as a powerhouse in Europe, but also as a powerhouse in the world, made a decision in the early 1900s to build a German navy equivalent to the powerful German army—seeking to attain the same prestige and reputation as Great Britain. This was alarming in the extreme to the British. Great Britain therefore sought an alliance with France in 1904—the Entente Cordiale—which was extended to include Russia in 1907. This diplomatic encirclement of the German Empire greatly alarmed both the kaiser and his military.

With Germany, Austria-Hungary, and Italy on one side and France, Great Britain, and Russia on the other, the stage was set for a colossal struggle between vast armies and tremendous firepower. All it needed was a spark, which the Balkans would provide.

5

This new ruler soon came into open conflict with his long-powerful chancellor, bringing about Bismarck's resignation in 1890. With Bismarck and his Euro-centered policies gone, an increasingly industrialized Germany began to flex its muscles around the world. The conflict between China and Japan was a prime opportunity for Germany to involve itself in Asian affairs, though it had no direct concern in the matter. More importantly, joining this international protest helped Germany to build a closer relationship with Russia, which *did* have direct concerns in the matter—it wanted Port Arthur, which had been contested in the Sino-Japanese War, since it was a warm-water port very close to Russia's eastern edge. Not only could Germany show solidarity with the Russians, but it could also encourage them to look more toward China and less toward the Balkans, which were becoming quite interesting to Germany. Indeed, the kaiser had already visited the Ottoman Sultan, declaring himself a friend to the Muslim Turks. This welcome offer of friendship from a European power soon brought about economic concessions for Germany and the right for them to build a "Berlin to Baghdad" railway line—a concept that was viewed with alarm by others in Europe who also had designs on the Balkans.

> *Hundreds of missionaries and thousands of Chinese Christians were martyred during this awful moment.*

Two years after China's defeat by Japan, two German missionaries were killed in Shandong Province on the northeastern coast of China. Seizing this as an excuse for military intervention, Germany immediately sent a fleet to seize Qingdao, a port city in Shandong. This was the beginning of *weltpolitik*, the new foreign policy of Kaiser Wilhelm II, in which Germany would aggressively seek "its place in the sun." The capture of Qingdao was the inadvertent beginning of a great scramble for China among the Western nations, as each sought to gain benefits to themselves from the obviously weakened giant. The fear of being partitioned, along with the recent humiliation by Japan, caused an uproar in China, leading to the murderous Boxer Rebellion of 1900–1901. Beginning as a violent anti-Christian movement, it quickly grew to include murder of any foreigners and destruction of all things foreign, since they were believed to be the source of China's current woes.

Hundreds of missionaries and thousands of Chinese Christians were martyred during this awful moment. Yet their deaths were not in vain. According to Dr. J. Edwin Orr, "The Chinese Christians had acquitted themselves bravely in their hour of martyrdom and persecution, so much curiosity and interest was aroused in the hearts of acquaintances. An itinerating bishop reported that all the churches were crowded to capacity, with increased opportunities of preaching." In fact, from this point, a prayer movement began, which led to a widespread awakening in China in 1906–7, and "extraordinary revival" throughout 1908–9.

> **?** To get an informal discussion started on this Key Concept, ask a simple leading question, such as, "Why do you think God sends revival?"

Worldwide Revivals— EXPLANATION

We need to first define what a revival means as described in these Units, since it is not the same as a "revival service" or a "tent revival" or "revival meetings" or any activity generated by Christians (including our human attempts to take back culture). Instead, it is something so far beyond human activity or planning, so far beyond the measure of an evangelistic endeavor, that were we to experience it, we would be like the first century disciples in the upper room on the Day of Pentecost—in utter awe at the stunning power of God's Spirit, without a shred of pride for our own participation in it. The leading historian of the revivals of the eighteenth through twentieth centuries, Dr. J. Edwin Orr, wrote, "An Evangelical Awakening is a movement of the Holy Spirit bringing about a revival of New Testament Christianity in the Church of Christ and in its related community. . . . The major marks of an Evangelical Awakening are always some repetition of the phenomena of the Acts of the Apostles, followed by the revitalizing of nominal Christians and by bringing outsiders into vital touch with the Divine Dynamic causing all such Awakenings—the Spirit of God."

So, then, *revival* is an unusual, supernatural occurrence that God does by His Spirit in His church, which also powerfully draws non-believers to the Lord. Historically, it happens from time to time and in different places around the world. Jesus had told His disciples, "But you shall receive power when the Holy Spirit has come upon you; and you shall be witnesses to Me. . . to the end of the earth" (Acts 1:8). This was fulfilled supernaturally in the book of Acts and in every true revival since then.

As we have noted thus far in *World Empires, World Missions, World Wars*, the Second Awakening took place in the early 1800s and the Great Prayer Revival began in the mid-1800s, both sweeping across much of the evangelized world. The worldwide revival

5

Boxer Rebellion

The revival in East Asia was not limited to China, however. One of the greatest revivals in history took place in Korea during this same time period. To set the stage, it is important to learn briefly about the Russo-Japanese War of 1904–5. When Japan returned the Liaodong Peninsula to China, Russia sought to acquire *concessions* (diplomatic term meaning "special privileges") to the peninsula. Russia particularly wanted access to the immensely important city of Port Arthur. Both Japan and Russia wanted to have control over the areas that had been at stake during the Sino-Japanese War—Korea and Manchuria (northern China). With both vying for the same territory, war was inevitable. The end result surprised many, since this became the first time in modern history that an Asian country defeated a European great power. In the treaty that provided terms for the end of this war, Russia agreed that "Japan possesses in Korea paramount political, military, and economical interests." For Koreans, the results of this war and treaty meant that they now were under the control of Japan, a frightening prospect that brought national indignation and outrage.

In the very midst of this turmoil, a spiritual awakening began in the city of Pyongyang, in the northern part of Korea. News had reached missionaries of revivals taking place in Wales and in India, with huge numbers of converts. This gave impetus for many to gather for prayer, crying out to God for this same grace to be seen in Korea. And, beginning in January of 1907, such an outpouring of God's Spirit was given that it resembled scenes from the book of Acts. Orr describes it in his book on early twentieth century revivals, *The Flaming Tongue*, like this:

From this point, a prayer movement began, which led to a widespread awakening in China in 1906–7, and "extraordinary revival" throughout 1908–9.

Discuss with your students what difference it could make in their own lives to consider that God, the Creator and Sustainer of life, prepares and comforts people before and after tremendous trials, through the outpouring of revival.

of the early 1900s was, according to Orr, "the most extensive Evangelical Awakening of all time, reviving Anglican, Baptist, Congregational, Disciple, Lutheran, Methodist, Presbyterian and Reformed churches, and other evangelical bodies throughout Europe and North America, Australaisa and South Africa, and their daughter churches and missionary causes throughout Asia, Africa and Latin America, winning more than five million folk to an evangelical faith in the two years of greatest impact in each country."

Why did God send revival at the turn of the twentieth century? Looking back through the lens of time may give us some understanding, though this is undoubtedly only a portion of what was in God's heart.

As we look at this time period, we can see that God sent revival in China between the period of the Boxer Rebellion of 1900–1901 and the revolution of 1911. Extraordinary revival came to Korea between the Russo-Japanese War of 1904–5 and the start of Japanese occupation in 1910. Revival came to South Africa and the African continent after the Boer War ended in 1902. Europe, which was soon to experience the utter devastation of World War I, saw unprecedented revival across national boundaries.

It seems evident that God was gathering the harvest beforehand and preparing His people for these unprecedented troubles—world wars, revolutions, conquests. Author F. C. Ottoman wrote, "As we look back over these extraordinary religious awakenings, which . . . so quickened the church and so effectively pressed the claims of God upon the consciences of multitudes, we cannot escape the conviction that God in gracious providence was reaping a spiritual harvest before He permitted the outburst of revolutionary forces that have overwhelmed the world."

5

It was customary for representatives of area churches to come from far and wide at the New Year for Bible study. In spite of tensions, a strange new spirit entered the meeting of fifteen hundred men. So many men wanted to pray that the leader told the whole audience: 'If you want to pray like that, all pray.' The effect was beyond description—not confusion, but a vast harmony of sound and spirit, like the noise of the surf in an ocean of prayer. As the prayer continued, an intense conviction of sin settled on the meeting, giving way to bitter weeping over their misdeeds. . . . An elder arose and confessed a grudge against a missionary colleague and asked for forgiveness. The missionary stood to pray but reached only the address to Deity, "Father!" when, with a rush, a power from without seemed to take hold of the meeting. The Europeans described its manifestations as terrifying. Nearly everyone present was seized with the most poignant sense of mental anguish; before each one, his sins seemed to be rising in condemnation of his life. . . . In meetings following, conviction of sin and reconciliation of enemies continued. . . . Not only was there deep confession, but much restitution. . . . The delegates to the Winter Bible Class went back to their homes and carried the revival to their various churches. Everywhere phenomena were the same. There was deep conviction of sin, followed by confession and restitution, a notable feature of all gatherings being the audible prayer en masse—a mode of intercession entirely new.

> *News of the Welsh revival in 1904 instigated prayer, not only in Korea, but in the four corners of the world.*

According to the Edinburgh Conference of 1910, "the Korean Revival . . . has been a genuine Pentecost," and Korean church membership quadrupled in one decade.

News of the Welsh revival in 1904 instigated prayer, not only in Korea, but in the four corners of the world. In the southern lands of Africa, where the brutal Boer War between British South Africa and the Boer states of Transvaal and the Orange Free State had just ended, a prominent Christian wrote, "What can the Church militant do to heal the sore between two brave peoples, and bring this land within the Kingdom of the King of Kings? A revival of true spiritual religion, reaching Boer and Briton alike, would do more towards raising the standard of national righteousness than can be readily imagined." When God answered prayer and sent revival to both Dutch Reformed and English churches, it brought not only new life but also profound healing between enemies. And revival was not limited to the English and Boers. God began to move among the African tribes, including the Zulu, Xhosa, and Sotho people. As we shall see in the next Unit, Rees Howells, a young Welshman who had been deeply moved by the Welsh revival, would be used by God in Africa during the time of WWI to bring a message of reconciliation to God and to others.

A political rift that would not be mended lay between the island of Cuba

5

and its colonial overlord, Spain. Though Cuba had been a Spanish colony since 1511, it was the introduction of sugarcane as a market crop that made it particularly profitable to the wealthy landowners. Since slavery was not abolished until 1886, landowners had been able to cheaply produce crops. By 1860, one-third of the world's sugar was produced in Cuba, using both African slaves and new levels of technology. A close neighbor to the United States, Cuba was seen as a very attractive addition, so the United States tried several times to buy the island from Spain from the 1860s onward.

Due to Napoleon's efforts in Europe and Simon Bolivar's in South America at the beginning of the nineteenth century, Spain had lost most of its massive colonial empire, so it was simply not interested in making a deal. Apart from a few outposts in Africa, only Cuba, Puerto Rico, the Philippines, and the island of Guam remained as Spanish colonies at the end of the century. But many Cubans, hampered economically and distressed politically by the corrupt and inefficient colonial administrators, wanted liberty and independence from Spain. Leading the way was José Marti, sometimes called the "Apostle of Cuban Independence."

By 1860, one-third of the world's sugar was produced in Cuba, using both African slaves and new levels of technology.

In 1895, Cuban exiles, including Marti, landed in their homeland with a revolutionary force to try to gain the much-desired freedom from Spain. Spanish repercussions were brutal, and as Americans heard about these atrocities, anti-Spanish sentiments grew in the United States. When the USS *Maine* mysteriously exploded while docked in Havana in February 1898, it brought about a furious storm of outrage against Spain. American public opinion, believing that this was a Spanish attack on American lives and property, forced President William McKinley to issue an ultimatum, demanding that Spain withdraw from Cuba. This action brought about the Spanish-American War, also known as the War of 1898. The "splendid little war," as it was called

USS Maine enters Havana Harbor

5

by American Ambassador John Hay, was quickly won by the United States, who captured not only Cuba and Puerto Rico, but, far away in the Pacific, the Philippine islands as well.

In the Treaty of Paris, Cuba received—on paper—independence, while America formally took Puerto Rico, Guam, and the Philippines. (Despite an earlier amendment promising that the United States would not annex Cuba, American soldiers continued to occupy the island.) It was America's hotly contested entrance into the world of imperial powers and widespread colonies. Though condemned by some who held that America was forsaking its guiding principles, other Americans would have agreed with a New York senator who said, "There is not a man here who does not feel four hundred percent bigger in 1900 now that he is a citizen of a country that has become a world power."

It is one thing to gain a colony; it's another thing entirely to govern it. Within three months, America began to experience the challenges and difficulties of this new imperialistic role as revolution broke out in the Philippines. The cause of distress in both "independent" Cuba and the colonized Philippines is not hard to find. As José Marti had written, "To change masters is not to be free." The revolution in the Philippines turned into a grueling, costly guerilla war, which increasingly disillusioned Americans about being an imperial power.

The revolution in the Philippines turned into a grueling, costly guerilla war, which increasingly disillusioned Americans about being an imperial power.

While this national debate was raging, the United States sought to acquire treaty rights for building a canal across the Isthmus of Panama. For those concerned with maintaining an American colony and commercial ventures in the Far East, a Panama canal would be a dream come true, drastically shortening a ship's traveling time from East to West and back. So, in 1904, work began on that massive Central American project. This was the same year that the Russo-Japanese war began in the East, and, on the other side of the world, an alliance of friendship was birthed between two old European enemies, France and England.

As the largest European colonizers of Africa, they had six years earlier nearly come to blows over conflicting plans. Britain had wanted to connect its massive string of colonies by building a railway line from south to north, while, at the same time, France had wanted to link its colonies from west to east by taking over a few more territories. This led to a brief confrontation called the Fashoda Incident in 1898, which was peacefully resolved the following year, in part because the two nations recognized there was a larger issue involved: the posturing of the German Empire was threatening to upset the balance of power. By 1904, each nation was well aware that they needed to join forces in order to keep Germany from becoming more powerful than it already was, so they reconciled their differences

5

and entered into a friendly partnership, known as the *Entente Cordiale* (or "friendly agreement"). Part of this conversation included France agreeing to British policies in Egypt, and Great Britain agreeing to French colonial aspirations in Morocco. France then negotiated a secret treaty with Spain, who currently held a tiny portion of Morocco but wished to increase it with the help of France, in exchange for allowing them to do what they wished.

France had not taken Germany into account when it laid its plans, however. As the French began to move toward setting up a *protectorate* in Morocco (which would have allowed them to largely control this North African country), Kaiser Wilhelm II sailed to the Moroccan city of Tangier and undiplomatically proclaimed his opinion that Morocco should be independent and free of colonial control. Since Germany had economic interests in this area of the world, there was an ominous warning in his appearance in Morocco. His aggressive statements launched the First Moroccan Crisis as international tensions began to skyrocket. The crisis was only resolved when an international conference was held with diplomats from the United States, Austria-Hungary, Russia, Italy, Great Britain, France, and Germany. The final agreement from this conference provided for the protection of German economic interests while giving France and Spain the right to certain "policing actions" in the port cities of Morocco. This crisis highlighted the growing conflict between the European nations over their worldwide interests, and was, indeed, a prelude to the war that was just over the horizon of the next decade.

In central China, a revolution caused the Qing (or Manchu) dynasty to fall after more than two hundred fifty years of rule.

Adding ever greater stress and pressure to the weakening diplomacy of these nations there would be one more international crisis between Germany, France, and England in 1911 over Morocco. That was only one of the crises of that year, however. In central China, a revolution caused the Qing (or Manchu) dynasty to fall after more than two hundred fifty years of rule. In its place, a short-lived Chinese Republic was established. In the Balkans, turbulence was about to break out into war, which would not only rearrange the political administration of these various nations, but would upset the critical balance of power in Europe.

Before this upset, however, the European nations continued to earnestly seek diplomatic means to prevent any one nation from growing too strong. The Entente Cordiale of 1904 between France and England was enlarged three years later by the addition of a most unlikely comrade, Russia. Despite the fact that these three had often been enemies—France had followed Napoleon into the disastrous War of 1812 in Russia, and England and France had fought against Russia during the Crimean War (1853–56)—and regardless of the opposing political goals they had often held, at this point it was absolutely critical to join forces against their more dangerous foe—Germany.

5

Dreadnought USS *New York* making full steam in 1915

Envisioning itself as a major player in world affairs, Germany had been in a naval arms race with England since the turn of the century. This was a significant change in thinking for the Germans, who had previously relied upon the invincible German army. Now, the possession of a large and powerful navy was seen as essential. Indeed, Admiral Tirpitz, the driving force behind the building of Germany's navy, remarked, "For Germany the most dangerous naval enemy at present is England. It is also the enemy against which we most urgently require a certain measure of naval force as a political power factor."

Great Britain was determined to not be outdone, since from the time of the Spanish Armada and the attempted Napoleonic invasion of Britain, history had proved over and over again that the Royal Navy was the very lifeline for this island empire. In 1909, the British Foreign Secretary told Parliament:

> When that program is completed, Germany, a great country close to our own shore, will have a fleet of thirty-three Dreadnoughts [the latest, most powerful battleship type]. The whole program . . . when completed . . . will be the most powerful fleet that the world has yet seen. That imposes upon us the necessity, of which we are now at the beginning . . . of rebuilding the whole of our fleet. That is what the situation is. What we do not know is the time in which we shall have to do it.

The time was shorter than anyone could have realized, and the soon coming war more horrific than anyone could have imagined. ◄

194 Alliances & Revivals (1860–1913)

You may choose to have your students read the article first and then listen to the audio recordings, or vice versa.

◉ Read the article

◉ Listen to the audio recordings in Listen to This

- The main concepts and chronological flow are contained in *What in the World?* Volume 3

- The life of artist and missionary Lilias Trotter, who ministered among the Muslims in Algeria, is described in *True Tales* Volume 3.

- Learn more about the revivals of the early 1900s in *Digging Deeper* Volume 3.

Phase 1

▶ **Listen to This**

What in the World? VOL. 3

DISC TWO:

» The Turn of the Century & Russia (track 8)

» The Balkan Wars (track 9)

DISC THREE:

» Russian Repressive Autocracy (track 1)

» Revival & Balkan Conflict (track 2)

True Tales VOL. 3

DISC TWO:

» Lilias Trotter—part 1 (track 6)

DISC THREE:

» Lilias Trotter—part 2 (track 1)

Digging Deeper VOL. 3

DISC TWO:

» The Welsh Revival (track 2)

» Across the Globe (track 3)

DISC THREE:

» Historic Rivalries (track 1)

» Pre-War Russia (track 2)

» Austro-Hungarian Empire (track 3)

| **Key People**
(Church) |
|---|
| **Amy Carmichael**
Rescuer of children in India |
| **Lilias Trotter**
Artist and missionary to Algeria |
| **William Borden**
Wealthy American who gave it all away to serve |
| **Rees Howells**
Welsh revivalist in Africa |
| **C. T. Studd**
Founder of Worldwide Evangelization Crusade |
| **Jonathan Goforth**
Missionary and revivalist in China |

Alliances & Revivals (1860–1913) **195**

◉ Read the Scriptures in Read For Your Life

The Scriptures are central to our understanding, our character, and our decisions. Therefore, we must give the greatest weight possible to them.

Help your students gain this perspective as they watch you handle the Scriptures with reverence and awe.

Discuss with your students what they are learning about God's ways in history, specifically how being a follower of Jesus impacts their view of nations, wars, and the immense troubles of the world.

KEY PEOPLE

The main characters in this Unit are listed in the Student Manual, along with a brief identifier, so that the students can familiarize themselves with these people.

◉ Recap the material with an activity

In different parts of the room, set up stations for the Eight Intelligences Recap Activities. Then allow students to work alone or together in small groups to accomplish THEIR CHOICE OF ONE of the following suggestions. At the start of the next class, ask for 3–4 groups of volunteers to share.

Homeschoolers: rather than setting up all eight stations, allow student(s) to choose which activity they would most enjoy, and do it.

Recap Suggestions:

Spatial: Create a poster with images, pictures, or designs that would help others to visually understand the early-twentieth-century European theory of the "balance of power."

Bodily Kinesthetic: In groups of three, choose one person to represent the Ottomans, one to be Russia, and one to be Austria-Hungary. The object of this recap is to conduct a historical wrestling match over who will control the Balkans. As you wrestle, remember this: the Ottoman Empire was considered the "sick man of Europe," Russia was considered to be powerful but not very advanced in technology or politics, and Austria-Hungary was recovering from a humiliating defeat by Prussia in the mid-1800s.

Interpersonal: In groups of two, each present an opposing position on whether America should have taken the Philippines, Puerto Rico,

---

Key People (World)

Nicholas II
Last czar of Russia

Edward VII
British king "Uncle of Europe"

Marie Curie
Polish-born French scientist

Wright brothers
Successful inventors of the airplane

Emperor Francis Joseph
Emperor of Austria, king of Hungary

Kaiser Wilhelm II
German emperor

Theodore Roosevelt
American president

▶ Read For Your Life

The Holy Bible

» **Biblical Response to Persecution** (such as in the Boxer Rebellion)—Matthew 5:10–12

» **Jesus's Promise to Those Who Follow Him** (consider the worldwide revival)—Mark 10:28–30

» **God's Wisdom and Power in Nations** (meditate on this while studying this time frame)—Daniel 2:20–22

» **The Results of Relying Solely on Human Reasoning** (ponder humanity's optimism for the future at the turn of the century)—Proverbs 14:12

▶ Talk Together

Opinion Column

» What did you find to be the most interesting aspect, or the most fascinating person, in this turn-of-the-century time period?

» When there is a need for change, often there are at least two ways of approaching it—either gradually or immediately. In Russia, how did the radicals' approach differ from the czar's? What do you think might have happened if the they could have worked together to bring about change for the good of the country?

» If you had been living in England during the time that Germany began building up its navy, what do you think might have been some of your concerns and the concerns of your government about this new development?

» The Ottoman Empire controlled the Balkan states for hundreds of years. What do you think might have been some of the reasons that the various countries in the Balkans began to seek independence from the Ottomans during the

---

and Guam (also occupying Cuba) at the end of the Spanish-American war. What reasons do you have for supporting your position? Try to convince the other person of the correctness of your view.

Musical: Imagine you are a participant in the Welsh Revival of 1904. Since Wales is known as a nation of singers, choose a song or hymn that you can sing to help describe your experience. If necessary, compose a new song of worship to the Lord that will describe the event in your country.

Linguistic: Retell one of the events in this Unit and explain in what ways

it contributed to, or prepared people for, the upcoming world war.

Math-Logical: Analyze the differences and similarities between the Triple Alliance (Germany, Austria-Hungary, and Italy) and the Triple Entente Cordiale (England, France, and Russia).

Intrapersonal: Consider and discuss in a small group how the Russians would have felt at the time of their defeat by Japan. How would this defeat impact their thoughts about the future? About the czar? About the church? Imagine this both from the perspective of one of the nobility or upper-level military leaders, and also as a factory worker or peasant.

1800s? Why would you have supported your country's independence if you had lived in the Balkans during this time?

» In the Russo-Japanese War of 1904–5, Russia was defeated by an Asian country that had just recently begun modernizing. In what ways do you think that a defeat at the hands of the Japanese might have been more damaging to the morale of the Russian government than if they had lost to a European power? What do you think this defeat might have indicated to the average Russian citizen?

» How does knowing that God sent life-changing revival to areas of the world that were in the midst of great tragedy and difficulty, such as Korea and China, affect your thinking about God's mercy and goodness expressed toward humanity? Does this change your view of God in any way? If so, how?

Critical Puzzling

» In Russia, Czar Alexander II began reforming the country in the areas of education, freeing the serfs, and beginning local government. What do you think the anarchists who killed him thought about these reforms? In what ways did the czar's death help the anarchist agenda? In what ways did it hurt it?

» Why was a "balance of power" so important in Europe? What was Napoleon's role in creating a need for this balance? For what purposes did the Triple Alliance and Triple Entente each form?

» What difference would an ice-free port have made for Russia and the Russian navy? In what ways might it have changed their political and military strategies? Why do you think the rest of Europe wanted to prevent Russia from gaining this?

» What similarities do you see between the military approach of Japan and that of Germany in the early twentieth century?

» Looking at a map, why do you think Austria-Hungary wanted to occupy Bosnia and Herzegovina? How might this occupation have benefited Austria-Hungary? Why might this occupation have been troublesome to Serbia?

» In what ways would the acquisition of the Philippines, Puerto Rico, Guam, and Cuba (though it was not formally annexed) have benefited the United States? How was this acquisition in stark contrast to America's former approach to other countries? What clues help us understand the attitudes of these countries toward being American colonies?

Naturalist: The German Empire under Kaiser Wilhelm II wanted its "place in the sun." Go outside and find something in nature that will illustrate what happens to a plant or tree that has its own place in the sun. Then share with others how your find is an example of the benefits the German Empire was seeking.

Or . . . Activity of Your Choice: What would you like to have your students do for a review activity concerning this week's introduction to Alliances & Revivals?

◉ Talk together

Individual Preparation

After completing their recap activities, students may begin to consider the questions in the Opinion Column and Critical Puzzling.

Class Discussion

Use the questions under Talk Together to get the students primed and to create a discussion environment in the classroom. You may also want to draw from the open-ended questions listed here.

? How do people or nations act toward someone who has humiliated them? What do you suppose French attitudes toward the German Empire might have been after the Franco-Prussian War of 1870? How might this lead to further conflict?

? When William Borden, heir to an enormous family fortune, decided to go as a missionary to the Muslims of China, it caused astonishment and dismay in America. Why might it be unusual for someone who will inherit millions of dollars to leave it all behind for the mission field? What are the unique temptations and arguments facing someone like William Borden or C. T. Studd (an English missionary who also came from a wealthy background)?

▶ **Resources for Digging Deeper**

Choose a few books that look interesting, or find your own.

TURN OF THE CENTURY

The Causes of World War I
Tony Allan • One of the titles in the 20th Century Perspectives series, this informative book will provide students with photos and articles covering the time period of this Unit as well as the next. **UE+**

The Twentieth Century CAMBRIDGE INTRODUCTION TO THE HISTORY OF MANKIND
Trevor Cairns • This is an excellent overview of the 1900s. Beginning with the early 1900s attitudes in Europe, Asia, and the United States, the book includes WWI, the post-war conditions, WWII, the Cold War, the breakup of colonization around the world, the Korean War, Vietnam, and the impact of our technical advances. It also contains detailed charts showing world events. Highly recommended! **UE+**

Incredible Century: A Pictorial History 1901–1970
R. J. Unstead • It is very interesting to see the twentieth century in pictures. This book gives a snapshot look at the major events of the 1900s from a secular perspective. While I disagree with the author's perspective on some issues, it is still true that a picture is worth a thousand words! **UE+**

THE BALKANS

The Balkans LIFE WORLD LIBRARY
Edmund Stillman • To study the history of the Balkans is to sort through many conquering countries, rival people groups, and various religious enmities. This book is an excellent overview of the history of the Balkans. **HS+**

Bulgaria ENCHANTMENT OF THE WORLD SERIES
Abraham Resnick • Bulgaria, on the eastern edge of the Balkans, has its own unique history. This book will provide students an appropriate introduction. **E+**

Albania ENCHANTMENT OF THE WORLD SERIES
David K. Wright • Albania's history is different from that of the other Balkan countries. This book, full of photos, will help students learn more about Albania and the Albanian people. **E+**

Greece ENCHANTMENT OF THE WORLD SERIES
R. Conrad Stein • Another in the series, this is an excellent "primer" for learning about Greece and the Greeks. **E+**

Yugoslavia
Carol Z. Rothkopf • Though the country is no longer called Yugoslavia, this book is a good introduction for children to the lands of Slovenia, Croatia, Bosnia and Herzegovina, Macedonia, Serbia, and Montenegro. It explains the different people groups involved, different languages and alphabets, and a bit of the history up to 1971 (when the book was written). **E+**

Romania ENCHANTMENT OF THE WORLD SERIES
Betty Carran • Another in the series, this is an excellent starting point for discovering more about Romania before the fall of Ceausescu. **E+**

◉ Choose books of interest/ internet search

Remember: Beware of Arrogance, Embrace Humility!

A list of possible books is given in the Student Manual. Encourage your students to look for books or videos on Alliances & Revivals from this list and from other sources. You may want to gather a selection of further resources prior to beginning Unit 5, or you may encourage the students to be treasure hunters and find them on their own. It would be helpful and time-saving before the Unit begins to check availability of these titles on your local library website.

RUSSIA

Russia: The Land

Greg Nickles • Learn more about this vast land, including its transition from czar to Soviet state to post-communism, in this excellent introduction to Russia for children. **UE+**

Nicholas II WORLD LEADERS PAST & PRESENT

George Vogt • A biography of the last "czar of all the Russias," this book is a fascinating glimpse into the lives of Nicholas and Alexandra. The errors in judgment, the misguided attempts to rule, and the unwieldy nature of the Russian government under the czar are all vividly portrayed. It makes one wonder, "What if?" **MS+**

THEODORE ROOSEVELT

Carry a Big Stick LEADERS IN ACTION SERIES

George Grant • Subtitled "The uncommon heroism of Theodore Roosevelt," this is an amazing biography of an astonishing man. Highly recommended! **MS+**

Theodore Roosevelt: An Initial Biography

Genevieve Foster • If you have read any of Genevieve Foster's historical books, you will know that children love her way of presenting history. This is a warm biography of an amazing man. **UE+**

Theodore Roosevelt: An American Original

Janet & Geoff Benge • One of the Heroes of History series, this is a well-told story full of colorful anecdotes for students about the president who was known as a "trust-buster" and who promised a "square deal" to the people during his election campaign. **UE+**

MARIE CURIE

Marie Curie: A Photographic Story of a Life

Vicki Cobb • This DK biography presents the fascinating life of the first person to receive two Nobel prizes (and the first woman to receive one!). **UE+**

The Story of Madame Curie

Alice Thorne • This is an excellent biography for younger students to read. Did you know that Marie Curie was Polish, and that because the Russian czar had forbidden higher education to Poles, she had to learn about science in secret? **E+**

FLIGHT

The Wright Brothers
A WORLD LANDMARK BOOK

Quentin Reynolds • Well written and interesting for children, this is the story of the brothers who worked together to make a machine that could fly. Excellent! **UE+**

The Wright Brothers: First in Flight

Tara Dixon-Engel & Mike Jackson • From newspaper publishing and running a bicycle shop, the Wright brothers moved on to one of the most puzzling questions of their day—discovering how man could fly. Learn about their success in this fascinating book. **UE+**

Wings: The Early Years of Aviation

Richard Rosenblum • What a delightful book! Along with captivating illustrations, this book is filled with fascinating bits and pieces of aviation history. **E+**

MISSIONARIES TO INDIA, AFRICA, & EAST ASIA

The Hidden Jewel TRAILBLAZER BOOKS

Dave & Neta Jackson · Historical fiction for children, this is the story of Amy Carmichael and the work she did in India. Highly recommended! **UE+**

Amy Carmichael CHRISTIAN HEROES THEN AND NOW

Janet & Geoff Benge · Wonderfully written, this series of Christian biographies is fascinating, factual, and historically accurate. Amy Carmichael was a missionary to India, ending up as "Mommy" to many young Indian orphans who had been rescued from temple prostitution. Highly recommended! **UE+**

A Chance to Die: The Life and Legacy of Amy Carmichael

Elisabeth Elliot · Author Elisabeth Elliot not only tells the story of Amy Carmichael's life, but also challenges us to greater trust in the Lord. **MS+**

John Hyde: The Apostle of Prayer MEN OF FAITH SERIES

Francis McGaw · "Praying Hyde" was the name of this missionary who prayed long and hard for India in the late 1800s. Learn more about the results of his prayers in this remarkable little book. **UE+**

Borden of Yale MEN OF FAITH SERIES

Mrs. Howard Taylor · Subtitled "The wealthy American whose sacrifice touched Egypt and the world for Christ," this is the story of a young man who counted all things as loss for the knowledge of Christ. He went to Egypt in 1913 for language school on his way to China. The untimely death of this fabulously wealthy man electrified the world with the claims of Christ. **MS+**

A Passion for the Impossible: The Life of Lilias Trotter

Miriam Huffman Rockness · Lilias Trotter was a missionary to Muslims in Algeria during the late 1800s and early 1900s. This book tells her fascinating story—including her potential career as a world-class artist, which she gave up to go to Algeria. **MS+**

Mask of the Wolf Boy TRAILBLAZER BOOKS

Dave & Neta Jackson · This is a historical fiction account of Jonathan and Rosalind Goforth, who lived through the Boxer Rebellion in China and went on to see a tremendous response to Jonathan's traveling evangelistic ministry. Excellent! **E+**

From Jerusalem to Irian Jaya: A Biographical History of Christian Missions

Ruth A. Tucker · This is the best book on the history of world missions available. Included are short biographies of missionaries all over the world, categorized by their geographical area of service. For this chapter read about Amy Carmichael (298–303), John R. Mott (319–325), and Pandita Ramabai (423–428). **UE+**

Rees Howells: Intercessor

Norman Grubb · Deeply impacted by the 1904 Welsh Revival, Rees Howells went to Africa, where he was used mightily by God in revival. The end of the book refers to the dramatic answers to his intercessory prayers during World War II. Life-changing! **MS+**

POSTIMPRESSIONISM

Vincent van Gogh WHY THEY BECAME FAMOUS

Sergio Bitossi, English adaptation by Vincent Buranelli · One of the most important painters of the 1800s, Vincent van Gogh was nonetheless one of the most tormented men of his age. This biography provides fascinating glimpses into his childhood, his career, and his search for meaning (including his attempts to preach the gospel to poor miners). **UE+**

LITERATURE

Freckles

Gene Stratton Porter · Written at the turn of the century, this is a well-loved story of a young man's life and adventures. **RA**

Anne of Green Gables

L. M. Montgomery · This classic story of a redhead named Anne should be required reading out loud! **RA**

Kim

Rudyard Kipling · Set in colonial India, this is Kipling's classic story about a street urchin, the cast-off son of a British soldier, and an old Indian man. **MS+**

VIDEO

The Wind and the Lion

This movie concerns an American citizen who was kidnapped in Morocco in the early 1900s. Hollywood substituted "Mrs. Pedicarris" for the actual "Mr. Pedicarris," but, apart from that, it is an intriguing look at international tensions just before WWI.

Warning: There are two scenes that might be too violent for younger children. **MS+**

Fiddler on the Roof

A classic musical for the family, this film gives a sense of what it was like for the Jews in Russia during this time. **AA**

What books did you like best?

_____

_____

_____

_____

The Internet also contains a wealth of information about Alliances & Revivals.

What sites were the most helpful?

_____

_____

_____

_____

_____

For more books, use these Dewey Decimal numbers in your library:

Balkans: 949.6

Russia: 947

Balance of power: 327

International relations: 327

General history of Europe: 940–944

Japan and China: 950–952

Art history: 709

Spanish-American War: 973.89

Airplane history: 533

5 Phase 1

▶ **Student Self-Evaluation** UNIT 5, PHASE 1

Dates and hours:_____

Key Concepts

Rephrase the four Key Concepts of this Unit and confirm your understanding of each:

- The Balkans

  _____

- Turn-of-the-Century Russia

  _____

- Upsetting the Balance of Power

  _____

- Worldwide Revivals

  _____

Tools for Self-Evaluation

Evaluate your personal participation in the discussions of this Phase. Bearing in mind that a good participant in a discussion is not always the most vocal participant, ask yourself these questions: Were you an
active participant? Did you ask perceptive questions? Were you willing to listen to other participants of
the discussion and draw out their opinions? Record your observations and how you would like to improve your participation in the future:

_____

_____

Every time period is too complex to be understood in one Phase of study. Evaluate your current knowledge of Alliances & Revivals. What have you focused on so far? What are your weakest areas of knowledge?

_____

_____

Based on the evaluation of this introduction, project ahead what you would like to study more of in the
following Phases.

_____

_____

◉ Conduct a review and evaluation

In this Phase of Unit 5, your students should have had the opportunity to explore Alliances & Revivals through reading, listening, thinking, and discussing by completing a selection from the following:

- informally discussed the Key Concepts;
- read the article;
- listened to the audio recordings;
- read the online articles;
- read the Scriptures;
- explored the recap activities;
- considered the Opinion Column and Critical Puzzling answers on their own;
- participated in class discussion;
- chosen books of interest or searched the Internet;
- completed their self-evaluation for this Phase.

Record student hours: _____

Assess student participation:

Create an evaluation system of your own, or refer to the evaluation rubric in the introduction, as a tool for assessing participation. The categories you will probably find most useful are

"Introduction," "Process: Teamwork," and *"Process: Originality."* To help students develop good discussion skills, encourage them to participate actively, ask content-based questions, and stay focused on the discussion at hand. Students demonstrate a higher level of discussion skills when they incorporate comments and questions from others into their own questions, and draw out opinions or ask for points of clarification from others.

Do not critique the self-evaluation page your student completes and do not direct the answers the student gives to the questions. Instead, allow sincere and personal completion of the evaluation, then discuss the

responses and incorporate those comments into your evaluation.

Determine a grade for this Phase, if using grades: _____

Teacher Self-Evaluation:

Evaluate your own use of materials and teaching opportunities: what worked and what did not; how effective was your time-management; how were your responses to the needs of your student; did you make your expectations clear; in what ways would you like to improve your approach for the next Unit? Incorporate suggestions from your students in your own evaluation *(this requires humility!)*.

Phase 2

▶ Research & Reporting

Explore one or more of these areas to discover something significant!

Turn of the Century

Choose one of these European nations, empires, or regions: Great Britain, France, Germany, Austria-Hungary, the Balkans, or Russia. Learn more about what was happening in this country, empire, or region during the turn of the century, who was allied with whom, what their special interests were, and how they became enmeshed in events just prior to the Great War.

The Ottoman Empire

Research and report on the decline of the Ottoman Empire. What were the internal reasons for this decline? The external reasons? What was the attitude of Europe toward the Ottoman Empire? What part did religion and geography play in these attitudes?

The Balkans

Study more on the Balkans and the Balkan Wars. What happened in the First and Second Balkan Wars? Who was fighting, who won, and what were the results? How did the Treaty of Bucharest in 1913 satisfy or dissatisfy the nations involved in the wars?

Nicholas II of Russia

Discover more about Nicholas II and Alexandra of Russia. How were they related to Queen Victoria? To Kaiser Wilhelm II? What strengths and weaknesses did they bring to the Russian throne? In what ways did Nicholas II misunderstand the attitudes of the military, the workers, and the peasants?

The Modernization of Japan

The development of Japan from a feudalistic society to a modern nation is a fascinating subject. Read more about the various means used by the Japanese government to make these significant changes in such a short time. In what ways did Japan mirror western nations? In what ways did it keep its own worldview and culture?

Political Alliances

Research and report on the Triple Alliance and the Triple Entente prior to World War I. Describe the form of commitment these alliances had, how they were formed, and what purposes they served. Were they defensive alliances, set up for protection, or offensive alliances? Did they change before the war?

Turn-of-the-Century Revivals

The Welsh Revival of 1904 and the Pyongyang (Korea) Revival of 1907 had a tremendous effect, not only on individuals, but on communities and nations as well. Study more about one of these revivals, or any of the revivals of the turn of the century in East Asia, India, South Africa, America, or Germany. Write about the central features of the revival and the impact it had upon the people involved.

◉ Choose a topic and begin research

Allow the students the freedom to choose one of the topics listed under research & reporting in the Student Manual, or to suggest their own area which they would like to research.

Motivating Suggestions:

Especially for Non-linguistic students, and those who are not motivated by written or oral reports, here are suggestions for alternative ways of reporting what has been researched.

Turn of the Century

Make a chart to show the most important aspects, such as their industries, their military, their political system, their colonies (if any), their view of other countries, their religion, their rulers, art and culture, geography and natural resources, daily life, etc.

You are a tour guide wishing to entice a group of potential time-traveling tourists to join you on a trip to your chosen country at the turn of the century. They need to be informed ahead of time about where they are going to go, political issues in the early 1900s, some of the famous historic people they might meet, and some of the most interesting sites in this nation. Prepare a meeting where you can share this fascinating information—with appropriate photos and images—to generate enthusiasm and interest. Be ready to sign them up on the spot!

The Ottoman Empire

As the Ottoman Empire, you are known as the "Sick Man of Europe"— though you still manage to hold on to most of your Balkan property. As a four-hundred-year-old empire, create a first-person presentation of your achievements, your current issues, and your concerns for the future. Be sure to explain the attitudes of Russia and Austria-Hungary toward you, as well as the attitudes of Great Britain and the German Empire.

Choose a piece of music, whether instrumental or vocal, classical or modern, that will depict the decline of the Ottoman Empire in the late 1800s and early 1900s. Create program notes for the audience, so that they will understand how this piece of music is connected to the Ottoman decline. Be prepared to answer questions from the audience after they have heard the piece!

The Balkans

Create a map that shows the geographic and political features of the Balkan Peninsula. Include the national boundaries, the mountain ranges, the valleys, the major cities, and the coastlines. You might wish to include languages, ethnicities, and religious distinctions, as well as showing the major routes through the Balkans from Asia to Europe and Europe to Asia. Put your map on display, and be prepared to answer questions from visitors. Some answers to prepare could include why Russia wanted to control this area (and why Europe did *not* want that); why Macedonia was such an important section of the Balkans geographically and politically; and which were the most powerful countries in the Balkans.

With a few other students playing the representatives of several Balkan nations, host a talk show where controversial subjects are discussed. This week's program, "An Insider's Look at the Balkan Wars," will give representatives from the various nations an opportunity to air their grievances and concerns. Be sure to ask what circumstances led to the First Balkan War. When that has been satisfactorily considered from all sides, ask what led to the Second Balkan War.

Nicholas II of Russia

Create an ad campaign to bolster Nicholas II's popularity with the people. Considering all the issues facing Nicholas, his family, and his country, create two or three memorable slogans that will be the centerpiece of this ad campaign. Consider print advertising (what images can you add to the slogan to really drive your message home?) and radio advertising (pair one slogan with a catchy tune so that everyone will start singing it).

Knowing that the Bolshevik Revolution is coming and that Nicholas II, Alexandra, and their children will soon be killed, journal your thoughts about the illusion of human power, the nature of our lives being a vapor, and the reality of eternity. What have you learned for your own life in the study of the lives of this ruler and his family?

The Modernization of Japan

Collect materials from the woods and fields to create a visual representation of the island nation of Japan. Then introduce other materials from the garage or house to represent its stunning growth into a fully industrialized, modernized nation. Be prepared to answer questions from interested observers concerning your creation.

---

5 Phase 2

The Boer War

Learn more about the Boer War of 1899–1902, Great Britain versus the Orange Free State and the Transvaal. What caused the war? Why was this region considered so valuable? What were the results of the war? Why did the British set up concentration camps? What were the results of the war for Africa, Great Britain, and the rest of the world?

Germany's "Place in the Sun"

Discover more about the change in German political theory from *realpolitik* to *weltpolitik*. How did this affect Germany's policies toward colonization? What was the impact on Germany's military? In what ways did this drive Germany to go to war?

The Spanish-American War

Research and report on the War of 1898, or Spanish-American War. Why did Cuba rise in revolt against Spain? What brought about American involvement in the war? Why did the American fleet sail to the Philippines? What were the results of the war?

Marie Curie

Learn about the life of Polish scientist Madame Curie. For what did she win two Nobel prizes? What was her field of study? What are some of the ways in which her discoveries have been utilized?

The Wright Brothers

Discover more about Orville and Wilbur Wright's flying machine. Report on how the Wright brothers approached the seemingly insurmountable problems of human flight, allowing them to succeed where so many others failed.

Create a collage to illustrate to an audience the rapid changing of Japan from a feudal to a modern nation. Include industry, the military, education, politics, imperialism, and any other transformations you have discovered.

Political Alliances

Using artistic materials such as clay, fabric, or papier-mâché, create sculptures that illustrate the similarities and differences between the Triple Alliance and Triple Entente Cordiale. The use of color, shape, and texture in identifying each nation and the manner in which they are connected to others need to provide visual insights into these political alliances.

Be prepared to answer questions of interested observers.

Compose a simple, rhythmic song for children, which they might use in playing jump rope games, to show who was connected to whom, as well as how and why.

Turn-of-the-Century Revivals

Create a flip chart or PowerPoint presentation to show where the revivals took place, along with the historic circumstances surrounding each revival, and some of unique aspects and results of each.

In a small group, decide what are the three most important points of this

▶ Brain Stretchers

Russo-Japanese War

Research and report on the Russo-Japanese War of 1904–5. What issue provoked this war? What was the result in Manchuria? In Japan? In Russia?

Compare Rulers

Compare and contrast Nicholas II with Peter the Great, then compare and contrast Nicholas II with Kaiser Wilhelm II. Show the governing abilities, leadership skills, family relations, military wisdom,

and diplomatic polices of each. Then evaluate whether Nicholas II could have prevented the revolution in Russia.

William Borden

Study the life of William Borden. What made him an unusual candidate for missions? What impact did his death in Egypt have on missions in Egypt? On the people of China whom he was preparing to serve?

Create Your Own Research Topic

_____

_____

_____

_____

worldwide revival. Then prepare a creative and memorable way your team can communicate these three points to younger children.

The Boer War

Imagine you are a Christian missionary ministering among African tribes in the Transvaal. As the war becomes increasingly bitter, with guerilla warfare and a scorched-earth policy, write a letter home to share your thoughts, prayers, and insights into this devastating situation. As a believer, how has this war affected your own thoughts about God's character and nature in contrast to man's sinfulness?

Create a three-person presentation about this war, representing the Boers, the British, and the Africans. Have each share a perspective on why this war is being fought, how it might have been avoided, and what the results of the war will mean to each of the people groups.

Germany's "Place in the Sun"

Compare and contrast the theories of _realpolitik_ under Bismarck and _weltpolitik_ under Kaiser Wilhelm II. Make a chart to show what they had in common and at what points these theories—and their accompanying actions—diverged. It might be illustrative to show how much international

tension and how much peace Germany experienced under each theory.

Create an action game for playing outside, in which players will experience what Germany meant by having "their place in the sun." Be sure to include an element of racing (since Germany was engaged in a naval arms race with England) and an element of wrestling (since Germany was trying to prove its strength in places like Morocco and China).

The Spanish-American War

José de San Marti wrote, "To change masters is not to be free." Artistically portray this in a painting, drawing, or collage, showing the specific setting of the Spanish-American War and its aftermath.

Set up a debate with a moderator, in the style of a televised political debate, in which one candidate will argue for America's step into imperialism while the other argues against what looks to be a departure from America's founding principles. Remember to give each debater opportunity to respond to statements made by the other.

Marie Curie

Consider what you have learned from the study of Marie Curie's life, and then journal your thoughts about how this study has impacted you personally. Are there lessons learned from her life that will have application in your own?

In the first-person character of Marie Curie, describe what childhood was like for you in Russian-controlled Poland, your educational experiences in Paris, the meeting of Pierre Curie and how that changed your life, and the scientific work to which you gave yourself.

The Wright Brothers

Write and illustrate a book for younger children that will help them learn the amazing story of these young men from Ohio and their flying machine. Be sure to include their background as bicycle mechanics, how they did their testing and experiments for flight in humble circumstances, and the obstacles they had to overcome in order to accomplish this seemingly impossible feat!

Gather materials with which you can build a simple miniature replica of the Wright brothers' glider used at Kitty Hawk. Then prepare an outdoor setting to explain to an interested audience just what the Wright brothers faced as they attempted to build a flying machine. What forces were they working with? Why did they spend so much time experimenting at Kitty Hawk? Be ready to answer questions!

The Boxer Rebellion

Considering the experiences of Christian missionaries and Chinese Christians who suffered under the Boxer Rebellion, choose a hymn (or write new lyrics for a well-recognized tune) that communicates a heavenly perspective when earthly tragedy strikes. Prepare a brief introduction to the events of the Boxer Rebellion for an audience (you might want to also prepare a PowerPoint presentation to give visual images of China), as well as a brief survey to be filled out after the event. After the introduction, invite the audience to sing the hymn together, then to reflectively fill out the survey. What response did they have? What did they learn? How has it impacted their thoughts about suffering and persecution?

You participated in the Boxer Rebellion, fearing for your beloved China and how drastically it had been weakened since the foreign devils

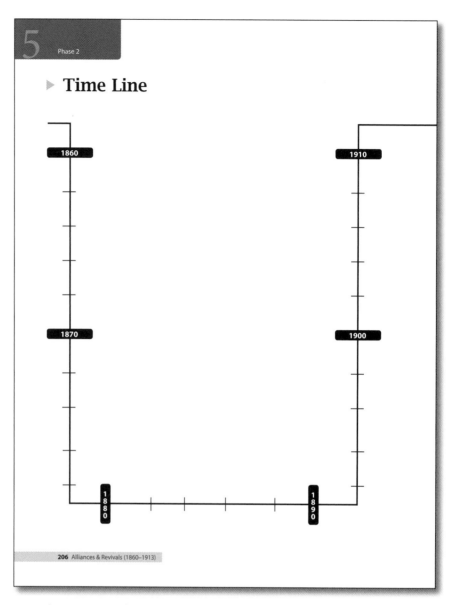

▶ Time Line

1860

1870

1880

1890

1900

1910

206 Alliances & Revivals (1860–1913)

arrived. Having seen firsthand that "the Chinese Christians had acquitted themselves bravely in their hour of martyrdom and persecution, so much curiosity and interest was aroused in the hearts of acquaintances," write a letter to the editor of your local newspaper. Share your thoughts about how this event has changed your perspective in ways you did not expect.

Amy Carmichael

Set up a display about Amy Carmichael's life in a museum devoted to Christian missionaries and their work. In addition to photographs, maps, and brief descriptions about Amy, you might want to include various objects to represent the significant and interesting features of her determined character and ministry. Be prepared to answer questions about this fascinating woman.

Choose the three or four most important facets of Amy Carmichael's work in India, and then prepare a series of pantomimes or choreographed actions to illustrate them. You might find it helpful as the segments change to choose appropriate music to create the ambience for telling the story.

Consider this for your time line

This time period is a time of striving and competing between nations; a time of acquiring and defending new imperial territories; a time of challenging the weaknesses of failing empires and dynasties. While it is the prelude to world-changing war, it is also the scene of God's great mercies and outpouring in worldwide revival. It is a brief moment in time in which to carefully consider the ways of man and the ways of God.

Key Events

- Russo-Turkish War
- Triple Alliance first signed
- Sino-Japanese War
- Spanish-American War
- Boxer Rebellion
- Panama Canal built
- Triple Entente signed
- First motorized airplane flight
- Russo-Japanese War
- Welsh Revival/ Pyongyang Revival
- Chinese Republic established
- First and Second Balkan Wars

Be sure to include the people listed in Key People in Phase 1.

Alliances & Revivals (1860–1913) **207**

"No king is saved by the multitude of an army;

A mighty man is not delivered by great strength.

A horse is a vain hope for safety;

Neither shall it deliver any by its great strength.

Behold, the eye of the LORD is on those who fear Him,

On those who hope in His mercy,

To deliver their soul from death,

And to keep them alive in famine."
Psalm 33:16–19

Talk with your students about how these verses give insight into the time period just before World War I. How were the nations, who were creating alliances and empires, striving to save and deliver themselves? What were the results? On the other hand, what were the experiences of those seeking the Lord during this same time period? What do your students learn from this scriptural perspective?

◉ Construct the time line

Read the information listed with the Key Events in the Student Manual. Dialogue with your students about the issues involved.

Find the dates for the Key People and Key Events listed.

Time Line Key

Key People in the Church

- Amy Carmichael: 1867–1951
- Lilias Trotter: 1853–1928
- William Borden: 1887–1913
- Rees Howells: 1879–1950
- C. T. Studd: 1860–1931
- Jonathan Goforth: 1859–1936

Key People in the World

- Nicholas II: 1868–1918
- Edward VII: 1841–1910)
- Marie Curie: 1867–1934
- Wilbur Wright: 1867–1912
- Orville Wright: 1871–1948
- Emperor Francis Joseph: 1830–1916
- Kaiser Wilhelm II: 1859–1941
- Theodore Roosevelt: 1858–1919

Key Dates

- Russo-Turkish War: 1877–1878
- Triple Alliance first signed: 1881
- Sino-Japanese War: 1894–1895
- Spanish-American War: 1898
- Boxer Rebellion: 1899–1901
- Panama Canal built: 1904–1914
- Triple Entente signed: 1907
- First motorized airplane flight: 1903
- Russo-Japanese War: 1904–1905
- Welsh Revival: 1904–1905
- Pyongyang Revival: 1907–1910
- Chinese Republic established: 1912
- First and Second Balkan Wars: 1912, 1913

▶ Words to Watch

revolution	aggressive	concessions	slavophile
revitalization	ethnicity	reform radicals	anarchy
incompatible	escalate	westernization	innovation
arms race	expedient	serfs	Russify
czar	reprisals	strategic	

Consider:

In this Unit there is a great emphasis on the changing shape of governments and political alliances, so it would be helpful to learn political terms and theories used to describe these changes. Here are a few to get you started.

balance of power	liberation	nihilism	occupy
colonialism	foreign policy	client state	ultimatum
Triple Alliance	jingoism	*weltpolitik*	
Triple Entente Cordiale	"peace with honor"	protectorate	

Other words you need to look up:

_____

_____

_____

_____

Here is one idea for making vocabulary study interesting and fun:

WORD AUCTION

In this vocabulary game, students are going to bid for as many vocabulary words as they can define and use appropriately. The winner will become Imperial Monarch for the Day, waited on hand and foot by the losers. Start by appointing one volunteer to be the auctioneer. Each bidder should be given paper and a pen or a word processor. When the auction begins, the auctioneer will start the bidding for the first word. If students wish to bid, they should indicate how much they are willing to pay: how many historical uses of that word can they make? For instance, if the word is czar, if a student can name three different czars and two different labels given to specific czars, then the bid would be five. If other students think they can top that, have them make a higher bid. When the bidding is finished, the top bidder must write out all of the usages of the word and submit it to the auctioneer. If the auctioneer is unsure of the correctness of any of the usages, the parent/teacher can be consulted. If the bidder fails to complete the bid, or uses a term incorrectly or non-historically, then the second-highest bidder for that word will have an opportunity. A great option would be to do all the auctioning and answering via email.

A list of definitions can be found at the back of this book in Appendix B.

◉ Practice vocabulary

You may find other words in this Unit that are especially appropriate for younger children. Feel free to substitute another vocabulary list for the one provided.

◉ Complete research projects and share in class or hand in

Create a safe environment for the presentations. Set ground rules prior to the presentations, so that students know how much time is available for each of them, and so that they know they will be honored and respected by all those observing.

▶ Student Self-Evaluation UNIT 5, PHASE 2

Dates and hours:_____

Research Project

Summarize your research question:

_____

_____

List your most useful sources by author, title, and page number or URL where applicable (continue list in margin if necessary):

_____

_____

Now take a moment to evaluate the sources you just listed. Do they provide a balanced view of your research question? Should you have sought an additional opinion? Are your sources credible (if you found them on your own)? Record your observations:

_____

_____

_____

Evaluate your research project in its final presentation. What are its strengths? If you had time to revisit this project, what would you change? Consider giving yourself a letter grade based on your project's merits and weaknesses.

_____

_____

_____

Letter grade: _____

You have just completed an area of specific research on the time of Alliances & Revivals. Now what would you like to explore in the upcoming Phases? Set some objectives for yourself.

_____

_____

_____

◉ Conduct a review and evaluation

In this second Phase of Unit 5, your students should have had the opportunity to explore Alliances & Revivals through researching, thinking, and reporting by completing a selection from the following:

- done a research project;
- learned the vocabulary;
- constructed a time line;
- created a project report on what was researched;
- completed their self-evaluation procedure for this Phase.

Record student hours: _____

Assess student effort in the research and reporting projects.

Create an evaluation system of your own, or refer to the evaluation rubric in the introduction, as a tool for assessing research and reporting. The categories you will probably find most useful are *"Introduction," "Task," "Process: Teamwork"* (if students are working together), along with Grammar, Format, and Spelling. As a tool for helping your students develop better research skills, pay attention to their evaluation of sources. Older students should learn how to make a "Sources Cited" list according to academic standards—refer them to English usage books or websites for formatting rules. Younger students should learn how to obtain a balanced view of their research subject; if they use more than one source they will get a bigger picture of what was happening. Encourage your students to make use of their self-evaluations for their next research projects, in order to practice good research skills.

Do not critique the self-evaluation page your student completes in the Student Manual—spelling errors are not to be considered in such an exercise. Students should feel free to humbly evaluate themselves without that added complexity. Instead, discuss with them the intention of their written comments and incorporate those into your evaluation.

Determine a final grade for this Phase: _____

Teacher Self-Evaluation:

Evaluate your own use of materials and teaching opportunities: what worked and what did not; how effective was your time-management; how were your responses to the needs of your student; did you make your expectations clear; in what ways would you like to improve your approach for the next Unit? Incorporate suggestions from your students in your own evaluation (*this requires humility!*).

Phase 3

▶ Maps and Mapping

Physical Terrain

» On a map showing the Balkan Peninsula, locate and label the mountain ranges and the major bodies of water that surround the peninsula.

» On a map of Eastern Asia, locate and label the Liaodong Peninsula, Japan, and Korea. Also label the major bodies of water in this area.

Geopolitical

» On the map of the Balkan Peninsula, locate and shade in different colors the nations of Greece, Macedonia, Bulgaria, Serbia, Albania, Bosnia and Herzegovina, Montenegro, Romania, Croatia, and Slovenia. Locate and label Austria, Hungary, Ukraine, and Russia.

» On the map of Eastern Asia, locate and shade in different colors Korea (both North and South) and the area of China known as Manchuria. Locate and label the Chinese cities of Qingdao and Lüshun (known formerly as Port Arthur) and the North Korean city of Pyongyang.

Explore

» *Worldwide Revival:* On a globe, locate the major places of revival (whether specific cities or general regions) in the first decade of the 1900s, including Wales, India, Korea, China, Germany, Japan, and South Africa. Then locate the major places of war in the first decade of the 1900s and up to WWI. What do you find significant about comparing these two sets of geographical and historical information?

» *Christian Outreach:* What is the status of evangelical outreach today in Russia? What opportunities and what difficulties face those who share the gospel in this area?

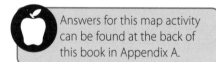

Answers for this map activity can be found at the back of this book in Appendix A.

◎ Create a map and discuss the issues in teams

The students each have an outline map in their manuals. They will be given assignments for drawing in the rivers, mountains, cities, and regional boundaries that are listed. For details on where these things are, please consult a historical atlas, an encyclopedia, or another source of geographic information.

Upper elementary students might be satisfied to accomplish only this portion:

• **Physical terrain:** This part of the mapping exercise will help students locate and mark the region of the Balkan Peninsula, which features prominently in this Unit and the next. Students will also locate the areas in East Asia that were part of the Russo-Japanese War and the Spanish-American War.

Middle school students might be satisfied to complete both the previous mapping exercise and this exercise:

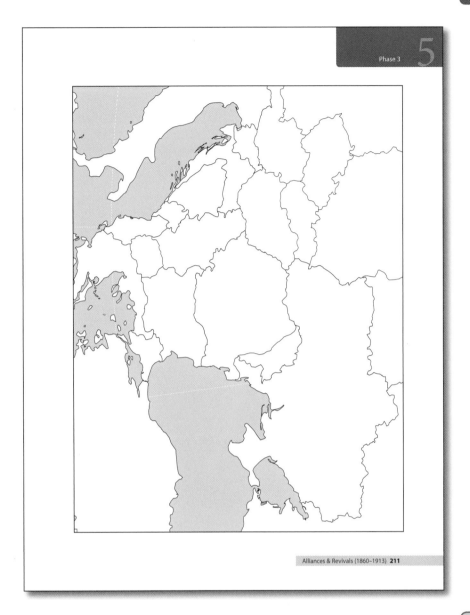

- **Geopolitical:** This section of the mapping exercise will provide the students an opportunity to locate and mark the various nations in the Balkans, as well as some of the cities and regions in China and Korea that are being studied in this Unit.

High school students might be satisfied to complete both the previous mapping exercises and at least one exploration topic of this exercise:

- **Explore** a selection from this portion of the mapping exercise in teams.

WORLDWIDE REVIVAL **?**

Students might find it helpful to create a chart or spreadsheet in which they can assemble the information and consider the geographical overlap of locations where revival brought new life and where war brought horrific devastation.

CHRISTIAN OUTREACH **?**

Students might wish to locate information about current missionary endeavors in Russia. If possible, to provide even more help and insight, interview someone who has worked in these fields.

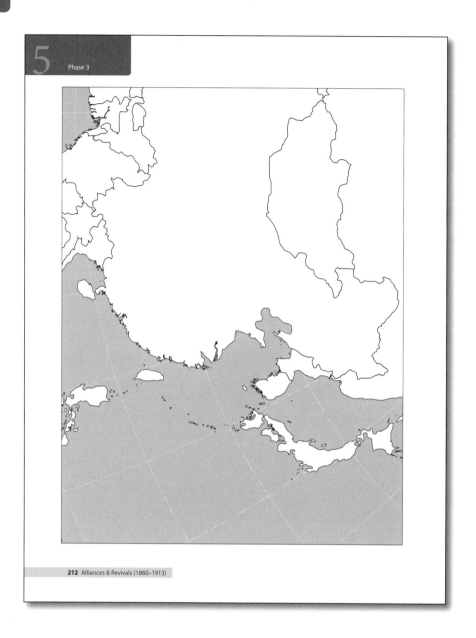

212 Alliances & Revivals (1860–1913)

▶ Art Appreciation

Wheat Fields with Cypresses by Vincent van Gogh

Van Gogh wrote to his brother that he desired in his art "to exaggerate the essential and to leave the obvious vague." Art historian A. W. Janson writes that, for Van Gogh, "it was the color, not the form, that determined the expressive content of his pictures." You can find a link to see this painting at the online resource page.

» What words could you use to describe this painting? How does this painting differ from the Impressionist paintings in the last Unit? In what ways did van Gogh exaggerate the essentials in this work? Would you agree with the art historian's viewpoint above that the colors, rather than the forms, were what van Gogh used to express this landscape? Explain your reasoning.

Still Life with Apples and Oranges by Paul Cézanne

Cézanne was one of the leading French painters of the late 1800s, moving art from Impressionism to Postimpressionism. One of his most- quoted statements, in which we see this movement away from Impressionism and toward something new, was, "I wish to make of Impressionism something solid and durable, like the art of the museums." You can find a link to see this painting at the online resource page.

» Describe what you see in as much detail as possible. Cézanne focused on geometric forms in his paintings, including spheroids and cylinders. In what ways does this seem to affect the painting? Does it look more realistic or more abstract?

> **CONSIDER:**
>
> The unsettling changes in art that had been made by the Impressionists were soon followed by the even more startling changes of the Postimpressionists (Gauguin, van Gogh, Cézanne, Seurat). They were no longer trying to copy nature— even fleetingly— but seeking to create their own expression of reality on the flat surface of the canvas.

The online resource page at www.HistoryRevealed.org contains many helpful Internet links to artwork, architecture, music, project helps, and more.

◉ Examine and discuss art and architecture

The online resource page at www. HistoryRevealed.org has links to view each of the items listed. Allow the students time to observe the paintings without any conversation, and then, when they are ready, engage them in some or all of the questions listed below or in the Student Manual.

Art Appreciation

Wheat Fields with Cypresses by Vincent van Gogh

Francis Schaeffer, in his book *The God Who is There*, writes of van Gogh and the other Postimpressionists:

> Each was a genius; they were very real human men, and each produced pictures which show their genius as artists. However, as we enjoy these pictures as art, appreciating their composition, their use of color and all the other things to admire, we must also see their place in the second step in the "line of despair." . . .What the philosopher was trying to do within the scope of the whole

> The optimism of philosophers, artists, economists, and scientists at the turn of the century would soon be crushed by the horror of WWI. Discuss with your students the impact of "losing hope in man." How is this impact different for those who have hope in God?

universe, they now tried to do on a limited scale on their canvases. . . . Van Gogh thought to make a new religion in which the sensitive people, the artists, would blaze the trail. For this purpose, he dreamt of starting an artistic community in Arles where he was living. He was joined by Gauguin, but after a few months they began to quarrel violently. Van Gogh's hope of his new religion was gone and soon after, he committed suicide. The death of hope in man had taken place in Van Gogh.

Still Life with Apples and Oranges by Paul Cézanne

Art historian Frederick Hartt wrote:

> Often the appearance of reality is neglected; the table, for example, has a tendency to disappear under the tablecloth at one level and emerge from it at another, and the two sides of a bottle or a carafe can be sharply different. Whether Cézanne did not notice such discrepancies in his search for just the right color to make a form go round in depth, or whether he decided on deformations consciously in the interests of abstract relationships of design, has never been convincingly determined. What is certain is that he cared for the subject only as arrangements of form and color.

Ask students to compare Cézanne's painting with Caravaggio's *Still Life with Fruit on a Stone Ledge* (painted in the early 1600s). How do these two paintings compare with one another? In this comparison, is there a sense of what is meant by "he cared for the subject only as arrangements of form and color"?

▶ Architecture

The architecture of Frank Lloyd Wright (1869–1959) was exhilarating to the architects of Europe when they first saw his designs presented in Wasmuth publications of 1910 and 1911. His "Robie House" in Chicago appeared exotic, almost Japanese, to the Europeans. Art historian Frederick Hartt described Wright as "an extraordinary man, a prophet of a new freedom and at the same time of a new discipline in architecture, a molder of form and space, and a genius who experienced the relationship between architecture and surrounding nature as has perhaps no other architect in history, so that his buildings seem literally to grow out of their environments." Wright described his view as "organic architecture," which meant buildings that are compatible with both their inhabitants and their environment.

Robie House designed by Frank Lloyd Wright

» You can see photos of this house at the online resource page. The Robie House was built in 1909 and is located on the campus of the University of Chicago. How would you describe this structure? Considering that neighboring houses of that era were built as Victorian-style structures, in what ways does this building seem compatible with its environment? The owner of the house had asked Wright to design a house that would shield his family from unwanted visitors. How does this structure fulfill his request?

» See photos of Wright's Kaufmann House, also known as Fallingwater, at the online resource page. Built in Bear Run, Pennsylvania, in 1936, and suspended over a waterfall, this house is another example of his organic architecture. In what ways is this home similar to Robie House? In what ways is it different?

The online resource page at www.HistoryRevealed.org contains many helpful Internet links to artwork, architecture, music, project helps, and more.

Architecture

Robie House designed by Frank Lloyd Wright

Alan Bowness, in *Modern European Art*, writes:

> The wide-spreading, hipped roofs and continuous strips of windows give it a low, horizontal emphasis. There is no ornamentation of any kind, nothing to detract from the impact of the building's sculptural forms. . . . The plan, with its multiple levels and easy flow between the rooms, confirms this aspect of spatial freedom. Wright's innovations make an interesting parallel with those of the cubist painters in this same year.

Links to two excellent websites that will provide a better understanding of the inside of the Robie House can be found at the online resource page.

Discuss with students what they think it would be like to live in this home. Would they like having no obvious front door? Would they enjoy the natural light that fills the space? What other observations do they have?

▶ Arts in Action

Select one or more, and let your artistic juices flow!

Postimpressionism Plates

» Create a unique three-dimensional piece of artwork in the style of Van Gogh. You will need:

- an inexpensive dinner or salad plate from a thrift shop or other source
- medium-weight, unprimed canvas fabric—large enough to cover plate
- craft glue
- several bright colors of acrylic paint
- paintbrush

» Cut or tear the canvas into smaller pieces, then layer and glue pieces onto the plate, overlapping them so that the plate is completely enveloped. Be as creative as you wish with the textures. Then, using a van Gogh painting as a visual reference, paint a scene on the plate. The canvas texture will add a unique aspect to your art project.

Still Life with Apples and Oranges

» Try your hand at creating a still life picture in the style of Paul Cézanne. One choice would be to paint, in geometric shapes, apples and oranges on a table. Another choice would be to cut out brightly colored construction paper in geometric shapes and arrange them on a background (poster board might be used as the background). Be inventive in your use of materials and the objects you include!

◉ Do an art project

Postimpressionism Plates

A link to a fantastic video and downloadable lesson plan of how to do this project can be found at the online resource page.

Still Life with Apples and Oranges

If students are interested in this project but would like to approach it with pre-printed materials, consider the project linked to at the online resource page.

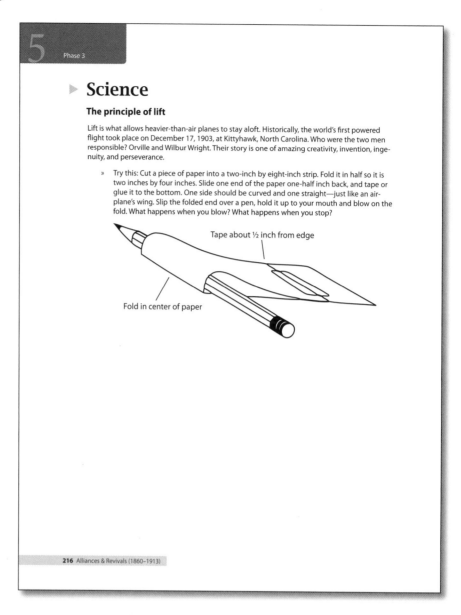

▶ Science

The principle of lift

Lift is what allows heavier-than-air planes to stay aloft. Historically, the world's first powered flight took place on December 17, 1903, at Kittyhawk, North Carolina. Who were the two men responsible? Orville and Wilbur Wright. Their story is one of amazing creativity, invention, ingenuity, and perseverance.

» Try this: Cut a piece of paper into a two-inch by eight-inch strip. Fold it in half so it is two inches by four inches. Slide one end of the paper one-half inch back, and tape or glue it to the bottom. One side should be curved and one straight—just like an airplane's wing. Slip the folded end over a pen, hold it up to your mouth and blow on the fold. What happens when you blow? What happens when you stop?

Tape about ½ inch from edge

Fold in center of paper

◉ Do a science experiment

The principle of lift, discovered in 1738 by Daniel Bernoulli, is that air has less pressure when it is moving. The faster it moves, the less pressure it exerts. When you blow air across the fold, the curve in the paper makes the air go further and faster than it does on the straight, underside of the paper. This means that there is less pressure on the top (moving faster over the curve) and more pressure on the bottom. That's what keeps a plane in the air!

▶ Music

The list of styles in musical eras includes baroque, classical, Romantic, impressionistic, twentieth century, and jazz. Igor Stravinsky's early compositions were the start of twentieth-century music. According to music historian Donald Grout, these compositions "exemplify nearly every significant musical tendency of the first half of the twentieth century." With "The Firebird," "Petrouchka," and "Rite of Spring"—three of the most influential compositions from the turn of the century—Stravinsky startled his audiences with the rhythmic drive and difficulty, the dynamic extremes, the unfamiliar melodic structure, and his powerful orchestral effects. These extremes in compositional style and orchestration became the new standard for the next three decades.

"The Firebird" by Stravinsky

Stravinsky, one of the most influential composers of the twentieth century, used traditional Russian music to create something that is the opposite of traditional in the Firebird suite.

» Watch this piece being performed (conducted by Stravinsky himself!) using the YouTube link at the online resource page. How does this music differ from Debussy or other nineteenth-century composers? What words could you use to describe this music?

Scott Joplin, an African-American composer, was considered to be the "King of Ragtime," a uniquely American musical form with syncopated rhythms. Ragtime, one of the genres leading to jazz, influenced many composers—including Igor Stravinsky!

"Maple Leaf Rag" by Scott Joplin

» You can find a link to listen to the music at the online resource page. As you listen to this famous piano rag, consider this: within ten years of being published, half a million copies of the sheet music were sold! How would you describe this music? Why do you think ragtime was so popular at this time in history?

▶ Cooking

This is an unusually tasty way to serve carrots. As you munch, talk about what you have learned of the Balkans.

Balkan Braised Carrots

6 tbsp buttersalt
2 tsp sugarfreshly ground pepper
12 carrots, thinly sliced1 ½ cups plain yogurt

4 green onions, cut into 1-inch pieces3 tbsp
fresh dill, chopped
cayenne pepper

Melt the butter in a saucepan. Add the sugar, carrot slices, and green onions. Cover and cook gently (braise) until carrots are tender, about 15 minutes. Season to taste with the spices. Add yogurt and dill, heat through (do not allow this to boil). Serve immediately. Serves 6.

◉ Listen to and discuss the music

Listen

Stravinsky's *The Firebird* (1910)

If your students are not familiar with the sounds of the experimentation or with the strident harmonies and rhythmic effects which twentieth century composers have been utilizing, then they will most likely be startled by the sound of Stravinsksy's music—much as the Parisian audiences of 1910–1913 were startled.

Scott Joplin's "Maple Leaf Rag"

Students can find a YouTube link at the online resource page to a recording of Scott Joplin himself playing "Maple Leaf Rag."

◉ Cook the food

Salata Sanatatea

2 cucumbers
1 large heart of lettuce
2 large apples
Juice from half a lemon
2 medium carrots
2 tbsp oil
2 tomatoes
Salt

Peel and thinly slice the cucumbers and apples. Wash and grate the carrots. Wash and tear the lettuce into small pieces. Mix all these with salt, lemon juice, and oil. Place in the salad bowl and decorate with tomato slices.

(Source: www.hnvn.com/recipes/archives/001244.html)

 You might also enjoy making this healthful salad from the Balkan country of Romania.

▶ Student Self-Evaluation UNIT 5, PHASE 3

Dates and hours:_____

Evaluate your projects

- List which of the activities listed in this Phase you did:

  _____

  _____

- Rate your enthusiasm: _____

  Explain: _____

  _____

- Rate the precision of your approach:_____

  Explain: _____

  _____

- Rate your effort toward the completion of the project: _____

  Explain: _____

- Ask yourself what worked and what did not. What would you do differently in the future, and what would you repeat?

  _____

  _____

- How did these hands-on activities enhance your knowledge of Alliances & Revivals? What made them worthwhile?

  _____

  _____

- In the first three Phases of this Unit, what aspect of the time period has most captured your imagination? What would you like to creatively pursue to conclude your study?

  _____

  _____

218 Alliances & Revivals (1860–1913)

◉ Conduct a review and evaluation

In this Phase, your students should have had the opportunity to explore Alliances & Revivals through various hands-on and creative sessions by completing a selection from the following:

- completed a mapping section;
- observed and discussed art & architecture;
- worked on an art project;
- experimented with a science project or taken a field trip;
- listened to music;
- tasted a food related to this Unit;
- completed their self-evaluation procedure for this Phase.

Record student hours: _____

Assess student involvement in the hands-on activities.

Create an evaluation system of your own or refer to the evaluation rubric in the introduction as a tool for assessing participation. The categories you will probably find most useful for evaluating projects are *"Task"* and *"Process: Teamwork."* Consider specifically the enthusiasm, the precision of approach, and the efforts toward improving skills and completing activities, rather than rating the project as compared to a masterpiece.

Do not critique the self-evaluation page your student completes in the Student Manual—it is acceptable for students to occasionally leave lines blank if a question does not apply. Instead, discuss with the student the intention of the written comments and incorporate those into your evaluation.

Determine a grade for this Phase, if using grades: _____

Teacher Self-Evaluation:

Evaluate your own use of materials: what worked and what did not? Consider your time management. Were you able to recognize and respond to your students' needs? Did you make your expectations clear? In what ways would you like to improve your approach for the next Unit? Incorporate suggestions from your students in your own evaluation (*this requires humility!*).

Phase 4

▶ In Your Own Way...

In this Unit, we have seen the world grow ever closer to war as the European Great Powers struggle to keep a balance of power; the Balkans come to center stage as they seek to expel their Ottoman overlord, during which Europe tries to both gain Balkan territory and bring "peace with honor"; Russia become a house divided between slavophiles, Westernizers, and anarchists—which will soon bring its centuries-old structure crashing down; in the East, Japan rise to become a modern military-industrial power, the overthrow of China's reigning dynasty, and Korea as the scene of both war and revival; the German Empire, ruled by a non-diplomatic kaiser, enter into a naval arms race with Great Britain, which looms as an impending threat to peace; supernatural revival result in the conversion of millions of people around the world in the first decade of the 1900s; America take long steps into imperialism and colonialism by gaining the Philippines, Puerto Rico, and Guam after the Spanish-American War; and the laborious task of building the Panama Canal. Now, choose a selection of these activities, or create your own, which will best express what you have learned from this Unit.

LINGUISTICS

Journalism

You are an official observer sent by the English government to report on the Balkan wars. Write several short, pithy telegrams describing what is taking place between the various countries of the Balkans and the Ottomans. Remember, though every word in a telegram is expensive, decisions will be made based on your reporting. Be short and to the point!

You have been hired by the *Christian Reporter* to discover how the work for the "evangelization of the world in this generation" is progressing. Your globe-trotting budget will allow you to visit as many sites of revival in the early 1900s as you wish, along with various missionary outposts.

Poetry

Finish this poem about the Triple Alliance and Triple Entente Cordiale:

They called it a "balance of power,"

Which made it a novel idea . . .

Prose

You entered the contest "Meet the Czarina at Home" and won an all-expenses-paid trip to Russia to meet Nicholas and Alexandra. Write a newsy letter to your parents telling them your observations of the court life of Russia.

Write a story for children about the Welsh Revival of 1904. Be sure to include such fascinating details as how policemen in certain towns had nothing to do because there was no crime after the revival, and how the pit ponies could no longer understand their bosses' language!

◉ Choose an area of expression

Students may work either individually or in teams.

Linguistics:

Journalism

Students interested in this journalism project may find inspiration by reading about the life of Januarius MacGahan, the American journalist in the Balkans, whose real life would make the most action-packed adventure Hollywood could devise. See the link at the online resource page.

Students may prefer to do this creative expression as a television reporter working from a script, rather than as a written journalistic piece. Be sure to film it in an interesting setting, with appropriate sound effects!

Poetry

Students might consider comparing the theory of balance of power to a children's teeter-totter (seesaw). With this in mind, illustrating the project like a nursery-rhyme book might make it more creative and exciting.

Prose

A fascinating real-life account of the Russian Court of Nicholas and Alexandra can be found in the book *Thirteen Years at the Russian Court* by Pierre Gilliard. It can be read online by going to the link at the online resource page.

Students who wish to write about the Welsh Revival might enjoy the book *Rees Howells: Intercessor* by Norman Grubb, or Wesley Duewel's book *Revival Fire*.

ART

Painting/Drawing

Draw a depiction of the Spanish-American War in Cuba. Most artists find it important to include Teddy Roosevelt leading the Rough Riders into the battle charge up San Juan Heights.

Graphic Design

Quick! Russian troops are at Constantinople, and your fellow British citizens are outraged! You will make a mint if you can design a T-shirt for sale that draws its inspiration from the wildly popular song:

We don't want to fight, but by Jingo if we do
We've got the ships, we've got the men, we've got the money too!

We've fought the Bear before, and while we're Britons true
The Russians shall not have Constantinople.

Cartooning

Draw a political cartoon showing how Russia's interest in gaining an ice-free port caused them to make friendly overtures to the people of the Balkans.

Fiber Art

Create a work of art whether through basketry, knitting, needlework, papermaking, quilting, sculpture, wearable art, or weaving. The focus of this piece is, through fiber art, to depict some aspect of the building of the Panama Canal.

MUSIC

Compose

Compose a song that will explain the many difficulties and disasters Russia was experiencing in this time, both internally and internationally. It might be interesting to use the melody of a Russian folksong as the basis for your composition.

Performance Practice

With your teacher's help, select an appropriate piece of music that expresses some particular aspect studied in this Unit that you found interesting.

Art:

Painting/Drawing

Students wishing to create an image of the Rough Riders might enjoy looking at Mort Kunstler's work *The Rough Riders*. You can find a link to this painting at the online resource page.

Graphic Design

Since the word "jingo" in this song gave rise to the term "jingoism," students might want to use only this word for the T-shirt while using as many other images as possible from the song.

Cartooning

Have students consider the geographical location of these Balkan countries in relation to Russia: Bulgaria, Serbia, Bosnia and Herzegovina, Montenegro, and Romania. Which would provide an ice-free port? Have students make a list of as many distinctive aspects of each of these countries as possible. From that list, they can then choose the most significant distinctive to create an image that will be a visual clue to identify the country.

Fiber Art

Students might find it helpful to visit the library or a local bookstore to look through various types of fiber art books—both design and "how-to"—to get ideas for what they might be able to do to replicate the Panama Canal.

Music:

Compose

You can find a link at the online resource page to an excellent website where you can hear Russian folk songs. You can listen to a very simple, slow example of each melody.

Performance Practice

For musical students, this selection may be a wonderful opportunity to express what they have learned. Make sure they select a piece that they have adequate time to prepare.

DRAMA

Comedy

Wilbur and Orville Wright made their original test flights at Kitty Hawk, North Carolina. Create a physical, comedic scene with the locals commenting on the highly unusual antics of these two determined brothers as they attempt to soar like birds.

Puppetry

Kaiser Bill is a puppet who knows what he wants and isn't afraid to take it. Uncle Ed, the British king, and Cousin Nicky over in Russia stand in his way, along with various other foreign friends. With the use of these puppets, tell the story of Wilhelm II's determination to find Germany's "place in the sun." Be sure to include the two Moroccan crises!

Drama

Through the use of drama, show Great Britain and France in their conflicting attempts to span the African continent. Be sure to include one of the most significant results of this conflict: the Entente Cordiale.

Prop Needs

_____

_____

Costume Ideas

_____

_____

Role/Player

_____

_____

Set Suggestions

_____

_____

Drama:

Comedy

Since the locals have never seen anything like this, what analogies might they use to describe what they are seeing? Encourage students to consider how to have the characters use familiar things to explain the unfamiliar. Look for things that might be unusual, because comedy is based on the unexpected. If the actors are saying things that the audience doesn't expect—an unusual metaphor, for example—it can be funny.

Puppetry

The political figures at this point in history were engaged in threat and violence, which is far easier to demonstrate easily and inoffensively with puppets. Research the puppets "Punch & Judy," because they established the modern concept of comic puppet violence. Encourage students to experiment with how, in the style of Punch & Judy, their characters can get what they want. *(Punch used a stick to beat on the other puppets.)*

Drama

Conflict and resolution is the basis of drama. Two people at cross purposes could be shown in a situation that parallels what was happening with Great Britain and France. This would allow them to explain the historic event without retelling the exact story. Students might want to work with the concept of metaphor: showing two people both wanting something, but, in the face of a looming threat, being more than happy to negotiate their differences.

Movement:

Pantomime

Students might find it very helpful to use a large map of Europe and the Balkans to chart the progress of the passengers on the train. Set up an environment: put the map on the wall of the train, just like they do on subways. Show the audience where you are traveling to on the map, and then, as you move from place to place, act differently. Experiment with different types of food, religious observances, and activities, depending on which region the train is traveling through. These might exemplify where you are and what is happening without words. Also feel free to develop characters. Who is traveling on the train? Are they wealthy, a family, a military, missionaries? If students wanted to do a group pantomime, each person could become a unique character and then each have a particular reaction to the same circumstances.

Dance

Students wishing to do this project might find it helpful to start with creating poses (like a human statue) associated with a certain attitude, phrase, or desire. Out of these poses, choose a few (depending on the age of the student, fewer for younger) and incorporate them into a dance for each perspective, for each character. If there were two dancers, one could dance the Harmonious Fists character and another the Revival character, and then they could dance together to show the contrast between these two attitudes.

Action

Encourage students to do research to find some of the physical elements of the culture. Then consider what can be done to represent these elements through physical postures. The question to ask is, "What behaviors does this culture have that are distinct from the other?" The object is to clearly define the characters through their physicality. Next, research the war to discover the most crucial battles and the surprises. From this list, condense the entire Russo-Japanese War into a series of crucial moments that will reflect the surprise and the effort of both sides.

MOVEMENT

Pantomime

You are on the first run of the Orient Express, the exotic new train route that travels from Paris to Istanbul. Pantomime your journey of 1883 through Europe, the Balkans, and the Ottoman Empire.

Dance

Choreograph a dance of the attitudes of the "Society of Righteous and Harmonious Fists," who led the Boxer Rebellion, and then contrast it with the attitudes of those who were being saved and forgiven during the revival which took place soon afterward in China.

Action

Through stylized action, with two or more students, recreate the Russo-Japanese War, which was fought on land and sea. Remember, this was the first time that an Asian country had been victorious over a European Great Power.

CONCEPTUAL DESIGN

A 3-D Diplomat

The Scenario

The Balkans are a mess. The Ottomans want to hold on to what they've got, Russia wants an ice-free port, Austria-Hungary wants Bosnia and Herzegovina, Germany wants a piece of the action, and England wants everyone to just settle down.

The Challenge

Create a three-dimensional map of the Balkans. Then, demonstrate your problem-solving diplomacy by redrawing the boundaries for each Balkan country, showing which country controls what.

The Rules

Be prepared to defend the reasoning behind your boundary lines and governmental authority, keeping in mind why the San Stefano, Berlin, London, Bucharest, and Constantinople treaties failed.

The Goal

Give the people groups of the Balkans what they want. Keep everyone else so well satisfied that they won't go to war.

CREATE YOUR OWN EXPRESSION

_____

_____

_____

_____

Conceptual Design:

The main problem with these other treaties is that they did not work! This exercise will allow students to think through ways they might learn from others' mistakes, improving the chance for peace. If students build a three-dimensional map—using papier-mâché, Lego® blocks, or other building materials, or if they use a three-dimensional computer modeling program—they will "see" the terrain far more effectively. This will help them understand the natural routes through the Balkans to Europe and Asia, which make it one of the most important pieces of real estate in the world.

● Share creative expressions in class

Create a safe environment for the presentations. Set ground rules prior to the presentations, so that students know how much time is available for each of them, and so that they know they will be honored and respected by all those observing.

▶ Student Self-Evaluation UNIT 5, PHASE 4

Dates and hours:_____

Evaluate your projects

- What creative project did you choose?
  _____

- What did you expect from your project, and how does the final project compare to your initial expectations?
  _____
  _____

- What do you like about your project? What would you change?
  _____
  _____

In Conclusion

Revisit the four Key Concepts from the beginning of this Unit. Explain how your understanding of and appreciation for each has grown over the course of your study.

- _____
  _____
- _____
  _____
- _____
  _____
- _____
  _____

Record your concluding thoughts on Alliances & Revivals:
_____
_____

◉ Conduct a review and evaluation

In this Phase of Unit 5, your students should have had the opportunity to express what they have learned about Alliances & Revivals through one or more various creative selections of their own choosing. These include:

- Linguistics;
- Art;
- Music;
- Drama;
- Movement;
- Conceptual Design.

Record student hours: _____

Assess student effort in the creative expressions, as individuals or as teams.

Create an evaluation system of your own, or refer to the evaluation rubric in the introduction, as a tool for assessing participation. The categories you will probably find most useful for evaluating their projects are *"Task," "Process: Teamwork," "Process: Originality,"* and Grammar, Format, and Spelling.

In this Phase especially, do not critique the self-evaluation page your student completes in the Student Manual—consider how the very soul of an artist has been exposed and vulnerable, so be encouraging and not belittling. Again, consider enthusiasm, precision of approach, and efforts toward improving skills and completing the activity, rather than rating the project as compared to a masterpiece. Instead, discuss with the student the intention of the written comments and incorporate those into your evaluation.

Determine a grade for this Phase, if using grades: _____

Teacher Self-Evaluation:

Evaluate your own use of materials and teaching opportunities: what worked and what did not; how effective was your time-management; how were your responses to the needs of your student; did you make your expectations clear; in what ways would you like to improve your approach for the next Unit? Incorporate suggestions from your students in your own evaluation (*this requires humility!*).

Take a moment now to evaluate the whole Unit. What would you like to remember if you taught this subject again? What do you recognize that your students gained most—either as students of history or as creative individuals? What did you learn about Alliances & Revivals or about teaching?

World War I & the Russian Revolution (1914–1918)

Pray with the students
at the beginning of each Unit.

Enthusiasm and delight
are the best ways to capture
a student's interest and
jump-start motivation, so:

» **For the Auditory Students:** To capture their attention at the very beginning of class, play a musical selection from the beginning of the war, such as "We Didn't Want to Fight," performed by Stanley Kirkby. (You can listen to this and other WWI selections by going to the link at the online resource page.

» **For the Kinesthetic Students:** Have the students warm up as class begins by doing an action like working together in pantomime to build trenches while ducking bullets.

» **For the Visual Students:** Provide a visual object to stimulate their interest in the new Unit, such as the portrait of Kaiser Wilhelm II by Albert Stricht.

» **For the hearts of all:** Pray with them at the beginning of the Unit, that God would help them discover what He has for each one to learn in this Unit.

◉ Learning Style Emphasis

Teachers can choose to have students do one or two activities, rather than the entire week's schedule. Please use what works for you in your unique setting.

	Week 1: Feeler	Week 2: Thinker	Week 3: Sensor	Week 4: Intuitor
	During this week, students will be introduced to World War I & the Russian Revolution, along with the appropriate Scriptures. You may follow this suggested schedule or adapt it to meet your students' needs:	Students will explore topics of interest through research and reporting, learn new vocabulary, and construct a time line relating to World War I & the Russian Revolution.	Students will gain cultural understanding through sensory activities as they explore interrelated subject areas through sensory activities pertaining to World War I & the Russian Revolution.	Students, through creative self-expression, using one or more creative activities, will present some aspect of what they have learned in the past three weeks relating to World War I & the Russian Revolution. Areas of expression include linguistics, art, music, drama, movement, and conceptual design.)
Monday	Informally discuss the Key Concepts Listen to the *What in the World?* audio recording(s)	Choose topic and begin research	Create a map and discuss the issues in teams	Choose an area of expression and begin work either individually or in teams
Tuesday	Read the article Listen to the other audio recording(s) Read the Scriptures		Examine and discuss art masterpieces & architectural structures	
Wednesday	Recap the material using activities Talk together	Practice vocabulary	Do an art project*	
Thursday	Conduct class discussion	Construct the tim eline	Do a science experiment or field trip**	
Friday	Choose books of interest/Internet search Conduct a review and evaluation	Complete research projects and share in class or hand in Conduct a review and evaluation	Listen to and discuss the music Cook the food listed in the recipe Conduct a review and evaluation	Share creative expressions in class Conduct a review and evaluation

*Art project will need to be planned ahead of time to acquire materials.

** Field trip will require extra planning time.

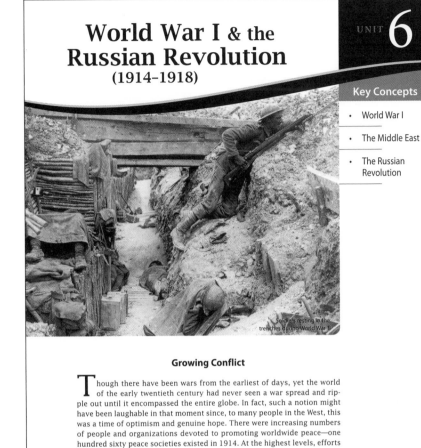

World War I & the Russian Revolution (1914–1918)

Key Concepts

- World War I
- The Middle East
- The Russian Revolution

Soldiers resting in the trenches during World War I

Growing Conflict

Though there have been wars from the earliest of days, yet the world of the early twentieth century had never seen a war spread and ripple out until it encompassed the entire globe. In fact, such a notion might have been laughable in that moment since, to many people in the West, this was a time of optimism and genuine hope. There were increasing numbers of people and organizations devoted to promoting worldwide peace—one hundred sixty peace societies existed in 1914. At the highest levels, efforts to create an international court, which could settle conflicts between countries without resorting to war, were pursued at The Hague Conventions in 1899 and 1907. A peaceful and prosperous Europe, with its interdependent financial investments and trade, made the thought of a European war seem utterly impossible—it wouldn't be worth the economic cost. Technology and

World War I & the Russian Revolution (1914–1918) **225**

◉ Informally discuss the Key Concepts with your students

KEY CONCEPTS Background Information

These are the main objectives of the Unit. As you proceed through the four weeks, your students will be given various ways of understanding each of these objectives. Explanations of these Key Concepts follow.

6

science were making huge differences in the world, creating labor-saving, time-saving devices—like Henry Ford's automobile. Tremendous nation-changing revivals, which had taken place during the first decade of the century, resulted in international missionary efforts to see the world evangelized in that generation. These revivals also impacted the perspective of Christians in Europe, as German and English pastors visited each other's countries to gain an understanding of being members of the same Body.

Europe's balance of power was still evident as the powerful nations of France, England, and Russia diplomatically allied themselves, attempting to compensate for the vast power of the treaty-bound nations of Austria-Hungary, Germany, and Italy. In the carefree summer of 1914, though a few political hot spots in the world still needed a bit of tidying up, it seemed that the idea of peace on earth and good will to all was just over the horizon.

In the carefree summer of 1914, it seemed that the idea of peace on earth and good will to all was just over the horizon.

As any good history book will tell you, though, peace was not what lay ahead. In order to grasp the immensity of the inconceivable, to see the struggle from the perspective of those living through it, and to better tell the story, the article for this Unit will be structured in four movements, as a sort of harsh-sounding, twentieth-century symphony of war, accompanied by tables noting some of what took place.

The Complex Relationships of the Orchestra

Though peace seemed to be likely, there were a few regions in 1914 that had the potential of erupting into conflict. The Balkans, in the southeastern corner of Europe, posed some of the most complex and interrelated diplomatic knots of contention in the world. As described in the previous Unit, the Balkans contained different religions, languages, ethnicities, and cultures. Of these various combinations, one group—the Southern Slavic people of the Balkans—had been more and more drawn to the idea of having their own nation, independent of Austria-Hungary and of the Ottoman Empire. Serbia, newly freed from Ottoman rule, was the undisputed victor of the recent Balkan wars and champion of the idea of independence for the Southern Slavs. Bulgaria, though a co-victor with Serbia in the first Balkan war, had lost all of its gains in the second, and was strongly motivated to retake lost territory—especially the strategic land of Macedonia, located at the top of the Aegean Sea. Bosnia and Herzegovina, a small country, had been annexed to its neighbor, the Austro-Hungarian Empire. This imperial giant contained within it three different Slavic peoples: the Bosniacs (Muslim), the Serbs (Orthodox), and the Croats (Catholic)—each with their own needs and concerns.

? To get an informal discussion started on this Key Concept, ask a simple leading question, such as, "What have you heard about World War I?"

World War I— EXPLANATION

Many adults today learned little during their school years about WWI, apart from the fact that it happened. For some, it was because the teacher never quite got to the end of the textbook and thus missed the war. For those in the United States, if they were told anything, it was that America had saved the day—end of story. This lack of knowledge is unfortunate, since the events of WWI and its aftermath are as relevant to today's headlines as the latest Middle East conflict. Indeed, the latest Middle East conflict is rooted in the events of WWI, as will be noted in the following Key Concept.

So, what are some of the reasons why WWI is so important to world history? Here are a few:

Huge disruption of many nations— When the war began, most of the major countries involved were governed in the same way as they had been for centuries. Pre-war Europe had nineteen monarchies and only three republics. By the time it ended, the great power autocracies had become a thing of the past, with four major empires having dissolved: the German Empire, the Austro-Hungarian Empire, the Russian Empire, and the

6

To the north of the Balkans, Austria-Hungary was allied with a military powerhouse—the German Empire, its northern neighbor. These two massive empires had on their eastern borders the immense and ponderous empire of Russia, which was slowly but surely increasing its military and industrial strength—and who was allied, not to its neighbors, but to former enemies, France and England. Significant to the events of 1914, both Austria-Hungary and Russia had long been drooling over the Balkan region. Austria-Hungary sought to protect its structural integrity by drawing all the Balkans' Southern Slavs into the Austrian fold, rather than having those living within its borders break away—potentially crumbling the empire. Russia sought to gain Istanbul for two important reasons. There was the sociological motivation to own the historic capital of Byzantium, since Russia considered itself to be the heir of the Byzantine culture. Also, there was removing the final barrier in Russia's development into the strongest, as well as largest, country in Eurasia through Istanbul's strategic access to the Mediterranean. Germany also sought a strong influence in the region because the Berlin-to-Baghdad railroad would run through the Balkans.

Both Austria-Hungary and Russia had long been drooling over the Balkan region.

On the southeastern corner of the Balkans lay the remainder of the Ottoman Empire's much-reduced European territory. Across the Bosporus, its expansive Asian lands stretched from Anatolia on the Mediterranean to the Caucasus on the Black Sea, and from Sinai to Mesopotamia. Despite its reputation as "the sick man of Europe," the Ottoman Empire had been recently energized by the Young Turk Revolution of 1908, setting a new sultan on the throne and improving the power and standing of the army. As was noted in the previous Unit, Germany had been building connections with the Ottomans for a number of years. This included helping them build a more workable military training program for officers, based on the German model, and becoming their source for military weaponry. And, in the southeast of the Ottoman Empire, the Russians and English played their "Great Game," trying to protect and expand their interests in Mesopotamia.

West of the Balkans across the Adriatic Sea was the recently formed nation of Italy, which had been ruled in part by the Austrian Hapsburgs since the Congress of Vienna in 1815. Though Italy had signed the Triple Alliance with Austria-Hungary and Germany, it had definite concerns about the four-hundred-mile border it shared with Austria-Hungary. There is even a term associated with this concern: "irredentism," the belief that all Italian-speaking territories should be included within the borders of the nation of Italy. One of the most significant of these places was Trieste, the main sea port of the Austro-Hungarian Empire. Located at the northeastern tip of the Adriatic, Trieste was seen by Italy as belonging rightfully to them.

Ottoman Empire. The number of republics in post-war Europe catapulted to fourteen, many of which were created out of these fallen empires.

Extremist governments—Through the sudden dissolving of these long-lived empires, the war also provided the necessary social and political upheavals for extremist governments to come into being. In Russia, Lenin established a communist (left-wing) government, based on a strict Marxist philosophy—which he sought to export to the world. In some of the post-war European republics, continuing inflation and dissatisfaction with the peace treaties gave rise to right-wing fascism, as will be seen in Hitler, Mussolini, and Franco. These new, virulent forms of government brought titanic changes to the world, as we will see over the next three Units.

Optimism turned to pessimism—In the early 1900s, human optimism was reaching an all-time high. The technologies of the Industrial Revolution were rapidly changing the world, making it seem as though the wildest technological dreams—such as man flying like a bird—could come true. With high hopes of man achieving worldwide peace on a scale never before seen and the economic and technological prosperity to go with it, it seemed as though humanity was at

6

The Tempo of Events

On June 28, 1914, the heir to the Austro-Hungarian Empire and his Czech wife were assassinated while visiting Sarajevo, capital city of Bosnia. The assassins, who had been trained by Serbian nationalists, were attempting to rid Bosnia of its Austro-Hungarian overlord so that the Southern Slavic people of Bosnia-Herzegovina could be joined to Serbia. Their success in assassinating Archduke Franz Ferdinand would soon provoke something much larger than they could have imagined.

Though this assassination of royalty was shocking to Europe's rulers, it was not that unusual. In the past few decades, many important political figures had been assassinated, as this was a favored method of some revolutionaries for forcing change. The Sarajevo tragedy was understood by the leaders of Europe to be one of those unfortunate events connected to the troubles in the Balkans, and, since Austria-Hungary seemed to be taking no action, tensions in early July evaporated. To all appearances, business was continuing as usual—Kaiser Wilhelm II even took his scheduled vacation.

Below the surface, however, decisions were being made. On July 6, Germany told Austria-Hungary that it supported their moving against Serbia, in effect giving them a signed blank check. Germany was convinced that if Austria-Hungary moved quickly in response to the killings, the Russian czar would not move to protect Serbia but would distance himself from Serbia, due to its apparent involvement in the killing of royalty, and that the rest of the world would understand and sympathize with Austria-Hungary for punishing Serbia. This was the opportune moment, Germany's leaders reasoned, for the Austrians to deal decisively with Serbia—to stop them from drawing away the Southern Slavs within the imperial border and initiating the breakdown of this widely divergent empire. Austria-Hungary was not known for decisiveness, however—they took nearly a month to present an ultimatum to Serbia. And when they finally did, it contained such outrageous demands that Europeans recognized it as merely a diplomatic ploy hiding their obvious intention to go to war with Serbia.

> *Below the surface, however, decisions were being made.*

As a side note, it is interesting to see that, though the European powers did not plan for war that summer, they had plans for conducting war should it ever come. Germany's military leaders, holding to a Darwin-influenced theory that nations had to struggle for their survival, believed that a war with Russia was going to be necessary in the not-too-distant future, and that it would undoubtedly draw France into the conflict as well. The German plan called for a quick, decisive victory against France so that the entire German army could hurry east to face the massive, slow-to-mobilize Russian army. They were not the only ones with a plan. The French, with the sting of the Franco-Prussian War still piercing their thoughts, had prepared something

last going to bring heaven to earth. By the end of the war, this optimism had given way to a dark pessimism and cynical disillusionment, fueled by traumatic memories of wrongs committed, collectively and individually, which opened the door for even more terrible events.

Seeds of future turmoil—The shifting boundaries of new nations, as empires broke apart at the end of the war, often left behind bitter rivalries and dissensions within these nations. Places such as Yugoslavia and Palestine had, within their new boundaries, the seeds of struggle that were destined to keep their regions in turmoil.

Unprecedented cost—The expense of fighting this war was approximately one hundred eighty-six billion dollars, far more than any previous war in history, and it left most of the major players deeply in debt. But the war had other and more grievous costs. By the time it was over, of the sixty-five million soldiers mobilized, nearly nine million had died, twenty-one million had been wounded, and nearly eight million had been taken prisoner. This means that more than half of WWI's military personnel became casualties. In addition, it is estimated that more than five million civilians died as a direct result of the war. This staggers the mind, and

called Plan XVII. The strategy was to go on the offensive at the outbreak of war and retake Alsace-Lorraine from the Germans. This now-German region remained so important to the French people that, forty years after its loss, the monument in Paris representing Alsace was still draped in black! Austria-Hungary had recently developed Plans B (Balkans) and R (Russia), which both focused on a limited war with Serbia. Russia had developed several plans over the years, but the most recent, Plan 19, called for an invasion of East Prussia, then continuing on to central Germany.

So much for worldwide peace and good will to all.

1914—First Movement: Allegro (Fast!)

War began like a series of falling dominoes. First, Austria declared war and started to mobilize against Serbia in response to the Sarajevo assassinations. Serbia, in alarm, called to its Orthodox big brother, Russia, for protection. Russia began to mobilize against Austria-Hungary, and as a precaution, against Austria-Hungary's ally, Germany. Germany demanded that Russia stop mobilization or suffer the consequences. Despite a flurry of telegrams between family members "Nicky" and "Willy" (the Russian czar and the German kaiser), Russia did not stop its mobilization, since Austria-Hungary was still mobilizing against Serbia. Here is a portion of Germany's official declaration of war with Russia:

> Russia having refused to comply with this demand, and having shown by this refusal that her action was directed against Germany, I have the honour, on the instructions of my Government, to inform your Excellency as follows: His Majesty the Emperor, my august Sovereign, in the name of the German Empire, accepts the challenge, and considers himself at war with Russia.

"His Majesty the Emperor, my august Sovereign, in the name of the German Empire, accepts the challenge, and considers himself at war with Russia."

Germany then turned to Belgium to request permission to take its army through Belgium's neutral territory, in order to confront France—Russia's ally—according to Germany's standard plan for war. Belgium refused permission. Germany declared war on Belgium, which brought Great Britain into the war. By August 12, the Triple Entente Cordiale members, or just Triple Entente (Great Britain, France, and Russia) were at war with two of the Triple Alliance members (Germany and Austria-Hungary). Serbia, with Austria-Hungary's attack, joined the Allies. Italy declared itself neutral in 1914, since its treaty called for support in war only in the case of defense, and Austria-Hungary's attack of Serbia was clearly an offensive move. The Triple Alliance became known as the Central Powers (located in Central

it shaped the perspective of those who lived through this war and who would fight in the next.

In order to help students better understand the events and effects of this war, charts have been included in the article for Unit 6 in the Student Manual that give a visual, short, bi-monthly, front-by-front synopsis of the war. The research required to create these charts revealed evidence that there has been a tremendous bias common among many descriptions of WWI. The bias can be clearly seen in older sources' description of the Balkan Front, the Italian Front, or the Caucasus Front as "sideshows." Yet "sideshow" hardly describes a theater of war where a million people die. This labeling is discovered by reading books specifically devoted to these fronts. They quite clearly portray the attitudes of superiority held by some of the leaders of the great powers and the ways they denigrated the importance and value of the people groups fighting at these fronts. These attitudes found their way into many of the general history books available, resulting in a bias that focuses mainly on the Western Front—to the point that the other areas of the war become obscured, keeping us from seeing the significance and connection between the far-flung elements of this tumultuous time. Please

6

Europe), while the Triple Entente was known as the Entente Powers or, more simply, the Allies. Both groups would increase their membership over the next four years: the Central Powers would add two more, the Ottoman Empire and Bulgaria; the Allies, in addition to Great Britain's Dominion colonies, would also add more than twenty countries across the globe, though not all would send troops to fight.

Unimaginably, this war dragged on for more than four Christmases, killing millions in the process.

Why did it grow from a limited conflict between Austria-Hungary and Serbia into a world war? That is the question many have sought to answer from the very beginning, and many theories have been produced. Some suggest that Europe's balance of power and its interwoven alliances dragged country after country into the abyss. Others see the land-grabbing, empire-building desires of the European countries, especially Germany, the newcomer to imperial splendor, as the cause of this runaway war. Among the newest theories, based on recently released primary sources from the various countries, is one suggesting that a relatively few people in positions of power in the German and Austro-Hungarian governments manipulated the situation so as to best benefit their own countries' needs.

Whatever the causes, no one in their wildest dreams expected the war to last more than a few months. They expected to tidy up the mess and get home by Christmas. As you will soon discover, there was nothing tidy about the unfolding drama, and the next several years would be spent on the *war fronts*: the places where armies clashed, whether in deserts, jungles, or the freezing mud of trenches. Unimaginably, this war dragged on for more than four Christmases, killing millions in the process.

Program Notes: Christians of Both Sides Respond

In August, Protestant German theologians and missionaries, including some who had attended the 1910 World Missionary Conference in Edinburgh, wrote "An Appeal to Evangelical Christians Abroad." They sought to prevent a rupture in the blossoming international fellowship—despite being on opposing sides of the war—and hoped their fellow Protestants in England and France could persuade their governments to protect German missions in Africa, keeping mission fields from becoming battlefields. In October, along with other German writers, composers, and academics, they wrote "An Appeal to the Civilized World." Here is a section from that appeal:

It is not true that Germany is guilty of causing this war. Neither the people, nor the government, nor the Kaiser wanted it. The German side did its utmost to prevent it. Documentary evidence of this truth is available for the world to see. During the twenty-six years of his reign,

Discuss with your students some of the effects of considering one's self or one's country as better, smarter, and more talented than anyone else's. Proverbs 16:18 says, "Pride goes before destruction, and a haughty spirit before a fall." In what ways might the great powers' pride and arrogance have affected the war? What application does this have to our own lives, and to the way we view our own countries? Pray with students that God would show them His ways and teach them His paths.

To get an informal discussion started on this Key Concept, ask a simple leading question, such as, "What do you know about the Middle East at the time of World War I?"

encourage your students to take the time to study these charts—they will help them grasp the dynamics of the various fronts, as well as what the uncertainties of the war felt like to the people of the time, who truly had no idea how or when it would end.

The Middle East— EXPLANATION

When the Ottoman Empire joined the Central Powers in October 1914, it meant that there would now be more fronts and battles in the war, requiring more soldiers, ammunition, and strategies. Though the British were not particularly concerned about the

abilities of an Ottoman army, the Allies were nevertheless determined to quickly eliminate the Ottomans from the war in order to pursue their prime goal of defeating Germany. They would learn at the Battle of Gallipoli that underestimating the Turkish soldier was a mistake.

How to accomplish this elimination was the topic of intense discussion, with plans ranging from capturing the Dardanelles and Istanbul to fostering a massive Arab revolt against the Turks—either of which would hopefully topple the Ottoman Empire and take them out of the war. Initially, the British government was not interested in acquiring any new territory

6

Wilhelm II has often enough shown himself to be the protector of peace, and even our opponents have often enough acknowledged this fact. Indeed, this very Kaiser, whom they now dare call an Attila, has been ridiculed by them for years, because of his steadfast efforts to maintain peace. Only when the great force that has long lurked about us attacked our people from three sides, only then did we rise up as one man. It is not true that we maliciously violated Belgian neutrality. France and England were demonstrably determined to violate it. Belgium was demonstrably in agreement with them. It would have been suicide on our part not to anticipate their move.

Many Germans also saw themselves as battling the cruel and oppressive Russian regime, which, in addition to its other barbarous acts, had been persecuting Russian Jews with a vengeful ferocity over the past several decades.

From the very beginning, each side had its own perspective on why it was engaged in this war. Sadly, with war propaganda on both sides actively working to shape perspectives, attitudes became so warped and twisted that even Christians were caught up in the rush to hate their enemies. Billy Sunday, the popular American evangelist, was quoted as saying, "If you turn hell upside down, you will find 'Made in Germany' stamped on the bottom." He so thoroughly accepted the propaganda, which depicted the Central Powers as utterly evil, that when America entered the war in 1917, he said, "Christianity and patriotism are *synonymous* terms."

That should make us stop and, like the Bereans of the New Testament, consider what is being said. Would the early Christians living in Rome have agreed with his words? And, beyond the controversial nature of that statement, we must observe that, in this furious moment of patriotism and war, there appears to have been no thought of how to obey the clear and simple command of Jesus in Matthew 5:44: "But I say to you, love your enemies." During WWI, church people, whether in the Central Powers or the Allies, seem to have seen their own side as righteous and to have vilified their country's enemy.

Despite the break in fellowship between the various European churches, care and compassion to the displaced, starving, wounded, and dying would come to play a huge part in offsetting the horrors of war through such organizations as the Young Men's Christian Association (YMCA) and the International Red Cross (IRC). An American who would later become president, Herbert Hoover, headed up a relief organization devoted to keeping the citizens of Belgium from starving to death. This international commission fed 11 million Belgians from 1914 to 1919, bringing food despite all the obstacles of war and despite the belligerent and defiant attitudes of military rulers of the Allies and Central Powers alike.

Japan had shown the world that it had the ability to score overwhelming victories on both land and sea against a much larger enemy

World War I & the Russian Revolution (1914–1918) **231**

or colonies that might come from the Ottoman's dissolution, though Britain's allies were very interested. One of the regions that would be up for grabs if the Ottoman Empire fell is what we call the Middle East, an expression that was not widely used until the summer of 1916. At the time of WWI, the countries that would come to be identified as part of the Middle East were located almost entirely within the Ottoman Empire—apart from the notable exception of Persia (Iran).

To understand how the Middle East has become such a tangled mess in the one hundred years since the war, it is helpful to understand how the twentieth-century story began. Great Britain was always defending her route to India, the "jewel" of the British Empire. There were those in the government who were concerned that their Muslim subjects in India might rise up in revolt if the Ottoman Sultan should call for a holy war. They knew from experience in the 1857 Indian Mutiny that it would be difficult to quell such an event—especially if the millions of Muslims under British control joined the revolution. Lord Kitchener, the greatest living British military hero *and* the War Minister, wanted to build a strong connection between Britain and the rulers of Arabia, who were

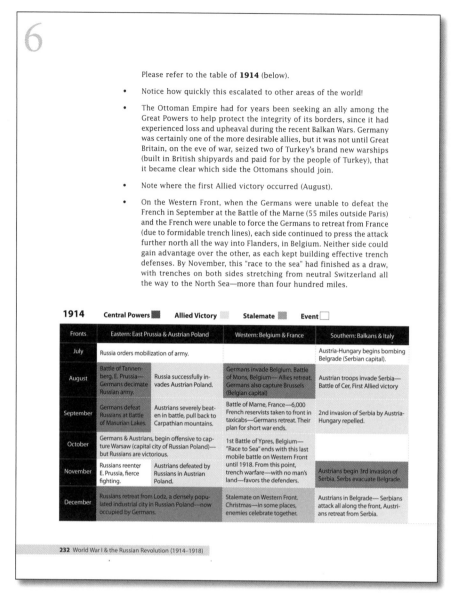

6

Please refer to the table of **1914** (below).

- Notice how quickly this escalated to other areas of the world!

- The Ottoman Empire had for years been seeking an ally among the Great Powers to help protect the integrity of its borders, since it had experienced loss and upheaval during the recent Balkan Wars. Germany was certainly one of the more desirable allies, but it was not until Great Britain, on the eve of war, seized two of Turkey's brand new warships (built in British shipyards and paid for by the people of Turkey), that it became clear which side the Ottomans should join.

- Note where the first Allied victory occurred (August).

- On the Western Front, when the Germans were unable to defeat the French in September at the Battle of the Marne (55 miles outside Paris) and the French were unable to force the Germans to retreat from France (due to formidable trench lines), each side continued to press the attack further north all the way into Flanders, in Belgium. Neither side could gain advantage over the other, as each kept building effective trench defenses. By November, this "race to the sea" had finished as a draw, with trenches on both sides stretching from neutral Switzerland all the way to the North Sea—more than four hundred miles.

1914   Central Powers ■   Allied Victory ▫   Stalemate ■   Event ☐

Fronts	Eastern: East Prussia & Austrian Poland		Western: Belgium & France	Southern: Balkans & Italy
July	Russia orders mobilization of army.			Austria-Hungary begins bombing Belgrade (Serbian capital).
August	Battle of Tannenberg, E. Prussia—Germans decimate Russian army.	Russia successfully invades Austrian Poland.	Germans invade Belgium. Battle of Mons, Belgium—Allies retreat. Germans also capture Brussels (Belgian capital)	Austrian troops invade Serbia—Battle of Cer, First Allied victory
September	Germans defeat Russians at Battle of Masurian Lakes.	Austrians severely beaten in battle, pull back to Carpathian mountains.	Battle of Marne, France—6,000 French reservists taken to front in taxicabs—Germans retreat. Their plan for short war ends.	2nd invasion of Serbia by Austria-Hungary repelled.
October	Germans & Austrians, begin offensive to capture Warsaw (capital city of Russian Poland)—but Russians are victorious.		1st Battle of Ypres, Belgium—"Race to Sea" ends with this last mobile battle on Western Front until 1918. From this point, trench warfare—with no man's land—favors the defenders.	
November	Russians reenter E. Prussia, fierce fighting.	Austrians defeated by Russians in Austrian Poland.		Austrians begin 3rd invasion of Serbia. Serbs evacuate Belgrade.
December	Russians retreat from Lodz, a densely populated industrial city in Russian Poland—now occupied by Germans.		Stalemate on Western Front. Christmas—in some places, enemies celebrate together.	Austrians in Belgrade—Serbians attack all along the front, Austrians retreat from Serbia.

232 World War I & the Russian Revolution (1914–1918)

seeking allies at the beginning of the war. Kitchener proposed that, if the Arabs actually threw off the Ottoman yoke, then Britain should support them in their "emancipation." In addition, he was concerned about a dark and ominous future for British India unless steps were taken to prevent a Muslim rebellion. As a solution to both concerns, he thought to encourage the ruler of Mecca, Hussein ibn Ali, to declare himself to be the new Muslim Caliph. In a marketing ploy worthy of Madison Avenue, Kitchener hinted that, with the historic city of Mecca in common to both Islam's founder and its current ruler, Hussein would be sure to win favor from the vast Arabic-speaking population within the Ottoman Empire. And, with Britain's naval firepower to control the coastline of the Arabian peninsula, it seemed to Kitchener and his aides that this was the best of all possible post-war worlds—a British-influenced Arabic Caliph. This was what was suggested to Hussein, despite the fact that there were other Arab contenders for such a position, including Ibn Saud, who was ruler over the eastern area of Arabia and a friend to Britain.

Unfortunately, what Kitchener communicated was not what he had intended. His misunderstanding of Islam led him to think that a Caliph

6

1915–16—Second Movement: Andante (Slow)

As 1915 began, the idea of a quick victory—for either side—was gone. The driving, moving battlefield of the Western Front slowed to a virtual standstill, and with it came a relentless pounding of the trenches as each side ferociously shelled and attacked. "Victories" were measured by yards, "battles" took months, and the true costs of this war were tallied in inconceivable numbers of dead, captured, and wounded. Belgium and northern France were looking more and more like scenes out of Dante's *Inferno*, and were, in fact, the inspiration for Tolkien's depiction of a realm where evil reigns. In 1968, he wrote about his experience on the Western Front in 1916: "I remember miles and miles of seething, tortured earth, perhaps best described in the chapters about the approaches to Mordor. It was a searing experience."

With this stalemate on the Western Front, the Allies sought to break the deadlock by opening a new front in the war, and for this they looked to the Dardanelle Straits. Capturing this strategic location could provide the Allies an opportunity to invade Istanbul, thereby taking the Ottoman Empire out of the war, and also permit the Allies to resupply Russia through the Straits to her ports on the Black Sea. In addition to these, the Central Powers and the Allies, who were always strategizing about ways to outflank and outgun each other, both sought to gain new allies in the Balkans. Hoping to draw others besides Serbia into war on the Allied side, Great Britain put into motion its plan to capture the Straits. Tragically, the

Ottoman Empire: Dardanelles, Caucasus, Iraq, Palestine		Africa/Asia: East Africa, West Africa, Pacific Islands, Eastern coast of China		Naval
		Allies capture German Togoland. Invade German Cameroon.	New Zealanders capture Western Samoa.	British fleet sets up blockade—also sinks three German cruisers in North Sea.
		Japan, Great Britain's ally, occupies German islands north of equator.	Australians capture northeastern New Guinea.	
Ottoman Empire joins Central Powers—a victory for Germany & Austria-Hungary. Turks bombard Russian port cities on the Black Sea. The war now enters a much larger phase.				
British bombard Dardanelles—its value strategically seen as Western Front stagnates	British troops land at port city of Basra, Iraq—just above the Persian Gulf.	Qingdao, German colony in China, captured by Japanese.		Germans sink two British cruisers off Chile, west coast of South America.
The Ottoman army attacks Russia in the Caucasus mountains. They are defeated, with massive casualties.				British sink three German cruisers off Falkland Islands, east coast of South America.

would be a spiritual authority only, and Hussein's tiny territory of Mecca would be all the physical land he would politically govern—just like Vatican City and the Pope. That is why he included in his message to Hussein in late 1914 these words, "It may be that an Arab of true race will assume the Khalifate at Mecca." Hussein read this British suggestion for him to become the new Caliph as an offer to make him the *political* as well as *spiritual* ruler of a vast Arabic kingdom.

As David Fromkin, author of *A Peace to End All Peace*, so clearly states:

> The British intended to support the candidacy of Hussein for the position of "Pope" of Islam—a position that (unbeknown to them) did not exist; while (unbeknown to them too) the language they used encouraged him to attempt to become ruler of the entire Arab world.

Thus, the first mistake was made.

Several months later, Hussein followed up with a letter demanding that Britain pledge to support his rule over most of Arabic-speaking Asia. He felt this was in keeping with what the British had promised earlier, yet it surprised the British a great deal. They had not realized what had been unintentionally communicated. When, however, the British heard

6

plan was formulated within their culture's biased and racist perspective. This caused them to falsely believe that that the Turkish defenders would be no match for the strength of the Allies. Thus, British troops (drawn largely from Australia and New Zealand) with French troops landed with the expectation that they would quickly move from the Gallipoli Peninsula (on the Dardanelle Straits) all the way to the prized city of Istanbul. The results were quite devastating to the Allies, as well as being tragically costly to both Allied and Turkish troops at Gallipoli. A new stalemate emerged when the Allied attackers could not gain the heights (necessary for victory) and the Turkish defenders could not force the Allies from the beaches (necessary for victory).

Though the Eastern Front was far more mobile than the Western, with battle lines moving forward and backward with great rapidity, still the armies there were chalking up increasing casualties, as well as tens of thousands of prisoners from both sides. Because Austria-Hungary had been unable to withstand Russian attacks, German troops from the West were sent to bolster Austrian troops beginning in May 1915. Together they launched a huge offensive, steadily pushing Russian troops out of Austrian Poland and into western Russia. These were dark days for the Allies. The following year, Russia, rearmed and reinvigorated, went on the offensive, blasting through the Austro-Hungarian lines—a crisis for the Central Powers.

> *In May, Italy entered the war as one of the Allies and proceeded to invade Austria-Hungary.*

In May, Italy entered the war as one of the Allies and proceeded to invade Austria-Hungary. The front that developed here (known as the Italian, Isonzo, or Soča Front) was nearly four hundred miles long, from the Swiss border to the Adriatic Sea, and was fought mainly in rocky and mountainous terrain. This was one of the deadliest fronts in the entire war, though it too, very soon deteriorated to a stalemate that lasted for two and a half years.

During the summer of 1915, in the Caucasus region, the Ottoman Empire sent a Turkish army to deport or exterminate the Armenians, who were thought to have assisted the Russian enemy as it invaded the area in the spring. It was, to a watching world, the systematic genocide of an ancient Christian culture, but they were unable to stop it—even the German protest had no effect.

On the Southern Front, Serbian troops faced the onslaught of armies from Germany, Austria-Hungary, and the newcomer Bulgaria in autumn of 1915. After valiantly defending their homeland and running out of supplies, the leadership made the decision to flee to the mountains of Albania in order to fight another day. In early 1916, a massive rescue operation was mounted by Italian, French, and British ships, transporting more than 150,000 Serb soldiers to the island of Corfu—the largest sea rescue operation in history

that Arab soldiers throughout the Ottoman army were dissatisfied with the way they were being treated by the Turkish government, they suddenly saw a way that Hussein could be used immediately, because the Arabs were ripe for revolution—or so they thought. Believing erroneously that there were tens or even hundreds of thousands of discontented Arab soldiers ready to join when Hussein launched his revolution, some British leaders were convinced that this could bring down the Ottoman Empire and change the war on the Western Front. Later, when the Arab Revolt began, it actually attracted only a few thousand.

But, in order to be able to promise Hussein land in Syria and Palestine, Britain had to gain permission from France. Part of this area—known to some, since the time of the Crusades, as "the France of the Near East"—was seen by the French as rightly belonging to them. It was with trepidation that two diplomats from Britain and France, Sykes and Picot, sat down to hammer out the details of winning Arab allegiance while still maintaining European plans in the Middle East. The Sykes-Picot agreement was a secret treaty, in which France would rule Lebanon and be the exclusive "influence" in Syria, while the British would take the two Mesopotamian

6

prior to WWII's Dunkirk evacuation. On Corfu, these exiles recovered and waited for the opportunity to retake their country.

In October 1915, the Allies landed a combined Franco-British force in Salonika (or Thessalonica, where the Apostle Paul preached), one of the largest sea ports in the Aegean, and recently claimed by Greece. The intention was to move these troops north to join in the fight to save Serbia, but they arrived too late. A controversial decision was then made by Allied high command to keep Salonika as an Allied outpost from which to attack the Central Powers, despite the disapproval of Greece's pro-German king (whose wife was Kaiser Wilhelm II's sister). Though invited by the Greek Prime Minister, who was pro-Allies, the Allied soldiers were not welcomed by all. One leader in Athens told the Allies, "You will be driven into the sea, and you will not have time even to cry for mercy." This Salonika/Bulgarian front, where Bulgarian troops faced Allied troops, bogged down into yet another stalemate, until a spectacular breakthrough in autumn 1918.

Program Notes: Beyond the Boundaries of War—Revival in Africa

In July of 1915, a couple sailed from England to South Africa to serve the Lord on the mission field. Rees Howells, a Welshman who had been deeply transformed by the Welsh Revival of 1904, and his wife, Elizabeth, intended to start with language study, as most new missionaries do. But when the local people learned that the Howells had come from the land of the Welsh Revival, they asked Rees to preach about revival (using interpreters). After six weeks of preaching, something new began to happen.

On Friday evening, when about a dozen of them had gathered in the Howells' house, Mrs. Howells taught them the chorus, "Lord, send a revival, and let it begin in me." The Spirit was upon them as they sang, and they continued the singing the next days in their gardens and elsewhere. As Mr. Howells listened to them, he recognized a sound he had heard in the Welsh Revival. "You know it when you hear it," he said, "but you can't make it; and by the following Thursday, I was singing it too. There was something about it which changed you, and brought you into the stillness of God." [from the book *Rees Howells, Intercessor* by Norman Grubb]

Ten thousand Africans were converted through the months of preaching.

From this small beginning, a tremendous revival came throughout South Africa, as Rees Howells was sent out to preach in many different cities, towns, and villages. Ten thousand Africans were converted, including the Queen of Swaziland, through the months of preaching from place to place. "In Johannesburg, for instance, Mr. Howells conducted great revival

provinces of Baghdad and Basra, and Palestine would come under a separate international administration. The British resumed correspondence with Hussein, agreeing in evasive language to an independent Arab kingdom (which the British intended to have under their authority, like Egypt) with imprecise boundaries described in such a way that they were subject to wide interpretation. Though Hussein did not fully accept the boundaries of the second correspondence, he agreed to raise the Arab revolt. What he thought he was getting was not even close to what France and Britain had written in their secret agreement.

This was the second mistake.

Yet there was another people group to consider, who would figure importantly in these negotiations about the post-war Middle East—the Jews. Exiled from Jerusalem since Rome destroyed it in AD 70, Jewish communities had spread to many parts of the world, especially Russia and Eastern Europe. Though allowed to practice their Jewish faith in these various nations, they were often the subject of racial discrimination and persecution. Beginning in the latter 1800s, Russia began a systematic plan to rid itself of its Jews by converting one-third to Orthodoxy, forcing one-third into exile, and

6

meetings for twenty-one days in one of the largest churches and it was packed every night. He had to speak through three interpreters, there were so many different tribes, but that did not hinder the Spirit breaking through and hundreds coming out every night for salvation." As is the case in all true revivals, there were no barriers of race or ethnicity as the Holy Spirit drew to Himself Zulu, Mpondo, Ngwane, Bomvana, British, and Dutch alike. Former enemies now became brothers and sisters in Christ.

It was a strategy untried by—and a lesson lost on—the warring nations of World War I.

Please refer to the tables of **1915** (below) and **1916** (p. 238).

- Note that the war took place not only on land, but on the sea and in the air as well.

- Be sure to observe what was taking place in Africa and Asia. Though not the same intensity as the battles on the European and Ottoman fronts, these were, nevertheless, impacting the people and nations where they were being fought.

1915 **Central Powers** ■ **Allied Victory** ▢ **Stalemate** ▨ **Event** ☐

Fronts	Eastern: East Prussia & Austrian Poland	Western: Belgium & France	Southern Balkans	Italy
Jan–Feb				
Mar–Apr	Russians capture Austrian fortress, providing a much needed victory for Allies. Highly publicized in the West, the fortress is held for only a few months.	During this year, Western Front remains stalemated, though localized battles continue. **Apr:** 2nd Battle of Ypres fought, the only major German attack in 1915, since many German troops are sent to the Eastern Front.	Expecting Allies to succeed at Dardanelles, Italy signs treaty w/Allies—in exchange for new borders at end of war.	
May–Jun	German strategy: Move soldiers from West to fight in East. They begin offensive drive with Austro-Hungarian troops to push Russia out of Austrian Poland, continues successfully for five months.	**May:** France launches new, though unsuccessful, attack on German lines, since they know that German troops have been moved to East. Germans use deadly poison gas for first time in battle—French used tear gas unsuccessfully prior to this.		Italy invades Austria-Hungary in what is now Slovenia. 12 Battles of the Isonzo River will be fought over more than two years. Eighteen miles gained in first two weeks, then stalemate until 1918. Nearly one million will die in what are among the most vicious mountain battles ever fought.
Jul–Aug				
Sep–Oct	Russian defeat in Poland & W. Russia. Czar Nicholas II takes personal command of Russian armies.	**Sep:** British use poison gas at Battle of Loos, but shifting winds cause up to 60,000 British casualties.	Bulgaria, joins Central Powers. **Oct:** Serbia invaded by combined Ger/A-H and Bulgarian troops. **Dec:** Remaining Serbians flee to Albanian coast.	
Nov–Dec	Winter causes a temporary end to fighting on Eastern Front. Massive Russian losses this year.			

236 World War I & the Russian Revolution (1914–1918)

killing the rest through government-encouraged pogroms (massacres).

Even in "civilized Europe," anti-Semitism was alive and well. A news reporter, Theodor Herzl, covering the story of a scandalous case of anti-Semitism in France, the Dreyfus Affair, was deeply concerned by this and other obvious anti-Semitism in sophisticated places such as France and the Austro-Hungarian Empire. Herzl, though seeing himself as a fully-assimilated Hungarian, was Jewish. As he pondered the significance of the rising anti-Semitism in the world, he began to dream of a Jewish homeland in Palestine, peopled with those who would leave their hostile host nations and return to their Promised Land. He was the one who gave birth to the modern political Zionism, which was an international movement for the return of the Jewish people to their homeland in Palestine.

Twenty years after the Dreyfus Affair, in 1916, a new British Prime Minister came to power who, unexpectedly, had a profound vision for the re-establishment of the Jews in the Holy Land. His background as a Nonconformist (non-Anglican Protestant) provided a rich biblical background for this vision. Indeed, as Fromkin

6

- Note that Britain's attempt to capture Baghdad, Iraq, led to its shocking humiliation—the surrender of British troops at Kut-al-Amara. Historian Martin Gilbert writes, "More men had surrendered to the despised Turk at Kut than had surrendered to the Americans at Yorktown."

- After a futile nine months of stalemate at Gallipoli, the Allied troops were successfully evacuated in December 1915. In eleven days, 35,268 troops were taken off the beaches, with few (some sources state without *any*) casualties.

- With huge Russian losses on the Eastern Front, the czar made the controversial decision to take personal command of his troops in late 1915. This decision was not popular with the Duma (the Russian parliament), and by the end of 1916—despite the brilliant success of the Brusilov Offensive—the Russian people had begun to react. The Russian Empire, ruled by the Romanov family for three hundred years, was about to collapse.

Ottoman Empire: Dardanelles, Caucasus, Iraq, Palestine		East Africa, West Africa, China	Naval	Air
Turks attack Suez Canal, defeated. After this attempt, British will send heavy reinforcements to protect the Suez Canal—their lifeline to India.		Japan presents 21 demands to China: either accept or face war.	German sub blockade of Great Britain—retaliation for British blockade—creates a lethal War Zone.	German Zeppelins bombard English coast: "Total War."
British troops begin moving up Tigris River, to capture oil wells of Iraq from Turks.	**Mar:** British fleet loses many ships to mines in Dardanelles. Decide to wait until troops can land.		British squadron sinks German cruiser off Chilean coast.	First dogfight of war, over Western Front. French pilot uses front-firing machine gun to shoot down enemy.
Russians successfully advance into E. Anatolia, which results in Turks systematically deporting and massacring Armenians—they are accused of assisting the Russian army. Up to one million die.	**Apr:** Allied troops (ANZAC—NZ/Australian, British, French) land at Gallipoli Peninsula to capture Istanbul. Though the Allies are expected to quickly take the peninsula, the Turks hold the heights and cannot be dislodged, nor can they dislodge the Allies from the beaches.	British South African troops capture Karibib railroad station in Southwest Africa. Germans surrender in Southwest Africa (Namibia).	Cruise liner *Lusitania* sunk by German U-boat (sub). 1,195 passengers killed. Cruise liner sunk by Germans off Irish coast. British sub attacks Constantinople, damages Galata Bridge.	German Zeppelins bombard suburbs of London. Allied aircraft bomb German city in retaliation.
On their way towards Baghdad, British capture small city of Kut-al-Amara, Iraq.	Stalemate through December.		In response to American demands, German subs stop sinking ships without warning.	German Zeppelins bomb London.
After pulling back from Battle of Ctesiphon, British are besieged at Kut-Al-Amara.	Evacuation of Allied troops from Gallipoli. Turks have successfully held against invaders.			

states, "He was only the latest in a long line of Christian Zionists in Britain that stretched back to the Puritans." With this perspective, it is easy to see how Lloyd George's government made possible the Balfour Declaration of 1917, which stated:

His Majesty's Government view with favor the establishment in Palestine of a national home for the Jewish people, and will use their best endeavors to facilitate the achievement of this object, it being clearly understood that nothing shall be done which may prejudice the civil and religious rights of existing non-Jewish communities in Palestine.

This was the third mistake.

In promising the Arabs an independent kingdom stretching across much of the Ottoman Empire, in agreeing to France's control of Syria and Lebanon, with an internationally controlled Palestine, and in now promising a Jewish homeland, they had committed themselves to fulfill mutually exclusive promises—an impossible situation.

Psalm 122:6 tells us to pray for the peace of Jerusalem. With your students, begin to pray for peace for that city, and for an openness to the gospel in the entire region of the Middle East.

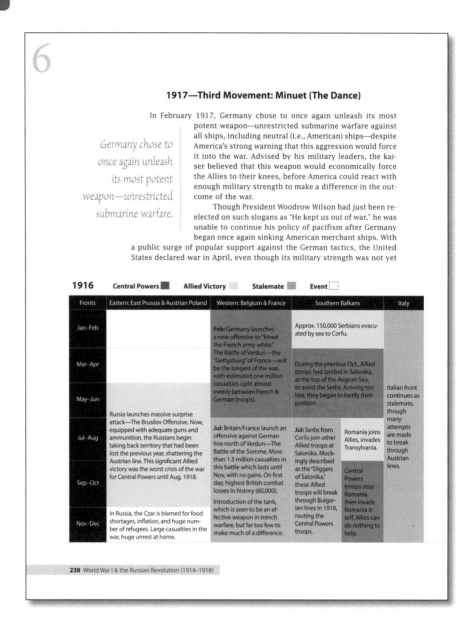

6

1917—Third Movement: Minuet (The Dance)

Germany chose to once again unleash its most potent weapon—unrestricted submarine warfare.

In February 1917, Germany chose to once again unleash its most potent weapon—unrestricted submarine warfare against all ships, including neutral (i.e., American) ships—despite America's strong warning that this aggression would force it into the war. Advised by his military leaders, the kaiser believed that this weapon would economically force the Allies to their knees, before America could react with enough military strength to make a difference in the outcome of the war.

Though President Woodrow Wilson had just been re-elected on such slogans as "He kept us out of war," he was unable to continue his policy of pacifism after Germany began once again sinking American merchant ships. With a public surge of popular support against the German tactics, the United States declared war in April, even though its military strength was not yet

1916   Central Powers ▮   Allied Victory ▯   Stalemate ▨   Event ☐

Fronts	Eastern: East Prussia & Austrian Poland	Western: Belgium & France	Southern Balkans	Italy
Jan–Feb		**Feb:** Germany launches a new offensive to "bleed the French army white." The Battle of Verdun—the "Gettysburg" of France—will be the longest of the war, with estimated one million casualties (split almost evenly between French & German troops).	Approx. 150,000 Serbians evacuated by sea to Corfu.	
Mar–Apr			During the previous Oct., Allied troops had landed in Salonika, at the top of the Aegean Sea, to assist the Serbs. Arriving too late, they began to fortify their position.	Italian front continues as stalemate, though many attempts are made to break through Austrian lines.
May–Jun	Russia launches massive surprise attack—The Brusilov Offensive. Now, equipped with adequate guns and ammunition, the Russians begin taking back territory that had been lost the previous year, shattering the Austrian line. This significant Allied victory was the worst crisis of the war for Central Powers until Aug, 1918.			
Jul–Aug		**Jul:** Britain/France launch an offensive against German line north of Verdun—The Battle of the Somme. More than 1.5 million casualties in this battle which lasts until Nov, with no gains. On first day, highest British combat losses in history (60,000).	**Jul:** Serbs from Corfu join other Allied troops at Salonika. Mockingly described as the "Diggers of Salonika," these Allied troops will break through Bulgarian lines in 1918, routing the Central Powers troops.	Romania joins Allies, invades Transylvania.
Sep–Oct		Introduction of the tank, which is seen to be an effective weapon in trench warfare, but far too few to make much of a difference.		Central Powers troops stop Romania, then invade Romania itself. Allies can do nothing to help.
Nov–Dec	In Russia, the Czar is blamed for food shortages, inflation, and huge number of refugees. Large casualties in the war, huge unrest at home.			

? To get an informal discussion started on this Key Concept, ask a simple leading question, such as, "What do you know about the Russian Revolution?"

The Russian Revolution— EXPLANATION

An autocrat is one who rules with absolute, unlimited power. In other words, he makes decisions that no one can overrule. It greatly helps in understanding the Russian Revolution to recognize that, when Czar Nicholas II took the reins of power in Russia in the late 1800s, he did so with an unshakeable belief in the God-ordained rightness of autocracy. His wife, German-born Alexandra (who had been raised since the age of six by her grandmother, Queen Victoria

of England), firmly believed in this as well. In their minds, to have Nicholas ruling as the autocratic czar of Russia was their Christian duty and responsibility. Many of the czar's ministers believed that Europe's troubles lay in its move toward democracy, free speech, and the people's participation in government. Thus, Nicholas II was surrounded by and counseled by people who believed that the best thing for Russia was to be governed by an autocrat.

However, as the twentieth century dawned, the Russian people were less and less pleased with this form of government, especially since it did not

up to the task. In fact, since Wilson's determination had been to remain neutral throughout the European struggle, America had focused on preparing itself for the global realities of life after the war. Seeing that the European theory of the balance of power had been destroyed in the trenches, America's most pressing future need would be to defend itself against whomever emerged as victor, whether Britain or Germany. To prepare for this future, the US Navy had been building a battleship fleet to rival Britain's. But at this moment, the Allies had no need for extra battleships. What they desperately and immediately needed was a vast infusion of manpower—armed and ready to fight—in the trenches of the Western Front. However, for the Americans to provide this would take more than a year of recruiting, equipping, and training. And in April 1917, no one knew whether the Allies would be able to hold the lines for one more year.

Though the Allies had planned a massive spring offensive for 1917, involving British, French, Russian, and Italian troops advancing against the Central Powers, it did not go as hoped—especially on the Eastern Front.

> *What they desperately needed was a vast infusion of manpower in the trenches of the Western Front.*

Ottoman Empire: Caucasus, Iraq, Palestine		East Africa, West Africa	Naval	Air
Three unsuccessful attempts to relieve besieged troops. **Apr:** British surrender at Kut-al-Amara, Iraq. Utter fiasco, coming shortly after the failed Allied attempt at Gallipoli.	Russian offensive in E. Turkey—from Lake Van to Black Sea, Russia captures important cities in the region, Erzurum and Trebizond.	Surrender of German Cameroon to Allies. Combined British-Belgian-Portuguese invasion of German East Africa begins.	German submarine campaign begins again. U-boats sink without warning all ships except passenger vessels—until May.	German fighter pilots begin new offensive approach against Allied planes at Verdun.
Arab Revolt proclaimed against Ottomans. Not as effective as anticipated. British fight Turks east of Suez canal—1st Allied victory against Ottoman Empire: Battle of Romani.		British occupy northern half of German East Africa—Tanzania, Rwanda, Burundi.	Battle of Jutland—only large naval battle of war. British lost more men/ships, won tactical victory.	French fighter pilots are formed into units, aggressively seek to engage German planes. The result is intense aerial combat, seen for the first time at Verdun, which leads to "ace" pilots—those who had downed a number of enemy pilots. The concept of air superiority, formation flying, and squadron-wing organization were all developed during the air battles over Verdun.
In Battle of Magdhaba, British continue pushing Turks from Sinai Peninsula.			British blockade causes widespread food shortages in Germany.	

provide them a legal means by which their voices could be heard—and the desire to participate and make their ideas known in government was increasingly attractive. Various groups were stirring up this desire and agitating for reform, proposing illegal and sometimes violent means to make their will known to the czar. One of the most powerful methods was in organizing city workers to leave their jobs unattended and go on strike.

In 1905, when a huge sea of protestors, led by an Orthodox priest, marched to the czar's palace to peacefully communicate their demands for better working conditions in the factories, the czar's guards became nervous and began shooting. When it was over, hundreds had been killed or wounded. This rift between the people and their czar, whom they had called "Little Father," greatly disillusioned many of the urban Russian people, provoking nationwide strikes and a huge outcry across the country. During this revolutionary moment, the czar unexpectedly modified his approach and granted what had been hoped for: a national representative assembly, to be called the Imperial Duma (a type of parliament that would bring input to governmental issues). This announcement

6

Russia, the Allies' sole Eastern European player, began to convulse in an upheaval that would not only remove it from the war, but would dramatically change the world.

Lenin passionately, even religiously, believed in Karl Marx's theories of communism.

It was not defeat in war that triggered this upheaval—it was hunger. The highly successful Russian offensive of 1916 had proved that Russia's military was stronger than that of the Austro-Hungarians; and, though Germany had continued to gain military victories against Russian troops, it could no longer place enough soldiers on the Eastern Front to withstand the seemingly limitless supply of Russian soldiers. Though news from the front was fairly good, and though the people still had the will to defend their land against the Germans, there were insurmountable troubles at home. Soaring prices and scarce food supply were causing severe hardships among heavily-burdened people who believed, whether accurately or not, that the czar's inefficient and corrupt government was the cause of their suffering. As workers in St. Petersburg ("Petrograd" during WWI) went on strike and a general revolution began, the czar was forced to abdicate his throne on March 15. In place of an autocratic ruler, a provisional (temporary) government was established. Within a short time, a man named Kerensky became the head of the government, working hard to both continue the war and feed the Russian people. But not everyone approved of this new form of government.

Loudest among the voices seeking to direct the new wind of change blowing through Russia was Vladimir Ilyich Ulyanov, or, as he called himself, Lenin. Lenin passionately, even religiously, believed in Karl Marx's theories of communism. He saw the ending of three hundred years of Romanov autocracy as the beginning of Marx's workers' revolution. There was to be no compromise with the provisional government because that would weaken the ongoing revolution. If done properly, this revolution would result in what Marx had envisioned—workers ruling the country and, eventually, the world. Because of this, Lenin fought strenuously against the provisional government, seeking its destruction. This wasn't too hard to accomplish, since the government was unsuccessful in battling either the problems at home *or* the Germans on the front. By November, with worsening food shortages in the cities and a crumbling army, Lenin's Bolshevik Revolution was able to seize power with one goal: firmly establishing the Marxist-Leninist Revolution throughout all of Russia. In order to do that, the Bolsheviks sought a peace treaty with Germany—which would mean the collapse of the Eastern Front.

Lenin

240 World War I & the Russian Revolution (1914–1918)

brought enormous anticipation, as people suddenly envisioned actually having a say in their government.

It is vital to remember, though, that the czar maintained a fundamental belief in autocracy, and had allowed the Duma only under pressure and against his better judgment. In fact, his attitude toward it was displayed when the government released specific details about how the Duma was expected to function: it would have only an advisory capacity (which meant the czar and his advisors could ignore it completely), and Duma members would come mainly from the nobility and upper levels of society. Hearing this, many rose up in protest, going on a strike that spread throughout the country—in essence shutting down the Russian Empire.

Once again, in order to prevent a revolution, the czar allowed changes to take place that were in direct contrast to what he believed. The Duma was given the power to actually make laws, historically an unprecedented act in Russia. Describing it as "this terrible decision" in a letter to his mother, the czar now became—at least on paper—a constitutional monarch.

The radical revolutionaries of Russia were stunned by this turn of events, as they saw that this new wind of freedom might keep Russia from

6

Stop and consider what the collapse of the Eastern Front meant to all those involved in the war. For the Allies, the Bolshevik Revolution was an utter disaster—eliminating the Allies' largest member, and the only one able to seriously distract the Central Powers from their relentless pounding on the Western Front. To them, it was potentially the beginning of a series of disasters that could culminate in their defeat. For Germany, however, this event was a godsend, a cause for celebrating. Freed from the immense drain of manpower and supplies required for the Eastern Front, Germany could now gather all of its troops, including highly trained storm troopers, and send them to the West.

It was a breathless race to see whether the vastly increased German forces on the Western Front could punch through Allied defenses before the new American ally could send enough troops to make a difference.

Please refer to the table of **1917** (p. 242).

- Note the building of the Hindenburg Line on the Western Front, which was so massive and well-prepared that the Germans believed it to be absolutely impenetrable.

- Note also that, in 1917, French soldiers mutinied on the Western Front, rebelling against their officers and against the ceaseless and futile slaughter of the battlefield.

- Be sure to observe that Greece finally joined the Allies, though Allied troops had been stationed at the Salonika Front since late 1915.

- Consider how the Battle of Caporetto on the Italian Front, which pushed the Allies back seventy miles, would have disheartened both the Allies and the Italian people as they observed the increasing momentum of the Central Powers' victories in the last months of 1917.

- For the Allies, the only good news at the close of 1917 came from the capture of Jerusalem in December by British troops under General Allenby. Though this Palestinian Front was not a main theater of the war, this victory brought a slight ray of hope as it ended the four-hundred-year rule of the Ottomans over Jerusalem.

Germany could now gather all of its troops, including highly trained storm troopers, and send them to the West.

Fourth Movement—Finale

As the new year of 1918 dawned, proposals for achieving peace were heard increasingly across the war-weary world. Best known of these was US President Wilson's "Fourteen Points," which set out his idealistic program for peace. This included a vision of the world that would be

experiencing a true Marxist-style revolution. Though they tried to keep the workers agitated and striking, the czar's action actually calmed the situation dramatically and the 1905 revolution faded away.

Sir Bernard Pares, a British observer, wrote, "There can be no doubt that economically the seven years from 1907 to 1914 were, so far, the most prosperous period in Russian history." Part of this prosperity came from Russia's growing industrial revolution. By 1914, its steel production equaled that of France and of Austria-Hungary. During this time, though the czar limited the Duma's power tremendously, other actions by his

ministers brought relief and hope to a large segment of the Russian population—several million peasants were enabled to own and farm their own land. The military, after its defeat in the Russo-Japanese War, was being modernized. The expectation of keen observers—including German military leaders—was that this modernization would make Russia's army the most powerful in the world.

Unfortunately, WWI came before Russia was ready. Though it could field an almost unlimited number of soldiers, it was still greatly lacking in training, equipment, and transportation. In a staggering statistic, of the twelve million soldiers mobilized, more

6

"fit and safe to live in; and particularly that it be made safe for every peace-loving nation." Even more significant was the concept that each of these nations would be able to "determine its own institutions, be assured of justice and fair dealing by the other peoples of the world as against force and selfish aggression." To many suffering through this conflict, especially the people of the Balkans and of the Austro-Hungarian Empire, this was, indeed, a vision of hope for the future. These Fourteen Points would become the standard for those seeking an "honorable" way to end the war.

For those watching in early 1918, it appeared likely it would be the Allies suing for peace with the victorious Central Powers, rather than vice versa. Consider what it looked like that winter: On the Eastern Front, negotiations for a settlement broke down in February because the German terms for peace were so harsh that the Bolsheviks simply could not accept them. Without missing a beat, the Germans took up arms again and marched farther and farther east. By the time the Brest-Litovsk peace treaty was signed in March, Germany had penetrated deep into Russia and was now in a position to dictate its own terms, regardless of Bolshevik sentiment. These

1917   Central Powers ■   Allied Victory □   Stalemate ▨   Event □

Fronts	Eastern: East Prussia & Austrian Poland	Western: Belgium & France	Southern Balkans	Italy
Jan–Feb				
Mar–Apr	**Mar:** Russia's czar is overthrown, and a new, provisional government is formed. The Allies view this event with alarm, while the Central Powers see that the Eastern Front may at last be ended.	Western Front continues as stalemate. Germans build a new, impenetrable system of trenches—the Hindenburg Line. **Late Feb–early Mar:** German troops retreat to this line.	Salonika front continues as stalemate. In Greece, though, a revolution occurs against the pro-German King Constantine (whose wife was the sister of Kaiser Wilhelm II).	Italian front continues as stalemate. **Oct–Nov:** Battle of Caporetto—Combined German & Austrian troops rout Italian troops, who retreat 70 miles to the Piave River (north of Venice). Italy rallies, unified in support of war. Allied Supreme War Council now formed to coordinate all theaters of the war.
May–Jun	Kerensky, Russia's new War Minister, believes that a victorious Germany would be disastrous for Russia, and that Russia must continue to aid its allies, so tries to continue the war.	**Apr:** The United States declares war on Germany, and exhausted French troops mutiny when commanded to attack German lines. French General Pétain calms his troops with his views on how the war should proceed: "We must wait for the Americans and the tanks." **Nov:** The Battle of Cambrai begins with 324 British tanks leading. Though the tanks broke through the line, the British could not hold their gains.	**Jun:** Constantine abdicates. **Jul:** The pro-Allies official who takes power declares war on Germany & Bulgaria.	
Jul–Aug	Russians launch offensive in Austrian Poland. Within three weeks, Russian troops are routed. The army begins to collapse.			
Sep–Oct				
Nov–Dec	**Nov:** Bolsheviks seize power. Lenin, a Marxist, is now in charge. He signs an armistice w/ Central Powers, ending fighting on Eastern Front and in the Caucasus—a huge blow to the Allies.			

than three-quarters of them became casualties (killed, wounded, or taken prisoner). The cost, in terms of human life and misery, is almost incalculable. As the country was struggling at home through the inescapable shortages and strains of war, the czar proved less and less able to give the necessary leadership and wisdom required. Beyond his own personal limitations, there was an even darker reason for his failure: the czar and his wife had fallen completely under the control of a manipulative, deceiving "monk" named Rasputin. They slavishly followed his counsel because they believed he had the power to help their beloved hemophiliac son.

As a result of their obedience to even the most senseless suggestions given by Rasputin, inept and corrupt ministers were appointed to various positions of governmental power, which took national conditions from bad to worse.

In what would become an unstoppable movement of the people—fed up with government corruption, hunger, and war—a series of unplanned events occurred that forever changed Russia and the world. In Petrograd, on March 8, 1917, a group of housewives, sick and tired of interminable food shortages, joined in a demonstration with ninety thousand workers who were on strike. Expressing

6

harsh terms included relinquishing seven provinces that had belonged to czarist Russia: the Caucasus, Poland, Finland, the Baltic provinces, Ukraine, Bessarabia, and Byelorussia. It is vital to note that within this relinquished territory lay one-third of Russia's population before the war, one-third of Russia's agricultural land, nine-tenths of its coalfields, and almost all of its oil production. The resources of Russia, which had been part of the Allies' strength, now belonged to their enemy.

On the Western Front, the month of March contained more grim news for the Allies. The first of the great German offensives of 1918 was launched against the British and French in France's central section of trench lines. Within four days, 45,000 Allied soldiers had been captured as the Germans successfully penetrated their defenses, crossing the Somme River before being stopped. As early as April, however, American troops were reaching the battlefield in increasing numbers, helping to stem the German tide. In that same month, a second massive German offensive was launched further north in Belgium, but British, French, and American troops again managed to hold the line.

Despite German successes, Austria-Hungary was beginning to shatter as its imperial borders splintered along national lines. In May, soldiers from divergent parts of the empire began to mutiny—Slovenians, Czechs,

Ottoman Empire: Caucasus, Iraq, Palestine		Africa/Asia: East Africa, China	Naval	Air
Mar–Apr: British army of Egypt launches offensive against Ottomans in Palestine. Two unsuccessful attempts against Gaza. **Jun:** General Allenby takes control. **Oct:** Third attempt is successful. This victory is the beginning of the end for Ottoman Empire. **Jul:** Arab guerillas, along with British Lieutenant Colonel T. E. Lawrence, capture port city of Aqaba from Ottomans, a seemingly impossible task. **Nov:** Britain publishes Balfour Declaration, promise of Jewish homeland in Palestine. **Dec:** The British capture Jerusalem, ending 400 years of Ottoman rule.	The new British government under David Lloyd George wants new advance prepared to move up the Tigris River. **Feb:** With more than 50,000 troops, the British retake Kut-al-Amara. **Mar:** Baghdad is taken—a morale-winning victory for British. **Sep:** By now the British have secured Baghdad, winning a victory on the Euphrates. Widespread famine in Persia begins in early 1917 with more than 9 million dead in two years.	China declares war against Germany & Austria-Hungary. Japan will not be the only Far East ally at war's end. Allies occupy all of German East Africa, though German garrison continues its attacks on Allied soldiers.	**Feb:** Germany launches unrestricted U-boat warfare, try to destroy Britain's economy and hasten the end of the war before America should decide to join the Allies. British Admiralty begins "convoy" system: in-bound merchant vessels escorted by Navy ships. Convoy system is so successful, outward bound ships from England now in convoys.	British institute the first "night bomber" squadron. **Apr:** By now the French have over 2,800 planes. Avg. life expectancy of pilot on Western Front—2 months. Germany launches first bomber aircraft raid against London, 162 people killed. First time an aircraft lands on a ship. Last raid by Zeppelins on Britain.

World War I & the Russian Revolution (1914–1918) **243**

their frustration, they carried simple signs reading, "We want bread." This mostly non-violent protest of the people was tolerated by the police, though carefully watched. The next day, an increasing number of workers on strike (perhaps 200,000) took to the streets. Though the czar's Cossacks (his greatly feared special troops) were called out, surprisingly, they did not attack the people. Though the military commander of Petrograd had more than enough soldiers stationed in the city to put down a revolution, he was unable to get them to disperse the masses, as many of them started up conversations with the strikers and carried their weapons in a non-aggressive manner. The next day, with even more people joining the strike, the police opened fire, killing a number of protestors. But, in an astonishing act, rather than running back to their homes, the people rushed toward the police and disarmed them, killing some in the process. On March 11, as the strike was growing larger and becoming potentially dangerous, a unit of soldiers fired into a large, milling crowd, killing and wounding many. That night, the soldiers in Petrograd must have made some serious decisions about what they would do when commanded to fire again on the people.

Ruthenians, and Serbs—each demanding independence from Austria-Hungary. The new, peace-loving emperor, Charles I, believed the solution was to establish a confederation in which each people group would govern itself under the umbrella of the empire. For many Austro-Hungarians, though, this limited autonomy was no longer sufficient. Full independence, as interpreted in Wilson's Fourteen Points, was their expectation and their strident demand.

At the end of May, the Germans launched yet another offensive against the Allies on the Western Front. During this assault, one French staff officer remarked on the effect of having the freshly arrived, eager-to-engage American troops in their midst: "We all had the impression that we were about to see a wonderful transfusion. . . . Life was coming in floods to re-animate the dying body of France." Despite this infusion of fresh courage, though, the German army had come terrifyingly close to Paris by early June. With the Allied lines battered so thin by these powerful German attacks, when General Ludendorff launched his offensive in mid-July, he wired the kaiser, "If the attack succeeds, the war will be over and we will have won it." The French Commander-in-Chief of the Allied troops, Marshal Foch, wired his government with a similar message: "If the present German attack succeeds, the war is over and we have lost it."

> "If the present German attack succeeds, the war is over and we have lost it."

However, just as ocean tides ebb and flow, now the tide of war began to flow in favor of the Allies. They launched vigorous counter-offensives, pushing the Germans back further and further. To their surprise, they discovered that the German troops had exhausted their reserves—and used up their best troops in the spring attacks—and now were unable to effectively hold the Allies back. The will to fight was ebbing away as the Germans experienced increasing losses.

On August 8, the Allies began in France what would become known as "The Hundred Days Offensive." It was so effective that by August 14, Ludendorff was recommending to the kaiser that Germany begin immediate negotiations for peace, though this advice was not followed. To further complicate Germany's efforts, Austria-Hungary, having lost an estimated 400,000 soldiers to desertion, notified Germany that it intended to begin peace negotiations at once, though it managed to continue until November.

At the Salonika Front in Greece, the Allies conceived a plan to begin a new offensive, attacking the Bulgarian lines at various points along the front. On September 14, Serbian and French guns began an assault on Bulgarian positions in the highest mountains of Macedonia. A German commander who was an eyewitness to this largest artillery assault in Balkan history described it as "an iron storm which soon developed into a hurricane." The next day, Serbian and French troops poured through Bulgarian lines, beginning the end of this front. As Misha Glenny writes in his book *The Balkans*, "Four years and one month after the Serbs had sustained the first casualties of

The next day, Monday, March 12, was the pivotal moment of the revolution as the soldiers changed sides, ignoring the orders of commanders and helping the people, even passing out weapons to them from their barracks. The police and army officers standing against the revolution were hunted down by soldiers and people alike, and the last barriers fell. When acquainted with the facts of the revolution, the czar abdicated.

For the next several months, two groups sought to run the country: the Duma—reluctant about the revolution—represented the moderate politicians, while the Soviet of Workers' and Soldiers' Deputies—demanding that Russia become a republic—represented the more radical leaders. The one able to bridge both groups was Alexander Kerensky, who eventually was made the head of Russia's Provisional Government, until it was toppled by the Bolshevik Revolution later that year. The victorious Bolsheviks were led by Vladimir Ilyich Ulyanov, or Lenin, a dedicated and brilliant disciple of Marx's communist theories. In a strange twist of history, it turns out that one of Lenin's teachers in his schoolboy days was actually the father of the one he would overthrow, Alexander Kerensky. There will be more in the next Unit on the Bolshevik Revolution.

the Great War in the Austro-Hungarian attack on Belgrade, the Allied Army of the Orient was engaged in a military operation, conceived by Serb military commanders, which would trigger Germany's defeat." This was also the opinion of Ludendorff, who later wrote, "August 8th was the black day of the German army in the history of this war. This was the worst experience that I had to go through, **except for the events that, from September 15th onwards, took place on the Bulgarian front and sealed the fate of the Quadruple Alliance**." (emphasis added) As a direct result of this attack, Bulgaria, the first of the Central Powers to fall, quickly sought an armistice with the Allies.

On October 2, the seemingly impenetrable Hindenburg Line on the Western Front was overrun by Allied troops. With this breakthrough in their defense, the Germans recognized that victory was no longer possible. However, they hoped to end the war in such a way that they would still retain the Alsace-Lorraine in France and the Polish districts in East Prussia. When the Germans sought an armistice with the US president in early October under these terms, Wilson—with the counsel and full agreement of France and Great Britain—rejected it. Thus, the war continued.

With this breakthrough in their defense, the Germans recognized that victory was no longer possible.

There was victory on another front, however, which caused one more Central Power to fall. With Britain's successful march through the Ottoman lands of Palestine and Mesopotamia, and with the Ottomans' seemingly indefatigable army beginning to break down, the Ottoman Empire sought an armistice with the Allies. The terms, which would prove to be unacceptable to the Turkish people, were nonetheless agreeable to the Ottoman Sultan, and the armistice was signed at the end of October.

By this point, the Austro-Hungarian Empire was collapsing. On the Italian Front, the Allies launched a new offensive, which pierced the Austrian lines and routed them in the process. In this debacle, more than three hundred thousand Austro-Hungarian soldiers were taken prisoner by the victorious Italians. The news at home was just as shocking. The day after the battle began, a Hungarian National Council was set up in Budapest to sever Hungary's connection to Austria. A few days later, an independent Czech State was proclaimed in Prague. Recognizing the futility of trying to continue a war while his empire was falling apart, Emperor Charles telegraphed this message to the kaiser: "My people are neither capable nor willing to continue the war. I have made the unalterable decision to ask for a separate peace and an immediate armistice." This armistice was signed on November 3.

The only theater of battle remaining in the war was now at the Western Front. In early November, the Americans launched a new offensive against the Germans, but when Germany tried to bring more troops from the East, the soldiers mutinied. Unable to continue the war under these conditions, a German delegation crossed into France to open armistice negotiations on

6

November 7. Back at home, the mutinies, the losses at the front, and the fact that many were near starvation brought Germany to the brink of revolution as various groups sought to bring radical change, even communist revolution, to the country. With this chaos in mind, the kaiser was advised by his closest aides that he must abdicate his throne or risk further revolution. The kaiser refused and even talked of leading his army to put down the revolution. Since his troops were no longer following him, it was pointed out to him that this idea would undoubtedly fail. In one of the strangest side-notes of the war, the German Chancellor announced publicly that the kaiser had, in fact, abdicated, and then went on to resign his own office.

On November 9, with the storm clouds of revolution swelling, the kaiser accepted his formerly announced abdication and went into exile in Holland. With his final removal from a position of power, the Allies willingly signed the armistice, which the Germans believed to be in accord with Wilson's Fourteen Points. On the Western Front, in the final note of this unimaginably tragic symphony, the armistice went into effect at the eleventh hour of the eleventh day of the eleventh month of 1918.

1918   Central Powers ■   Allied Victory ▢   Stalemate ▨   Event ▢

Fronts	Eastern: East Prussia & Austrian Poland	Western: Belgium & France	Southern Balkans	Italy
Jan–Feb	Germany, in peace treaty, demands territory from Russia, who says, "no." Germany continues war, invades Ukraine.	Stalemate continues. US President proposes 14 points for permanent world peace.		
Mar–Apr	**Mar:** Treaty of Brest-Litovsk ends Eastern Front. Collapse of Front allows Germany to send troops to Western Front.	Germany, with numerical superiority, now launch three offensives. They gain 40 miles on the Somme,10 miles at Battle of Lys, and in 3rd Battle of Aisne, come to within 55 miles of Paris.	Salonika front continues as stalemate.	Italian front continues as stalemate. **Jun:** Austrian-Hungarian troops attack Italian front, beaten back.
May–Jun	Ongoing civil war in Russia between Bolsheviks and anti-Bolsheviks (1918–1920).		Romania signs harsh treaty—favors Germany	
Jul–Aug	Former Czar Nicholas II and his family are murdered by Bolsheviks. Volunteer allied troops sent to N. Russia/Siberia.	French halt final German offensive. **Aug 8:** Allied "Hundred Days Offensive."		
Sep–Oct		**Sep:** Germans retreat to Hindenburg line. Allies continue offensive, more than 1 million American troops now fighting. **Oct:** German commander Ludendorff resigns.	**Sep 15:** Serbian & Allied forces attack—shatter Bulgarian lines. **Sep 29:** Bulgaria signs Armistice.	**Oct 23:** Battle of Vittorio Veneto, Italians shatter Austrian lines.
Nov–Dec		Germans in general retreat. **Nov 11:** Germany signs Armistice.		**Nov 3:** Austria-Hungary signs Armistice.

Four empires had irretrievably fallen as a result of this war. Russia's Romanov dynasty, which had proudly ruled for three hundred years, ended piteously as the czar and his family were murdered by Bolsheviks. Austria-Hungary's Hapsburg dynasty, which had governed the Holy Roman Empire, the Austrian Empire, and, finally, the Austro-Hungarian Empire for more than three hundred fifty years, found itself banned from Austria after the war. Germany's Hohenzollern dynasty, which had first ruled Brandenburg-Prussia and then the German Empire for five hundred years, ended in a Dutch exile. And, finally, as a result of WWI, the Ottoman Empire, which beginning in 1299 grew to encompass much of the Balkans, Western Asia, and North Africa, found itself being partitioned by the victorious Allies. This would result, as we will see in the next chapter, in a Turkish revolution that would bring an utter end to an empire that had survived for more than six hundred years.

As the smoke cleared from the battlefields, multitudes rejoiced at their newfound peace. Unfortunately, the symphony of this "war to end all wars" would become the mere prelude to the next—and still more terrible—war.

Please refer to the table of **1918** (p. 246).

Ottoman Empire: Caucasus, Iraq, Palestine			Africa/Asia: East Africa	Naval/Air
Feb: Jericho is captured, begins 7-month occupation of Jordan valley.		Turks successfully battle against Armenian troops in E. Turkey, recapturing Trebizond and Erzerum.		
With German offensive on Western Front, London recalls 90,000 of Allenby's troops. At same time, many Ottoman troops removed from Palestine to serve in Caucasus.	**Mar:** British capture Hit in Euphrates River valley.			**Apr:** Royal Air Force is formed—first separate air service in military.
	May: Continuing to move north, British capture Kirkuk.	Armenians sign peace treaty with Ottomans.		
		British detachment reaches Baku.		
Sep 19: Battle of Megiddo, Ottomans retreat. **Oct 1:** British take Damascus unopposed.	**Oct 29:** Battle of Sharqat: Final action of war in Mesopotamia. **Oct 30:** Ottoman Empire signs Armistice.	Ottoman Army captures Baku oil fields, Azerbaijan		**Oct 21:** Unrestricted U-boat warfare ceases. **Oct 29:** Mutiny of German sailors at Kiel leads to open revolution.
			Nov 25: Last members of German East African garrison surrender.	**Nov 9:** Abdication of Kaiser announced.

6

- Note that the end of the war on the Eastern Front did not result in peace for revolutionary Russia.

- Consider how Germany benefited not only from the peace treaty with Russia, but also from the peace treaty with Romania, who signed over their oil fields to Germany.

- It is fascinating to consider Serbia's epic struggle in this war—from being the first country invaded, to its courageous defense of its homeland, to the soldiers' winter flight through the Albanian mountains, to their rescue by Allied ships and evacuation to the island of Corfu, and the pivotal part it played on the Salonika Front with the resulting fall of the first Central Power nation.

- Note that the September 19 Battle of Megiddo in Palestine is also referred to as the Battle of Armageddon, since it took place at the site of Armageddon (or Megiddo).

The longest-lasting campaign of the war ended on November 25 (long after the armistice) when the last German soldiers in East Africa surrendered. Their story is one of the most memorable military adventures of the war and brought much honor to those Germans who had fought, and then eluded, Allied troops for the entire war. One officer with the Nigerian Brigade said of these Germans, "To the very end they kept their tails up, and fought a one-sided contest with indomitable courage and exemplary dash, and they never failed to leave their mark on their opponents." ◀

248 World War I & the Russian Revolution (1914–1918)

You may choose to have your students read the article first and then listen to the audio recordings, or vice versa.

◉ Read the article

◉ Listen to the audio recordings in Listen to This

- The main concepts and chronological flow are contained in *What in the World?* Volume 3

- The life of T. E. Lawrence, popularly known as Lawrence of Arabia, is described in *True Tales* Volume 3.

- Learn more about the African and Italian fronts in WWI on *Digging Deeper* Volume 3.

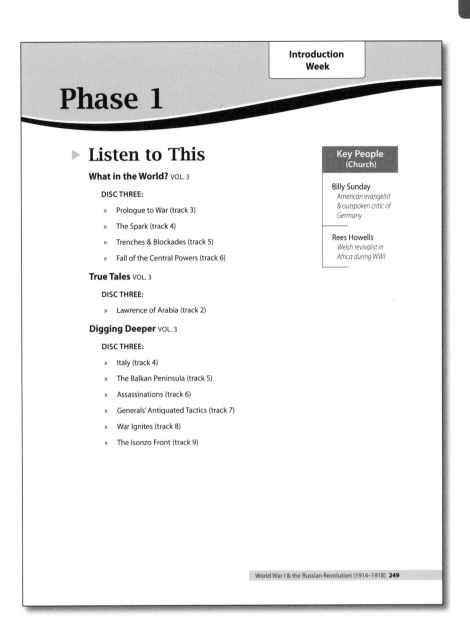

Phase 1

▶ **Listen to This**

What in the World? VOL. 3

DISC THREE:

» Prologue to War (track 3)

» The Spark (track 4)

» Trenches & Blockades (track 5)

» Fall of the Central Powers (track 6)

True Tales VOL. 3

DISC THREE:

» Lawrence of Arabia (track 2)

Digging Deeper VOL. 3

DISC THREE:

» Italy (track 4)

» The Balkan Peninsula (track 5)

» Assassinations (track 6)

» Generals' Antiquated Tactics (track 7)

» War Ignites (track 8)

» The Isonzo Front (track 9)

**Key People
(Church)**

Billy Sunday
*American evangelist
& outspoken critic of
Germany*

Rees Howells
*Welsh revivalist in
Africa during WWI*

World War I & the Russian Revolution (1914–1918) **249**

◉ Read the Scriptures in Read For Your Life

The Scriptures are central to our understanding, our character, and our decisions. Therefore, we must give the greatest weight possible to them.

Help your students gain this perspective as they watch you handle the Scriptures with reverence and awe.

Psalm 27:3 says, "Though war may rise against me, in this I will be confident." Discuss with your students what it means to actually and actively put our trust and faith in the Lord even when troubles (including war) overwhelm us.

Key People (World)

Paul von Hindenburg
German field marshall in WWI

Ferdinand Foch
Marshal of France, Supreme Commander of Allied Forces

Philippe Pétain
French commander, one of the most successful of WWI

David Lloyd George
British prime minister during WWI

Woodrow Wilson
US president: "Keeping the world safe for democracy"

Erich Ludendorff
German "First Quartermaster General"

Vladimir Lenin
Leader of Bolshevik Revolution

Chaim Weizmann
Jewish Zionist

E. Lawrence
British officer involved in Arab Revolt

▷ Read For Your Life

The Holy Bible

- » **Biblical Response to Those Suffering in War** (whether soldiers or civilians)—Psalm 27:3–5

- » **God's Role in Ending Wars** (consider WWI, the stalemates and the surprising ending)—Psalm 46:8–9

- » **Biblical Response When Others Seek Evil and Provoke War** (consider to whom we look)—Psalm 140:1–2

- » **The Value of Having Wise Counsel** (consider the Allies in WWI before 1918, when each worked separately and often at cross-purposes)—Proverbs 15:22

▷ Talk Together

Opinion Column

- » What did you find to be the most interesting aspect, or the most fascinating person, during World War I?

- » Imagine you were living in Austria-Hungary when the heir to the throne, Archduke Francis Ferdinand, was assassinated in Bosnia-Herzegovina by a Serbian nationalist. What do you think your attitude would be toward Serbia? If you were a citizen of Serbia instead, how do you think you would view Austria-Hungary?

- » In your opinion, why do you think WWI was such a long war? In what ways do you think it changed the world?

- » Consider a different outcome for WWI. What do you think might have happened in Europe if Germany had been successful in quickly defeating France, as it had so carefully planned to do? What do you think might have happened in the world if Germany had won the war in mid-1918, as most people expected it would?

- » What do you think it would have been like to live in Russia during the war, before the Russian Revolution? Do you think you would have been patriotic to your homeland? In what ways might the high casualties among the Russian army have caused you to question Czar Nicholas II?

KEY PEOPLE

The main characters in this Unit are listed in the Student Manual, along with a brief identifier, so that the students can familiarize themselves with these people.

◉ Recap the material with an activity

In different parts of the room, set up stations for the Eight Intelligences Recap Activities. Then allow students to work alone or together in small groups to accomplish THEIR CHOICE OF ONE of the following suggestions. At the start of the next class, ask for 3–4 groups of volunteers to share.

Homeschoolers: rather than setting up all eight stations, allow student(s) to choose which activity they would most enjoy, and do it.

Recap Suggestions:

Spatial: Create two propaganda posters, one that communicates the "righteous cause" of the Allies and the other communicating the "self-defense" of the Central Powers.

Bodily Kinesthetic: Become a series of "living statues," depicting stop-action poses of soldiers at each of the fronts.

Interpersonal: In groups of two, consider the deteriorating situation in July 1914 between the Triple Alliance and the Entente Cordiale. Discuss the issues and anticipated developments the leadership of each combatant would have been facing when considering whether to go to war.

Musical: Play music from WWI, such as the selections suggested at the beginning of the Unit, and think about what you have learned so far about the "war to end all wars." Then list the four most important facts you have learned.

Linguistic: Write a simple description of World War I in your own words.

Math-Logical: Chart the sequence of events from the assassination of Archduke Franz Ferdinand through Great Britain entering the war.

Intrapersonal: Consider whether the things you have learned about WWI thus far have changed, challenged, or strengthened your perspective on war. Journal your thoughts.

Naturalist: First obtaining permission, dig a small trench outside and add water to make it muddy. Then share what you think would have been some of the difficulties soldiers faced in the trenches. (Alternatively, make some mud, bring it inside in a container, and share your thoughts.)

Or . . . Activity of Your Choice: What would you like to have your students do for a review activity concerning this week's introduction to World War I & the Russian Revolution?

Critical Puzzling

» As Austria-Hungary mobilized against Serbia, why do you think Russia decided to mobilize its troops? What purpose was served when Germany declared war on Russia? Why do you think Germany chose to invade neutral Belgium? It is interesting to consider that many of Europe's leaders did not think that Great Britain would enter a war in which it had no personal interest. What motives do you think Great Britain may have had for entering the war?

» Why do you think Italy, though bound by treaty to Germany and Austria-Hungary, chose to remain neutral at the outbreak of WWI? What might have changed its position, resulting in Italy joining the Allies?

» At the outbreak of the war, Britain set up a very effective naval blockade. What impact might this have had on Germany? What types of products might have become unavailable because of this blockade? The Germans chose to retaliate with a submarine blockade of Great Britain and France, sinking merchant ships carrying products to these nations. What do you think might have been the pros and cons discussed before taking this approach? Do you think Germany made a wise decision?

» In what ways was this a different type of war than had been fought in the past? How do you think the invention of the machine gun, the tank, and the airplane changed the way this war was conducted?

» Winston Churchill, as First Lord of the Admiralty, authorized a plan for the Allies to take the Dardanelles, which would have opened Istanbul for capture and provided a direct supply route through the Black Sea to Russia. ANZAC (Australian and New Zealander) soldiers, along with French and British troops, fought the Turks at Gallipoli, but they lost disastrously. What attitudes do you think caused the Allies to take the risk of battling on Turkey's "doorstep"?

» What purpose do you think it served for Britain to capture Jerusalem from the Ottomans in 1917?

◉ Talk together

Individual Preparation

After completing their recap activities, students may begin to consider the questions in the Opinion Column and Critical Puzzling.

Class Discussion

Use the questions under Talk Together to get the students primed and to create a discussion environment in the classroom. You may also want to draw from the open-ended questions listed here.

Why do you think that both sides in the war chose to develop and use chemical warfare? What do you think had changed in the world that made this seem acceptable? **?**

T. E. Lawrence is one of the more interesting personalities of this war. How unusual do you think it was for a British soldier to lead Arab guerrilla fighters? In what ways do you think the efforts of Lawrence and the Arabs made a difference in the Allied war effort? **?**

Why do you think Germany helped Lenin get back to Russia even though Germany and Russia were at war? What do you think they would have hoped to receive from Lenin if they helped him? What was the effect of Lenin's return? How did this affect the war on the Eastern Front? The Western Front? **?**

6 Phase 1

▶ Resources for Digging Deeper

Choose a few books that look interesting, or find your own.

WORLD WAR I

The War to End All Wars

Russell Freedman • Written by a Newbery Medal winner, this is a profound and vivid portrayal of the immensity and destruction of WWI. **MS+**

World War I DK EYEWITNESS BOOKS

Simon Adams • Excellent resource for a visual and informative look at the multifaceted interest points of the war. **UE+**

The Story of the First World War

Colonel Russell Reeder • A basic "primer" of WWI, this fascinating book uses interesting stories to help students understand the various details of fighting a war on more than one front with many nations involved. **UE+**

World War I AMERICA'S WARS SERIES

Gail B. Stewart • This is a description of WWI from the perspective of the Americans. It shows the war effort (including no longer permitting steel ribs to be used in corsets!), the relationship between the kaiser and President Wilson, and the impact of the United States entering the war on the side of the Allies. **UE+**

World War One: An Illustrated History in Colour, 1914–1918

Robert Hoare • This book is worth the search. Filled with pictures, maps, and brief descriptions of different facets of the war, it is a fantastic overview of the "war to end all wars." **UE+**

America's First World War: General Pershing and the Yanks A WORLD LANDMARK BOOK

Henry Castor • This biography of the man in charge of the American soldiers sent to WWI shows why his job was not enviable—he had to bring the "doughboys" up to battle standards, making sure they were adequately led and provisioned. **UE+**

In Flanders Fields: The Story of the Poem by John McCrae

Linda Granfield • This is an excellent children's book for giving a sense of reality to the fighting in World War I. It is not so graphic that children would have nightmares, but it does convey the sense of horror and loss for the soldiers in this war. **E+**

THE AIR WAR

Flying Aces of World War I A WORLD LANDMARK BOOK

Gene Gurney • This book contains fascinating accounts of the best fighter pilots of several nations during the first war to use airplanes—WWI. Meet the men who changed the nature of battles with the use of their machines. Absolutely riveting. **UE+**

Sky Battle: 1914–1918

David C. Cooke • This is the story of the development of the airplane as a weapon of war—from the spindly contrivance of wood and muslin found in the first airplanes to deadly machines. Well-written and well-researched. **UE+**

Remember: Beware of Arrogance, Embrace Humility!

◉ Choose books of interest/ internet search

A list of possible books is given in the Student Manual. Encourage your students to look for books or videos on World War I & the Russian Revolution from this list and from other sources. You may want to gather a selection of further resources prior to beginning Unit 3, or you may encourage the students to be treasure hunters and find them on their own. It would be helpful and time-saving before the Unit begins to check availability of these titles on your local library website.

THE MIDDLE EAST

Lawrence of Arabia STERLING POINT BOOKS

Alistair MacLean • T. E. Lawrence was one of the most colorful personalities of WWI. Though he labored in a war far from the European trenches and without important military rank, his participation in the Arab Revolt helped to defeat the Ottoman Empire. Absolutely fascinating! **UE+**

Chaim Weizmann WORLD LEADERS PAST & PRESENT

Richard Amdur • This is the biography of a Russian Jew who studied science in Germany, moved to England, and, by his scientific assistance to the British during WWI, gained the Balfour Declaration of 1917—which guaranteed the Jews a national homeland in Palestine. Chaim Weizmann, a fascinating personality, was the first elected president of the new nation of Israel. **MS+**

RUSSIA

The First Book of the Soviet Union

Louis L. Snyder • An excellent book for introducing to children the history of Russia and the Communist Revolution, it includes a fascinating description of Lenin's return to Russia through German lines. **UE+**

Russia CULTURES OF THE WORLD

Oleg Torchinsky • Learn about Russia, its history, its geography, and the culture of the Russian people. Since the book was written after the breakup of the USSR, it includes information about the current situation. Fascinating! **UE+**

Vladimir Lenin WORLD LEADERS PAST & PRESENT

John Haney • This biography of the man who brought communism to Russia puts together all of the elements involved—his exile, the provisional government set up after the abdication of the czar, the "Red" army fighting the "White" army, the October Revolution, and more. **MS+**

Mosaic: A Child's Recollections of the Russian Revolution

Valentina Antonievna Seletzky • As the young daughter of a military officer and his wife before the Bolshevik Revolution, the author shares her memories of life in pre-Communist Russia, their escape across Siberia, and their voyage to America. This book provides a unique and innocent glimpse into a rich and historic culture, one that ended with Lenin. [Author's note: There is a brief mention of a fortune-telling tradition at Christmas time, along with a child's look at some of the upper-class social mores of the time.] **HS**

LITERATURE

The Secret Adversary

Agatha Christie • Dame Agatha writes a mystery about Tommy and Tuppence, which begins with the sinking of the *Lusitania*. A classic mystery. **MS+**

Cheaper by the Dozen

Frank B. Gilbreth, Jr., & Ernestine Gilbreth Carey • Efficiency! That's the word around which this American family functions. A great read-aloud classic! **AA**

VIDEO

Sergeant York

The true story of Sergeant York is amazing! As a Christian, he was not sure whether it was right to go off to war. The movie shows how he resolved this issue, and what the incredible results were. **UE+**

Lawrence of Arabia

This award-winning movie is a Hollywood depiction of T. E. Lawrence and the Arabs who fought against the Germans in WWI. There are some graphic depictions of violence and the movie leaves you with the impression that Lawrence was insane at times. His family disagreed with the interpretation of the director, and historians now recognize that much of what is believed about Lawrence's exploits is unverifiable, as he was his own source. Despite all that, it still is fascinating to watch. **MS+**

Blood and Oil: The Middle East in World War I

A film by Marty Callaghan · A recent documentary, this DVD is a remarkable compilation of various expert views on the subject, along with photos, film clips, maps, and a fast-paced story of the intrigues and events of this region of the war. Excellent! [Author's note: There are a few brief, disturbing images of lifeless bodies, from actual video footage.] **MS+**

For more books, use these Dewey Decimal numbers in your library:

Airplanes: 623.7; 629.133

WWI: 940.3

Infantry, air, and naval warfare: 356–359

General histories— Russia: 947.0; Germany: 943; France: 944

Tanks: 623

Submarines: 940.9

Balfour Declaration: 956.9

What books did you like best?

_____

_____

_____

_____

The Internet also contains a wealth of information about World War I & the Russian Revolution.

What sites were the most helpful?

_____

_____

_____

_____

▶ Student Self-Evaluation UNIT 6, PHASE 1

Dates and hours:_____

Key Concepts

Rephrase the three Key Concepts of this Unit and confirm your understanding of each:

- World War I

  _____

- The Middle East

  _____

- The Russian Revolution

  _____

Tools for Self-Evaluation

Evaluate your personal participation in the discussions of this Phase. Bearing in mind that a good participant in a discussion is not always the most vocal participant, ask yourself these questions: Were you an active participant? Did you ask perceptive questions? Were you willing to listen to other participants of the discussion and draw out their opinions? Record your observations and how you would like to improve your participation in the future:

_____

_____

Every time period is too complex to be understood in one Phase of study. Evaluate your current knowledge of World War I & the Russian Revolution. What have you focused on so far? What are your weakest areas of knowledge?

_____

_____

Based on the evaluation of this introduction, project ahead what you would like to study more of in the following Phases.

_____

_____

◉ Conduct a review and evaluation

In this Phase of Unit 6, your students should have had the opportunity to explore World War 1 & the Russian Revolution through reading, listening, thinking, and discussing by completing a selection from the following:

- informally discussed the Key Concepts;
- read the article;
- listened to the audio recordings;
- read the online articles;
- read the Scriptures;
- explored the recap activities;

- considered the Opinion Column and Critical Puzzling answers on their own;
- participated in class discussion;
- chosen books of interest or searched the Internet;
- completed their self-evaluation for this Phase.

Record student hours: _____

Assess student participation:

Create an evaluation system of your own, or refer to the evaluation rubric

in the introduction, as a tool for assessing participation. The categories you will probably find most useful are *"Introduction", "Process: Teamwork"* and *"Process: Originality"*. To help students develop good discussion skills, encourage them to participate actively, ask content-based questions, and stay focused on the discussion at hand. Students demonstrate a higher level of discussion skills when they incorporate comments and questions from others into their own questions, and draw out opinions or ask for points of clarification from others.

Do not critique the self-evaluation page your student completes and do not direct the answers the student gives to the questions. Instead, allow sincere and personal completion of the evaluation, then discuss the responses and incorporate those comments into your evaluation.

Determine a grade for this Phase, if using grades: _____

Teacher Self-Evaluation:

Evaluate your own use of materials and teaching opportunities: what worked and what did not; how effective was your time-management; how were your responses to the needs of your student; did you make your expectations clear; in what ways would you like to improve your approach for the next Unit? Incorporate suggestions from your students in your own evaluation (*this requires humility!*).

◉ Choose a topic and begin research

Allow the students the freedom to choose one of the topics listed under research & reporting in the Student Manual, or to suggest their own area which they would like to research.

Motivating Suggestions:

Especially for Non-linguistic students, and those who are not motivated by written or oral reports, here are suggestions for alternative ways of reporting what has been researched.

Causes of WWI

Prepare a televised interview using three students: the interviewer, the spokesperson for Austria-Hungary, and the spokesperson for Germany. Allow each spokesperson to air concerns about what the neighboring country is doing.

Create a poster for each cause of WWI you have studied. Craft each poster so that it will tell the issue, the location, the personalities or cultures, and the results. Use maps, visual images, time lines, and short captions.

WWI in 1914

Create a PowerPoint presentation to help viewers understand the beginning of WWI's flow of events. Charts, diagrams, and maps will be invaluable as you explain your findings.

Act 1: Prior to the outbreak of WWI, as a German military staff officer, prepare a presentation for the kaiser to explain Germany's Schlieffen Plan. *Act II:* Now prepare a brief summary of what actually took place in France when Germany invaded, taking a suitably chastened attitude.

The Western Front

Set up a museum for visitors to learn about the Western Front. Create a few replicas of items used, a diorama of the trenches, and pictures with explanations of the hardships endured.

Phase 2

▶ Research & Reporting

Explore one or more of these areas to discover something significant!

Causes of WWI

Research and report on the various causes of WWI, including Austria-Hungary's view on Serbian nationalism and German concerns about the Russian army's plan for modernization.

WWI in 1914

Discover the date and reason each participant entered the war in the summer and fall of 1914. Also, learn more about how the strategic plans for defeating the enemy, which each nation had been creating before the war, actually played out.

The Western Front

Learn more about some aspect of the Western Front, such as the "race to the sea," the construction of trenches, the years-long stalemate, the Hindenburg Line, the use of poison gas, no-man's-land, "going over the top," or the way that the machine gun changed the strategy of battle.

The Eastern Front

Study more about the Eastern Front. Where was it located? Where did Russia attack Germany and Austria-Hungary? How successful were each of these countries in repelling Russian troops? Learn about the successful 1915 German offensive and the successful 1916 Brusilov offensive, where each side appeared—for a time—to be winning.

The Russian Revolution

Research and report on the Russian Revolution of 1917, including the revolution in March and the Bolshevik revolution in October. What factors led to the March revolution? How did the Bolsheviks gain power in October? Learn more about why Russia signed a peace treaty in which they relinquished one-third of their land to Germany.

America's Changing Involvement

Study and write about America's participation in World War I. What was America's original position toward the war? In what ways did America support the war effort? Why did America enter the war on the side of the Allies? What was involved in bringing American troops to the actual fronts? What effect did their joining the war have on the Allies? On the Germans?

The Naval War

Study how Britain and Germany used their navies in this war, including submarines. Be sure to show the British blockade of Germany, and the "underwater blockade" Germany used in retaliation. Discover the reason why the Germans seldom brought their surface ships out of port during this war, and the results when they did.

The Air War

Research and report on the use of dirigibles (zeppelins) and planes during World War I. Read about the way zeppelins were used by Germany, and the results. Describe the way airplanes became an offensive tool with the addition of machine guns and bombs. Be sure to include stories of the pilot "aces" from both sides in the war, and display the types of medals that were won.

Gallipoli

Learn more about the Allies' plan to capture the Dardanelles, and why Winston Churchill was blamed for what transpired at Gallipoli. Describe the ongoing efforts by the ANZAC, French, and British soldiers to capture the high ground, as well as Mustafa Kemal Atatürk's leadership in its successful defense. Consider the sea evacuation of December 1915 to January 1916—what had been

---

In a small group, decide what are the five most significant points that younger students should understand about the Western Front. Then, plan how the group could actually teach these points to a group of six-year-olds. Use as many of the five senses as possible as you teach.

The Eastern Front

Create a papier-mâché topographic map of the Eastern Front. You can find a link at the online resource page to show you how. Then demonstrate to an audience the location of East Prussia, Galicia, and the Carpathian mountain range, and explain the part each of these locations played in this front.

Create an outdoor obstacle course that will help others learn about the Eastern Front. With rope, set up these regional locations: East Prussia, Galicia, Austria-Hungary, Germany, and Russia. Next, mark these specific cities with an object: Berlin, Vienna, Warsaw, Krakow, and Petrograd. Then chart the obstacle course twice: 1) the route a victorious Russian army would take from Petrograd to Berlin and Vienna, and 2) the route a victorious German/Austro-Hungarian army would take to Petrograd from Berlin and Vienna.

The Russian Revolution

Choose two pieces of music: one to represent the March Revolution, in which the people united to

ain, its sinking of merchant ships, and, in 1917, its unrestricted submarine warfare. The second person will be a British Royal Navy destroyer, explaining its blockade of Germany, its Battle of Jutland, and its convoy system.

Create a rhythmic chant about WWI's naval war, including the blockades, the underwater war, the convoys, the Battle of Jutland, and the German naval mutinies.

The Air War

Write and illustrate a children's book showing the development and use of airplanes and Zeppelins in WWI. Since this is for children, focus on the amazing growth of technology in these aircraft rather than their increased ability to bring destruction.

Before a live audience, interview a German ace pilot about what fighting the war is like in an airplane. Second, interview one of the Allied aces to discover if he has any differences in perspective.

Gallipoli

Set up two areas representing the obstacles faced by Allied soldiers and by Turkish soldiers at Gallipoli. Each area should exhibit replicas of artifacts that will help viewers understand life at this front. In addition, create some sort of visual aid to explain why the Allied soldiers were unable to gain the heights, and why the Turkish soldiers were unable to dislodge Allied soldiers from the beaches. Give tours of the Gallipoli Front, explaining what happened.

The Australian and New Zealand soldiers (ANZACs) who fought on this front were treated as heroes in their own countries, even though the campaign ended in failure. Beginning April 25, 1916, Australia and New Zealand began holding "ANZAC Day" celebrations. Plan one for your friends and family, with as many of the traditions included as possible. To learn more about these traditions, see the link at the online resource page.

---

anticipated in terms of casualties, and what were the surprising results?

The Arab Revolt

Discover more about the personalities of those involved in the Arab Revolt, including Hussein, Sharif of Mecca; his eldest son, Faisal; and British officer T. E. Lawrence. Describe the development of the revolt and the part it played in WWI.

Tank Technology

Study and write about the development of the tank during World War I. What was Winston Churchill's contribution to this new weapon? Discover why it was so uniquely suited to WWI, and what part it played during the war.

The Balfour Declaration of 1917

Research and report on the reasons for Great Britain's Balfour Declaration, promising a Jewish homeland in Palestine, and how this conflicted with the promises made to Hussein earlier in the war. Learn about the rising tide of anti-Semitism in Europe and Russia, and how this led to political Zionism.

The Italian Front

Learn more about Italy's entry into the war, how "irredentism" played a part in this decision, and why Italy invaded Austria-Hungary. Find out how Mussolini was involved in this front. Describe the difficult conditions under which all of the participants fought and lived.

Serbia's Story

Discover how Serbia successfully defended itself against Austria-Hungary—until Bulgaria joined the Central Powers. Learn about the Serbians' flight across the Albanian mountains in winter, their rescue by Allied ships in a massive evacuation by sea from the Albanian coastline in early 1916, and the part they played at Salonika.

The End

Research and report on the end of World War I. Learn more about why Bulgaria signed an armistice; why the Ottoman Empire signed; why the Austro-Hungarians signed; and why Germany finally signed. What new developments or changes in circumstances brought these different Central Powers to peace talks?

▶ Brain Stretchers

German Colonies

Research and report on the fascinating story of what happened to German colonies when WWI began. Be sure to learn about Germany's colony in China, its colonies in the Pacific Islands, and its far larger colonies in Africa. The longest front of the entire war was in German East Africa!

Ottoman Empire

Discover the results of the Ottomans' entrance into the war. What was the impact on Palestine, Mesopotamia, and the Caucasus? Be sure to read about the Turkish move to grab the Suez Canal, the British move to grab oil-rich provinces of Mesopotamia, the British capture of Jerusalem, and what led to the Armenian Massacre of 1915.

Create Your Own Research Topic

_____

_____

_____

---

overthrow the czar, and the other to represent the Bolshevik Revolution, in which Lenin overthrew the Provisional Government. Explain the differences between these two.

Imagine you are an Orthodox Christian factory worker in Petrograd in March of 1917. Many of your fellow workers are angry about the czar, the obvious corruption of his government, the horrible losses in the war, and the crushing lack of food in the city. Journal your thoughts and prayers for your country during this explosive moment.

America's Changing Involvement

Hold a formal debate in America during January 1917. The resolution for debate is "America should continue the policy of non-interventionism as instructed by our Founding Fathers, despite Germany's provocation." One team will argue for this position, while the other team will argue against it.

Create an ad campaign to keep America out of the war. Or, conversely, create an ad campaign to bring America into the war. Remember that ads appeal to our emotions, not our reason, so structure your campaign with this in mind.

The Naval War

With two people, create a first-person presentation for a live audience. One person will be a German submarine, explaining its blockade of Great Brit-

The Arab Revolt

Create a game of strategy based on the Arab Revolt. The dangers of raising a revolt are that the Ottoman Empire might send an army to crush you, other Arab leaders might refuse to follow your lead, European leaders might disdain you and break their promises, and you may lose it all. The reward could be a chance to rule an independent, united Arab kingdom.

Prepare to tell the events of the Arab Revolt as a storyteller, from the astounding capture of Aqaba from the Ottomans to the exploits of the Arab soldiers who, with T. E. Lawrence, attacked the Hejaz Railway. If you can wear an Arabic costume during your presentation, so much the better!

Tank Technology

Draw diagrams of the interior and exterior of a tank, labeling any significant items. Then prepare a short talk in which you explain how the tank was developed, what part it was expected to play in trench warfare, and how it performed during WWI.

Using a flip chart or PowerPoint, compare and contrast the use of the tank in WWI with the other new strategic marvels used in the war, such as the airplane and the machine gun.

The Balfour Declaration

Write a Jewish-style folksong about the longing to return to the Holy Land. Include the phrase that has been spoken every year for hundreds of years at the end of the Passover Seder, "Next year in Jerusalem."

Create a collage to illustrate to an audience the colliding hopes of the Arabs and the Zionist Jews during WWI, both of whom had received promises from the British government.

The Italian Front

You are an Italian patriot who believes your current boundaries are unacceptable and weak. Convince your audience that you are justified in invading Austria-Hungary, showing why you switched from being a member of the

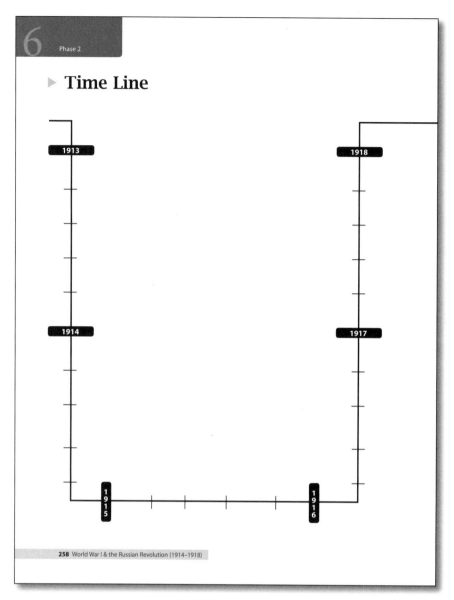

Triple Alliance to become allied with Britain, France, and Russia.

As an Italian reporter, discover the perspective of the common man about this war that is being forced on your country. Write what you learn, including the part Mussolini has played.

Serbia's Story

Set up a dramatic outdoor scene, and with a small group re-enact the story of Serbia's actions in the war. Include the various geographic obstacles they faced, the difficulties they encountered, and their successes.

Consider what it was like to live in Serbia through WWI, and then write

out your thoughts. What insights have you gained for yourself?

The End

Prepare a PowerPoint presentation to compare and contrast the end of the war for each of the Central Powers. Include the part each of the Allied nations fighting on various fronts played in these decisions.

Hold a memorial service for the Ottoman Empire, the German Empire, the Russian Empire, and the Austro-Hungarian Empire—each of which perished as a result of WWI. Include a program for each attendee that describes the most important facts from the "life" of these empires.

Consider this for your time line
Though seldom considered today, this "Great War" changed the shape of the world in many ways. Beyond the obvious disappearance of four empires by war's end, it is sobering to consider the number of civilian and military casualties, the extraordinary devastation and destruction in the regions where the war was fought, and the loss of nearly an entire generation of men from many of the great power nations. As we will see in the following units, many of the conflicts that have taken place from that time until the present have their roots in WWI.

Key Events

- Assassination of Francis Ferdinand
- Battle of the Marne
- Battle of Tannenberg
- Gallipoli
- Armenian Massacre
- Battle of Verdun
- Battle of Somme
- British surrender at Kut-al-Amara
- Russian Revolution
- British take Jerusalem
- American troops at Western Front
- Allied "Hundred Days Offensive"
- German Armistice

Be sure to include the people listed in Key People in Phase 1.

Psalm 27:13 says, "I would have lost heart unless I had believed that I would see the goodness of the Lord in the land of the living." Talk with your students about the impact that hope has on a person and a nation. Discuss the difference between putting one's hope in man's abilities and putting one's hope in the God of the universe.

◉ Construct the time line

Read the information listed with the Key Events in the Student Manual. Dialogue with your students about the issues involved.

Find the dates for the Key People and Key Events listed.

Time Line Key
Key People in the Church
- Billy Sunday: 1862–1935
- Rees Howells: 1879–1950

Key People in the World
- Paul von Hindenburg: 1847–1934
- Ferdinand Foch: 1851–1929
- Philippe Pétain: 1856–1951
- David Lloyd George: 1863–1945
- Woodrow Wilson: 1856–1924
- Erich Ludendorff: 1865–1937
- Vladimir Lenin: 1870–1924
- Chaim Weizmann: 1874–1952
- T. E. Lawrence: 1888–1935

Key Dates
- Assassination of Francis Ferdinand: June 28, 1914
- Battle of the Marne: September 5-12, 1914
- Battle of Tannenberg: August 23–30, 1914
- Gallipoli: April 25, 1915–January 9, 1916
- Armenian Massacre: 1915
- Battle of Verdun: February 21–December 18, 1916
- Battle of Somme: July 1–November 18, 1916
- British surrender at Kut-al-Amara: April 29, 1916
- Russian Revolution: 1917
- British take Jerusalem: December 30, 1917
- American troops at Western Front: June 1917
- Allied "Hundred Days Offensive": August 8–November 11, 1918
- German Armistice: November 11, 1918

Words to Watch

trenches	assassinate	ultimatum	stalemate
provisional govern-ment	impenetrable	propaganda	attrition
	relief (charity)	neutral	genocide
mobilize	irredentism	resupply	armistice
aviation	front (in war)	belligerent	autocracy
convoy			

Consider:

The vocabulary you will find in the study of World War I includes a number of "isms," of which these are but a few.

Bolshevism	militarism	socialism
nationalism	pacifism	capitalism

Other words you need to look up:

_____

_____

_____

_____

Here is one idea for making vocabulary study interesting and fun:

CREATE-A-PHRASE

Your job is to take each of these vocabulary words and assign it a phrase that captures its essential meaning. For example, "trenches" could become "the hopeless shelter of WWI soldiers."

A list of definitions can be found at the back of the book in Appendix B.

◉ Practice vocabulary

You may find other words in this Unit that are especially appropriate for younger children. Feel free to substitute another vocabulary list for the one provided.

◉ Complete research projects and share in class or hand in

Create a safe environment for the presentations. Set ground rules prior to the presentations, so that students know how much time is available for each of them, and so that they know they will be honored and respected by all those observing.

▶ Student Self-Evaluation UNIT 6, PHASE 2

Dates and hours:_____

Research Project

Summarize your research question:

_____

_____

List your most useful sources by author, title, and page number or URL where applicable (continue list in margin if necessary):

_____

_____

Now take a moment to evaluate the sources you just listed. Do they provide a balanced view of your research question? Should you have sought an additional opinion? Are your sources credible (if you found them on your own)? Record your observations:

_____

_____

_____

Evaluate your research project in its final presentation. What are its strengths? If you had time to revisit this project, what would you change? Consider giving yourself a letter grade based on your project's merits and weaknesses.

_____

_____

_____

Letter grade: _____

You have just completed an area of specific research on the time of World War I & the Russian Revolution. Now what would you like to explore in the upcoming Phases? Set some objectives for yourself.

_____

_____

_____

◉ Conduct a review and evaluation

In this second Phase of Unit 6, your students should have had the opportunity to explore World War 1 & the Russian Revolution through researching, thinking, and reporting by completing a selection from the following:

- done a research project;
- learned the vocabulary;
- constructed a time line;
- created a project report on what was researched;
- completed their self-evaluation procedure for this Phase.

Record student hours: _____

Assess student effort in the research and reporting projects.

Create an evaluation system of your own, or refer to the evaluation rubric in the introduction, as a tool for assessing research and reporting. The categories you will probably find most useful are *"Introduction"*, *"Task"*, *"Process: Teamwork"* (if students are working together), along with Grammar, Format, and Spelling. As a tool for helping your students develop better research skills, pay attention to their evaluation of sources. Older students should learn how to make a "Sources Cited" list according to academic standards—refer them to English usage books or websites for formatting rules. Younger students should learn how to obtain a balanced view of their research subject; if they use more than one source they will get a bigger picture of what was happening. Encourage your students to make use of their self-evaluations for their next research projects, in order to practice good research skills.

Do not critique the self-evaluation page your student completes in the Student Manual—spelling errors are not to be considered in such an exercise. Students should feel free to humbly evaluate themselves without that added complexity. Instead, discuss with them the intention of their written comments and incorporate those into your evaluation.

Determine a final grade for this Phase: _____

Teacher Self-Evaluation:

Evaluate your own use of materials and teaching opportunities: what worked and what did not; how effective was your time-management; how were your responses to the needs of your student; did you make your expectations clear; in what ways would you like to improve your approach for the next Unit? Incorporate suggestions from your students in your own evaluation (*this requires humility!*).

Phase 3

▶ Maps and Mapping

Physical Terrain

» Locate and label the Baltic Sea, the North Sea, the English Channel, the Adriatic Sea, the Aegean Sea, the Black Sea, and the Dardanelle Straits.

» Locate and label these mountain ranges: the Carpathians, the Caucasus, the Alps.

Geopolitical

» The following are the countries where the Western, Eastern, Southern, and Ottoman fronts were located, though many were under different names during this time. Locate and label these modern-day nations: Belgium, France, Germany, Russia, Hungary, Poland, Serbia, Bulgaria, Greece, Italy, Slovenia, Turkey, Iraq, Syria, and Israel.

» Mark and label these cities that were pertinent to the events of WWI: Sarajevo, Berlin, Vienna, Paris, Brussels, St. Petersburg (Petrograd), Belgrade, Warsaw, Krakow, Thessaloniki (Salonika), Trieste, Istanbul, Basra, Baghdad, Damascus, and Jerusalem.

Explore

» *Worldwide Revival:* On a globe, locate the major places of revival (whether specific cities or general regions) in the first decade of the 1900s, including Wales, India, Korea, China, Germany, Japan, and South Africa. Then locate the major places of war in the first decade of the 1900s and up to WWI. What do you find significant about comparing these two sets of geographical and historical information?

» *Christian Outreach:* What is the status of evangelical outreach today in Russia? What opportunities and what difficulties face those who share the gospel in this area?

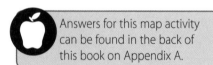

Answers for this map activity can be found in the back of this book on Appendix A.

◉ Create a map and discuss the issues in teams

The students each have an outline map in their manuals. They will be given assignments for drawing in the rivers, mountains, cities, and regional boundaries that are listed.

For details on where these things are, please consult a historical atlas, an encyclopedia, or another source of geographic information.

Upper elementary students might be satisfied to accomplish only this portion:

- **Physical terrain:** This part of the mapping exercise will help students locate and mark the major bodies of water and mountain ranges involved in WWI.

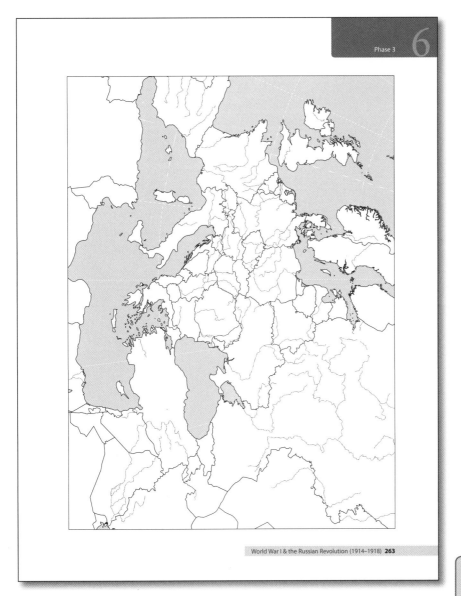

Middle school students might be satisfied to complete both the previous mapping exercise and this exercise:

- **Geopolitical:** This section of the mapping exercise will provide the students an opportunity to locate and mark the various nations in which the battles of WWI were fought, as well as the cities that were central to the conflict. (Know-

ing these will greatly assist students in understanding the war.)

High school students might be satisfied to complete both the previous mapping exercises and at least one exploration topic of this exercise:

- **Explore** a selection from this portion of the mapping exercise in teams.

THE GEOGRAPHICAL THEATERS OF WAR

Students might find it helpful to make a simple map for each front they study on which they label the various terrains. This will help the student to better grasp the difficulties faced by each side as they sought to overcome the obstacles of terrain. Precipitation and temperature charts will help to complete their understanding.

CHRISTIAN OUTREACH

Students might wish to locate information about current missionary endeavors in the Middle East. If possible, to provide even more help and insight, interview someone who has worked in these fields.

As we consider with our students how Dadaism was an artistic protest against the futile destruction of WWI, our hearts should be moved with sympathy. And yet, as we consider the means by which these artists protested—creating the artistic absurdity of Dadaism—we recognize that they were also expressing the view that life itself is meaningless. This false view of the world must be examined in light of biblical truth. Proverbs 8 4–8:would be an excellent plumb line with which to start:

"To you, O men, I call, and my voice is to the sons of men. O you simple ones, understand prudence, and you fools, be of an understanding heart. Listen, for I will speak of excellent things, and from the opening of my lips will come right things; for my mouth will speak truth; wickedness is an abomination to my lips. All the words of my mouth are with righteousness; nothing crooked or perverse is in them."

◉ Examine and discuss art and architecture

The online resource page at www. HistoryRevealed.org has links to view each of the items listed. Allow the students time to observe the paintings without any conversation, and then, when they are ready, engage them in some or all of the questions listed below or in the Student Manual.

Art Appreciation

Tu m' by Marcel Duchamp

Francis Schaeffer, in his book *How Should We Then Live*, wrote:

Dada carried to its logical conclusion the notion of all having come about by chance; the

▶ # Art Appreciation

Tu m' by Marcel Duchamp (1918)

One of the best-known artists of the WWI-influenced Dada style of art, Marcel Duchamp had previously experimented with Cubism. As WWI enveloped much of Europe, he began exhibiting ready-made objects (which he signed as the artist) to refute the idea of art expressing meaning. This painting was one of his last. You can find a link to see this painting at the online resource page.

» Remembering that this is not supposed to mean anything, how would you describe it? What images can you identify? In French, the expression "Tu m' . . ." means "You _____ me." The viewer must supply the verb. It has been suggested that Duchamp was saying of painting, "You bore me." What verb would you supply for the title?

I and the Village by Marc Chagall (1911)

Chagall was a Russian-born Jewish painter, and was among the most successful artists of the twentieth century. Studying and working in Paris, he returned home in 1914 to marry the love of his life, and was trapped by the closing of the borders at the outbreak of war. You can find a link to see this painting at the online resource page.

» This was painted three years before WWI. How would you describe this vision of his Russian village? What scenes and objects can you identify? Compare this painting to Duchamp's *Tu m'*. In what ways are they similar? In what ways are they different?

CONSIDER:
During WWI, a group of anti-war, anti-Western civilization artists formed a group with an artistic style known as "Dada" (chosen specifically because it is a meaningless word.) With the stalemate and senseless destruction on the Western Front, this style was "a protest against the entire fabric of European society, which could give rise to and condone the monstrous destruction of the war" (Frederick Hartt). Dadaism powerfully expressed a worldview philosophy of meaninglessness and absurdity, leading eventually to surrealism.

The online resource page at www.HistoryRevealed.org contains many helpful Internet links to artwork, architecture, music, project helps, and more.

result was the final absurdity of everything, including humanity. The man who perhaps most clearly and consciously showed this understanding of the resulting absurdity of all things was Marcel Duchamp. . . . The chance and fragmented concept of what *is* led to the devaluation and absurdity of all things. All one was left with was a fragmented view of a life which is absurd in all its parts. . . . Thus art itself was declared absurd.

I and the Village by Marc Chagall

Chagall wrote of his works:

I do not understand them at all. They are not literature. They are only pictorial arrangements of images which obsess me. . . . The theories which I make up to explain myself and those which others elaborate in connection with my work are nonsense. . . . My paintings are my reason for existence, my life, and that's all.

Ask students what they like or dislike about Chagall's *I and the Village*. Have them share their thoughts concerning Duchamp's attitude toward painting and meaning as expressed in *Tu m'*; then compare this attitude with Chagall's.

▶ Architecture

Walter Gropius, a German-born architect, was one of the pioneers of modern architecture. Recognizing that factories were here to stay, he nevertheless believed that an architect and designer could "breathe a soul into the dead product of the machine." A few years before WWI, Gropius, in collaboration with Adolph Meyer, designed the steel-framed glass facade of a German factory that produced shoe lasts. During the war, Gropius served as a cavalry officer on the Western Front, receiving the Iron Cross for bravery.

The Fagus Works at Alfeld, Germany designed by Walter Gropius

» You can find a link to see this building at the online resource page. This building, which shows the steel and glass exterior walls, is an excellent example of early modern architecture. How would you describe this structure? Imagine if you had been a worker at this factory. What do you think the impact of the walls of glass would have had on your everyday work experience?

▶ Arts in Action

Select one or more, and let your artistic juices flow!

Expressing Worldview

Since Dadaism was such an effective artistic means of conveying the worldview message that there is no meaning in the world, consider how you might express your Christian worldview—which proclaims that life does have meaning—through art.

» Using sculpture, painting, mosaics, or whichever medium of art you prefer, create and title an artwork that expresses a Christian worldview. You may choose to do a Biblical scene, a historical scene, a nature scene, or a contemporary scene. Remember, the point is to communicate the biblical truth that life has a purpose, meaning, and a Loving Designer.

Scenes from Your Life

» Marc Chagall's painting *I and the Village* contains various images and scenes of his home village, rendered with rich and interesting colors. Consider how you might create a drawing or painting that would contain an image or scene from your hometown. A crayon etching is one way to create a vibrant and interesting piece.

World War I & the Russian Revolution (1914–1918) **265**

The online resource page at www.HistoryRevealed.org contains many helpful Internet links to artwork, architecture, music, project helps, and more.

into the dead product of the machine." In what ways does this building reflect this concept?

◉ Do an art project

Architecture

The Fagus Works at Alfeld, Germany designed by Walter Gropius

Architect Kevin Havens wrote:

Steel and glass construction was replacing traditional stone and brick masonry just prior to the war. More importantly, all ornament, or reference to classicism, was being completely removed and replaced with a more pure expression of a steel frame in-filled with abundant glass . . . a most shocking departure from what had been built in the past century. The WWI era was not a time for prolific building, and is, perhaps, best remembered (from an architectural perspective) as an intellectual and social caldron from which radically new building technologies and aesthetic philosophies would emerge that ushered in the age of Modernism.

The Fagus Works factory's website is excellent for seeing the factory, which continues to produce shoe lasts (the site is in German, but the photos are fascinating!). You can find a link at the online resource page.

Discuss with students their thoughts about the design of this factory and Gropius's desire to "breathe a soul

Expressing Worldview

This is more than a mere exercise for this Unit. It could be the start of a thoughtful career in the arts, in which your student seeks to express the reality of life as seen through the lens of Christianity. An excellent resource to for helping students learn to express their worldview through art is "Eight Secrets to Teaching Art in the Home." A link to this article can be found at the online resource page

Scenes from Your Life

A link to a YouTube video about how to create a crayon etching can be found on the online resource page. "Leona's Art Class" is very well done

▶ Science

During WWI, Frenchman Paul Langevin developed an underwater ultrasonic source for submarine detection. Though "SONAR" (an acronym of SOund Navigation And Ranging) was not available to the Allies in WWI, it was secretly brought up to full functioning capability during the interim years and used successfully during WWII.

Active sonar sends out an underwater pulse of sound, a "ping." When it hits something, the sound echoes back. This echo allows the sonar operator to determine how far away the object is, since the speed of sound in salt water is known for a variety of conditions. For example, suppose the temperature, depth, and saltiness of the water indicate that sound will travel at 4,800 feet per second. If it took two seconds to hear the echoing "ping," the echo traveled 4,800 feet to get to the object and 4,800 feet to get back. Do this series of three experiments to learn more about underwater sonar.

» First, observe what a sound wave looks like! Using a Slinky, have one person hold one end while you hold the other end across a table. Stretch it loosely, then jerk your end toward your friend. Watch what happens. Continue to jerk it forward and back to allow many waves to form. And, amazingly, the Slinky clumps up and stretches out just like air or water does when it carries a sound wave!

» Second, learn about the way sound travels through water. In a swimming pool, have a friend listen to you make a sound while you are both underwater. Then make the same sound above water. Does being underwater make the sound louder and clearer? An optional way to try this experiment is to take two rocks with you into the bathtub. When your ears and hands are submerged under the water, try clicking the rocks together. Next, try clicking the rocks together when both your ears and hands are above the water. Which medium—air or water—allows the sound to travel more loudly and clearly? Sound waves actually travel through the water more than four times faster than through the air!

» Third, learn more about echoes. Cliffs are ideal for this experiment, but you may also want to try it in a large, empty gym or against the side of a brick building. Loudly say a word or make a sound. Then count the number of seconds it takes before you hear an echo. Divide the seconds by two, then by five to get the distance to the cliffs in miles. (Divide by two because the sound traveled twice—to the cliffs and then back to your ears. Divide by five because sound travels roughly one-fifth of a mile per second in air at the temperatures generally experienced near the surface of the earth.) You need to be a least forty feet away in order for your ears to have time to hear the echo.

◉ Do a science experiment

A fascinating link showing how air carries a sound wave can be found at the online resource page.

▶ Music

The music of Ralph Vaughan Williams stands in stark contrast to the art of the Dadaists. An English composer of the early twentieth century, his style reflects a different use of music than that of Stravinsky and other expressionistic composers. It is very serious and technically very professional, artful, and beautiful, yet it was something the average concert-goer could enjoy without feeling assaulted musically. Vaughn Williams said, "The composer must not shut himself up and think about art, he must live with his fellows and make his art an expression of the whole life of the community."

"Pastoral" Symphony by Vaughan Williams

Vaughan Williams, a brilliant composer, served during WWI as a private with the Royal Army Medical corps—when he was forty-two years old. He conceived this piece of music while at a battlefield in France: "It's really wartime music—a great deal of it incubated when I used to go up night after night with the ambulance wagon at Ecoivres and we went up a steep hill and there was a wonderful Corot-like landscape in the sunset—it's not really lambkins frisking at all as most people take for granted." You can find a link to listen to the music at the online resource page.

　　» After listening to this symphony, talk together about the sounds of war that can be heard amidst the beauty. Do you hear purpose and meaning in this music? In what ways does this express a different worldview than the Dadaists?

"Le Tombeau de Couperin" by Ravel

Maurice Ravel was a French composer who also served during WWI, as an ambulance driver in the French army. He had been composing a suite for piano in 1914, just before the onset of war. Completing it in 1917, after his discharge, he dedicated each of its six movements to friends who had died in the war. You can find a link to listen to the music at the online resource page.

　　» This beautiful music is one of the earliest examples of twentieth century Neoclasssicism. Considering the trauma of Ravel's having served in the war, what message does this piece bring to you?

◉ Listen to and discuss the music

Listen

Vaughan Williams's "Pastoral" Symphony (1922)

Critiqued as "the best English orchestral music of this century," this piece of music is a beautiful, moving lament for those who died in WWI.

You can find a link to a YouTube video of a portion of this symphony, but students interested in hearing music composed about the war might find it more satisfying to hear it in its entirety. Check online for MP3 downloads (there are free, short samples to hear) or your local music store.

Ravel's "Le Tombeau de Couperin" (1914–1919)

Ravel originally composed this for piano, then arranged four of the movements for orchestra. It was in this form that it was first heard in public early in 1920.

A YouTube video of Vlado Perlemuter playing this piece on the piano can be found at the online resource page. It is astonishing to watch someone play this complex music! There is also a link to hear an orchestral recording.

▶ Cooking

This is a simple recipe you can make that comes from the Ukraine. It is wonderful on a cold winter day!

Ukrainian Piroshki

Sour Cream Pastry:
1¾ cup flour
½ tsp baking powder
¼ tsp salt
¼ cup butter, cold
1 egg, lightly beaten
½ cup sour cream

Glaze:
1 beaten egg

Mushroom Filling:
3 green onions, chopped
½ pound mushrooms, chopped
2 tbsp butter
2 tsp flour
1½ tbsp sour cream
4 tsp fresh dill
pinch allspice, salt, black pepper
1 hard-boiled egg, chopped

Prepare the pastry by sifting the dry ingredients into a large bowl. Cut the butter into the flour until it is the consistency of cornmeal. In a separate bowl, beat eggs and sour cream until smooth. Blend into the flour mixture. Gently knead the dough on a floured board until smooth. Shape into a ball, cover and chill for one hour.

Sauté the green onions and mushrooms in the butter until golden. Remove onions and mushrooms from pan, and reserve. Melt remaining 1 tablespoon in pan, sprinkle the flour into the melted butter and stir over medium heat for about a minute. Blend in the sour cream, remove from heat. Add the previously sautéed vegetables, and add the spices and chopped eggs, mixing well.

Preheat oven to 400ºF. Roll out the dough to 1/4-inch thickness on a lightly floured board. Cut into three-and-a-half-inch rounds. Place a heaping tablespoon of filling in the center of each round. Fold into crescent shapes and pinch the edges to seal. Place on greased baking sheet. Brush with egg glaze and bake until golden, about 15 to 20 minutes.

Makes approximately 18 piroshkis.

◉ Cook the food

Alternate meat filling

Students might prefer to use this meat filling in making piroshkis:

½ onion, chopped
2 tbsp canola oil
½ pound lean ground beef
Salt and pepper to taste
1 hard-boiled egg, chopped

Sauté the onion in oil for 5 minutes, then add the ground beef. Cook until the meat is browned; drained well. Add spices. Cool and add chopped eggs.

Fill pastry as directed in the Student Manual recipe.

▶ Student Self-Evaluation UNIT 6, PHASE 3

Dates and hours:_____

Evaluate your projects

- List which of the activities listed in this Phase you did:

  _____

  _____

- Rate your enthusiasm: _____

  Explain: _____

  _____

- Rate the precision of your approach:_____

  Explain: _____

  _____

- Rate your effort toward the completion of the project: _____

  Explain: _____

  _____

- Ask yourself what worked and what did not. What would you do differently in the future, and what would you repeat?

  _____

  _____

- How did these hands-on activities enhance your knowledge of World War I & the Russian Revolution? What made them worthwhile?

  _____

  _____

- In the first three Phases of this Unit, what aspect of the time period has most captured your imagination? What would you like to creatively pursue to conclude your study?

  _____

  _____

World War I & the Russian Revolution (1914–1918) **269**

◉ Conduct a review and evaluation

In this Phase of Unit 6, your students should have had the opportunity to explore World War I & the Russian Revolution through various hands-on and creative sessions by completing a selection from the following:

- completed a mapping section;
- observed and discussed art & architecture;
- worked on an art project;
- experimented with a science project or taken a field trip;
- listened to music;
- tasted a food related to this Unit;

- completed their self-evaluation procedure for this Phase.

Record student hours: _____

Assess student involvement in the hands-on activities.

Create an evaluation system of your own or refer to the evaluation rubric in the introduction as a tool for assessing participation. The categories you will probably find most useful for evaluating projects are *"Task"* and *"Process: Teamwork."* Consider specifi-

cally the enthusiasm, the precision of approach, and the efforts toward improving skills and completing activities, rather than rating the project as compared to a masterpiece.

Do not critique the self-evaluation page your student completes in the Student Manual—it is acceptable for students to occasionally leave lines blank if a question does not apply. Instead, discuss with the student the intention of the written comments and incorporate those into your evaluation.

Determine a grade for this Phase, if using grades: _____

Teacher Self-Evaluation:

Evaluate your own use of materials: what worked and what did not? Consider your time management. Were you able to recognize and respond to your students' needs? Did you make your expectations clear? In what ways would you like to improve your approach for the next Unit? Incorporate suggestions from your students in your own evaluation (*this requires humility!*).

Phase 4

▶ In Your Own Way…

In this Unit, we have seen the assassination of Austria-Hungary's heir to the throne develop into a conflict which drew one nation after another into an inconceivable world war, with destruction on a scale never before seen. Russians and Germans, Austro-Hungarians and Serbs, Turks and Armenians, Arabs and British, Africans and Japanese, Australians and New Zealanders, Indians and Bulgarians, Romanians and Czechs, Montenegrins and Slovakians, Slovenians and Greeks, Italians and Belgians, French and Americans—all fought during this war. From the mud to the desert to the jungle to the mountains, from East to West and North to South, from the depths of the sea to the heights of the heaven, this war was the costliest in terms of human life and economics that had ever been fought. Four empires fell, and one experienced a new type of upheaval—the Russian Revolution. Now, choose a selection of these activities, or create your own, which will best express what you have learned from this Unit.

LINGUISTICS

Journalism

Write a strong letter to the editor of the *British Times*, in which you share your outrage over your country's foolish attempt to capture Baghdad—which led to the surrender at Kut-al-Amara. Since you want others to be moved by your opinion, do your research and carefully craft your letter.

You are an ace reporter for the highly controversial magazine *The Military Exposé*. The use of the newly invented airplane has everyone in suspense—is it strictly for observation, or might it be used as an aggressive military weapon? Uncover the facts and tell the story!

Poetry

Write a ballad to tell the tale of the events leading up to the Balfour Declaration of 1917.

Prose

Write a short, action-packed account of Serbia's part in WWI. Illustrations and maps would be a great accompaniment to this.

You belong to an Arab tribe that has actively recently joined the revolt against the Turks. Consequently, you are now fighting the Germans. Write a letter home to your family, who are concerned for your safety. Cheer them up with an anecdote about your exploits, being sure to include something about T. E. Lawrence, the very unusual British soldier who is working with you.

◉ Choose an area of expression

Students may work either individually or in teams.

Linguistics:

Journalism

Students crafting this opinion piece would do well to learn more about the differences between the British government in India and the British government in London concerning policies in Mesopotamia. One key to unlocking this incident is to examine the British capture of Basra at the beginning of the war. You can find a link to an article at the online resource page.

The development in WWI of the airplane as a strategic military tool is a fascinating story. An excellent, 48-page resource (Chapter 1: The Early Years of Military Flight) can be freely downloaded as a PDF from the Royal Air Force website. A link is that the online resource page.

Here's a sample of what you will find: "It was said that in 1913 an instruction to the infantry went something like: 'If you cannot find a hedge, hide yourself under your blanket and make a noise like a mushroom.'"

Poetry

Students who are interested in this project would find it helpful to learn more about the anti-Zionism of some of the wealthier and more prominent Jews in England and France. Help students answer the question, "Why did some Jews want the British government to help them gain a homeland in Palestine, while others firmly opposed this move?"

Prose

Serbia's part in the war is controversial: the western view of this Balkan nation at the beginning of the war was that they were a nation of Slav revolutionaries, assisting in the assassination of Austria-Hungary's heir to the throne. The Serbian view was quite different, as they sought to keep from being swallowed up by Austria-Hungary—who had the well-earned reputation of gobbling up small nations and people groups.

PBS.org has some interesting background information on T. E. Lawrence, Prince Feisal, and the Arab Revolt. The link is at the online resource page.

ART

Painting/Drawing

Create a painting or drawing that will illustrate life on the Western Front during the war.

Graphic Design

The German government has hired your marketing firm to create an ad campaign to attract its citizens to become sailors in the new submarines. Since the idea of staying underwater for long periods of time—while dodging surface ships who will be trying to destroy you— is not the most attractive idea to sane people, you are going to have to really use some creative, persuasive techniques. Go for it!

Cartooning

Draw a political cartoon of how necessity was the mother of invention when it came to the tank in WWI.

Mixed Media Art

Using mixed media, create a work of art that conveys your thoughts on WWI in such a way that it tells the truth, but also brings hope and beauty. This may reflect either a general or specific aspect of the war.

MUSIC

Compose

As an ANZAC solider (or, conversely, as a Turkish soldier), compose a rousing camp song about Gallipoli, including the sense of monotony in doing the same thing over and over again. You might include a soldier's view of how to end this stalemate.

Performance Practice

With your teacher's help, select an appropriate piece of music expressing some particular aspect studied in this Unit that you found interesting.

Art:

Painting/Drawing

Encourage students interested in choosing this artistic piece to do an online image search for "Western Front trenches." There are some excellent photos, though some will undoubtedly be from the movie *All Quiet on the Western Front*.

Graphic Design

The German term for this underwater boat is "Unterseeboot." Students who do an online image search for this term will find some fascinating book covers and photos to aid them in their marketing quest.

Cartooning

The British were not the only ones working on a tank design during WWI. You can find a link to images of a Russian model, which proved to be unworkable, at the online resource page.

Mixed Media Art

Students might find it helpful to visit an Australian website to learn more about the possibilities of creating art with mixed media. A link can be found at the online resource page.

Music:

Compose

To give students an idea of what a camp song might include, have them check out the Scout Songs link at the online resource page.

Performance Practice

For musical students, this selection may be a wonderful opportunity to express what they have learned. Make sure they select a piece that they have adequate time to prepare.

DRAMA

Drama

Dramatize the story of how Lenin gained power during the Bolshevik Revolution. Remember, from his exile in Switzerland he was returned home on a train through the "good graces" of the Germans—the warring enemies of his country.

Comedy

Create a comedic skit showing two French soldiers in Paris hurrying to catch a taxi to take them to the Battle of the Marne. Though the soldiers know that time is of the essence, they are faced with a problem: the savvy taxi driver's handbook does not explain how to figure the extra fare for driving in hazardous conditions to a battle zone—which would be a necessary consideration in this particular situation.

Puppetry

Use puppets to tell a slapstick version of the back-and-forth flow of this war—moments of hope for one side soon crushed by the other and then reversed. Your goal is to depict through puppetry a very brief overview of the war, so that children and adults alike will understand it.

Prop Needs

_____

_____

Costume Ideas

_____

_____

Role/Player

_____

_____

Set Suggestions

_____

_____

Drama:

Drama

The students need to decide whose point of view to tell the story from. Whose story is it? Do they want to tell the Germans' story? The Bolsheviks' story? The Russian soldiers' story? A personal story will emerge dependent upon who is telling the story, the person through whose eyes you are seeing the facts. Every story is told through a point of view, sometimes several points of view; but for this project it would be easiest to just pick one. Or, take two opposing points of view and use them in conflict, so that the audience understands there is more than one point of view on this. Is it a German politician and a Russian politician? It will change the dramatic narrative, even if it doesn't change the facts of the story.

Comedy

What's at stake here? When you're dealing with conflict and characters getting what they want or need, you talk in terms of "high stakes." In comedy, the stakes are as high as or higher than in tragedy, and that's what makes it funny. What are the circumstances for these soldiers? How badly do they need to get to the front, and how fast? Contrast it with the taxi driver: how much does he want to live versus how much money is it worth to risk driving to a battle? Explore how to increase the stakes for all characters to increase the conflict, as this will make it increasingly funny.

Puppetry

One tool in comedic theater is breaking expectations. In this instance, using the puppets to create a slapstick means that when you do something (for instance, crush a puppet), they don't do what you expect (remain crushed)—they bounce back, breaking your expectations. You expect a certain action to cause a certain effect, but it doesn't happen. Experimenting with breaking expectations and cause and effect can help to enhance the comedy.

MOVEMENT

Pantomime

You are America. Pantomime your approach to this European conflict, and how this approach gets revised and developed over the course of four years. Remember to show your participation on the battlefield during the last few months of the war.

Dance

Choreograph a dance that shows the changing attitudes of everyday people on both sides of the conflict, from their first excitement and anticipation of a short, victorious war to their stunned amazement at the carnage of the stalemates and the seemingly endless nature of it, and finally the breathtaking high drama and unexpected end of it.

Action

Through stylized action with at least two students, show eight of the most important events from June through November of 1914.

CONCEPTUAL DESIGN

The Mess: Lovingly Prepared, Beautifully Served

We all know that war is ugly. The ugliness of death and destruction was magnified in the trenches of WWI through the unrelieved mud, bugs, rats, stench, and bombed-out landscape. Since frontline soldiers live there for long stretches of time, someone at HQ came up with the bright idea of relieving some of the drab and boring environment. They want *you* to design a mess kit and MREs (Meals Ready to Eat) that will bring a touch of home—a bit of beauty—to the trenches. You have been hired to put together a sample kit and MRE for the soldiers of your nation. Remember, the food must be dried, canned, or packaged. For the beautifying mess kit: eating utensils, table linens, and decorations—anything you can think of that is mass-producible, colorful, beautiful, and inexpensive could be included. Your insight just might inspire these folks to finish up and come home!

CREATE YOUR OWN EXPRESSION

_____

_____

_____

_____

Movement:

Pantomime

Because there is a changing, developing progression in America's approach to the war, express the American standpoint using some sort of time line. It would be helpful to bring in other media to help show the sequence. Use written words to indicate America's involvement through the different phases of the war. Find music that metaphorically expresses it. Find or create art that does as well. Then put them all together, so you have a rich environment in which to work. Now, with this richness to help, express America's view through movement.

Dance

It might be really interesting to experiment with different genres of movement to express these various attitudes. A student might show the initial excitement as hip-hop, the drawn-out stalemates as ballet, and then the unexpected resolution as a modern dance. Using different forms of dance may provide the contrast; then find ways to blend them. Music might assist this—develop a musical collage of different sounds for different genres of movement.

Action

Transitioning between these scenes is going to be the challenge. Encourage students to find creative ways to move from one scene to the next using repetition, contrast, stillness, overlapping, tempo (speed, rate), or sound (either sound they make themselves or external sound cues). The question to ask is, "How do I get from 1 to 2 to 3 . . . to 8 in such a way that the transitions are not interruptions but help tell the story?"

Conceptual Design:

Encourage students to work with a budget (since price *is* an object), a nutritional guide (it must promote health), and perhaps a color wheel to make it as aesthetically pleasing as possible.

◉ Share creative expressions in class

Create a safe environment for the presentations. Set ground rules prior to the presentations, so that students know how much time is available for each of them, and so that they know they will be honored and respected by all those observing.

◉ Conduct a review and evaluation

In this Phase of Unit 6, your students should have had the opportunity to express what they have learned about World War I & the Russian Revolution through one or more various creative selections of their own choosing. These include:

- Linguistics;
- Art;
- Music;
- Drama;
- Movement;
- Conceptual Design.

Record student hours: _____

Assess student effort in the creative expressions, as individuals or as teams.

Create an evaluation system of your own, or refer to the evaluation rubric in the introduction, as a tool for assessing participation. The categories you will probably find most useful for evaluating their projects are *"Task," "Process: Teamwork," "Process: Originality,"* and Grammar, Format, and Spelling.

In this Phase especially, do not critique the self-evaluation page your student completes in the Student Manual—consider how the very soul of an artist has been exposed and vulnerable, so be encouraging and not belittling. Again, consider enthusiasm, precision of approach, and efforts toward improving skills and completing the activity, rather than rating the project as compared to a masterpiece. Instead, discuss with the student the intention of the written comments and incorporate those into your evaluation.

Determine a grade for this Phase, if using grades: _____

Teacher Self-Evaluation:

Evaluate your own use of materials and teaching opportunities: what worked and what did not; how effective was your time-management; how were your responses to the needs of your student; did you make your expectations clear; in what ways would you like to improve your approach for the next Unit? Incorporate suggestions from your students in your own evaluation (*this requires humility!*).

Take a moment now to evaluate the whole Unit. What would you like to remember if you taught this subject again? What do you recognize that your students gained most—either as students of history or as creative individuals? What did you learn about World War I & the Russian Revolution or about teaching?

---

6 Phase 4

▶ Student Self-Evaluation UNIT 6, PHASE 4

Dates and hours:_____

Evaluate your projects

- What creative project did you choose?
  _____

- What did you expect from your project, and how does the final project compare to your initial expectations?
  _____
  _____

- What do you like about your project? What would you change?
  _____
  _____

In Conclusion

Revisit the three Key Concepts from the beginning of this Unit. Explain how your understanding of and appreciation for each has grown over the course of your study.

- _____
  _____
  _____

- _____
  _____

- _____
  _____

Record your concluding thoughts on World War I & the Russian Revolution.

_____
_____
_____
_____

Fascism & Fundamentals
(1915–1938)

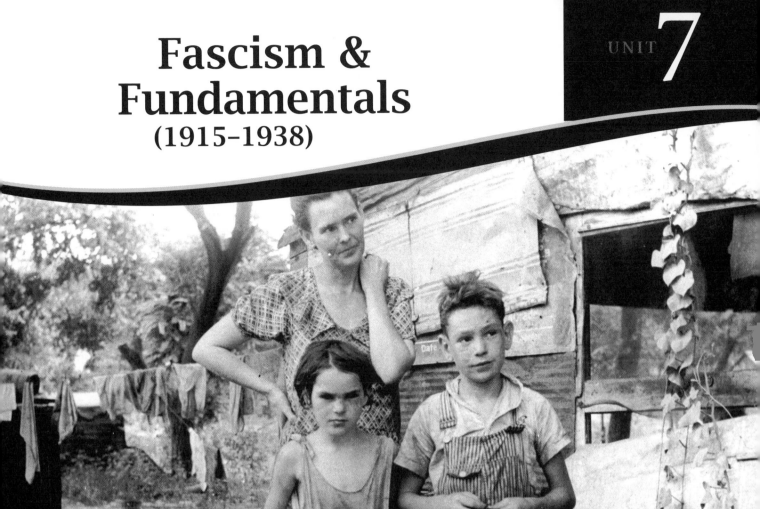

Pray with the students
at the beginning of each Unit.

Enthusiasm and delight
are the best ways to capture
a student's interest and
jump-start motivation, so:

» **For the Auditory Students:** To capture their attention at the very beginning of class, listen to a musical selection that inspired Nazi Germany—from one of the Ring operas composed by German composer Richard Wagner—such as the famous theme "Ride of the Valkyries." (A link can be found at the online resource page.)

» **For the Kinesthetic Students:** Have the students warm up as class begins by physically demonstrating the Wall Street crash and the collapse of the economy in the Great Depression.

» **For the Visual Students:** Play the trailer from the movie *Chariots of Fire*, the story of Olympic champion and devout Christian, Eric Liddell. (A link can be found at the online resource page.)

» **For the hearts of all:** Pray with them at the beginning of the Unit, that God would help them discover what He has for each one to learn in this Unit.

◉ Learning Style Emphasis

Teachers can choose to have students do one or two activities, rather than the entire week's schedule. Please use what works for you in your unique setting.

	Week 1: Feeler	Week 2: Thinker	Week 3: Sensor	Week 4: Intuitor
	During this week, students will be introduced to Fascism & Fundamentals, along with the appropriate Scriptures. You may follow this suggested schedule or adapt it to meet your students' needs:	Students will explore topics of interest through research and reporting, learn new vocabulary, and construct a time line relating to Fascism & Fundamentals.	Students will gain cultural understanding through sensory activities as they explore interrelated subject areas through sensory activities pertaining to Fascism & Fundamentals.	Through creative self-expression, using one or more creative activities, students will present some aspect of what they have learned in the past three weeks relating to Fascism & Fundamentals. Areas of expression include linguistics, art, music, drama, movement, and conceptual design.
Monday	Informally discuss the Key Concepts Listen to the *What in the World?* audio recording(s)	Choose topic and begin research	Create a map and discuss the issues in teams	Choose an area of expression and begin work either individually or in teams
Tuesday	Read the article Listen to the other audio recording(s) Read the Scriptures		Examine and discuss art masterpieces & architectural structures	
Wednesday	Recap the material using activities Talk together	Practice vocabulary	Do an art project*	
Thursday	Conduct class discussion	Construct the time line	Do a science experiment or field trip**	
Friday	Choose books of interest/Internet search Conduct a review and evaluation	Complete research projects and share in class or hand in Conduct a review and evaluation	Listen to and discuss the music Cook the food listed in the recipe Conduct a review and evaluation	Share creative expressions in class Conduct a review and evaluation

*Art project will need to be planned ahead of time to acquire materials.

** Field trip will require extra planning time.

Fascism & Fundamentals (1915–1938)

UNIT 7

Key Concepts

- Reshaping the Political Map
- Totalitarian Regimes
- Christianity Between the Wars

Family during the Great Depression. Credit: Dorothea Lange.

The Approaching Storm Clouds of War

In order to understand the time between WWI and WWII—with the emergence of powerful, hate-filled, racist rulers bent on wars of conquest— we must discover what life was like in the days, months, and years following the last battle. More so than in any war that had come before, the nations who fought in WWI, both victors and defeated foes, were in precarious positions—economically and governmentally, through depopulation and insecurity. Here is but a glimpse of the unsettled and hazardous conditions they faced:

- Germany, defeated on paper but not in mind, was faltering under a political tsunami of communists, socialists, monarchists, and liberal democrats all vying for control as a result of the kaiser's abdication.

Fascism & Fundamentals (1915–1938) **275**

◉ Informally discuss the Key Concepts with your students

KEY CONCEPTS Background Information

These are the main objectives of the Unit. As you proceed through the four weeks, your students will be given various ways of understanding each of these objectives. Explanations of these Key Concepts follow.

7

- France was devastated and depopulated, burning with fear and anger against Germany, who had destroyed so many of its citizens and soldiers, as well as its industries and agricultural land.

- Great Britain was suffering economic distress and colonial agitation due to many diverse aspects of the war—not least of these being that Indian soldiers, who had fought valiantly as equals in the war, now sought equality at home.

- Russia was convulsing under a civil war between the "Red" Bolshevik army and the "White" monarchist/Allied/non-communist army, while continuing to face starvation-level famine.

- The Ottoman Empire, dismantled by the Allies, found itself invaded by Greeks bent on capturing as much territory as possible. They were countered by Turkish revolutionaries who eventually won not only this small war but their own republic.

- Austria-Hungary was being divided into smaller and smaller portions, reducing mighty Austria to only six and a half million people. The breakup had begun even before the armistice—Czechoslovakia having been recognized by the Allies as an "Allied Nation," Poland having been promised independence, and the Southern Slavs banding together in hopes of a peace treaty to grant them statehood.

- Even the United States—the least affected Ally—was facing a staggering load of debt at war's end after providing huge loans and vast quantities of supplies during the war. The US was also facing increasing racial tensions and unrest for much the same reasons as Britain: Native Americans and African-Americans, who had fought during the war in Europe as equals with white Americans, experienced rising levels of discrimination and racism at home.

Two months after fighting ended on the Western Front, diplomats and leaders gathered in Paris to create the treaty that would govern a vastly changed world.

Two months after fighting ended on the Western Front, diplomats and leaders gathered in Paris to create the treaty that would govern a vastly changed world. The problem was that those around the diplomatic table had come with different agendas, different requirements, and different attitudes: everything from France's belligerent "Make them pay!" to Wilson's "Let's all get along," to Japan's "It's time for racial equality." The blueprint many had counted upon, believing it would be the foundation of the peace treaty, was President Wilson's Fourteen Points. This included, of course, the plan to form the League of Nations, which would become the new place and structure for international disputes to be peacefully resolved.

? To get an informal discussion started on this Key Concept, ask a simple, leading question, such as, "In what ways do you think WWI reshaped Europe and the Middle East?"

Reshaping the Political Map—EXPLANATION

At the end of the war, many areas of Europe and the Middle East were in shambles—some specifically due to the devastation of battles fought in their territory, and others due to the breakup of the centuries-old Ottoman, Austro-Hungarian, and Russian empires. In Asia, the difficulties were increasing. China, superficially ruled as a Republic yet actually divided among various warlords, was seeing a rise of communism similar to Russia's. Japan, one of the victorious allies, seeing China as within its own sphere of influence (much as the European empires had been modeling) continued an unrelenting pressure on the crumbling nation.

As the empires collapsed, many competing political philosophies rushed in to fill the void—including democracy, communism, anarchy, and, eventually, fascism. It was a troubled, sometimes terrifying, time for those living in these lands, as violence and revolution proliferated.

It was under these conditions that diplomats from around the world gathered in Paris to hammer out the Treaty of Versailles. It was increasingly obvious to the diplomats who were sanctioned to "resolve" the problems, particularly international boundaries and economics, that they faced significant limitations in what they could actually accomplish. In addition to the chaos and disintegration of the former empires, the victors no longer had massive armies with which to force their terms, nor did their nations have any remaining desire for war. And, unlike treaties of the past, where an absolute monarch could make unilateral decisions regardless of the views of the nation, now the democratically elected leaders of Great Britain, France, and the United States knew that they would have to answer to the voters of their

One of the items not specifically addressed in the Fourteen Points concerned who was going to pay for the war. Every European nation involved had spent much more than it had on hand (remember, no one had envisioned a long, drawn-out war), and had to go into debt in order to finance the four ruinous years of destruction. (Germany finally finished paying nearly $36 billion, the WWI debt assigned by the Allies, on October 3, 2010!) Debt causes troubles, and massive debt eventually caused massive economic troubles, as we shall see worldwide in the Great Depression. Thinking of their incredible debt, the massive destruction in their nation, and the deeply disturbing potential of future conflict because of a still proud and powerful Germany next door, France went into the peace conference with an agenda to cripple their enemy economically and militarily. Britain's concerns were a bit broader—the danger of a communist revolution moving beyond the borders of Russia and into Europe. They maintained that if Germany was not completely crippled by the forthcoming peace treaty, perhaps its government could become a buffer for the Western European countries against the communists. Woodrow Wilson took the opposite approach from France, more of a "parenting approach": first, discipline Germany, and then let it be reconciled to its neighbors. His greatest hopes for the future and for international peace were in the yet-untried League of Nations.

Debt causes troubles, and massive debt eventually caused massive economic troubles, as we shall see worldwide in the Great Depression.

In addition to the plans and goals of the "big three"—France, Britain, and the United States—many other people and nations, including representatives from the Balkans, the Middle East, and Asia, came with high hopes to Paris, believing that they would find new solutions to old problems and justice for all concerned. There were hopes and expectations beyond merely drawing boundary lines in Europe and the Middle East. But, on many issues, the desires of one group conflicted with the expectations of another, as seen, for example, in Britain's contradictory promises to both Arabs and Jews. Among the competing concerns of the great powers, these other difficulties were frequently not resolved at the peace table, but were actually intensified.

For instance, the highly distinguished representatives of Japan came with one overriding objective, expressed by the leading Tokyo newspaper in this way: "Above all our Peace Envoy must not forget to persuade the Conference to agree to the relinquishment of the principle of **racial discrimination**, which if allowed to exist would continue to be a menace to the future peace of the world." (emphasis added) As one of the acknowledged industrial and military powers, and as one of the victorious allies of WWI, Japan believed it had a voice that would be heard and respected as the world came together to form the League of Nations. And, though the European and American powers did not realize it at the time, the Japanese

respective nations for the decisions made at this peace conference.

Beyond the obvious issues regarding the future of Germany, the diplomats wrangled over redrawing the map of Europe and the Middle East. To be decided at the bargaining table were the fates of the nations which would become Poland, Czechoslovakia, Yugoslavia, Saudi Arabia, Palestine, Syria, Iraq, and Lebanon.

Here are some of the issues facing them.

Poland, which had been divided between Russia, Prussia, and Austria in the late 1700s, was now reunited into one independent nation—but this was not tidily done. In order to give Poland direct access to the sea, the Treaty of Versailles split East Prussia from the rest of Germany, creating a "Polish corridor." The awkwardness of this arrangement is obvious—several million Germans living in a "foreign" country. This would be one of the trouble spots Adolf Hitler would inflame when he came to power.

In Central Europe, the Czechs and Slovaks, who had lived formerly under the Austro-Hungarian flag, wanted to unite as an independent nation. At the treaty table, they were granted their "historic frontiers," including Bohemia. Unfortunately, the drawing of what turned out to be artificial boundaries did not take into account the three and a half million German-speaking Austrians who were now enfolded into a Slavic nation, nor did it recognize that many Ukrainians (Ruthenes) would now be separated from their own homeland. Again, this would be an area of trouble upon which Hitler would seize—when the opportune moment arrived.

On the western side of the Balkan peninsula, a new nation was proclaimed on December 1, 1918— before the diplomats even gathered for the peace conference. The Kingdom of the Serbs, Croats, and Slovenes included also Bosnia and Herzegovina, Montenegro, and Dalmatia.

7

diplomats were the spokesmen for other non-white people in the world—Africans, East Indians, and Asians.

It seemed that the time had finally arrived for racial equality to become the way nation dealt with nation and people with people. The League of Nations, which would set its rules during the peace conference, appeared to be the perfect vehicle for accomplishing this mission, especially since President Wilson had publicly expressed interest in the rights of religious, national, and racial minorities. Tragically, the Japanese request for racial equality—even after it had been reduced to the simplest language possible, an amendment guaranteeing "the principle of equality of nations and just treatment of their nationals"—was refused by Wilson. President Wilson, Chairman of the International Commission, negotiating the amendments to the League, refused to include the equality amendment, despite its passing by a majority of votes! What many European, British, and American leaders did not realize at the time was that this dismissal of racial equality would come back to haunt them, not only in their far-flung colonies but also in the rising tide of racial unrest in their own backyards.

> *It seemed that the time had finally arrived for racial equality to become the way nation dealt with nation and people with people.*

In Acts 17:26, the Bible states something that has profound implications for this issue of racial equality: "And He has made from one blood every nation of men to dwell on all the face of the earth." Though there are certainly different people groups—with different languages, cultures, characteristics, religions, and geographic locations—the only "race" is the human race. Applying that truth to the way we think about others, Ken Ham and A. Charles Ware in the book *One Blood, One Race* state, "We all need to treat every human being as our relative. We are of one blood. All of us are equal in value before our Creator God."

Though the commission delegates in their halls of power did not hold to that high biblical view of equality, far away in the Central American nation of Guatemala, a missionary working with his wife among the Cakchiquel Indians did. Cameron Townsend, a young American sent in 1917 to sell Spanish Bibles in the Guatemalan countryside, had discovered that the people he was seeking to serve did not speak—or read—Spanish. These non-Spanish-speaking native people were considered inferior and less intelligent, and they were treated accordingly. Townsend, however, after spending time with one of the Cakchiquel Christians, recognized that the real issue was simply that the Cakchiquel language was unwritten. As a result, there were no books available in their native language, and no schools where reading and writing could be taught. This had kept the Cakchiquel from reading not only the Bible, but also a variety of books on medicine, farming, and education—whatever might have benefited them in the twentieth century.

278 Fascism & Fundamentals (1915–1938)

The diplomats did not create this new nation—and, in fact, kept addressing them throughout the conference as "Serbia"—yet, when the Treaty of Versailles was presented, representatives of this new nation were among the signers. A decade later, the name would be changed to Yugoslavia.

Perhaps the most challenging diplomacy of all was the question of who would rule in the Middle East. The Arabs, who had been promised some form of independence in trade for joining the Allied war effort, came to the peace conference with high anticipation. The Zionists, who had been promised a Jewish homeland in Palestine, greatly desired to see the promise fulfilled. The third group seeking land in the Middle East, the British and French, had secretly agreed to a division of the former Ottoman Empire at war's end. There was no way for each to have the fullness of what had been hoped. The diplomats at the peace conference tried to provide a solution that would work, but in fact, it only inflamed the problems. The Arabs, hoping for true independence, ended with only Saudi Arabia as an independent state. The other Arab lands would go under British and French control: Palestine and Mesopotamia became virtual colonies—known as mandates—of

7

Without any background in the science of linguistics (which was a new and developing study of human language), Cameron Townsend took on the monumental task of learning the nuances of the Cakchiquel language, creating an alphabet for them, translating the Bible into the heart-language of this people group, and developing a primer in order to teach the people to read their own language. From the richness of his experience came the formation of the Summer Institute of Linguistics (SIL) and Wycliffe Bible Translators, which continue to send workers to translate languages and serve ethnic minorities on six continents. Cameron Townsend is remembered as a "stimulator of linguistic research among ethnic minorities and champion of their cultural dignity."

What a contrast to the attitudes found among the most powerful delegates at the Treaty of Versailles and the League of Nations! Even the British Foreign Secretary, Lord Balfour, whose declaration had promised a Jewish homeland in Palestine, had particular prejudices that jaundiced his point of view. During the deliberations for the League of Nations, he was quoted as saying that the "all men are created equal" proposition of the US Declaration of Independence "was an eighteenth century proposition which he did not believe was true. He believed it was true in a certain sense that all men of a particular nation were created equal, but not that a man in Central Africa was created equal to a European."

Consider the vast change of attitude in Great Britain from the spiritual and political climate one hundred years prior. In the early 1800s, William Wilberforce and the evangelicals known as "The Clapham Sect" had worked tirelessly to persuade the British Parliament to outlaw the African slave trade—despite its massive revenue gain for the nation. They succeeded against all odds in 1807. By 1919, however, the attitudes of Britain's political leaders had reverted. A significant reason for this was the far-reaching influence of Social Darwinism.

According to Paul Gordon Lauren in his book *Power and Prejudice*,

> Through the efforts of such Social Darwinists as the English publicist Herbert Spencer in *The Principles of Sociology* and his compatriot Thomas Huxley . . . the biological theories of Darwin were applied to the human social and political realm and then popularized through most of the Western

Cameron Townsend (Uncle Cam)—Reprinted with permission from JAARS.org

Cameron Townsend is remembered as a "stimulator of linguistic research among ethnic minorities and champion of their cultural dignity."

the British, while Syria and Lebanon became French mandates.

As for the question of how the conflict between Jews and Arabs concerning Palestine would be handled, the preamble of the British Mandate included these words: "in favour of the establishment in Palestine of a national home for the Jewish people, it being clearly understood that nothing should be done which might prejudice the civil and religious rights of existing non-Jewish communities in Palestine." How to allow one without prejudicing the rights of the other would become a diplomatic nightmare, as it remains to this day. And, as with so many other areas of unrest, Hitler would manage to exacerbate anti-Semitic animosities with an infusion of his own virulent and potent hatred of the Jews.

7

world. By the last decade of the nineteenth century these ideas had created a powerful intellectual atmosphere and acquired enough prestige to command widespread attention and thus influence many others to come. . . . The stature of such a viewpoint could buttress all kinds of opinions with the dignity of scientific truth. It offered a scientific explanation for those who wanted to understand nature, a rationalization for rugged individualism and competition, an excuse for immigration quotas and imperialism, and a justification for viewing racial struggles as a fundamental part of "immutable" natural law and the "inevitable" unfolding of biological destiny.

The pseudo-scientific concept of "survival of the fittest" among nations and people groups not only justified racism toward those considered to be inferior, but, as we shall see in the next Unit, it unleashed a horrific destruction on those who were considered to be a threat to the "pure" bloodline. Those deemed inferior were said to be lower on the Darwinian "ladder of race," which had light-skinned people at the top and dark-skinned people at the bottom, with other skin colors in between. Those who deemed themselves at the very top were German leaders, who saw pure Germans as the master or *Aryan* race.

Those who deemed themselves at the very top were German leaders, who saw pure Germans as the master or Aryan race.

Noticeably absent from the peace talks in Paris were representatives of Russia, the Allied member who only a few years earlier had undergone political upheaval. As J. A. S. Grenville states in *A History of the World in the Twentieth Century*, "Lenin's Russia was openly hostile both to the victors and the vanquished of 1918. They were all, in Lenin's eyes, imperialist bourgeois powers ripe for revolution." Lenin, who had successfully taken power in the 1917 October Revolution, combined the political theories of Karl Marx with his own political philosophy into Marxist-Leninist communism. Stated simply, communism viewed "workers" as good (as opposed to "employers," who were bad), so the ultimate vision was that of a workers' paradise where there would be no owners—everything would be held in common. Note that this was different from the biblical description in Acts 2:44–45, where believers sold what they owned and divided it among those who had need out of a heart of love and compassion. The biblical account was of a people who freely and willingly gave at a specific moment in time to share with other believers. In communism, the idea was that everyone would share, whether they wanted to or not, and no one would be allowed to own anything.

As you might imagine, this idea was popular with those who had been laboring under awful conditions in factories (though extremely unpopular with those who owned businesses!). However, as Russian author Alexandr

? To get an informal discussion started on this Key Concept, ask a simple, leading question, such as, "What similarities do you think there are between communism and fascism?"

Totalitarian Regimes— EXPLANATION

It is fascinating to discover the many similarities there are in two forms of government—one on the far left, the other on the far right—that view themselves as extremely different from one another and are quite hostile to each other. We can better understand this puzzle as we consider the word *totalitarian*. This descriptive political term means a form of government that does not allow people to have individual freedoms (no freedom of religion, freedom of speech, freedom of the press, etc.) and that actively enforces the submission of all aspects of an individual's life to the authority of the government through force and repression. In the early 1920s, Mussolini used the term *totalitario* to describe his vision of a new form of government in Italy: "All within the state, none outside the state, none against the state." Within two decades after WWI, two oppressive totalitarian types of government—communism and fascism—were in place to engulf the world. That was a chilling moment that would directly give rise to WWII and, after that, the Cold War.

So what did they have in common? Here is an overview.

7

Solzhenitsyn later wrote, "This was March 1918—only four months after the October Revolution—all the representatives of the Petrograd factories were cursing the Communists, who had deceived them in all their promises . . . [and] had given orders to machine gun the crowds of workers in the courtyards of the factories who were demanding the election of independent factory committees." It was not, nor would it ever become, a paradise for workers—or anyone else, for that matter. With communism's utter rejection of any form of religion, being fully and completely founded on atheism, it would not be possible. Paradise is the domain of the Creator God and is the promise of heaven. Without Him, whether on earth or in heaven, there is no paradise.

In this godless regime, the importance of each individual was denied, since they were grouped together and considered valuable as "the workers" or worthless as "the owners." In direct contrast to the view of Scripture that each person has worth, that "even the very hairs of our head are numbered," Marxist-Leninist communism devalued the individual, opening the door to extraordinary acts of violence. After an assassination attempt on his life in 1918, Lenin established the use of "Red Terror"—mass arrests and executions—to purposely search for and punish political enemies. The unbridled use of terror—against whomever was considered to be a threat, including those who simply disagreed with or criticized the leader—actually became the policy of the state. To those who would exclaim, "That is wrong!" Solzhenitsyn explains: "Communism has never concealed the fact that it rejects all absolute concepts of morality. It scoffs at good and evil as indisputable categories. Communism considers morality to be relative. Depending upon circumstances, any act, including the killing of thousands, could be good or bad. It all depends upon class ideology, defined by a handful of people." As the people of Russia began to understand that they were now in the grip of yet another tyrant, many rose up and fought unsuccessfully against communism in the Russian Civil War, which claimed millions of lives. After Lenin died in 1924, Joseph Stalin eliminated rivals one after another, until he could take undisputed control of the country. With that, Marxist-Leninist communism moved to a new level of oppression.

> *Paradise is the domain of the Creator God and is the promise of heaven. Without Him, whether on earth or in heaven, there is no paradise.*

Joseph Stalin

- Dictatorial leadership (with a charismatic leader who held complete control)
- Single, centralized, political party (no dissenting parties allowed)
- Ruthless use of terror (against any and all who were perceived as a threat)
- Use of secret police
- Propaganda and censorship (using and controlling the press to control ideas)
- Controlled economy (while communistic government owned all forms of business and industry in its nation, fascism controlled those who owned business and industry in its nation)
- Integrated all social, economic, and political structures under the state to create the "ideal community"
- Hostility to organized religion (while communism was atheistic, fascism jealously clung to a hero-worship of the leader)

How did they differ? Here is an overview.

Communism

- Left-wing ideology (a radical, worldwide program to dismantle democratic and monarchist

7

Mussolini implemented many of the same strategies Lenin and Stalin had used in controlling the population: the use of terror, censorship, propaganda, and police supervision.

With the worldwide scope of communist philosophy—believing that soon the entire world would experience its own overthrow of capitalism and embrace the final "stage" of humanity, that is, communism—the Russians were quite eager, as had been the French armies of the late 1700s, to export their revolution far beyond their own borders. The organization dedicated to this was known as the "Third International," the "Communist International," or simply "Comintern." Spreading propaganda, stimulating revolution, and supplying eager workers to the cause, Russian communists were seen by most other nations in the world as a loathsome menace to be stamped out, though many downtrodden and dissatisfied workers heard the message with joy.

It was the fear of this spread of communism in Europe that opened the door to fascism. The term *fascism* (referring to an ancient Roman symbol of authority) was used by the Italian journalist-politician Mussolini when he founded his fascist movement in 1919. Though the fascists were extremely radical in their views (including a devotion to war and violence), yet with their expressed hatred of Marxism and their protection of farms and factories from communist instigators, they suddenly became very popular across a wide sweep of Italians, including the Catholic Church. They

Benito Mussolini

were perceived as protecting Italy not only from the communists, but also from the atheism of the communists—which would have been very important to many, even if they were not quite comfortable with some of the violent actions, revolutionary attitudes, and anti-religious beliefs of the fascists. However, when Mussolini made a pretense of dropping some of these troubling ideas, he was able to gain ever more support from the Italian people—resulting in the king appointing him prime minister in 1922. Then, as the strongest man in Italy, Mussolini was able to gather to himself the reins of power. In doing so, he implemented many of the same strategies Lenin and Stalin had used in controlling the population: the use of terror, censorship, propaganda, and police supervision.

Perhaps the most telling aspect of fascism (and certainly, to a Christian, the most troubling) was how it functioned as a secular religion, elevating Mussolini—as it would also

282 Fascism & Fundamentals (1915–1938)

governments in favor of the working class)

- Emphasized the working class
- Held the utopian goal of a classless society
- Saw revolution as the required means of change (sought to export revolution for this purpose)
- Worked to overthrow traditional values and institutions
- Based on an atheistic worldview

Fascism (including Italian Fascism and German Nazism)

- Right-wing ideology (a radical, nationalist program to gather all power into the hands of the central government)
- Emphasized the unity of the nation (such as doing everything to benefit the "German master race")
- Viewed foreign ideas and people as corrupting influences
- Held the utopian goal of the fascist society (as example, the "thousand-year rule of the Third Reich")

7

elevate Hitler—to a godlike position. People began, in effect, to worship him. In 1925, one fascist author wrote of Mussolini, "A century from now, history may tell us that after the war a **Messiah** arose in Italy who began speaking to fifty people and ended up evangelizing a million; that these first disciples then spread through Italy and with their faith, devotion and sacrifice conquered the hearts of the masses." The noted scholar Peter Godman described Mussolini as wishing "to be regarded as a new Augustus, a second Caesar. . . . The task demanded a superman. Against the paradise that Mussolini aimed to establish on earth were pitted the demonic forces of liberals, democrats, socialists, communists, and (later) Jews. Yet he would triumph against these foes of mankind, for he was not only Caesar Augustus, but also the **Savior**." Lest there be any doubt in our minds regarding Mussolini's own perspective, consider his quote, "Fascism is a **religion**. The twentieth century will be known in history as the century of Fascism." (emphasis added in each)

Isn't it fascinating to consider that paradise was the goal for both communism, which believed in a godless atheism, and fascism, which worshipped a false savior? Each of these systems—maintaining power through terror, violence, propaganda, and the loss of freedoms—claimed to be *the* solution to the woes of humanity, promising a utopia on earth. How could this be? Why did people fall for this kind of thinking? Just as it was in Bible times, so it was in the 1920s and '30s, and so it is today. If we don't seek the truth, we will be deceived by a lie. Jesus described for His disciples what this would look like: "For many will come in My name, saying, 'I am the Christ,' and will deceive many. . . . Then many false prophets will rise up and deceive many. And because lawlessness will abound, the love of many will grow cold" (Matthew 24:5, 24:11–12). It would grow colder than ice in the hearts of many during these years leading up to WWII, especially in the nations where fascism or communism flourished.

Even in the church, false ideas began to arise and take root. From the time of the Reformation, *Sola Scriptura* had been the foundation of Protestant theology. Until this point, when the divine revelation of the Scriptures was attacked, the threats had come from beyond the church, from non-Christian thinkers such as Enlightenment philosophers. But now a new type of threat to Christianity was being advanced—attacks against Scripture were coming from inside its own sanctuaries. Prior to WWI, Protestants had generally held to the authority of Scripture and the unity of the body of Christ. Indeed, there were numerous examples of cooperation across interdenominational boundaries in missions and evangelism, and Bible societies were prevalent for the translation and distribution of Scripture throughout the

Each of these systems—maintaining power through terror, violence, propaganda, and the loss of freedoms—claimed to be the solution to the woes of humanity, promising a utopia on earth.

- Had a romanticized view of their ancient past (in the case of Italy—ancient Rome; in the case of Germany—ancient German sagas, exemplified by Wagnerian operas)

- Allowed private property and capitalist enterprise, but with extremely tight controls

- Superficially reaffirmed traditional values (but at its core it usurped "family values" and replaced them with "state values")

- Superficially unopposed to Catholicism/Christianity, though in practice, any who would not bow to fascism—especially priests and pastors—were threatened or eliminated.

Christianity Between the Wars—EXPLANATION

From the time of the early church, there were those who challenged the good news: God became flesh and dwelt among us, took our sin upon Himself as He died on the cross, and was raised from the dead to eternal life. Historically, the challenges have risen inside as well as outside the church, from the obvious persecutions of Roman emperors to the subtle enticements of Gnostic heresies, and on and on to the present. Though the specific issues changed from era to era, the battle for a true

? To get an informal discussion started on this Key Concept, ask a simple, leading question, such as, "In what ways was Christianity challenged in the years between the wars, and in what areas was the vibrant truth of Christianity clearly seen?"

7

world. However, after the war, the new wave of thinking among European Protestant theologians—a questioning of whether the source of the Scriptures was divine revelation—hit the church in full force. In *The Two Kingdoms*, this conflict is described:

> If God revealed Himself in Christ and redeemed humanity from sin, there must be submission to this authoritative revelation. But now to what must one submit and how much must one believe? . . . The liberal response was to affirm the new situation, whereas the conservatives rejected it. On the American scene this set the stage for a bruising culture war in the 1920s known as the fundamentalist-modernist contro-versy. The conservatives challenged the tenets of modern-ism with prophetic courage and showed that such things as the theory of evolution and the documentary hypothesis of Scripture were incompatible with biblical Christianity.

This division between modernism and fundamental-ism split many Protestant denominations in the United States. As modernists gained control of church leader-ship, those holding to biblical inerrancy often broke away and began new denominations, such as the Orthodox Presbyterian Church, the General Association of Regular Baptists, and the Southern Methodist Church. Highly respected seminary professor J. Gresham Machen, author of *Christianity and Liberalism*, left his teaching position at Princeton seminary, which had fallen to modernist theology, to start the conservatively-based Westminster Theological Seminary. Beyond denominational boundaries, many interdenominational organizations working on the mission field and university campuses were also splin-tered down the modernist-fundamentalist line.

A belief in biblical inerrancy involved more than internal church disputes. Many Christians in America were deeply concerned at the perceived impact Darwinism and the teaching of evolution—which was contrary to a plain reading of Scripture—was having on democracy and moral-ity. Though many today scoff at this, considered in the historic setting of the 1920s and 30s, Darwinism actually was having a powerful effect on the thinking of commu-nist and fascist governments of the era, as they justified their use of terror, violence, and racism based on the concept of "survival of the fittest." Since these totalitarian governments, with their Social Darwinism theories firmly in place, despised democracy, it is not surprising that some in democratic countries might have suggested that Darwinism was a threat to their own form of government. With this in mind, American fundamentalists were able

Many Christians in America were deeply concerned at the perceived impact Darwinism and the teaching of evolution— which was contrary to a plain reading of Scripture—was having on democracy and morality.

and vibrant biblical Christianity has been constant.

During the era between WWI and WWII, the battle continued as new and forceful ideas arose in the church within the ranks of Christian philoso-phers and theologians.

To lay a foundation for understand-ing why these new ideas had such power, consider two things. First, the "war to end all wars" had impacted the way people viewed the world, bringing to many a cynical, disillu-sioned, and pessimistic attitude. For them, the ideas of a loving God and a moral universe had become utterly meaningless. Secondly, beyond the

emotional and philosophical angst of war, an attitude of intellectual arro-gance, based on a new age of science and technology, gained ground—any concept that could not be verified mathematically or scientifically was considered to be old-fashioned and childish. With these intertwined at-titudes of pessimism and arrogance, a new view of Scripture was devel-oped that diminished its authority. Theologians began to question the previously held belief that the Bible was "divine revelation," inspired by God and inerrant in its transmission to man. This, of course, had huge im-plications for the church. If the Bible does not mean what it says, then

what do we know concerning Christi-anity? What happens to the message of the gospel and the motivation to share it?

Dr. Francis Schaeffer, in *The Great Evangelical Disaster*, wrote the follow-ing:

> But what was really at stake? It was the gospel itself. We are not talking about minor variations in the interpretation of second-ary doctrines. We are not talking about denominational differ-ences. The things being denied by the liberals were at the heart of the Christian faith—the authority of the Bible, the deity

to convince several states to ban the teaching of human evolution in public schools, but this stand was challenged in the 1925 Scopes Trial in Tennessee. Though they won the battle in court, the fundamentalists lost the war in the eyes of the public—thanks largely to the media's portrayal of Bible-believing Christians as uneducated country bumpkins.

At the same time that Christians in the West were struggling over the issue of inerrancy, missionaries in the East were striving to overcome the backlash of racism in their sending nations. When the United States passed an immigration law in 1924, according to author Paul Gordon Lauren it "slammed the door to Asians and most other non-whites, reducing the number of immigrants from Japan to zero." Even Stephen Jay Gould, a noted evolutionist, was appalled by this policy, describing it as "one of the greatest victories of scientific racism in American history." The United States was not the only government to move in this direction, as European and British commonwealth countries also tightened immigration restrictions based on "racial purity" during this time period. The effect of Social Darwinism, with its pseudo-scientific approach, caused tremendous suffering for those deemed less valuable and inferior. Less obviously, it brought destruction of soul to those who prided themselves in their light skin color. And, in the case of India, it brought about a movement for independence.

The leader of this movement was Mahatma Gandhi, known as the Father of India. Recognizing the futility of violence in the quest for independence, he championed the use of non-violent civil disobedience by the masses, which proved over a few decades to be an irresistible force against which the British government had no effective power. When an American missionary/evangelist to India, E. Stanley Jones, asked Gandhi what missionaries could do to "see Christianity naturalized in India, so that it shall be no longer a foreign thing identified with a foreign people and a foreign government, but a part of the national life of India," Gandhi provided a fascinating insight. From Jones's book, *The Christ of the Indian Road*:

> He very gravely and thoughtfully replied: "*I would suggest, first, that all of you Christians, missionaries and all, must begin to live more like Jesus Christ.*" He needn't have said anything more—that was quite enough. I knew that looking through his eyes were the three hundred millions of India, and

The effect of Social Darwinism, with its pseudo-scientific approach, caused tremendous suffering for those deemed less valuable and inferior.

Mahatma Gandhi

of Christ, the meaning of salvation. Harry Emerson Fosdick, pastor of the First Presbyterian Church of New York and one of the most influential spokesmen of modernism, was a clear example. In his famous sermon, "Shall the Fundamentalists Win?" given in 1922, he explained what the liberal means by the return of Christ.

"The liberals," Fosdick preached, "say 'Christ is coming!' They say it with all their hearts; but they are not thinking of an external arrival on the clouds. They have assimilated as part of divine revelation the exhilarating insight that these recent generations have given to us, that development [i.e., modern progress] is God's way of working out His will. . . . When they say that Christ is coming, they mean that, slowly it may be, but surely, His will and principles will be worked out . . . *in human institutions.*"

Here we have what is at stake—the denial of the work of Christ and the actual return of Christ; the "new revelation" of modern thought replacing the Bible; salvation as the modern progress of human institutions. This is heretical denial of the gospel, and is directly related to the Enlightenment view of the perfectibility of Man. (emphasis added)

In response to this new way of viewing the Scriptures and Christianity, Bible-believing British and American scholars rose to defend the historic view. One of the key strategies was the publication of *The Fundamentals*, containing ninety articles by respected scholars and teachers, which affirmed and defended these "essential fundamentals of the faith":

- The inspiration and inerrancy of the Bible

- The deity of Christ and His virgin birth

7

speaking through his voice were the millions of the East saying to me, a representative of the West, and through me to the very West itself, *"If you will come to us in the spirit of your Master, we cannot resist you."* Never was there a greater challenge to the West than that, and never was it more sincerely given.

"Second," he said, *"I would suggest that you must practice your religion without adulterating or toning it down."* This is just as remarkable as the first. The greatest living non-Christian asks us not to adulterate it or tone it down, not to meet them with an emasculated gospel, but to take it in its rugged simplicity and high demand. But what are we doing? As someone has suggested, we are inoculating the world with a mild form of Christianity, so that it is now practically immune against the real thing. Vast areas of the Christian world are inoculated with a mild form of Christianity, and the real thing seems strange and impossible. As one puts it, "Our churches are made up of people who would be equally shocked to see Christianity doubted or put into practice." I am not anxious to see India take a mild form—I want her to take the real thing.

"Third, I would suggest that you must put your emphasis upon love, for love is the center and soul of Christianity." He did not mean love as a sentiment, but love as a working force, the one real power in a moral universe, and he wanted it applied between individuals and groups and races and nations, the one cement and salvation of the world. . . .

"Fourth, I would suggest that you study the non-Christian religions and culture more sympathetically in order to find the good that is in them, so that you might have a more sympathetic approach to the people." Quite right. Certainly we should be sincerely grateful for any truth found anywhere, knowing that it is a finger post that points to Jesus, who is the Truth."

The Great Depression began as the stock market collapsed in the United States.

The swirling currents of international racism, fascism, and communism, and the church controversies over inerrancy amidst the gleeful decadence of America's mid-1920s prosperity, came into sharp focus four years later, as a new headline captured the attention of Americans and Europeans alike: "Wall Street Crash!" What would become an unprecedented catapult into international financial disaster and grinding poverty for millions, the Great Depression began as the stock market collapsed in the United States. The effects rippled out across the globe, impacting nation after nation.

Though the actual causes were very complex and continue to be debated, we can look at the basic outlines of the problem in order to better

- The substitutionary atonement of Christ's death
- The literal resurrection of Christ from the dead
- The literal return of Christ

From that scholarly beginning, the Fundamentalist movement in the United States began to organize and challenge modernism in the churches and the culture. Thus the 1920s battle between modernist and fundamentalist was engaged, leading eventually to the Scopes Trial in Tennessee. As far as public opinion in America regarding the Fundamentalist view was concerned, the Scopes Trial proved to be the battle that lost the war.

Under the successful assault of modernism in the US, not only were the Scriptures viewed in a new light, but also the motivation for sharing the life-changing message of Christ's redemption began to wane. Many Christian organizations that had been focused on evangelism, such as the Young Men's Christian Association, began to shift their focus. A summary of YMCA history published in 1936 reported: "The purpose of developing a vital Christian faith had taken the place of the desire to win men to Christ. . . . Similarly, Bible study underwent not merely a transformation, but virtually disappeared. At the beginning of the decade there were

almost thirty thousand students in Bible study classes; by its end, only four thousand."

Despite this challenge to the faith, biblical Christianity continued to grow in various places of the world. Dr. J. Edwin Orr, historian of Protestant revivals in the eighteenth, nineteenth, and twentieth centuries, wrote:

In the 1920s and 1930s, when the Western world enjoyed a postwar boom and suffered an unprecedented economic depression, and evangelism therein—with rare exceptions—was cramped by a debilitating malaise of

understand the dynamics of the 1930s. One of the immense and lingering troubles after WWI was that governments continued to owe huge amounts of money, which had been borrowed in order to finance their efforts to win the war. In the case of Germany, the issue was that they were required by the Treaty of Versailles to make huge *reparations* (payments for damages caused by war). Since the Germans at the time were unable to pay their yearly reparation bill, the Allies constantly readjusted downward the amount the Germans would pay. That meant the Allies had less money to pay on their own loans to the United States. The US was, in the meantime, giving huge short-term loans to Germany. Looking back, it is obvious that this was not a sustainable plan. But with the financial boom of the Roaring Twenties in the United States, money seemed nearly limitless.

If workers can't earn an income, they won't have money for food or shelter. If a vast number of workers can't earn an income, that nation will be eager for a leader who will solve the problem.

When the United States began to experience financial difficulties with the crash of the Wall Street stock market in 1929, it called for immediate repayment of short-term loans—such as those Germany had been using to rebuild its nation. Since there was no money to pay these loans, Germany suffered a virtual collapse of its economy, resulting in thirty percent unemployment by 1932. That means one out of every three German workers could not find a job. That scenario was played out to a lesser degree in other nations of the world, including Great Britain at fifteen percent and the United States at twenty-three percent unemployment during that same year.

Adolf Hitler

If workers can't earn an income, they won't have money for food or shelter. If a vast number of workers can't earn an income, that nation will be eager for a leader who will solve the problem. In the case of the United States, the voters turned out Herbert Hoover (who had come to the presidency only months before the stock market collapse) and elected Franklin Roosevelt, who promised them a "new deal."

In the case of Germany, voters looked increasingly to the German Fascist party, which was called the National Socialist, or *Nazi*, party, with its *Führer*, the strong and confident Adolf Hitler. The Nazis' political platform was quite simple: blame the Jews, the communists, and democracy for German troubles. With mind-numbing rhetoric, Hitler promised the

---

churchly anemia, the younger churches of Asia and Africa experienced surge after surge of spiritual power, issuing in revival of true believers, restoration of backsliders and nominal church members, the awakening of the masses round about, and folk movements as well as healthy indigenous evangelism.

Of this time in China, he reported:

Among Protestants, there were two constituencies in all China—those who considered the Scriptures the revelation of God and those who appreciated them as literature; those who believed in prayer and those who taught that prayer had only a subjective value. The latter had no message.

A revival of unprecedented impact began in China in 1927 and continued for twelve years until 1939. This revival took place during the highly tumultuous years when the Nationalists were battling against the Communists in China, as well as during the initial time of the Japanese invasion of China. It was an indigenous movement, with Chinese preachers and teachers traveling throughout the vast country to witness of the saving grace of Jesus Christ. One man, known throughout the world as Andrew Gih, formed the Bethel Evangelistic Band with a group of other dedicated young men. Fearless under fire, these Chinese preachers traveled and preached in areas that were experiencing the devastation of civil war—and they certainly gained a hearing!

The Bethel Band received a pathetic call to a church in Hinghwa which had endured persistent persecution from the Communists. A great congregation had been scattered, and, when a faithful few gathered, shouting agitators would interrupt the pastor, seize the pulpit, and blaspheme the Name before an unwilling audience.

the Depression-stricken, debt-ridden, out-of-work people a re-establishment of a proud and prosperous Germany. What they did not see was what simmered just below his public image—blatant lies, venomous hatred, and an appetite for violence that within a dozen years would destroy tens of millions in the raging inferno of WWII.

Hitler did what he said he would do, however. He put the people of Germany back to work, reducing unemployment year by year until everyone had a job—but many of the jobs involved rearming the nation for war. With income, adequate food and shelter, even vacations made possible by the Third Reich, the German people swiftly became a reinvigorated nation who willingly followed their leader wherever he wanted to go.

What did the Christians think of Hitler and the Nazi program? Surprisingly, many in the beginning saw him as the defender of Germany against godless communism. Church historian J. Edwin Orr had the opportunity to preach on revival in Germany during a brief visit in 1935. This is what he recounted in his book *Prove Me Now*:

> One opinion which has remained in my mind—it was reiterated often enough—is the claim that the great majority of believers in Germany welcome the advent of Adolf Hitler and National Socialism.
>
> "You see," said one pastor, "Germany was being undermined more and more by Communists, and truly dark days lay ahead for the Fatherland. I am not a National Socialist, but I felt that, when Hitler smashed Communism, God had delivered Germany from a terrible menace."
>
> "Was the menace not exaggerated?"
>
> "No! You can have no idea how much we dreaded a Communist revolution. One of my friends has seen a 'black list' compiled by local Communists in readiness for the coming uprising. The 'black list' contained his name, and my name, and the names of many other pastors."
>
> "A roll of honor?" I queried, ironically.
>
> "Well," he gave a short laugh, "we were all to be quickly disposed of—murdered—so that terror would fall upon the whole Christian community."
>
> "So you think that Hitler's coming to power has benefited the religious life of Germany?"
>
> "In every way except one—yes! That exception exists solely because the more militant Nazis want to merge all German denominations into one great German Church. This the Evangelicals have strongly resisted. But the resistance has been a blessing in itself, for it has knitted them together in bonds hitherto unrealised."

The evangelists found a church, seated for 3000, covered with posters denouncing Christianity. The meetings began without interference on weekdays, but by the time a revival had moved two thousand people, the Communists came to break up the meeting. There was such power in the service that they hesitated, interested in spite of themselves, and one of their number went forward with others seeking peace with God. (*Evangelical Awakenings in Eastern Asia* by J. Edwin Orr)

In India, a young Sikh by the name of Sundar Singh became a Christian and chose to share the gospel with his fellow countrymen as a Christian "sadhu" (a term used for India's holy men, generally Hindu, who lived simply and traveled from place to place). As was the case in China, the impact of hearing the gospel from an indigenous preacher was powerful. Sundar Singh, who was always barefoot—even while crossing the Himalayas—took the simple message of Jesus to different areas of India and into Tibet. Eventually the doors opened for him to speak to people in Burma, Singapore, Japan, China, England, the US,

Australia, New Zealand, Switzerland, Germany, Holland, Sweden, Norway, and Denmark. His message, though not always well received, was nonetheless unforgettable.

Revival also came to Africa during the 1920s and 30s. Perhaps the most spectacular results could be seen in Rwanda beginning in 1936.

It seemed as though the Holy Spirit with His unseen hand gathered together the hospital staff, men from the nearby village, and others in a room with the hospital. They prayed and sang, and some were smitten down

7

"Over one hundred pastors were imprisoned last week," I said.

"That is so. But I know Niemöller and also many of his friends who were arrested. They will agree with what I have said about the advent of National Socialism."

Many enthusiastic Christians in Germany consider National Socialism to be pro-Christian. I do not. I cannot reconcile it with my ideas of Christianity. But I think that Germany may find that it is a blessing in disguise. Persecution or difficulties of other kinds tend to make Christians more real.

Orr's final remark would prove to be prophetic. Eventually, those who professed Christianity in Germany would split over Nazi doctrines. The pro-Nazis joined the "German Christians" movement, while others who courageously renounced the Nazis, such as Martin Niemöller and Dietrich Bonhoeffer, began the "Confessing Church."

Far more important to Hitler than enticing Christians to his side was the plan to gather German children to himself and to Nazi ideology. His desire, and soon his decree, was that all of the German youth in the Reich must belong to the Hitler Youth. This movement existed for the purposes of training all of the children of the nation to be good Nazis, teaching them to see the world through the lens of a *master race*, which was, they believed, the German (Aryan) people. The oath taken by ten year old boys in Hitler's youth program was the following:

In the presence of this blood banner, which represents our Führer, I swear to devote all my energies and my strength to the savior of our country, Adolf Hitler. I am willing and ready to give up my life for him, so help me God.

And, tragically, the God to whom these children made their appeal for help was no longer the Judeo-Christian God. Reinhold Kirsten, in his autobiography *Blood and Honor*, describes what it was like to be the son of a German pastor during the time of Nazi Germany.

When I began the third grade, our religion teacher announced that he would not tell us those stories about the cruel Jewish God or that meek and mild Jesus. Instead he would teach us about our original gods—Thor and Zeus and others, the gods of the old Germanic tribes from which our nation sprang. I was appalled. Even in my youthful understanding, this was going too far. That was, perhaps, the earliest recollection I have of direct teaching about a super race. But the Reich used every means available to promote the doctrine. At our Monday night Hitler Youth meetings, we heard dreadful stories of so-called

Far more important to Hitler than enticing Christians to his side was the plan to gather German children to himself and to Nazi ideology.

Pray with your students about what it means to believe and to live the Word—to not only talk the Talk but walk the Walk. Or, as the Apostle Paul says, "Walk worthy of the Lord." Colossians 1:10

under a tremendous conviction of sin. Revival swept into the girl's school, and similar manifestations came from five different centers across the mission. Everywhere the mysterious power of the Holy Spirit was at work.

. . . The famous East African revival, which began in Rwanda in June 1936, rapidly spread to the adjacent countries of Burundi, Uganda, and the Congo, then further around. The Holy Spirit moved upon mission schools and spread to churches and whole communities, producing deep repentance and changed lives.

Anglican Archdeacon Arthur Pitt-Pitts wrote in September 1936: "I have been to all the stations where this Revival is going on, and they all have the same story to tell. The fire was alight in all of them before the middle of June, but during the last week in June, it burst into a wild flame which, like the African grass fire before the wind, cannot be put out."

That East African revival continued for 40 to 50 years and helped to establish a new zeal for enthusiastic holiness in African Christianity. It confronted demonic strongholds and began

to prepare churches to cope with the horrors of massacres and warfare of later years. (*Flashpoints of Revival* by Geoff Waugh)

When we hear that God's Word is not to be trusted, we need to look beyond the rhetoric and examine the reality. The fact is, He continues to redeem and change lives, including yours and mine.

7

Jewish barbarities. Official speeches, magazines, news-papers, pictures, laws, acts of government—all helped to infuse in me the concept of the pure, strong, superior Aryan, in contrast to the weak, depraved, and inferior Jew.

Anti-Semitism, a racism specifically targeted against Jews, permeated every aspect of life in Germany, even making its way through the doors of many German churches. Astonishingly, the pro-Nazi German Christians would have been in agreement with the philosopher who wrote, "Whoever claimed that Jesus was a Jew was either being stupid or telling a lie. . . . Jesus was not a Jew." In these highly influential and racist writings of Houston Stewart Chamberlain, the Jesus of the Bible was replaced with a Jesus who was Aryan, a member of the Master Race.

Standing in stark relief, the Light of the World—Jesus, the Jewish Messiah—would remain the ever-present Beacon of Hope for those who would look.

Chamberlain was a man who believed Hitler was going to be the sav-ior of Germany. After a personal meeting in 1923, the elderly Englishman-turned-German—who had previously influenced Kaiser Wilhelm II—wrote to Hitler, "You have mighty things to do. . . . My faith in Germanism had not wavered an instant, though my hope—I confess—was at a low ebb. With one stroke you have transformed the state of my soul. That in the hour of her deepest need Germany gives birth to a Hitler proves her vitality." Chamberlain promptly joined the Nazi party, joining others who were mesmerized by Hitler's darkly magnetic personality.

The psalmist describes so clearly a man like Hitler, whom the world would soon fear: "He has put forth his hands against those who were at peace with him; He has broken his covenant. The words of his mouth were smoother than butter, but war was in his heart; his words were softer than oil, but they were drawn swords" *(Psalm 55:20–21).*

The darkness of the Third Reich was just beginning. The depth of suffering and horrors into which the world would be plunged was beyond human comprehension. But that is not the end of the story, nor even the full perspective of the event. Standing in stark relief, the Light of the World—Jesus, the Jewish Messiah—would remain the ever-present Beacon of Hope for those who would look. The psalmist continues, "Cast your burden on the Lord, and He shall sustain you. He shall never permit the righteous to be moved. But You, O God, shall bring them down to the pit of destruction; Bloodthirsty and deceitful men shall not live out half their days; But I will trust in You" (Psalm 55:22–23). ◀

You may choose to have your students read the article first and then listen to the audio recordings, or vice versa.

◉ Read the article

◉ Listen to the audio recordings in Listen to This

- The main concepts and chronological flow are contained in *What in the World?* Volume 3

- Learn more about the time be-tween the wars in *Digging Deeper* Volume 3.

Phase 1

▶ Listen to This

What in the World? VOL. 3

DISC THREE:

» Economic Chaos & Great Depression (track 7)

» Fascist Italy & Militant Japan (track 8)

» Hitler's Germany & Revivals (track 9)

DISC FOUR:

» Jewish Palestine & German Conquests (track 1)

Digging Deeper VOL. 3

DISC TWO:

» Dr. J. Edwin Orr (track 4)

» Between the Wars (track 5)

▶ Read For Your Life

The Holy Bible

» **Biblical Warning Against Pride** (consider, for instance, the nationalistic pride of the fascists)—Proverbs 8:13, 16:18

» **God's View of the Jews and His Response to Those Who Would Plunder Them**—Zechariah 2:8

» **The Significance of Evangelism** (consider the impact of modernism)—Romans 10:14–15

» **The New Testament Explanation and Defense for Racial Equality**—Acts 17:26–27

**Key People
(Church)**

Gresham Machen
Founder of Westminster Theological Seminary

Sundar Singh
Christian sadhu to India

E. Stanley Jones
Evangelist to India's intellectuals

Cameron Townsend
Founded Wycliffe Bible Translators

Eric Liddell
Olympic athlete & missionary to China

Isobel Kuhn
Missionary to the Lisu people of China

For fascinating background information, be sure to listen to track 3 from the Bonus CD, The History of Geology & Darwin: 1750-1925.

◉ Read the Scriptures in Read For Your Life

The Scriptures are central to our understanding, our character, and our decisions. Therefore, we must give the greatest weight possible to them.

Help your students gain this perspective as they watch you handle the Scriptures with reverence and awe.

In a time when Social Darwinism was accepted—while the biblical explanation of origins (including the Scriptural view of racial equality) was denied—many atrocities and acts of violence were committed on the basis of "race." It is vital that we know and believe the truth in God's Word, and that we daily live it out in a way that reflects the heart of God as revealed in Jesus.

KEY PEOPLE

More of the main characters in this Unit. They are listed in the Student Manual, along with a brief identifier, so that the students can familiarize themselves with these people.

◉ Recap the material with an activity

In different parts of the room, set up stations for the Eight Intelligences Recap Activities. Then allow students to work alone or together in small groups to accomplish THEIR CHOICE OF ONE of the following suggestions. At the start of the next class, ask for 3–4 groups of volunteers to share.

Homeschoolers: rather than setting up all eight stations, allow student(s) to choose which activity they would most enjoy, and do it.

Recap Suggestions:

Spatial: Make a collage of the various results of the Treaty of Versailles, using magazines, photos, drawings, maps, or whatever illustrates the new countries and new tensions arising from the end of WWI.

Bodily Kinesthetic: Have one student toss a ball to the next student while stating an interesting fact from this Unit. How fast a pace can you sustain?

Interpersonal: In groups of two or three, discuss the effects on world events of today's political/economic situation and compare them with the effects of the Great Depression. Talk together about how these current events are similar and how they are different from the events of the 1930s.

Musical: In a small group, create a rhythmic chant about the life of

---

Key People (World)

Kemal Ataturk
First president of Turkish Republic

Benito Mussolini
Fascist dictator of Italy

Chiang Kai-shek
Chairman of Nationalist Gov't of China

Adolf Hitler
Nazi leader of the Third Reich

Albert Einstein
German theoretical physicist

▶ Talk Together

Opinion Column

» Who was the most interesting person, or what was the most fascinating aspect, in this time between the wars?

» After WWI, the Treaty of Versailles left many dissatisfied. If you had been a diplomat at the proceedings, what changes to the treaty would you have suggested? What would have been the most important issues for you?

» Imagine you were visiting Cameron Townsend as he was translating the Bible into the Cakchiquel language. What questions would you have for him? Why do you think that their Spanish-speaking neighbors thought the Cakchiquel Indians were inferior? In what ways would the work of Cameron Townsend change that image? How does this reflect the heart of God?

» Imagine you were living in Germany during the early 1930s, when the worldwide Depression had eliminated nearly one-third of the jobs in your nation. Suddenly, a political leader is talking about putting everyone back to work and restoring the glory of your country. What kind of questions would you have about his plan? What concerns would you have if you heard Hitler's "platform"?

» In your opinion, do you believe it was a providential act of God that began opening a homeland for the Jews in Palestine? How were the German Jews affected by this after Hitler began his anti-Semitic campaign? How do you think the Arabs in Palestine viewed the increasing numbers of Jewish immigrants to Palestine?

Cameron Townsend or the work of Wycliffe Bible Translators.

Linguistic: In a small group, debate the Modernist-Fundamentalist controversy among Christians in the 1920s to 1930s. What reasons would churches have to split over this issue?

Math-Logical: Answer the question: Prior to WWII, what made Hitler so attractive to Germany?

Intrapersonal: Write a journal entry reflecting on the popularity of anti-Semitism in Nazi Germany. Consider the cost of living out the biblical command to love (as described in the life

of Jesus and in 1 Corinthians 13) while your culture is demanding otherwise.

Naturalist: Go outside and choose a plant that represents fascism and a separate plant that represents communism. Share in a small group the reasons that you chose these plants, and give a comparison/contrast of the characteristics that make them good representatives of these two political systems.

Or . . . Activity of Your Choice: What would you like to have your students do for a review activity concerning this week's introduction to Fascism & Fundamentals.

Critical Puzzling

» In fascist thinking, war was a good thing. Mussolini wrote, "War alone brings up to its highest tension all human energy and puts the stamp of nobility upon the peoples who have courage to meet it." In what ways do you think this vision of nobility would affect fascist leaders and their followers? In what ways is this different from the biblical view?

» Given that one of the biblical Ten Commandments requires us to worship no other gods, what results might you expect to find in a country where the ruler was essentially worshipped? Historically, what causes and effects do you see in the nations of Stalin, Hitler, and Mussolini relating to worshipping a man instead of God?

» In what ways did modernism in the church address the issues of the day? What did they have to remove from Christianity in order to be acceptable to the culture? In what ways did evangelicalism, or Fundamentalism, address those same issues?

» What was the benefit to Marxist-Leninist communism in exporting revolution? What were the potential problems with this policy?

» Why do you think Hitler blamed all of Germany's problems on the Jews and the communists? Why do you think many Germans were ready to accept this view? Do you see any similarities anywhere in the world today? What is the potential outcome of this kind of blame and hatred?

» How did Darwinian evolution fuel the idea of racism? What effect do "scientific studies"—whether legitimate or otherwise—have on the way people think? What were some of the results of this pseudo-scientific approach to people of different skin colors? Though Social Darwinism has been discredited, racism still exists. What examples of racism can you see in your nation today?

◉ Talk together

Individual Preparation

After completing their recap activities, students may begin to consider the questions in the Opinion Column and Critical Puzzling.

Class Discussion

Use the questions under Talk Together to get the students primed and to create a discussion environment in the classroom. You may also want to draw from the open-ended questions listed here.

> How would you explain the difference between a healthy pride in one's own nation and the unhealthy pride of fascism? Where does one draw the line between healthy and unhealthy pride? What might be the results of this type of thinking? Do you see evidences today of fascism in your own country? **?**

> What do you think would be the effect of indoctrinating children at a very young age to believe the doctrines of fascism/Nazism/communism? What is the difference between teaching children the truths of the Bible and teaching them lies? What is the eventual impact on the individuals and on the nation? **?**

▶ # Resources for Digging Deeper

Choose a few books that look interesting, or find your own.

HITLER

The Rise and Fall of Adolf Hitler WORLD LANDMARK BOOK

William L. Shirer • The author, William Shirer, also authored *The Rise and Fall of the Third Reich*, which is one of the preeminent books about Nazi Germany. He has scaled down the level of difficulty for this children's biography and has succeeded magnificently in portraying one of the scariest people in world history. Highly recommended! **UE+**

Hitler and the Germans CAMBRIDGE TOPIC BOOK

Ronald Gray • The rise of Nazism in Germany is one of the main topics of this book. It shows the development of this nationalistic trend and the atrocities which resulted from it. WWII only makes sense as we understand the

philosophies undergirding and supporting the Nazi mentality. **MS+**

Hitler

Albert Marrin • Described as "the most fascinating and frightening man in history," Hitler's story is told in this excellent biography. **UE+**

Adolf Hitler WORLD LEADERS PAST AND PRESENT

Russell A. Berman • Hindenburg, the legendary German general of WWI, was twice elected president of the Weimar Republic. By his appointment, Hitler became Chancellor of Germany in 1933, positioning him to take complete control of the country when Hindenburg died. This excellent book is not only a biography but also shows the state of affairs in Germany between the two world wars. **MS+**

EINSTEIN

Albert Einstein GROUNDBREAK SERIES

Struan Reid • With brief explanations of Einstein's scientific theories, this excellent biography highlights the life and times of one the most important scientists of the twentieth century, including the fact that his Jewish ancestry made him unacceptable to the Nazis—a boon to the free world! **UE+**

Albert Einstein

Elma Ehrlich Levinger • This is an extremely interesting biography of one of the greatest physicists of history. Though not a practicing Jew, German-born Einstein helped Chaim Weizmann raise money for the Hebrew University in Palestine. He supported pacifism until Hitler went to war. And to help stop Nazi Germany, he suggested to President Roosevelt that the United States start a program to build the atomic bomb. Did you know that Einstein was on the Nazi's "hit list"? **UE+**

THE TURKISH REPUBLIC

Kemal Ataturk WORLD LEADERS PAST AND PRESENT

Frank Tachau • Ataturk (which means "Father of the Turks") was the military commander who held back the Allies during their disastrous attempt to take the Gallipoli peninsula in WWI. He led his nation in repelling the Greeks who invaded after WWI,

eventually becoming the first president of the Turkish Republic. **MS+**

Focus on Turkey WORLD IN FOCUS SERIES

Anita Ganeri • Learn about the history, geography, and culture of Turkey, including some of the issues facing the Turkish Republic today. **UE+**

 # Choose books of interest/ internet search

Remember:

Beware of Arrogance,

Embrace Humility!

A list of possible books is given in the Student Manual. Encourage your students to look for books or videos on Fascism & Fundamentals from this list and from other sources. You may want to gather a selection of further resources prior to beginning Unit 3, or you may encourage the students to be treasure hunters and find them on their own. It would be helpful and time-saving before the Unit begins to check availability of these titles on your local library website.

INDIA

Ghandi: A Photographic Story of a Life

Amy Pastan • A DK biography, this is an excellent introduction to the life and work of the man known as the "Father of India." **UE+**

Ghandi WORLD LEADERS PAST AND PRESENT

Catherine Bush • This is a biography of the man who helped end British rule in India through the use of passive resistance. It is astonishing to consider how effective this method was in demonstrating to the British that they could no longer administrate

this part of the Empire. Though violence between different religious groups did accompany the birth of independence in India, the process of actually gaining independence was remarkably free of violence. **MS+**

Jawaharlal Nehru WORLD LEADERS PAST AND PRESENT

Lila Finck and John P. Hayes • A fascinating look at India's first prime minister and one of the prime movers in India's bid for independence, this biography also shows how Nehru ably functioned as a world statesman on India's behalf. **MS+**

CHINA

The Rise of Modern China 20TH CENTURY PERSPECTIVE SERIES

Tony Allan • Learn about the struggle between the nationalists and communists of China, how they joined for a time to fight against the Japanese invasion, and reasons for the success of the Communist Party. Fascinating! **UE+**

The Man who Changed China: The Story of Sun Yat-sen A WORLD LANDMARK BOOK

Pearl Buck • If you have ever wondered how China went from the Boxer Rebellion to the Communist Revolution,

this book will bring a helpful understanding. Sun Yat-sen spent almost his entire life trying to bring democracy to his beloved China. It required the revolutionary act of overthrowing the Qing (or Manchu) Dynasty. **UE+**

Sun Yat-sen WORLD LEADERS PAST AND PRESENT

Jeffrey Barlow • To understand modern China, one must understand what happened after the Qing Dynasty. Sun Yat-Sen was a major factor in helping the country move from an imperial government to one more representative of the people. This book shows the transition—and why he is known as the "father" of his country. **MS+**

THE GREAT DEPRESSION

The Great Depression WITNESS TO HISTORY SERIES

Nathaniel Harris • The Great Depression was not only an American economic crisis—it affected nearly the entire

world. This excellent introduction will give students an understanding of some of the factors leading to the stock market crash, some of the major international effects, and the part WWII played in ending the Depression. **UE+**

WYCLIFFE BIBLE TRANSLATORS/CAMERON TOWNSEND

Cameron Townsend: Good News in Every Language

Janet and Geoff Benge • The story of Cameron Townsend is riveting, as we discover how one man's persevering obedience to God can change the world. Highly recommended! **UE+**

OLYMPIC ATHLETES IN THE 1920s–'30s

Eric Liddell: Something Greater than Gold

Janet and Geoff Benge • One of the Christian Heroes: Then & Now series, this is an excellent biography of the 1924 Olympic gold medalist who shocked the world by refusing to run on Sunday and went on to become a missionary in China. **UE+**

Eric Liddell: Pure Gold

David McCasland • More than an interesting story, this book will challenge readers to a greater level of service and a higher degree of trust in God as they witness Eric Liddell's remarkable life. Highly recommended! **MS+**

Jesse: The Man Who Outran Hitler

Jesse Owens with Paul Neimark • At sixty-four years of age, Jesse Owens returned to his childhood faith. In this book, which he described as his "spiritual autobiography," you will discover not only Jesse Owens's remarkable accomplishment at the 1936 Olympics in Berlin, but also the challenges he faced in his life.

President Carter said of him, "A young man who possibly didn't even realize the superb nature of his own capabilities went to the Olympics and performed in a way that I don't believe has ever been equaled since." **HS**

Jesse Owens: Young Record Breaker CHILDHOOD OF FAMOUS AMERICANS

M. M. Eboch • Though written for younger students, this is an excellent introduction to the African American athlete whose prowess confounded Hitler's theories of racial superiority in the 1936 Olympics. **E+**

Athens to Atlanta: 100 Years of Glory

Lee Benson, Doug Robinson, Dee Benson • A look at the Olympics from 1896–1996, this coffee table book includes information about the 1924 Paris Olympics where Eric Liddell competed, as well as the 1936 Berlin Olympics where Jesse Owens (an African-American competitor) completely ruined Hitler's plans for showing the superiority of the Aryan race! **UE+**

ISOBEL KUHN

Nothing Daunted: The Story of Isobel Kuhn

Gloria Repp • Based on the autobiographical writings of a missionary to the Lisu people of China, this compelling story of a courageous Christian woman encourages us to trust the One who is utterly faithful. **MS+**

Isobel Kuhn: On the Roof of the World

Janet and Geoff Benge • One of the Christian Heroes: Then & Now series, this is an excellent introduction for younger students to one of the great Christian missionaries to China. **UE+**

CHRISTIAN HISTORY

The 100 Most Important Dates in Church History

A. Kenneth Curtis, J. Stephen Lang, and Randy Petersen • Beginning with the year 64 in Rome and continuing to 1976, this book is filled with short descriptions of events and people within the church. For this chapter, read about the first Christian radio broadcast, Cameron Townsend with the Summer Institute of Linguistics, and the Fundamentals of Christianity, which launched the Fundamentalist movement. **UE+**

CLASSIC FICTION

The Unpleasantness at the Bellona Club

Dorothy Sayers • Dorothy Sayers was one of the great mystery writers of the twentieth century. This classic is a particular favorite because of the unexpectedly happy conclusion. **MS+**

VIDEO

Chariots of Fire

This is the incredible story of Eric Liddell and his Christian witness at the 1924 Paris Olympics. For the whole family!

What books did you like best?

_____

_____

_____

_____

The Internet also contains a wealth of information about Fascism & Fundamentals.

What sites were the most helpful?

_____

_____

_____

_____

For more books, use these Dewey Decimal numbers in your library:

Third Reich: 943

Turkish Republic: 956

Communism: 320.5; 329.9

Nonviolent civil disobedience: 322; 303

The Great Depression and the New Deal: 973.9

Olympic Games: 796

Fascism: 320.5; 329.9

Penicillin: 615.329; 610.9

Bible linguistics: 266.00

Anti-Semitism: 301.45; 572.2; 323.14

Nazism: 943.086

European History: 940–949

League of Nations: 341.1

Treaty of Versailles: 940.3

Scopes Trial: 44.7; 345.7

▷ **Student Self-Evaluation** UNIT 7, PHASE 1

Dates and hours:_____

Key Concepts

Rephrase the three Key Concepts of this Unit and confirm your understanding of each:

- Reshaping the Political Map

  _____

- Totalitarian Regimes

  _____

- Christianity Between the Wars

  _____

Tools for Self-Evaluation

Evaluate your personal participation in the discussions of this Phase. Bearing in mind that a good participant in a discussion is not always the most vocal participant, ask yourself these questions: Were you an active participant? Did you ask perceptive questions? Were you willing to listen to other participants of the discussion and draw out their opinions? Record your observations and how you would like to improve your participation in the future:

_____

_____

Every time period is too complex to be understood in one Phase of study. Evaluate your current knowledge of Fascism & Fundamentals. What have you focused on so far? What are your weakest areas of knowledge?

_____

_____

Based on the evaluation of this introduction, project ahead what you would like to study more of in the following Phases.

_____

_____

_____

◉ Conduct a review and evaluation

In this Phase of Unit 7, your students should have had the opportunity to explore Fascism & Fundamentals through reading, listening, thinking, and discussing by completing a selection from the following:

- informally discussed the Key Concepts;
- read the article;
- listened to the audio recordings;
- read the online articles;
- read the Scriptures;
- explored the recap activities;
- considered the Opinion Column and Critical Puzzling answers on their own;
- participated in class discussion;
- chosen books of interest or searched the Internet;
- completed their self-evaluation for this Phase.

Record student hours: _____

Assess student participation:

Create an evaluation system of your own, or refer to the evaluation rubric in the introduction, as a tool for assessing participation. The categories you will probably find most useful are "Introduction," "Process: Teamwork," and "Process: Originality." To help students develop good discussion skills, encourage them to participate actively, ask content-based questions, and stay focused on the discussion at hand. Students demonstrate a higher level of discussion skills when they incorporate comments and questions from others into their own questions, and draw out opinions or ask for points of clarification from others.

Do not critique the self-evaluation page your student completes and do not direct the answers the student gives to the questions. Instead, allow sincere and personal completion of the evaluation, then discuss the responses and incorporate those comments into your evaluation.

Determine a grade for this Phase, if using grades: _____

Teacher Self-Evaluation:

Evaluate your own use of materials and teaching opportunities: what worked and what did not; how effective was your time-management; how were your responses to the needs of your student; did you make your expectations clear; in what ways would you like to improve your approach for the next Unit? Incorporate suggestions from your students in your own evaluation (this requires humility!).

Phase 2

▶ Research & Reporting

Explore one or more of these areas to discover something significant!

Fascism

Investigate the beginnings of fascism, its underlying philosophies and worldview. Be sure to consider the fascist governments of Italy, Germany, and Spain.

Czechoslovakia

Research and report on the country of Czechoslovakia, which was created out of the former Austro-Hungarian Empire. Be sure to include a description of the Sudentenland and why this was important to Hitler's plans, along with what happened in the Munich Agreement. Describe Chamberlain and Dadier's participation in the Munich Agreement, contrasting it with Churchill's pronouncement of doom.

Cameron Townsend/Wycliffe Bible Translators

Research and report on the life and work of Cameron Townsend, the founder of Wycliffe Bible Translators and the Summer Institute in Linguistics. How did his work in linguistics change the world? How has this impacted world missions?

Hitler/Mussolini

Research and report the life and dictatorship of either Adolf Hitler or Benito Mussolini. Include early life, military experience during World War One, and rise to a position of power in the government. For Hitler, learn more about his belief in Aryan supremacy and his unrelenting hatred toward the Jews, the Slavs, and those who were mentally or physically handicapped. For Mussolini, be sure to include the changing nature of his diplomacy with the Catholic Church and the pope.

The Rise of Modern China

Learn about the growth of nationalism in China under Sun Yat-sen, the overthrow of the Qing dynasty, the warlord period, and the struggle between the nationalists and communists before the Japanese invasion. Be sure to include the impact of the war with the Japanese upon these two military groups, as well as upon the people of China.

Poland

Research and report on the country of Poland, concentrating most of your focus on independence after World War One, the difficulties of the Polish Corridor, and why both Germany and Russia eagerly coveted the land.

Gandhi

Research and report on the life and philosophy of Mahatma Gandhi and how he affected the British Empire in India. Indicate the areas where Gandhi's form of protest was effective, and where it was not. In what ways did Gandhi influence areas of the world beyond India?

Eric Liddell

Eric Liddell was a true Christian hero—not just for his refusal to run on Sunday during the 1924 Olympics, but also in how he lived his life. Discover more about his childhood, his education, his athletics, and his missionary service in China.

◉ Choose a topic and begin research

Allow the students the freedom to choose one of the topics listed under research & reporting in the Student Manual, or to suggest their own area which they would like to research.

Motivating Suggestions:

Especially for Non-linguistic students, and those who are not motivated by written or oral reports, here are suggestions for alternative ways of reporting what has been researched.

Fascism

Create a flipchart where you can compare and contrast the fascist governments of Italy, Germany, and Spain. Visually assist your audience to understand the information through the use of appropriate colors, symbols, and images. Be prepared to answer questions.

Choose a piece of music that will express some aspects of fascism, whether a recording or personal performance. Prepare program notes for your audience on fascism, and prior to playing the music, explain why this selection particularly represents fascism for you. Be prepared to answer questions afterwards.

Czechoslovakia

Create a series of drawings, paintings, or other images to illustrate what the democratic state of Czechoslovakia was like prior to WWII. Be sure to include the various people groups within its boundaries, especially the Germans of the Sudentenland region—since their existence outside of German borders had a special appeal to Hitler.

Do a first-person presentation of Winston Churchill that will clearly express his contrary opinion of the Munich Agreement. Be sure to give preparatory background on how Czechoslovakia had come into existence as a democratic country, as well as what will be the likely outcome of Hitler's latest outrage.

Cameron Townsend/ Wycliffe Bible Translators

Create and illustrate a book for younger students that will help them come to know the life and work of "Uncle Cam" and his impact on world missions and Bible translation.

Imagine you are a Cakchiquel Indian watching Cam Townsend labor for years to learn your language so that he might translate the Bible into Cakchiquel. Journal the effect this would have on you, how it would speak of the value of the Bible, and the assurance you would gain to learn that God spoke your language!

The Rise of Modern China

In a large outdoor area, set up a small-scale version of China. Be sure to indicate where the NW, NE, SW, and SE corners of the country are located. Then with three teams of players—one to represent the nationalists, one to represent the communists, and one to represent the Japanese invasion force—set up a series of athletic games that will depict the political struggle. The object for the players is to learn the major events of the time period between the early 1900s and 1949.

Compose a song about the rise of modern China, including the overthrow of the last dynasty, the short-lived Chinese Republic, the conflict between nationalist and communist forces, and the impact of Japan's actions.

Hitler/Mussolini

Using two students, have one act as a television news reporter and the other as one of the fascist dictators. Conduct an interview before a live audience, with a prepared set of questions. Decide prior to the interview whether this will function as "propaganda" for the dictator, or whether it will be an investigative interview to reveal what the rhetoric hides.

Consider what it would have been like to be a citizen of either Italy or Germany when a fascist dictator came to power. Write your thoughts about what you are witnessing in your nation, your concerns about future events under fascist leadership, and the results of your search through the Scripture and before God in prayer regarding your responsibility as a Christ-follower in this environment.

Poland

Draw a map of Poland after the Treaty of Versailles that includes the Polish Corridor. With the use of colors and images, not only show Poland's boundaries with Russia and Germany, but demonstrate how historically they both had been very interested and aggressive neighbors.

Create a poster to depict the history of Poland, highlighting events between WWI and WWII.

Gandhi

Using the political issues in India during Gandhi's life, create a series of posters with each one containing a symbol of one issue (for example, a

---

Fundamentalism

Study the beginning of the Fundamentalist movement in the church in America. What was the situation in America and Europe when *Fundamentals of Christianity* was published? How did the Fundamentalist movement seek to address the issues raised by modernist thinkers?

Kemal Ataturk

Research and report on the rise of Turkey as a modern nation from the ashes of the Ottoman Empire. Describe the life, philosophy, and work of Kemal Ataturk who was known as the "Father of the Turkish Republic."

Isobel Kuhn

Study and write about Isobel Kuhn, the Canadian woman who became a missionary to the Lisu people of China. Include a description of the way life changed as the Lisu church began to grow.

Jesse Owens

Jesse Owens was an African-American athlete who won four gold medals in the 1936 Olympics in Berlin, despite Nazi propaganda of the superiority of the Aryan master race. Research and report on his life in America, the effect his Olympic victory had upon Hitler, and what life held for him after his return home—including the way in which US presidents honored him.

Anti-Semitism/Zionism

Learn more about anti-Semitism and Zionism. Study anti-Semitism, especially during the time frame of WWI, the interwar period, and WWII. Where was anti-Semitism the most common? The least common? Where were the largest settlements of Jews during the 1930s? In correlation to this, study the Zionist movement, which began in the late 1800s. Be sure to include the effect on Palestine of the Balfour Declaration in the 1920s–1930s.

Albert Einstein

Study the life of Albert Einstein, as well as the scientific theories he developed. What were his views on war? What were his views on Hitler? Why did he move to the United States? What impact did he have on US military strategy?

---

mound of salt or a spinning wheel), with images to express corresponding events. Include a short amount of text to explain the effect on both rulers and ruled. Be prepared to answer questions from interested observers.

In a small group, decide the effectiveness of mass non-violent civil disobedience, especially concerning Gandhi's approach in India. In what ways was this very successful? In what ways was it not successful? What can be learned from this example?

Eric Liddell

Compare and contrast the life of Eric Liddell with that of a contemporary athlete of your choosing. Consider athletic ability, service to others, attitude toward oneself (arrogant or humble), personal integrity, and any other marker by which a life could be judged.

Induct Eric Liddell into the Athletes of History Hall of Fame with an official ceremony. Prepare a description of his accomplishments and why he has been chosen to be included in this prestigious group, along with a display of mementos of his life. You will want to invite others to attend the actual ceremony, which may include scenes from *Chariots of Fire*.

also differences in economy, tourism, religious freedom, and education.

Isobel Kuhn

The Lisu people of China were considered in the 1930s to be vastly inferior to the Chinese. Times and political climates have changed, so now create an advertising campaign to bring a truer and healthier vision of the Lisu, based on what John and Isobel Kuhn learned during their years of working with them.

Set up an area to become a museum dedicated to honoring the ministry of John and Isobel Kuhn. You will want to include various objects to represent the type of work they accomplished, photos or images to represent the people they worked with, and a map showing where they lived and worked. Then become an informative tour guide, taking groups through the museum and answering questions.

Jesse Owens

Compose a rousing song to celebrate the Olympic achievements of Jesse Owens in Berlin—in the face of the myth of Aryan supremacy. You might wish to include verses retelling the difficulties he faced when he returned to America.

Create a diorama of the spectacular gold-medal achievements of Jesse Owens in the 1936 Berlin Olympics. Be sure to include the element of surprised disappointment that his victory brought to the Nazis.

Anti-Semitism/Zionism

Set up a political debate, with a moderator (a strong one), between an Arab nationalist and a Jewish settler in Palestine. The debate will focus on the impact of the Balfour Declaration and the British Mandate for the Arabs and Jews. Remember to give each debater opportunity to respond to statements made by the other.

Create a time line of anti-Semitism in Nazi Germany, showing the ongoing series of events and legislation that

---

▶ Brain Stretchers

Fascism and Nazism

Compare and contrast fascism and Nazism with communism; with democracy. How are they different? How are they the same? Show what life is like for the common person under each of these regimes.

Theory of Relativity

Research and report on Einstein's theory of relativity in the sciences being wrongly applied to philosophy. Show how the absolute standards of right and wrong were considered no longer appli-cable due to this theory, and explain what Einstein believed about this misapplication.

Great Depression

Study the Great Depression and its international effect on countries and their economies. Compare and contrast this with the Soviet Union during the same time, noting that many contemporary observers believed communism was proving to be a better system due to its economic stability during this decade long depression.

Create Your Own Research Topic

_____

_____

_____

_____

Fundamentalism

Recreate the Scopes Trial of 1925, rethinking the strategies of the Fundamentalists in court and in the media. How could this have been done in such a way as to both win the case in court _and_ to positively influence public opinion?

Prepare the OpEd piece for presentation at the beginning of the weekly talk show _Christianity Under Fire._ This week's topic: why the Fundamentalist/Modernist controversy of the 1920s is still relevant nearly one hundred years later.

Kemal Ataturk

Go outside to collect items that will represent the rise of the Turkish Republic and the most important experiences of Ataturk's life in connection with this momentous event. Then use these items for illustrations as you present to an audience a fast-paced and interesting account of what transpired as the Ottoman Empire was replaced.

Create a chart that lists the differences between the secular republic of Turkey, with its Muslim majority, and the Islamic republics of the Middle East. Consider not only the differences in legislation and lifestyle, but

made life increasingly difficult for German Jews.

Albert Einstein

Make a collage of the life and work of Einstein, using magazines, photos, and drawings. Include those events and scientific theories that you found to be most significant for the world. Be prepared to answer questions about the issues represented in the collage.

Conduct an interview with Einstein on the radio. Ask him his thoughts on Hitler, on war, on the atom bomb, and whatever else would be interesting to a listening audience.

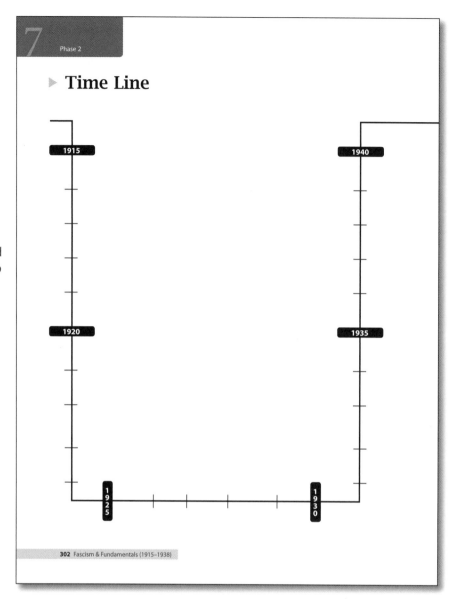

▶ **Time Line**

302 Fascism & Fundamentals (1915–1938)

◉ Construct the time line

Read the information listed with the Key Events in the Student Manual. Dialogue with your students about the issues involved.

Find the dates for the Key People and Key Events listed.

Consider this for your time line

This is a time of great political upheaval and chaos in numerous lands, and a time when many suffer hunger and unemployment due to the Great Depression. It is an era of growing racism and anti-Semitism, with frightening visions for the future. There is also, however, an amazing new wave in missions as Wycliffe Bible Translators begin the task of bringing the Bible into the heart languages of people groups around the world.

Key Events

- Treaty of Versailles
- Red Army victorious in Russian Civil War
- League of Nations formed
- Mussolini's March on Rome
- Turkish Republic proclaimed
- USSR formed
- Scopes Trial
- Collapse of US Stock Market
- Hitler appointed German Chancellor
- Summer Institute of Linguistics begun
- Nazis repudiate Treaty of Versailles
- Ethiopia (Abyssinia) invaded by Italy
- Spanish Civil War
- Nazis march into Austria
- Munich Conference

Be sure to include the people listed in Key People in Phase 1.

Hebrews 4:12 says, "For the word of God is living and powerful, and sharper than any two-edged sword, piercing even to the division of soul and spirit, and of joints and marrow, and is a discerner of the thoughts and intents of the heart." Talk with your students about the significance of this moment in time, as the inerrancy of the Bible comes under attack in some regions of the world, while others devote their lives to translating the Bible to distant people groups.

Time Line Key

Key People in the Church

- Gresham Machen: 1881–1937
- Sundar Singh: 1889–1929
- E. Stanley Jones: 1884–1973
- Cameron Townsend: 1896–1982
- Eric Liddell: 1902–1945)
- Isobel Kuhn: 1901–1957

Key People in the World

- Mahatma Gandhi: 1869–1948
- Kemal Ataturk: 1881–1938
- Benito Mussolini: 1883–1945
- Chiang Kai-shek: 1887–1975
- Adolf Hitler: 1889–1945
- Albert Einstein: 1879–1955

Key Dates

- Treaty of Versailles: June 28, 1919
- Red Army victorious in Russian Civil War: 1921
- League of Nations formed: June 28, 1919
- Mussolini's March on Rome: October, 1922
- Turkish Republic proclaimed: October, 1923
- USSR formed: December, 1922
- Scopes Trial: 1925
- Collapse of US Stock Market: 1929
- Hitler appointed German Chancellor: 1933
- Summer Institute of Linguistics begun: 1934
- Nazis repudiate Treaty of Versailles: 1935
- Ethiopia (Abyssinia) invaded by Italy: October, 1935
- Spanish Civil War: July 17, 1936–April 1, 1939
- Nazis march into Austria: March, 1938
- Munich Conference: September 28–29, 1938

▶ Words to Watch

fascism	purge	inflation	fundamental
Nazism	anti-Semitism	terrorist	reparations
plebiscite	nationalistic	Zionism	translation
Comintern	factions	Aryan	linguistics
chancellor	atrocities	Stock Market	appeasement
Marxism-Leninism	violation	repudiate	non-violence

Consider:

Many words which may be unfamiliar to English-speakers from this time period are derived from German, because they were part of the Nazi terminology. Here are some of the most important to know (including a few English translations):

Reich	Drang nach Osten	Volk ohne Raum	Endsieg
Blitzkrieg	Führerprinzip	Sieg Heil	Kristillnacht
Anschluss	Gleichschaltung	Untermensch	

Other words you need to look up:

_____

_____

_____

_____

Here is one idea for making vocabulary study interesting and fun:

A PLAY ON WORDS

Using the vocabulary words, write a short skit that depicts some event or circumstance from this era. If desired, the skit could be acted out either by actors or puppets.

A list of definitions can be found at the back of the book in Appendix B.

◉ Practice vocabulary

You may find other words in this Unit that are especially appropriate for younger children. Feel free to substitute another vocabulary list for the one provided.

◉ Complete research projects and share in class or hand in

Create a safe environment for the presentations. Set ground rules prior to the presentations, so that students know how much time is available for each of them, and so that they know they will be honored and respected by all those observing.

▶ Student Self-Evaluation UNIT 7, PHASE 2

Dates and hours:_____

Research Project

Summarize your research question:

_____

_____

List your most useful sources by author, title, and page number or URL where applicable (continue list in margin if necessary):

_____

_____

Now take a moment to evaluate the sources you just listed. Do they provide a balanced view of your research question? Should you have sought an additional opinion? Are your sources credible (if you found them on your own)? Record your observations:

_____

_____

_____

Evaluate your research project in its final presentation. What are its strengths? If you had time to revisit this project, what would you change? Consider giving yourself a letter grade based on your project's merits and weaknesses.

_____

_____

_____

Letter grade: _____

You have just completed an area of specific research on the time of Fascism & Fundamentals. Now what would you like to explore in the upcoming Phases? Set some objectives for yourself.

_____

_____

_____

◉ Conduct a review and evaluation

In this second Phase of Unit 7, your students should have had the opportunity to explore Fascism & Fundamentals through researching, thinking, and reporting by completing a selection from the following:

- done a research project;
- learned the vocabulary;
- constructed a time line;
- created a project report on what was researched;
- completed their self-evaluation procedure for this Phase.

Record student hours: _____

Assess student effort in the research and reporting projects.

Create an evaluation system of your own, or refer to the evaluation rubric in the introduction, as a tool for assessing research and reporting. The categories you will probably find most useful are *"Introduction," "Task," "Process: Teamwork"* (if students are working together), along with Grammar, Format, and Spelling. As a tool for helping your students develop better research skills, pay attention

to their evaluation of sources. Older students should learn how to make a "Sources Cited" list according to academic standards—refer them to English usage books or websites for formatting rules. Younger students should learn how to obtain a balanced view of their research subject; if they use more than one source they will get a bigger picture of what was happening. Encourage your students to make use of their self-evaluations for their next research projects, in order to practice good research skills.

Do not critique the self-evaluation page your student completes in the Student Manual—spelling errors are not to be considered in such an exercise. Students should feel free to humbly evaluate themselves without that added complexity. Instead, discuss with them the intention of their written comments and incorporate those into your evaluation.

Determine a final grade for this Phase: _____

Teacher Self-Evaluation:

Evaluate your own use of materials and teaching opportunities: what worked and what did not; how effective was your time-management; how were your responses to the needs of your student; did you make your expectations clear; in what ways would you like to improve your approach for the next Unit? Incorporate suggestions from your students in your own evaluation *(this requires humility!)*.

The Hands-On Week

Phase 3

▶ Maps and Mapping

Physical Terrain

» Locate and label on a map of central Europe the Sudeten mountain range and the Bohemian Forest and the Elbe river of Czechoslovakia. Also, locate and label the Oder, Bug, and Vistula rivers of Poland.

» Locate and label on a map of the Middle East the Taurus mountain range of the Turkish Republic. Locate and label the Hejaz mountains of Saudi Arabia, as well as the desert known as "The Empty Quarter." Also, locate and label the Tigris and Euphrates rivers.

Geopolitical

» Locate and label on a map of Europe the countries which emerged from the ashes of WWI: Poland (including the Polish Corridor), Czechoslovakia, Yugoslavia. Also, locate the small country of Austria (which was formerly the heartland of the mighty Austro-Hungarian empire).

» Locate and label on a map of the Middle East the countries (some of which functioned under the British or French Mandates) which emerged from the disintegration of the Ottoman Empire: The Turkish Republic, Saudi Arabia, Palestine, Syria, Transjordan, Lebanon, Iraq.

Explore:

» *Germans Outside Germany:* Hitler used the excuse of Germans under foreign rule to invade Austria and Czechoslovakia. Learn more about the settlements of Germans outside the borders of the Weimar Republic (what remained of Germany after WWI). Where were they located? How large were the settlements of German-speakers outside Germany?

» *Christian Outreach:* What is the status of evangelical outreach today in Central Europe? What opportunities and what difficulties face those who share the gospel in these areas?

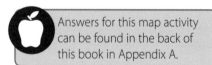

Answers for this map activity can be found in the back of this book in Appendix A.

◉ Create a map and discuss the issues in teams

The students each have an outline map in their manuals. They will be given assignments for drawing in the rivers, mountains, cities, and regional boundaries that are listed. For details on where these things are, please consult a historical atlas, an encyclopedia, or another source of geographic information.

Upper elementary students might be satisfied to accomplish only this portion:

• **Physical terrain:** This part of the mapping exercise will help students locate and mark the mountain ranges and rivers of Central Europe—areas Hitler coveted for Germany. It will also help students locate and mark the mountain ranges and rivers of the countries of the Middle East that emerged from the Ottoman Empire.

Middle school students might be satisfied to complete both the previous mapping exercise and this exercise:

- **Geopolitical:** This section of the mapping exercise will provide the students an opportunity to locate and mark the new countries that

arose at the end of WWI, including countries in Europe and the Middle East.

High school students might be satisfied to complete both the previous mapping exercises and at least one exploration topic of this exercise:

- **Explore** a selection from this portion of the mapping exercise in teams.

GERMANS OUTSIDE GERMANY

Students might find it helpful to create a spreadsheet of the data they compile on German settlements in countries beyond German borders. Then, create a map to show what Hitler was considering as the Treaty of Versailles was renounced.

CHRISTIAN OUTREACH

Students might wish to locate information about current missionary endeavors in Central Europe. If possible, to provide even more help and insight, interview someone who has worked in these fields.

◉ Examine and discuss art and architecture

The online resource page at www. HistoryRevealed.org has links to view each of the items listed. Allow the students time to observe the paintings without any conversation, and then, when they are ready, engage them in some or all of the questions listed below or in the Student Manual.

Art Appreciation

Tenement Flats by Millard Sheets

From December of 1933 to June of 1934, the US hired nearly 4,000 out-of-work artists and commissioned them to create more than 15,000 paintings, murals, prints, and other pieces of art. The Smithsonian American Art Museum has compiled a series of paintings from the Federal Works of Art Project, called *1934: A New Deal for Artists*, which will be touring the United States from 2011 to 2014. To view the art online, see the link at the online resource page.

▶ Art Appreciation

Tenement Flats by Millard Sheets

In 1934, during the height of the Great Depression, thousands of artists were hired by the US Government under the Public Works of Art Project (PWAP) to create art depicting America. One of the better known of these artists was a California painter named Millard Sheets. You can find a link to see this painting at the online resource page.

» These tenements were in the Bunker Hill neighborhood of downtown Los Angeles, California. Look closely at the painting and answer theses questions: What are the women doing? How is life portrayed at the bottom of the hill in comparison to the top of the hill? What message may the artist have been trying to communicate?

States of Mind: The Farewells by Umberto Boccioni

Boccioni, an Italian artist, was a signer to the "Technical Manifesto" of Futurist painting, which demanded that "all subjects previously used must be swept aside in order to express our whirling life of steel, of pride, of fever, and of speed." The Italian Futurists became identified with Italian Fascism since they both promoted Italian nationalism and violence—including war. You can find a link to see this painting at the online resource page.

» The setting is a crowded train station. What words could you use to describe this painting? The artist was seeking to convey far more than a picture of a place—he wanted to evoke particular sounds, movement, emotions, even smells. The Futurist Manifesto included this phrase: "We will sing of the great crowds agitated by work, pleasure, and revolt . . . the gluttonous railway stations devouring smoking serpents." Knowing that, take your time to consider the painting again. What does it convey to you?

Unique Forms of Continuity in Space by Umberto Boccioni

This masterpiece is Boccioni's major sculptural work. It portrays a figure striding powerfully through space, expressing great vitality and velocity. You can find a link to see this sculpture at the online resource page.

» In what ways does this sculpture exemplify the Futuristic concepts of "steel, pride, fever and speed"? How would you describe this sculpture?

CONSIDER:

The founder of Italian Futurism was Filippo Marinetti. In 1909, he published the Futurist Manifesto, which glorified war, reckless speed, and aggressive violence while attacking morality, women, and that which honored antiquity (including libraries and museums). Marinetti founded the Futurist Political Party in 1918, which was soon absorbed into Mussolini's Fascist Party.

The online resource page at www. HistoryRevealed. org contains many helpful Internet links to artwork, architecture, music, project helps, and more.

Discuss with students the realities of the Great Depression in America, where one-third of the US population was unemployed and agriculture was suffering the droughts of the Dust Bowl. How might this Public Works of Art Project, which was part of FDR's New Deal, have influenced not only the artists but also the citizens of America?

States of Mind: The Farewells by Umberto Boccioni

Futurism, disdaining Italy's past, sought instead to awaken a hunger in modern man for the power and speed of modern technology. With its elevation of violence, aggression, rashness and explosive speed, its hatred of women, and its utter egotistical humanism, Italian Futurism appealed especially to young men— many of whom would, after WWI, join the Italian Fascist party.

Unique Forms of Continuity in Space by Umberto Boccioni

Boccioni began studying sculpture in 1912 and found it to be such an expressive medium for his artwork that he declared, "These days I am obsessed by sculpture! I believe I have glimpsed a complete renovation of that mummified art."

Ask students whether this figure appears to be masculine or feminine.

The online resource page at www.HistoryRevealed.org contains many helpful Internet links to artwork, architecture, music, project helps, and more.

Art has a power to move people, as it embodies and conveys a way of looking at the world. This power can work either for good or for evil, depending on the worldview it rests upon. Talk with your students about the correlation they see between the art of futurism and the politics of fascism. Pray together about how God might raise up artists in this day who will have the giftings and the foundation for creating powerful art that will communicate the reality of God and His redemption.

With their answers in mind, begin a discussion of what might happen to a culture when it becomes popular for men to philosophically hate women. How does a biblical view of creation— of the significance of both Adam and Eve—impact this discussion?

This sculpture is depicted on the Italian-issue twenty-cent euro coin.

Architecture

Città Nuova, designs by Antonio Sant'Elia

Just before WWI, Sant'Elia conceived a futuristic and visionary approach to urban architecture—what cities of the future should look like. His buildings of steel, glass, and reinforced concrete were not only possible due to modern advances in building technology, but they also provided the structure for the fast-paced modern life of a city. Central to the city would be massive stations for trains and airplanes, as well as a network of roads and subways underground—which would allow for rapid movement of people and vehicles. Professor and author Esther da Costa Meyer described it this way: "Traffic assumes a role analogous to that of water in a fountain."

Discuss with your students their thoughts about the degree to which Sant'Elia's vision for future urban architecture—which was shocking in its day—has been realized. Ask them, "Which aspects do you observe that have been incorporated in cities you have experienced?"

▶ Architecture

The architecture designs of Antonio Sant'Elia, an Italian Futurist, were a gateway to the future of modern urban architecture. He wrote, "We are no longer the men of the cathedrals, the palaces, the assembly halls but of big hotels, railway stations, immense roads, colossal ports, covered markets . . . demolition and rebuilding schemes. We must invent and build the city of the future, dynamic in all its parts . . . and the house of the future must be like an enormous machine."

Città Nuova, designs by Antonio Sant'Elia

» You can find a link to drawings of Sant'Elia's modern "New City" at the online resource page. Notice the significance of skyscrapers which were to be the basic structure upon which the city would be centered, emphasizing man's technological achievements. It may not be obvious in the drawings, but there were no natural features such as fountains of water, parks, or trees included in his renderings. How would you describe these drawings? In what way does this architectural style reflect the artistic philosophy of Italian Futurism? If this New City had been built according to the architect's design, what do you think it would have been like to live there?

▶ Arts in Action

Select one or more, and let your artistic juices flow!

American Art

» Imagine you have just been hired by the Federal Works of Art Project to artistically depict scenes of America. Choose a landscape, a cityscape, an everyday occurrence, a holiday celebration, or whatever would typify America during the 1930s. Then, in whatever medium you prefer—whether collage, drawing, painting, photography, etc.—create an art piece. Be sure to give it an engaging title!

◉ Do an art project

American Art

Encourage students to look through the works of art included in the Smithsonian American Art Museum's traveling exhibition *1934: A New Deal for Artists*, which can be found online (as noted above), in order to gain a better idea of the type of scenes historically painted by artists during 1934.

▶ Science

» In 1928, a revolutionary discovery was made by Alexander Fleming that would eventually save so many lives that it seemed almost miraculous. Where was this discovery made? In a moldy dish! Penicillin, the first of the antibiotic medicines, was, at first glance, an unlikely miracle drug, since it came from a simple mold. However, when Fleming, a medical researcher, examined a dish where bacteria he was trying to grow for medical research purposes had been contaminated by mold, he saw that near this mold, all of the bacteria were dead. With careful observation and experimentation, he discovered that this mold would kill many disease-causing bacteria. Since then, doctors have used it to treat illnesses such as staph infections, meningitis, strep throat, pneumonia, and even some cases of diphtheria. It took another dozen years to create penicillin in great enough quantities to be medically useful, but this amazing breakthrough in medicine was worth waiting for.

» Create your own mold! Using an aluminum pan at least two inches deep and six inches square, fill the pan with about one inch of soil or compost. On top of the soil, add a layer of strawberries (or tomato slices) and old bread. Lightly water this layer. Cover the pan with plastic wrap, sealing it tightly with a large rubber band. Place the pan in a warm, dark place for a day or two. Check to see if the mold is growing. If not, add a bit more water and try it again. Keep it covered so that the mold is not released or disturbed. Observe it every day or two, charting or sketching the changes you find. Be sure to carefully handle the disposal of the soil and mold after the successful completion of your experiment. This would be great stuff to add to you compost pile!

▶ Music

Dmitri Shostakovich, one of the most important Russian composers during the Soviet era, composed this piece in 1937, near the height of the Stalinist Purge of 1936–38. He composed this symphony shortly after government officials denounced him—which carried with it chilling possibilities. The first performance saved his career. One reviewer wrote, "The symphony is a work of extraordinary profundity by a mature artist who has successfully overcome the childhood diseases of leftism. This is indeed a joyous occasion." Reinstituted into the ranks of Communist faithfuls, Shostakovich continued composing music for Soviet Russia for more than three decades. Intriguingly, the possibility exists that all was not as it seemed. After Shostakovich's death, news came to the West that he actually was a secret dissident and opposed to the Soviet regime. You can find a link to listen to the music at the online resource page.

Symphony no. 5 in D minor, op. 47 by Shostakovich

» After listening to this symphony, talk together about the imagery created through the music. In what ways does this music reflect Russia? Communism? Militarism?

◉ Do a science experiment

Students interested in the growth of fungus, bacteria, and molds might find it fascinating to watch time lapse movies—especially the mold growing on strawberries—from Cornell University's Plant Pathology department. You can find a link at the online resource page.

◉ Listen to and discuss the music

Listen

Shostakovich's "Symphony no. 5 in D minor, op. 47"

After his death, Shostakovich's supposed memoir was published. It was purported to have been dictated to someone and then smuggled to the West in the 1970s. In this memoir, *Testimony*, Shostakovich describes living a double life. Appearing as a good communist functionary in public, he actually was a secret dissident—encoding his true thoughts and feelings in certain compositions. In this fifth symphony, it may be that the finale—which appears to be triumphant—is, instead, his ironic mockery of what was expected. At least one former Soviet musician declared that this irony "is obvious to any Russian." However, no one can be certain whether Shostakovich actually authored this testimony of dissidence, which leaves us with little but tantalizing clues.

The online resource page has links to a YouTube video of an excellent portion of Bernstein's version of this symphony, as well as the complete version.

► Cooking

In this Unit, we have had the opportunity to learn about Gandhi and India's struggle for independence. What a wonderful excuse to try a delicious curry!

Chicken Curry

Authentic curry recipes will instruct you to make your own curry powder from a number of spices. Try it sometime! Generally, we just use a good curry powder from the grocery store.

1 Tbsp butter	½ cup chopped onion
¾ tsp salt	2 cups cold milk
1 cup finely chopped, pared apple	1 clove garlic, minced
2 to 3 tsp curry powder	2 cups diced cooked chicken
1 cup sliced celery	2 Tbsp cornstarch (you may substitute
¾ cup cold chicken broth	cooked turkey or tofu, if desired)

In a large frying pan, melt butter. Add apple, celery, onion, and garlic. Cook until onion is tender. Combine cornstarch, curry powder, salt, and broth in a bowl, whisking until smooth. Stir into onion mixture, add milk. Cook and stir until mixture thickens. Stir in chicken and heat through. Serve over hot rice, and offer any combination of these condiments: mango chutney, coconut, raisins, chopped peanuts, chopped green onions, chopped hard-boiled eggs, bananas.

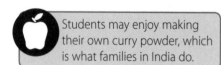

Students may enjoy making their own curry powder, which is what families in India do.

◉ Cook the food

Curry Powder

3 Tbsp coriander seeds
1 tsp cumin seeds
½ tsp mustard seeds
10 green cardamom pods
½ tsp black peppercorns
4 small dried red chiles (2 tsp ground Paprika may be substituted)
½ tsp turmeric powder
½ tsp ground ginger
½ tsp cinnamon
½ tsp salt

Crack open the cardamom pods and remove the seeds, discard the husks. In a dry skillet, gently and individually heat each type of seed, the peppercorns, and chiles for a few seconds—just until they start to release a tantalizing aroma. Remove from heat and let cool. Grind the whole seeds, peppercorns, and chiles using a spice or coffee grinder, or use a mortar and pestle. Add the other ground spices to the mix, and store in a tightly closed jar in a cool, dark place.

▶ Student Self-Evaluation UNIT 7, PHASE 3

Dates and hours:_____

Evaluate your projects

- List which of the activities listed in this Phase you did:

  _____

  _____

- Rate your enthusiasm: _____

  Explain: _____

  _____

- Rate the precision of your approach:_____

  Explain: _____

  _____

- Rate your effort toward the completion of the project: _____

  Explain: _____

  _____

- Ask yourself what worked and what did not. What would you do differently in the future, and what would you repeat?

  _____

  _____

- How did these hands-on activities enhance your knowledge of Fascism & Fundamentals? What made them worthwhile?

  _____

  _____

- In the first three Phases of this Unit, what aspect of the time period has most captured your imagination? What would you like to creatively pursue to conclude your study?

  _____

  _____

◉ Conduct a review and evaluation

In this Phase of Unit 7, your students should have had the opportunity to explore Fascism & Fundamentals through various hands-on and creative sessions by completing a selection from the following:

- completed a mapping section;

- observed and discussed art & architecture;

- worked on an art project;

- experimented with a science project or taken a field trip;

- listened to music;

- tasted a food related to this Unit;

- completed their self-evaluation procedure for this Phase.

Record student hours: _____

Assess student involvement in the hands-on activities.

Create an evaluation system of your own or refer to the evaluation rubric in the introduction as a tool for assessing participation. The categories you will probably find most useful for evaluating projects are *"Task"* and *"Process: Teamwork."* Consider specifically the enthusiasm, the precision of approach, and the efforts toward improving skills and completing activities, rather than rating the project as compared to a masterpiece.

Do not critique the self-evaluation page your student completes in the Student Manual—it is acceptable for students to occasionally leave lines blank if a question does not apply. Instead, discuss with the student the intention of the written comments and incorporate those into your evaluation.

Determine a grade for this Phase, if using grades: _____

Teacher Self-Evaluation:

Evaluate your own use of materials: what worked and what did not? Consider your time management. Were you able to recognize and respond to your students' needs? Did you make your expectations clear? In what ways would you like to improve your approach for the next Unit? Incorporate suggestions from your students in your own evaluation (*this requires humility!*).

Phase 4

▶ In Your Own Way…

In this Unit, we have seen the aftereffects of the Treaty of Versailles; the victory of the Bolsheviks in the Russian Civil War; the rise of fascism in Italy and Germany; the pioneering work of Cameron Townsend; the growing conflict between China and Japan; the idolizing of Mussolini and Hitler; the Modernist/Fundamentalist controversy; growing anti-Semitism and racism; the Great Depression; a movement toward independence for India; the gathering storm clouds of war; and the challenges facing those who followed Christ. Now, choose a selection of these activities, or create your own, that will best express what you have learned from this Unit.

LINGUISTICS

Journalism

You have the extreme honor of interviewing the great German general and current president of the Weimar Republic, Paul von Hindenburg. He has just appointed a new chancellor for Germany, one Adolf Hitler. Find out for the readers of your magazine, *The Republic Reporter*, just who is this new chancellor and why has von Hindenburg appointed him? Be sure to include the president's view on the future.

For your highly controversial television news program, *What's the Point?*, interview Cameron Townsend about his commitment to translate the Bible into the previously unwritten language of the Cakchiquel people of Guatemala. Though your initial intent may be to show your viewers an outlandish waste of time, the actual interaction with Cam Townsend may reshape the interview.

Poetry

Write an epic poem from the biblical (and eternal) perspective concerning the Nazis program to blame, vilify, and eliminate the Jews.

Prose

Write a short story for children about Isobel Kuhn, a missionary in the late 1920s to the Lisu people of China.

As a British soldier stationed in India, write a letter home to your folks describing the new "nonviolent or passive resistance" movement being headed up by a lawyer named Gandhi. Describe your personal experience with this effective technique as it is being used in the bid for Indian independence.

◉ Choose an area of expression

Students may work either individually or in teams.

Linguistics

Journalism

Students interested in writing the journalistic piece with President von Hindenburg would find it helpful to consider three facts: he was actually a monarchist (as opposed to one who believes in a democracy); he was fearful of communism (which was still a looming possibility); and, after a long life serving his country, he was now showing some signs of senility.

For a downloadable resource on Cameron Townsend's life and work, see the link at the online resource page. Click on "longer biographical sketch."

Students who choose the *What's the Point* project will find the data contained in this bio very helpful.

Poetry

Suggest to students who are interested in crafting this epic poem that they read and ponder Zechariah 2:8–9: "For thus says the Lord of hosts: 'He sent Me after glory, to the nations which plunder you; for he who touches you touches the apple of His eye. For surely I will shake My hand against them, and they shall become spoil for their servants. Then you will know that the Lord of hosts has sent Me.'"

Prose

For a fascinating glimpse into the life of Isobel Kuhn through the eyes of Elisabeth Elliot, see the link at the online resource page.

Students who wish to write the letter about what was happening in the movement for independence in India should consider these quotes from Gandhi:

> Passive resistance is a method of securing rights by personal suffering; it is the reverse of resistance by arms.

ART

Painting/Drawing/Collage

Create an artistic image that will highlight some of the results of worshipping anything other than God, including a human political leader such as Hitler, Mussolini, or Stalin.

Graphic Design

Your advertising company has just been hired to create a full page ad for the nation's newspapers. With the Scopes Trial courtroom as the setting, make a monkey out of the theory of Social Darwinism with its ladder ranking of racial superiority. You might want add a cameo of Hitler (who really believed in this concept) somewhere in the ad.

Sculpture

Capture artistically the rise of the Turkish Republic from the ashes of the Ottoman Empire. Be sure to show the struggle involved in this event, and, if possible, the new path Kemal Ataturk chose for his country.

MUSIC

Performance Practice

With your teacher's help, select an appropriate piece of music expressing some particular aspect studied in this Unit that you found interesting.

Passive resistance is an all-sided sword; it can be used anyhow; it blesses him who uses it and him against whom it is used.

Passive resistance, unlike nonviolence, has no power to change men's hearts.

The sword of passive resistance does not require a scabbard.

Art:

Painting/Drawing

Students may prefer to envision this from either an earthly perspective—showing the devastation wrought to people and nations when Hitler, Mussolini, and Stalin became objects of devotion—or from a heavenly perspective, with eternity in mind.

Graphic Design

Look through a number of political cartoons, observing the exaggeration they use in order to gain the desired effect. In this exercise, you are attempting to influence people's opinion against something growing in popularity during the 1920s, so look for areas to exaggerate the unpleasant realities of Social Darwinism in order to wake people up.

Sculpture

In order to better understand Kemal Ataturk's vision, students could learn about Kemalism, which is the term for the six fundamental concepts of the new Turkish Republic: republicanism, populism, secularism, reformism, nationalism, and statism.

Music

Performance Practice

For musical students, this selection may be a wonderful opportunity to express what they have learned. Make sure they select a piece that they have adequate time to prepare.

Drama

Drama

Great drama is frequently marked by recurring themes. Students might consider the relationship of Eric Liddell with China: a European born in China, and, after his university work

> Here is a principle in comedy: the closer you get to breaking the rule, the greater the tension, but if you actually break the rule, thereby releasing the tension, it will produce consequences. The element that will provide tremendous comedy in this situation is figuring out what the characters can and cannot do. Can the Modernists just kick him off the platform, or not? Can he say Modernism is bad, or not? Encourage students to consider which cultural rules apply in this situation, how far these rules can be strained before the situation breaks, and what the consequences will be if the rules are broken.

and Olympic success, returning to China. Every drama also incorporates an underlying thread that weaves through the story. Decide upon the thread for this narrative, whether home or running or belonging or value, and craft the narrative around it. There is a significance to each of our lives because God has designed us for His plans and purposes. Eric Liddell lived out the unique story that God had prepared for him.

Comedy

These two positions are on opposing sides concerning the inerrancy of Scripture, which is not funny, but the possibilities in creating these scenes are ripe with humor. Students might choose to recreate Barry Foster's message and the Modernists' reaction or to enact the scene backstage when the Modernists discover they've invited the wrong guy and are trying to figure out what to do now.

Puppetry

Set up a series of short scenes taking place in different locations at different times. Since there will be very little time for action, the stage picture—which would be all the visible elements that the audience can see arranged on the stage—will

DRAMA

Drama

Dramatize the story of Eric Liddell. You might choose to include scenes from any of these areas of his life: childhood in China, school in Great Britain, 1924 Olympics in Paris (with his "awful" running style!), and missionary work in China.

Comedy

There has been a slight mix-up on the part of an elderly secretary. A little known Fundamentalist preacher named Barry Foster (a fictional character) was mistakenly sent the invitation intended for renowned Modernist preacher Harry Fosdick (a historical character). The invitation is to address the prestigious audience gathered at the 1922 American Modernist convention.

Puppetry

After the Treaty of Versailles, a group of puppets are confused as to where Czechoslovakia, Poland, and the Kingdom of Serbs, Croats, and Slovenes are actually located. With the magic of time-lapse puppetry, take them on a journey through these newly created countries.

Prop Needs

_____

_____

Costume Ideas

_____

_____

Role/Player

_____

_____

Set Suggestions

_____

_____

_____

become very significant. An example of this would be from the balcony scene in Romeo and Juliet. Juliet is set above Romeo as the beginning stage picture, then he has to climb to the balcony, which changes the stage picture. This actually tells the story more effectively than if they were both on the ground. Since this would be a very helpful device for this puppet show, encourage students to consider setting up very different stage pictures between the puppets and their environment. Suggest a series of signs (incorporating images and words) to assist students in transitioning from location

to location. The faster the transition, the funnier it will be.

Movement

Mime

Pantomime is physical recreation of actual movement.

Mime is a romanticized, heightened, expressive version.

A pantomime of this would be a literal action—you could pantomime Hitler promising these good things, then have him pantomime shooting people, and finally, show the German civilians reacting to this. That would be pantomime.

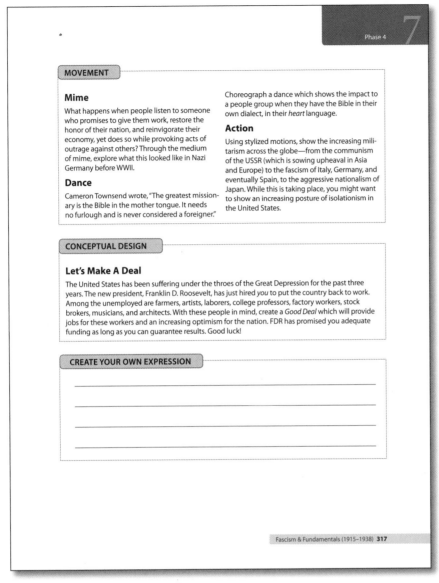

MOVEMENT

Mime

What happens when people listen to someone who promises to give them work, restore the honor of their nation, and reinvigorate their economy, yet does so while provoking acts of outrage against others? Through the medium of mime, explore what this looked like in Nazi Germany before WWII.

Dance

Cameron Townsend wrote, "The greatest missionary is the Bible in the mother tongue. It needs no furlough and is never considered a foreigner."

Choreograph a dance which shows the impact to a people group when they have the Bible in their own dialect, in their *heart* language.

Action

Using stylized motions, show the increasing militarism across the globe—from the communism of the USSR (which is sowing upheaval in Asia and Europe) to the fascism of Italy, Germany, and eventually Spain, to the aggressive nationalism of Japan. While this is taking place, you might want to show an increasing posture of isolationism in the United States.

CONCEPTUAL DESIGN

Let's Make A Deal

The United States has been suffering under the throes of the Great Depression for the past three years. The new president, Franklin D. Roosevelt, has just hired *you* to put the country back to work. Among the unemployed are farmers, artists, laborers, college professors, factory workers, stock brokers, musicians, and architects. With these people in mind, create a *Good Deal* which will provide jobs for these workers and an increasing optimism for the nation. FDR has promised you adequate funding as long as you can guarantee results. Good luck!

CREATE YOUR OWN EXPRESSION

_____

_____

_____

_____

---

flags of these nations. Then, for the movement, experiment with moving the flags through space with different tempo, attitude, rhythm, size, and direction. It might be helpful for students to envision a grid on the floor, which would be a geometric floor pattern. To utilize the grid, imagine the different nationalities as specific chess pieces on a giant chessboard. Now consider the different directions they might move. Are they a rook, so only right angle moves are allowed? Or, perhaps they are a bishop, a pawn, or a knight, which would determine the way a nation could move. Experiment with how characters move across the grid, as this will be visually helpful.

Conceptual Design:

Let's Make a Deal

Make lists of the kinds of products each of these types of laborers and disciplines could produce. Next, imagine a visionary project that would incorporate products from all of these laborers. Finally, pitch the idea to FDR, Congress, and the laborers. As you put all the pieces together to create the pitch, remember two things: 1) people will work harder if you motivate them to want to contribute; and 2) you need to restore their faith in America's economic solutions, its political system, and in themselves as a necessary and integral part of society.

◉ Share creative expressions in class

Create a safe environment for the presentations. Set ground rules prior to the presentations, so that students know how much time is available for each of them, and so that they know they will be honored and respected by all those observing.

Mime, on the other-hand, would be finding non-literal ways to express the story. Students could depict the pain of not having work, of having their culture dishonored, and of living in dire poverty, then experiencing the jubilation of this promise of redemption, and, finally, showing the tension in their consciences at the increasingly obvious plight of a brutalized minority.

Dance

Dance is the most expressive version of mime. A lyrical dance is a story-telling dance that might look similar to mime—the expressive gestures and the heightened physicality, with movements that are less literal and more abstract. Students choosing

this creative expression could use extremes of physical position to indicate heightened emotion. For instance, when someone is surprised, to lean backward slightly would be a change in physical position. In dance, taking this to an extreme would be actually bending over backward to indicate surprise. To be most effective, students should be encouraged to find ways to express delight, pleasure, longing, resolution, and joy that incorporate extreme physical positions and rhythms.

Action

For students doing this action scene, encourage them to first find and recreate the actual historical

◉ Conduct a review and evaluation

In this Phase of Unit 7, your students should have had the opportunity to express what they have learned about Fascism & Fundamentals through one or more various creative selections of their own choosing. These include:

- Linguistics;
- Art;
- Music;
- Drama;
- Movement;
- Conceptual Design.

Record student hours: _____

Assess student effort in the creative expressions, as individuals or as teams.

Create an evaluation system of your own, or refer to the evaluation rubric in the introduction, as a tool for assessing participation. The categories you will probably find most useful for evaluating their projects are *"Task," "Process: Teamwork," "Process: Originality,"* and Grammar, Format, and Spelling.

In this Phase especially, do not critique the self-evaluation page your student completes in the Student Manual—consider how the very soul of an artist has been exposed and vulnerable, so be encouraging and not belittling. Again, consider enthusiasm, precision of approach, and efforts toward improving skills and completing the activity, rather than rating the project as compared to a masterpiece. Instead, discuss with the student the intention of the written comments and incorporate those into your evaluation.

Determine a grade for this Phase, if using grades: _____

Teacher Self-Evaluation:

Evaluate your own use of materials and teaching opportunities: what worked and what did not; how effective was your time-management; how were your responses to the needs of your student; did you make your expectations clear; in what ways would you like to improve your approach for the next unit? Incorporate suggestions from your students in your own evaluation (*this requires humility!*).

Take a moment now to evaluate the whole unit. What would you like to remember if you taught this subject again? What do you recognize that your students gained most—either as students of history or as creative individuals? What did you learn about Fascism & Fundamentals or about teaching?

> ## Student Self-Evaluation UNIT 7, PHASE 4

Dates and hours:_____

Evaluate your projects

- What creative project did you choose?

  _____

- What did you expect from your project, and how does the final project compare to your initial expectations?

  _____
  _____

- What do you like about your project? What would you change?

  _____
  _____

In Conclusion

Revisit the three Key Concepts from the beginning of this Unit. Explain how your understanding of and appreciation for each has grown over the course of your study.

- _____
  _____
- _____
  _____
- _____
  _____

Record your concluding thoughts on Fascism & Fundamentals.

_____
_____
_____
_____

318 Fascism & Fundamentals (1915–1938)

World War II & Miraculous Deliverances (1939–1945)

Pray with the students at the beginning of each Unit.

Enthusiasm and delight are the best ways to capture a student's interest and jump-start motivation, so:

» **For the Auditory Students:** To capture their attention at the very beginning of class, play a musical selection from World War II, such as "The Boogie Woogie Bugle Boy of Company B." You can find a link at the online resource page to a video clip of the Andrews Sisters singing their hit song in Abbot and Costello's movie, *Buck Privates*.

» **For the Kinesthetic Students**: Have the students warm up as class begins by marching. Since there were different styles of marching during WWII— the Germans used the "goose step" march, while the Allies used a traditional form—perhaps your students would enjoy the challenge of creating a new type of march.

» **For the Visual Students:** Bring a picture to class of the Big Three (Churchill, FDR, Stalin) meeting at Yalta, February of 1945.

» **For the hearts of all:** Pray with them at the beginning of the Unit, that God would help them discover what He has for each one to learn in this Unit.

◉ Learning Style Emphasis

Teachers can choose to have students do one or two activities, rather than the entire week's schedule. Please use what works for you in your unique setting.

	Week 1: Feeler	Week 2: Thinker	Week 3: Sensor	Week 4: Intuitor
	During this week, students will be introduced to World War II & Miraculous Deliverances, along with the appropriate Scriptures. You may follow this suggested schedule or adapt it to meet your students' needs:	Students will explore topics of interest through research and reporting, learn new vocabulary, and construct a time line relating to World War II & Miraculous Deliverances.	Students will gain cultural understanding through sensory activities as they explore interrelated subject areas through sensory activities pertaining to World War II & Miraculous Deliverances.	Students, through creative self-expression, using one or more creative activities, will present some aspect of what they have learned in the past three weeks relating to WWII & Miraculous Deliverances. Areas of expression include linguistics, art, music, drama, movement, and conceptual design.)
Monday	Informally discuss the Key Concepts Listen to the *What in the World?* audio recording(s)	Choose topic and begin research	Create a map and discuss the issues in teams	Choose an area of expression and begin work either individually or in teams
Tuesday	Read the article Listen to the other audio recording(s) Read the Scriptures		Examine and discuss art masterpieces & architectural structures	
Wednesday	Recap the material using activities Talk together	Practice vocabulary	Do an art project*	
Thursday	Conduct class discussion	Construct the time line	Do a science experiment or field trip**	
Friday	Choose books of interest/Internet search Conduct a review and evaluation	Complete research projects and share in class or hand in Conduct a review and evaluation	Listen to and discuss the music Cook the food listed in the recipe Conduct a review and evaluation	Share creative expressions in class Conduct a review and evaluation

*Art project will need to be planned ahead of time to acquire materials.
** Field trip will require extra planning time.

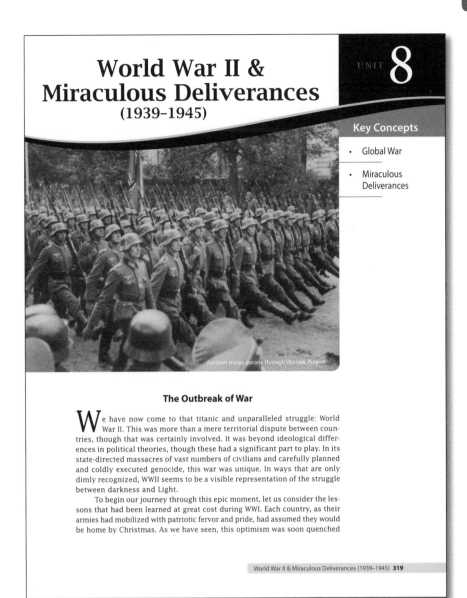

World War II & Miraculous Deliverances
(1939–1945)

Key Concepts

- Global War

- Miraculous Deliverances

German troops parade through Warsaw, Poland

The Outbreak of War

We have now come to that titanic and unparalleled struggle: World War II. This was more than a mere territorial dispute between countries, though that was certainly involved. It was beyond ideological differences in political theories, though these had a significant part to play. In its state-directed massacres of vast numbers of civilians and carefully planned and coldly executed genocide, this war was unique. In ways that are only dimly recognized, WWII seems to be a visible representation of the struggle between darkness and Light.

To begin our journey through this epic moment, let us consider the lessons that had been learned at great cost during WWI. Each country, as their armies had mobilized with patriotic fervor and pride, had assumed they would be home by Christmas. As we have seen, this optimism was soon quenched

World War II & Miraculous Deliverances (1939–1945) **319**

◉ Informally discuss the Key Concepts with your students

KEY CONCEPTS Background Information

These are the main objectives of the Unit. As you proceed through the four weeks, your students will be given various ways of understanding each of these objectives. Explanations of these Key Concepts follow.

8

by the mind-numbing horrors of a *war of attrition* (reducing an army through sustained attack) where millions died. The first lesson learned: don't go to war unless absolutely necessary, and only with the greatest reluctance, because the cost in human lives and shattered economies is entirely too high. The second lesson, learned in the trenches: create an impregnable line which would hold back the enemy, since defenders suffered fewer losses and attackers were nearly always at their mercy in a stationary war. The third lesson Germany had learned to its great dismay: do not fight a war on two fronts. With enemies on either side, you will not be able to marshal all of your resources to win on either front. As they had learned in WWI, trying to fight between two fronts is a lose-lose proposition. Despite this knowledge, a mix of new factors and old forces would eventually cause Germany to forget the lessons.

Mussolini and Hitler, who formed the Rome-Berlin Axis, both preached to their nations a doctrine of war.

In the previous Unit, we learned that one of the tenets of fascism was a belief in the value of war—that it was a glorious undertaking allowing humanity to struggle for the survival of the fittest. Mussolini and Hitler, who formed the Rome-Berlin Axis, both preached to their nations a doctrine of war, though it would bear bitter fruit. However, with memories of WWI clearly etched in the public mind, other European and American political leaders sought to do everything within their means to pull back from the brink of war—despite the menacing gestures of Adolf Hitler and his Nazi war machine. The United States, attempting to reestablish its prior position of political isolationism, passed a series of Neutrality Acts in the 1930s to insure that America would not be drawn again into a foreign war.

On 25 October 1936, the Axis between Germany and Italy was formally declared.

Great Britain and France, the most powerful European opponents of fascism, sought to pacify Hitler's unrelenting demands through what is known as *appeasement*. Seeking to pacify Hitler as he furiously claimed the right to rule over Germans regardless of current international boundaries, the British and French did nothing to stop Hitler when he goose-stepped into Austria in March 1938. He swallowed the German-speaking nation whole, despite the provision of the Treaty of Versailles specifically forbidding merging Germany and Austria into one nation. Six months later, with ever increasing appetite, Hitler required that the German-speaking western region of Czechoslovakia be allowed to join Nazi Germany—or else. In a meeting with Hitler, Mussolini and the prime ministers of Great Britain

320 World War II & Miraculous Deliverances (1939–1945)

? To get an informal discussion started on this Key Concept, ask a simple, leading question, such as, "What countries do you think were involved in World War II?"

Global War— EXPLANATION

It can be hard to fathom how many nations and individuals were affected by WWII. Often, in connection with this war, we read about Germany, Great Britain, Japan, and the United States. However, numerous nations were invaded and many supplied soldiers to the cause. To better understand this, consider the following list and those countries affected, whether as the aggressor or the invaded.

Hitler's aggression: 1936–38

Germany, Austria, Czechoslovakia

Invasion of Poland and its aftermath: 1939

Germany, USSR, Poland, Estonia, Latvia, Lithuania, Finland

Blitzkrieg in Western Europe: 1940

Germany, Denmark, Norway, Holland, Belgium, Luxembourg, France, Iceland (occupied by Britain)

Battle of Britain: 1940–41

Germany, Great Britain

War in North Africa: 1940–43

Italy, Germany, Great Britain, Libya, Egypt, Tunisia, Morocco, Algeria

8

and France signed the Munich Agreement. It formally permitted Germany to acquire the Sudetenland, which contained not only a large number of German-speaking people but the industrial centers and defense fortifications of Czechoslovakia, as well. Though this small nation was free to reject their decision and defend itself from Nazi attack, the Munich Agreement stated decisively that they would be on their own—their former allies would no longer come to their aid. In October 1938, the feat was accomplished when Germany *occupied* the region (took control of the area through military conquest), but as many had feared, that was not sufficient to satisfy Hitler's appetite. The following March, he consumed the remainder of Czechoslovakia.

These were acts of international bullying, using intimidation and threat to gain what was desired. However, to many in Western Europe, the land lost in the eastern part of Europe seemed to be of no significant importance. To those with limited vision, the loss of Czechoslovakia was a small price to pay for peace and not comparable to losing a Western European country like Belgium or France. By allowing Hitler to have what he wanted, war was avoided and peace was prolonged.

The Nazi menace was now contained, or, at least, that was the great hope.

At that moment, as "peace in our time" was being wildly celebrated by many in Great Britain, it may have seemed that, with the occupation of Austria and Czechoslovakia, the Nazis would have to be satisfied. Great Britain and France had guaranteed Poland's borders, and if Hitler marched much further east, he would run right into Stalin—who had proven at least to his own people to be as diabolical a bully as Hitler, if not greater. And Hitler would surely not dare to try these tactics in the West, since the heavily fortified and impregnable Maginot Line of France, which covered the entire border between France and Germany, would stop him in his tracks. The Nazi menace was now contained, or, at least, that was the great hope.

This optimistic outlook shattered when a *non-aggression pact* (treaty to avoid war) was signed in August 1939, between two most unlikely allies: the Nazi leadership of Germany and the communist leadership of the Soviet Union. Suddenly, the communists were no longer a threat to the Nazis in the East, and the Nazis were no longer protecting Western Europe from communism. Fears of what this might mean to all of Europe escalated, but the country most immediately concerned in this new threat was Poland, who dwelt between the two voracious nations. Armed with old-fashioned weapons, horses, and nineteenth century ideas of battle, the Polish army was no match for the September 1 invasion by the Nazis, with their finely honed strategy of *blitzkrieg* (lightning war) utilizing the most up-to-date weapons, tanks, and airplanes. Recognizing that this assault broke Hitler's previous promises, Great Britain's prime minister issued an ultimatum to warn that, if they did not withdraw, Britain and France would fulfill their pledge to defend Poland. On September 3, they declared war on Germany.

World War II & Miraculous Deliverances (1939–1945) **321**

War in East Africa: 1940–41

Italy, Ethiopia, Italian Somaliland, Eritrea, Kenya, Sudan, British Somaliland

Invasion of Balkans: 1940–41

Italy, Germany, Bulgaria, Albania, Greece, Yugoslavia

War in Russia: 1941–44

Germany, Romania, Hungary, Finland, Slovakia, USSR

War in Pacific: 1941–45

Japan, US, China, Britain, Australia, Dutch East Indies (Indonesia), Malaya, New Guinea, Ceylon (Sri Lanka), India, Philippines, Timor, Hong Kong, Singapore

War in Asia: 1940–45

Japan, Laos, French Indochina (Vietnam, Cambodia), Thailand

War in Middle East: 1940–45

Italy, Palestine (Israel), Britain, USSR, Iran, Iraq, Syria, Lebanon

War in Mediterranean: 1943–45

Britain, US, Sicily, Italy

Normandy Invasion: 1944

France, Germany, Britain, US, Canada

Beyond these, there were also a number of nations who provided soldiers for the battlefields, including Bahrain, Brazil, Fiji, Nepal, New Zealand, Oman, Rhodesia (Zimbabwe), South Africa, and Transjordan.

8

Please refer to the table **Axis Actions Leading to Outbreak of War** (below).

War Begins in Europe and North Africa

Hitler's angry response to this declaration of war was one of blame and resentment toward Britain. In proclamations to the German people and to the army, he said, "Great Britain has for centuries pursued the aim of rendering the peoples of Europe defenseless against the British policy of world conquest . . . . The British Government, driven on by those warmongers whom we knew in the last war, have resolved to let fall their mask and to proclaim war on a threadbare pretext."

Though England had pledged to aid Poland, France had specifically promised, in the Franco-Polish Military Convention of May 19, 1939, "France will launch an offensive action against Germany with the bulk of her forces, starting on the fifteenth day after the first day of the general French mobilization." This offensive was not launched, much to the bitter dismay of the Polish people. This was partly because the French were fearful of experiencing a return of the nightmare of WWI, and partly because by September 15 the Polish army was nearly defeated and western Poland was effectively in Nazi hands.

In a surprising move that stunned the world, the Soviet Union invaded eastern Poland on September 17. Aware that this action would cause a diplomatic firestorm, the Soviets considered how they could justify themselves

Axis Actions Leading to Outbreak of War

Country	1931–1933	1934–1935	1936
Germany	**1931:** German millionaire finances Nazi party with 800,000 members. **1933:** Hitler appointed Chancellor, granted dictatorial powers. **1933:** Boycott of Jews begins.	**1934:** Hitler is voted Führer. **1935:** Enactment of Nuremberg Laws against Jews.	Germany remilitarizes the Rhine, breaking Treaty of Versailles—France & England do nothing.
Italy		**1935:** Italy invades Ethiopia in a brutal display of power, despite League of Nations declaring Italy to be the aggressor and imposing sanctions.	Mussolini & Hitler form Rome-Berlin Axis. Ethiopia is annexed by Italy.
Japan	**1931:** Japan seizes a city in Manchuria, in northern China, and begins to extend its domination. **1932:** Japan sets up "protectorate" over Manchuria, now called Manchukuo. America protests. **1933:** Japan withdraws from League of Nations.	**1934:** Japan renounces treaties with US (1922 & 1930) limiting naval armament.	Germany signs Anti-Comintern Pact with Japan (anti-communism).

322 World War II & Miraculous Deliverances (1939–1945)

? To get an informal discussion started on this Key Concept, ask a simple, leading question, such as, "Is God's presence seen even in very difficult times, such as WWII?"

Miraculous Deliverances— EXPLANATION:

There were a number of instances when nations battling Nazi and Japanese aggression during WWII experienced such amazing protection and "coincidences" that people of the time termed the situations "miraculous."

Though it is impossible for us as finite humans to thoroughly plumb the depths of God's miracles in human history, there is much we can discover about His ways in various events as we examine unusual timing, weather factors, out-of-character decisions, and the right people being in the right place at the right time.

Here are a few examples of this during certain events of World War II:

Dunkirk—essential to Britain's survival

The sea: According to Walter Lord, author of *The Miracle of Dunkirk*, "The English Channel is usually rough, rarely behaves for very long. Yet a calm sea was essential to the evacuation, and during the nine days of Dunkirk the Channel was a millpond. Old-timers still say they have never seen it so smooth."

and not appear to be co-aggressors with the Nazis. Among captured German papers from WWII was a dispatch from the Soviet Foreign Minister, V. Molotov, in which he wrote, "The Soviet Government intended to justify its procedure as follows: The Polish State had disintegrated and no longer existed; therefore, all agreements concluded with Poland were void; third powers might try to profit by the chaos which had arisen; the Soviet Government considered itself obligated to intervene to protect its Ukrainian and White Russian brothers and make it possible for these unfortunate people to **work in peace**." (emphasis added) This was the fourth time that Russia and Germany had partitioned Poland, but this occupation would provide the time and place for the unbelievable: the systematic destruction of the Jews (and others considered to be "sub-humans") on a scope never envisioned before.

In a surprising move that stunned the world, the Soviet Union invaded eastern Poland on September 17.

The Soviets, in a secret agreement with the Nazis, were authorized to move beyond the boundaries of eastern Poland and to take—with German approval and support—the Baltic nations of Estonia, Latvia, and Lithuania. From that position of strength, they launched an attack on Finland, who did not tamely submit to Russian occupation but fought vigorously to hold on to their lands. This "Winter War" was ultimately won by the USSR, but the poor showing by the Soviet military gave Hitler hope that, when he chose to attack the communist state—his ultimate enemy—the Nazis would easily triumph.

In the meantime, people in the West were incensed over the victories Hitler and Stalin were winning in Poland, the Baltic states, and Finland. It

1937	1938	1939
Germany & Italy assist nationalistic forces under General Franco in Spain during the Spanish Civil War, which begins in 1936 and continues until 1939.	**Mar:** Germany takes Austria in what is known as the Anschluss. **Sep:** Munich Agreement between Germany, France, and England allows Germany to have Sudetenland in Czechoslovakia. **Oct:** Germany occupies Sudetenland.	**Mar:** Germany takes the rest of Czechoslovakia. **Aug:** Non-aggression pact between Germany & USSR includes a division of Eastern Europe between them. **Sep:** Hitler invades Poland, beginning WWII.
Italy joins Anti-Comintern Pact with Germany and Japan. Italy withdraws from League of Nations.	Anti-Jewish laws enacted in Italy.	**Apr:** Italy invades Albania.
Japan, under new premier, begins aggressive war policy. It seizes Beijing, Shanghai, Nanjing, Tianjin, and Hangzhou—massacring Chinese civilians in Nanjing during the process. Japanese planes sink US gunboat in Chinese waters.	Japanese retake Qingdao and occupy Guangzhou and Hankou.	US cancels Japanese trade agreement of 1911, leaving Japan economically vulnerable because it depends heavily upon foreign imports and exports.

The sky: Cloud cover protected the beaches of Dunkirk for much of the evacuation.

Hitler: He ordered the panzers to stop only ten miles from Dunkirk, when nothing could have stopped them from completely cutting off an escape by sea for the BEF and French forces. Walter Lord remarked, "If Hitler was secretly trying to let the British go home, he was slicing it awfully thin. He almost failed and caught them all."

The Luftwaffe: At this point in the war, the fighter pilots' job was simply to cover the bombers, not to strafe the beaches. Because of this, thousands

more survived to come home than would have been possible.

Midway—turning point of the war in the Pacific

Lack of vital information prior to June 4: Japanese reconnaissance of Pearl Harbor canceled due to refueling site difficulties, and submarine patrols delayed due to maintenance issues in Japan.

Failed air search on June 4: One Japanese ship's catapult (to launch planes) experienced mechanical difficulties, delaying the launch for thirty vital minutes. Another scouting plane from a different ship was forced to return due to engine difficulties.

8

was clear that the Nazis and Soviets were the aggressors in this war, but it was not entirely clear what they would dare to do next. Many of Hitler's stated plans (written in his autobiography, *Mein Kampf*) dealt with the need for "living space" in the East for German farmers, which, supposedly, he had now acquired. In addition, Hitler had sworn time and time again to respect the neutrality of the Netherlands, Belgium, and Luxembourg. If the neutrality of these buffer states was going to be respected, and with the powerful French Maginot Line in place, the Germans had no obvious entry point into France—though it was doubtful that Hitler would stand upon ceremony if he decided to invade the West.

In fact, one month after Finland had submitted to the Soviets, the Germans moved swiftly north to capture Denmark and Norway. The Danish king surrendered immediately to the Nazis, while his brother, the Norwegian king, refused. The Norwegians provided a staunch resistance to the German invasion, holding out in certain regions of the country for two months, until Norwegian troops in the north finally surrendered to the Nazis.

> *One month after Finland had submitted to the Soviets, the Germans moved swiftly north to capture Denmark and Norway.*

With Austria, Czechoslovakia, Poland, Denmark, and a hopelessly outgunned Norway in his hands, Hitler turned to his next objective. The small nations standing between the Nazis and France were but a mere appetizer for the main French course. Belgium, like any small animal confronted with a hungry predator, tried to avoid provoking Hitler to attack. They stiffly held to their neutrality. The Netherlands, regarded as "Fortress Holland" with its water barriers and fortified eastern front, was believed to be well defended. The total number of French, British, Dutch, and Belgian divisions and tanks was nearly equal to the German divisions and tanks massing across the border, yet three things would prove to be fatal flaws in the way the West prepared for Hitler's attack: 1) neutrality, 2) lack of unified command, and 3) outdated theories of battle.

First, neutrality—as a neutral country, Belgium could not have foreign troops staged within her borders. They had to keep the formidable British and French armies waiting just across the border in France until Hitler attacked, though this would greatly delay desperately needed help to fend off the invasion. Second, command—significantly, while the Germans were being commanded by those who had formulated a brilliant and unexpected plan of attack, the western Allies were merely trying to hold back the deluge, whenever or wherever it came. Third, theories—the French, British, Dutch, and Belgian military commanders were still operating under WWI ideas, not recognizing that tanks, airplanes, and mechanized forces were about to transform the rules of war.

On May 10, the day that Winston Churchill became the new prime minister of Great Britain, the expected attack occurred on Belgium, Luxembourg,

Unbelievable timing: Just as the Japanese air carriers were refueling and rearming their aircraft—an effort that would take only a few minutes—a squadron of dive-bombers from the USS Enterprise found them, destroying three air carriers in six minutes.

El Alamein—turning point of the war in the West

Water in the desert: From the book *Rees Howells: Intercessor* comes an amazing story:

> Between Rommel's men and Alexandria were the remnants of a British army—fifty tanks, a few score field guns, and about 5,000 soldiers. The sides were equally matched, with the Germans holding the advantage, because of their superior 88mm guns. Both armies were near exhaustion from heat, dust and lack of water. The battle was grim. In the words of Major Rainer: "The sun was almost overhead, and our men were fast reaching the end of their endurance, when the Nazis broke. Ten minutes more and it might have been us.
>
> "Slowly, sullenly the Mark IV tanks lumbered back from their battle smoke. And then an incredible thing happened: 1,100 men of

8

and the Netherlands, despite Hitler's promises to respect their neutrality. While the French and British armies rushed across the border to confront the enemy divisions smashing through Belgian defenses, the Nazis did what no one had foreseen—they moved their tanks across Luxembourg through the heavily wooded and hilly Ardennes Forest to the border of France. Conventional strategy considered the Ardennes to be just an extension of the Maginot Line because this terrain would be too densely forested and difficult for tanks. The Nazis' decision to cross there was a brilliant strategy. Simply stated, the Allies, who had not foreseen this possibility, did not have a sufficient deterrent waiting on the other side to stop them. William Shirer, eyewitness journalist to WWII and the author of *The Rise and Fall of the Third Reich*, wrote of this moment:

Winston Churchill—prime minister of Great Britain

> May 14, the avalanche broke. An army of tanks unprecedented in warfare for size, concentration, mobility and striking power, when it had started through the Ardennes Forest from the German frontier on May 10 stretched in three columns back **for a hundred miles** far behind the Rhine, broke through the French Ninth and Second armies and headed swiftly for the Channel, behind the Allied forces in Belgium. This was a formidable and frightening juggernaut. Preceded by waves of Stuka dive bombers . . . this phalanx of steel and fire could not be stopped by any means in the hands of the bewildered defenders. (emphasis added)

The French and British armies in Belgium were now trapped between two powerful German armies. When the Belgians laid down their arms and surrendered to the Nazis, it appeared that all was lost. In fact, on May 15, Churchill received a call from the French prime minister, who declared, "We have been defeated! We are beaten!" The mobile German tanks, known as *panzers*, that had blazed across the west to the English Channel were now only ten miles from Dunkirk, the last remaining Channel port from which the Allies might evacuate—and no defense stood between them. Yet, in the midst of what looked like certain defeat, something absolutely amazing occurred—the evacuation of nearly the entire British Expeditionary Force from Dunkirk, along with more than one hundred thousand other Allied soldiers, despite attempts by the Nazis to stop it.

The French and British armies in Belgium were now trapped between two powerful German armies.

the 90th Light Panzer Division, the elite of the Afrika Korps, came stumbling across the barren sand with their hands in the air. Cracked and black with coagulated blood, their swollen tongues were protruding from their mouths. Crazily they tore water bottles from the necks of our men and poured life-giving swallows between their parched lips."

Major Rainer then goes on to give this reason for their surrender. The Germans had been twenty-four hours without water when they overran the British defenses and found a 6-inch water pipe. They shot holes in it and drank deeply. Only when they had taken great gulps did they realize that it was **sea** water! The pipe had only just been laid and Major Rainer had started to test it. Fresh water, however, was never used for tests on pipes—it was too precious. "Two days later it would have been full of fresh water . . . . The Nazis didn't detect the salt at once, because their sense of taste had already been anesthetized by the brackish water they had been used to, and by thirst.

8

Lifeboats evacuating Allied soldiers at Dunkirk

At the time, this was acknowledged far and wide as a miracle because the circumstances which allowed these Allied soldiers to escape certain capture seemed unexplainable by human reasoning. It was certainly beyond the understanding of the German soldiers fuming angrily and helplessly at Hitler's demand that they suddenly stop their panzers ten miles short of success. However, in the book *Rees Howells: Intercessor*, by Norman Grubb, a window into the power of prayer is given against the backdrop of this miraculous moment in history. At the Bible College of Wales, as students and faculty sought God in prayer and intercession on behalf of the trapped Allied soldiers and for England, who would be open and helpless with this army captured, Rees Howells told those gathered on May 20, "The next 24 hours will be the crisis in this great battle. They are ready to take our country at any moment. Even before lunchtime the history of the world may be changed. Such a thing as this has not happened to us before, and you do not know how much faith is needed. We are coming to the Lord this morning and telling Him our eyes are on Him today. Unless He intervenes, we are lost."

> *At the Bible College of Wales, students and faculty sought God in prayer and intercession on behalf of the trapped Allied soldiers and for England.*

Mr. Howells, who had long experience of praying for difficult, even impossible, situations, was well equipped at this point to pray according to 1 John 5:14–15 for the situation developing at Dunkirk: "Now this is the confidence that we have in Him, that if we ask anything according to His will, He hears us. And if we know that He hears us, whatever we ask, we know that we have the petitions that we have asked of Him." Because he had come to a place of such experience with God, he had faith to believe that, through prayer and intercession, God could actually change an individual's—or a nation's—life.

Though there is much about this subject that is beyond our understanding, yet we have clues from Scripture. Jesus described for us the significance of faith in releasing the dynamic power of prayer when He said in Matthew 17:20, "For assuredly, I say to you, if you have faith as a mustard seed, you will say to this mountain, 'Move from here to there,' and it will move; and nothing will be impossible for you." As the *intercessors* (those who petition God on behalf of others) at the Bible College of Wales learned during WWII, and as all who have experienced praying and interceding can attest, God does hear and answer prayers. His answers seldom come, though, in the way or the timing that we expect. He is not, after all, a vending machine dispensing candy-wrapped answers for our dollar's worth of

The surrender of those 1,100 crack soldiers may have been the deciding incident in the battle." Such an incredible happening as this cannot be treated as a mere coincidence. Assuredly the hand of Almighty God is in evidence once more, coming to our aid when weighty issues are in the balance.

D-Day in Normandy— Operation Overlord

Opposing views: Runstedt, the German Commander-in-Chief of the West, and Rommel, Field Marshal in charge of defending the Atlantic coast, disagreed on the right approach to an Allied invasion. Runstedt thought they should defeat the Allies on the field, Rommel thought they should prevent the Allies from gaining the beaches. Hitler chose a

8

prayer, but the Creator and Redeemer, the One described in Romans 11:33: "Oh, the depth of the riches both of the wisdom and knowledge of God! How unsearchable are His judgments and His ways past finding out!"

While Great Britain's army was saved, France fell before the onslaught of the Nazi blitzkrieg. On June 22, after six weeks of fighting, the French government agreed to German terms for an armistice. This quick defeat was utterly shocking to the rest of the world. According to British military expert B. H. Liddell Hart in his book on the Second World War, France had the ability to mobilize five *million* trained men. With its size, strength, and its planned defenses, France had been seen as the only army on the continent who could stand against the Nazi menace. Remember that during WWI, despite the unrelenting slaughter on the battlefields of France, for four years the French army had held the line against Germany. Now, unbelievably, in less than two *months*, the war was over for the French. The armistice directed that France be divided into "Occupied" territory in the north (including Paris and the entire Atlantic coast) and "Unoccupied" territory in the south (including its colonial territories) with the capital at Vichy. From June 1940 to November 1942, WWI hero Marshal Pétain and his Vichy government cooperated and collaborated with the Nazis. Eventually, the Germans occupied the entire nation.

While Great Britain's army was saved, France fell before the onslaught of the Nazi blitzkrieg.

After only a matter of weeks, Great Britain was the last European power left to fight. International diplomatic pressure mounted for them to come to peaceful terms with Germany in order to bring about a quick end to the war. When the King of Sweden, a neutral, urged Churchill toward a negotiated peace with Hitler, Churchill replied, "Before any such requests or proposals could even be considered, it would be necessary that effective guarantees by deeds, not words, should be forthcoming from Germany which would ensure the restoration of the free and independent life of Czechoslovakia, Poland, Norway, Denmark, Holland, Belgium and above all, France."

It is fascinating to consider that, according to William Shirer who was resident in Berlin during the summer of 1940, "as I recall those summer days, everyone, especially in the Wilhelmstrasse and the Bendlerstrasse, was confident that the war was as good as over." In fact, Hitler and the German High Command had no plans in place for dealing with a combative Great Britain since they were certain it would not want to continue to fight a hopeless battle. However, by mid July, when Great Britain was not showing any willingness to come to Hitler's peace table, the Nazis began to look toward forcing their

Nazi officers parading in the deserted Foch avenue, Paris, France (1940).

"compromise" between the two—which made it impossible for either of these men to do their job.

Sleeping on the job: Hitler demanded that he be consulted before bringing in reinforcements in case of an invasion. However, he slept until late in the morning on D-Day—and his staff would not wake him up!

The deceiver deceived: Hitler would not release the 1st SS Panzer Corps from Paris to head for Normandy until the end of the day—he thought the landings were just a trick to turn the Nazis' eyes away from the real invasion force.

Fooled by the weather: Rommel, the man who wanted to stop the Allies on the beaches, thought that the stormy weather would keep the Allies from invading on June 6. Therefore, he took a quick trip to Germany to confer with Hitler and attend his wife's birthday.

Away from their posts: The German commander of that part of Normandy was in Brittany, the commander of the reserve panzer corps was in Belgium, and another key commander was also away from his unit.

Take the time to talk with your students about God's work in the world, even during times of catastrophe and terror. Recount to one another some of the specific ways each of you have seen God's provision, His timing, or His answers to prayer. This might be an excellent time to encourage students to keep a prayer journal, in which they record their specific prayers and God's specific answers.

8

hand. The German Navy Commander-in-Chief was convinced "that Britain can be made to ask for peace simply by cutting off her import trade by means of submarine warfare, air attacks on convoys and heavy air attacks on her main centers."

Though they were the dominant sea power in the world, the island nation lagged behind Germany in air power—and it was in the air that Hitler looked first to bend Great Britain to his will. The Battle of Britain, though terrifying to many in England, did not succeed according to Hitler's plans. The British kept a stiff upper lip; the children, hidden away in the country, played pretend war games; and British pilots and coastal radar operators kept a round-the-clock vigil over their nation. After several months of bombing raids, Hitler—like Napoleon before him—recognized the difficulty of trying to subdue Britain and cancelled the invasion plans for the moment.

> *After several months of bombing raids, Hitler recognized the difficulty of trying to subdue Britain and cancelled the invasion plans for the moment.*

The other battle which held out more promise for the Germans was the Battle of the Atlantic, where German submarines began the work of cutting off Britain's supply line of food and armaments, sinking merchant ships and their escorts as rapidly as possible. This battle continued to the bitter end, though after May 1943, the Allies began to get the upper hand.

In the meantime, Great Britain was the only Western European democracy left in this struggle against Hitler. Many in the United States, during the summer of 1940, believed that the British would need to come to terms with the Nazis and end the war as quickly as possible. This was a comforting thought for the pacifists and for those who believed isolationism to be the best policy for America. However, others in the country recognized that Hitler had world-wide dominion in his sights. They sought to wake the country up to the dangers of war-mongering fascism, which would not be satisfied with merely swallowing Europe.

Wanting to join in the fascist military triumphs of Nazi Germany but determined to wage his own *magnificent war*, Mussolini attacked the British colony of Somaliland in Africa in August, British-held Egypt in September, and Greece in October. This was a mistake, as, in each case, he found that his armies were not able to gain the glorious victory he had envisioned. In fact, he was defeated, sooner or later, by everyone he attacked.

Authors John Harrison and Richard Sullivan, in their book *A Short History of Western Civilization*, wrote about Italy's attacks in Africa:

> To meet this threat, Churchill made one of the most daring and farsighted military moves in history. Believing Suez to be the most strategic spot in the world in a global war, he sent half of Britain's scarce supply of tanks and artillery [Britain had left much of its land armaments in Dunkirk during the evacuation of June 1940] around Africa to Egypt while the

8

Nazis stood poised across the channel for the invasion of Great Britain . . . . During the winter of 1940–41 the fascist armies moving on Egypt were completely destroyed by light mobile British forces. Mussolini's bubble had burst with a feeble plop. Henceforth he was hardly more than a prisoner of the German forces that were sent to save him.

While Mussolini was seeking to revive the glory of ancient Rome through war, Hitler was busy drawing Balkan and Eastern European countries into partnership with the Axis powers. For their own unique reasons, several countries (Romania, Hungary, Slovakia, Bulgaria, and Yugoslavia) surrendered to the pressure of Hitler's forceful demands. But in the case of Yugoslavia, the army revolted against this. A new leader, the seventeen-year-old King Peter, was declared to have come of age, and as a strong anti-Nazi, he opposed the pact with Hitler.

This minor revolt against the Nazis infuriated Hitler. Having already committed to two Mediterranean actions—assisting the Italians in Libya with General Rommel's Afrika Korps and aiding Italy by invading Greece—Hitler decisively added a new name to his hit list, Yugoslavia. Marching through the Balkan peninsula, the Nazis quickly gained victories over the Greeks and Yugoslavs. And, yet, since they did not conquer the hearts of the people in these lands, a fierce resistance, which would eventually tie up large numbers of Axis soldiers, began to take root in fertile soil.

Please refer to the table **War in Europe/Africa** (p. 330).

A fierce resistance, which would eventually tie up large numbers of Axis soldiers, began to take root in fertile soil.

General Rommel

A Global Conflict

What motivated Hitler? Though complex, twisted, and a deceiver of epic proportions, yet one foundational determination remained crystal clear throughout his career: he had an obsessive hatred of Jews and communists; he was determined to put an end to their existence. Slavic peoples, such as the Poles, Czechs, and Russians, were considered only slightly better, fit to be slaves to their Aryan masters. It would be in Poland that all this hatred and prejudice would focus on its final solution.

Shortly after the 1939 invasion of Poland, Hitler informed his staff about the future of this captive nation. Quoting from the diary of Franz Halder, head of the German Army General Staff: "We have no intention of rebuilding Poland . . . . Not to be a model state by

8

German standards. Polish intelligentsia must be prevented from establishing itself as a governing class. Low standard of living must be conserved . . . . Cheap slaves . . . . Total disorganization must be created! The Reich will give the Governor General the means to carry out this devilish plan." The Governor General, Hans Frank, by May 1940, was able to show just how this goal was being accomplished, having already murdered thousands of Polish intellectuals. He justified this by claiming Hitler's orders, "The men capable of leadership in Poland must be liquidated. Those following them . . . must be eliminated in their turn. There is no need to burden the Reich

War in Europe/Africa

Axis Victory ■ **Allied Victory** ▢ **Soviet Victory** ▢ **Event** ☐

Fronts	Eastern		Western	Southern
Sep–Dec 1939	**Sep 1:** Hitler invades western Poland, campaign lasts 4 weeks. **Sep 28:** Warsaw surrenders. **Oct 6:** Nazis annex W. Poland.	**Sep 17:** USSR invades eastern Poland. **Oct 6:** USSR takes E. Poland. **Oct 10:** Baltic nations accept USSR. **Nov 30:** USSR attacks Finland.	**Sep 3:** UK & France declare war on Germany; US remains neutral. **Sep 10:** 158,000 troops in British Expeditionary Force to France. **Sep–Mar:** Dubbed "Phony War" by journalists.	
Jan–May 1940	Western Poland under control of Nazis, who quickly begin forcing Jews into Jewish ghettos and building concentration camps.	**Feb 1:** USSR launches new assault on Finland. **Mar 6:** Finland sues for peace.	**Apr:** Germans take Denmark, begin invasion of Norway—Br & Fr troops join Norwegian troops, but Allies decide to evacuate. **May:** Germany begins Western Offensive against Belgium (2 weeks) & Netherlands (4 days); BEF rescued from Dunkirk (abandon equipment).	
Jun–Dec 1940		USSR controls Baltic and eastern Poland, under terms of German-Soviet non-aggression pact.	**Jun:** Germans launch new offensive into France (6 weeks). **Jun 10:** Mussolini declares war on UK & France. **Jun 22:** Armistice between France & Germany (Vichy Regime in S. France).	**Oct:** Italy attacks Greece, defeated by Greek forces. **Nov:** Hitler draws Romania, Hungary, Slovakia into Axis.
Jan–May 1941			Much of European continent now under the control of the Nazis.	**Mar:** Bulgaria & Yugoslavia join Axis—Yugoslavian coup d'état reverses this. **Apr:** Germans take Yugoslavia (11 days) & Greece (3 weeks). **May:** Germans successfully invade island of Crete (1 week).

330 World War II & Miraculous Deliverances (1939–1945)

8

with this . . . no need to send these elements to Reich concentration camps."
This was just the beginning of terrors in Poland.

Part of the philosophical theory behind invading eastward was to create "living space" for German farmers. In order to do that, nearly all of the Jews and many of the Poles were driven from their homes in areas annexed by Germany. Jewish *ghettos* (isolated or segregated areas) were set up in various places around the region, and the Jews of Poland and, increasingly, ofoccupied Europe were forced into them. This herding of Jews into confined and controlled spaces would make it much easier for the Nazis when the day came to eliminate them.

African	Naval	Air
	Six-year Battle of the Atlantic begins as German U-boats sink a liner, British naval ships, and merchant ships.	
	By end of March: U-boats have sunk more than 400 British, Allied, and neutral ships.	**Jan**: British coastal command airplanes are fitted with radar detection sets—to be used to find German U-boats. **May**: Luftwaffe flies more than 1,000 sorties in support of Western Offensive.
Aug: Italy overruns British Somaliland. **Sep**: Italy attacks Egypt from Libya, threatening British interests in Suez Canal. **Jun**: British attack Vichy forces in Syria, defeat them in 6 days. **Dec–Feb '41**: British offensive against Italians in Libya. First land victory of British against Axis in WWII.	**By end of December**: U-boats in Battle of Atlantic have sunk nearly 900 British, Allied, and neutral ships.	**Jul–May '41**: Battle of Britain—German bombing campaign before invasion. **Jul 10–Aug 12**: Ports & shipping. **Aug 13–Sep 6**: Airfields & factories. **Sep 7–end Sep**: Air raids on cities. **Oct–May '41**: *The Blitz*—Night bombings of London & industrial centers.
Mar–Apr: German Gen. Rommel recaptures Libya—except Tobruk, which is held by Australian troops. **May**: Rommel breaks through British lines and reaches El Alamein, 200 miles from Suez Canal.	**Mar**: Battle of Cape Matapan near Greece; Italy routed by British ships. **May**: The *Bismarck* sunk by British.	**Feb–Mar**: RAF begin regular night bombings of industrial targets in Germany.

World War II & Miraculous Deliverances (1939–1945) **331**

8

Corrie ten Boom

At the time of the invasion, the Jewish population in Poland was three and a half million—one of the largest concentrations of Jews in the world. Tragically, more than three million of these Polish Jews would die through the Nazi *Holocaust*. This planned destruction of Jews, Gypsies, and others included massacres, starvation, and death marches, as well as the thoroughly evil but efficiently planned concentration and extermination camps in Poland, Germany, and throughout German occupied Europe.

The Holocaust was brutality and cruelty beyond what civilization had ever envisioned. It was a diabolical hell on earth for millions of people. It is vital for us to not minimize the reality of the Holocaust. And it is even more vital that we recognize the reality of Scripture. Psalm 139:7–8 says, "Where can I go from Your Spirit? Or where can I flee from Your presence? If I ascend into heaven, You are there; if I make my bed in hell, behold You are there."

One who experienced both of these in full measure and wrote about it for future generations was Corrie ten Boom. An elderly Dutch woman arrested with her family for helping Jews, Corrie described her experience of God's reality as she and her sister Betsie went through unspeakable Nazi horrors. In her book *Tramp for the Lord*, she explained being transferred from a prison in Holland to Ravensbrück, the women's extermination camp in Germany.

This was the notorious women's death camp itself, the very symbol to Dutch hearts of all that was evil. As we stumbled down the hill, I felt the little Bible bumping on my back. As long as we had that, I thought, we could face even hell itself. But how could we conceal it through the inspection I knew lay ahead?

It was the middle of the night when Betsie and I reached the processing barracks. And there, under the harsh ceiling lights, we saw a dismaying sight. As each woman reached the head of the line she had to strip off every scrap of clothes, throw them all onto a pile guarded by soldiers and walk . . . past the scrutiny of a dozen guards into the shower room. Coming out of the shower room she wore only a thin regulation prison dress and a pair of shoes.

Our Bible! How could we take it past so many watchful eyes?

"Oh, Betsie!" I began—and then stopped at the sight of her pain-whitened face. As a guard strode by, I begged him in

8

German to show us the toilets. He jerked his head in the direction of the shower room. "Use the drain holes!" he snapped.

Timidly Betsie and I stepped out of line and walked forward to the huge room with its row on row of overhead spigots. It was empty. . . . A few minutes later we would return here stripped of everything we possessed. And then we saw them, stacked in a corner, a pile of old wooden benches crawling with cockroaches, but to us the furniture of heaven itself.

In an instant I had slipped the little bag over my head and, along with my woolen underwear, had stuffed it behind the benches.

And so it was that when we were herded into that room ten minutes later, we were not poor, but rich—rich in the care of Him who was God even of Ravensbruck. . . .

Before long, we were holding clandestine Bible study groups for an ever-growing group of believers, and Barracks 28 became known throughout the camp as "the crazy place, where they hope."

Yes, hoped, in spite of all that human madness could do. We had learned that a stronger power had the final word, even here.

Corrie and Betsie, living through the nightmare of the Holocaust, learned experientially that "there is no pit so deep that He is not deeper still!"

While the concentration camps and Jewish ghettos were being built, occupied, and put to their dreadful purposes, Hitler turned his malevolent eye toward his other hatred: the communists. Actually, for him they were one and the same, as he considered all Jews to be Bolsheviks (communists). Having successfully secured the European continent, he turned from the difficulties of dealing with unyielding Britain and set his sights on the USSR, despite the non-aggression pact he had so recently signed with Stalin.

On June 22, 1941, the Nazis, fresh from their victories over Greece, Yugoslavia, and Crete, launched *Operation Barbarossa*. Without warning, and to Stalin's surprise, a blitzkrieg invaded the USSR, following the same formula as had been used to such great effect in Poland and Western Europe. To many observers, it seemed that nothing could stop the German war machine—more than three million Soviet troops were taken prisoner between June and December 1941. Winston Churchill in his WWII memoirs wrote:

> Almost all responsible military opinion held that the Russian armies would soon be defeated and largely destroyed. . . . A general retirement took place on the whole twelve-hundred mile Russian

Corrie and Betsie, living through the nightmare of the Holocaust, learned experientially that "there is no pit so deep that He is not deeper still!"

8

front south of Leningrad for about four or five hundred miles. The strength of the Soviet Government, the fortitude of the Russian people, their immeasurable reserves of manpower, the vast size of their country, the rigors of the Russian winter, were the factors which ultimately ruined Hitler's armies. But none of these made themselves apparent in 1941.

What the Nazis did not know was that something had changed in their successful formula. Many historians believe that Hitler's brief swoop into the Balkans actually delayed the Nazi invasion force just long enough that they were caught unprepared in Russia by the coldest European winter of the 20th century. Some believe that the shortage of roads and abundance of mud slowed the German mechanized advance through Russia enough to prevent victory. Others point to Hitler's choice to divide his troops toward three different objectives: north, through the Baltic region to Leningrad; south to the Crimea; and directly east to Moscow. Though the Crimea was successfully occupied, Leningrad held out against the Nazis in what would become one of the epic stories of WWII, lasting 900 days until the Red Army finally lifted the siege in January 1944. And the capture of Moscow, having been significantly delayed by the Battle of Smolensk, remained a Nazi dream rather than an actual fact. In the winter of 1941–42, German officers could just make out the buildings of Moscow through their binoculars, but that was as close as they ever got. When Soviet Siberian soldiers, well equipped for winter warfare, attacked the Germans on December 5, they were able within a month to push the invaders back as much as one hundred sixty miles.

Though the Crimea was successfully occupied, Leningrad held out against the Nazis in what would become one of the epic stories of WWII.

Before this battle outside Moscow began, Germany still appeared to the rest of the world to be invincible. Hitler had announced on October 3, 1941, "I declare today, and I declare it without any reservations, that the enemy in the East has been struck down and will never rise again." Believing that the certainty of German victory over the Soviet Union provided the perfect and opportune moment for their own war program, Japan—without a declaration of war—attacked the United States at its Pacific naval base, Pearl Harbor, on the island of Oahu. December 7, 1941, was, in the words of President Roosevelt, "a day which will live in infamy." Shocked to the depth of its core, the outraged nation was now fully united behind the president in his determination to go to war.

On December 11, Germany and Italy joined Japan by declaring war on the United States. To the relief of Churchill, this brought America into a full-fledged partnership as an ally with Great Britain and her dominions. The Japanese, who were part of the Axis Powers, continued their victorious

8

surge through the Pacific, taking island after island and region after region in Asia. Within a few months, they had captured British, American, Dutch, and Australian territories, from Burma to New Guinea to the Solomon Islands. Despite the Japanese aggressiveness to create their own empire in East Asia, Churchill and Roosevelt agreed that their first priority was to defeat Hitler and Nazi Germany.

The globe was now inflamed by war on land, sea, and air. The major theaters of the war were located in Western Europe and the Mediterranean, in the Soviet Union, and, now, in the Pacific. Despite what appeared to be temporary setbacks by the Nazis in the Soviet Union, the year 1942 dawned bright for the Axis Powers and overcast for the Allies in Asia, Europe, and Africa. The first break in Allied gloom did not come for six months, until the American Navy gained their first victory at sea over the Japanese Imperial Fleet in June, at the Battle of Midway. Though this was a pivotal Allied win—eventually recognized to be the turning point in the Pacific war—the war was not over, not by a long shot. The Japanese navy was still strong. In fact, it had more *air carriers* (a large naval vessel designed as a mobile air base) in the Pacific than the Americans did.

From our vantage point today, visible cracks can be seen in the Axis armor—though, to be sure, it was not obvious to the people living in 1942. One of these cracks can be found when we consider that the movements of war by Germany, Italy, and Japan were conceived and implemented in isolation, being neither planned nor coordinated with each other. Hitler usually did exactly what was in his heart to do, neither communicating with nor inviting the others to share in his exploits, as was the case with the Italians and the Japanese, as well.

> Despite the Japanese aggressiveness to create their own empire in East Asia, Churchill and Roosevelt agreed that their first priority was to defeat Hitler and Nazi Germany.

On the other hand, the Allies—Great Britain with its dominion nations, the US, and, in a completely unanticipated arrangement, the USSR—actively cooperated with each other, planning their strategies in coordination. In some ways this was easy, since the Western Allies had enjoyed an ongoing friendship for decades, strengthened increasingly as Hitler's menace grew. However, the new alliance with the Soviet Union was bizarre, given that they had essentially been enemies until the Nazis invaded the USSR. Churchill, recounting his first meeting with Stalin wrote, "I pondered on my mission to this sullen, sinister Bolshevik State . . . which, until Hitler appeared, I had regarded as the mortal foe of civilized freedom. . . . We had always hated their wicked regime, and, till the German flail beat upon them, they would have watched us being swept out of existence with indifference and gleefully divided with Hitler our Empire in the East."

Their first ground-breaking conference was held in Moscow, August 1942. Stalin and Churchill were there, along with FDR's representative,

8

Averell Harriman. During the conference, Stalin learned that the Second Front in France, which he so eagerly desired in order to redirect Hitler's attention from the East to the West, was not scheduled to be launched until 1943 at the earliest. Instead, Great Britain, with the agreement of the United States, offered to attack North Africa in Operation Torch. In Churchill's view, it would be like attacking a crocodile in his soft and vulnerable underbelly. This was little consolation to Stalin who was currently facing the crocodile's teeth in the renewed onslaught of the powerful Nazi war machine, which had begun a new eastern advance in June 1942. Rapidly closing in on the southern city of Stalingrad, the Nazis seemingly had victory in their sights just weeks after Stalin had met with the Allies. The Soviets, however, made a courageous stand, refusing to give up the city. After months of fierce battle, including brutal house-to-house fighting, they managed to encircle the German Sixth Army in early 1943—capturing 300,000 Nazi soldiers, much to Hitler's fury.

Only sixty-five miles from Alexandria, the Afrika Korps was within striking distance of the strategically important Suez Canal.

While the Allied High Command worked on preparations for Operation Torch in French North Africa, General Rommel and his Afrika Korps continued to battle brilliantly against them. After staging a dramatic advance and equally dramatic retreat during 1941, he pursued the British Eighth Army during the summer of 1942 eastward through the desert all the way to El Alamein, in what has been described as a "near rout." Only sixty-five miles from Alexandria, the Afrika Korps was within striking distance of the strategically important Suez Canal. The British fleet actually prepared to evacuate the Mediterranean lest it become trapped, and Churchill flew to the desert to see with his own eyes what was needed to avoid this catastrophic defeat.

In *The Rise and Fall of the Third Reich*, William Shirer wrote of this moment:

British infantry manning a sandbagged defensive position near El Alamein

It seemed to many a startled allied statesman, poring over a map, that nothing could now prevent Rommel from delivering a fatal blow to the British by conquering Egypt and then, if he were reinforced, sweeping on northeast to capture the great oil fields of the Middle East and then to the Caucasus to meet the German armies in Russia, which already were beginning their advance toward that region from the north. It was one of the darkest moments of the war for the Allies and correspondingly one of the brightest for the Axis.

Looking back, we know what happened, that the British managed to gain victory over Rommel

8

at the Battle of El Alamein. But what was it like for those living through the uncertainty and fearfulness of the Nazis' seemingly unstoppable movements? One man who knew firsthand the disastrous experience the British faced as Rommel pushed them back through the desert wrote of it in the book *Shaping History Through Prayer and Fasting*. Derek Prince, who later became internationally known through his books and teaching, was a young Christian with the British forces in North Africa. He described it this way, "During the long and demoralizing retreat . . . God laid on my heart a burden of prayer, both for the British forces in the desert and for the whole situation in the Middle East. . . . I searched in my heart for some form of prayer that I could pray with genuine faith and that would cover the needs of the situation. After a while, it seemed that the Holy Spirit gave me this prayer, 'Lord, give us leaders such that it will be for Your glory to give us victory through them.'"

"Now this is not the end. It is not even the beginning of the end. But it is, perhaps, the end of the beginning."

Churchill eventually appointed B. L. Montgomery to be field commander at this epic moment in North Africa. Montgomery restored morale for his discouraged soldiers, instilled tremendous discipline in their ranks, and made sure that he had superior numbers before attacking Rommel—all of which made a huge difference when the Battle of El Alamein was fought. Derek Prince attributed the change in fortune—from near rout to clear victory—to God's response to specific prayer. And, fascinatingly, Montgomery often attributed his successes on the battle field to "divine providence."

On November 10, 1942, speaking of El Alamein, Churchill said, "The Germans have received back again that measure of fire and steel which they have so often meted out to others. Now this is not the end. It is not even the beginning of the end. But it is, perhaps, the end of the beginning." This first major Allied victory on land was a turning point of the war in the Mediterranean/Western European theater.

Please refer to the table **Global War** (p. 338).

The Turning Tide

It is fascinating to consider the way totalitarian governments functioned in the midst of the uncertainty of battles and defeats. Stalin and Hitler—who were poles apart in their political theories—both viewed retreat or surrender as treason, and issued harsh orders to "fight to the last man," demanding punishment for those who would not. In Asia, Japan held this same viewpoint, though it was not a policy of leaders. It was, instead, a deeply-held cultural belief—to fight to the death because surrender was shameful. This profoundly influenced Japanese soldiers and civilians alike, and made a huge difference in how prisoners-of-war held by the Japanese were treated.

8

The issue of retreat and surrender became increasingly important to the Axis nations as they began to increasingly face defeat on many fronts. In November 1942, the Western Allies finally opened a Second Front by launching Operation Torch in French North Africa. Though opening an Allied Front in Africa was not acceptable to Stalin (he demanded an invasion of France), Churchill's plan carried the day. Under the command of US General Eisenhower, an Anglo-American force was landed in Vichy-held Morocco and Algeria. Though there was initial resistance by French Vichy troops, they soon signed an armistice with the Allies. (In retaliation for this, Hitler sent his troops to occupy the Vichy-controlled part of France.) As the Allied invasion force moved eastward, British troops under Montgomery were pushing Rommel westward across Libya to Tunisia. They converged in Tunisia

Global War — **Axis Victory** ■ **Allied Victory** ■ **Stalemate** ■ **Event** □

Fronts	Eastern	Western	African
Jun–Dec 1941	**Jun 22:** Germany attacks USSR—Operation Barbarossa—with more than 150 divisions. One division moves south, occupies Crimea. **Sep 8:** Blockade of Leningrad (till Jan '44) **Oct:** German troops reach outskirts of Moscow, brutal winter begins.	**German-occupied territories in Europe:** Denmark, Netherlands, Belgium, Northern France, Serbia, Montenegro, Albania, Greece, western USSR. **Vassal states:** Norway, Vichy France, Croatia. **Axis partners w/Germany:** Italy, Slovakia, Hungary, Romania, Bulgaria, Finland. **Dec 11:** Germany & Italy decare war on US **Dec:** "Nacht und Nebel"—enemies of state deported & imprisoned (Jews, Communists, and other "inferior"races).	**Nov 18:** British begin 2nd invasion of Libya. **Nov–Dec:** British drive Rommel's forces back across Libya to western border. **Nov 27:** British successfully conquer Italian East. **Dec 10:** British relieve besieged Tobruk.
Jan–Jun 1942	**Spr:** New offensive to the Don, Volga, and Caucasus regions.	**Jan:** Wannsee Conference—"Final Solution" agreed upon. European Jews to be systematically exterminated.	**Jan:** Rommel recaptures half of the ground lost in a swift 17-day campaign. **May:** Rommel resumes his offensive in the Libyan desert. **Jun:** Rommel captures Tobruk, two days later, he enters Egypt—one of the darkest moments for Allies in the war.
Jul–Oct 1942	**Aug 25:** Hitler orders capture of Stalingrad. Soviet troops successfully hold city through autumn.		**Oct 23:** Battle of El Alamein in Egypt; Britain is victorious. Winston Churchill wrote after the war: *"Before Alamein we never had a victory. After Alamein, we never had a defeat."*

in February 1943, with the Afrika Korps trapped in between—surrendering to the Allies in May.

February 1943 was also a significant month in the Pacific theater of war. After six months of fierce battle for the strategic island of Guadalcanal, in the Southern Solomons, the Japanese evacuated their forces from the island. This marked the moment when the Allies were able to move from *defensive* to *offensive* operations in the Pacific.

It was an important month in the Soviet theater, as well. Despite Hitler's furious orders to the contrary, the German Sixth Army in Stalingrad surrendered in February 1943. It was the beginning of the end for the German war machine. Now, instead of their blitzkrieg armies slicing quickly and powerfully through Soviet lines, the Nazis found themselves being relentlessly pushed out of the USSR and, in time, all the way across Eastern Europe. The myth of Hitler's invincibility was exposed for all the world to see, as

Asian	Naval	Air
Jul: Japanese take French Indochina. US embargo on oil to Japan threatens to cripple it. **Dec 7:** Japanese surprise attack on Pearl Harbor. **Dec 8:** America enters the war. **Dec 25:** Hong Kong falls to Japan.	**Battle of the Atlantic:** In 1941, almost 1,300 British, Allied, & neutral ships have been sunk. In 1942, U-boats are found ranging as far as along N. & S. American coasts, including Gulf of Mexico, as well as along western African. **Aug:** Churchill & Roosevelt meet for first time aboard naval ship off coast of Newfoundland; they issue "Atlantic Charter."	**Jul:** Despite major attacks by RAF bombers, little damage done—accurate bombing is a problem.
Jan 23: Japanese attack northern New Guinea, gain control. **Feb 15:** Singapore falls to Japanese forces. **May 6:** Last American troops in Philippines surrender to Japan. **June:** Japanese occupy western Aleutians. **By mid-1942,** Japan's "Greater East Asia Co-Prosperity Sphere" included: Greater Japan—Japan, Taiwan, Korea. **Japanese Protectorates:** Manchukuo, Inner Mongolia, Nanjing China, Thailand, Burma & Philippines. **Under Japanese Economic & Military control:** French Indochina. **Japanese Occupation:** northern New Guinea, Solomon Islands, former British & Dutch possessions in Malaysia & Indonesia.	**May:** Battle of Coral Sea in Pacific; stopped Japanese—first serious setback. **Jun:** Battle of Midway Allied victory—turning point of war in Pacific.	**Jan–Feb:** RAF attacks on ships & naval facilities. **Apr–May:** RAF bombing raids against German industrial centers & cities—not very effective. **May 30:** 1,000 RAF bombers attack Cologne.
Aug 7: American forces land at Guadalcanal; fierce fighting for months to gain control of island. **Sep:** Japanese come within 30 miles of Port Moresby, New Guinea. US General MacArthur sends troops to stop them.		**Jul:** USAF bombing crews take part in bombing enemy airfields in Europe for first time.

World War II & Miraculous Deliverances (1939–1945) **339**

8

Germany became involved in two things Hitler had never dreamed possible: a war on two fronts and a war of attrition. Just as had been learned in the lessons of WWI, these two elements drained Germany of irreplaceable manpower and resources. From this time, the nearly limitless resources of the USSR and its allies began to arrive on the eastern battlefield.

Despite the German humiliation at Stalingrad, the war was far from over. It became a long and brutal wrestling match that would yet last more than two years. Though the Nazis were unable to win any further victories in the East, they still resisted doggedly and determinedly every step backward in retreat—all the way to Berlin.

The Allies, continuing to build momentum from their victory on the North African Front, made plans to take the next step in the Mediterranean theater. That something was in the works was obvious to Germany and Italy, who sought feverishly to minimize their risks. Recognizing that Italy's losses in North Africa and the imminent Allied invasion somewhere in the Mediterranean might topple Mussolini's government, Hitler was hesitant to commit a large number of German troops too deeply in southern Italy and its islands. There was a certain danger that, if Mussolini was ousted and Italy switched sides, Hitler's forces could be trapped—and he could ill afford the loss of more troops and equipment.

The Allies took their first step back onto European soil when they invaded Sicily on July 10, 1943.

Despite all of Hitler's strategizing, however, the Allies took their first step back onto European soil when they invaded Sicily on July 10, 1943. Many factors were involved in the success of this invasion, a very significant one being the huge numbers of crack German and Italian troops who had been captured in North Africa in May. It is highly uncertain whether the Allies would have been able to grab and keep their toehold in Sicily and into Italy soon after that if these soldiers had remained to defend the southern gateway into Europe.

However, one of the most fascinating and unlikely factors in the successful capture of Sicily was Operation Mincemeat. In preparation for the landings on Sicily, the Allies successfully convinced the Nazis that the coming attack would NOT take place on Sicily—the most obvious location. They planted false information on a dead body disguised as an Allied soldier, which was then very carefully situated to wash up on a Spanish beach into Axis hands. These bogus Allied documents detailed the invasion of Sardinia and Greece, rather than Sicily. When Hitler heard about the documents, he was convinced that they must be legitimate. Because of this new information, German troops were redirected away from Sicily to reinforce Greece, Sardinia, and Corsica, which meant fewer casualties during the initial landings of Allied troops. It seemed significantly encouraging to the Allies that the Sicilians greeted them as *liberators* not as enemies. It indicated that the Fascist government of Mussolini was in serious trouble.

The successful landing of the Allies on Sicily did, in fact, have tremendous repercussions on the Axis. Mussolini was dismissed from power on July 25 and arrested. On September 3, British and Canadian troops began landing on the toe of Italy, just as the new Italian government signed a secret armistice with the Allies. The slow and arduous reconquest of the European mainland from the south had begun.

Please refer to the table **Allies Turn the Tide** (p. 342).

Victory for the Allies!

The year 1944 was to be a year of liberating breakthroughs and discouraging setbacks, the year when hope turned increasingly into certainty for an Allied victory. From Russia to Europe to the Pacific, mile by mile, city by city, and island by island, the Allies pushed relentlessly against the Axis powers. While the Allies rapidly increased the output of tanks, ships, planes, and trained soldiers, the Axis powers were finding their own supplies to be rapidly dwindling. And in a war of attrition, which was the case on many of these battlefields, the one with the most supplies usually wins.

The Allied victories for this year began in January, when the Nazi's siege of Leningrad—nine hundred days!—was finally lifted by the Soviet Army. The epic struggle of nearly three million determined civilians, who willingly chose scarcity and difficulty rather than surrender, was concluded victoriously. It cost them more than six hundred thousand lives.

> By taking back lands conquered by the Japanese after Pearl Harbor, it was becoming increasingly possible to threaten Japan itself.

In the Pacific, the Allies had discovered that they could make tremendous tactical progress against the Japanese by *island-hopping*—instead of battling for every island, they would bypass some, engaging only certain Japanese-held areas that they needed to control. By doing this, the Allies could isolate these powerful areas and render them harmless, all the while continuing to drive toward bigger objectives, like the Philippines. In late 1943, Admiral Chester Nimitz steamed across the Central Pacific, capturing tactical spots in the Gilbert and Marshall island groups, as General Douglas MacArthur pursued the plan of island-hopping or leapfrogging over entrenched enemy locations on the north coast of New Guinea (on the southern borders of the war). With the Japanese dogma that surrender was treasonous and death far more honorable, each of the islands that the Allies attacked were successfully captured only with shocking violence and loss of life. Regardless of the cost, however, the islands had to be taken in order to move the war nearer to Japan. By taking back lands conquered by the Japanese after Pearl Harbor, it was becoming increasingly possible to threaten Japan itself.

8

On the other side of the world, the Allies faced a difficult situation in Italy. Though the Italians had done an about-face and joined with the Allies, still Hitler's troops were able to quickly take control and hold most of this mountain-studded country. B. H. Liddell Hart, in *History of the Second World War*, writes, "The sequel to the invasion of Italy had been very disappointing. In four months the Allied forces had advanced only seventy miles beyond Salerno—mostly in the first few weeks—and were still eighty miles short of Rome. Alexander himself described the process as 'slogging up Italy.' But a more general description that came to be used in the autumn was 'inching.'" As the new year began, Allied forces, including Free French, Polish, Canadian, Kiwi, British, and American soldiers, sought to break through the Nazi-held boundary across the mountainous terrain of southern Italy, known as the Gustav Line. The Gustav Line was perfectly suited for defense and seemed impossible to cross.

Allied High Command's strategic plan for a major Italian breakthrough had, by this time, been replaced with a smaller aim—to tie up as many

Allies Turn the Tide

Axis Victory ▮   Allied Victory ▯   Stalemate ▨   Event ☐

Fronts	Eastern	Western	African
Nov–Dec 1942	**Nov:** Heavy fighting in Stalingrad & Caucasus; Soviets gaining ground over Germans. **Nov 19:** Russians begin offensive in Stalingrad, begin to encircle German 6th army.	**Nov 11:** In retaliation for Allied troops taking French Morocco & Algeria, Hitler occupies Vichy France. Now all of France under direct German control.	**Nov 8:** Allies open a 2nd front in N. Africa; occupy Morocco & Algeria. **Nov 9:** German troops move into Tunisia. **Nov 30:** Germans halt Allied invasion of Tunisia.
Jan–Jun 1943	**Feb 2:** After 2 month siege, German 6th Army in Stalingrad surrender to Soviets. **Feb 21:** Germans launch new offensive.	Continental Europe remains under Axis control.	**May 13:** German Afrika Korps caught in the Allied pincer move—east from Egypt and west from Algeria—are unable to evacuate; surrender in Tunisia. **Jun:** Allies control islands between Sicily and Tunisia.
Jul–Dec 1943	**Jul:** Soviet offensive spreads across Eastern Front. **Dec 14:** Soviets begin winter offensive. **Jul:** German offensive—Battle of Kursk, greatest tank battle of war—Germans can't break through.	**Jul 10:** Invasion of Sicily begins; Mussolini is overthrown & arrested. **Sep 9:** Allied forces land at Salerno, Italy, after new Italian govt announces armistice with Allies. Hitler sends 30 divisions into Italy—entrenched 40 miles north of Naples at "Gustav Line." **Nov 28–Dec 1:** Tehran Conf: US & Britain agree to open second front in western Europe to relieve USSR.	Allies successful in Africa.

German troops as possible in Italy so they would not be available to fight at the new front opening soon in Normandy. By this time, Allied commanders had become intent on mustering more than a million soldiers, landing craft, and assorted supplies for Operation Overlord, the coming invasion of Western Europe across the English channel. This meant that many men and supplies were shipped from their Italian stations up to England, leaving the Italian campaign somewhat short-handed for the task of capturing Rome and driving northward. Despite the challenges, and in a controversial move, US General Mark Clark was able to bring the American Fifth Army to the outskirts of Rome by June 4, 1944.

Two days later, Clark's victory was eclipsed by the D-Day invasion of Normandy. Planning for this invasion of France had begun shortly after the evacuation of troops at Dunkirk, nearly four years prior, and in the months leading up to D-Day, extensive work planning, gathering, training, stockpiling—and trying to hide all this from the enemy—had been taking place in England. Though the preparations were as thorough as could possibly be done, success was by no means assured.

Asian	Naval	Air
Mid-Nov: Allies have driven Japanese back to the coast of southeastern New Guinea.	Total U-boat strength at 400 by end of '42—up from 250 in Jan '42, and despite 86 lost to Allies.	
Fighting continues at Guadalcanal.	**Nov 27:** In Toulon, French warships scuttled to prevent seizure by Germans.	
Jan 23: Allies secure southeastern New Guinea. **Feb 9:** End of Japanese resistance at Guadalcanal. **Jun:** Allied two-pronged drive up the Solomons & New Guinea coast. Japanese work to reinforce their positions in the Solomon Islands and northern New Guinea. **Apr–Jun:** Japanese unsuccessful in destroying Allied air & naval power in the Solomons & New Guinea.	**Mar:** Battle of the Atlantic peaks as U-boats successfully attack even well defended convoys. More than 2,000 British, Allied, & neutral ships have been sunk in the first five months of 1943.	**Jan 16:** Royal Air Force bombs Berlin; first use of Target Indicator marker bombs. **Mar–Jul:** RAF bombers begin campaign of strategic bombing in Battle of the Ruhr. "Bomber Command had stopped Speer's armaments miracle in its tracks". (author Adam Tooze)
Oct: Allies retake New Georgia Island after months of intense fighting. **Nov:** Allied beachhead secured on Bougainville island, which allows Allies to cut supply line of Japanese in remaining Solomon islands. It becomes painfully clear to the Allies that the war in the Pacific will be a long and fierce struggle, with high casualties.	With the help of British code-crackers, the Allies finally have accurate knowledge of German Navy & U-boat operations. This, with the changing of their own codes, allows Allies to challenge Germany in Battle of Atlantic.	**Aug:** USAF bombers raid German industrial factory in daylight—ineffective & costly mission, as Luftwaffe shoots down significant percentage. **Nov:** Start of 4-month Allied bombing campaign against Berlin.

8

Consider these facts: the Germans had held the Atlantic coastline for four years; they were certain to know that an invasion would be launched from England to a place on the Atlantic coast of Europe; and they had the time and the means to fortify this coastline—including mining the beaches and setting up huge obstacles to fend off the landing craft of an invasion. In addition, the Germans had fifty-eight divisions in the West, ten of which were highly mobile panzer divisions—a quelling thought to Allied optimists. And consider this, on the planned date for the invasion, June 5, a fierce storm with gale force winds was whipping through the English Channel. Though weather reports indicated that the storm would lighten later in the evening and through the night hours, no one was certain whether the invasion forces—traveling across the English channel in an armada of ships—would actually be able to land their troops on the Normandy beaches. Finally, consider the solemn reality that, if they did arrive, the first group of invaders would be only six divisions by sea and three divisions by air. With another potential storm brewing, these soldiers could be left stranded on a hostile coast without backup for days. With the unexpected difficulties experienced over the past several months in Italy, the Allies knew that this venture was a tremendous risk. It is sobering to recognize that they did not have a single backup plan in case of failure. B. H. Liddell Hart says of this moment, "At the outset, the margin between success and failure was narrow. The ultimate triumph has obscured the fact that the Allies were in great danger at the outset, and had a very narrow shave."

"At the outset, the margin between success and failure was narrow. The ultimate triumph has obscured the fact that the Allies were in great danger at the outset, and had a very narrow shave."

It was General Dwight Eisenhower, Supreme Allied Commander of the invasion, who made the final decision to launch in the early hours of June 6. Landing at five different beaches along sixty miles of the Normandy coast, 150,000 troops, 1,500 tanks, and thousands of motorized vehicles were disembarked. Of the troops, two divisions were British, two were American, and one was Canadian. Before the ships arrived, more than 13,000 Allied paratroopers were dropped behind enemy lines in order to secure vital areas. Though fighting was fierce, and in some places nearly impossible to overcome, by the end of June 6, Eisenhower knew that his troops were on the mainland to stay. Joseph Stalin, who knew well the benefit to his own troops if this western invasion succeeded, wrote to Churchill, "As is evident, the landing, conceived on a grandiose scale, has succeeded completely. My colleagues and I cannot but admit that the history of warfare knows no other like undertaking from the point of view of its scale, its vast conception, and its masterly execution."

The success of D-Day was the turning point of the war in Europe. Because of Hitler's raging order to stand and fight to the last man, the

8

Landing at Normandy

bulk of his mechanized forces at Normandy, along with 200,000 German soldiers, were captured. Though there were many battles yet to be fought, the eventual outcome was clear: victory for the Allies.

A coming victory over Japan was visible by mid-1944, after the Battle of the Philippine Sea and the capture of Saipan. The naval engagement, which took place near the Mariana Islands on the eastern extreme of the Philippine Sea, was the largest aircraft carrier battle of WWII. The Japanese had hoped to destroy the US Pacific fleet in this action, but when the battle was over, the Japanese navy had been decimated and much of its airpower destroyed. The neighboring land battle for the island of Saipan, the most costly to that point in the Pacific war in terms of casualties, was a significant victory for the Americans. From the Marianas, B-29 bombers could bring the war directly to the homeland of Japan. Lieutenant General Holland M. Smith, Commander of the US Fleet Marine Force in the Pacific, said, "I have always considered Saipan the decisive battle of the Pacific offensive . . . the naval and military heart and brain of the Japanese defense strategy." It was on this island, when retreat was impossible and surrender dishonorable, that thousands of Japanese soldiers launched themselves against US troops in the largest *banzai* (suicide) attack of the war. The Americans were learning, to their great dismay, that the Japanese, even the civilians, would kill themselves before surrendering. This was a bitter revelation to Allied leaders as they began to recognize the cost of invading Japan: an unimaginable loss of life, both Allied and Japanese.

The success of D-Day was the turning point of the war in Europe.

8

At the start of the year, when the homelands of Germany and Japan began to be ravaged, the war intensified unbelievably in its ferocity. In Europe, with Soviet troops racing from the East and Allied troops from the West, Hitler's thousand year Reich was shattering before his very eyes. The massive destruction of German cities, like Dresden and Hamburg, through Allied bombing raids, was bringing the war to Germans who had not expected devastation in the Reich, having trusted in Hitler's promise of invincibility. In Japan, citizens in Tokyo and other cities experienced the fury of incendiary bombs dropped by B-29 bombers, igniting the mostly wooden structures of the cities and turning them into firestorms.

The Axis powers were not the only ones to experience terror from the skies, however. Toward the end of 1944, in the naval Battle for Leyte Gulf, Japan unleashed a new weapon that was formidable and highly unpredictable: *kamikaze* (suicide) pilots in planes filled with explosives sought to strike Allied warships as pilot-driven bombs. Many were shot down before they could crash onboard a ship, but others made it through ship defenses and wreaked havoc.

Throughout the war, Allied political leaders met from time to time to discuss how they might best coordinate, cooperate, and strategize as they confronted the military strength of the Axis powers. US President Franklin Roosevelt, British Prime Minister Winston Churchill, and Soviet dictator Joseph Stalin had an extraordinary season of working together—to the point of addressing each other as friends. But as the war was coming close to its end, they faced an insurmountable difficulty. What would the post-war world look like? Which political systems would be established after the Nazis and the Japanese were defeated? Stalin indicated willingness to allow elections in newly liberated nations, but in reality, he was only agreeable to this idea if newly elected governments were pro-Soviet. He was quite determined that communism should be the "free choice" in each country he liberated. FDR and Churchill, on the other hand, demanded free and fair elections—regardless of the outcome—for each of the nations involved, beginning with Poland and continuing through Central and Eastern Europe.

Tragically, as the Soviet soldiers raced in, there was nothing the Western Allies could do to stop them from imposing a harsh totalitarian police state upon those they liberated—apart from going to war. To give a clear example of the true "choice" given to those in the path of the Soviet advance, it is instructive to note that German citizens and soldiers alike were desperate to have US and British troops arrive in their area ahead of the Soviet troops. German soldiers traveled for days to be able to surrender to British or American troops. In Paris, though liberated by the Western Allies, a struggle for power unfolded between French Communists and

Kamikaze (suicide) pilots in planes filled with explosives sought to strike Allied warships as pilot-driven bombs.

346 World War II & Miraculous Deliverances (1939–1945)

8

nationalists under Charles de Gaulle. In Greece, British troops, who were landed to support Greek nationalists, found themselves involved in battle against communist insurgents after the Nazis had fled. J. A. S. Grenville states, "The realities of Soviet 'freedom' were already apparent before the war with Germany was even won. A division of Europe was emerging between the Soviet-controlled territory of Eastern, central and south-eastern Europe and the West."

By spring 1945, as the Soviet military was marching toward Berlin and the Western Allies were about to cross the Rhine river into Germany, Hitler demanded that his soldiers continue fighting this hopeless war. In fact, on March 19, he commanded that "the battle should be conducted without consideration for our own population," and instructed German workers to destroy "all industrial plants, all the main electricity works, waterworks, gas works" together with "all food and clothing stores." When challenged about this monstrous order, Hitler said, "If the war is lost, the German nation will also perish. So there is no need to consider what the people require for continued existence." Fortunately, Germans ignored these final directives. On April 30, when Soviet troops had surrounded Berlin and all hope for a last-minute reprieve was gone, Hitler committed suicide. Quickly, Germany arranged for a surrender, which was signed on May 7, 1945, ending the war in Europe.

On April 30, when Soviet troops had surrounded Berlin and all hope for a last-minute reprieve was gone, Hitler committed suicide.

All eyes now turned to the islands of the Pacific and the raging war that still continued there. For the Japanese—despite the knowledge that they could no longer hope to win the war, despite the bombing raids that were devastating Japan (three million residents of Tokyo were homeless due to the incendiary bombing raid in March 1945), despite the dramatic losses of Japanese ships, planes, and pilots, and despite the Allies advancing ever nearer with each captured island—there was no stopping the war. Surrender was treason. For the Allies—despite their successes in bombing Japanese cities, despite their successes in capturing even the most entrenched islands held by Japanese soldiers, despite the inevitability of victory—there was no easy way to end the war. And the longer it continued, the more people would die.

In April 1945, President Roosevelt collapsed and died unexpectedly. Vice President Harry Truman took his place, becoming one of the Big Three leaders of the war, at a time of very difficult decisions. With all of the facts and figures of a continuing and horrific war before him, President Truman gave the order to drop the atomic bombs on Japan—a decision which

Atomic explosion at Nagasaki, August 9, 1945

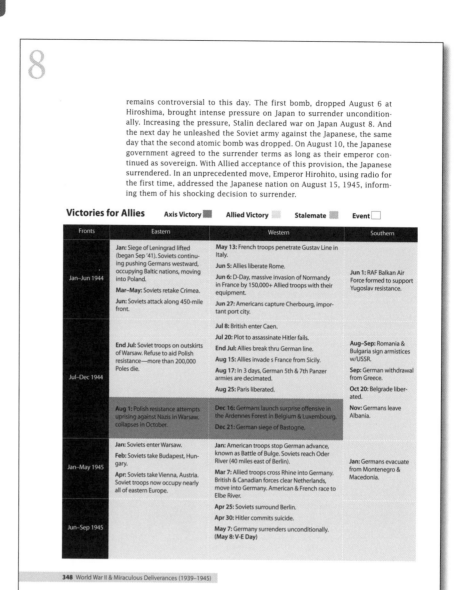

8

remains controversial to this day. The first bomb, dropped August 6 at Hiroshima, brought intense pressure on Japan to surrender unconditionally. Increasing the pressure, Stalin declared war on Japan August 8. And the next day he unleashed the Soviet army against the Japanese, the same day that the second atomic bomb was dropped. On August 10, the Japanese government agreed to the surrender terms as long as their emperor continued as sovereign. With Allied acceptance of this provision, the Japanese surrendered. In an unprecedented move, Emperor Hirohito, using radio for the first time, addressed the Japanese nation on August 15, 1945, informing them of his shocking decision to surrender.

Victories for Allies   Axis Victory ▓   Allied Victory ░   Stalemate ▓   Event ☐

Fronts	Eastern	Western	Southern
Jan–Jun 1944	**Jan:** Siege of Leningrad lifted (began Sep '41). Soviets continuing pushing Germans westward, occupying Baltic nations, moving into Poland. **Mar–May:** Soviets retake Crimea. **Jun:** Soviets attack along 450-mile front.	**May 13:** French troops penetrate Gustav Line in Italy. **Jun 5:** Allies liberate Rome. **Jun 6:** D-Day, massive invasion of Normandy in France by 150,000+ Allied troops with their equipment. **Jun 27:** Americans capture Cherbourg, important port city.	**Jun 1:** RAF Balkan Air Force formed to support Yugoslav resistance.
Jul–Dec 1944	**End Jul:** Soviet troops on outskirts of Warsaw. Refuse to aid Polish resistance—more than 200,000 Poles die.	**Jul 8:** British enter Caen. **Jul 20:** Plot to assassinate Hitler fails. **End Jul:** Allies break thru German line. **Aug 15:** Allies invade s France from Sicily. **Aug 17:** In 3 days, German 5th & 7th Panzer armies are decimated. **Aug 25:** Paris liberated.	**Aug–Sep:** Romania & Bulgaria sign armistices w/USSR. **Sep:** German withdrawal from Greece. **Oct 20:** Belgrade liberated. **Nov:** Germans leave Albania.
	Aug 1: Polish resistance attempts uprising against Nazis in Warsaw. collapses in October.	**Dec 16:** Germans launch surprise offensive in the Ardennes Forest in Belgium & Luxembourg. **Dec 21:** German siege of Bastogne.	
Jan–May 1945	**Jan:** Soviets enter Warsaw. **Feb:** Soviets take Budapest, Hungary. **Apr:** Soviets take Vienna, Austria. Soviet troops now occupy nearly all of eastern Europe.	**Jan:** American troops stop German advance, known as Battle of Bulge. Soviets reach Oder River (40 miles east of Berlin). **Mar 7:** Allied troops cross Rhine into Germany. British & Canadian forces clear Netherlands, move into Germany. American & French race to Elbe River.	**Jan:** Germans evacuate from Montenegro & Macedonia.
Jun–Sep 1945		**Apr 25:** Soviets surround Berlin. **Apr 30:** Hitler commits suicide. **May 7:** Germany surrenders unconditionally. (**May 8:** V-E Day)	

348 World War II & Miraculous Deliverances (1939–1945)

◉ Read the article

◉ Listen to the audio recordings in Listen to This

The main concepts and chronological flow are contained in *What in the World? Volume 3*

Learn more about espionage and D-Day in WWII on *Digging Deeper Volume 3.*

8

Please refer to the table **Victories for Allies** (below).

It was over. Six years of war had finally ended. Though estimates vary, the death toll of this war was more than forty million civilians and twenty million military personnel, making it the deadliest war in history. It was not merely battles between opposing nations' soldiers, however. The Holocaust claimed the lives of more than six million Jews when Hitler's personal vendetta—and his "Final Solution"—became official Nazi policy. As the war ended, millions were displaced refugees, homeless and hungry. And yet, as hopeless and dismal as it seems, this is not the end of the story. There remains One who writes His story in the lives of people and nations—a story of hope, of courage, and of new life. We will gain more glimpses of His ways in our world in the next, and final, Unit. ◀

Asian	Naval	Air
Jun: Allied forces go on offensive in Burma. By end of month, Japanese army is defeated near Rangoon. **Jun 19:** Largest aircraft carrier battle: Japanese lose 400 planes; Americans lose 130 in Battle of Philippine Sea.	**Jun:** More than 2,800 warships, amphibious & landing craft, ferry vessels take part in Operation Overlord—D-Day.	**Feb:** Allies bomb railroads in occupied Europe, in preparation for D-Day. **May:** Allies bomb coastal radar sites. **Jan:** Little Blitz—5 month Luftwaffe campaign against London.
Sep: Japanese forces capture airfields in south China, disrupting Allied plans to build airfields to bomb Japan.	**Aug:** Nearly 900 warships & landing craft take part in "Operation Dragoon"—Allied invasion of southern France through Mediterranean.	**Oct 14:** Operation Hurricane—highest number of sorties in 24 hours by RAF Bomber Command.
Oct 23–26: Battle of Leyte Gulf, largest naval battle of war; Japan's fleet nearly destroyed.		**Sep 17–25:** "Market Garden"—Allied airborne invasion of Holland fails.
Mar: Manilla retaken by Allies. **Feb–Mar:** Battle of Iwo Jima; Allies victorious after some of the fiercest fighting of Pacific war. **Apr–Jun:** Battle for Okinawa, an island considered part of Japan's homeland.	**Apr 1:** Greatest amphibious operation of the Pacific war begins as Allies land on Okinawa. Mass kamikaze attacks by Japanese planes against ships & troops continue until June.	**Mar 24:** "Varsity"—Allied crossing of Rhine, includes 1500 aircraft & 1300 gliders. Successful. **Jan 1:** Last major air raid against Allied airfields.
Aug 8: Russia declares war on Japan, invading Manchuria. **Aug 15:** Emperor Hirohito broadcasts Japan's surrender over radio– VJ-Day. **Sep 2:** MacArthur formally accepts Japan's unconditional surrender.	**Jul–Aug:** US 3rd Fleet & British Pacific Fleet bombard Japan by sea & air.	**Aug 6:** To prevent more than 1 million Allied casualties on invading Japan, the US drops an atomic bomb on Hiroshima, killing 80,00 people. **Aug 9:** 2nd "A" bomb dropped; 40,000 die in Nagasaki.

World War II & Miraculous Deliverances (1939–1945) **349**

◉ Read the Scriptures in Read For Your Life

The Scriptures are central to our understanding, our character, and our decisions. Therefore, we must give the greatest weight possible to them.

Help your students gain this perspective as they watch you handle the Scriptures with reverence and awe.

When our world collapses, when unthinkable difficulties invade, when darkness closes in, does the Bible have anything to say to us? (Psalm 94:17–19). To Jewish families in concentration camps, Christian pastors in Germany, English children evacuated to the countryside, was there a perspective in Scripture that would have made a difference? (Habakkuk 3:17–19). After reading the Scriptures through, talk and pray with your students about the reality of living in a fallen world, where tragedies can and do occur—and the even truer reality of eternity with God, where there will be no more crying, no more sorrow, no more pain (Revelation 21:4).

◉ Recap the material with an activity

In different parts of the room, set up stations for the Eight Intelligences Recap Activities. Then allow students to work alone or together in small groups to accomplish THEIR CHOICE OF ONE of the following suggestions. At the start of the next class, ask for 3–4 groups of volunteers to share.

Homeschoolers: rather than setting up all eight stations, allow student(s) to choose which activity they would most enjoy, and do it.

Recap Suggestions:

Spatial: Create a mural, choosing colors for the background that speak to you of WWII, then draw images or cut out magazine photos to show some aspect of what you have learned about the events, places, and personalities associated with the war.

Bodily Kinesthetic: Set up different sections of a room to represent various fronts involved in WWII. Then, as a tour guide, take groups to each of these geographic locations, describing what is happening in each section. (How could you creatively show the Battle of the Atlantic and the Battle of Britain?)

Interpersonal: In a small group, discuss at what point Great Britain and France should have stood up to Hitler. Was it over the reoccupation of the Rhineland? The occupation of Austria, the Sudetenland, or Czechoslovakia? Should they have gone to war over Poland? What reasons can you use to justify your position?

Phase 1

Key People (Church)

Dietrich Bonhoeffer
German pastor, executed by Nazis

Martin Niemoller
German pastor & Nazi prisoner

Corrie ten Boom
Hider of Jews & survivor of concentration camp

Gladys Aylward
Missionary to China

▶ ## Listen to This

What in the World? VOL. 3

DISC FOUR:

» Miracle at Dunkirk (track 2)

» Battle of Britain (track 3)

» Pearl Harbor, Midway, El Alamein (track 4)

» D-Day & the Atom Bomb (track 5)

Digging Deeper VOL. 3

DISC THREE:

» Rommel, Italy, and the War's End (track 10)

» The Visible War (track 11)

▶ ## Read For Your Life

The Holy Bible

» **Crying Out to God for Deliverance from Oppressors and from Troubles**—Psalm 54:1–4; Psalm 88; Psalm 102:1–13

» **Perspective on the Judgment of God on Evil Laws** (consider Hitler)—Psalm 94:20–23

» **The Value of Counsel in Time of War** (consider the Allies working together)—Proverbs 20:18, 24:6; Ecclesiastes 3:8

» **Spiritual Perspective for Believers in Time of War**— Ephesians 6:12–18; 2 Corinthians 10:4

Musical: Choose (or compose) a song that expresses your thoughts about WWII. Will you choose a military march, a song of loss, a song of courage?

Linguistic: Write a short, pithy letter to be delivered to every ship owner in England, requesting their help with the evacuation at Dunkirk. It must inspire patriotism and courage, without begging or whining.

Math-Logical: List five reasons why the Axis powers were victorious until mid-1942. Next, list five reasons why the Allies were able to win the war in 1945. Compare and contrast these

reasons. How close was the contest, in your opinion?

Intrapersonal: Write your thoughts about which personality from WWII you would wish to be, whether political, military, or courageous civilian. What are your reasons for that choice?

Naturalist: The British Seventh Armored Division, fighting in North Africa, became known as the "Desert Rats." Learn more about the small, jumping rodent, the jerboa, which became the emblem of this division. Find video footage online of jerboas, as well as information about the soldiers of the British 7th Armored

▶ Talk Together

Opinion Column

» Who did you find to be the most interesting person, or the most fascinating aspect, of World War II?

» Many historians believe that Hitler could have been stopped—and WWII prevented—if his violations of the Treaty of Versailles had been punished. What is your opinion? *There are two things to keep in mind as you consider the answer. First, painful lessons had been learned from the four years of devastating war in WWI, lessons that continued to affect the opinions of the West. Secondly, think about a child who is not corrected when he does something wrong and then compare Hitler to that child. With those things in mind, share your opinion.*

» World War II was a time known as the Holocaust, when unthinkable atrocities were committed against many ethnic people groups, particularly the Jews. Why do you think people allowed the Holocaust to happen? The price for harboring Jews was imprisonment, and, potentially, death. If you had been living in Germany or the Nazi-occupied countries of Europe during this time, what do you think your response would have been when Jews were being rounded up for deportation? Are there situations in the world today that are similar to this situation? Are there ways you can help protect those who are being destroyed in "ethnic cleansing"? In what ways could you and your family make a difference?

» Hitler signed a non-aggression pact with the Soviet Union in August 1939. In your opinion, how might this benefit Germany? How might it benefit the Soviet Union? In what ways might Poland be affected by this pact? Why do you think the British Prime Minister threatened war with Germany if Hitler invaded Poland, since he had done nothing when Germany consumed Austria and Czechoslovakia?

» In what ways was the rescue of Allied soldiers from Dunkirk a miracle? How does this situation demonstrate the power of God in human history? Do you think the soldiers might have been aware of God's intervention during this time? What are your reasons? If you had been one of the soldiers, what would you have prayed for? Describe any instance in your life when you have seen God answer your prayers.

Key People (World)

Adolf Hitler
Nazi Leader of the Third Reich

Benito Mussolini
Fascist dictator of Italy

Hideki Tojo
Japanese prime minister

Winston Churchill
British prime minister

Franklin Roosevelt
American president

Joseph Stalin
Communist dictator

Erwin Rommel
Nazi's "Desert Fox"

Bernard Montgomery
British Commander, Victor at El Alamein

Dwight Eisenhower
American General, Supreme Commander of Allied Forces Europe

Douglas MacArthur
American General, Supreme Commander, SW Pacific Area

World War II & Miraculous Deliverances (1939–1945) **351**

Division. In what ways does the jerboa typify the British Desert Rats

Or . . . Activity of Your Choice: What would you like to have your students

do for a review activity concerning this week's introduction to World War II & Miraculous Deliverances?

◉ Talk together

Individual Preparation

After completing their recap activities, students may begin to consider the questions in the Opinion Column and Critical Puzzling.

Class Discussion

Use the questions under Talk Together to get the students primed and to create a discussion environment in the classroom. You may also want to draw from the open-ended questions listed here.

?

After Germany attacked Poland, France and England declared war on Germany. Then for the next several months, neither France nor England made any military moves against Germany, nor Germany against them. This period of time—with inactivity in the West—is called the "phony war." Why do you suppose neither side attacked? What kind of attitude do you think the people in Europe had about the war during this time? Do you think the rest of Europe was prepared for what Germany was about to launch? What are your reasons?

?

Gladys Aylward was a small, poorly educated English servant girl who believed that God had called her to China. After her admittance to the China Inland mission school (which trained people in England for missionary work in China), she was informed that she was too old and too ignorant to learn Chinese. Though this was a huge obstacle, it did not deter her from going. What character qualities do you see in Gladys that made it possible for her to keep going, despite the obstacles? How does her story challenge you today?

» In North Africa, the battle of El Alamein began in October of 1942. Looking back on this battle, Winston Churchill later said, "Before Alamein we never had a victory. After Alamein we never had a defeat." Imagine you had been living in England during the first two years of the war without seeing any major victories for the Allies. What would have been your thoughts at the success of this battle? What do you think the effect of hope can be on an individual or nation when facing a terrible trial, especially one that is long-lasting?

» When Hitler ended the bombing of Britain, he turned eastward. How did Operation Barbarossa become one of his greatest mistakes? In what ways was this military operation similar to Napoleon's fight with Russia during the War of 1812? Why do you think Hitler attacked Russia?

» The development of the atomic bomb ushered the world into the "Atomic Age"—for good and for evil. Given the statistics of fighting in the Pacific, Japan's cultural view of surrender, and the estimated number of lives that would be lost in attacking the Japanese homeland, if you had been the US president in 1945, what decision would you have made concerning the dropping of the atomic bombs? Explain your reasoning. What alternative solution might you suggest?

Critical Puzzling

» The leader of Czechoslovakia, the democratic country under discussion at the Munich Conference of 1938, was not invited to attend this conference, despite the fact that it was the fate of his country being discussed. Why do you think British Prime Minister Neville Chamberlain proclaimed, "Peace in our time," after this conference? Who was supposed to live in peace as a result of this? What message did this conference send to the people of Eastern Europe?

» After Hitler successfully defeated France, Belgium, Holland, Norway, and Denmark with his blitzkrieg of 1940, he fully expected England to recognize the impossibility of continuing a war single-handedly. Why do you think Hitler believed they would sign a treaty recognizing his victories in Europe, and why do you think they refused? What part did Winston Churchill play in this decision?

» In the book *Rees Howells: Intercessor*, the author describes the level of intense prayer offered up to God on behalf of Great Britain during the Battle of Britain, including the fact that Rees Howells believed God answered prayer concerning even the focus of the air attacks. Though stressful to British citizens, the change from bombing of airports and military installations to bombing civilian targets enabled Great Britain to withstand Hitler. In what ways does this situation in history encourage you to pray for your own country?

» Why do you think the Japanese wanted to liberate other Asian people from European and American colonization? In retrospect, do you think the Asians wanted to be liberated by the Japanese? What are your reason(s)? Why do you think America was perceived at this time as the main stumbling block to Japanese goals in the Pacific?

» The battle at Midway was a turning point in the war in the Pacific. In what ways do you consider the events at Midway to be unusual, even miraculous? What did each side hope to accomplish at Midway? What do you think might have been the result of Japan winning this battle? In what ways might this have affected the outcome of WWII?

» Consider the logistical and tactical difficulties facing the Allies as they prepared for the invasion of Normandy (D-Day). Why weren't Allied soldiers already on the European Continent? What kinds of obstacles did they face? What were some of the supplies they needed to get ashore? How difficult do you think it was for Hitler's soldiers to defend the coastline? And, looking back, what mistakes do you think were made by the German High Command?

> ## Resources for Digging Deeper

Choose a few books that look interesting, or find your own.

WORLD WAR II

World War II—Battles and Leaders

Aaron R. Murray, editor • From DK, this excellent little book provides a brief overview of each of the major aspects of a very complicated war. **UE+**

World War II

H.P. Willmott, Robin Cross, Charles Messenger • Far more detailed than the title listed above, this extraordinary book provides timelines, maps, photos, articles, and quotes. [Author's note: There are some graphic photos from concentration camps.] Older students interested in WWII would find this title to be an excellent resource on the war. **MS+**

The Great Depression and World War II

George E. Stanley • One of a series entitled "A Primary Source History of the United States," this provides a uniquely American perspective on the major historic events from 1929—1949, particularly America's involvement in WWII. **UE+**

World War II for Kids

Richard Panchyk • Filled with interviews and stories, along with craft projects for children, this is a unique and valuable resource for studying WWII. **UE+**

BATTLE OF BRITAIN & WINSTON CHURCHILL

The Battle of Britain A WORLD LANDMARK BOOK

Quentin Reynolds • A first person account of the bombing of Britain by Hitler's Germany, this book is a perfect introduction to the "never give in" spirit of the British. **UE+**

Winston Churchill A WORLD LANDMARK BOOK

Quentin Reynolds • The author writes, "As a war correspondent in London during the worst days of the blitz, I saw what one great human being—namely, Winston Churchill—could do to hold together a nation literally on the verge of being annihilated." This is a fantastic biography, well written, which gives some of the amazing details of the life of Churchill. **UE+**

Never Give In LEADER IN ACTION SERIES

Stephen Mansfield • According to Henry Kissinger, "Our age finds it difficult to come to grips with Churchill.

The political leaders with whom we are familiar generally aspire to be superstars rather than heroes. The distinction is crucial. Superstars strive for approbation; heroes walk alone. Superstars crave consensus; heroes define themselves by the judgment of a future they see it as their task to bring about. Superstars seek success in a technique for eliciting support; heroes pursue success as the outgrowth of their inner values." As the author states, "Winston Churchill was a hero." **UE+**

Winston Churchill WORLD LEADERS PAST AND PRESENT SERIES

Judith Rodgers • This is an excellent biography of one of the greatest statesmen of the twentieth century. The photographs are fascinating! Highly Recommended! **MS+**

◉ Choose books of interest/ internet search

Remember:
Beware of Arrogance,
Embrace Humility!

A list of possible books is given in the Student Manual. Encourage your students to look for books or videos on World War II & Miraculous Deliverances from this list and from other sources. You may want to gather a selection of further resources prior to beginning Unit 8, or you may encourage the students to be treasure hunters and find them on their own. It would be helpful and time-saving before the Unit begins to check availability of these titles on your local library website.

SEA BATTLES & RESCUES

The Battle for the Atlantic A
WORLD LANDMARK BOOK

Jay Williams • Because England is an island nation, Hitler planned to prevent any supplies bound for England from coming through by using his submarines and navy ships, while at the same time bombing the British to bring them to their knees. He was so successful at sea early on that Winston Churchill proclaimed it "the Battle of the Atlantic." This book describes in fascinating detail this ongoing battle. **UE+**

The Sinking of the Bismarck A
WORLD LANDMARK BOOK

William L. Shirer • At the moment of England's greatest peril in WWII, when the Nazis had succeeded in destroying many British merchant and naval ships, the most powerful ship in the world was put into German service—the *Bismarck*. This book details the incredible story of how the British, against all odds, were able to sink her. **UE+**

The Miracle of Dunkirk

Walter Lord • As stated on the jacket, "This is the story of the greatest rescue of all time." Winston Churchill called the rescue of 338,000 Allied soldiers from the beaches of Dunkirk "a miracle of deliverance." Though this is a secular book, it is filled with incidents that can only be explained by the supernatural intervention of God. **HS+**

Midway: Battle for the Pacific A
WORLD LANDMARK BOOK

Captain Edmund L. Castillo, USN • Landmark books provide remarkable detail in an understandable format. This title gives a blow-by-blow description of the Battle of Midway, the turning point in the War of the Pacific. Even more importantly, the battle is analyzed, helping the reader to learn why the Japanese, with vastly superior numbers, lost to the US. Fascinating! **UE+**

Miracle at Midway

Charles Mercer • The author served as an intelligence officer in the Pacific during WWII and his experience brings the "miracle" at Midway to life! **MS+**

Carrier War in the Pacific AMERICAN HERITAGE JUNIOR LIBRARY

Stephen W. Sears • Admiral Isoroku Yamamoto, commander in chief of the Imperial Japanese Navy, in 1942 wrote, "In the last analysis, the success or failure of our entire strategy in the Pacific will be determined by whether or not we succeed in destroying the US fleet, more particularly, its carrier task forces." This book tells the story of the war waged on sea and in the air. **UE+**

THE RUSSIAN FRONT

Siege of Leningrad WORLD AT WAR SERIES

R. Conrad Stein • This is a fantastic series for children about World War II. The siege of Leningrad is one of the most amazing stories of the war—a city under siege by the Nazis for almost nine hundred days! **UE+**

WAR IN THE PACIFIC

The Bombing of Pearl Harbor LANDMARK EVENTS IN AMERICAN HISTORY SERIES

Michael V. Uschan • Written for younger students, this is a well-rounded account of the dramatic event which pushed the United States into WWII. **E+**

From Pearl Harbor to Okinawa A WORLD LANDMARK BOOK

Bruce Bliven Jr. • Subtitled, The War in the Pacific, 1941–1945, this provides upper elementary students a very readable account of the war from the Japanese attack on Pearl Harbor to the Japanese surrender. **UE+**

Thirty Seconds Over Tokyo A WORLD LANDMARK BOOK

Captain Ted W. Lawson • Written by one of the pilots who dropped bombs on Tokyo shortly after Pearl Harbor, this is a tense accounting of one of the US's greatest morale-boosters in WWII. Can't-put-it-down suspense! **UE+**

Hirohito WORLD LEADERS PAST & PRESENT SERIES

Karen Severns • This is a biography of the Japanese emperor at the time of WWII. What a fascinating look behind the scenes! **MS+**

The Flying Tigers A WORLD LANDMARK BOOK

John Toland • Did you know that the war in the Pacific actually began in 1937? That was when Japan attacked China. This book recounts the incredible story of the American pilots who, through their daring and skill, kept China from being completely overrun. **UE+**

Fall of Singapore WORLD AT WAR SERIES

R. Conrad Stein • The fall of Singapore was the worst defeat in England's history and also the beginning of the end of European colonial empires in the East. Fascinating! **UE+**

Guadalcanal Diary

Richard Tregaskis • This was written by a war correspondent who had firsthand experience of the battle for the island of Guadalcanal (one of the Solomon Islands). This battle was one of the turning points of the war in the Pacific. **UE+**

JAPANESE-AMERICAN INTERNMENT

Farewell to Manzanar

Jeanne Wakatsuki Houston and James D. Houston • Jeanne Wakatsuki was born in America to Japanese parents who lived in California. As a young girl, Jeanne, along with more than 110,000 other Japanese-Americans, was placed in an internment camp for the duration of the war. Learn what it was like from this eyewitness account. Highly Recommended! **MS+**

Journey to Topaz

Yoshiko Uchida • A fictional account of a Japanese-American family placed into an internment camp during WWII, this is a moving and thought-provoking story. **UE+**

D-DAY

Invasion: The Story of D-Day

Bruce Bliven, Jr. • This book shows the intense drama of D-Day from an eyewitness account, photos, and factual information about the equipment and methods used to storm the beaches. Riveting! **UE+**

Remember D-Day: The Plan, the Invasion, Survivor Stories

Ronald J. Drez • A National Geographic title, this fascinating book provides a clear and understandable depiction of the largest amphibious invasion in history. Highly Recommended! **UE+**

D-Day: The Invasion of Europe AMERICAN HERITAGE JUNIOR LIBRARY

Al Hine • This is a blow-by-blow accounting of one of the most significant events of WWII. The Allies could have been forced back into the sea by the Nazis—this book explains why that did not happen. **UE+**

THE RESISTANCE/ESCAPE/CONCENTRATION CAMPS

Twenty and Ten

Claire Huchet Bishop • The incredible true WWII story of French people at a school under German occupation who decide to hide ten Jewish refugee children. There is also a video of this story entitled *Miracle at Moreaux*. Highly recommended! **RA**

Sky: A True Story of Resistance During World War II

Hanneke Ippish • Hanneke Ippish was born in Holland, the daughter of a Protestant minister. In 1945, she was incarcerated for working with a Dutch resistance organization during WWII. This book is the true story of her experiences—and it its truly incredible! **UE+**

Rescue in Denmark

Harold Flender • From the introduction: "In October 1943, the Nazis decided to round up Denmark's eight thousand Jews for shipment to the death camps. The entire country acted as an underground movement to ferry the eight thousand to Sweden. It was one of the few times that Eichmann had been frustrated. He visited Copenhagen in a rage—but to no avail. The Jews were saved." This is one of the most amazing stories from WWII! **MS+**

The 100 Most Important Dates in Church History

A. Kenneth Curtis, J. Stephen Lang, and Randy Petersen • Beginning with the year 64 in Rome and continuing to 1976, this book is filled with short descriptions of events and people within the church. For this Unit read about Dietrich Bonhoeffer. **UE+**

The Hiding Place

Corrie ten Boom • This is the autobiography of an amazing woman who learned to trust God. She and her family aided the Dutch resistance effort and helped to hide Jews in Holland during WWII. The family was caught and sent to a concentration camp. Only Corrie was released—to a worldwide ministry which endured for decades. This book changed my life. **UE+**

Corrie ten Boom CHRISTIAN
HEROES THEN AND NOW

Janet & Geoff Benge • Wonderfully written, this series of Christian biographies is fascinating, factual, and historically accurate. Corrie ten Boom's life is a tremendous testimony of God's grace in the midst of overwhelming troubles. **UE+**

Surviving Hitler: A Boy in the Nazi Death Camps

Andrea Warren • Based on a true story, this is one fifteen-year-old Jewish boy's account of what it took to survive in a concentration/labor camp. One of the most potent aspects of this story is Jack's profound decision not to hate his captors. Highly Recommended **MS+**

Escape from Warsaw

Ian Serraillier • Historical fiction about three children separated from their parents in Warsaw during WWII. They set out to try to find their father in Switzerland with tremendous courage and faith. **UE+**

The Story of the Trapp Family Singers

Maria Augusta Trapp • This is the story which inspired the movie *The Sound of Music*. It is very interesting to get a glimpse into the life of a family whose husband and father had fought on the side of Kaiser in WWI, and in WWII, takes his family away from everything they had ever known. (A Catholic family, the Trapp history is written from a practicing Catholic perspective.) Fascinating! **MS+**

Journey to America

Sonia Levitin • This historical fiction book, a winner of the National Jewish Book award, tells the story of a mother and three young daughters who flee Germany in 1938. The father has gone on ahead to make it possible for the family to come to America. **UE+**

WWII SPECIFICS

Air War Against Hitler's Germany AMERICAN HERITAGE JUNIOR LIBRARY

Stephen W. Sears • Filled with photos, maps, and illustrations, this excellent book describes the battle in the air between the Allies and Nazi Germany. **UE+**

The Seabees of World War II A
WORLD LANDMARK BOOK

Commander Edmund L. Castillo, USN • Written by the "King Bee" of the seabees, this is an amazing story of people who accomplished unbelievable engineering feats during WWII. The author writes, "Trying to capture the Seabees on paper is a little like trying to describe a wildcat that has the skill of a master mechanic, the tenacity of a bulldog, the speed of lightning, the ingenuity of Thomas Edison, the humor of Bob Hope, and the dedication to duty of John Paul Jones." **UE+**

The Story of the Paratroops A
WORLD LANDMARK BOOK

George Weller • Paratroopers played a very important part in WWII. Learn how a Dutch sniper quite possibly saved England by shooting the leader of the German paratroopers at the beginning of the war! **UE+**

Nisei Regiment WORLD AT WAR SERIES

R. Conrad Stein • During WWII, a regiment of soldiers was formed, all of whom were Japanese-American. Their accomplishments were astounding! **UE+**

The Story of Atomic Energy A
WORLD LANDMARK BOOK

Laura Fermi • Written by the widow of the physicist who built the first uranium pile (to see if it were possible to cause an atomic chain reaction), this fascinating book not only shows the development of atomic theory, it also sets this story into its moment of history. The race to build the first atomic bomb in WWII led to the many peaceful uses of atomic energy, as well. **MS+**

GLADYS AYLWARD

Gladys Aylward CHRISTIAN
HEROES THEN AND NOW

Janet & Geoff Benge • Wonderfully written, this series of Christian biographies is fascinating, factual, and historically accurate. Gladys Aylward went to China as a missionary, though she flunked missionary school! Learn more about her and the way God was able to use this "small woman" in this excellent book. **E+**

Gladys Aylward: The Little Woman

Christine Hunter • A wonderful introduction to the amazing story of a true heroine, this book is a fascinating, page-turning account of Gladys Aylward's life. **UE+**

Flight of the Fugitives TRAILBLAZER BOOKS

Dave & Neta Jackson • Historical fiction for children, this is the story of Gladys Aylward and her mission in China before and during WWII. **E+**

The Small Woman

Alan Burgess • Wonderfully told, this biography of Gladys Aylward also gives an authentic flavor of China before the Communist Revolution. **UE+**

WARRING IN PRAYER

Rees Howells: Intercessor

Norman Grubb • Deeply impacted by the 1904 Welsh Revival, Rees Howells then went to Africa and was used mightily by God in revival there. The end of the book refers to the dramatic answers to his intercessory prayers during World War II. Life-changing! **MS+**

AUDIO

Bonhoeffer: The Cost of Freedom

This production from Focus on the Family is stirring. Follow the life of Dietrich Bonhoeffer, a German theologian, from childhood to his execution just before the end of WWII. His life, his integrity, and his willingness to stand for what was right will change your life. Highly recommended! **MS+**

VIDEO

The Longest Day

This movie feels like a documentary in its depiction of D-Day. The German soldiers speak German with English subtitles! It shows the tenseness, the slender thread by which the Allies hung on in certain places, and the remarkable string of mistakes made by the Germans. Excellent! **UE+**

Midway

There are numerous movies made about WWII. You may find some excellent documentaries of WWII, and some other Hollywood movies that are reasonably accurate. This one is a good depiction of the battle of Midway—if you can overlook the Hollywood additions to the story! It really shows how the Japanese made the wrong decisions about whether to put torpedoes or bombs on their planes. [Disclaimer: Albeit mild by 21st century standards, this film about the military includes a certain amount of swearing.] **MS+**

The Inn of the Sixth Happiness

The story of Gladys Aylward, this movie is somewhat romanticized for Hollywood but it is an excellent portrayal of the conditions Gladys faced. **UE+**

For more books, use these Dewey Decimal numbers in your library:

Aerial combat: 940.5442; 5449

Aircraft carrier: 359.9483

Battles: 940.542

Military machines: 623

Manhattan Project: 355

Holocaust Nazism: 940.531

World War 2: 940.53

Japan: 952

History of Pacific Islands: 995; 996

Military science: 355

Mounted forces & warfare: 357

Sea (Naval) forces & warfare: 359

Missions: 266

What books did you like best?

_____
_____
_____

The Internet also contains a wealth of information about World War II & Miraculous Deliverances.

What sites were the most helpful?

_____
_____
_____

◉ Conduct a review and evaluation

In this Phase of Unit 8, your students should have had the opportunity to explore the rise of World War II & Miraculous Deliverances through reading, listening, thinking, and discussing by completing a selection from the following:

- informally discussed the Key Concepts;
- read the article;
- listened to the audio recordings;
- read the online articles;
- read the Scriptures;
- explored the recap activities;
- considered the Opinion Column and Critical Puzzling answers on their own;
- participated in class discussion;
- chosen books of interest or searched the Internet;
- completed their self-evaluation for this Phase.

Record student hours: _____

Assess student participation:

Create an evaluation system of your own, or refer to the evaluation rubric in the introduction, as a tool for assessing participation. The categories you will probably find most useful are

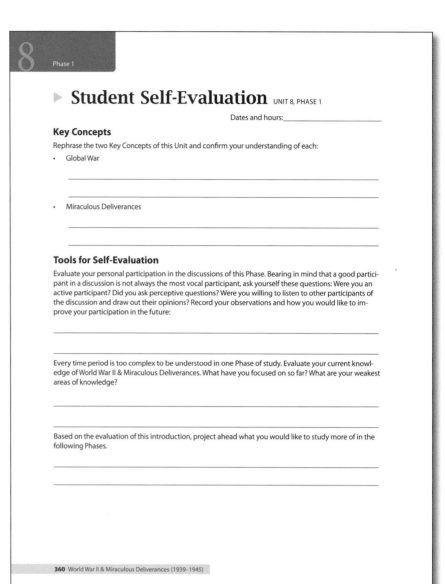

8 Phase 1

▷ **Student Self-Evaluation** UNIT 8, PHASE 1

Dates and hours:_____

Key Concepts

Rephrase the two Key Concepts of this Unit and confirm your understanding of each:

- Global War

- Miraculous Deliverances

Tools for Self-Evaluation

Evaluate your personal participation in the discussions of this Phase. Bearing in mind that a good participant in a discussion is not always the most vocal participant, ask yourself these questions: Were you an active participant? Did you ask perceptive questions? Were you willing to listen to other participants of the discussion and draw out their opinions? Record your observations and how you would like to improve your participation in the future:

Every time period is too complex to be understood in one Phase of study. Evaluate your current knowledge of World War II & Miraculous Deliverances. What have you focused on so far? What are your weakest areas of knowledge?

Based on the evaluation of this introduction, project ahead what you would like to study more of in the following Phases.

360 World War II & Miraculous Deliverances (1939–1945)

"Introduction," "Process: Teamwork," and "Process: Originality." To help students develop good discussion skills, encourage them to participate actively, ask content-based questions, and stay focused on the discussion at hand. Students demonstrate a higher level of discussion skills when they incorporate comments and questions from others into their own questions, and draw out opinions or ask for points of clarification from others.

Do not critique the self-evaluation page your student completes and do not direct the answers the student gives to the questions. Instead, allow sincere and personal completion of the evaluation, then discuss the

responses and incorporate those comments into your evaluation.

Determine a grade for this Phase, if using grades: _____

Teacher Self-Evaluation:

Evaluate your own use of materials and teaching opportunities: what worked and what did not; how effective was your time-management; how were your responses to the needs of your student; did you make your expectations clear; in what ways would you like to improve your approach for the next Unit? Incorporate suggestions from your students in your own evaluation (this requires humility!).

Phase 2

▶ Research & Reporting

Explore one or more of these areas to discover something significant!

WWII

Research and report on the various causes of WWII, potentially including the impact of the Treaty of Versailles on Germany, the worldwide economic depression, the failure of the League of Nations to deter international aggression, the rise of totalitarian governments, and the worldview of Adolf Hitler.

Battle of Britain

Research and report on the bombing of Britain during the Battle of Britain. Show the strategy of the Germans, how this changed over time, and the defenses of the British. Include Winston Churchill's policy towards Hitler.

Dunkirk

The rescue of 338,000 Allied soldiers from the shores of Dunkirk is one of the most amazing military operations in history. Research and report on what transpired in Belgium and France to require this rescue, who was involved, and how the Germans responded.

Invasion of USSR

Research and report on Operation Barbarossa, the Nazi invasion of the USSR. What relationship did Nazi Germany and Communist Russia have prior to this event? How did this operation differ from the invasion of Western Europe? What were the results?

War in North Africa

Learn more about the war in North Africa. What part did Italy play? Why did Germany become involved? How did Rommel turn the tide? What effect did Montgomery have on the British troops? In what ways did the Allied invasion of French North Africa impact the situation?

Pearl Harbor

Study the bombing of Pearl Harbor by Japan. Include details on why this surprise attack was deemed necessary by the Japanese, what strategies were used to accomplish it, the results on the US Navy, and the effect it had upon US involvement in WWII.

Internment Camps

After the bombing of Pearl Harbor, the US government set up internment camps for Japanese-American citizens. Research and report on these camps. What was their purpose? Was there evidence that supported the decision to build these camps? What was the effect upon the Japanese-Americans who were confined?

Battle of Midway

Learn more about the Battle of Midway. It might be helpful to create a diagram showing the Japanese fleet, Midway Island, and the US ships. Explain the significance of the decision to rearm the Japanese planes with torpedoes. Why was this naval battle the turning point of the war in the Pacific?

◉ Choose a topic and begin research

Allow the students the freedom to choose one of the topics listed under research & reporting in the Student Manual, or to suggest their own area which they would like to research.

Motivating Suggestions:

Especially for Non-linguistic students, and those who are not motivated by written or oral reports, here are suggestions for alternative ways of reporting what has been researched.

WWII

In a group of two or three, discuss your research on the events, political theories, and personalities leading up to WWII. What are the major reasons for WWII, in your opinion? What actions do you think could have been taken, if any, that might have prevented war?

Create a video clip (or perform live): as an international journalist, interview everyday people on the streets of Berlin, London, and Paris in August 1939.

What are their attitudes toward a possible war? Is this different from the stated goals of their country's leaders?

Battle of Britain

Create an ad campaign to bolster courage during the Battle of Britain. You might want to quote part of Winston Churchill's famous words from June 1940:

> We shall fight with growing confidence and growing strength in the air, we shall defend our island, whatever the cost may be. We shall fight on the beaches, we shall fight on the landing grounds, we shall fight in the fields and in the streets, we shall fight in the hills; we shall never surrender.

Create a diorama to display in miniature some of the most significant events of the Battle of Britain. Remember, this was the first major military campaign to be fought solely with air forces, so planes will be a dominant feature in your diorama!

Dunkirk

Write and illustrate an exciting children's book of the miracle at Dunkirk. Be sure to include the astonishing features of this noted WWII event, including the order to halt the Nazi panzers only miles from Dunkirk, the stillness of the English Channel during the rescue, and the extraordinary conglomeration of sea-going vessels used for the evacuation.

Design an outdoor action game portraying the amazing events of the rescue at Dunkirk. One team will represent the German Panzers, Luftwaffe, and Army, while the other will be the British Expeditionary Force, the French Army, and the British Navy (with help from assorted smaller vessels). The object of the game is to teach others more of this high-action, real-life drama, using whatever actions and sound effects would be appropriate.

Invasion of USSR

Compare and contrast the Nazi invasion of the USSR with the Nazi invasion of Western Europe. Use diagrams, charts, maps, and whatever might assist you in communicating to your audience. Be prepared to explain why the Nazis were not successful in Operation Barbarossa.

As a television journalist, prepare a special on Operation Barbarossa. For this piece, it would be very interesting to set up interviews with Adolf Hitler, Joseph Stalin, and, perhaps, Winston Churchill. What reasons does Hitler have for invading? Is Stalin surprised? What does Churchill think of this new move on the part of the Nazis?

War in North Africa

Create a flip chart or PowerPoint presentation, which will provide an overview of the war in North Africa. There were several campaigns during this time, from Italy's initial assault to the Nazi surrender in Tunisia, so prepare something to show the sequence of events. It might be helpful to consider what the greatest needs were for soldiers battling in North Africa, such as fresh water and fuel, and how this impacted the war.

Imagine you were a soldier (either Axis or Allies) in North Africa during WWII. Write down your personal thoughts about the effect of fighting under a general who inspires confidence as opposed to fighting under one who does not. If you are an Axis soldier, how does Rommel inspire you? Or, if you are an Allied soldier, how does Montgomery inspire you? What can you learn from their example?

Pearl Harbor

You are Admiral Isoroku Yamamoto, commander of Japan's Combined Fleet. Please explain why you planned the attack on Pearl Harbor, why the US was not informed of Japan's intention to go to war, and what your fears are for the future of your homeland. You will be talking to a hostile crowd, so prepare your remarks carefully.

D-Day

D-Day was the beginning of the collapse of the Third Reich. Research and report on what was involved in planning and executing this military invasion. Include the strategies used to fool the Germans as to place and time for the invasion. Why was D-Day necessary?

The Holocaust

Research and report on the concentration camps used by the Nazis. What was the purpose of these camps? What was the Final Solution? Which groups of people were considered to be valueless in Nazi Germany?

The Resistance

Study the underground "Resistance" during WWII. What did people in the Resistance do? How did they affect the war effort? In what ways did the political leanings of people in the Resistance impact the effect? How did the Nazis fight the Resistance?

Saving the Lipizzans

Learn the unusual story of the WWII rescue of the Lipizzan stallions in Czechoslovakia. These famous Spanish Riding School horses, whose trained movements go back to the time of the ancient Greeks, were at risk of potential destruction by the approaching Soviet army at the time of their rescue.

Navajo Code Talkers

Discover the fascinating story of the Navajo Code Talkers during WWII. What was their mission? How successful were they? How were they honored after the war?

The War in China

Research and report on the war in China. Include information about Japan's strategies for defeating China and how China responded. Who were the Flying Tigers and what part did they play in defense of China? How were China's internal struggles between Nationalist and Communist forces affected by the war with Japan?

Gladys Aylward

Gladys Aylward, a little British parlormaid, was the first European to become a Chinese citizen. Learn more about her life. In your report, show the difficulties she faced in getting to the mission field, as well as the work she did in China.

Atomic Bomb

Research and report on the Manhattan Project. Show the purposes atomic energy has for the military and how it was used to quickly bring about the end of the war in the Pacific. Contrast this with the peacetime uses of atomic energy.

Create a collage of the bombing of Pearl Harbor, including scenes in Japan, the Pacific, Hawaii, and Washington, DC. Be sure to depict the response of the US to this attack.

Internment Camps

Design an advertising campaign to free Japanese-American civilians from their internment camps. Remember that fear and racism have been the major factors in imprisoning over one hundred thousand people, many of whom are fellow US citizens. Your task is to show the country that what they have believed is false and to set it on a path to right the wrongs. Go get 'em!

Create a chart to compare the imprisonment of Japanese-Americans in American internment camps with imprisonment of Jews in Nazi concentration camps. In what ways were they similar? In what ways were they different? Be sure to include the reasons why the American camps were opened versus the reason the Nazi camps were opened, and the reasons why they each closed.

Battle of Midway

Create a papier-mâché map of Midway Island and the surrounding Pacific. Then, using physical objects to represent the ships and planes of each side, demonstrate to a watching audience the events of the Battle of Midway. Be prepared to answer questions!

Choose a piece of music that expresses some aspect of what you have learned of the Holocaust. Prepare program notes for your audience with information on the Holocaust, and then, prior to playing a recording of your selected music, explain to your audience why you chose this particular piece and what it represents to you. Be prepared afterwards to answer questions.

The Resistance

Design a board game for the Resistance in which players will seek to outwit the Nazi forces. Possibilities for causing as much trouble as possible to these occupiers of your country include propaganda, not cooperating with Nazi rules (as in the actual case of Denmark helping its Jews to escape to Sweden), disinformation (false information deliberately spread by rumors in order to influence public opinion or obscure the truth), hiding crashed Allied pilots, and even outright warfare. Accessing a radio, extra rations, or a weapon will help players but will also put them in greater danger. The goal is to defeat the Nazis.

You have the opportunity, in January, 1944, to secretly interview one or two people (preferably a young man and a young woman) in the French Resistance. Prepare questions to ask which will not put them at risk but will help your live audience to grasp the perils and possibilities of their task. Remember, rumors on the street indicate that the Allied invasion can't be very long in coming! Be sure to ask them their thoughts on that.

Saving the Lipizzans

Present an interesting and informative talk as the curator of the Spanish Riding School museum. Your topic today: "Saving Historic War Horses from War."

Write new lyrics to an old cowboy song, such as "Red River Valley" or "Streets of Laredo," to memorably tell the story of the rescue of the Lipizzans during WWII.

▶ Brain Stretchers

German Blitzkrieg
Study the military tactics of the German blitzkrieg, its origin in English military theory, how it worked, why Allied armies in Western Europe were unable to withstand it, and why the blitzkrieg failed against the Soviet Union.

Maginot Line
Discover why France considered the Maginot Line to be impenetrable to Hitler's forces, including its construction, defenses, and troops. Discover what the Germans did to render the Maginot barrier useless.

Invasion of Sicily
Learn more about the Allied invasion of Sicily and Italy. What strategies did the Allies use in preparation for the invasion of Sicily? What particular geographic location was chosen for the invasion of Italy, and what were the limitations of this location? Why were the Allies stopped at Monte Cassino for so many months?

Nazism
There has been a resurgence of Nazism recently. Study and analyze the reasons for this return to a violent, defeated political philosophy. Devise a Christian response to those involved.

Heavy Water Factory
One of the more fascinating stories of WWII concerns the "heavy water" factory in Norway, which Hitler wanted to exploit for the purposes of building an atomic bomb. Research and report on the work of the Allied soldiers from Norway who were assigned the job of stopping him.

Create Your Own Research Topic

_____

_____

_____

_____

Using a flip chart or PowerPoint presentation, show the development of the war in the Pacific from the time of Pearl Harbor until the Battle of Midway. Demonstrate why this battle was the turning point in the Pacific.

D-Day

You are a British spy who has been assigned the task of infiltrating the Nazi coastal patrol. After collecting as much data as possible regarding the Nazis' preparations to withstand an Allied invasion of Europe, report your findings to your superior officers, along with your suggestions for safeguarding D-Day.

Rewrite history. D-Day will not take place in France, it will be launched in Norway. Write your battle plan, the goal of the mission, the obstacles to overcome, and the results. Use the actual events of D-Day as a model for your rewrite. How would this have affected the outcome of the war?

The Holocaust

Imagine you had been an inmate at Ravensbrück concentration camp with Corrie ten Boom and had survived. Journal your thoughts about the truth that Corrie and Betsie taught: "There is no pit so deep, that God's love is not deeper still." How would that affect your perspective concerning the concentration camp? What does it teach you about life in the twenty-first century?

Navajo Code Talkers

Write a story for younger children about the Navajo Code Talkers, the absolutely vital work they did during the war in the Pacific, and the uniqueness of their ancient language—their code was never broken by the Japanese.

Create your own museum to honor the Navajo Code Talkers. Though their work had been done extraordinarily well—successful and significant—it was considered to be an ongoing military secret, one that might be used again. Thus, no one knew what they had done for more than two decades. These heroes were unrecognized. You can change that at your museum. [Author's note: Perhaps, because of what you learned in this experience, you will want to make a donation to the actual Code Talkers museum. You can find a link at the online resource page.]

The War in China

Make a map of China during WWII, using colors to differentiate between the areas held by Japan, the areas held by Nationalist forces, and the areas held by Communist forces. Be prepared to answer questions, as people examine your map, about the events of WWII in China.

Set up a debate with a moderator, in the style of political debates, between Nationalist leader Chiang Kai-shek and Communist leader Mao Zedong concerning China's battle with Japan and their battle with each other. Remember to give each debater opportunity to respond to statements made by the other.

Gladys Aylward

Since much of Gladys's adventures took place outdoors, on mountainsides, in caves, and with mule-trains, set up a space outside that will depict the amazing story of her life. Carefully prepare the site with props, action games, improvised caves/mountains, and whatever else will help make this come alive for your audience. Then take groups of people through the site explaining her work, along with the war in China.

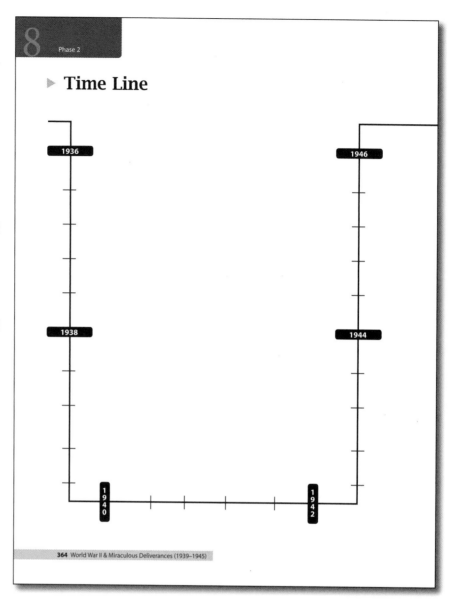

▶ Time Line

1936
1938
1940
1942
1944
1946

364 World War II & Miraculous Deliverances (1939–1945)

Compare and contrast Gladys Aylward's life with the life of Hudson Taylor, founder of the China Inland Mission. Consider this: as they were both missionaries to China, in what ways did each of their lives impact the Chinese? In what ways did each of their lives impact the people of their home country? It might be helpful to create a chart to show what these two had in common and in what areas their lives were different.

Atomic Bomb

Imagine being a US Marine who has been fighting on Iwo Jima when news of the atomic bomb at Hiroshima breaks. Conversely, imagine being a Japanese civilian living in the shattered city of Tokyo when the same news is reported. Write your thoughts about each of these two very different perspectives. Pray and consider this: what might it mean to your life to always seek to understand the other person's perspective?

As a news journalist, interview President Harry Truman concerning his controversial decision to drop the A-bomb. Ask the hard questions and listen for his responses. What do you hope your audience will understand after this interview?

Consider this for your time line

This time period covers the most lethal war in human history, with more soldiers and civilians killed and wounded than in any other war. As more and more nations enter the fight, the contest grows to global proportions. And, with communist Russia on the side of the Allies, it is far more complicated than merely totalitarian regimes against freedom-loving democracies. As you create your timeline, thoughtfully consider the perspective of WWII in light of David's words, "Man is like a breath; his days are like a passing shadow."

Key Events	
• Japanese invasion of China	• German surrender at Tunisia
• Occupation of Czechoslovakia	• Rome liberated
• Invasion of Poland	• D-Day
• Invasion of Western Europe	• Battle of Philippine Sea
• Invasion of Balkans	• Warsaw uprising
• Invasion of USSR	• Battle of the Bulge
• Bombing of Pearl Harbor	• Germany surrenders
• Battle of Midway	• Battle of Iwo Jima
• Battle of El Alamein	• Atomic bombs dropped
• German surrender at Stalingrad	• Japan surrenders

Be sure to include the people listed in Key People in Phase 1.

World War II & Miraculous Deliverances (1939–1945) **365**

Psalm 90:12 says, "So teach us to number our days, that we may gain a heart of wisdom." Talk with your students about eternity, in light of what they have seen in WWII. What spiritual wisdom can they glean from this time period?

- Bernard Montgomery: 1887–1976
- Dwight Eisenhower: 1890–1969
- Douglas MacArthur: 1880–1964

Key Dates

- Japanese invasion of China: July, 1937
- Occupation of Czechoslovakia: August, 1968
- Invasion of Poland: September, 1939
- Invasion of Western Europe: May, 1940
- Invasion of Balkans: April, 1941
- Invasion of USSR: June, 1941
- Bombing of Pearl Harbor: December 7, 1941
- Battle of Midway: June, 1942
- Battle of El Alamein
  - » 1st battle: July, 1942
  - » 2nd battle: October–November, 1942
- German surrender at Stalingrad: February, 1943
- German surrender at Tunisia: May, 1943
- Rome liberated: June, 1944
- D-Day: June 6, 1944
- Battle of Philippine Sea: June, 1944
- Warsaw uprising: started August, 1944
- Battle of Bulge: December, 1944–January, 1945
- Germany surrenders: May, 1945
- Battle of Iwo Jima: February–March 1945
- Atomic bombs dropped
  - » Hiroshima: August 6, 1945
  - » Nagasaki: August 9, 1945

Japan surrenders: September 2, 1945

◎ Construct the time line

Read the information listed with the Key Events in the Student Manual. Dialogue with your students about the issues involved.

Find the dates for the Key People and Key Events listed.

Time Line Key

Key People in the Church

- Dietrich Bonhoeffer: 1906–1945
- Martin Niemoller: 1892–1984
- Corrie ten Boom: 1892–1983
- Gladys Aylward: 1902–1970

Key People in the World

- Adolf Hitler: 1889–1945
- Benito Mussolini: 1883–1945
- Hideki Tōjō: 1884–1948
- Winston Churchill: 1874–1965
- Franklin Roosevelt: 1882–1945
- Joseph Stalin: 1878–1953
- Erwin Rommel: 1891–1944

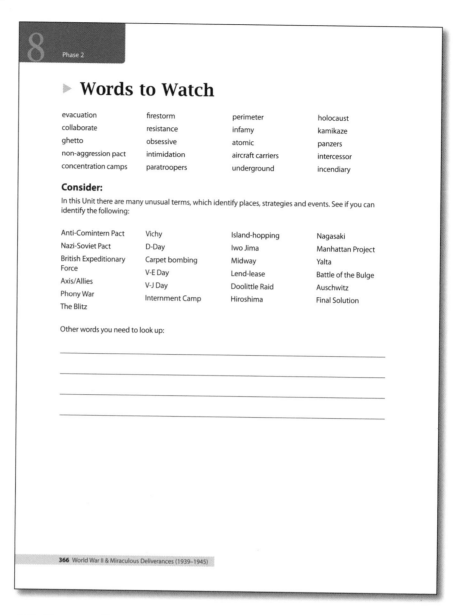

▶ Words to Watch

evacuation	firestorm	perimeter	holocaust
collaborate	resistance	infamy	kamikaze
ghetto	obsessive	atomic	panzers
non-aggression pact	intimidation	aircraft carriers	intercessor
concentration camps	paratroopers	underground	incendiary

Consider:

In this Unit there are many unusual terms, which identify places, strategies and events. See if you can identify the following:

Anti-Comintern Pact	Vichy	Island-hopping	Nagasaki
Nazi-Soviet Pact	D-Day	Iwo Jima	Manhattan Project
British Expeditionary Force	Carpet bombing	Midway	Yalta
Axis/Allies	V-E Day	Lend-lease	Battle of the Bulge
Phony War	V-J Day	Doolittle Raid	Auschwitz
The Blitz	Internment Camp	Hiroshima	Final Solution

Other words you need to look up:

_____

_____

_____

_____

Here is one idea for making vocabulary study interesting and fun:

CROSSWORDS!

Design a crossword puzzle for these WWII vocabulary words. Be sure to use clues that are derived from their usage in war.

A list of definitions can be found at the back of the book in Appendix B.

◉ Practice vocabulary

You may find other words in this Unit that are especially appropriate for younger children. Feel free to substitute another vocabulary list for the one provided.

◉ Complete research projects and share in class or hand in

Create a safe environment for the presentations. Set ground rules prior to the presentations, so that students know how much time is available for each of them, and so that they know they will be honored and respected by all those observing.

> ## Student Self-Evaluation UNIT 8, PHASE 2

Dates and hours:_____

Research Project

Summarize your research question:

_____

_____

List your most useful sources by author, title, and page number or URL where applicable (continue list in margin if necessary):

_____

Now take a moment to evaluate the sources you just listed. Do they provide a balanced view of your research question? Should you have sought an additional opinion? Are your sources credible (if you found them on your own)? Record your observations:

_____

_____

Evaluate your research project in its final presentation. What are its strengths? If you had time to revisit this project, what would you change? Consider giving yourself a letter grade based on your project's merits and weaknesses.

_____

_____

Letter grade: _____

You have just completed an area of specific research on the time of World War II & Miraculous Deliverances. Now what would you like to explore in the upcoming Phases? Set some objectives for yourself.

_____

_____

_____

◉ Conduct a review and evaluation

In this second Phase of Unit 8, your students should have had the opportunity to explore World War II & Miraculous Deliverances through researching, thinking, and reporting by completing a selection from the following:

- done a research project;
- learned the vocabulary;
- constructed a time line;
- created a project report on what was researched;
- completed their self-evaluation procedure for this Phase.

Record student hours: _____

Assess student effort in the research and reporting projects.

Create an evaluation system of your own, or refer to the evaluation rubric in the introduction, as a tool for assessing research and reporting. The categories you will probably find most useful are *"Introduction," "Task," "Process: Teamwork"* (if students are working together), along with Grammar, Format, and Spelling. As a tool for helping your students develop better research skills, pay attention to their evaluation of sources. Older students should learn how to make a "Sources Cited" list according to academic standards—refer them to English usage books or websites for formatting rules. Younger students should learn how to obtain a balanced view of their research subject; if they use more than one source they will get a bigger picture of what was happening. Encourage your students to make use of their self-evaluations for their next research projects, in order to practice good research skills.

Do not critique the self-evaluation page your student completes in the Student Manual—spelling errors are not to be considered in such an exercise. Students should feel free to humbly evaluate themselves without that added complexity. Instead, discuss with them the intention of their written comments and incorporate those into your evaluation.

Determine a final grade for this Phase: _____

Teacher Self-Evaluation:

Evaluate your own use of materials and teaching opportunities: what worked and what did not; how effective was your time-management; how were your responses to the needs of your student; did you make your expectations clear; in what ways would you like to improve your approach for the next Unit? Incorporate suggestions from your students in your own evaluation (*this requires humility!*).

Phase 3

▶ Maps and Mapping

Physical Terrain

» On a map of Europe and North Africa, locate and label the English Channel, the British Isles, the Normandy coast of France, the island of Sicily, the Scandinavian Peninsula, the North Sea, the Mediterranean, and the Atlantic Ocean.

» On a map of Eastern Asia and the western Pacific, locate and label these islands in the Central Pacific Theater: Hawaiian Islands, Marshall Islands, and Caroline Islands. Next, locate and label these islands that were in the Southwestern Pacific Theater: Solomon Islands, the Philippines, Indonesia, and New Guinea. Also, locate and label the islands of Japan. What kind of climate and vegetation are typical of these islands?

Geopolitical

» On the map of Europe and North Africa, locate and shade the area of Europe under direct or indirect Nazi control from June 1940 until D-Day. Locate and label Dunkirk, St. Petersburg (Leningrad), Warsaw, Berlin, Paris, and London.

» On the same map, locate and shade in different colors, the North African colonies of Italy (Libya), and of France (Morocco, Algeria, Tunisia). Next, locate and shade in a separate color, Egypt (which was under the influence of Great Britain). With different colored arrows for the Allies and the Axis, show the movement of the war in North Africa.

» On the map of Eastern Asia and the western Pacific, locate and label Pearl Harbor, Midway, Singapore, Hong Kong, Guadalcanal, Saipan, Okinawa, Iwo Jima, Hiroshima, Nagasaki, and Tokyo. With different colored arrows for the Allies and the Axis, show the movement of the war in the Pacific.

Explore:

» *Prized Location:* Learn more about why both Germany and the Soviet Union would find Poland to be such a prized strategic geographic location during WWII.

» *V-E Day, V-J Day:* Discover the geography of success in the war in Europe and/or the war in the Pacific. In Europe, from the time of D-Day until Germany surrendered, what was the geographic strategy of the Allies in the West and the East? In the Pacific, what was the geographic strategy of the Allies in moving towards the Japanese homeland?

» *Christian Outreach:* What is the status of evangelical outreach today in the Pacific islands? What opportunities and what difficulties face those who share the gospel in these areas?

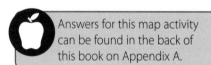

Answers for this map activity can be found in the back of this book on Appendix A.

◉ Create a map and discuss the issues in teams

The students each have an outline map in their manuals. They will be given assignments for drawing in the rivers, mountains, cities, and regional boundaries that are listed. For details on where these things are, please consult a historical atlas, an encyclopedia, or another source of geographic information.

Upper elementary students might be satisfied to accomplish only this portion:

• **Physical terrain:** This part of the mapping exercise will help students locate and mark the geographic areas affected by WWII, including Europe, North Africa, East Asia, and the Pacific islands.

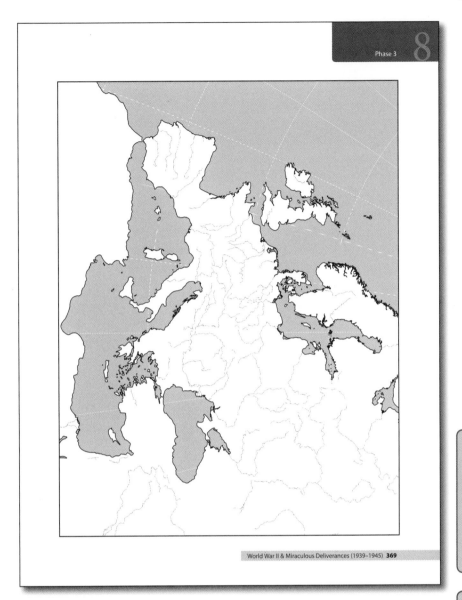

World War II & Miraculous Deliverances (1939–1945) **369**

Middle school students might be satisfied to complete both the previous mapping exercise and this exercise:

- **Geopolitical:** This section of the mapping exercise will provide the students an opportunity to locate and mark the area of Europe controlled by the Nazis, the geography of the war in North Africa, and the specific battle zones in Eastern Asia and the Pacific.

High school students might be satisfied to complete both the previous mapping exercises and at least one exploration topic of this exercise:

- **Explore** a selection from this portion of the mapping exercise in teams.

PRIZED LOCATION ?

Students might find it helpful to look at a topographical map, as well as a map showing natural resources, of Poland, eastern Germany, and western Russia. In what ways did Poland possess what both Germany and the Soviet Union wanted?

VE DAY, V-J DAY ?

Students interested in this project might find it helpful to choose one theater of the last days of war, whether Germany or Japan. From this point, encourage them to learn more about the mobility and supply issues of the advancing Allies and the defense issues of the Axis.

CHRISTIAN OUTREACH ?

Students might wish to locate information about current missionary endeavors among Pacific islanders. If possible, to provide even more help and insight, interview someone who has worked in these fields.

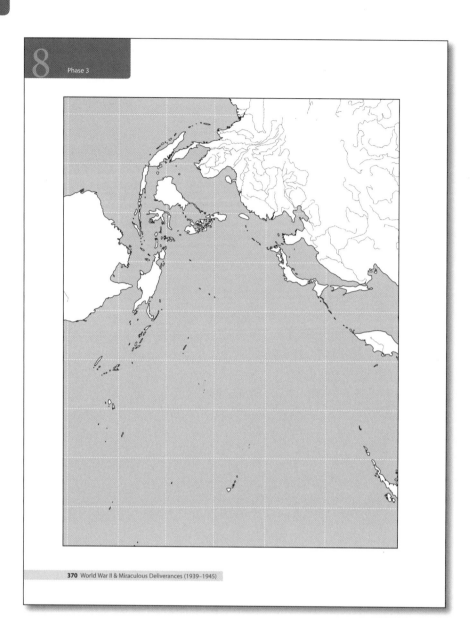

370 World War II & Miraculous Deliverances (1939–1945)

Art Appreciation

Four Freedoms (a series of four paintings) by Norman Rockwell, 1943

In 1941, US President Franklin Roosevelt presented his State of the Union address to Congress. In this speech, he specifically identified four essential human rights: freedom of speech, freedom of worship, freedom from want, and freedom from fear. These were incorporated into the Atlantic Charter created by Roosevelt and Churchill, and later became part of the charter of the United Nations. You can find a link to see these paintings at the online resource page.

» What words could you use to describe them? Norman Rockwell was famous as an *illustrator* rather than as a fine artist. In what ways do these paintings reflect that? In what ways did Rockwell capture the meaning of FDR's speech?

We Can Do It! by J. Howard Miller, circa 1942

Often referred to as **Rosie the Riveter**, this WWII poster was created by an American graphic design artist hired by Westinghouse Company. Today, it is one of the best-known posters of WWII, but during the war it was only one of many. You can find a link to see this poster at the online resource page.

» Describe what you see. Knowing this was created for propaganda purposes during WWII, what do you think was the purpose (and potential effect) of this poster?

> **CONSIDER:**
> The National Archives of the United States produced an exhibit in 1994 entitled *Powers of Persuasion*. Quoting from this exhibit: "Guns, tanks, and bombs were the principal weapons of World War II, but there were other, more subtle forms of warfare as well. Words, posters, and films waged a constant battle for the hearts and minds of the American citizenry just as surely as military weapons engaged the enemy. Persuading the American public became a wartime industry, almost as important as the manufacturing of bullets and planes. The Government launched an aggressive propaganda campaign with clearly articulated goals and strategies to galvanize public support, and it recruited some of the nation's foremost intellectuals, artists, and filmmakers to wage the war on that front . . . quotes from popular songs and sayings attest to the success of the campaign that helped to sustain the war effort throughout the world-shaking events of World War II."

> The online resource page at www.HistoryRevealed.org contains many helpful Internet links to artwork, architecture, music, project helps, and more.

◉ Examine and discuss art and architecture

The online resource page at www.HistoryRevealed.org has links to view each of the items listed. Allow the students time to observe the paintings without any conversation, and then, when they are ready, engage them in some or all of the questions listed below or in the Student Manual.

Art Art Appreciation

Four Freedoms (a series of four paintings) by Norman Rockwell, 1943

This is part of the text of FDR's speech, in which he describes the four human freedoms:

> In the future days, which we seek to make secure, we look forward to a world founded upon four essential human freedoms.

> The first is freedom of speech and expression—everywhere in the world.

> The second is freedom of every person to worship God in his own way—everywhere in the world.

> The third is freedom from want—which, translated into universal terms, means economic understandings which will secure to every nation a healthy peacetime life for its inhabitants—everywhere in the world.

> The fourth is freedom from fear—which, translated into world terms, means a world-wide reduction of armaments to such a point and in such a thorough fashion that no nation will be in a position to commit an act of physical aggression against any neighbor—anywhere in the world.

> That is no vision of a distant millennium. It is a definite basis for a kind of world attainable in our own time and generation. That kind of world is the very antithesis of the so-called new order of tyranny which the dictators seek to create with the crash of a bomb.

> —Franklin D. Roosevelt

We Can Do It! by J. Howard Miller, circa 1942

With a total commitment to war, the US found that it lacked enough able-bodied workers at home during WWII. The need was to create an atmosphere where women were expected to do their part for the war—including working in industries formerly considered to be "men's work."

This is an actual quote from the Office of War Information, in the *Basic Program Plan for Womanpower*:

> These jobs will have to be glorified as a patriotic war service if American women are to be persuaded to take them and stick to them. Their importance to a

nation engaged in total war must be convincingly presented.

Architecture

Reich Chancellery designed by Albert Speer, 1938

Architect Kevin Havens writes,

Hitler admired the timeless classicism of the Roman Empire and clearly modeled his own Third Reich vision on the notion of millennial longevity. But his view, as articulated by Speer and other contemporaries, deliberately robbed classicism of one of its most important qualities: humanizing scale and ornament. The Greeks and Romans spent generations developing a complex system of proportion and decoration that told a very human story of artisan skill and continuity of craft. Hitler hijacked the political association of power and domination from the ancients but eschewed the very elements (the fingerprints if you will) that made these structures sophisticated human creations.

The architecture of the Third Reich was stripped of delicate scale elements that citizens could admire from the pedestrian vantage point and left only the large scale features that communicate intimidation, centralization of power, and severe discipline. It always strikes me as a "military" type of expression that primarily conveys force but no compassion. In contrast, the architecture of Rome (even with the brutality of the Caesars) was interwoven with deeply artistic intentions. The architecture was a record of the Roman culture and an emerging republic. This took centuries to develop. As the old adage goes: "Rome wasn't built in a day"... but evidently it was Hitler's intention to create a new Roman Empire literally overnight.

His reinvention of Neoclassicism was like a counterfeit copy: superficial in likeness and bankrupt in content.

A link to an excellent online resource, with images and text, can be found at the online resource page.

Discuss with your students the way architecture can express a culture and its philosophy. What impact does Christianity have on this discussion? How could it shape the architecture of a culture?

▶ Architecture

The architecture of the Third Reich—immense, powerful, and soulless—reflected Hitler's view of himself as the world's leader, Nazism as the correct political theory, and Germany as the center of the universe. Consider what his favored architect, Albert Speer, wrote of Hitler: "Just as he determines the will and nature of the movement, so also he determines the simplicity and purity of its buildings, their strength of expression, the clarity of the thinking, the quality of the material, and most importantly, the new inner meaning and content of his buildings. Building is not merely a way of passing time for the Führer, rather a serious way of giving expression in stone to the will of the National Socialist movement."

Reich Chancellery designed by Albert Speer, 1938

» Though it was destroyed by the Soviet army as they came into Berlin, many photos remain. You can see a photo of the Reich Chancellery at the online resource page. It cost over one billion dollars in today's currency and took four thousand workers working in shifts twenty-four hours per day to finish in just under one year. How would you describe this building? In what ways would this building have reflected to visitors the characteristics of the Nazi regime?

▶ Arts in Action

Select one or more, and let your artistic juices flow!

"Human Freedoms" Art

» In the style of Rockwell, and using any one (or all) of the four human freedoms referred to in FDR's speech, create a work of art which will depict a meaningful image of this freedom for today's culture. You might choose to make a collage, do an illustration, use photography, or some other form of visual art.

Propaganda Poster Art

» Create your own poster in the style of J. Howard Miller's *We Can Do It!* Choose the issue on which you wish to influence others, decide what is the most important point to communicate, brainstorm what visual images will work most effectively, and colorfully create the poster. Have fun!

◉ Do an art project

"Human Freedoms" Art

Encourage students to think about images that would convey these freedoms in such a way that it would speak deeply to people of very different cultures:

- Freedom of speech
- Freedom of worship
- Freedom from want
- Freedom from fear

▷ Science

One of the technologies with the greatest potential for damage developed during WWII was rocketry. Germany was trying to gain the ability to launch long-range ballistic missiles against her enemies, while the Allies were also working on this technology. Unfortunately for the Allies, the Germans had a scientist named Wernher von Braun working for them. Von Braun's interest was in space exploration, but the same rockets that would allow man to travel in space would also benefit the military who used them for weaponry. It was a blessing to the Allies that Germany did not develop the V-2 (guided missile) until the closing days of WWII—otherwise the outcome of the war might have been very different.

» Learn the Newtonian principle behind rockets! Isaac Newton said that for every action there is an opposite and equal reaction. How does this work in rocketry? Try this: Blow up a long (not a round) balloon and let it go. Why does it fly forward?

» When you blow up a balloon and hold the end shut, all the air stays inside the balloon, so there is no overall action. But, when you let go of the end, the action of the air rushing out in one direction causes an equal reaction in the other direction. To see it more clearly, thread a long piece of fishing line through a straw. Tie each end of the fishing line to chairs placed across the room from each other, making sure that the fishing line is taut. Blow up a long balloon, and, holding the neck securely so no air escapes, have someone else tape the balloon to the straw in a couple of places. Now let go of your balloon—in other words, launch your "rocket."

What does freedom from want, for instance, mean to someone living in Somalia? Or, what does freedom of worship mean to someone living in France?

Propaganda Poster Art

For an excellent "primer" on propaganda posters used by the US during WWII, visit the Powers of Persuasion link at the online resource page.

◉ Do a science experiment

Feel free to choose one of these projects. If students love science, they might want to consider doing all of them!

For students interested in rocketry, encourage them to read more about Robert Goddard and Wernher von Braun, two of the most important rocket scientists in history.

NASA has an amazing booklet, *Rockets Teacher's Guide with Activities*, that is available free online. You can find a link at the online resource page.

The online resource page at www.HistoryRevealed.org contains many helpful Internet links to artwork, architecture, music, project helps, and more.

◉ Listen to and discuss the music

Listen

Bartok's *Concerto for Orchestra*

In the book *The Gift of Music*, by Jane Stuart Smith and Betty Carlson, Bartok is described as one of history's most important *ethnomusicologists* (discovering and preserving musical expression of a tribe or of a local culture). The authors wrote:

> . . . what Bartok called "peasant music" greatly influenced his composing. His originality developed as a result of this discovery. "The use of borrowed materials has nothing to do with the artistic results of a piece," he said. "After all Shakespeare, Moliere, Bach and Handel borrowed. Everybody has his roots in the art of some former time." He succeeded in transmitting folk music into something universal.

This profoundly important, influential musician and composer was also one who rejected his Roman Catholic roots, first turning to atheism and later to Unitarianism.

▶ Music

Bela Bartok was one of the most significant and influential composers of the twentieth century. His most important works were composed from 1930 to 1945. Bartok was from Eastern Europe (born in what was then Hungary, now Romania) and was vocal in his denunciation of Nazi Germany. He fled Hungary in 1939 because of the "robbery and murder of Nazism," ending up eventually in New York.

The music of Bartok derives much of its melodic line and rhythmic irregularities from the folk songs and gypsy music which he spent years collecting in Eastern Europe. There is a tremendous sense of driving rhythmic energy in this music. Harmonically, it is challenging to the ear because Bartok used chords and harmonies that were either derived from Eastern European sources or made up to follow his own system. You may have heard musicians talking about how a piece of music was written in a particular "key" (like, the "Key of A"). Bartok expanded that concept, incorporating such a variety of harmonic techniques that the notion of the "key" is all but lost. You will notice that his music sounds different from the music of other composers we have studied!

Concerto for Orchestra by Bartok (1943)

You can find a link to listen to the music at the online resource page. This piece was composed while he was dying of leukemia and is, for some, the most popular of his works today. How would you describe this music? How is it different from the other composers you have studied?

For further study in this time period, follow the phenomenon of musical theater that swept the world, beginning in the 1940s. Some good examples would be *Oklahoma* or *Brigadoon*.

▶ Cooking

Douglas MacArthur, at his forced departure from Corregidor Island during WWII, told the people of the Philippines, "I shall return." And you will return to these treats over and over once you try them!

Camote Frito—Deep-Fried Sweet Potato Chips

2 pounds sweet potatoes (it's easier if they are long and cylindrical)   Powdered sugar

CAUTION: *Adult supervision required!*

Peel the sweet potatoes and cut them crosswise into paper-thin slices. Drop the slices into a bowl filled with cold water and let them soak for about 15 minutes.

Pour oil into a deep fryer or large, heavy saucepan to a depth of 2 to 3 inches and heat it until it reaches a temperature of 375° on a deep-frying thermometer.

Just before frying, drain the slices and pat them completely dry. Fry the potatoes in three batches—slowly immersing them into the hot oil. Fry for 3 to 4 minutes, or until they turn a golden color. As they brown, transfer the slices to paper towels to drain. Serve warm, sprinkled lightly with powdered sugar. Enjoy!

◉ Cook the food

Though not quite the same as the deep-fried Camote Frito, these sweet potato chips provide a much healthier version of the Filipino favorite.

2 sweet potatoes (sliced 1/8-inch thick or less)
1 tbsp canola oil
Powdered sugar

Preheat oven to 400°F. Lightly oil two baking sheets, then place the sliced sweet potatoes—without overlapping—on the sheets. Brush the slices with oil.

Bake the potato chips until they just begin to brown on the edges, approximately twelve to fifteen minutes. Remove from oven, dust with powdered sugar, and serve immediately.

▷ Student Self-Evaluation UNIT 8, PHASE 3

Dates and hours:_____

Evaluate your projects

- List which of the activities listed in this Phase you did:

  _____

  _____

- Rate your enthusiasm: _____

  Explain: _____

  _____

- Rate the precision of your approach:_____

  Explain: _____

  _____

- Rate your effort toward the completion of the project: _____

  Explain: _____

  _____

- Ask yourself what worked and what did not. What would you do differently in the future, and what would you repeat?

  _____

  _____

- How did these hands-on activities enhance your knowledge of World War II & Miraculous Deliverances? What made them worthwhile?

  _____

  _____

- In the first three Phases of this Unit, what aspect of the time period has most captured your imagination? What would you like to creatively pursue to conclude your study?

  _____

  _____

World War II & Miraculous Deliverances (1939–1945) **375**

◉ Conduct a review and evaluation

In this Phase of Unit 8, your students should have had the opportunity to explore World War II & Miraculous Deliverances through various hands-on and creative sessions by completing a selection from the following:

- completed a mapping section;
- observed and discussed art & architecture;
- worked on an art project;
- experimented with a science project or taken a field trip;
- listened to music;
- tasted a food related to this Unit;

- completed their self-evaluation procedure for this Phase.

Record student hours: _____

Assess student involvement in the hands-on activities.

Create an evaluation system of your own or refer to the evaluation rubric in the introduction as a tool for assessing participation. The categories you will probably find most useful for evaluating projects are *"Task"* and *"Process: Teamwork."* Consider specifically the enthusiasm, the precision of approach, and the efforts toward improving skills and completing activities, rather than rating the project as compared to a masterpiece.

Do not critique the self-evaluation page your student completes in the Student Manual—it is acceptable for students to occasionally leave lines blank if a question does not apply. Instead, discuss with the student the intention of the written comments and incorporate those into your evaluation.

Determine a grade for this Phase, if using grades: _____

Teacher Self-Evaluation:

Evaluate your own use of materials: what worked and what did not? Consider your time management. Were you able to recognize and respond to your students' needs? Did you make your expectations clear? In what ways would you like to improve your approach for the next Unit? Incorporate suggestions from your students in your own evaluation (*this requires humility!*).

◉ Choose an area of expression

Students may work either individually or in teams.

Linguistics:

Journalism

The British press called it the *sitzkrieg* because it seemed to be a case of sitting around worrying rather than actually fighting. When it finally came, however, we now know that it was far worse than anyone had anticipated. Encourage students to consider what it would be like to have a potential catastrophe on your front doorstep, which then appears to be only a false alarm, until suddenly, the catastrophe occurs. [Author's note: This is what it was like while we lived close to Mt. St. Helens just before the mountain erupted. People were unaware of how much destruction was about to be unleashed.]

Ernie Pyle, a Pulitzer Prize winning reporter during WWII, wrote articles in a casual style that brought to light the viewpoint of the common soldier. Encourage students interested in this project to read some of his writings, many of which have been compiled into books—learn from a master!

Poetry

Encourage students interested in writing a poem about Dunkirk to

consider the rhythm of the line, especially as it is being read aloud. Look for ways to repeat patterns of rhythm in the poem, from one line to the next. It might be helpful to think of this in terms of giving a musical feel to the spoken word. A link to an excellent online source can be found at the online resource page.

Prose

Winston Churchill said, "In wartime, truth is so precious that she should always be attended by a bodyguard of lies." Students doing this project might find it helpful (and intriguing) to read or watch *The Man Who Never Was*, by Ewen Montagu. This is the true story of how the British completely deceived the Germans regarding the invasion of Sicily. Having learned what worked in this first deception, they will have to find completely new ideas for what to try now, for this far more significant invasion.

Ask students to consider whether the soldier they are representing believes the Nazi ideas or is he, rather, a German Christian who was simply drafted into the military. That will make a considerable difference in how the letter is written and the type of information that is included!

Phase 4

> The Expression Week

▶ In Your Own Way…

In this Unit, we have seen: the might of Hitler's military power—the blitzkrieg— unleashed on Europe and the Soviet Union; the Battle of Britain; Italian and German forces attacking in North Africa; Japan's surprise bombing at Pearl Harbor; America's entry into the world war; Churchill, Roosevelt, and Stalin working together against Hitler; war in the Pacific; war in the Atlantic; war on land, sea, and air; the Holocaust; island-hopping and carpet-bombing; D-Day and the Battle of the Bulge; victory in Europe; atomic bombs and victory in the Pacific. It has been total war filling the globe, with tragedy and terror following in its wake. Throughout the darkness of this time, however, we have seen again and again glimpses of God's love shining through. Now, choose a selection of these activities, or create your own, which will best express what you have learned from this Unit.

LINGUISTICS

Journalism

As a reporter for the national newspaper *France Today*, you have been assigned to interview your fellow citizens during what is being termed the "Phony War." Are the people you interviewed concerned about Germany's intentions? Help your readers by getting the scoop on this puzzling issue!

You are with the American Marines as they hop from island to island in the Pacific theater of the war. Writing for the American magazine *Saturday Evening Post*, describe what it's like for these soldiers as they face Japanese forces at each location. What is it they hope, and what is it they fear?

Poetry

Finish this poem about the sea evacuation of Dunkirk:

Our circumstance hopeless,

We despaired on the beach …

Prose

The Allies have asked you, a noted intelligence specialist, to make a plan to deceive the Germans about Operation Overlord (the plans for the D-Day invasion). Knowing that the Germans are expecting some sort of invasion, it is up to you to point them in the wrong direction. Remember, though, they were fooled once at the invasion of Sicily, so it won't be easy to fool them a second time. Good luck!

As a German soldier with Rommel's forces in North Africa, write a letter home to your family describing your experiences chasing Allies. You might want to include what you have heard through the grapevine about the new British commander, Montgomery.

376 World War II & Miraculous Deliverances (1939–1945)

ART

Painting/Drawing

WWII is a study in the truth of Corrie ten Boom's words: "There is no darkness so great that God's love is not greater still." Create a painting, or series of paintings, which will visually present this truth in the historic setting of this war.

Graphic Design

Create a modern day T-shirt to be sold in the stores of St. Petersburg (Leningrad): "I survived the 900-day siege!" Since this was a Russian triumph over the German military, be sure to include visual clues that will tell—or, at least, allude to—the story.

Cartooning

The German blitzkrieg blazed across Western Europe like the lightning for which it was named. Yet, it was not successful in the invasion of Russia. Create a two-to-three frame political cartoon of this technologically mobile marvel, and what slowed it down.

3-D Art

Using art tape and paper or cardboard, create a three-dimensional memorial to the victims of the Holocaust.

MUSIC

Compose

As a British soldier, compose a marching song about the battle of El Alamein. Remember Churchill's insightful words, *"Before Alamein we never had a victory. After Alamein, we never had a defeat."*

Performance Practice

With your teacher's help, select an appropriate piece of music which expresses some particular aspect studied in this Unit that you found interesting.

World War II & Miraculous Deliverances (1939–1945) **377**

Art:

Painting/Drawing

Encourage students interested in creating this painting to decide which scenes from WWII they wish to depict, and then to consider more than one way of visually showing God's love lighting the darkness of war. From these scenes and these possibilities, create as powerful an image as possible.

Graphic Design

Survivor T-shirt designs are common. What is uncommon is communicating a story—especially a newsworthy one—and telling it well. Encourage students to look for the kind of visual images that will immediately identify "Russian versus Nazi," and then to weave these, along with the slogan, into an eye-catching design.

Cartooning

Ask students what elements—geographical, technical, human—contributed to the success of the blitzkrieg in the West. How could these be turned into caricatures for a political cartoon? In the same way, what elements—geographical, technical, human—contributed to failure in the East? Again, how could these be turned into caricatures? With all of the caricaturized elements at hand, students will be prepared to make a visual statement about what happened in Russia.

3-D Art

Encourage students to consider what three-dimensional object(s) could represent some aspect of the Holocaust for viewers. For instance, there is a memorial in the US of a vast collection of buttons in a huge glass sculpture to commemorate those killed in the Holocaust. It depicted in a very small way the fact that the Nazis stole from each of their victims all of their earthly belongings—including their clothes and buttons.

Music:

Compose

Marching songs always contain a definite and regular rhythm—that is what allows everyone to successfully march together. Encourage students to work with an even 1-2 or a 1-2-3-4 rhythm as they either write new music or simply write new words for an older tune.

Performance Practice

For musical students, this selection may be a wonderful opportunity to express what they have learned. Make sure they select a piece that they have adequate time to prepare.

Drama:

Reality Theater

For students interested in this dramatic presentation, encourage them to do character research. Attempt to recreate the character of Corrie ten Boom as accurately as possible, with the emotional, empathetic connection to bring her character to life. Character research incorporates learning the person's biography, culture, and geography, studying personal habits of behavior or thought through documentation and recordings. At the same time, the actor must fill the gaps in the action of the historical record with imagined circumstances—which the student dreams up—thereby creating a personal connection to, and ownership of, their role as this historic figure.

Comedy

For this skit, encourage students to embrace exaggeration—it makes for great comedy. Students might want to begin the skit by having the main actor decide that the way to identify the mystery island is to announce that there is a problem of some sort at Midway. Then, recreate the scene where he tries to come up with the right kind of problem to fake. It must be a problem significant enough to be announced in Japanese communication, but not so bad that it will cause them to call off the attack. He must have a plan for convincing his commanding officer to go along with this, too. Find the many—and humorous—possibilities, discard the ridiculous, and settle on the best.

DRAMA

Reality Theater

The Christian TV program *Miracles Today* has asked you to interview Corrie ten Boom about her recent experiences in a German concentration camp. Be sure to ask her about the bottle of vitamins!

Comedy

The Battle of Midway was the result of code-breaking, courage and, as Christians would attest, *providence*. The story of the code-breaking, however, contains great potential for comedy. Set up the scene: one person, working with cryptographers in Hawaii, comes up with a crazy idea of how to identify which mystery island Japan is planning to attack—fake a problem on Midway, report it openly, and wait for the Japanese to swallow the bait.

Puppetry

Using puppets, reenact the story of Gladys Aylward's life, including her failure at the missionary school in London, traveling adventures across Siberia, unusual work for the Mandarin, and the famous rescue of the orphaned children during the war.

Prop Needs

_____

_____

Costume Ideas

_____

_____

Role/Player

_____

_____

Set Suggestions

_____

_____

378 World War II & Miraculous Deliverances (1939–1945)

Puppetry

For students interested in creating a puppet show of Gladys Aylward's life, encourage them to use signs, images, and words to denote location—these will aid in creating quick transitions. Another means of making transition with great capacity for comedy is to open the curtain and reveal the new situation.

Movement:

Pantomime

The performer is attempting to communicate through physical actions something unfamiliar to the audience's eye. The actor requires a second perspective, an outside perspective, to evaluate the clarity of the performance. That is why a director would be of great value for this project. There are different roles in developing a theatrical production: writer, actor, director. In this case, the writer will probably also be the actor. In deciding on the appropriate series of physical actions, the student is writing not just a script, but a physical script. The director's job in this case will only be to point out what's not clear in the presentation. (The writer may choose to ask the director for ideas on how to clarify it, but it's not the director's job in this case to tell the actor what to do.)

in place of ships if you reenact the Battle of the Philippine Sea. In this example, a paper clip with an upside down thumbtack could represent an aircraft carrier; a paper clip with a match could be a destroyer. All of the variations of paper clips will be noted in your key. The key must allow the observer to identify every model at a glance, so draw a picture of the symbol and what military item it represents. Note: keep it simple!

Conceptual Design:

Design a Dollar

Create a shoebox to hold all your good ideas. It can be figurative, like a folder on your computer desktop, or it can be a literal shoebox. Its function is to store all of the images you find that might work for this project. Encourage students to research as many images as possible in a designated amount of time. If there is an image they like, they should save it to (or in) their shoebox. It might be a picture cut out of a magazine or an online image. Once they have spent the designated amount of time researching and collecting images for their shoebox, have them sort through the shoebox and pick their favorite image. This process allows the artist the imaginative scope of several ideas without choosing one immediately, allowing the opportunity for inspiration without the pressure of selection—until they feel they have enough resources to glean from.

◉ Share creative expressions in class

Create a safe environment for the presentations. Set ground rules prior to the presentations, so that students know how much time is available for each of them, and so that they know they will be honored and respected by all those observing.

MOVEMENT

Pantomime

You are one of the Allied paratroopers on D-Day. With pantomime, create a distinct example of each of the many physical actions involved in this momentous twenty-four hour period, from packing your bags in England to fulfilling your mission in Normandy. Be prepared to answer questions from an intrigued audience about the experiences of the paratroopers!

Dance

Choreograph a dance of the Big Three—Churchill, FDR, Stalin. What are the distinctive character traits of each that you wish to depict through dance? Consider how you might best express the ways that their ideas flowed together, and the ways in which they conflicted.

Miniature Action

There were many notable battles in this war, such as the Battle of Kursk (the biggest tank battle in WWII) and the Battle of the Philippine Sea (the largest aircraft carrier battle in history). Choose a battle (one of these or another of your choosing) then set up a miniaturized version of this event. Be sure to include the appropriate geographic elements, whether land, island, sea, or air!

CONCEPTUAL DESIGN

Design a Dollar

Never forget! Your award-winning design is intended to provide to democracy-loving people of your nation an emotionally moving, visual reminder of the price of defending freedom in WWII. Whether you work with currency or coin, remember, you have the front AND the back.

CREATE YOUR OWN EXPRESSION

_____

_____

_____

_____

Dance

This is a dance where the character traits and intellectual ideals of these three leaders are examined. Encourage students interested in this project to learn about the way many choreographers utilize Rudolf Laban's *Effort Actions*. He was a theater professional who devised this system of describing physical energy dynamics, which include dab, punch, flick, glide, and a few others you can look up on Wikipedia. The student's job will be to create logical associations with these metaphorical *effort actions*. Determine the traits and ideals of each of these world leaders and correlate them with particular movements incorporating effort actions. Students should be able to explain why they chose these particular actions, and how these are associated with the Big Three.

Miniature Action

The use of a *key* will be of critical importance in this project because, unless you work for a metal factory, you will not be able to recreate these military vehicles in this scale with proper materials. A key explains the relationship between the model and the actual military unit it represents. It will allow for a great degree of "shorthand" in your model building, based on the materials at hand. For example, paper clips can be used

◉ Conduct a review and evaluation

In this Phase of Unit 8, your students should have had the opportunity to express what they have learned about World War II & Miraculous Deliverances through one or more various creative selections of their own choosing. These include:

- Linguistics;
- Art;
- Music;
- Drama;
- Movement;
- Conceptual Design.

Record student hours: _____

Assess student effort in the creative expressions, as individuals or as teams.

Create an evaluation system of your own, or refer to the evaluation rubric in the introduction, as a tool for assessing participation. The categories you will probably find most useful for evaluating their projects are *"Task," "Process: Teamwork," "Process: Originality,"* and Grammar, Format, and Spelling.

In this Phase especially, do not critique the self-evaluation page your student completes in the Student Manual—consider how the very soul of an artist has been exposed and vulnerable, so be encouraging and not belittling. Again, consider enthusiasm, precision of approach, and efforts toward improving skills and completing the activity, rather than rating the project as compared to a masterpiece. Instead, discuss with the student the intention of the written comments and incorporate those into your evaluation.

Determine a grade for this Phase, if using grades: _____

Teacher Self-Evaluation:

Evaluate your own use of materials and teaching opportunities: what worked and what did not; how effective was your time-management; how were your responses to the needs of your student; did you make your expectations clear; in what ways would you like to improve your approach for the next Unit? Incorporate suggestions from your students in your own evaluation (*this requires humility!*).

Take a moment now to evaluate the whole Unit. What would you like to remember if you taught this subject again? What do you recognize that your students gained most—either as students of history or as creative individuals? What did you learn about World War II & Miraculous Deliverances or about teaching?

▶ Student Self-Evaluation UNIT 8, PHASE 4

Dates and hours: _____

Evaluate your projects

- What creative project did you choose:

  _____

- What did you expect from your project, and how does the final project compare to your initial expectations?

  _____

  _____

- What do you like about your project? What would you change?

  _____

  _____

In Conclusion

Revisit the two Key Concepts from the beginning of this Unit. Explain how your understanding of and appreciation for each has grown over the course of your study.

- _____

  _____

- _____

  _____

Record your concluding thoughts on World War II & Miraculous Deliverances.

_____

_____

_____

_____

_____

_____

380 World War II & Miraculous Deliverances (1939–1945)

Early Cold War & Renewed Vision
(1945–1955)

Pray with the students at the beginning of each Unit.

Enthusiasm and delight are the best ways to capture a student's interest and jump-start motivation, so:

» **For the Auditory Students:** Listen to a gospel music recording from the 1940s or 50s, such as the Swan Silvertones singing "Mary Don't You Weep."

» **For the Kinesthetic Students:** Invite students to physically demonstrate the effect on people from both sides of an "Iron Curtain."

» **For the Visual Students:** Find a photographic image depicting the Berlin Airlift, or watch a YouTube video of what was known as Operation Little Vittles. See the online resource page.

» **For the hearts of all:** Pray with them at the beginning of the Unit, that God would help them discover what He has for each one to learn in this Unit.

◉ Learning Style Emphasis

Teachers can choose to have students do one or two activities, rather than the entire week's schedule. Please use what works for you in your unique setting.

	Week 1: Feeler	**Week 2: Thinker**	**Week 3: Sensor**	**Week 4: Intuitor**
	During this week, students will be introduced to the Early Cold War & Renewed Vision, along with the appropriate Scriptures. You may follow this suggested schedule or adapt it to meet your students' needs:	Students will explore topics of interest through research and reporting, learn new vocabulary, and construct a time line relating to the Early Cold War & Renewed Vision.	Students will gain cultural understanding through sensory activities as they explore interrelated subject areas through sensory activities pertaining to the Early Cold War & Renewed Vision.	Students, through creative self-expression, using one or more creative activities, will present some aspect of what they have learned in the past three weeks relating to the Early Cold War & Renewed Vision. Areas of expression include linguistics, art, music, drama, movement, and conceptual design.)
Monday	Informally discuss the Key Concepts Listen to the *What in the World?* audio recording(s)	Choose topic and begin research	Create a map and discuss the issues in teams	Choose an area of expression and begin work either individually or in teams
Tuesday	Read the article Listen to the other audio recording(s) Read the Scriptures		Examine and discuss art masterpieces & architectural structures	
Wednesday	Recap the material using activities Talk together	Practice vocabulary	Do an art project*	
Thursday	Conduct class discussion	Construct the time line	Do a science experiment or field trip**	
Friday	Choose books of interest/Internet search Conduct a review and evaluation	Complete research projects and share in class or hand in Conduct a review and evaluation	Listen to and discuss the music Cook the food listed in the recipe Conduct a review and evaluation	Share creative expressions in class Conduct a review and evaluation

*Art project will need to be planned ahead of time to acquire materials.
** Field trip will require extra planning time.

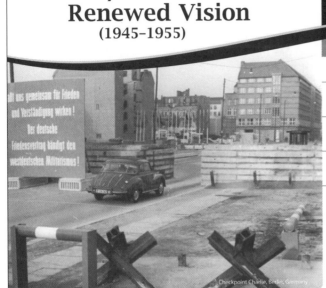

Early Cold War & Renewed Vision (1945–1955)

UNIT **9**

Key Concepts

- Europe divided

- Communism in Asia

- America's Perspective

- New Challenges to the Church

Checkpoint Charlie, Berlin, Germany

What's in a name? As we consider the post-war years of 1945–1953, this famous question from Shakespeare's *Romeo and Juliet* will guide us to look beneath the surface, past the rhetoric and beyond the statistics, to discover the human faces and national fears in the rubble of WWII. Foundational to understanding how the world changed after the war, new names, such as *Cold War, Displaced Person, Containment, Arms Race,* and even such familiar names as *Communist* and *Democratic*, need to be considered in their post-WWII context. As we examine the political—oftentimes explosive—conflicts developing in Europe, Asia, Africa, and the Middle East from 1945–1953, along with East-West tensions between the former Allies, we will gain deeper understanding not only of this historic time, but of issues the world still faces today.

Before the end of WWII, Allied leaders had already agreed about what to do in Germany to end its war-begetting culture: *denazification,*

Early Cold War & Renewed Vision (1945–1955) **381**

◉ Informally discuss the Key Concepts with your students

KEY CONCEPTS Background Information

These are the main objectives of the Unit. As you proceed through the four weeks, your students will be given various ways of understanding each of these objectives. Explanations of these Key Concepts follow.

9

disarmament, and *democratization*. First was "denazification," meaning that, in an unprecedented move, Nazi leaders must be put on trial for "crimes against humanity." "Disarmament" meant the German military machine must be dismantled, including its strong industries capable of turning out panzers and V-rockets. "Democratization" meant Germans must be shown a new democratic political form, without the dictatorial control of a *kaiser* or *führer*, which would allow them to live peaceably among their European neighbors.

After V-E day, as the Allies straddled the country of their fallen enemy, Germany was broken into four zones of occupation: Soviet, American, British, and, somewhat surprisingly, French. Each of the four viewed this occupation from a unique perspective and with a specific agenda.

The Soviets' agenda was the most demanding because, of all the Allies, they had experienced the greatest loss. With estimates of twenty-four million dead, even greater numbers made homeless, and the massive destruction of factories and railroads by invading Nazis, the USSR was intent on protecting itself and regaining its vigor. This would be accomplished partially through reparations and partially through dismantling German industries to ship home, insurance that the Germans would be unable to rearm militarily.

The French, also repeat victims of German aggression, wanted to keep this large and competitive neighbor as harmless as possible—ideally allowing France to control the prime industrial areas of the Ruhr valley. For both the Soviets and the French, a nation of German farmers was far more palatable than a nation of German soldiers.

The British, who had nearly bankrupted their economy to fight the war, wanted Germany to become productive, profitable, and able to pay their own way as soon as possible. And the Americans, though committed to German occupation for a time, were anxious to cross the Atlantic and go home.

These were not the only differences, however. Despite the temporary forced alliance during WWII, the Soviet Union and the West (the non-communist nations) continued to hold remarkably different political and philosophical viewpoints, making them utterly suspicious of one another's motives. As we will soon see, these differences led to escalating hostilities and a new form of war.

> *After V-E day, as the Allies straddled the country of their fallen enemy, Germany was broken into four zones of occupation.*

Displaced Persons in Europe

Before this new version of war came to pass, however, an immediate challenge faced the Allies. In the everyday lives of people living in the devastated areas of Europe, the pressing issue was survival: finding

? To get an informal discussion started on this Key Concept, ask a simple, leading question, such as, "What do you know about the Iron Curtain in Europe?"

Europe Divided— EXPLANATION

After the successful Allied landing at Normandy, as Hitler's war machine began to crumble, Western Allied forces pushed from Europe's Atlantic coast to Germany while Soviet forces pushed toward Germany from the east. Each side, as they raced to Berlin, liberated the nations across their path, which had so recently been occupied by the Nazis. This meant that while the Western European countries experienced a renewal of their freedom after the war, the countries of Eastern and Central Europe experienced a continuing restriction of freedom—control by right-wing totalitarianism now shifted to control by left-wing totalitarianism.

Germany was the focus for the Allies, both Soviet and Western. As the aggressor in two world wars in the space of twenty-five years, Germany was considered to be militaristic in the extreme and likely to restart its warmongering capability. Because of this, the Allies had agreed on the necessity of occupying the nation, of putting on trial the Nazi leaders, of reeducating the population, and of controlling its potential to manufacture armaments of war. Dividing the nation into four zones, the Allies set about trying to accomplish these goals while, at the same time, making sure the German people neither starved to death nor succumbed to mass epidemics (like the influenza epidemic after WWI).

In the American, British, and French zones, located in the western region of Germany, Allied leaders worked to find political leaders who would be capable of taking Germany into a democratic form of government, rather than continuing a totalitarian form. The Allies anticipated that re-educating the population would be a long-term process, that it might take an entire generation before a peace-loving Germany would emerge. However, with the bitter experience of defeat and a sense of betrayal by Hitler and his Nazis, it turned out to only be a short time before Germans in the western zone were engaging in the political process, freely choosing their own leaders in a multi-party election in 1946.

9

adequate food, clothing, and shelter. As we look back at this moment from the removed perspective of several decades, it is important to not skip over the plight of multiplied millions who had become homeless and were now struggling to exist.

Why were there so many? Obviously, those whose homes were destroyed in the Allied bombing of Germany were now seeking shelter. But beyond that, there were also people known as *Displaced Persons* (or refugees) who found themselves a long way from home. Many people, forcibly taken by the Nazis from other countries and transported to slave-labor or concentration camps, were suddenly released by the Allies. A vast number of prisoners of war were set free from Nazi prison camps. Separated from their families and often broken in body, soul, and spirit, these survivors were desperate to return home, find what remained of their families, and begin rebuilding their lives. Many, however, could no longer go back to what they had called home for fear of execution by the Soviets. Another stream of refugees were Germans who had been living in Poland, East Prussia, and Czechoslovakia. At war's end, they were furiously driven out of their former dwellings and sent back to a devastated and divided Germany that had little to offer. And, while many Eastern Europeans had fled to the west as the Soviet army approached, many more for the next decade and a half would flee Soviet domination, until the building of the Berlin Wall in 1961 closed the door. This shattering war resulted in a virtual explosion of suffering, with estimates of between eleven and twenty *million* Displaced Persons in Western Europe.

WWII resulted in a virtual explosion of suffering, with estimates of between eleven and twenty million Displaced Persons in Western Europe.

Camps were set up for these refugees by the occupying Allies, the United Nations, and charitable organizations who sought to deal with the problem. Though, over time, many of these people returned to their countries of origin, a Church World Service brochure in 1948 said that there yet remained 850,000 in camps who could never go home.

These 850,000 are today's DP—the hard core of irrepatriables [persons who cannot go home]. They are Poles, Latvians, Lithuanians, Estonians, Yugoslavs, Greeks, Ukrainians, Czechoslovaks. Brought into Germany as slave laborers and concentration camp inmates, they cannot return to their Soviet-dominated lands because of fear of political and religious persecution. This is the third year since "liberation" that 850,000 DPs continue to live in DP camps. The United States has promised that none of them would be forced to go back to Soviet-dominated countries to face enslavement or death. . . . Fifty per cent of all DPs are women and children. . . . All religions and denominations are represented among the DPs. Four out of five are Christian.

Talk with your students about Christianity behind the Iron Curtain. The testimonies of Brother Andrew (*God's Smuggler*) and Richard Wurmbrand (*Tortured for Christ*) vividly depict the kind of mind control exerted under atheistic Communism. Together, pray earnestly that God would break through any boundaries set up by man to keep out the Word of God and the truth of the gospel.

1952, more than 16,000 refugees fled to West Berlin. This open door would shut dramatically in 1961, when East Germany built the Berlin Wall to keep its people from deserting.

The Berlin Wall was the symbol of the *Iron Curtain*, or the political division, between the Soviet-controlled countries and the democratically established countries of Europe. Behind the Iron Curtain lay the Eastern and Central European nations that were held captive by Stalin until communist-controlled governments could be put in place. Some of these countries—Estonia, Latvia, Lithuania—had simply (and illegally) been absorbed into the Soviet Union without Allied approval at the end of WWII. Some had sided with the Allies during the war, but despite this fact, when the Soviet troops entered, freedom to choose their own political system was gone. These were Poland, Czechoslovakia, Yugoslavia, and Albania. Those who sided with the Nazis—Hungary, Romania, and Bulgaria—came under even greater measures of control. With the exception of Yugoslavia, these Iron Curtain countries, stretching from the Baltic to the Balkans, were utterly dominated by the Soviet Union from 1948 until the fall of Communism.

The Soviets, with their zone located in the eastern portion of Germany, went about their business as determinedly as the Allies in the western zones—under an entirely different agenda. With the firmly held doctrine that communism was the next step in the evolution of politics and economics, the Soviets sought to reeducate the people in their zone with Stalin's version of Marxism-Leninism. In the Soviet zone, political parties were reestablished in 1945, but when the communists were not able to win a majority of seats during the election of 1946, they found other less pleasant means of taking control.

Though Berlin was located in the eastern Soviet zone, it was divided up among the four occupying Allies. This city would be the site of one of the earliest and most confrontational showdowns between the Soviets and the West when the Soviets cut off all means of supply to the western sectors. As mentioned on the audio CDs, the Berlin Airlift, from June of 1948 until May of 1949, allowed the West to care for the people of Berlin without using military force against the Soviets. This tiny island of Western democracy, isolated in a sea of Soviet tyranny, proved to be very attractive to Germans living in the east. In one month alone, August

9

Corrie ten Boom, directed by God to return to Germany after the war with a message of hope and forgiveness, was able, with a group of friends, to convert a former concentration camp into a place of refuge. In a chapter of her book *Tramp for the Lord*, Corrie describes some of the challenging and difficult aspects of life for displaced persons: "The camp was crowded. Some rooms were jammed with several families. Noise and bedlam were everywhere as families, many without men because they had been killed in the war, tried to carry on the most basic forms of living." Corrie found that because of her own deep personal loss in the war, she could communicate at a heart level the great need to forgive. She had learned firsthand that when we forgive, we begin to heal.

Corrie found that because of her own deep personal loss in the war, she could communicate at a heart level the great need to forgive.

In the midst of the chaos and confusion of the DP camps, people like Corrie devoted themselves to serving the immense needs of the overwhelmed refugees. Though tragedy, loss, and suffering were common experiences, yet the grace of God was visible through the loving care of His people. In describing what she saw taking place in individual lives, Corrie quoted from one of Fanny Crosby's hymns:

Down in the human heart, crush'd by the tempter,
Feelings lie buried that grace can restore;
Touched by a loving heart, wakened by kindness
Chords that were broken will vibrate once more.

Displaced Persons in Palestine

The heartache of being homeless and displaced was not limited to the European continent, however. In the primed powder keg of the Middle East, Arab farmers and Jewish settlers each had laid claim to the land known as Palestine. Each side, with historic reasons for their claim, viewed the other with increasing hostility as the fires of *nationalism* (both Arab and Jewish) intensified. Shortly after the end of WWII when the unspeakable atrocities of the Holocaust were exposed to a stunned world, creating a Jewish state in Palestine suddenly seemed a just and righteous cause to the international community—except to the Arabs, especially those who had lived on the land for countless generations. As in all hotly disputed politics, each side viewed the other with increasing distrust and loathing. It was not uncommon for Arabs to suspiciously view Jews as tools of Western imperialism and for Jews to arrogantly view Arabs as backward and ignorant. Fear, rhetoric, and violence created an ever-widening gap between these two groups, while the idea of a shared land and common government became completely unworkable in the fury of opposing nationalist agendas.

384 Early Cold War & Renewed Vision (1945–1955)

Communism in Asia— EXPLANATION

What were the factors that made communism so attractive to many people in China, Vietnam, and North Korea? Part of the answer is in the vision of communism's economic paradise held out to the workers, or, in this case, to the peasants of a nation. Part of the answer can be found in how diligently the Communists fought against the Japanese during WWII. And the answer can also be discovered in considering the factor of colonialism in Asia. It is obvious that the vast country of Russia became communist under far different circumstances and background than did the countries of Asia, which would follow in its footsteps. Russia, though never quite comfortable with the West and constantly in competition with it, had never suffered the humiliation of being carved into pieces by Western European nations as China had been; had never suffered the indignities of colonization that Vietnam had experienced. Korea, which had been under Japanese occupation for thirty-five years, shared the burning desire of these nations to no longer be under the control of others. This was an intense nationalism, born out of the experiences of colonization, exploitation, and racism.

It is interesting to note that communism, in its classic form, was not about nationalism. In fact, it required that its adherents lay aside their loyalty to their own nation and embrace the political, economic, and social theories of the international communist community. This view was firmly held by Stalin, and he sought to remove anyone from leadership positions in any of his satellite nations if they would not follow him implicitly, with total, unquestioning obedience.

This is what makes studying the interaction between the Asian style

9

Great Britain, still acting under the post-WWI mandate to govern Palestine, sought to pacify the Arabs by banning immigration of Jews. Rather than bringing peace, however, this merely inflamed and internationalized the situation, making it a concern for many nations besides those directly involved. As desperate Jews, disregarding the British ban, fled Europe for illegal immigration to Palestine, many were caught by British patrol boats and either returned to Europe or put into barbed-wire enclosed internment camps on Cyprus. This was a public relations disaster—many nations openly voiced their disapproval. For the British, it was a lose-lose proposition. No matter what they did in Palestine, they made hostile enemies among both Jews and Arabs, each bent on exacting revenge on the British and each other. And in the midst of it, the British incurred the world's disdain.

Finally, Great Britain brought the unsolvable problem to the United Nations, formed by the Allies at war's end to provide peaceful solutions to international conflicts. On November 29, 1947, a majority of members in the UN General Assembly voted to partition the land of Palestine into two states—one for Jews and one for Palestinian Arabs—with Jerusalem as an international city. While the Jews accepted partition (reasoning that it was a start, and better than nothing), the Arabs utterly refused it.

Jewish and Arab leaders alike were fully aware that to create a new state of Israel would require massive changes to the status quo and would open the possibility of ever-increasing encroachment on Arab land. Many Arabs believed the Jews would behave in their partitioned area like the proverbial camel, continually moving further and further into the tent—until completely dominating the tent. As early as 1916, a Zionist writer, Israel Zangwill, indicated, "if we wish to give a country to a people without a country, it is utter foolishness to allow it to be the country of two peoples . . . a different place must be found either for the Jews or for their neighbors." For the Jews, the vision was to create a place of safety, of belonging, for their people, a place where every Jew in the world would be safe and welcome. With Hitler's systematic murder of six million Jews in the Holocaust, the vision had become an urgent need. For the Arabs, this was not a vision but a nightmare. From their perspective, the establishment of a Jewish nation meant setting a foreign Westernized state right in the Middle East, just as Arab nations were actively seeking independence from all European colonizers. And, on the humanitarian level, where their health, prosperity, and daily living were affected, it would force Palestinian Arabs to make the agonizing decision to either relocate away from their own homeland or to exist under a foreign government.

On November 29, 1947, a majority of members in the UN General Assembly voted to partition the land of Palestine into two states—one for Jews and one for Palestinian Arabs—with Jerusalem as an international city.

Early Cold War & Renewed Vision (1945–1955) **385**

J. Edwin Orr, the noted historian of revivals in the 19th and 20th centuries, wrote in the book *Evangelical Awakenings in Eastern Asia*, "It is interesting to note that the Chinese Communists borrowed and perverted some of the methods of phenomenal revival used in the China-wide movement of the 1930s in their attempt to bring about submission to the will of Mao. Instead of Scripture as a court of appeal, they presented the words of Mao. Instead of the accusations of conscience, they used perjured accusers of the brethren. Instead of confession of sin against God, they promoted confessions of opposition to Mao. Instead of restitution of property misappropriated and the reconciliation of enemies, they called for reeducation in Maoist thought and the denunciation of declared 'enemies' of the regime, whether guilty or not." Consider with your students the way this counterfeit system supplanted biblical concepts. What examples of this are seen in the world today? How does this affect people?

of communism and the Soviet style so fascinating; the Asian experience is so different from the experiences of the Eastern and Central European countries that were Soviet satellites. It can be most clearly seen in the example of China under Mao. Though the Chinese viewed the Soviets as the ones who had brought forth the "truth" of communism to the world, they were not willing to let the Soviets utterly control or dictate their actions. Mao was prepared to walk his own path, considering what he thought was best for China, regardless of Soviet directions. Eventually these two countries would come to view each other with hostility and

suspicion, believing that the other was not properly communistic.

North Korea had its unique approach. Seeking aid from both the Soviets and Chinese in preparation of the war against South Korea, Kim Il Sung found that the Soviets would only provide armaments and advice—not troops—as they were fearful of pushing the United States too far. China was not currently interested in the Korean War because its focus was on retaking the island of Formosa from Chiang Kai-shek. That changed dramatically, however, when American troops crossed the 38th parallel. At that point, the Communist Chinese were deeply concerned they might

lose an important and necessary buffer zone between them and the Americans, whom they believed to be imperialists. This was such a pivotal issue that they were willing to send a million Chinese soldiers into battle to stop the Americans.

Despite the differences between communism in Asia and the Soviet Union, there were many similarities. Terror, secret police, forced distribution of land, nationalization of factories and businesses, propaganda, the cult of personality, and fervent atheism that sought to destroy religions of any sort were all part of the bondage that settled suffocatingly on these nations.

9

When five countries of the Arab League attacked the new state of Israel six months later, on May 14–15, 1948, it resulted in a war from which hundreds of thousands of Palestinians fled, joining the ranks of displaced persons and suffering the brutal challenges of living long-term in refugee camps. [Author's note: After Israel's War of Independence, 750,000 Jews living in Arab countries were evicted from their homes and made their way to Israel. There, over time, they would be assimilated into the new nation. It was not the same story for the Palestinian refugees who, for the most part, remained refugees on the borders of neighboring Arab nations.]

Post-WWII Asia

Continuing eastward, it is interesting to consider how Japan, the other vanquished WWII enemy, fared after its surrender. With Japan's previous decades of military aggression, many anticipated that it would continue to be a major Allied concern in the post-war world. Surprisingly, however, Japan's recovery from war took a far different path than Germany's. The answer to this puzzle can be partly explained by the manner in which it was treated after the war. Rather than being divided as Germany had been, Japan remained a whole nation. And since Soviet soldiers had never entered Japan in the closing days of the war, they were not permitted to share its occupation. The occupation became the sole responsibility of US troops placed under the command of General Douglas MacArthur. The effect—and unexpected benefit—was that Japan did not become a center of contention in the East-West political struggle. However, three other Asian nations—Vietnam, China, and Korea—would soon become key sites in that escalating conflict.

With Japan's previous decades of military aggression, many anticipated that it would continue to be a major Allied concern in the post-war world.

In order to grasp the shape of things to come, we need to reexamine the experiences of most Asian countries in the previous hundred years. The unifying experience among these diverse countries was that they had lived under the burden and humiliation of Western colonization—and they deeply resented it, which should not come as a surprise. Nearly two hundred years prior, the American Revolution showed the lengths people would go to in order to gain their liberty, their freedom from an oppressive colonial master. From this common perspective, we begin to understand why many in Asia would work so hard to throw off their colonial rulers. Tragically, though, nations that replaced Western-dominated imperialism with Soviet-inspired communism soon found they had exchanged the old master for a new and merciless tyrant.

Vietnam, also known as French Indo-China, had long been part of France's colonial empire. Along with the infrastructure of government,

---

? To get an informal discussion started on this Key Concept, ask a simple, leading question, such as, "How did Americans view the Cold War?"

America's Perspective— EXPLANATION

In 1945, at the end of the war, President Truman had only been in office for a matter of months. The challenge before him was to try to follow the path Roosevelt had staked out in previous meetings with Stalin and Churchill. Unfortunately, Stalin had a different interpretation of those meetings, and with his army occupying a large portion of Europe, Truman was now left with a messy situation.

At first, the main issue on America's mind was to bring the troops home, leaving only the bare minimum needed to keep the Germans in check.

But, as time went on and tensions increased, American leaders began to wonder what the Soviets actually thought. In February 1946, one of the on-site experts, George Kennan, sent an 8,000-word telegram to Washington with his analysis of the situation. Here, in part, is what he wrote:

> In summary, we have here a political force committed fanatically to the belief that with US there can be no permanent modus vivendi, that it is desirable and necessary that the internal harmony of our society be disrupted, our traditional way of life be destroyed, the international authority of

9

schools, and hospitals, the French had also brought the knowledge of their own French Revolution to the Vietnamese. This, combined with the heady theories of Marxist-Leninist doctrine, gave many students a profound desire to see their nation exist without the crushing burden of colonial overlords. During WWII, Vietnam was invaded and occupied by the Japanese, then ruled by a hated collaboration of Japanese officers and French Vichy administrators. Vietnamese Communists in the north, led by a charismatic leader, Ho Chi Minh, stoutly resisted this occupation. When the Japanese surrendered on August 14, Ho Chi Minh moved quickly to take control of the major cities, proclaiming the independent Democratic Republic of Vietnam on September 2, 1945.

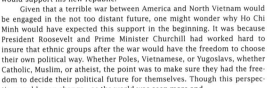

Ho Chi Minh

Since Ho Chi Minh was quoting from the American Declaration of Independence and the French Declaration of the Rights of Man in proclaiming independence and since he was joined by American OSS officers, he believed the United States would support his new republic.

Given that a terrible war between America and North Vietnam would be engaged in the not too distant future, one might wonder why Ho Chi Minh would have expected this support in the beginning. It was because President Roosevelt and Prime Minister Churchill had worked hard to insure that ethnic groups after the war would have the freedom to choose their own political way. Whether Poles, Vietnamese, or Yugoslavs, whether Catholic, Muslim, or atheist, the point was to make sure they had the freedom to decide their political future for themselves. Though this perspective would soon change—as the world was seen more and more in terms of Communism versus Democracy—yet in 1945, America's major concern in Southeast Asia was to remove the burden of colonialism.

France quickly moved to regain power in Vietnam, assisted at first by the British who utilized Japanese soldiers—the former occupying army—to help them gain control. Americans stood by, watching with fury. MacArthur said, "If there is anything that makes my blood boil it is to see our allies in Indo-China and Java deploying Japanese troops to reconquer . . . people we promised to liberate." When the French army strength in Indo-China was deemed sufficient, the British withdrew. Despite ongoing diplomatic negotiations on the part of the French and Ho Chi Minh, war for Indo-China broke out in December 1946. Increasingly, Vietnam was divided in two, with the Communists holding the north and French forces holding the south. And, with the changing

In 1945, America's major concern in Southeast Asia was to remove the burden of colonialism.

our state be broken, if Soviet power is to be secure. This political force has complete power of disposition over energies of one of world's greatest peoples and resources of world's richest national territory, and is borne along by deep and powerful currents of Russian nationalism. In addition, it has an elaborate and far flung apparatus for exertion of its influence in other countries, an apparatus of amazing flexibility and versatility, managed by people whose experience and skill in underground methods are presumably without parallel in history. Finally, it is seemingly inaccessible to considerations of reality in its basic reactions. For it, the vast fund of objective fact about human society is not, as with us, the measure against which outlook is constantly being tested and re-formed, but a grab bag from which individual items are selected arbitrarily and tendentiously to bolster an outlook already preconceived.

Kennan believed that the Soviet Union would respond only to force and would withdraw if confronted with strong resistance. The impact of his insights was significant. In 1947, the US instituted the Truman Doctrine, which declared America's commitment to use as much force as necessary to counter all forms of Soviet aggression. In that same year, the United States offered the Marshall Plan to the war-weakened nations of Europe. This plan proposed a massive financial contribution—thirteen billion dollars—to assist in Europe's recovery from the destruction of WWII. In the minds of American leaders, this would hopefully prevent any more nations in Europe from falling to the communists.

Slowly but surely, the apparatus for the Cold War was set in place. Action and reaction, by both Soviets and Americans, created increasing tension as each sought to outdo the

9

tides of political reality, the war in Vietnam was viewed not as a war for a colony's independence, but part of an overall communist strategy for world dominion. In opposing communism, America would become the financial backer and weapons supplier of the French until France's utter humiliation and acknowledged defeat in 1954.

The West versus the Soviets

In order to understand these "changing tides of political reality," we need to consider the vast difference between the Soviet perspective on the world and the West's perspective. The Soviet government was a thoroughly Marxist-Leninist form of *communism*, meaning the leaders of this totalitarian system controlled the media and policies without tolerating criticism, and the government owned and controlled the basic means of production in industry and agriculture—including the workers. The West was *democratic*, meaning the people had individual rights and a voice in their government, and *capitalist*, which is an economic system controlled largely by individuals and private companies instead of by the government. Lenin, the father of Soviet-style communism, had stated decades earlier that as long as both capitalism and communism existed, "we cannot live in peace, one or the other will triumph." In other words, until communism completely filled the world—which Marx believed to be historically inevitable—there would be a constant state of antagonism, even war, between the Soviets and the capitalist West. Stalin also held that view. In 1927, he said:

> *Lenin, the father of Soviet-style communism, had stated decades earlier that as long as both capitalism and communism existed, "we cannot live in peace, one or the other will triumph."*

In the course of further development of international revolution there will emerge two centers of world significance: a socialist center, drawing to itself the countries which tend toward socialism, and a capitalist center, drawing to itself the countries that incline toward capitalism. Battle between these two centers for command of world economy will decide the fate of capitalism and of communism in the entire world.

This perspective directly affected the Soviet leader's post-WWII attitude. While Great Britain and the US were planning ways to insure free elections in liberated Europe, increase trade for all, and solve international conflicts through peaceful negotiations at the UN, the Soviet Union was anticipating that the West was preparing for war. J. A. S. Grenville, in his book *A History of the World in the Twentieth Century*, states:

During the years from 1945 to 1948, Stalin brought Eastern and central European politics and societies under Soviet

other in preparation, in influence, in espionage. American fears of espionage grew in intensity after it was learned that the actions of a treasonous atomic scientist had helped the Soviet Union create an atomic bomb. This led to the "red scare" hysteria of the McCarthy era, a time when many Americans were accusing each other of being communist, and Senator McCarthy was using his influence to search for evidence of communist infiltration. Many lost their good reputation and were harmed by these accusations because, whether true or false, just being accused ruined a person's chance for employment.

The Soviet threat was perceived as a clear and present danger in American halls of power. This can be readily seen in this quote from a report presented to the president in January 1953, by the Chairman of the National Security Resources Board:

National Security Resources Board advice to the President . . . has emphasized the attainment of the United States goal of world peace through realistic preparedness in the atomic age. Such preparedness provides the basic deterrent to war.

We must have in being sufficient retaliatory and defense

9

control. He was obsessed by the fear that eventually the capitalist powers would take advantage of their superiority to attack the Soviet Union, which therefore had only a few years in which to prepare.

While leaders of Western nations were subject to being dismissed from their positions by the unpredictable opinions of voters, as had recently occurred in Britain when Churchill was voted out and Attlee was elected, Stalin was in an entirely different position. As the dictator of a totalitarian, one-party political system, he ruthlessly controlled those under him. In the book *The Two Kingdoms: The Church and Culture Through the Ages*, Stalin's rule is described as "even more brutal than Hitler's, involving the forced collectivization of farms, police terror, slave labor camps, purges of rivals. . . . He brought into Communism the 'cult of the personality.'"

As had been the case with Hitler, the cult of personality meant that Joseph Stalin was actually worshipped by many, with a religious-style fervor. An example of this can be seen in a speech given by Nikita Krushchev in 1937:

> These men lifted their villainous hands against Comrade Stalin. By lifting their hands against Comrade Stalin, they lifted them against all of us, against the working class . . . against the teaching of Marx, Engels, Lenin. . . . Stalin is our hope, Stalin is the beacon which guides all progressive mankind. Stalin is our banner. Stalin is our will. Stalin is our victory.

As had been the case with Hitler, the cult of personality meant that Joseph Stalin was actually worshipped by many, with a religious-style fervor.

With Stalin as the undisputed center of the Soviet communist universe, it becomes clear why there was such a brutal suppression of any conflicting religious or political ideas throughout the lands dominated by the Soviet Union.

Because Stalin was obsessed by fear that his former allies were conspiring to attack the USSR, he brought a new level of terror to the multiplied millions in the Soviet Union, those who had just survived the horrors of the Nazis and WWII. Stalin used his devoted followers in the Communist Party to extract every bit of labor possible from the masses of workers and peasants in the Soviet Union, imprisoning and often executing any who were thought to be resistant to or hindering communism in any way. He emphasized the building up of heavy industry—which would be necessary to produce war machines—to the detriment of agricultural production. He pushed Soviet scientists to develop the atomic bomb, which was successfully accomplished and tested in August 1949, shocking American leaders who thought their sole ownership of nuclear weapons would deter the Soviets from any serious military moves. And Stalin sought to protect his vast nation by creating buffer states between the Soviet Union and the West. These were the *satellite*

Early Cold War & Renewed Vision (1945–1955) **389**

capabilities to meet an aggressor successfully at any time he might choose to strike. We must be alive to the fact that the ready strength of the United States for years to come may be the decisive block between the Kremlin and world conquest. We must be continuously aware of the implications of the danger we face, and must soundly develop our resources to deal with them.

The Cold War was, in American eyes, a battle they must not lose.

New Challenges to the Church—EXPLANATION

Despite the tremendous revivals of the early 1900s, Bible-believing Christians found that, especially after the tragic losses of the first World War, the Scriptures were coming more and more under fire by liberal theology. As we have seen in a previous unit, Fundamentalism was brought forth as an attempt to combat the attack on a literal interpretation of Scripture. This struggle—between the view of the Bible as authoritative and historically accurate versus the liberal view of the Bible—grew in intensity. To complicate things, a new

To get an informal discussion started on this Key Concept, ask a simple, leading question, such as, "In what ways do you think the years following WWII impacted the Christian church?"

9

nations of Central and Eastern Europe, from Estonia in the north to Bulgaria in the south, bound under the heavy-handed domination of communism.

These activities did not go unnoticed by the West. In fact, the more Stalin prepared to defend against a strike from the West, the more they tried to figure out what kind of villainy he was brewing. Make no mistake, Stalin qualified as a villain, whose regime had murdered more than twenty million of its own people. Was this man now preparing his military to launch an aggressive strike against the West? That was the urgent question for which America wanted an answer.

One man prepared to give that answer was Deputy Chief of the US Mission in Moscow, George Kennan. An academically and professionally trained expert on Russia, Kennan's "long telegram" of 1946 and published article in 1947 had profound impact in America. Consider what it meant to leaders of the "land of the free" when they read, "In foreign countries Communists will, as a rule, work toward **destruction of all forms of personal independence, economic, political or moral**." (emphasis added)

> *America would follow a policy of containment, as they sought to contain Soviet aggression by standing strong against it.*

His analysis suggested to them that they were dealing with a system whose core values were subversive and dangerous, whose leader would not play fair on the international "playing field." This became the new American perspective. It was a dramatic shift from what had been the immediate post-WWII attitude of trying to work with the Soviets. From now on, America would follow a policy of *containment*, as they sought to contain Soviet aggression by standing strong against it. Though in later years Kennan would disavow the militaristic response his writing generated among America's leaders, the Long Telegram, as it was known, nevertheless provided exactly what President Harry Truman needed in formulating a response to the Soviets' ongoing and aggressive behavior in Turkey and Greece. On March 12, 1947, he proposed a policy to the US Congress which would become known as the Truman Doctrine. In essence, he was committing the United States to preventing the Soviet Union from inciting communist revolutions and restricting democracy—opposing them anywhere and at any cost.

This commitment caused the American government to actively prepare for a struggle of global proportions. It would require an unprecedented approach, with new strategies at home and abroad, if the US was to succeed against a relentless enemy who refused to live in peace. Thus, only four months after his presentation to Congress, Truman signed the National Security Act of 1947 which established the Department of Defense, the Central Intelligence Agency (CIA), and the National Security Council.

Unbelievably, only a few years after the end of the most destructive war in history, the stage was now set for a new kind of war, a *Cold War*,

390 Early Cold War & Renewed Vision (1945–1955)

---

view emerged after WWII known as *neo-orthodoxy* (which uses much of the same biblical terminology as held by evangelicals, but without the high view of the inspiration and inerrancy of Scripture).

Immediately after the war ended, the newly installed communist government of Romania brought together Christian pastors and called upon them to announce in a nationwide broadcast their loyalty to the new regime. One man, hearing the denunciations of Christianity required by these new rulers, decided it was better to suffer the reproach of Christ than to sit safely on the sidelines. Richard Wurmbrand spoke up that

night, telling the truth of the gospel to the people of his nation and, at the same time, exposing the lies of the communists. This defiance would cost him years of tremendous suffering in prison, though it would eventually result in the highly influential book *Tortured for Christ* and the powerful international organization Voice of the Martyrs.

In 1947, Francis Schaeffer, an American pastor from St. Louis, went on a fact-finding tour in the rubble of Europe to discover the state of Christianity in nations which had been under Nazi control. What he learned of the increasing trend in Europe toward neo-orthodoxy deeply affected

9

which would develop between the two great powers—the US and the USSR—and the nations that would align themselves with either side. Rather than a traditional war of soldiers firing guns at enemy lines, it would become a form of war unknown before this time—a war of intrigues, espionage, posturing, threats, propaganda, and a massive nuclear arms race (the effort to quickly develop and produce more and more powerful weapons). It would divide much of the world between the Western Bloc and the Soviet Bloc; it would array the military commitments of NATO (North Atlantic Treaty Organization pact signed in 1949) against the Warsaw Pact (mutual defense treaty signed in 1955 between the Soviet Union and its European satellites). The Cold War would be seen in the West as the Free World standing up to Soviet bullying and aggression. It would be pictured by the Soviets as defending themselves and their neighbors against capitalist imperialism. It would continue to be the dominating and overarching global battle through which everything else was evaluated by the two great powers (or superpowers) for nearly forty-five years until the Soviet Union was finally dissolved.

The Cold War would be seen in the West as the Free World standing up to Soviet bullying and aggression.

A Third Perspective—Non-Alignment

There was yet another political perspective at work among the international community, *Non-alignment*. It had different needs and voiced different concerns than either the Soviets or the West. Before defining this term, we need to understand the background of the many developing nations who had lived under Western colonial rule and were now demanding independence. In order to "see through their eyes," we must recognize that, in spite of the positive changes which had come to colonized lands in the form of education, law and order, better health care, and increasing industries, there were many negative and unjust elements.

Two of the most troubling were, first, enriching the colonizer while impoverishing the native people through depletion of a colony's natural resources, and second, racism—perhaps the most painful and destructive element—one which was common to all people groups under Western rule. Though by no means the approach of every Westerner, yet there were many European and American administrators, businessmen, and, distressingly, sometimes even Christian missionaries, who considered native people as less than themselves . . . less intelligent, less capable, less important.

To gain a glimpse of what it was like for people living under this ethnic shaming, listen to the words of Jawaharlal Nehru, the man who would become India's first prime minister in 1947:

him. After much prayer and a definite sense of being led by the Lord, the Schaeffers moved to Switzerland the next year. In addition to other labors, they prepared "Children for Christ" materials for churches to use throughout Europe. These materials were a means of presenting the truths of Scripture in a way that was effective, lively, and life-changing. Eventually, the Schaeffers began the ministry of L'Abri, where people from all nations and all walks of life—especially those who were not satisfied with the answers of the world—could come to ask deep and penetrating questions about Christianity in a place where it was both believed and lived. The answers they found began to ripple out across the world, and Francis Schaeffer became known as the "missionary to the intellectuals."

In America, the war had caused the nation to recover dramatically from the Great Depression. Instead of "Brother, can you spare a dime?", the melody of the land changed to "Happy days are here again," as the economy boomed. The growing materialism, however, shifted many people's focus from the eternal to the here and now, with a nationwide emphasis on gaining as much of the pleasures of life as possible. Into this self-satisfied and weed-choked mentality, God sent a young man

9

The idea of a master race is inherent in imperialism. There was no subterfuge about it; it was proclaimed in unambiguous language by those in authority . . . generation after generation, and year after year, India as a nation and Indians as individuals were subjected to insult, humiliation, and contemptuous treatment. . . . The memory of it hurts, and what hurts still more is the fact that we submitted for so long to this degradation.

With the upheaval of WWII, and the shattering of Europe's strength, many colonies in Asia and Africa believed that their moment had at last come.

With the upheaval of WWII, and the shattering of Europe's strength, many colonies in Asia and Africa believed that their moment had at last come. Two days after the Japanese surrender, Indonesia declared its independence from the Dutch, though it took four years of guerilla fighting before the Dutch would formally acknowledge its independence. Two years after WWII, the British departed from the colony they had termed their "jewel in the crown," now partitioned into India and Pakistan—both gaining not only independence but, tragically, a deepening of ethnic and religious strife. Soon after, on the Gold Coast of Africa, the Africans of Ghana were successful in gaining their independence in 1951 from Great Britain. And in 1952, Egyptian officers, resentful of the continuing military presence of the British, overthrew the British-supported monarchy of King Farouk and established a republic the following year.

President Tito of Yugoslavia, a communist leader who successfully resisted Soviet control, eventually joined with the leaders of these former colonies (Indonesia, India, Ghana, and Egypt) to generate a new structure of cooperation that would be known as *Non-alignment*—neither of the Western Bloc nor the Soviet Bloc. This Third Bloc of non-aligned nations had a perspective of hostility toward what they viewed as imperialism, colonialism, and racism (largely attributed to America and the West), and of resistance toward foreign aggression, domination, and interference in their nations (largely attributed to the Soviets). Though this non-aligned movement would not be formally set up for several more years, the concerns were first voiced in 1953 by India's delegation to the United Nations.

In the eyes of those now throwing off the yoke of colonialism, Christian missions had been equated with Western imperialism. Instead of God's good news for every tribe and nation, many nations were identifying Christianity as an instrument of the West and identifying it with colonizing political and economic aims. When one recognizes that these former colonies were developing political and economic aims of their own and held their own traditional religions and belief systems, it becomes easier to understand why Christianity was seen as something Western rather than as universal truth for all cultures. Despite the untold sacrifice and commitment made

392 Early Cold War & Renewed Vision (1945–1955)

from North Carolina who combined the calling of an evangelist with a fiery delivery. Billy Graham, a Youth for Christ preacher, took Los Angeles by storm in 1949 when he preached at a crusade which was extended for weeks. When the American media decided that Graham's message and his impact on Hollywood celebrities was newsworthy, the entire nation was introduced to him. Billy Graham would continue to bring a simple gospel message across the country, and, eventually, across the world. Millions responded to his presentation in subsequent decades, and millions more heard the salvation message.

In 1949, when the Communist People's Republic of China was proclaimed, foreign missionaries became unwelcome in the land they had come to serve. Viewed as agents of Western imperialism, members of organizations such as the China Inland Mission were hounded out of China with increasing hostility and hatred. Though Chinese Christians were still somewhat free to gather in churches, it became more and more difficult as communism tightened its atheistic grip on the country. Eventually, an underground church would develop in China, while a Three-Self Patriotic Movement (subservient to the government) would maintain a

9

by thousands who had left their homes to serve the people of developing nations with the love of Christ, the immensely successful propaganda campaign to depict Christianity as "the tool of imperialism" eroded much of the work of the past decades. As early as 1924, the Young China Association declared, "We strongly oppose Christian education which destroys the national spirit of our people and carries on a cultural program in order to undermine Chinese civilization."

While the non-aligned countries viewed missionaries with deepening suspicion, communist victors of the Chinese civil war held this distortion of Christianity as a vital doctrine.

China's Communist Revolution

As noted in a previous unit, Japan had launched a major attack against China in 1937, heralding the beginning of Japan's aggressive war in the Pacific.

It has been noted by many that war makes for strange bedfellows. Despite the bitter Chinese civil war that had been taking place for years between the left-wing Communists and right-wing Nationalists (known as Kuomintang), they temporarily ended their fighting to present a united front against their common enemy, Japan.

When Japan attacked Pearl Harbor, China entered the war on the side of the Allies. In another strange alliance, China, in spite of its basic distrust and resentment of the West, would nonetheless ally itself with these powerful enemies of Japan in a classic case of "the enemy of my enemy is my friend." As full-fledged Allies, the Chinese were now eligible to receive military arms and financial assistance under the Land-Lease program from the United States, just as other Allies were receiving.

The Chinese were now eligible to receive military arms and financial assistance under the Land-Lease program.

When the war ended with the Japanese surrender, it signaled a new phase in the struggle between the Kuomintang and the Communist Party. Unable to agree on a coalition government, the civil war was renewed in 1946—but the numbers had changed drastically. The Communists had grown massive through the years of the war, while the army of the Kuomintang had perceptibly shrunk. However, with American military and financial aid continuing to the Kuomintang, it seemed at first that they would manage to succeed. Even the Soviets, though obviously interested in acquiring a new communist neighbor, seemed to think that Chiang Kai-shek might be the better leader on which to gamble, and thus, officially recognized the Kuomintang government. In C. P. Fitzgerald's book *The Birth of Communist China*, he writes:

Early Cold War & Renewed Vision (1945–1955) **393**

public presence of sorts. Many would suffer for their faith, in ways past our comprehension. Perhaps the most challenging issue for Christianity in China can be understood in this quote from a communist in the book *God's Smuggler*. In visiting the People's Republic of China in 1965, Brother Andrew asked to see a church in an agricultural area. The commune leader responded, "In the communes, sir, you will find no churches. You see, religion is for the helpless. Here in China we are not helpless any more."

That, however, is not the end of the story. Though no one knows for sure how many Christians there currently are in China, the estimate is as high as 80 million believers (according to David Aikman, author of *Jesus in Beijing*). And Christianity appears to be flourishing in a land that once tried to eradicate it.

God's message has not changed, despite the challenges of the twentieth century. His heart for the peoples of the world and His continuing purposes can be glimpsed in the story of Jim Elliot. In 1952, Jim and his coworker, Pete Fleming, traveled to Ecuador for the express purpose of reaching an unreached people group—the Waodani. Though it would take four years of preparation, they would eventually make contact. In the tragedy that followed, as Jim and Pete, along with

9

Mao Zedong

Both Russia and America doubted the competence of the Chinese side which they backed; the Americans knew Chiang was weak, his regime corrupt, his economy unsound, but it might be that the Communists were, after all, only a peasant movement incapable of taking and ruling cities. The Russians knew that the Communists had a purely agrarian background, that they had no support from the few industrial workers in China, with whom they had long been out of touch . . . their Marxist purity was at least somewhat suspect, since Mao's peasant policy had been the foundation of his power. Chiang was no doubt weak, too, but he might not be too weak to hold on for many years yet. The Chinese Revolution was not cut to a Russian pattern and so might not be the real thing; best to treat it with caution until the situation clarified.

In the end, the corruption of Chiang Kai-Shek's government so alienated the people of China—including a vast number of the Kuomintang soldiers, who eagerly surrendered—that the Communist Party won the loyalty of peasants, soldiers, and scholars alike. On October 1, 1949, in the historic city of emperors, Beijing, Mao Zedong proclaimed a new nation, the People's Republic of China. The symbolism of using Beijing was not lost on the population. Mao was instituting a new reign, one which would surpass in totalitarian control any empire the Chinese had ever known.

This new nation would be thoroughly communist in its approach, with a staunch and active atheism as its foundation, indeed, its new religion. Consider C. P. Fitzgerald's analysis:

In Chinese Communist writing, the October Revolution in Russia becomes the equivalent of the Birth of Christ for the Christian.

In Chinese Communist writing, the October Revolution in Russia becomes the equivalent of the Birth of Christ for the Christian. From that great event the world is changed, salvation becomes possible, the apostles of the Communist creed, Lenin, Stalin (and in Chinese eyes Mao Zedong) begin their evangel. . . . Russia, the land of the Revolution, is the Holy Land of the Communist.

Mao gave full praise to the power of communism when he said, "We have fought our foreign enemies and those within and without the party. Thanks be to Marx, Engels, Lenin, and Stalin. They gave us weapons, but these were not machine guns, they were the principles of Marxism-Leninism." Though all religions in China—apart from atheism—were now suspect and came under increasing pressure, Christianity, with its ties to the West, was under particular scrutiny. The Chinese Communists, fully committed

Nate Saint, Ed McCully, and Roger Youderian, literally laid down their lives that the Waodani might know Christ, God worked in such a powerful way that the tribal people were reached and the world was moved.

Finally, despite communism's avowed intention to remove religion, particularly Christianity, and replace it with atheism, God raised up Brother Andrew. This was a man whom God could use to "strengthen that which remains." In 1955, Brother Andrew was called by God to encourage the Body of Christ behind the Iron Curtain, in lands where communism was trying to crush the churches. One of the primary missions of Brother Andrew and those joining him was to bring Bibles into lands where Bibles were scarce . . . and beloved. Consider his experience, as told in the biography, *Brother Andrew*, by Dan Wooding:

The Soviet Union was the next country on my agenda. And it was there that I met a Russian Christian who made a deep

9

to communist doctrine and hostile to imperialism, were terrifyingly ruthless against those who would dare to hold allegiance to any other system. With this perspective driving them on, they saw the dismantling of biblical Christianity as an issue of patriotism.

In his book *Jesus in Beijing*, David Aikman describes that in 1954, the Religious Affairs Bureau director, He Zhenxiang,

> . . . made it clear that Christian theology itself could now be modified and altered at will by the authorities. Calling the process "infusing Marxist-Leninist thought into the positive doctrines of religion," He declared, "The positive values of patriotism should take the place of negative religious propaganda. We Communists can accept as reasonable certain parts of the Bible, which Christians use, but we must also pay attention to the doctrines that they preach. If we infuse those doctrines with our Marxist-Leninist thought, then they will have positive influence and can serve our cause." He made it clear that the parts of the Bible he objected to were the Ten Commandments, anything supernatural, and anything about the days leading up to the Second Coming of Christ.

The Chinese Communists were terrifyingly ruthless against those who would dare to hold allegiance to any other system. They saw the dismantling of biblical Christianity as an issue of patriotism.

The Korean War

In the early years of the Cold War, Asia proved to be one of the most significant regions in the struggle between communism and the West.

As Mao consolidated his 1949 victory in the civil war, the vast and populous country of China became thoroughly communist-controlled. This was largely good news for the Soviet Union, its massive northern neighbor, regarded as the "Holy Land of Communism." It was also good news for Kim Il Sung, the leader of the Democratic People's Republic, the communist government of North Korea.

As mentioned in a previous unit, the people of Korea had suffered under Japanese occupation since 1910—a hateful condition that did not end until 1945. With Soviet troops having entered Japanese-controlled Manchuria just days before the end of the war, they were the closest Allied army to Korea. It had been determined that the Soviets should disarm the Japanese in the northern part of the peninsula, north of the 38th parallel, while US troops would disarm them in the south, as all eyes were still focused on the potential for the Japanese to renew the fighting.

In the North, the Soviets installed Kim Il Sung, a trained and committed communist, as the new leader. In the South, the thoroughly anti-communist

impression on me. Joseph told me that he had been in a labor camp for ten years for his faith. As we talked, he revealed that while in the camp he had made a most unusual Bible. "Andrew," he said, "my job in the camp was to empty cement bags. I had managed to get hold of a pencil and would rip off pieces of the thick brown bags and write on them the Bible verses I could remember. I managed to fill twelve pages with these verses, and often when I was alone in a quiet corner, I would be joined by other Christians. Then I would open my shirt and pull out the 'cement-bag Bible' hidden under it and we would read the verses together."

"How I loved that Bible," he told me as his eyes filled with tears.

With the fall of communism and the crumbling of the Berlin Wall in 1989, many doors for the gospel opened into formerly closed lands. However, there are new challenges—new "closed doors" which seek to restrict people from learning of Jesus. Pray with your students about the issues they see facing the church around the world today.

9

and US-backed Syngman Rhee took control. Though the uniting of Korea into one nation was the original intent of the Allies, once these opposing leaders came into power on either side of the 38th parallel, there would be only one realistic path to unification: war.

Only five years after the end of WWII, on June 25, 1950, the world was stunned when Kim Il Sung sent his North Korean soldiers into South Korea in an aggressive move to take the whole peninsula by force. This action—a sudden firestorm early in the Cold War—brought the world to the brink of global war.

It is instructive to consider why this was the case. In French Indo-China, France was battling a losing war with the Vietnamese communists. China had just been declared a communist nation by Mao. In both of these instances, the Americans had supplied arms and money to those fighting against communism. But in this instance, the American perspective shifted dramatically. It was not known, yet, how much the Soviet Union and China had been involved in planning or providing for Kim Il Sung's attack, but in America it was considered quite likely that Stalin was actually masterminding this move in a global communist strategy.

Truman's decision was to fight a "limited war" on Korean soil, with no nuclear weapons used.

As Truman reviewed the events that had led to WWII—particularly the ineffectiveness of appeasement—he considered North Korea's attack with a war-hardened perspective. Believing he was dealing with the same issue in this instance, Truman determined to immediately send in the US military to bolster the South Korean army.

Sending in American troops, even under UN authorization, created a potentially flammable situation, since Russia and China, these two communist and anti-American giants, were Korea's close neighbors. In fact, if America's commanding officer, Douglas MacArthur, had had his way, it would have been just that—inflamed with nuclear arms. South Korean, American, and other UN forces faced not only the North Koreans but eventually the Chinese—and, if things escalated, the Soviets. MacArthur's idea of total war, with no holds barred, would have ensured that this would become a global fight to the death between Communism and the West. Instead, Truman's decision was to fight a "limited war" on Korean soil, with no nuclear weapons used. Though limited, it would prove nonetheless to be an extremely brutal war, with four million casualties.

The World, The Church

In the watershed year of 1953, the hot spot of the Cold War in Korea finally ended its fighting at the signing of an armistice between North and South. That was not the only highlight of that year, however. Joseph Stalin, the greatly feared and highly idolized dictator of the Soviet Union, died,

You may choose to have your students read the article first and then listen to the audio recordings, or vice versa.

◉ Read the article

◉ Listen to the audio recordings in Listen to This

- The main concepts and chronological flow are contained in *What in the World?* Volume 3

- Hear the story of Jim Elliot and his mission to the Waodani in *True Tales* Volume 3.

- Discover more about the incredible drama of the Korean War and the high tension during the early days of the Cold War in Europe in *True Tales* Volume 3.

- Learn more about the revivals of the mid-twentieth century in *Digging Deeper* Volume 3.

9

eventually to be replaced by Nikita Krushchev. In an interesting timing of events, President Truman, a Democrat who was known as being tough on Communist Russia, was replaced by the newly elected President Dwight Eisenhower, a Republican whose party would become increasingly zealous in uncovering communists in America.

Dwight D. Eisenhower

While both Truman and Eisenhower would, in their opposition to atheistic communism, emphasize that America was a Christian nation, the church in America, as in other parts of the world, was facing unprecedented challenges. With the modernist interpretation of Scripture becoming the standard in mainline churches of Europe and America, and with the increasingly secular "scientific" mindset among educated people who looked with incredulity at Christian doctrines, Christianity appeared to be rapidly declining. Where atheism became the enforced policy of totalitarian regimes, Christians suffered greatly and it was not known whether Christianity itself would survive.

And yet, things are not always as they seem. To a materialistic and secular American culture, God was preparing a young man from North Carolina, Billy Graham, who would present the gospel message with such clarity and power that evangelical Christianity took on a sudden burst of energy. To the European intellectuals, God was preparing an American couple, Francis and Edith Schaeffer, who would give "honest answers to honest questions" in such a way as to astound their hearers with dynamic truth and vibrant love of Christianity. And, finally, to those believers who were crushed under the communist boot, God was preparing a young Dutchman, Brother Andrew, to minister behind the Iron Curtain, bringing hope and Bibles to the countries closed by Communism. It was a call of God, as Revelation 3 states, to "strengthen those things which remain."

Just as believers needed God's strength and help in the 1950s, so it remains today. Regardless of what we face, either now or in the future, it is imperative that we hold fast the reality of God's goodness, His power, His faithfulness, His love, and His salvation. His Word so clearly tells us the outcome: "Now to Him who is able to do exceedingly abundantly above all that we ask or think, according to the power that works in us, to Him be glory in the church by Christ Jesus to all generations, forever and ever. Amen" (Ephesians 3:20–21).◀

◉ Read the Scriptures in Read For Your Life

The Scriptures are central to our understanding, our character, and our decisions. Therefore, we must give the greatest weight possible to them.

Help your students gain this perspective as they watch you handle the Scriptures with reverence and awe.

Pray that your students will gain greater insight into God's eternal purposes as they consider the international turmoil of the decade following WWII, and gain personal understanding of God's faithfulness in answer to prayer.

◉ Recap the material with an activity

In different parts of the room, set up stations for the Eight Intelligences Recap Activities. Then allow students to work alone or together in small groups to accomplish THEIR CHOICE OF ONE of the following suggestions. At the start of the next class, ask for 3–4 groups of volunteers to share.

Homeschoolers: rather than setting up all eight stations, allow student(s) to choose which activity they would most enjoy, and do it.

Recap Suggestions:

Spatial: Create a three-dimensional representation of the *distinct* divide between the Soviet Bloc and the Western Bloc, between those on each side of the Iron Curtain—the Soviets and the "Free World."

Bodily Kinesthetic: In small groups, play charades depicting one of this Unit's Key People in the Church as they go out to minister to the people where God has called them. With one student acting, have the others in the group guess which person they represent.

Interpersonal: In pairs, discuss what you think are the three most important points of this time period in history. If there is more than one pair, take a few minutes to share with other groups to discover whether they chose the same three points.

Musical: Write new lyrics to a slave song (such as "Swing Low, Sweet Chariot") to describe the persecution faced by believers in communist lands, as well as God's mercy and provision for them.

Phase 1

Key People (Church)

Brother Andrew
Dutch missionary, serving behind Iron Curtain

Jim Elliot
Martyred missionary to the Waodani people

Francis and Edith Schaeffer
Founders of L'Abri; missionaries to Intellectuals

Billy Graham
American evangelist, known through crusades, radio, and TV

Nate Saint
Martyred missionary aviation pilot

Betty Greene
Helped to found Missionary Aviation Fellowship

▶ Listen to This

What in the World? VOL. 3

DISC FOUR:

» Cold War & the Iron Curtain (track 6)

» Brother Andrew & the Berlin Airlift (track 7)

» Communist China & Korean War (track 8)

» Decolonization & Israel (track 9)

True Tales VOL. 3

DISC THREE:

» Korean War (track 3)

» Cold War (track 4)

» Jim Elliot (track 5)

Digging Deeper VOL. 3

DISC TWO:

» World War II and Billy Graham (track 6)

» The Promise of Revival (track 7)

DISC THREE:

» The Hidden War (track 12)

» Enigma (track 13)

398 Early Cold War & Renewed Vision (1945–1955)

Linguistic: Create a ten-word slogan that captures the essence of the Arab-Israeli conflict.

Math-Logical: Analyze the effect that President Truman's decision for a limited war in Korea had upon Korea, China, the USSR, the US, and the world. Next, analyze what some of the repercussions would have been if General MacArthur had been given permission to conduct the war in his own way.

Intrapersonal: Imagine you are a Displaced Person living in a refugee camp three years after the end of WWII. Your homeland is now occupied by the Soviet forces, and to return would probably mean your death. Either in a small group or on paper, share your thoughts about what is most important to you, your daily goals in the camp, and what will help you rise above your present situation.

Naturalist: Put together a representative sampling of military food rations for soldiers of the different nations at war in this Unit, including Vietnam, Korea, China, Russia, the United States, and France. Each group of soldiers will have very distinct tastes, so be sure to label each group of rations appropriately.

Or . . . Activity of Your Choice: What would you like to have your students do for a review activity concerning this week's introduction to Early Cold War & Renewed Vision?

▶ Read For Your Life

The Holy Bible

» Prophecies Concerning Restoration of People of Israel from Captivity (considered by some to be promises concerning modern Israel)—Psalm 126; Isaiah 43:5–6; Jeremiah 46:27–28

» Loving Your Enemies (consider Corrie ten Boom after WWII)—Matthew 5:43–48

» Eternal Perspective on Life (consider Jim Elliot)—John 12:24–26, 15:13

▶ Talk Together

Opinion Column

» What was the most interesting aspect, or the most interesting person, of this Unit, whether from the Cold War, the rebirth of Israel, the communist revolution in China, the Korean War, or post-WWII missions?

» Why do you think the Soviet Union and the West moved away from being allies to being enemies after WWII ended? What do you think might happen if nations use the same word—such as *democratic*—to mean opposite things?

» If you had been a refugee in Germany at the end of WWII, what zone of occupation would you have tried to get to, or which would you have avoided? Why?

» Imagine you had been a Jew living in Palestine on May 14, 1948. How would you feel about the declaration of Israel as a nation? Now, imagine you had been an Arab living in Palestine on May 14, 1948. How would this change your previous answer?

Key People (World)

Harry Truman
US president

David Ben-Gurion
Israel's first prime minister

Gamal Abdel Nasser
Egyptian president

Konrad Adenauer
Chancellor of Federal Republic of Germany

Kwame Nkrume
Ghana's first prime minister

Ho Chi Minh
Prime minister and president of North Vietnam

Jawharlal Nehru
India's prime minster after independence

Josip Tito
Communist prime minister of Yugoslavia

Mao Zedong
First Chairman of the Communist Party of China

Kim Il Sung
Communist prime minister of North Korea

◉ Talk together

Individual Preparation

After completing their recap activities, students may begin to consider the questions in the Opinion Column and Critical Puzzling.

Class Discussion

Use the questions under Talk Together to get the students primed and to create a discussion environment in the classroom. You may also want to draw from the open-ended questions listed here.

? The United Nations was formed after World War II to provide an international forum for keeping peace in the world and to provide humanitarian assistance where needed. In what ways do you think the UN has fulfilled its original goals? How do you think the Cold War impacted the UN?

? Why do you think that Jews and Arabs were not willing to share the land and a common government? What would be the fears for Jews? What would be the fears for Arabs?

» Why do you think the Communist countries did not allow Bibles to be imported or openly brought into their lands? Why was it critically necessary for the churches under Communist regimes to have Bibles? Do you think it was right for Brother Andrew to smuggle Bibles into these closed countries? Explain your reasons. How does this impact the way you value having access to your own Bible?

Critical Puzzling

» When you consider the difference between the end of WWI and WWII, in what ways did they differ? How were the enemies of the Allies treated after each of these wars? Describe the difference. How did this affect Japan and Germany? Do you think the Allies were wiser after WWII in the treatment of their defeated foes?

» *Cold War* is the term used to describe the high level of tension between the Communist bloc countries and the West after World War II. What are some of the reasons that East and West did not engage in another full scale world war but fought "limited" wars, such as in Korea and Vietnam, instead? In what ways has that situation changed today?

» As colonies in Asia and Africa began gaining their independence after WWII, both the Western Bloc and the Eastern Bloc sought to have influence and gain alliances with these new nations. However, many chose to walk a third path of non-alignment. Why do you think this might have been a more attractive option for former European colonies? What impact did decolonization have upon Christian missions?

» In what ways do you think the Holocaust might have influenced the vote at the United Nations for the partition of Palestine? Do you think the vote would have been different if it had been delayed by ten years? Explain your reasons.

» General Douglas MacArthur, an American hero, was fired by President Truman during the Korean War. MacArthur, who believed that the correct approach was winning the war regardless of the cost, continued to publicly criticize Truman's policy of limited war. This was a highly controversial decision at the time, leading initially to calls for Truman's impeachment. Considering the situation in the early Cold War, who do you think had the greater wisdom? What do you think would be the effect on the United States if a military leader could control the president's actions?

» Why do you think China became a Communist country? What struggles did people have in China prior to Mao Zedong? How did life for the people of China change after the Revolution? How were the China Inland Mission and other missionary organizations in China affected by the Communist Revolution? What happened to the churches and Christians in China?

▶ Resources for Digging Deeper

Choose a few books that look interesting, or find your own.

THE COLD WAR

The Cold War 20TH CENTURY PERSPECTIVES

David Taylor • This is an excellent primer on the many aspects of the Cold War, including events and headline personalities in Europe, Asia, and America. **UE+**

The Berlin Wall: How it Rose and Why it Fell

Doris M. Epler • This excellent book traces the history of the Cold War in Germany, beginning with WWII. It includes the Berlin airlift and the famous speech made by President John F. Kennedy in Berlin just months before his assassination. **UE+**

Konrad Adenauer WORLD LEADERS PAST & PRESENT

Edythe Cudlipp • Elected Chancellor of the Federal Republic of Germany in 1949, Adenauer's life of service to Germany spans from before the first world war until 1963. This biography helps to show what transpired in this country after the end of WWII. **MS+**

KOREAN WAR

The Korean War 20TH CENTURY PERSPECTIVES

Michael Burgan • The Korean War was a complex and controversial "police action" and was one of the major hot spots in the Cold War. Learn more about its various controversies and sudden upheavals in this engaging book. **UE+**

The Korean War: Limits of American Power PERSPECTIVES ON HISTORY SERIES

Karl E. Valois • With a brief overview of the war for introduction, this short book provides selected primary source documents of the Korean War, including excerpts from speeches, letters, and writings of Truman, MacArthur, and other notables. **MS+**

The War in Korea A WORLD LANDMARK BOOK

Robert Leckie • The Korean War, 1950–1953, is explained in an understandable way in this excellent account. The emerging role of the United Nations becomes evident in the story of this war. **UE+**

The Military History of the Korean War

S. L. A. Marshall • Written for children by a brigadier general operations analyst in Korea, this is a well-written, fascinating description of the Korean War. **UE+**

Korea ENCHANTMENT OF THE WORLD SERIES

Sylvia McNair • This series of books gives a brief overview of the country's history, its geography, and culture. An excellent primer for discovering more about Korea and the Korean people. **E+**

◉ Choose books of interest/ internet search

A list of possible books is given in the Student Manual. Encourage your students to look for books or videos on the Early Cold War & Renewed Vision from this list and from other sources. You may want to gather a selection of further resources prior to beginning Unit 9, or you may encourage the students to be treasure hunters and find them on their own. It would be helpful and time-saving before the Unit begins to check availability of these titles on your local library website.

Remember:

Beware of Arrogance,

Embrace Humility!

COMMUNIST REVOLUTION IN CHINA

The Rise of Modern China 20TH CENTURY PERSPECTIVE SERIES

Tony Allan • Listed also in Unit 7, this book will provide an excellent background to understanding the struggle between the nationalists and Communists of China, as well as reasons for the eventual success of the Communist Party. Fascinating! **UE+**

Mao Zedong WORLD LEADERS PAST & PRESENT

Hedda Garza • This is the man who made China an influential world power. He was a Communist revolutionary. He said, "A revolution is not a dinner party, or writing an essay, or painting a picture, or doing embroidery; it cannot be so refined, so leisurely and gentle, so temperate, kind, courteous, restrained, and magnanimous. A revolution is an insurrection, an act of violence by which one class overthrows another." This attitude explains much of what took place in China after 1949. **MS+**

Chiang Kai-Shek WORLD LEADERS PAST & PRESENT

Sean Dolan • Chiang Kai-Shek worked under Sun Yat-Sen, and after Sun Yat-Sen's death, he became the head of the Guomindang (Nationalist Party) in 1925. After WWII, through the corruption of his government and his strong-arm tactics toward dissenters, he lost China to the Communists under Mao Zedong. An excellent biography. **MS+**

China's Long March: 6,000 Miles of Danger

Jean Fritz • Jean Fritz is a noted children's author, and this book is a wonderful example of her ability to tell a story. She traveled to China in 1986 to talk to survivors of the Long March (when the Communist Chinese fled to the mountains). This book is their story. **UE+**

The Long March: Red China Under Chairman Mao

Don Lawson • This is a fantastic book! Beginning with the trial of the Gang of Four (including Mao's widow), it describes Mao's childhood, the Long March, the Communist Revolution, Mao's mistakes, and the impact he had upon China. **UE+**

Green Leaf in Drought-Time

Isobel Kuhn • Subtitled The Story of the Escape of the Last CIM Missionaries from Communist China, this amazing book provides a glimpse of God's hand, His ways, and His timing in the lives of His children as they go through extreme difficulties. Highly recommended! **MS+**

Every Good Gift: Sufficient Grace in Time of Need

Linda Baker Kaahanui • Read first-hand accounts of Chinese Christians during the early years of Communist rule in this sobering, encouraging, and challenging book. **HS**

THE UNITED NATIONS

The United Nations in War and Peace A WORLD LANDMARK BOOK

T. R. Fehrenbach • If you can locate this book, it is an excellent "primer" of world events after the end of WWII (up to 1965) written from the perspective of the development of the United Nations. Learn about the Cold War, the Partition in Palestine, the Korean War, the Suez Canal Crisis, the Hungarian revolt, the Cuban missile crisis, and the start of the Vietnam War. Highly recommended! **UE+**

MODERN ISRAEL & ARAB CONFLICT

The Mirage of Peace

David Aikman • The Middle East is complex, and to begin to understand the issues one must look beyond today's headlines and into its history. Uniquely positioned and gifted to sort out this complexity, Dr. Aikman has provided this remarkable resource as an overview of the region's history, nation by nation. Highly recommended! **HS**

Scars of War, Wounds of Peace: The Israeli-Arab Tragedy

Shlomo Ben-Ami • The author of this book was trained as a historian at Oxford University and served for a time as Israel's Foreign Minister. Heavily involved in negotiations and peace talks, Ben-Ami brings a wealth of understanding of the viewpoints of both sides. The most balanced book available on the subject! **HS**

The Arab-Israeli Conflict

Tony McAleavy • Published by Cambridge University Press, this book shows the development of the multi-faceted struggle in the Middle East. Though it contains excellent information and some primary source document excerpts, it is not the evenly balanced and careful reporting of the book listed above. Watch for the author's bias in the quotes and questions. **MS+**

Ben-Gurion and the Birth of Israel A WORLD LANDMARK BOOK

Joan Comay • David Ben-Gurion, born in Poland in 1886, moved to Palestine in 1906 along with many other Jewish settlers. His life revolved around the building up and establishing of Israel as a nation. He was, in fact, the one who announced the establishment of Israel to the world in 1948, as the Arab nations were beginning to attack Tel-Aviv. **UE+**

David Ben-Gurion WORLD LEADERS PAST & PRESENT

John J. Vail • Another in this excellent series of biographies for older students, this title focuses on the man known as the founding father of his country. Highly recommended! **MS+**

Israel CULTURES OF THE WORLD SERIES

Jill duBois • This series of books gives a brief overview of the country's history, its geography, and culture. An excellent "primer" for discovering more about modern-day Israel and the people who live there—Arabs and Jews. **E+**

AFRICAN INDEPENDENCE

Haile Selassie WORLD LEADERS PAST & PRESENT

Askale Negash • Emperor of Ethiopia from 1920 until 1974 (in exile from 1936–1941), this was one of the most remarkable leaders in the 20th century. Considered the elder African statesman during the decolonization of much of Africa, his influence was critically important. Excellent! **MS+**

Kwame Nkrumah WORLD LEADERS PAST & PRESENT

Douglas Kellner • The founder of modern Ghana and one of the architects of the pan-African movement (to end colonial rule), Nkrumah was a significant player in African politics. Decolonization in Africa is a multi-faceted study, involving economics, politics, tribal loyalties, and military rule. This book and the one listed above will give the student a good foundation for learning about decolonization. **MS+**

Assassins in the Cathedral TRAILBLAZER BOOKS

Dave & Neta Jackson • This is a historical fiction account of Festo Kivengere, bishop in Uganda during Idi Amin's rule. Though the setting is later than the scope of this Unit, it will help your student not only understand some of the difficulties faced by the African countries with warring tribes coexisting side by side, but it will show the profound importance of forgiveness. Excellent! **UE+**

BROTHER ANDREW

God's Smuggler

Brother Andrew • This autobiography is one of the most profound books our family has ever read. Highly recommended! **UE+**

Brother Andrew: God's Secret Agent

Janet & Geoff Benge • One of the Christian Heroes series by YWAM Publishing, this is an excellent and compelling look at the life and work of Brother Andrew. Unlike the other two titles, this book actually identifies Brother Andrew's family and his village in Holland. **UE+**

Brother Andrew MEN OF FAITH SERIES

Dan Wooding • Subtitled The remarkable story of the man who has come to be known as God's Smuggler, this is the biography of a man used by God to penetrate the communist countries of the world with Bibles for the persecuted church. **UE+**

MISSIONS

Nate Saint: On a Wing and a Prayer

Janet & Geoff Benge • Nate Saint was the missionary aviator who flew the group of missionaries (including Jim Elliot) to reach the Auca (Waodani) Indians. His powerful testimony is movingly portrayed in this excellent book. Highly recommended! **UE+**

Jungle Pilot

Russell T. Hitt • This is the updated edition of the missionary classic about the martyrdom of Nate Saint. Included are photos, plus a new epilogue written by Nate's son, Stephen, who returned to the jungles of Ecuador to report the remarkable progress in the work with the Waodani (named Auca by their enemies). Highly recommended! **UE+**

Jim Elliot: One Great Purpose

Janet & Geoff Benge • Wonderfully written, this title in the Christian Heroes series is fascinating, factual, and historically accurate. Jim Elliot was an American missionary in Ecuador, who gave his life so that the Waodani (Auca) Indians might know Jesus. Highly recommended! **UE+**

Through Gates of Splendor

Elisabeth Elliot • Jim Elliot's story has motivated many people to live a sacrificial life for the sake of Jesus. He was an American missionary who wanted to live his life fully for Jesus, regardless of the cost. He was martyred in 1956 while attempting to reach an isolated tribe in Ecuador—the Auca Indians. This powerful book was written by his widow. **MS+**

Dayuma: Life under Waodani Spears

Ethel Emily Wallis • If you are going to read about Jim Elliot or Nate Saint, you MUST read this book! It tells what happened among the Waodani (Auca) after the martyrdom of the missionaries in 1956. **UE+**

Betty Greene: Wings to Serve

Janet & Geoff Benge • One of the founders of Mission Aviation Fellowship, Betty Greene was a remarkable woman whose life was devoted to serving God and His people through flying. This is an amazing and fascinating account of her story. **UE+**

From Jerusalem to Irian Jaya: A Biographical History of Christian Missions

Ruth A. Tucker • This is the best book on the history of world missions available. Included are short biographies of missionaries all over the world, categorized by their geographical area of service. For this chapter read pages 352–360, 386–391, 464–467. Highly recommended! **UE+**

FRANCIS & EDITH SCHAEFFER

Francis & Edith Schaeffer
WOMEN & MEN OF FAITH SERIES

L. G. Parkhurst, Jr. • Subtitled Christian missionary apologists who challenged a world of skeptics to faith, this is the biography of two of the most influential Christians of the twentieth century. **UE+**

L'Abri

Edith Schaeffer • The autobiographical story of how God took an American couple to Europe immediately after WWII to begin a ministry to skeptics and intellectuals. Life-changing! **UE+**

Tapestry

Francis & Edith Schaeffer • One of the most treasured books on my shelf, this is the story of Francis and Edith Schaeffer. Told in rich detail, her book describes how God worked mightily in their lives to provide a refuge, a l'abri, for a world disillusioned by war and liberal theology. It is out of print, but worth the search. Highly recommended! **MS+**

LITERATURE

The Chronicles of Narnia

C. S. Lewis • Classic literature for children and adults alike, they are allegorical stories of the Kingdom of God. These books were set partially during the time of WWII and shortly afterward. Wonderful for reading aloud! **RA+**

What books did you like best?

_____

_____

_____

The Internet also contains a wealth of information about the Early Cold War & Renewed Vision.

What sites were the most helpful?

_____

_____

_____

For more books, use these Dewey Decimal numbers in your library:

DNA: 570

Rocketry, space travel: 387, 629

Cold War: 909, 973, 959; Berlin: 943.155, 940.554; Iron Curtain: 940.554

China: 915.0

Sub-Saharan Africa: 916.7; Uganda, Kenya: 967.61; Congo: 967.51

General History of Africa: 960; Southern Africa: 968

US History: 973.6–973.7

Non-alignment: 327

India: 954.03; Pakistan: 954.91

Israel/ Palestine, Mid-East: 956.9

Modern communism: 335.43

Yugoslavia: 949

Korea: 951.9

Displaced Persons: 940

United Nations: 341.23

Waodani/Waorani/ Auca: 986.6

◉ Conduct a review and evaluation

In this Phase of Unit 9, your students should have had the opportunity to explore the Early Cold War & Renewed Vision through reading, listening, thinking, and discussing by completing a selection from the following:

- informally discussed the Key Concepts;
- read the article;
- listened to the audio recordings;
- read the online articles;
- read the Scriptures;
- explored the recap activities;
- considered the Opinion Column and Critical Puzzling answers on their own;
- participated in class discussion;
- chosen books of interest or searched the Internet;
- completed their self-evaluation for this Phase.

Record student hours: _____

Assess student participation:

Create an evaluation system of your own, or refer to the evaluation rubric in the introduction, as a tool for as-

---

▶ Student Self-Evaluation UNIT 9, PHASE 1

Dates and hours:_____

Key Concepts

Rephrase the four Key Concepts of this Unit and confirm your understanding of each:

- Europe Divided

_____

- Communism in Asia

_____

- America's Perspective

_____

- New Challenges to the Church

_____

Tools for Self-Evaluation

Evaluate your personal participation in the discussions of this Phase. Bearing in mind that a good participant in a discussion is not always the most vocal participant, ask yourself these questions: Were you an active participant? Did you ask perceptive questions? Were you willing to listen to other participants of the discussion and draw out their opinions? Record your observations and how you would like to improve your participation in the future:

_____

_____

Every time period is too complex to be understood in one Phase of study. Evaluate your current knowledge of the Early Cold War & Renewed Vision. What have you focused on so far? What are your weakest areas of knowledge?

_____

_____

Based on the evaluation of this introduction, project ahead what you would like to study more of in the following Phases.

_____

_____

_____

---

sessing participation. The categories you will probably find most useful are *"Introduction," "Process: Teamwork,"* and *"Process: Originality."* To help students develop good discussion skills, encourage them to participate actively, ask content-based questions, and stay focused on the discussion at hand. Students demonstrate a higher level of discussion skills when they incorporate comments and questions from others into their own questions, and draw out opinions or ask for points of clarification from others.

Do not critique the self-evaluation page your student completes and do not direct the answers the student gives to the questions. Instead, allow

sincere and personal completion of the evaluation, then discuss the responses and incorporate those comments into your evaluation.

Determine a grade for this Phase, if using grades: _____

Teacher Self-Evaluation:

Evaluate your own use of materials and teaching opportunities: what worked and what did not; how effective was your time-management; how were your responses to the needs of your student; did you make your expectations clear? Incorporate suggestions from your students in your own evaluation *(this requires humility!)*.

Phase 2

▶ Research & Reporting

Explore one or more of these areas to discover something significant!

Postwar Germany/Japan

Research and report on Germany and/or Japan since the end of WWII. In what ways did these nations change after WWII? What were the similarities in their postwar experience? What were the differences? In what ways did the development in West Germany and Japan differ from East Germany in terms of politics, economics, and culture?

Displaced Persons

Discover the story of those left homeless, helpless, and far from home at the end of WWII. What were the various reasons to explain why so many people were stranded in Germany or in transit from one country to another, in the early postwar years? What happened to these refugees?

Truman Doctrine/Marshall Plan

Learn more about the circumstances surrounding Truman's announcement of America's new approach to communism worldwide and the reasons for the Marshall Plan in Europe. How did these two American policies affect the world? How did they affect America?

Cold War

Research and report on the Cold War, the Iron Curtain, the Berlin Airlift and/or the Berlin Wall. List the countries in the Soviet Bloc and the countries in the Western Bloc (also known as the Free World). What were the major differences between these two sets of countries politically, economically, religiously, and culturally? What part did propaganda and espionage play in the Cold War?

Brother Andrew/Open Doors Ministry

Study the life and ministry of Brother Andrew. What were the specific parameters of his ministry? Learn more about the obstacles he faced, God's miraculous provision and protection, and how the church behind the Iron Curtain was strengthened.

India's Independence

Research and report on the way India was partitioned at independence into India and Pakistan, which was separated into East Pakistan and West Pakistan. What was the reason for partition? What difficulties were encountered by these nations during independence? Discover the challenges Pakistan, Bangladesh (formerly East Pakistan), and India have faced in the decades since independence.

African Independence

Study and write about the history of any of the African countries since its independence. One point to keep in mind: in Africa, the national boundaries of many of the countries were artificially drawn by European rulers in the 1800s, without regard to historical tribal boundaries. This has caused continuing deadly and unresolved conflicts between people groups.

Early Cold War & Renewed Vision (1945–1955) **407**

◉ Choose a topic and begin research

Allow the students the freedom to choose one of the topics listed under research & reporting in the Student Manual, or to suggest their own area which they would like to research.

Motivating Suggestions:

Especially for Non-linguistic students, and those who are not motivated by written or oral reports, here are suggestions for alternative ways of reporting what has been researched.

Postwar Germany/Japan

Compare and contrast postwar Germany with postwar Japan. Make a chart or PowerPoint presentation that examines their common experiences and where their experiences diverged. You might, instead, choose to compare and contrast West Germany with East Germany.

Set up a museum with two sections: one to show life in East Germany and one for West Germany. Include as many artifacts and photos as pos-

sible to help visitors understand the significant differences between them in everyday life, as well as hopes for the future. Then take groups through, pointing out the most interesting aspects and answering questions.

Displaced Persons

With the use of photographs, paint, and three-dimensional objects, create a collage that will help viewers to grasp what life was like for individuals living in a Displaced Person camp.

Write a children's story about Corrie ten Boom's description of renovating an old concentration camp to become a place of refuge for Displaced Persons. Include some of her stories of people's lives being transformed.

Truman Doctrine/ Marshall Plan

Using a large map of the world, a pointer, and colored pins, show an audience the geographic magnitude of the Soviet occupation of Central and Eastern Europe at the end of WWII. Next, show which nations were fighting internally against communists in 1947. With this information, explain what the Truman Doctrine meant, why it was a change in American policy, and how it provided the foundation for a response to North Korea's invasion of South Korea. You might also show where the Marshall Plan was accepted and where it was refused.

Host a live TV show, and interview Harry Truman on his views of communism, why he created the Truman Doctrine, and his thoughts on whether this was effective and appropriate. The second guest on the program is George Marshall, author of the Marshall Plan. Ask him why this assistance was offered to the Soviets and its satellite countries and whether the US Senate would have approved funding the Soviets in 1947! Also, discover how this plan differed from previous plans. In what ways were the European countries involved beyond merely receiving the financial support?

Cold War

Outside, divide the yard into two sections, an East and a West. Gather similar items into each section, but distribute and arrange them to represent the differences in life under the Soviet Bloc and the Western Bloc. Take tours of interested viewers and help them grasp the dynamics of the Cold War. You might even create a Berlin Wall or an Iron Curtain!

Imagine you were living in West Berlin during the time of the Berlin Airlift. Write an opinion piece to submit to the West Berlin newspaper, detailing your thoughts about why West Berlin is in its current situation, how your city is in the center of the Cold War, and your thoughts about those people and nations who are flying in supplies.

Brother Andrew/Open Doors Ministry

Create a "film score" of music to represent Brother Andrew's life, whether original music or another composer's. Once you have selected the appropriate music, pair this music with images of his life and ministry, in either a PowerPoint or video presentation.

In a small group, discuss whether you believe smuggling Bibles into closed countries is appropriate for Christians to do. Using Brother Andrew's ministry as a starting point, evaluate this activity in light of the Scriptures.

India's Independence

Create two first-person presentations which will give a glimpse into India's partition and independence. One presentation will be as a Hindu, explaining why partition is wrong for India, and your thoughts about how this will affect your country. The second presentation will be as a Muslim, explaining why partition is necessary, and the difficulties your family members have faced as Muslims in a predominantly Hindu nation.

Create an ad campaign for India's independence *without* partition. Your firm has been hired by friends of Gan-

Israel as a Nation

Learn more about the reestablishment of Israel as a nation in 1948 and its history since that moment. Include information on the UN vote for Partition, the announcement of independence by Israel, the attack by Arab nations, and subsequent wars. It would be helpful to also learn about the political structure, economy, and culture of Israel since 1948.

Palestinian Refugees

The issue of displaced Palestinian Arabs, who have had no homeland since 1948, is complex and sobering. Discover the reasons given by each side for the Palestinians fleeing their homes. Why were they not allowed back into Israel? Why were they not allowed to settle in other Arab lands (except in refugee camps)? Show the effects of living permanently in refugee camps, the political solutions that have been tried, and whether there has been any success in these attempts.

Communist China

Research and report on the Communist Revolution in China. Include the struggle between Chiang Kai-Shek's Nationalist Party and Mao Zedong's Communist Party, the Long March, and the results of the revolution. Discover what was beneficial and what proved to be harmful to the various classes of people in China after the revolution. How was the Christian church in China affected?

Korean War

Learn more about the Korean War. Why was Korea divided in two at the end of WWII? For what reasons was Korea occupied by two different allies? Why did the war begin? What part did the UN play in this war? How was the fighting ended? What are the ongoing tensions between North Korea and South Korea?

United Nations

Research and report on the United Nations. In what ways was the UN different from the League of Nations? When and by whom was the United Nations formed? What are its purposes? How are member nations able to influence and affect situations in the world? Has it been effective?

Missionary Aviation

Missionaries around the world often depend on the ministry of "jungle pilots." The service of the pilots is often both dangerous and exciting. Discover information about missionary aviation, including when this type of ministry began, what the circumstances were, who was involved, and where. Be sure to investigate Missionary Aviation Fellowship, JAARS (Jungle Aviation And Radio Service), and, for new advances, I-TEC (Indigenous People's Technology and Education Center).

The Waodani

Learn more about the Waodani people (known as "Auca" by their enemies) and how the gospel has transformed their culture. Be sure to include the martyrdom of the five missionaries who first made contact with them, the work of Rachel Saint and Elisabeth Elliot, and the continuing work in the jungles of Ecuador.

dhi who wish to use the power of advertising for communicating Gandhi's vision to people throughout India. Images, slogans, and musical jingles would all be appropriate for this campaign. And, remember, Gandhi is considered the Father of India, so make use of as many visual reminders as possible of his campaign for independence from the British.

African Independence

Choose one African nation and set up a room to represent the chronology of this country from medieval times to the present. Use props to demonstrate the various tribal groups, experiences of the nation under colonial-

ism, and what has happened since independence. Then act as a walking tour guide, taking groups into the room, and explaining the significance to the nation of each of your displays. A few suggestions for this might be Uganda, Democratic Republic of the Congo (DRC), or Kenya.

Create a chart listing the differences between America's independence and a particular African nation's independence. Include not only the actual years surrounding independence, but also chart the differences in what has happened in the decades since. Explain to your viewers why this African nation has had vastly different experiences than

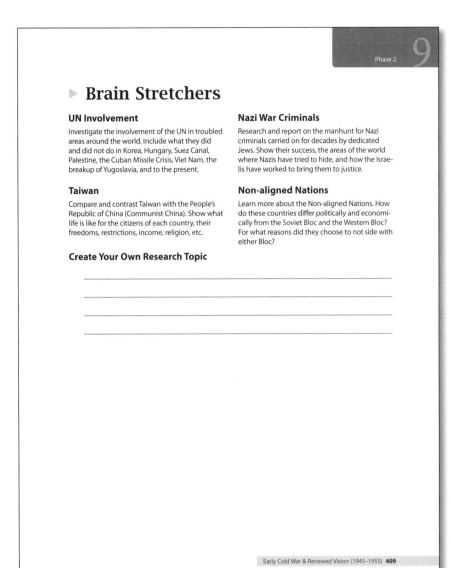

▶ Brain Stretchers

UN Involvement

Investigate the involvement of the UN in troubled areas around the world. Include what they did and did not do in Korea, Hungary, Suez Canal, Palestine, the Cuban Missile Crisis, Viet Nam, the breakup of Yugoslavia, and to the present.

Taiwan

Compare and contrast Taiwan with the People's Republic of China (Communist China). Show what life is like for the citizens of each country, their freedoms, restrictions, income, religion, etc.

Nazi War Criminals

Research and report on the manhunt for Nazi criminals carried on for decades by dedicated Jews. Show their success, the areas of the world where Nazis have tried to hide, and how the Israelis have worked to bring them to justice.

Non-aligned Nations

Learn more about the Non-aligned Nations. How do these countries differ politically and economically from the Soviet Bloc and the Western Bloc? For what reasons did they choose to not side with either Bloc?

Create Your Own Research Topic

_____

_____

_____

_____

America's, even though its majority population is Christian (such as in the DRC and Uganda).

Israel as a Nation

Using Israeli folk music as a guide, compose a Jewish-style song, with each verse describing an element of modern Israel's history since 1948. You might choose to focus mainly on the events surrounding modern Israel becoming a nation, or instead, list each of Israel's wars beginning with its first war for survival in 1948.

In groups of two, script an interview with Prime Minister David Ben-Gurion in which you will ask him his thoughts on Israel, on the Arab world's response to Israel as a nation, the flight of Arab Palestinians, and his refusal to allow them back into the country after fighting ceased. After practicing the skit, perform it for an audience. Search online, since many of his actual comments about these issues are available! And, remember, there is much controversy regarding the Arab/Israeli conflict, so be prepared to answer hostile questions with gentle wisdom, humility, and grace.

Palestinian Refugees

Create a PowerPoint presentation or in which you can depict not only the statistics of life in Palestinian refugee camps, but also include the pathos of real people living permanently in a temporary holding spot.

Imagine you were a Palestinian living with your family in a refugee camp. In a journal, consider these questions: What are your personal hopes and fears as you consider your life? What is your attitude toward Israel? What is your attitude toward countries, such as the US, who support Israel? What do you think of the Arab nation who hosts your refugee camp but will not allow you to settle among them as a citizen? What possibilities do you dream for a peaceful ending of the refugee camps?

Communist China

Design a mural that portrays the Communist Revolution in China and its affect upon the people of China. Be sure to include culturally and artistically appropriate images to convey the story. Be available to offer helpful comments as people view your creation.

Compare and contrast Mao Zedong's rule of China with imperial rule, such as the Dowager Empress who presided over the Boxer Rebellion. In what ways did Mao break with imperial rule? In what ways did he maintain its privileges and power? You might also want to include in your chart the experience of the people of China under both these rulers. In what ways did life change under Chinese communism? In what ways did it stay the same?

Korean War

Create a three-dimensional map of Korea, which includes the major mountain ranges, major rivers, major cities, and the location of the 38th parallel. Then, layer on arrows and dates to show the flow of the Korean War through the peninsula. Be prepared to answer questions as visitors view the map.

Evaluate which are the most important scenes and high-drama events for young children to know about the Korean War, and then write and illustrate a First Picture Book about this hotspot in the Cold War. Remember that young children need simple sentences and should not be exposed to graphic violence—a challenge in describing this war!

United Nations

There are differing opinions on the value of the UN, with some seeing it as a force for good while others view it as having potential to do harm. Make a presentation of your findings on the history of the UN, along with the many areas in which it works, including help with refugees, emergency food distribution, peacekeeping efforts, and gathering data about poverty. As part of your presentation, explain why people hold such strong views on it today, both positively and negatively, including the demographics of those who hold each position. Note which issues governed by the UN have been and continue to be controversial.

Create a model UN where you can debate the post-WWII crisis of millions of Displaced Persons. With a small group of students, each one representing a different country in the UN, come together to present a speech regarding your country's willingness to assist in this emergency situation. Consider these questions: What resources does your country have to offer? How can each of these countries formulate a plan that will quickly make a difference in Europe? To prepare for this experience, each student will need to learn the UN rules on debates and policy. Learn about the culture of the country you will represent. Then dress and act like someone from that country during the debate. Don't break character until the entire presentation is over! The website of the United Nations Association of the United States has a tremendous amount of information for those interested in this project. A link can be found at the online resource page.

Missionary Aviation

Tell the story of the early days of Missionary Aviation Fellowship, in character as either Betty Greene or Nate Saint. Include as many props as

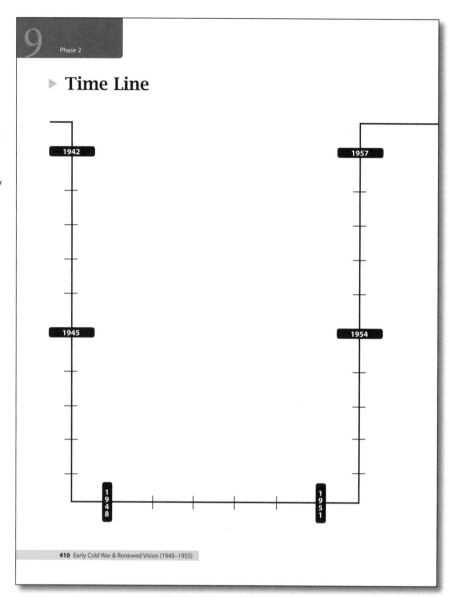

▶ Time Line

1942

1957

1945

1954

1948

1951

410   Early Cold War & Renewed Vision (1945–1955)

possible to make this presentation as incredible for your audience as the true story in real life. Talk about the issues faced by missionary pilots, as well as some of the amazing benefits provided by missionary aviation.

Outside, create a display which will depict aspects of flying and missions. It might be interesting to create a miniature dirt runway, built to scale, and a replica of a missionary's jungle residence. Describe for viewers some of the day-to-day challenges for missionaries and missionary pilots. Answer the question: In what ways does the work of missionary pilots advance the preaching of the gospel?

The Waodani

Imagine you have been temporarily taken up to heaven and have been given permission to film an interview with the five men who were martyred by the Waodani people in 1956. Discuss with Jim Elliot, Nate Saint, Ed McCulley, Peter Fleming, and Roger Youderian their thoughts about what happened on that decisive day. Given the heavenly perspective, as well as the knowledge that many of the Waodani eventually became believers, do each of these men believe their sacrifice was worthwhile? Next, while you're there, interview Rachel Saint (Nate's sister) who lived among the Waodani in order to share the good

Consider this for your time line

In the first decade after WWII, despite the recent experience of unfathomable destruction, the world did not settle back into a time of peace. Instead, the emerging Cold War pitted groups of nations against other nations with the newly honed weapons of espionage, propaganda, and an escalating nuclear capacity. The most highly populated nation on the planet became communist, which continued to build tension throughout the Cold War. Involving both of the communist giants, North Korea launched an invasion against South Korea, which brought the world to the brink of nuclear war. And yet, in the midst of violence, oppression, and war, the God of peace moved mightily through His people—those whose names we know and those whose names only God knows—as they faithfully obeyed Him.

Key Events

- UN formed
- Truman Doctrine
- Berlin Airlift
- India's Independence
- French Indo-China War
- The New Nation of Israel
- North Atlantic Treaty Organization (NATO)
- Warsaw Pact
- Yugoslavia ousted from Soviet Bloc
- Communist Revolution in China
- Korean War

Be sure to include the people listed in Key People in Phase 1.

Jesus said in Matthew 10:39: "He who finds his life will lose it, and he who loses his life for My sake will find it." Jim Elliot wrote, "He is no fool who gives what he cannot keep to gain that which he cannot lose." Talk with your students about what this means to them, and in what ways Jim Elliot's life has challenged them to serve Jesus.

- Francis Schaeffer: 1912–1984; Edith Schaeffer: b. 1914
- Billy Graham: b. 1918
- Nate Saint: 1923–1956
- Betty Greene: 1920–1997

Key People in the World

- Harry Truman: 1884–1972
- David Ben-Gurion: 1886–1973
- Gamal Abdel Nasser: 1918–1970
- Konrad Adenauer: 1876–1967
- Kwame Nkrume: 1909–1972
- Ho Chi Minh: 1890–1969
- Jawharlal Nehru: 1889–1964
- Josip Tito: 1892–1980
- Mao Zedong: 1893–1976
- Kim Il Sung: 1912–1994

Key Dates

- UN. formed: October, 1945
- Truman Doctrine: 1947
- Berlin Airlift: June, 1948–May, 1949
- India's Independence: 1947
- French Indo-China War: 1945–1954
- The New Nation of Israel: 1948
- North Atlantic Treaty Organization: NATO): 1949
- Warsaw Pact: 1955
- Yugoslavia ousted from Soviet Bloc: 1948
- Communist Revolution in China: 1949
- Korean War: 1950–1953

news with them. What is her perspective on these events, both on the mens' deaths and the Waodanis' lives?

Compose an epic poem or original song about the Waodani people and the means by which God brought them the message of salvation in Jesus. Be sure to focus on how these people—the most feared among all the Amazon tribes—were precious to the heart of God, and the depths of love that His people held for the Waodani, that they would share Him even at the cost of their lives.

◉ Construct the time line

Read the information listed with the Key Events in the Student Manual. Dialogue with your students about the issues involved.

Find the dates for the Key People and Key Events listed.

Time Line Key

Key People in the Church

- Brother Andrew: b. 1928
- Jim Elliot: 1927–1956

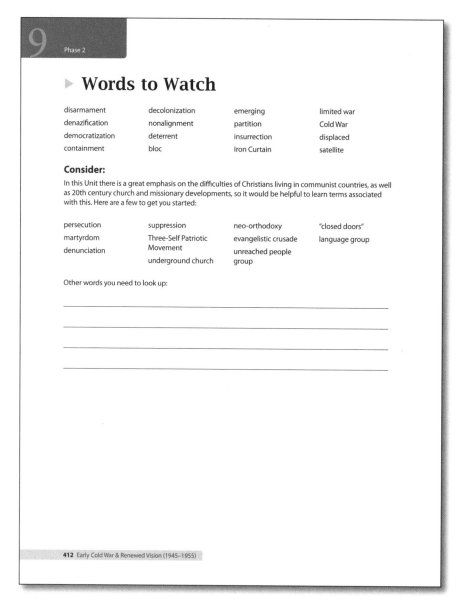

▶ Words to Watch

disarmament	decolonization	emerging	limited war
denazification	nonalignment	partition	Cold War
democratization	deterrent	insurrection	displaced
containment	bloc	Iron Curtain	satellite

Consider:

In this Unit there is a great emphasis on the difficulties of Christians living in communist countries, as well as 20th century church and missionary developments, so it would be helpful to learn terms associated with this. Here are a few to get you started:

persecution	suppression	neo-orthodoxy	"closed doors"
martyrdom	Three-Self Patriotic Movement	evangelistic crusade	language group
denunciation	underground church	unreached people group	

Other words you need to look up:

_____

_____

_____

_____

Here is one idea for making vocabulary study interesting and fun:

SING A SONG OF SYLLABLES!

To the nursery rhyme tune of "Sing a Song of Six-Pence," compose a rhyming song that will define the Words to Watch in this Unit. You may define more than one word per stanza, if it seems appropriate.

A list of definitions can be found at the back of the book in Appendix B.

◉ Practice vocabulary

You may find other words in this Unit that are especially appropriate for younger children. Feel free to substitute another vocabulary list for the one provided.

◉ Complete research projects and share in class or hand in

Create a safe environment for the presentations. Set ground rules prior to the presentations, so that students know how much time is available for each of them, and so that they know they will be honored and respected by all those observing.

▷ Student Self-Evaluation UNIT 9, PHASE 2

Dates and hours:_____

Research Project

Summarize your research question:

_____

_____

List your most useful sources by author, title, and page number or URL where applicable (continue list in margin if necessary):

_____

_____

Now take a moment to evaluate the sources you just listed. Do they provide a balanced view of your research question? Should you have sought an additional opinion? Are your sources credible (if you found them on your own)? Record your observations:

_____

_____

_____

Evaluate your research project in its final presentation. What are its strengths? If you had time to revisit this project, what would you change? Consider giving yourself a letter grade based on your project's merits and weaknesses.

_____

_____

_____

Letter grade: _____

You have just completed an area of specific research on the time of the Early Cold War & Renewed Vision. Now what would you like to explore in the upcoming Phases? Set some objectives for yourself.

_____

_____

_____

◉ Conduct a review and evaluation

In this second Phase of Unit 9, your students should have had the opportunity to explore the Early Cold War & Renewed Vision through researching, thinking, and reporting by completing a selection from the following:

- done a research project;
- learned the vocabulary;
- constructed a time line;
- created a project report on what was researched;
- completed their self-evaluation procedure for this Phase.

Record student hours: _____

Assess student effort in the research and reporting projects.

Create an evaluation system of your own, or refer to the evaluation rubric in the introduction, as a tool for assessing research and reporting. The categories you will probably find most useful are *"Introduction," "Task," "Process: Teamwork"* (if students are working together), along with Grammar, Format, and Spelling. As a tool for helping your students develop better research skills, pay attention to their evaluation of sources. Older students should learn how to make a "Sources Cited" list according to academic standards—refer them to English usage books or websites for formatting rules. Younger students should learn how to obtain a balanced view of their research subject; if they use more than one source they will get a bigger picture of what was happening. Encourage your students to make use of their self-evaluations for their next research projects, in order to practice good research skills.

Do not critique the self-evaluation page your student completes in the Student Manual—spelling errors are not to be considered in such an exercise. Students should feel free to humbly evaluate themselves without that added complexity. Instead, discuss with them the intention of their written comments and incorporate those into your evaluation.

Determine a final grade for this Phase: _____

Teacher Self-Evaluation:

Evaluate your own use of materials and teaching opportunities: what worked and what did not; how effective was your time-management; how were your responses to the needs of your student; did you make your expectations clear? Incorporate suggestions from your students in your own evaluation (*this requires humility!*).

> **The Hands-On Week**

Phase 3

▶ Maps and Mapping

Physical Terrain

» On a map of the Middle East, locate and label these four general terrains in modern Israel and the disputed Palestinian Territories: the coastal plain along the Mediterranean, the central highlands (including the Judean and Galilean hills), the Jordan Rift Valley, and the Negev Desert. Also label the major bodies of water: the Mediterranean Sea, the Jordan River, the Sea of Galilee, and the Dead Sea.

» On a map of Eastern Asia, locate and label the island of Taiwan. Also, locate and label the Korean Peninsula. Label the major bodies of water surrounding these two land forms: the Sea of Japan, the Yellow Sea, and the East China Sea.

Geopolitical

» On the map of the Middle East, locate and shade in different colors Israel, the disputed Palestinian Territories (the West Bank and the Gaza Strip), and the Golan Heights (which Israel claims but which the international community considers part of Syria). Also locate and label the Arab countries surrounding the region.

» On the map of Eastern Asia, locate and label North Korea and South Korea, China, and Russia. Next, locate and label the DMZ on the 38th parallel between North Korea and South Korea, the Yalu River, and the cities of Pyongyang, Busan (formerly Pusan), Inchon, and Seoul.

Explore

» ***Missionary Aviation Fellowship:*** On a world map, locate and label where MAF located its bases in the first decade of its existence. Discover the geographical challenges for missionaries in these areas, and determine why providing pilots and airplanes in remote locations made such a difference.

» ***Christian Outreach:*** What is the status of evangelical outreach today in North Korea? What extreme difficulties face those who share the gospel in this area? In South Korea, which is now one of the largest missionary-sending nations, discover the vast outreach of Korean missionaries to other countries.

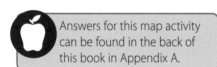

Answers for this map activity can be found in the back of this book in Appendix A.

◉ Create a map and discuss the issues in teams

The students each have an outline map in their manuals. They will be given assignments for drawing in the rivers, mountains, cities, and regional boundaries that are listed. For details on where these things are, please consult a historical atlas, an encyclopedia, or another source of geographic information.

Upper elementary students might be satisfied to accomplish only this portion:

- **Physical terrain:** This part of the mapping exercise will help students locate and mark the terrain of Israel and the disputed Palestinian territories, as well as identifying where Taiwan, the Korean Peninsula, and the major bodies of water surrounding them are located.

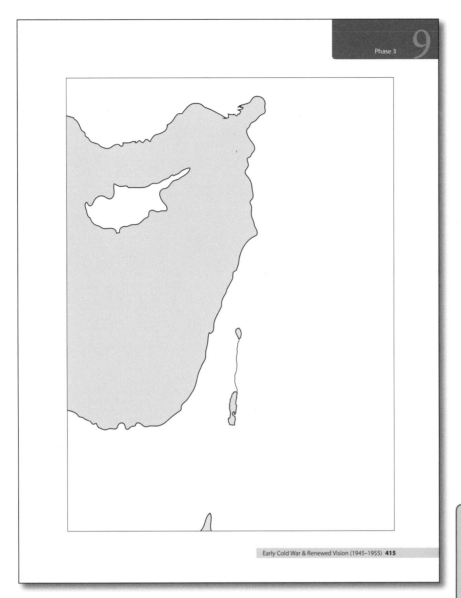

Middle school students might be satisfied to complete both the previous mapping exercise and this exercise:

- **Geopolitical:** This section of the mapping exercise will provide the students an opportunity to locate and mark the specific geographic locations of the areas which have been a prominent part of Arab/Israeli wars and which continue to

be disputed between Israel and the Palestinians. Also, students will discover the geographic locations of the major events of the Korean War.

High school students might be satisfied to complete both the previous mapping exercises and at least one exploration topic of this exercise:

- **Explore** a selection from this portion of the mapping exercise in teams.

MISSIONARY AVIATION FELLOWSHIP

Students might find it helpful to visit MAF's website to learn more of the specifics about what they have accomplished and where they are located. See the link at the online resource page.

CHRISTIAN OUTREACH

Students interested in this project might find it interesting to learn about Franklin Graham's opportunity to preach in North Korea. See the online resource page for a link to an article by Samaritan's Purse.

Also, it is eye-opening to search online for your country's requirements and suggestions for visiting North Korea.

416 Early Cold War & Renewed Vision (1945–1955)

▶ Art Appreciation

Number 1, 1950 (Lavender Mist) by Jackson Pollock, 1950

After the war, a new group of artists began creating a style of art known as abstract expressionism. The best known of these artists was Jackson Pollock, who, rather than using a paint brush, usually preferred to spatter or drip paint. With huge canvases tacked to the floor, Pollock could move freely, dripping, spilling, and throwing paint in what has been termed "Action Painting." He described that he felt "nearer, more a part of the painting, since this way I can walk round it, work from the four sides and literally be in the painting." Though it appears to be the creation of chance effects, Pollock said, "When I am painting, I have a general notion as to what I am about. I **can** control the flow of the paint: there is no accident, just as there is no beginning and no end."

» You can find a link to see this painting at the online resource page. What words could you use to describe this painting? How does it differ from the art of the 1800s? As you look at this painting, what is your response to the results of "Action Painting"? What philosophical view of the world does this painting suggest?

Number 61 (Rust and Blue) by Mark Rothko

Rothko's paintings, also abstract expressionism, provide a dramatic contrast to Pollock's work. Rather than creating a painting filled with random, abstract movement, Rothko "subdued the aggressiveness of Action Painting so completely that his pictures breathe the purest contemplative stillness," according to H. W. Janson in *History of Art*.

» You can find a link to see this painting at the online resource page. Describe what you see in as much detail as possible. How does it differ from the painting by Pollock? Many people find that Rothko's paintings, which are quite large, move them deeply. Why might this be so?

> **CONSIDER:**
> In his book *The God Who Is There*, Francis Schaeffer quotes from an article in *The New Yorker*. "Painters like the late Jackson Pollock in America . . . have nevertheless sought in the accidents of throwing or dripping paint a key to creation beyond the reach of the artist's conscious mind and will." Schaeffer's analysis: "In other words, this is not merely self-expression: it is . . . the hope that through the art form the impersonal universe will somehow speak as the artist works."

> The online resource page at www.HistoryRevealed.org contains many helpful Internet links to artwork, architecture, music, project helps, and more.

◉ Examine and discuss art and architecture

The online resource page at www.HistoryRevealed.org has links to view each of the items listed. Allow the students time to observe the paintings without any conversation, and then, when they are ready, engage them in some or all of the questions listed below or in the Student Manual.

Art Appreciation

Number 1 (Lavender Mist) by Jackson Pollock, 1948

A link to a fascinating video clip of Pollock actually creating one of his paintings can be found at the online resource page.

Ask students their thoughts about Pollock's comment, "I want to express my feelings, rather than illustrate them. Technique is just a means of arriving at a statement." What statement do you believe Pollock was making through his technique?

Number 61 (Rust and Blue) by Mark Rothko

A moving YouTube video of Rothko's work at the Tate Modern in London

The gift of being able to create is something our Creator God has shared with humanity. And, just as His creation reflects His character, so our human creations reflect us. Ephesians 5:1 tells us, "be imitators of God as dear children." How does that imitation, that obedience to His Word, affect our artwork? What are the implications of this for Christian artists?

can be found using the link a the online resource page.

Art historian Simon Schama comments on the video:

> If some of those portals are blocked, others open into the unknown space Rothko talked about, the place that only art can take us. Far away from the buzzing static of the moment, and towards the music of the spheres. . . . To be taken towards the gates that open onto the thresholds of eternity, to feel the poignancy of our comings and our goings, our entrances and our exits, our births and our deaths. Womb, tomb, and everything in between. Can art ever be more complete, more powerful?

Ask students about the way art affects them personally. Have they ever seen a painting that brought them to tears or gave them greater understanding of life? What is their response to Schama's comments? In what ways could modern art be seen in our culture as replacing religious belief?

[Author's note: When I sat in the Rothko room at the Tate Modern and quietly considered the paintings, I was moved to tears. Within them was an inexpressible depth, and, to my eyes, a sorrow. Though not a spiritual experience, it was emotional in a quiet and contemplative way.]

Architecture

Unités d'Habitation designed by Le Courbusier, completed 1952

Architect Kevin Havens writes that the international style:

> . . . proposed that buildings should honestly express their construction and not be a nostalgic notion of past societies. As a result, buildings could employ large expanses of glass and could support large column-free spaces because of what technology had become capable of achieving. The avant-garde architects and philosophers of this period also eschewed dependencies on the past, such as the ornament and intricate detail found with the historic styles. They sought to "liberate" architecture from both the cultural and political symbolism of tradition and to substitute a fresh vision for the future. In fact some of the aesthetic inspirations for the International Style came not from architecture but from new transportation technologies, like ocean liners and aircraft design. The expression was truly "international" in that it expressed no particular culture but rather an Ideal.

The International Style was born out of this climate of protest against historic styles and was initially quite politically charged. Le Corbusier in fact wrote an architectural manifesto early in his career entitled "Architecture or Revolution." He saw modernism as an imperative for civilization to move forward. What Le Courbusier's philosophy overlooked was the desperate need for people to be connected together in living, working, closely knitted communities . . . not the overcrowded "housing islands" modern urban planners were *designing* . . .

It is an interesting illustration of how philosophy, literature, art and architecture all conspire at various times in history to inform each other about what is "right." *All people* breath the "air of their time" and think accordingly. [What a contrast to the timeless wisdom of Scripture!]

A link to an excellent online resource for viewing the *Unité d'Habitation* in Marseille can be found at the online resource page.

▶ Architecture

In Unit six, we saw the German style of architecture made famous by Walter Gropius. Originally known as the Bauhaus movement, it was the beginning of a time of architectural experimentation made possible by new building technologies, such as reinforced concrete structural frames. A sharp break from traditional, historic architectural styles, this built upon a philosophy of moving into the future rather than revering the past. After WWII, this architectural approach, now termed the "international style," was widely popular as it drew its inspiration from modern technology. With the devastation caused by WWII, the reconstruction of Europe gave the architects of this style many opportunities to work on projects on an extensive scale. The international style can be characterized by geometric shapes, sometimes white wall, and a flat roof. The use of reinforced concrete (concrete with steel rods in it to strengthen the structure) enabled the architects to create huge structures with an abundance of windows.

Unités d'Habitation designed by Le Courbusier, completed 1952

One of the most important architects of this style was Le Courbusier. His "Unités d'Habitation" were apartment buildings for 1,600 people concentrated in one tower block surrounded by parks. The original building was located in Marseille, France, while others based on this design were built in Berlin and other cities. The advertising slogan for this was, "a revolutionary event, sun, space, and greenery. If you want to raise a family in privacy, in silence and in natural surroundings . . . ."

> » You can find a link to see photos of Le Courbusier's Unités d'Habitation at the online resource page. How would you describe this structure? Does this look like a place one could live "in natural surroundings"? Explain your reasoning.

Seagram Building designed by Mies van der Rohe, completed 1958

Ludwig Mies van der Rohe, with Gropius and Le Courbusier, pioneered modern architecture and is considered to be the master of glass and steel architecture. The monumental Seagram Building in New York City is considered to be the finest skyscraper in the international style.

> » You can find a link to see photos of the Seagram Building at the online resource page. Mies described his buildings as "skin and bones" architecture. Would you agree? How would you describe this building? Compare it to the Chrysler Building, built in 1930, and the Empire State Building, built in 1931. What differences do you see between the Seagram Building and these two built less than thirty years earlier?

Seagram Building designed by Mies van der Rohe, completed 1958

It is fascinating to discover that Mark Rothko was commissioned to create paintings for the Four Seasons restaurant in the Seagram Building, only to later refuse the commission. Several of the paintings Rothko had painted for the restaurant were given to the Tate Modern in London.

Dialogue with your students about their views on the impact of the International Style on modern architecture. How does liberating architecture from its historic base and from tradition affect us today?

► Arts in Action

Select one or more, and let your artistic juices flow!

Action Painting

» Outdoors, set up an appropriate place for painting in the style of Jackson Pollock. You will need butcher paper, plenty of cardboard, rubber balls of various sizes, a large stick, and several colors of paint (tempera or acrylic). Tape a long piece of butcher paper to the cardboard. Consider which aspects are under your control (color, general plan, equipment, distance) and which aspects are not (gravity, details, overlap). There are several decisions to be made: limited colors or all the colors; balls, sticks, or both; only certain balls or all the balls; limited coverage or extensive coverage; sequence and pattern or playfully random and overlapping. Do approach the painting from all four sides, as Pollock did. When you are finished, give your work a title, let it dry completely, then set it up on an easel or wall.

Contemplative Creations

» In the style of Rothko, create a painting, fiber art, or a sculptured piece that will provide an oasis of quiet and calm for the viewer. You might use blocks of color in soothing tones, whether painted on canvas, layered fabric quilted or pieced together, or three-dimensional objects arranged in a simple way. Then consider the best setting for the finished art, as the environment will enhance or detract from your work.

The online resource page at www.HistoryRevealed.org contains many helpful Internet links to artwork, architecture, music, project helps, and more.

◉ Do an art project

Action Painting

For a slightly different approach to action painting, check out the link to the Splash and Splatter project at the online resource page.

Contemplative Creations

Encourage students to learn more about the visual elements, especially color and shape, which lend themselves to soothing and calming the viewer. As they complete their art project and choose a setting, it would be fascinating to consider auditory and kinesthetic elements that are calming as well.

Talk together about the following questions.

How would you define art?

How would you define Christian art?

Using your definitions, would this Action Painting or Contemplative Creation qualify as either art or Christian art? What philosophy or worldview do you think this reflects?

[Author's note: For those students who did the Action Painting, this discussion is not intended to negate the fun of playing with sticks and balls in paint! It is, however, intended to encourage students to consider the significance of serious art on a culture.]

▶ Science

The Discovery of DNA

In 1953, the most important advance of the 20th century in biology took place when Francis Crick and James D. Watson of the University of Cambridge published a paper on the structure of DNA. Their ground-breaking conclusion was that DNA is a three-dimensional double helix, and in the paper, they were able to satisfactorily explain all the bonds that hold it together. This opened the door to understanding genetics.

» Try this: You can actually do an experiment that will extract DNA from split peas and allow you to see the DNA! This is what you will need:

½ cup dried split peas	2 tbsp liquid dish soap
¼ tsp salt	¼ tsp meat tenderizer
1 cup water	Rubbing alcohol, chilled

In a blender, blend on high speed the split peas, salt, and water until it is the consistency of thin soup. This will separate the pea cells.

Next, strain the mixture into a clear glass and vigorously stir in the liquid dish soap. Let this sit for five to ten minutes. This will break down the cell membrane and nucleus, which will release the DNA from inside the cell.

Now, *very gently* stir the meat tenderizer into the glass. This will remove the proteins that coat the DNA.

Finally, with the glass slightly tilted, *slowly* pour the chilled rubbing alcohol down the inside until there is an equal amount of alcohol to mixture. The white stringy clumps are the DNA of the peas!

◉ Do a science experiment

A link to an excellent website that shows this experiment with photos and detailed explanations can be found at the online resource page.

You can alos view an animated video clip of a DNA strand.

Music

Francis Poulenc (1899–1963) was a French composer who is considered to be one of the major liturgical composers of the twentieth century. The story of how Poulenc, who was known to his friends as a light-hearted, witty, frivolous man, came to be writing such powerful religious music in the latter part of his life is fascinating. In 1936, a close friend was killed in an automobile accident. Poulenc later said, "The horrible snuffing-out of this musician so full of vitality had absolutely stupefied me. Ruminating on the frailty of our human condition, I was once again attracted to the spiritual life . . . . You now know the true source of inspiration for my religious works."

"Mass in G Major" by Poulenc

» Listen to Poulenc's "Mass in G Major." You can find a link at the online resource page. This music is ethereal and calm, in contrast to Poulenc's "Gloria," which musically expresses exultation. How would you compare this music to the music of other composers? How does it compare to the music sung in your church?

Cooking

In studying about Korea in this Unit, we have the opportunity to sample some of its wonderful food!

Barbecued Short Ribs

3 pounds beef short ribs, trimmed of fat and gristle

Marinade:

2 tbsp fresh ginger root, peeled & minced	½ cup soy sauce
2 cloves garlic, crushed	¼ cup sugar
¼ cup tahini (sesame seed paste)	6 green onions, chopped

Combine marinade ingredients in a gallon plastic bag. Add ribs to marinade and seal the bag. Turn to distribute marinade evenly. Let stand two to four hours in the refrigerator, turning bag occasionally.

Preheat oven to 375 degrees F, or fire up the charcoal grill. Place ribs on a roasting rack or on the grill. Reserve marinade. Roast ribs for 40 minutes, turning meat often and basting with the marinade. If cooking in the oven, raise oven heat to 450 degrees F and continue cooking until they are crisp, about five minutes. Serves 4 to 6.

◉ Listen to and discuss the music

Listen

Poulenc's "Mass in G Major"

Poulenc's music, rich and original, was based on the great masters of the past—Bach, Mozart, Chopin, Tchaikovsky, Puccini, Debussy, and others. Jane Stuart Smith, in *The Gift of Music*, writes: "It was not that he had no ideas himself, but because of his love for the music of these composers he made their music become a part of his. The music of Poulenc is as personal as any composed in this century."

The online resource page has links to hear portions of each section of Poulenc's "Mass in G Major."

◉ Cook the food

One of the mainstays of Korean food is kimchi (fermented vegetables), which is traditionally eaten at breakfast, lunch, and dinner. There are many different types of kimchi, but the most common is one made from Napa cabbage and red pepper flakes. You can purchase kimchi at a store, or you can try your hand at making it at home. There are many online sources for recipes, and their authors often say they enjoy kimchi most when it is fresh!

9 Phase 3

▶ Student Self-Evaluation UNIT 9, PHASE 3

Dates and hours:_____

Evaluate your projects

- List which of the activities listed in this Phase you did:

  _____

  _____

- Rate your enthusiasm: _____

  Explain: _____

  _____

- Rate the precision of your approach:_____

  Explain: _____

  _____

- Rate your effort toward the completion of the project: _____

  Explain: _____

  _____

- Ask yourself what worked and what did not. What would you do differently in the future, and what would you repeat?

  _____

- How did these hands-on activities enhance your knowledge of the Early Cold War & Renewed Vision? What made them worthwhile?

  _____

  _____

- In the first three Phases of this Unit, what aspect of the time period has most captured your imagination? What would you like to creatively pursue to conclude your study?

  _____

  _____

  _____

422 Early Cold War & Renewed Vision (1945–1955)

◉ Conduct a review and evaluation

In this Phase of Unit 9, your students should have had the opportunity to explore the Early Cold War & Renewed Vision through various hands-on and creative sessions by completing a selection from the following:

- completed a mapping section;
- observed and discussed art & architecture;
- worked on an art project;
- experimented with a science project or taken a field trip;
- listened to music;
- tasted a food related to this Unit;
- completed their self-evaluation procedure for this Phase.

Record student hours: _____

Assess student involvement in the hands-on activities.

Create an evaluation system of your own or refer to the evaluation rubric in the introduction as a tool for assessing participation. The categories you will probably find most useful for evaluating projects are *"Task"* and *"Process: Teamwork."* Consider specifically the enthusiasm, the precision of approach, and the efforts toward improving skills and completing activities, rather than rating the project as compared to a masterpiece.

Do not critique the self-evaluation page your student completes in the Student Manual—it is acceptable for students to occasionally leave lines blank if a question does not apply. Instead, discuss with the student the intention of the written comments and incorporate those into your evaluation.

Determine a grade for this Phase, if using grades: _____

Teacher Self-Evaluation:

Evaluate your own use of materials: what worked and what did not? Consider your time management. Were you able to recognize and respond to your students' needs? Did you make your expectations clear? Incorporate suggestions from your students in your own evaluation (*this requires humility!*).

Phase 4

The Expression Week

▶ In Your Own Way…

In this Unit, we have seen the lingering effects of WWII in the humanitarian efforts for Displaced Persons and in the massive rebuilding of Europe and Japan, the start of nearly half a century of Cold War, the drama of the Berlin Airlift, the international division of nations as the Soviet Union led the Eastern Bloc of communist countries while the United States led the Western Bloc of democracies, the non-aligned nations who sided with neither, the newly won independence of nations in Asia and Africa, the emergence of modern Israel and the ongoing tragedy of Palestinian refugee camps, the victory of communism in China, the stalemate of the Korean War, and the extraordinary efforts of God's people to minister in difficult places. Now, choose a selection of these activities, or create your own, which will best express what you have learned from this Unit.

LINGUISTICS

Journalism

Berlin is in the spotlight, as the Soviets have denied any access to the city by land or water, have refused to feed anyone outside the Soviet zone of Berlin, and now have cut electricity. Tensions are high, rumors are wild. You would love to capture the big story of the Berlin Airlift, but unfortunately you are only a junior reporter in your news agency and that is outside your beat. Depressingly, you have been assigned to see if there is possibly a "human interest" story worth printing. Don't despair! That is going to be your ticket to the big-time—getting the scoop on Operation Little Vittles and the Candy Bombers!

Find someone who fought in the Korean War or in a subsequent war and then interview that person. Ask about their experiences, what they learned, how it changed their lives. Write up the interview and submit it to your local newspaper, an organization's newsletter, or student magazine.

Poetry

Finish this poem about the decolonization of Africa, from the point of view of an African patriot.

In the mists of morning, the masters are unmasked

Emptying empires, ebbing like the sea …

Prose

Write a children's story about Brother Andrew, God's Smuggler. Tell in simple terms of his adventures and how God directed him to bring Bibles into closed countries, beginning with nations behind the Iron Curtain.

It's November 1947, and the vote for Partition has just been taken at the United Nations. It's now official. Israel will become a nation! As a British soldier and Christian believer stationed in Israel, you are in the right place at the right time, seeing unbelievable events unfold around you. However, it is an unstable time to be living in Jerusalem, and your parents back home are quite worried. It's time to write them a letter to let them know what's happening. Help them understand the current situation between the Jews, Palestinian Christians, and Palestinian Muslims, and what you're hearing on the street concerning the future—especially as Britain prepares to withdraw its troops.

◉ Choose an area of expression

Students may work either individually or in teams.

Linguistics:

Journalism

Students interested in writing a newspaper account of Operation Little Vittles will find great sources online, particularly at the PBS website link provided at the online resource page.

Here is an excerpt of a journalistic piece, written in July 1990, by David LaChance in the *Union News*:

Halvorsen was known as "the Candy Bomber" on both sides of the Atlantic, but the West German children also called him "Uncle Wiggly Wings," because he would wiggle the wings of his C-54 transport plane as a signal before unloading his candy cargo. Halvorsen said the idea of dropping candy came to him after he had met a group of German children outside the fence of Tempelhof Airport . . . . "They spoke with me for about an hour, and gave me a real appreciation for freedom," he said. Turning to leave, he suddenly realized that the children, unlike youngsters in other countries in war-torn Europe, had not asked him for any candy or gum. They were so grateful for the shipments of food, he said, "They wouldn't lower themselves to being a beggar. That just blew my mind." He fished in his pocket and found two sticks of gum. Those he broke in half and gave to four of the children, while the others were happy to simply sniff the wrapper, he said.

The idea then came to him to drop candy during his next delivery run. The crowds of children grew larger with each trip, and "Operation Little Vittles" was born.

Now there's a great start for a human interest piece!

According to an Internet source, there are more than five million Korean War veterans alive in 2012. For students in the US wanting to interview a Korean vet, one suggestion would be to contact the local Veterans of Foreign Wars or, online through the link at the online resource page. For students outside the US whose country participated in the Korean War, check with the Veterans Affairs of your nation.

Poetry

Students interested in creating a poem of Africa would find a wealth of inspiration in the poetry of Somalia, which was granted partial independence in 1950, and full independence in 1960. Poetry is a central aspect of Somali culture. Not something stowed away in books for academics, rather it is part of the day-to-day fabric of their lives. Poetry is used for telling history, describing current events, communicating ideas, in reconciliation, and even in political debates! Known as a "nation of poets," Somalis believe that nothing important is said unless it's poetry; and nothing is important unless it's said in poetry.

Since Somalia, like many African nations, is an oral culture—meaning that poetry is spoken rather than read—they use the power of *alliteration* (to repeat a particular sound in a series of words or phrases) in their poetry.

Many languages used alliteration in poetry, such as this one in old English.

"The Vision of William Concerning Piers the Plowman" by William Langland (about AD 1362–1393)

A feir feld full of folk ‖ fond I per bit-wene,

Of alle maner of men, ‖ þe mene and þe riche,

Worchinge and wandringe ‖ as þe world askeþ.

In modern spelling:

A fair field full of folk ‖ found I there between,

Of all manner of men ‖ the mean and the rich,

Working and wandering ‖ as the world asks.

Prose

Reading Brother Andrew's *God's Smuggler* would be highly recommended for students interested in this project. In addition, YWAM Publishing's Christian Heroes book on Brother Andrew brings a valuable perspective on Andrew's ministry. Online, there are many YouTube videos of Brother Andrew speaking, but one in particular might be of use for students in this project. You can find a link at the online resource page.

Ask students to do the work of researching BOTH Jewish and Arab reaction to the UN plan for partition, recognizing that, in order to do justice to the situation, one must learn what *each* side says of itself and what it says of the other. Significantly, Proverbs 18:17 says, "The first one to plead his cause seems right, until his neighbor comes and examines him."

The following reproduces the student page:

ART

Painting/Drawing

Create a painting, a series of paintings, or a collage that will provide a visual window into the Cold War. Include the various ways the Western Bloc and Eastern Bloc waged war, such as propaganda and espionage. Remember, this war is cold, not hot!

Graphic Design

Start a trend in fashion and politics. Design a talking T-shirt that presents reasons for non-alignment, and then present these colorful shirts to dissatisfied delegates for the 1953 United Nations barbecue. Casual wear has been specified, and talking T-shirts have never before been seen, so make your point, but be diplomatic!

Cartooning

Draw a political cartoon from the American point of view and a second cartoon from the Soviet point of view. In each, the subject is the Truman Doctrine. The heroes and villains of the cartoons, however, will depend upon who is cheering whom.

Shadow Box

Create a shadow box to artistically represent the story of the Waodani people and the missionaries who, through death and life, brought the liberating message of God's redemption to them. Fashion the box with several interior spaces, then gather the articles you wish to display.

MUSIC

Medley

The United Nations has fifty-one original member states, representing a wide range of cultures and languages. Splice together excerpts of typical melodies (samples) from several of these divergent nations. You will be raising awareness for your listeners of just how diverse is the membership of the UN. Be as creative and "techy" as possible!

Performance Practice

With your teacher's help, select an appropriate piece of music which expresses some particular aspect studied in this Unit that you found interesting.

Art:

Painting/Drawing

For a painting or collage of the Cold War, students might find it helpful to do an online search for images of the Cold War. Next, have them to consider various ways in which they could visually communicate the metaphorical nature of "cold" in the term "Cold War."

Graphic Design

The non-alignment movement was focused on developing nations that were striving to walk in the middle between the Soviet Bloc and the Western Bloc. Students might look for ways to incorporate symbolic images to express this "in the middle" feel in their designs. The five national leaders who founded the movement in 1961 were from Egypt, Ghana, India, Indonesia, and Yugoslavia. Cultural images from these nations might provide an additional source for the design.

Cartooning

In 1947, President Truman, referring to the civil war in Greece being fought between nationalists and Communists, indicated that the Truman Doctrine was "the policy of the United States to support free people who are resisting attempted subjugation by armed minorities or by outside pressures." Encourage students

Drama:

Comedy

The process of generating physical comedy takes place during rehearsal, discovering through trial and error what is actually funny. Encourage students to create the environment of a military kitchen in order to start generating ideas. Suggest they choose several items of food, which they will need to contain, as well as containers, maybe some unlikely containers. Flour, eggs, milk, frozen peas sitting in tipsy bowls or flimsy bags all have great comic potential, as they will easily explode, break, spill or roll without much effort. Begin slowly and systematically "containing" the food, recording the ideas and noting the difficult parts. Then do it faster, and again, faster. Adding the extreme comic pacing to the ridiculous orders will bring out the humor. The urgency leads to mistakes, and that can be funny; creating chaos in an attempt to bring order, that is funny. Eventually, they will discover where urgency creates chaos (like the flour going all over the actor instead of into the container).

Puppetry

Students will have to decide what it is that the foolish puppet is unwilling to relinquish and how to make that comical. For instance, a foolish puppet is allergic to cats but wants to hold on to a stuffed kitten, or a puppet wants to hold forever a memorable, though melting, ice cube. Once the concept is worked out, then consider the importance of props, both action props, and story props. An action prop has some physical behavior, like a spring compressed and then springing, or a can of hair spray spraying. A story prop, like a stuffed animal, doesn't do anything, but as a prop, it can be made to respond to the actor. For this puppet show, find props that repel the puppet, like springs that jump away, a stuffed kitten that provokes an allergy, an ice cube that melts, or a can of hairspray that keeps spraying the puppet in the face.

DRAMA

Comedy

Create a comedy of errors in which a cook in the US Army accidentally receives the wrong orders. The high level military directive requires that the new policy of "containment" be put into practice immediately. The cook, having no idea that these orders were meant for someone in military intelligence, tries desperately to comply—in the kitchen—with comedic results.

Puppetry

Jim Elliot, who was known to be both a passionate follower of Jesus and one who enjoyed playing, understood wisdom when he said, "He is no fool who gives what he cannot keep to gain that which he cannot lose." With this in mind, create a humorous puppet show for children with a foolish puppet who seeks to hold onto something he cannot keep. Let that struggle develop until a gentle voice of wisdom brings light.

Drama

Present dramatically the unseen world of refugee camps. Whether your focus is the European Displaced Persons camps or Palestinian refugee camps, demonstrate what day-to-day life is like, the types of issues faced, and the struggle to retain hope and dignity while you are living permanently in overcrowded and deplorable conditions.

Prop Needs

Costume Ideas

Role/Player

Set Suggestions

to take the time to read George Kennan's Long Telegram, as it would be very helpful for this project. Also, it will be important to examine Soviet reaction to the West, particularly in the crisis leading to the Berlin Airlift.

Shadow Box

Students will want to decide beforehand how many different objects they want to display, and then create that number of interior "rooms." Create an outside shell, and then divide it into interior spaces. Using cardboard might require an extra layer, or tri-wall material. Tape the shadow box together, prime and paint it. Next, set up each of the spaces artistically to tell the story of the Waodani and the gospel.

Music:

Medley

Students might enjoy downloading samples of folk or ethnic music from a wide selection of UN nations, and then, using audio software, assembling the samples into a United Nations medley.

Performance Practice

For musical students, this selection may be a wonderful opportunity to express what they have learned. Make sure they select a piece that they have adequate time to prepare.

Drama

Students could go about this using either a character-driven story or a plot-driven story. Character-driven is focused on the emotions, thoughts, and behaviors of a small group of characters who become important to the audience. The empathy connection is most important, helping an audience to understand that these characters are similar to them. It is necessary to give time for the characters' thoughts, emotions, and behaviors to connect with the audience. Plot-driven is concerned with what happens. Though it can involve any number of people, what is most important is the dramatic arc: an inciting incident that creates conflict, events that increase the conflict, attempts to resolve the conflict, and the denouement.

Movement:

Mime

For students who wish to create this mime, it is an opportunity to use a lot of expression in the body—to artistically portray hope and need, to physically express the emotions the Plan represented to the people of Europe. Combine the physical actions of contortion (twisting, bending, flexing) and extension (moving from a bent to a straight position) to portray these emotions. Consider using a non-musical sound track. For instance, rhythms, speech, and chaotic noise might represent this historic period and provide a directive auditory environment.

Dance

Dancers who choreograph this piece might find that using costumes could make a dramatic difference. Encourage students to find ways to incorporate the process of changing costumes into the dance itself: don't stop dancing to put on a costume, instead, make putting on the costume as peoples' lives change part of the dance. One costume item that would be symbolic would be long red scarves.

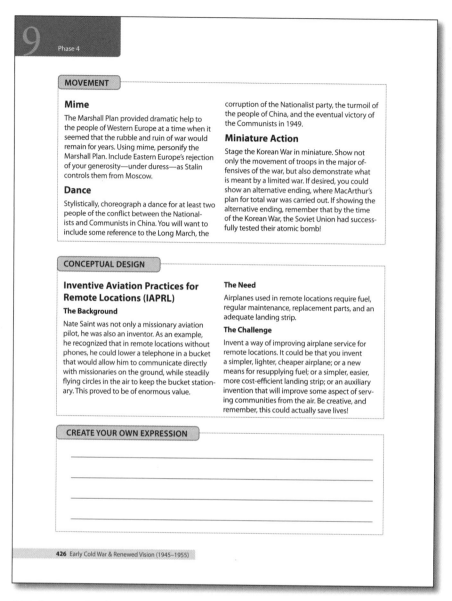

MOVEMENT

Mime

The Marshall Plan provided dramatic help to the people of Western Europe at a time when it seemed that the rubble and ruin of war would remain for years. Using mime, personify the Marshall Plan. Include Eastern Europe's rejection of your generosity—under duress—as Stalin controls them from Moscow.

Dance

Stylistically, choreograph a dance for at least two people of the conflict between the Nationalists and Communists in China. You will want to include some reference to the Long March, the corruption of the Nationalist party, the turmoil of the people of China, and the eventual victory of the Communists in 1949.

Miniature Action

Stage the Korean War in miniature. Show not only the movement of troops in the major offensives of the war, but also demonstrate what is meant by a limited war. If desired, you could show an alternative ending, where MacArthur's plan for total war was carried out. If showing the alternative ending, remember that by the time of the Korean War, the Soviet Union had successfully tested their atomic bomb!

CONCEPTUAL DESIGN

Inventive Aviation Practices for Remote Locations (IAPRL)

The Background

Nate Saint was not only a missionary aviation pilot, he was also an inventor. As an example, he recognized that in remote locations without phones, he could lower a telephone in a bucket that would allow him to communicate directly with missionaries on the ground, while steadily flying circles in the air to keep the bucket stationary. This proved to be of enormous value.

The Need

Airplanes used in remote locations require fuel, regular maintenance, replacement parts, and an adequate landing strip.

The Challenge

Invent a way of improving airplane service for remote locations. It could be that you invent a simpler, lighter, cheaper airplane; or a new means for resupplying fuel; or a simpler, easier, more cost-efficient landing strip; or an auxiliary invention that will improve some aspect of serving communities from the air. Be creative, and remember, this could actually save lives!

CREATE YOUR OWN EXPRESSION

_____

_____

_____

Miniature Action

Encourage students to create a three-dimensional map to show the Korean War effectively, unless they are using a projector onto a screen. A link to an incredible online resource for free topographical maps of the Korean War can be found at the online resource page.

Conceptual Design:

Inventive Aviation Practices for Remote Locations (IAPRL)

Regardless of whether a student has chosen to do this particular project, everyone should visit the website of the Indigenous People's Technology and Educational Center (i-tec) to learn the amazing inventions that are being created to serve people in remote locations worldwide. A link can be found at the online resource page.

◉ Share creative expressions in class

Create a safe environment for the presentations. Set ground rules prior to the presentations, so that students know how much time is available for each of them, and so that they know they will be honored and respected by all those observing.

▶ Student Self-Evaluation UNIT 9, PHASE 4

Dates and hours:_____

Evaluate your projects

- What creative project did you choose?

  _____

- What did you expect from your project, and how does the final project compare to your initial expectations?

  _____

- What do you like about your project? What would you change?

  _____
  _____

In Conclusion

Revisit the four Key Concepts from the beginning of this Unit. Explain how your understanding of and appreciation for each has grown over the course of your study.

- _____
  _____

- _____
  _____

- _____
  _____

- _____
  _____

Record your concluding thoughts on the Early Cold War & Renewed Vision.

_____
_____
_____

Early Cold War & Renewed Vision (1945–1955) **427**

◉ Conduct a review and evaluation

In this Phase of Unit 9, your students should have had the opportunity to express what they have learned about the Early Cold War & Renewed Vision through one or more various creative selections of their own choosing. These include:

- Linguistics;
- Art;
- Music;
- Drama;
- Movement;
- Conceptual Design.

Record student hours: _____

Assess student effort in the creative expressions, as individuals or as teams.

Create an evaluation system of your own, or refer to the evaluation rubric in the introduction, as a tool for assessing participation. The categories you will probably find most useful for evaluating their projects are *"Task," "Process: Teamwork," "Process: Originality,"* and Grammar, Format, and Spelling.

In this Phase especially, do not critique the self-evaluation page your student completes in the Student Manual—consider how the very soul of an artist has been exposed and vulnerable, so be encouraging and not belittling. Again, consider enthusiasm, precision of approach, and efforts toward improving skills and completing the activity, rather than rating the project as compared to a masterpiece. Instead, discuss with the student the intention of the written comments and incorporate those into your evaluation.

Determine a grade for this Phase, if using grades: _____

Teacher Self-Evaluation:

Evaluate your own use of materials and teaching opportunities: what worked and what did not; how effective was your time-management; how were your responses to the needs of your student; did you make your expectations clear? Incorporate suggestions from your students in your own evaluation (*this requires humility!*).

Take a moment now to evaluate the whole unit. What would you like to remember if you taught this subject again? What do you recognize that your students gained most—either as students of history or as creative individuals? What did you learn about the Early Cold War & Renewed Vision or about teaching?

Unit 1: Europe

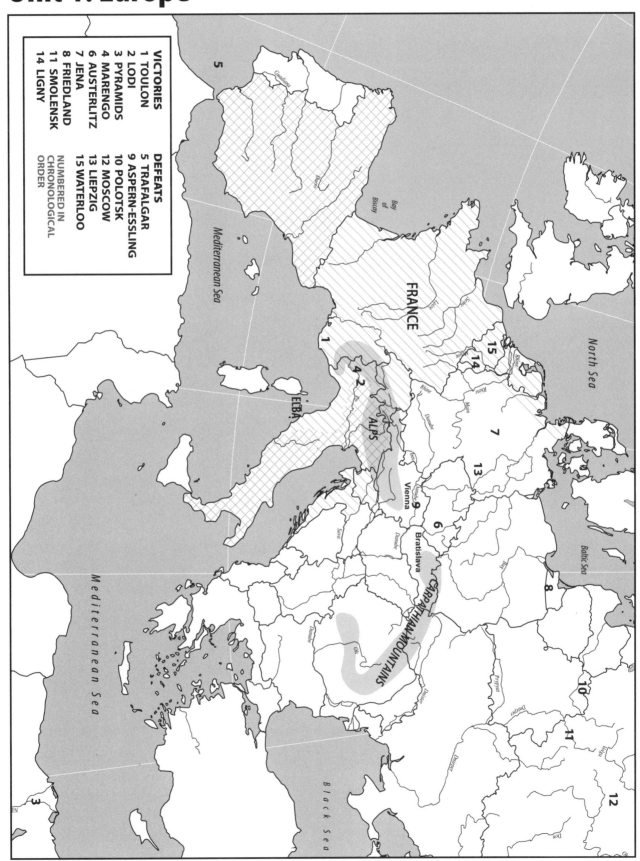

VICTORIES
1 TOULON
2 LODI
3 PYRAMIDS
4 MARENGO
6 AUSTERLITZ
7 JENA
8 FRIEDLAND
11 SMOLENSK
14 LIGNY

DEFEATS
5 TRAFALGAR
9 ASPERN-ESSLING
10 POLOTSK
12 MOSCOW
13 LIEPZIG
15 WATERLOO

NUMBERED IN
CHRONOLOGICAL
ORDER

Unit 1: Map of India

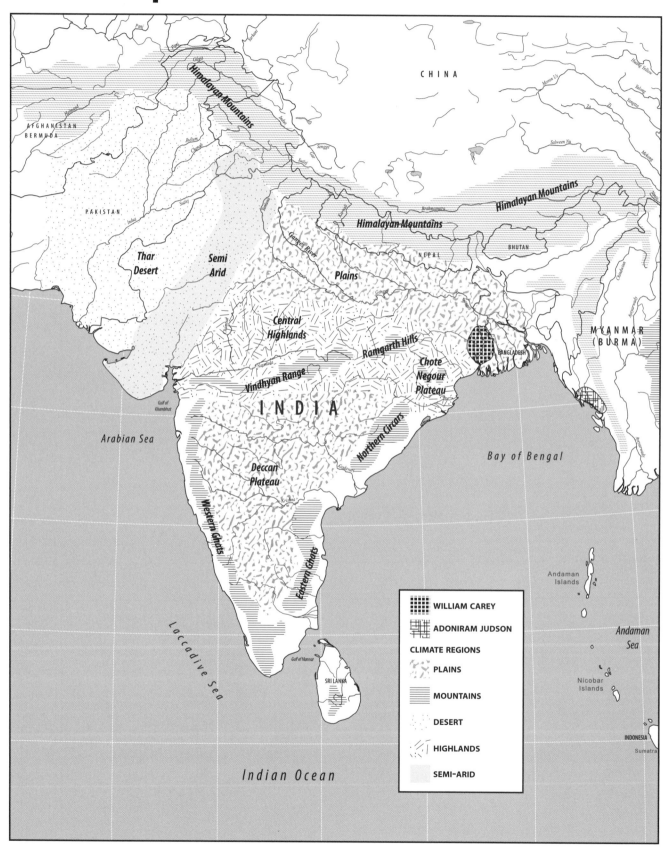

CHINA

AFGHANISTAN
BERMUDA

PAKISTAN

Himalayan Mountains

Himalayan Mountains

Himalayan Mountains

NEPAL

BHUTAN

Thar
Desert

Semi
Arid

Plains

Central
Highlands

Ramgarth Hills

Chote
Negour
Plateau

BANGLADESH

MYANMAR
(BURMA)

Vindhyan Range

INDIA

Gulf of
Khambhat

Arabian Sea

Deccan
Plateau

Northern Circars

Bay of Bengal

Western Ghats

Eastern Ghats

Andaman
Islands

Laccadive Sea

Andaman
Sea

Gulf of Mannar

SRI LANKA

Nicobar
Islands

INDONESIA

Sumatra

Indian Ocean

	WILLIAM CAREY
	ADONIRAM JUDSON
CLIMATE REGIONS	
	PLAINS
	MOUNTAINS
	DESERT
	HIGHLANDS
	SEMI-ARID

Unit 2: Map of Europe

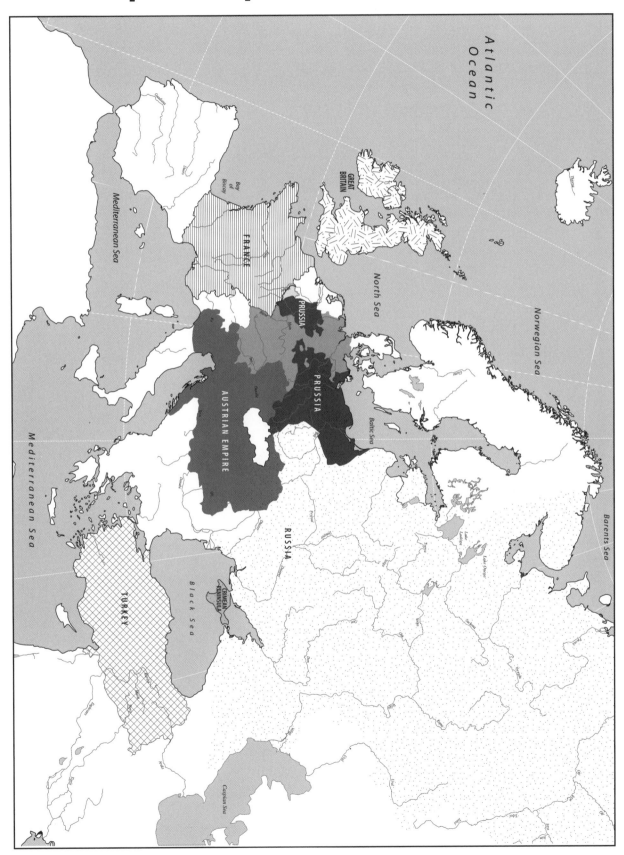

Unit 2: Central and South America

North
Atlantic
Ocean

Colorado

Ohio

Mississippi

Rio Grande

Sierra Madre Occidental

Chihuahuan Desert

Sierra Madre Oriental

Gulf of
Mexico

MEXICO

Sierra Madre del Sur

BAHAMAS

CUBA

PUERTO
RICO

JAMAICA

HAITI

DOM.
REP.

ST KITTS & NEVIS

ANTIGUA & BARBUDA

DOMINICA

ST LUCIA

BARBADOS

BELIZE

HONDURAS

GUATEMALA

EL SALVADOR

NICARAGUA

Caribbean Sea

ST VINCENT & THE GRENADINES

GRENADA

PANAMA

COSTA RICA

TRINIDAD & TOBAGO

VENEZUELA

FRENCH GUIANA

SURINAME

GUYANA

COLOMBIA

Japurá

Negro

ECUADOR

Amazon

Juruá

Purus

Madeira

Amazon

Teffé

Xingu

B R A Z I L

PERU

Juruena

Iténes

BOLIVIA

PARAGUAY

South Pacific Ocean

CHILE

Uruguai

Salado

URUGUAY

ARGENTINA

South
Atlantic
Ocean

	WON INDEPENDENCE
///	PORTUGUESE
≡	SPANISH

Falkland Islands

South Georgia

Unit 3: Map of Africa

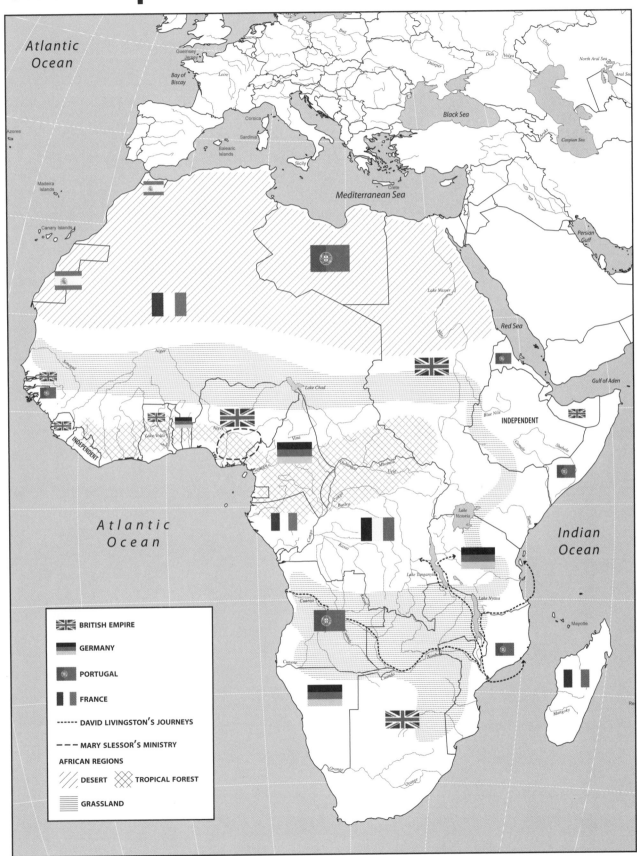

BRITISH EMPIRE

GERMANY

PORTUGAL

FRANCE

- - - - - DAVID LIVINGSTON'S JOURNEYS

- - - MARY SLESSOR'S MINISTRY

AFRICAN REGIONS

DESERT   TROPICAL FOREST

GRASSLAND

Unit 3: Map of the World

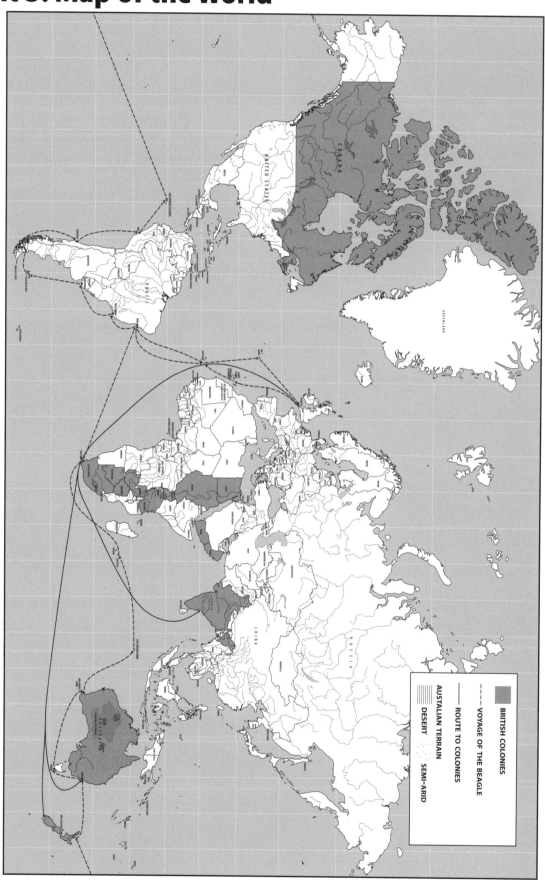

Unit 4: Map of China

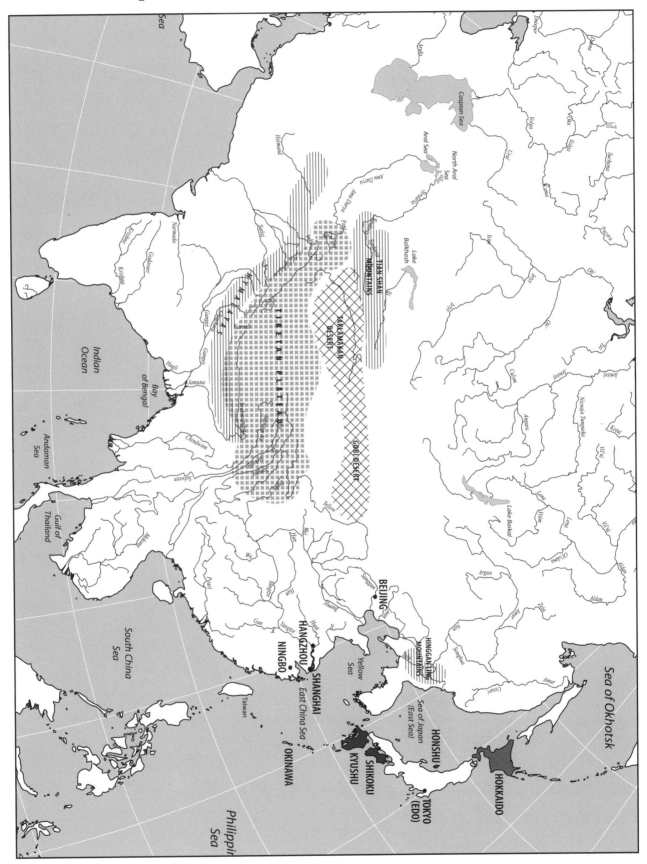

Unit 4: Map of Europe

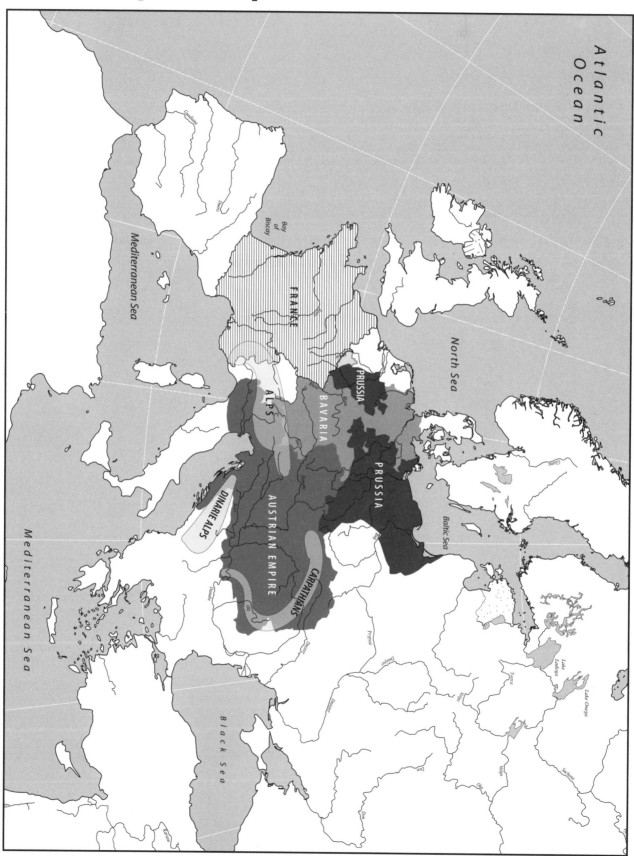

Unit 5: Map of the Balkans

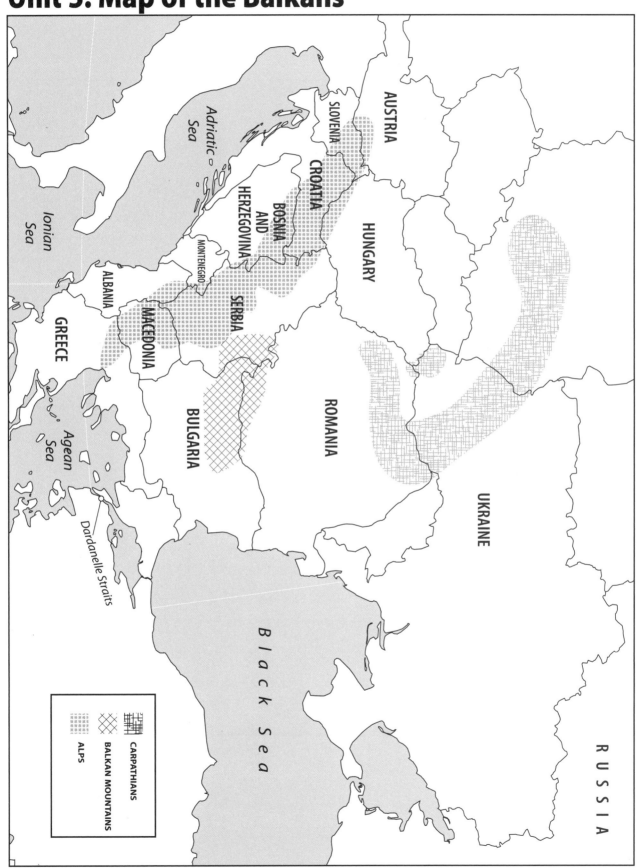

AUSTRIA

SLOVENIA

CROATIA

BOSNIA AND HERZEGOVINA

MONTENEGRO

ALBANIA

MACEDONIA

SERBIA

HUNGARY

Adriatic Sea

Ionian Sea

GREECE

Agean Sea

Dardanelle Straits

BULGARIA

ROMANIA

UKRAINE

Black Sea

RUSSIA

CARPATHIANS

BALKAN MOUNTAINS

ALPS

Unit 5: Map of Eastern Asia

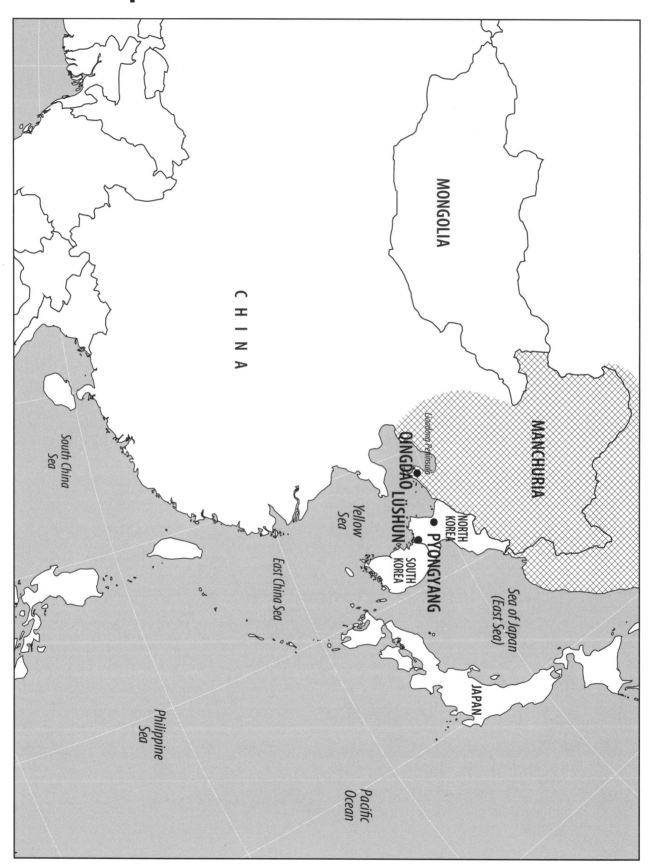

Unit 6: Map of Eastern and Western Europe

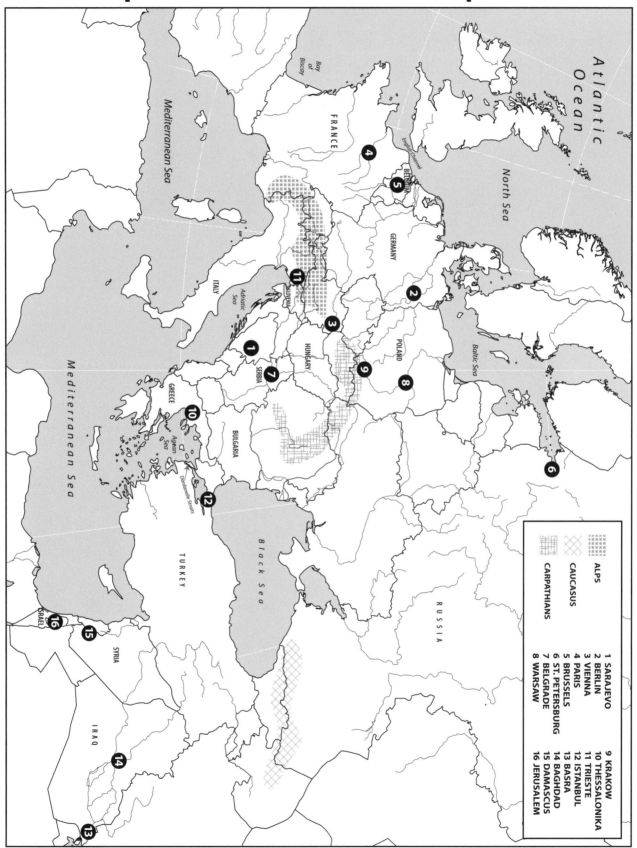

1 SARAJEVO	9 KRAKOW
2 BERLIN	10 THESSALONIKA
3 VIENNA	11 TRIESTE
4 PARIS	12 ISTANBUL
5 BRUSSELS	13 BASRA
6 ST. PETERSBURG	14 BAGHDAD
7 BELGRADE	15 DAMASCUS
8 WARSAW	16 JERUSALEM

ALPS

CAUCASUS

CARPATHIANS

Unit 7: Map of Central Europe

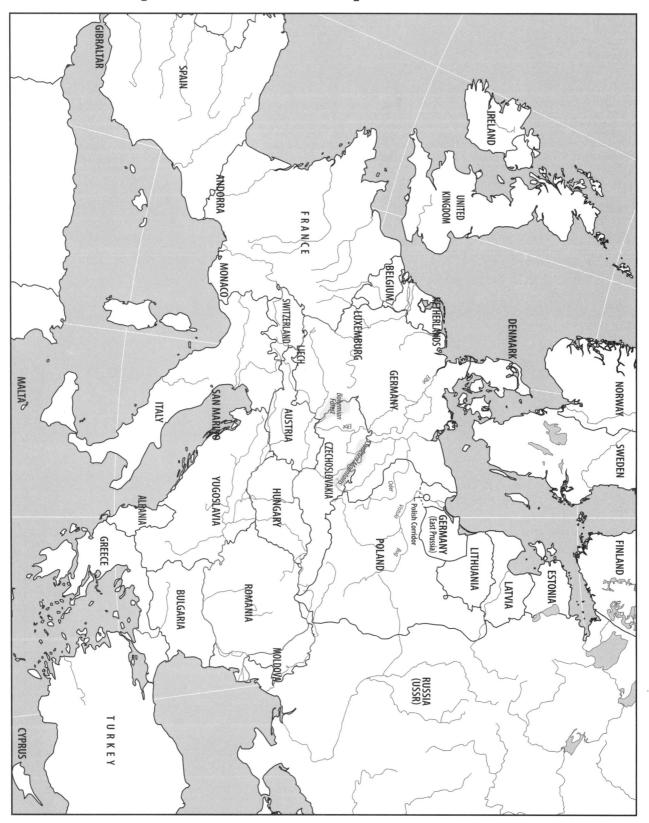

Unit 7: Map of the Middle East

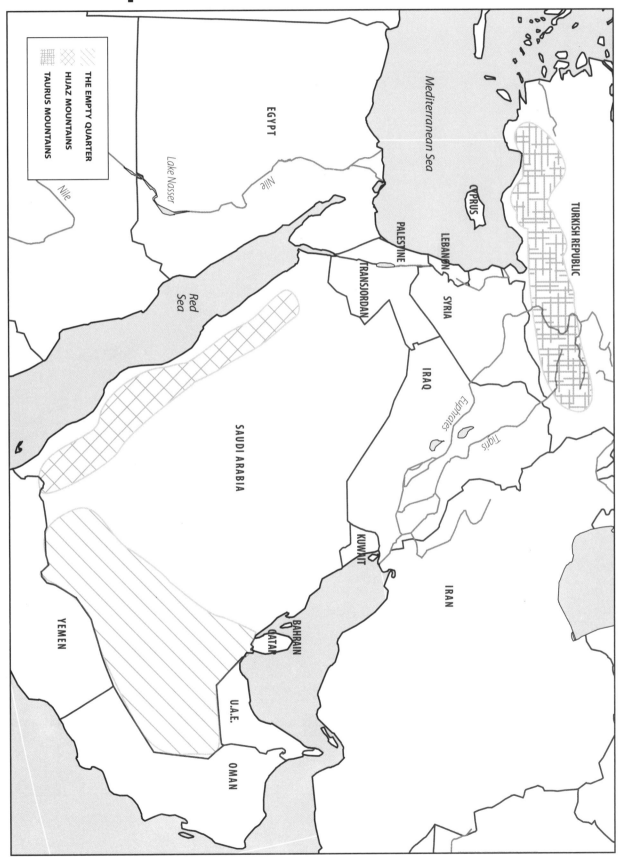

THE EMPTY QUARTER
HIJAZ MOUNTAINS
TAURUS MOUNTAINS

EGYPT

Mediterranean Sea

Lake Nasser

Nile

Nile

CYPRUS

TURKISH REPUBLIC

PALESTINE

TRANSJORDAN

LEBANON

SYRIA

IRAQ

Red Sea

Euphrates

Tigris

SAUDI ARABIA

KUWAIT

IRAN

YEMEN

BAHRAIN

QATAR

U.A.E.

OMAN

Unit 8: Map of Europe and North Africa

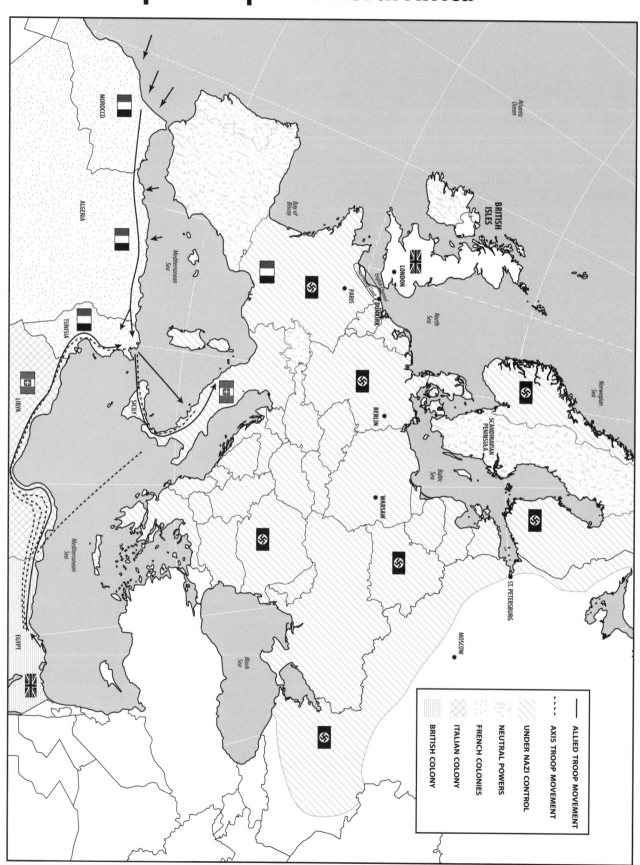

Unit 8: Map of Eastern Asia and Western Pacific

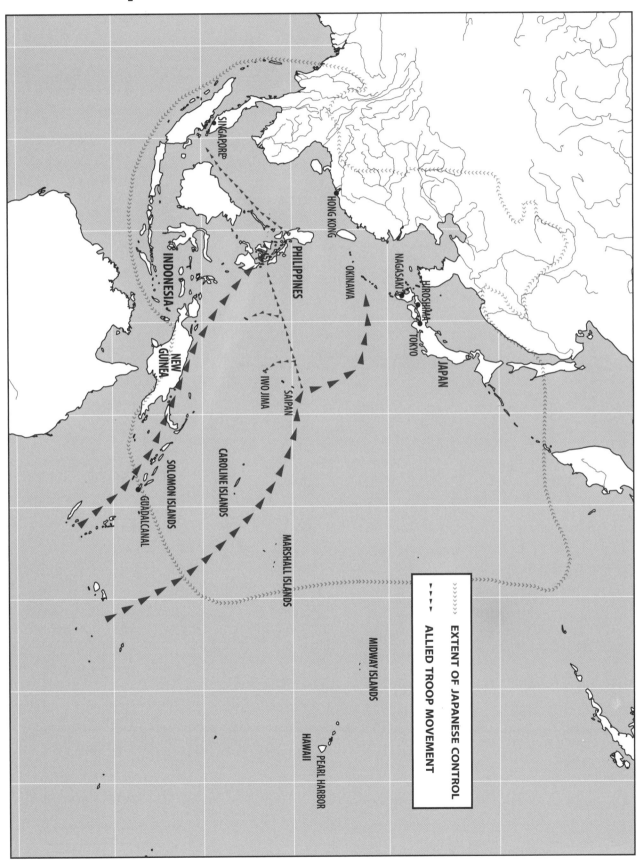

SINGAPORE

HONG KONG

INDONESIA

PHILIPPINES

OKINAWA

NAGASAKI

HIROSHIMA

TOKYO

JAPAN

NEW GUINEA

IWO JIMA

SAIPAN

SOLOMON ISLANDS

CAROLINE ISLANDS

GUADALCANAL

MARSHALL ISLANDS

MIDWAY ISLANDS

HAWAII

PEARL HARBOR

EXTENT OF JAPANESE CONTROL

ALLIED TROOP MOVEMENT

Unit 9: Middle East

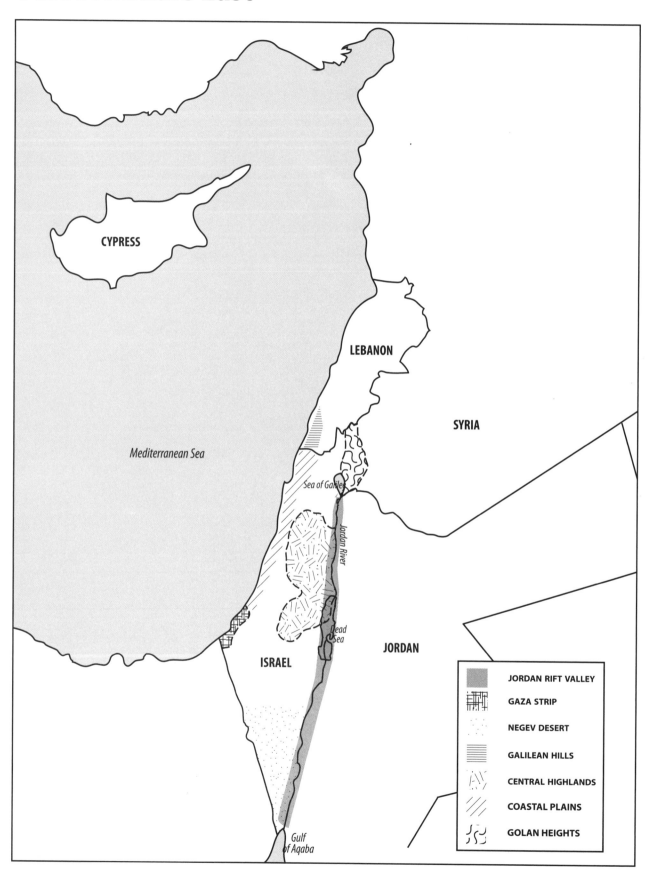

CYPRESS

LEBANON

SYRIA

Mediterranean Sea

Sea of Galilee

Jordan River

Dead Sea

JORDAN

ISRAEL

Gulf of Aqaba

	JORDAN RIFT VALLEY
	GAZA STRIP
	NEGEV DESERT
	GALILEAN HILLS
	CENTRAL HIGHLANDS
	COASTAL PLAINS
	GOLAN HEIGHTS

Unit 9: Eastern Asia

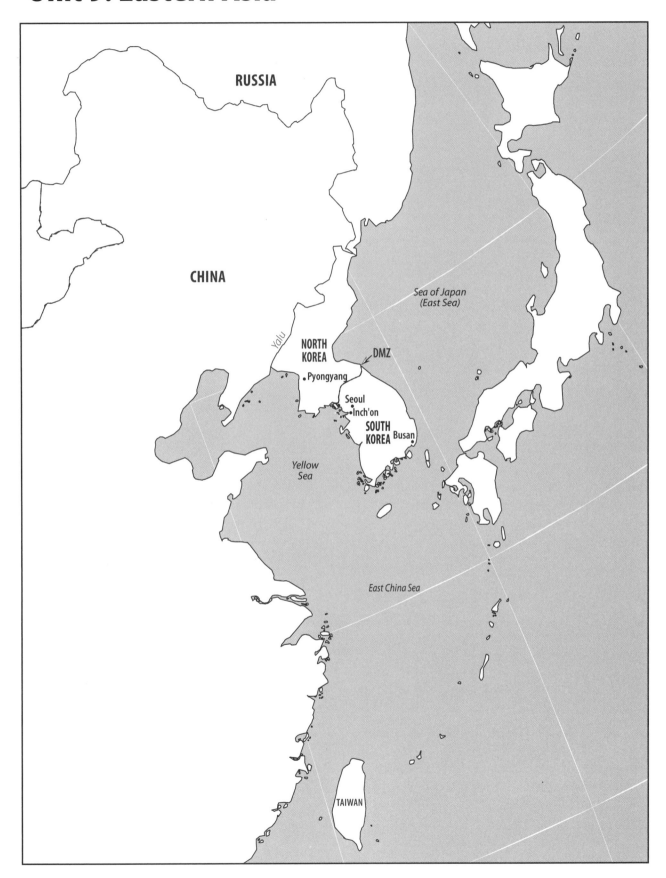

RUSSIA

CHINA

Sea of Japan
(East Sea)

Yalu

NORTH
KOREA

DMZ

•Pyongyang

Seoul
•Inch'on

SOUTH
KOREA Busan

Yellow
Sea

East China Sea

TAIWAN

The following definitions will help you with a quick definition in case your student is not certain which of the various possibilities is to be used in the context of each Unit.

Unit 1

abdication—a formal renunciation and relinquishment of a throne or high office and the powers and responsibility entailed by it; when a ruler steps down from the throne and gives up their place of authority

abolition—the act of ending slavery

alliance—a formal association or written agreement between two or more nations to advance their common interests and causes

annexation—the incorporation of a country or other territory into the domain of an existing political unit such as a country, state, or city. The taking over of a country or territory by another country or state

capitulate—to give up all resistance, surrender, and accept agreed upon terms

coalition—an alliance/group of people or nations that forms for a specific purpose or cause

coup—political takeover in which leadership/power changes hands

despotism—a system of government in which the ruler exercises absolute power, especially in a cruel and oppressive way

dictator—ruler with absolute power and authority who is not effectively restricted by a constitution or laws

diplomacy—the conducting of negotiations between nations including such things as alliances, treaties, and agreements

dissolution—the annulment or termination of a formal, legal bond or contract, or the disbanding of an assembly the ending of an agreement; the disbanding of a group/organization

exile—forced removal from one's country

nepotism—favoritism shown to relatives or close friends by those in power, particularly in the form of appointment to an office. When people in power appoint their relatives to positions in government

occupation—the invasion, conquest, and exercise of governmental control over a nation or territory by a foreign army

Quasi-War—an undeclared war between the United States and the French Republic from 1798 to 1800 fought mostly in the Caribbean as American naval ships engaged French naval ships

society—a voluntary association of individuals working/meeting together because of common interests and striving toward common goals

tactical—relating to the use of military maneuvers, particularly small-scale actions serving a larger purpose

tactician—a person who is skilled in the planning and execution of military maneuvers/tactics

vanquish—to defeat or conquer in battle and subdue completely

Unit 2

canal—artificial waterway used for travel, shipping, or irrigation

censorship—the practice of banning or limiting access to any information or books deemed objectionable or dangerous

charcoal—a dark or black porous carbon produced primarily by charring wood in a kiln, from which air is excluded. It is used for fuel and in various mechanical, artistic, and chemical processes. A dark carbon usually produced by burning wood; it was once used primarily for fuel

concession—granting, yielding, or conceding of a privilege; or the acknowledgment of something as correct, as in conceding the point in an argument

confederation—a league or alliance of independent nations or states whose central authority is usually confined to common defense and limited political cooperation. A league of independent states with a common central authority

industrialized—converted to industrialization; the development of large scale manufacturing activity

invention—A new device, method, or process originated after study and experimentation

liberal—favoring proposals for reform, open to new ideas for progress; not limited by traditional, orthodox, or authoritarian attitudes or dogmas

liberate—to set free from slavery, oppression, or foreign control

manufacture—to make a raw material into a finished product, especially by means of a large-scale industrial operation

mechanization—using machinery to perform tasks or to assist humans in performing their tasks

orphanage—an institution for the housing and care of children without parents

reactionary—characterized by reaction against radical

political or social change; marked by extreme conservatism

repression—the act of forcible subjugation to quell any opposition or disagreement. The use of force to keep people under control

slum—a heavily populated area of a city, characterized by poverty and poor housing, usually run down and dilapidated. The section of a city that is usually old and run down, where poor people primarily live

smelting—fusing or melting of ore in order to separate the impurities from metal

status quo—existing condition or state of affairs; the way things currently are

telegraph—an apparatus for transmitting messages or signals to a distant place by means of an electric device consisting of a sending instrument and a distant receiving instrument connected by a conducting wire

textiles—fabrics made by knitting or weaving; cloth

urbanize—taking on the characteristics of the city or of city life

Unit 3

accession—act of coming into possession of a right, title, or office; often used in terms of a king or queen coming into possession of their throne

caste—any of the hereditary social divisions into which Hindu society is traditionally divided, each caste being excluded from social interactions with the others. A social class which is a part of Hindu society; each class level has specific duties and privileges; classes are not allowed to interact with one another

civil as in "civil war"—relating to citizens and their interactions with one another or with the state

colonization—the act of establishing a colony; any people or territory separated from but subject to a ruling power

communism—a system of government in which a single, totalitarian political party holds power, claiming to be able to make progress toward a higher social order. The state plans and controls the economy, all property is owned collectively, and all goods are equally shared by the people. A system of government where people live and work in communities. The land, homes, tools, etc. belong to the community, not to the people. All goods are shared equally among everyone

compromise—a settlement of differences by mutual concessions; an agreement reached by giving up certain conflicting demands and settling for something less than what was originally wanted

emancipation—the act of freeing from restraint or bondage, particularly a slave

equality—the condition of being equal in value and of having the same political, social, and economic rights

eugenics—the study or practice of trying to improve the qualities of the human species by discouraging reproduction by persons having undesirable traits and encouraging reproduction by persons presumed to have inheritable desirable traits. The belief that the human race can be made better by only allowing the "best" people to have children and keeping those who are sick or disfigured from having children

evolution—the theory of the origin of species that holds that all organisms have grown and developed from past simpler organisms and that new kinds of animals arise and are perpetuated by natural selection. The theory that all plants and animals (including humans) started out as very simple life forms and have gradually developed over long periods of time into the complex life forms we see today

exhibition—a large scale public display of art objects or industrial or agricultural products

free trade—trade between countries, free from governmental restrictions or duties (such as quotas or protective tariffs)

ideology—the set of ideas and beliefs that form the basis of a political, economic, or other system

imperialism—the policy of a nation to extend its rule or authority over foreign countries by the establishment of economic and political hegemony, or by acquiring and holding colonies. The practice of a larger country growing stronger by taking over poorer or weaker countries that have important resources

indigenous—naturally originating in and characteristic of a particular region or country; native

malaria—a disease characterized by cycles of chills, fever, and sweating, which is transmitted to the human bloodstream by the bite of an infected mosquito

naturalism—the belief that everything which occurs in the world can be explained by natural causes, and that the natural is therefore all that exists; there is no supernatural creation, control of the world, or eternal significance for life

racism—the belief that differences among the many human races determine cultural and individual achievement and that certain races are therefore superior. The belief that certain races are better and more successful than other races

sovereignty—the authority and right of a state or people to govern itself/themselves independently

trek—a slow or difficult journey, especially one made on foot

Unit 4

commerce—the buying and selling of goods, particularly on a large scale, between cities or nations

depose—to remove from an office or a position of power, particularly to remove from a throne

electricity—the electric current/charge that is created by the attraction of atomic particles (electrons and protons) with opposite charges and the repulsion of particles with the same charge. The electric charge created by positive and negative particles in the air

empire—an extensive territory made up of a number of peoples or nations which are ruled by a single emperor or empress

ethnocentric—operating/acting on the belief that one ethnic group, nation, or culture (usu. one's own) is superior to all others

exploit—to selfishly and unethically use someone or something to achieve one's own purposes

foreign devils—a derogatory term used by the Chinese to refer to foreigners especially during the Opium Wars and the later Boxer Rebellion

ignominious—something that is disgraceful or degrading and deserving of public shame

indemnity—something paid by way of compensation for something damaged or lost

isolationism—the policy of isolating one's country from the affairs of other nations by declining to enter into alliances, economic commitments, international wars, etc., and seeking to devote the entire efforts of one's country to its own advancement

lucrative—something that can make money and lead to a lot profit or wealth

pasteurization—the process of heating a food or beverage, such as milk, to a specific temperature for a specific period of time in order to kill microorganisms that could cause disease or spoilage

phonograph—a device which reproduces sound. The sounds are mechanically transcribed in a spiral groove on a circular disk or cylinder, then a stylus on the device follows the groove in the revolving disk or cylinder and transmits vibrations which are converted into sound

prowess—superior or exceptional skill, strength, or courage, especially in battle

realpolitik—political realism or practical politics, especially policy based on power rather than on ideals; exemplified by such statesmen as Bismarck

spartan—characteristic of the Spartans, who were famous for being warlike, rigorously self disciplined, brave, stoical, severe, and frugal

telephone—an instrument that converts voice and other sound signals into a form that can be transmitted across distances and that also receives and reconverts waves into sound signals

unification—the act of joining together as one unit, as when two countries unify to become one nation

vaccine—a preparation of weakened microorganisms introduced into the body to produce immunity to a specific disease by causing the formation of antibodies. A small portion of a virus which is put into the body to help the body produce disease fighting mechanisms and prevent the person from getting the disease again

workhouse—an public institution where poor people did unpaid work in return for food and shelter

Unit 5

aggressive—characterized by unprovoked attacks, invasions, or the like; militantly forward or menacing; tending to start a fight or quarrel

anarchy—political or social disorder due to an absence of any governmental control or rule of law

arms race—continued competition between countries to achieve superiority in quantity and quality of military arms

concessions—benefits or privileges granted by a government, such as the right to use land for a specific purpose, or the right to engage in a certain activity for profit

escalate—to increase or intensify quickly; to become more serious or to become worse

ethnicity—a person's cultural background or where they came from

expedient—tending to promote some proposed or desired object; useful for one's own purpose, advantage, or interest

incompatible—unable to be joined together or exist together; contrary or opposed in character

innovation—something newly introduced; new or different method, device, or custom

radicals—those who favor drastic political, economic, or social reforms; those who go against social norms

reform—to correct or improve something and cause it to be better; to remove defects and put an end to wrong

reprisal—payback; retaliation against someone, for injuries received, by the infliction of equal or greater injuries

revitalization—bringing of new life and vigor; the returning to productivity and prominence

revolution—a sudden, radical change in society or the political system, often accompanied by violence

Russify—to make something Russian in character or quality

serf—a person in a condition of servitude, required to render services to a landowner; particularly agricultural laborers in 18th- and 19th-century Russia and eastern Europe

slavophile—a person advocating the supremacy of Slavic culture over western European influences; particularly referring to mid-19th century Russian intellectuals who favored traditional cultural practices over Western innovations in religion and politics

strategic—important or essential in relation to an objective, a plan of action, or a military maneuver

Unit 6

armistice—an agreement made by warring parties to temporarily cease fighting; a truce

assassinate—to kill someone suddenly or secretively, especially for political reasons

attrition—wearing down; especially a weakening of resistance due to continuous pressure, stress, or harassment

autocracy—government by a single person who has unlimited power and authority

aviation—the science of designing, producing, and operating aircraft/airplanes

belligerent—eager to fight, warlike, aggressive, hostile

convoy—a fleet of ships sailing together for mutual protection or with a protective escort of armed ships

front (in war)—a contested armed boundary between opposing forces, such as the Western Front in WWI; it can be a local front, or a tactical front

genocide—the deliberate and systematic extermination of a national, racial, political, or cultural group. The killing of all people belonging to a certain race, religion, or culture

impenetrable—impossible to enter, penetrate, pass, or break through

irredentism—the belief that territory culturally or historically related to one's nation should be recovered and again incorporated into one country; particularly, a 19th-century Italian political party that advocated the incorporation of regions adjacent to Italy and inhabited largely by Italians but under foreign control

mobilize—to organize, bring together, and prepare for active service or emergency; particularly preparing military troops for use in battle

neutral—belonging to neither one side nor the other; not aligned with, supporting, or favoring either side in a war or controversy

propaganda—materials that are deliberately spread in order to promote certain ideas, political movements, or people, or in order to criticize and slander opposing people or movements

provisional government—an emergency or temporary government set up to take the place of a government that has collapsed or been overthrown

relief (charity)—help or assistance (including money, food, or medical aid) given to the poor in times of need and distress

resupply—to provide with fresh supplies, particularly weapons and ammunition

stalemate—a situation in which two opposing forces find that further action is impossible or futile and neither side can win

trenches—long, narrow ditches dug by soldiers for cover and concealment, with the removed earth heaped up in front to serve as a protection from enemy fire and attack

ultimatum—a final uncompromising demand made by one party, which, if rejected by the other party, will usually lead to a break in relations and the use of force

Unit 7

anti-Semitism—an attitude or policy of prejudice, hatred, and hostility toward Jewish people

appeasement—the act of giving or conceding something to a potentially hostile power in order to keep the peace

Aryan—member or descendant of the early speakers of Indo-European languages; in Nazi terms, a member of the master race; a non-Jew

atrocities—actions which are shockingly inhumane, wicked, and ruthless; particularly acts of extreme cruelty against prisoners or civilians in wartime

chancellor—any of various officials of high rank, especially the chief minister of state in certain parliamentary governments, such as Germany

Comintern—short for Communist International; an international Communist organization founded by Lenin in 1919 to promote communist revolution in countries other than the USSR

factions—small groups that have broken off from a larger body due to disagreements on policies or modes of action, etc.

fascism—a governmental system led by a dictator with complete power and characterized by suppression of opposition through terror, regulation of all industry, and an emphasis on aggressive nationalism and usually racism

fundamental—a basic principle, rule, or doctrine that serves as the groundwork and basis of a system; an essential part

inflation—a progressive increase in the general prices of goods brought about by growing demand or the decline of the purchasing power of money due to a surplus of available currency an increase in the price of goods

linguistics—the science of language, including the study of the structure, development, etc. of a particular language and its relationship to other languages

Marxism-Leninism—important contribution to Marxism by Lenin of a precise political formula for seizing political power through revolutionary means

nationalistic—devoted to the interests or culture of one's nation; committed to obtaining national independence and the right to self government

Nazism—German form of fascism as defined by Adolf Hitler; the major characteristics included a policy of racist nationalism, national expansion, and state control of the economy

non-violence—the refusal to use any violent means in order to gain political or social aims, especially when protesting against oppression, injustice, discrimination, etc.

plebiscite—a direct vote of the people on an important political issue

purge—getting rid of what is unwanted; especially the removal of opponents from a state or a political party

reparations—payments required from a defeated nation for damages caused by war

repudiate—to refuse to recognize, or to reject as having no authority or binding force

Stock Market—the market where stocks and bonds are traded

terrorist—a person who frightens and terrorizes others as a means to a political end

translation—the act of taking something written or spoken in one language and changing it into another language

violation—a breaking or infringement of a law, agreement, treaty, etc.

Zionism—a Jewish movement that arose in the late nineteenth century in response to growing anti-Semitism; it sought to reestablish a Jewish homeland in Palestine. Today, Zionism continues to support the development of the state of Israel

Unit 8

aircraft carrier—warship designed as a mobile, floating air base with long flat decks on which aircraft can take off and land at sea

atomic—pertaining to or using atomic energy that is created by reactions within an atom's nucleus (either nuclear fission or fusion)

collaborate—to work together and cooperate; particularly to work with or for an enemy, especially an enemy occupying one's country

concentration camps—prison camps where political prisoners or ethnic minorities are kept, usually under harsh conditions; in particular the camps established by the Nazis for the persecution and extermination of Jews and other minorities

evacuation—the removal of people from a threatened or dangerous area; often an area about to be invaded or bombed by an enemy

firestorm—an intense fire over a large area, such as one initiated by an atomic explosion, that is sustained and spread by rushing winds

ghetto—a section of a city inhabited primarily by a minority group of the same race or religion, often as a result of discrimination or social or economic restrictions; formerly, in most European countries, the section of the city where all Jews were required to live

holocaust—a massive and complete slaughter; specifically, the systematic mass killing of European Jews in Nazi concentration camps incendiary—a weapon, device, or bomb designed to start fires; particularly various versions of firebombs that were used during WWII

infamy—disgrace and extreme dishonor resulting from an evil and criminal act that is publicly known

intercessor—a person who entreats the favor of someone on behalf of someone else; particularly one who prays to God on behalf of another

intimidation—the use of fear and threats of violence to frighten someone into submission or compliance

kamikaze—one of a group of Japanese pilots trained to perform suicidal missions by crashing their aircraft, loaded with explosives, into an enemy target, especially a warship

non-aggression pact—a treaty between two or more nations agreeing to avoid war or armed conflict and to henceforward resolve their disputes through peaceful negotiations

obsessive—extreme, excessive; motivated by and continually occupied with a persistent overriding idea

panzers—German armored vehicles, mainly tanks, especially those used in WWII

paratrooper—a soldier trained to attack or land in combat areas by parachuting from airplanes; a parachute jumper

perimeter—the outer limits of an area; a fortified boundary that protects a troop position

resistance—the act of opposing or withstanding something and refusing to give in; also an underground organization engaged in a struggle for national liberation in a country under military occupation

underground—hidden or secretive; an undercover organization planning activities to overthrow a government, or an occupying military force

Unit 9

bloc—a group of nations that share common interests and are acting together in international affairs, such as the Soviet bloc

Cold War—a state of political tension and intense economic, military, and ideological rivalry between nations which falls short of military conflict; especially the rivalry which existed between the United States and the Soviet Union after WWII

containment—an act or policy of restricting an opposing nation from growing territorially or from influencing other nations ideologically

decolonization—the act of freeing a colony and allowing it to become independent and self-governing; the process of eliminating colonialism

democratization—the act of making a country democratic, operating on the basis of political equality for all

denazification—the process of removing Nazis from official positions and removing Nazi elements and influences from government and culture

deterrent—something that prevents or blocks, particularly a military superiority of defense or retaliation that keeps an enemy from attacking

disarmament—reduction or limitation of the size, equipment, armament, etc., of the military force of a country as laid out by a treaty

displaced—moved or put out of the usual or proper place, especially forced to leave one's homeland

emerging—newly formed, or just coming to maturity and prominence

insurrection—an open rising up against an established government/authority; rebellion

Iron Curtain—the military, political, and ideological barrier established between the Soviet bloc and western Europe from 1945 to 1990 that prevented all communication and interaction

limited war—a war conducted with less than a nation's total resources, as in without using atomic weapons, and restricted in aim to less than total defeat of the enemy, or restricted to a small area of the world

nonalignment—a political policy of not aligning oneself with any other nation in its ideological course or objectives; particularly refusing to make any pre-commitment to a particular side in a conflict of power

partition—something that divides or separates, such as a wall

satellite—an object launched into space to orbit Earth or another celestial body

About the Author

Diana Waring has been fascinated by history since she was old enough to discover that World War II had ended ten years prior to her birth in Germany. As a child, she always wanted to understand the chronological march of kings, the connection between momentous events—especially wars—and the international tapestry of fascinating people throughout the ages. The first glimmers of understanding came in a rapid-fire African history course at college, but the full explosion of light dawned when she began teaching world history side by side with the Bible to her three children. It was at that point, with the research required to answer their innumerable questions, that all the pieces began to fall in place. The contagious excitement of discovery led to her speaking and writing about history.

While writing this book, Mrs. Waring lived in the Pacific Northwest with her husband and dog. She now resides in Indiana, when she is not visiting her adult children or traveling around the world to educate teachers and parents on the wonders of learning.